LYNCHBURG COLLEGE
SYMPOSIUM READINGS

CLASSICAL SELECTIONS ON GREAT ISSUES

SERIES ONE
VOLUME V

WAR AND PEACE

Aquinas
Grotius
Vattel
Thucydides
Dante
Machiavelli
Sun Tzu
Clausewitz
Mahan
Tolstoy
Mackinder
Crowe
Hawtrey
Horne
Bowman
Laotse
James
Woodward
Eisenhower

UNIVERSITY
PRESS OF
AMERICA

ii

SERIES ONE

SYMPOSIUM READINGS

Lynchburg College in Virginia

Compiled and Edited by the
following faculty members of Lynchburg College:

Kenneth E. Alrutz, A.M., University of Pennsylvania; Assistant
Professor of English

Virginia B. Berger, M.A., Harvard University; Associate Professor
of Music

Anne Marshall Bippus, Ed.D., University of Virginia; Associate
Professor of Education

James L. Campbell, Ph.D., University of Virginia; Associate Professor of English

Robert L. Frey, Ph.D., University of Minnesota; Professor of
History

James A. Huston, Ph.D., New York University; Dean of the College,
Professor of History and International Relations

Shannon McIntyre Jordan, Ph.D., University of Georgia; Instructor
in Philosophy

Jan G. Linn, D.Min., Christian Theological Seminary; Assistant
Professor, College Chaplain

Peggy S. Pittas, M.A., Dalhousie University; Associate Professor
of Psychology

Clifton W. Potter, Jr., Ph.D., University of Virginia; Professor
of History

Julius A. Sigler, Ph.D., University of Virginia; Professor of
Physics

Phillip H. Stump, Ph.D., University of California at Los Angeles;
Assistant Professor of History

Thomas C. Tiller, Ph.D., Florida State University; Dean of Student
Affairs, Professor of Education

Copyright © 1982 by

University Press of America, Inc.

P.O. Box 19101, Washington, D.C. 20036

Printed in the United States of America

ISBN (Perfect): 0-8191-2471-0
ISBN   (Cloth): 0-8191-2470-2

Library of Congress Catalog Card Number: **82-45154**

ACKNOWLEDGEMENTS

The following copyrighted materials have been used with the permission of the copyright holders:

From *The Art of War* by Sun Tzu. c.1963, Oxford University Press.

From *War and Peace*, "1812" by Leo Tolstoy. c.1942, Oxford University Press.

From *The Wisdom of Laotse*, by Laotse. c. 1948, Random House, Inc.

From *Beach Red* by Peter Bowman. c.1945, Random House.

The authors acknowledge with appreciation the permissions granted by these holders of the respective copyrights.

INTRODUCTION

War has been an overwhelming problem for mankind from the earliest times. What are its causes? Is there any hope of eliminating war as an instrument of national policy? Can it at least be restricted in its scope and violence? Is it realistic to attempt to distinguish between just and unjust wars? What implications might this have for national policy and for individual action? Can rules of morality be applied to the conduct of war and to relations among nations generally? What are the conditions of peace?

The attempts which statesmen, warriors, philosophers, theologians, and common people have made through the ages to find solutions to these questions provide some perspective for our own attempts. So far no one has come up with any effective and lasting solutions. On the other hand, they have been able to maintain sufficient restraint at least to allow us to survive. Whether this still can be done in the nuclear age is another question.

In any event, war must not be thought about in isolation. Always it must be related to the vital interest and policies which called it into being.

CONTENTS

ix

Thomas Aquinas, THE SUMMA THEOLOGICA: "OF WAR"

Hugo Grotius, CONCERNING THE LAW OF WAR AND PEACE

Emeric de Vattel, THE LAW OF NATIONS

1. What was the attitude of Thomas Aquinas on just and unjust wars? Compare with the position of Vattel.

2. What does Grotius consider to be the sources of international law?

3. What is the point of Grotius' reference to the Melian Dialogue in Thucydides?

4. Do you believe that restraints can be put upon war by means of international law? How or why not?

5. Compare Vattel's view of the nature of international law with that of Grotius.

6. What does Vattel consider to be the rights and duties of states?

7. What would be Vattel's position on Israel's 1981 preemptive strike on Iraq's nuclear facility?

8. In time of war, what are the rights and duties of neutral states?

9. According to Vattel, what are the conditions for neutral trade with belligerents in time of war?

A leader of 13th century Scholasticism in philosophy, theology, and teaching, Thomas Aquinas was a major force in systematizing Latin Christian theology and in teaching its tenants to a following of students. The Scholastic Method of proposing an open question followed by arguments for one side or the other, together with a series of objections with responses, and a conclusion, is found in his great theological work *Summa Theologica* (1266-73). He draws largely on Augustine in his comments on just and unjust wars.

WE must now consider war, under which head there are four points of inquiry: (1) Whether some kind of war is lawful? (2) Whether it is lawful for clerics to fight? (3) Whether it is lawful for belligerents to lay ambushes? (4) Whether it is lawful to fight on holy days?

ARTICLE I. *Whether It is Always Sinful To Wage War?*

We proceed thus to the First Article: It seems that it is always sinful to wage war.

Objection 1. Because punishment is not inflicted except for sin. Now those who wage war are threatened by Our Lord with punishment, according to Matt. 26. 52: *All that take the sword shall perish with the sword.* Therefore all wars are unlawful.

Obj. 2. Further, Whatever is contrary to a Divine precept is a sin. But war is contrary to a Divine precept, for it is written (Matt. 5. 39): *But I say to you not to resist evil;* and (Rom. 12. 19): *Not revenging yourselves, my dearly beloved, but give place unto wrath.* Therefore war is always sinful.

Obj. 3. Further, Nothing, except sin, is contrary to an act of virtue. But war is contrary to peace. Therefore war is always a sin.

Obj. 4. Further, The exercise of a lawful thing is itself lawful, as is evident in exercises of the sciences. But warlike exercises which take place in tournaments are forbidden by the Church, since those who are slain in these trials are deprived of ecclesiastical burial. Therefore it seems that war is a sin absolutely.

On the contrary, Augustine says in a sermon on the son of the centurion:[1] "If the Christian Religion forbade war altogether, those who sought salutary advice in the Gospel would rather have been counselled to cast aside their arms, and to give up soldiering altogether. On the contrary, they were told: 'Do violence to no man; . . . and be content with your pay' (Luke 3. 14). If he commanded them to be content with their pay, he did not forbid soldiering."

I answer that, In order for a war to be just, three things are necessary. First, the authority of the sovereign by whose command the war is to be waged. For it is not the business of a private person to declare war, because he can seek for redress of his rights from the tribunal of his superior. Moreover it is not the business of a private person to summon together the people, which has to be done in wartime. And as the care of the common weal is committed to those who are in authority, it is their business to watch over the common weal of the city, kingdom or province subject to them. And just as it is lawful for them to have recourse to the material sword in defending that common weal against internal disturbances, when they punish evil-doers, according to the words of the Apostle (Rom. 13. 4): *He beareth not the sword in vain: for he is God's minister, an avenger to execute wrath upon him that doth evil;* so too, it is their business to have recourse to the sword of war in defending the common weal against external enemies. Hence it is said to those who are in authority (Ps. 81. 4): *Rescue the poor: and deliver the needy out of the hand of the sinner;* and for this reason Augustine says (*Contra Faust.* xxii, 75):[2] "The natural order conducive to peace among mortals demands that the power to declare and counsel war should be in the hands of those who hold the supreme authority."

Secondly, a just cause is required, namely that those who are attacked should be attacked because they deserve it on account of some fault. Therefore Augustine says (Q. x, *super*

Jos.):[3] "A just war is usually described as one that avenges wrongs, when a nation or state has to be punished, for refusing to make amends for the wrongs inflicted by its subjects, or to restore what it has seized unjustly."

Thirdly, it is necessary that the belligerents should have a right intention, so that they intend the advancement of good, or the avoidance of evil. Hence Augustine says (*De Verb. Dom.*):[4] "True religion does not look upon as sinful those wars that are waged not for motives of aggrandisement, or cruelty, but with the object of securing peace, of punishing evildoers, and of uplifting the good." For it may happen that the war is declared by the legitimate authority, and for a just cause, and yet be rendered unlawful through a wicked intention. Hence Augustine says (*Contra Faust.* xxii):[5] "The passion for inflicting harm, the cruel thirst for vengeance, an unpacific and relentless spirit, the fever of revolt, the lust of power, and such things, all these are rightly condemned in war."

Reply Obj. 1. As Augustine says (*Contra Faust.* xxii):[6] "To take the sword is to arm oneself in order to take the life of anyone, without the command or permission of superior or lawful authority." On the other hand, to have recourse to the sword (as a private person) by the authority of the sovereign or judge, or (as a public person) through zeal for justice, and by the authority, so to speak, of God, is not to *take the sword*, but to use it as commissioned by another, and so it does not deserve punishment. And yet even those who make sinful use of the sword are not always slain with the sword, but they always perish with their own sword, because, unless they repent, they are punished eternally for their sinful use of the sword.

Reply Obj. 2. Precepts of this kind, as Augustine observes (*De Serm. Dom. in Monte,* i),[1] should always be borne in readiness of mind, so that we be ready to obey them, and, if necessary, to refrain from resistance or self-defence. Nevertheless it is necessary sometimes for a man to act otherwise for the common good, or for the good of those with whom he is fighting. Hence Augustine says (*Ep. ad Marcellin.*):[2] "Those whom we have to punish with a kindly severity, it is necessary to handle in many ways against their will. For when we are stripping a man of the lawlessness of sin, it is good for him to be vanquished, since nothing is more hopeless than the happiness of sinners, whence arises a guilty impunity, and an evil will, like an internal enemy."

Reply Obj. 3. Those who wage war justly aim at peace, and so they are not opposed to peace, except to the evil peace, which Our Lord *came not to send upon earth* (Matt. 10. 34). Hence Augustine says (*Ep. ad Bonif.* clxxxix):[3] "We do not seek peace in order to be at war, but we go to war that we may have peace. Be peaceful, therefore, in warring, so that you may vanquish those whom you war against, and bring them to the prosperity of peace."

Reply Obj. 4. Manly exercises in warlike feats of arms are not all forbidden, but those which are inordinate and perilous, and end in slaying or plundering. In olden times warlike exercises presented no such danger, and hence they were called exercises of arms or bloodless wars, as Jerome states in an epistle (cf. Veget., —*De Re Milit.* i).[4]

ARTICLE 2. *Whether It Is Lawful for Clerics and Bishops To Fight?*

We proceed thus to the Second Article: It seems lawful for clerics and bishops to fight.

Objection 1. For, as stated above (A. 1), wars are lawful and just in so far as they protect the poor and the entire common weal from suffering at the hands of the foe. Now this seems to be above all the duty of prelates, for Gregory says (*Hom. in Ev.* xiv):[5] "The wolf comes upon the sheep, when any unjust and rapacious man oppresses those who are faithful and humble. But he who was thought to be the shepherd, and was not, leaveth the sheep, and flieth, for he fears lest the wolf hurt him, and dares not stand up against his injustice." Therefore it is lawful for prelates and clerics to fight.

Obj. 2. Further, Pope Leo IV writes (xxiii, qu. 8, can. *Igitur*):[6] "As adverse tidings had frequently come from the Saracen side, some said that the Saracens would come to the port of Rome secretly and covertly; for which reason we commanded our people to gather together, and ordered them to go down to the sea-shore." Therefore it is lawful for bishops to fight.

Obj. 3. Further, It seems to be the same whether a man does a thing himself, or consents to its being done by another, according to Rom. 1. 32: *They who do such things, are worthy of death, and not only they that do them, but they also that consent to them that do them.* Now those, above all, seem to consent to a thing, who induce others to do it. But it is lawful for bishops and clerics to induce others to fight, for it is written (xxiii, qu. 8, can. *Hortatu*)[7] that "Charles went to war with the Lombards at the instance and entreaty of Adrian, bishop of Rome." Therefore they also are allowed to fight.

Obj. 4. Further, Whatever is right and meritorious in itself is lawful for prelates and clerics. Now it is sometimes right and meritorious to make war, for it is written (xxiii, qu. 8, can. *Omni timore*)[8] that "if a man die for the true faith, or to save his country, or in defence of Christians, God will give him a heavenly reward." Therefore it is lawful for bishops and clerics to fight.

On the contrary, It was said to Peter as representing bishops and clerics (Matt. 26. 52): *Put up again thy sword into the scabbard* (Vulg., —*its place*). Therefore it is not lawful for them to fight.

I answer that, Several things are requisite for the good of a human society, and a number of things are done better and quicker by a number of persons than by one, as the Philosopher observes,[9] while certain occupations are so inconsistent with one another, that they cannot be fittingly exercised at the same time; hence those who are assigned to important duties are forbidden to occupy themselves with things of small importance. Thus according to human laws, soldiers who are assigned to warlike pursuits are forbidden to engage in commerce.

Now warlike pursuits are altogether incompatible with the duties of a bishop and a cleric for two reasons. The first reason is a general one, because, namely, warlike pursuits are full of unrest, so that they hinder the mind very much from the contemplation of Divine things, the praise of God, and prayers for the people, which belong to the duties of a cleric. Therefore just as commercial enterprises are forbidden to clerics, because they entangle the mind too much, so too are warlike pursuits, according to II Tim. 2. 4: *No man being a soldier to God, entangleth himself with secular business.* The second reason is a special one, because, namely, all the clerical Orders are directed to the ministry of the altar, on which the Passion of Christ is represented sacramentally, according to I Cor. 11. 26: *As often as you shall eat this bread, and drink the chalice, you shall show the death of the Lord, until He come.* Therefore it is unbecoming for them to slay or shed blood, and it is more fitting that they should be ready to shed their own blood for Christ, so as to imitate in deed what they portray in their ministry. For this reason it has been decreed[1] that those who shed blood, even without sin, become irregular. Now no man who has a certain duty to perform can lawfully do that which renders him unfit for that duty. Therefore it is altogether unlawful for clerics to fight, because war is directed to the shedding of blood.

Reply Obj. 1. Prelates ought to withstand not only the wolf who brings spiritual death upon the flock, but also the pillager and the oppressor who work bodily harm; not, however, by having recourse themselves to material arms, but by means of spiritual weapons, according to the saying of the Apostle (II Cor. 10. 4): *The weapons of our warfare are not carnal, but mighty through God.* Such are salutary warnings, devout prayers, and, for those who are obstinate, the sentence of excommunication.

Reply Obj. 2. Prelates and clerics may, by the authority of their superiors, take part in wars, not indeed by taking up arms themselves, but by affording spiritual help to those who fight justly, by exhorting and absolving them, and by other like spiritual helps. Thus in the Old Testament (Jos. 6. 4) the priests were commanded to sound the sacred trumpets in the battle. It was for this purpose that bishops or clerics were first allowed to go to war; and it is an abuse of this permission, if any of them take up arms themselves.

Reply Obj. 3. As stated above (Q. XXIII, A. 4, reply 2) every power, art or virtue that pertains to the end, has to dispose that which is directed to the end. Now, among the faithful, carnal wars should be considered as having for their end the Divine spiritual good to which clerics are deputed. Therefore it is the duty of clerics to dispose and counsel other men to engage in just wars. For they are forbidden to take up arms, not as though it were a sin, but because such an occupation is unbecoming their persons.

Reply Obj. 4. Although it is meritorious to wage a just war, nevertheless it is rendered unlawful for clerics, by reason of their being assigned to works more meritorious still. Thus the marriage act may be meritorious; and yet it becomes reprehensible in those who have vowed virginity, because they are bound to a yet greater good.

ARTICLE 3. *Whether It Is Lawful To Lay Ambushes in War?*

We proceed thus to the Third Article: It seems that it is unlawful to lay ambushes in war.

Objection 1. For it is written (Deut. 16. 20): *Thou shalt follow justly after that which is just.* But ambushes, since they are a kind of deception, seem to pertain to injustice. Therefore it is unlawful to lay ambushes even in a just war.

Obj. 2. Further, Ambushes and deception seem to be opposed to faithfulness even as lies are. But since we are bound to keep faith with all men, it is wrong to lie to anyone, as Augustine states (*Contra Mend.* xv).[2] Therefore, as "one is bound to keep faith with one's enemy," as Augustine states (*Ep. ad Bonifac.* clxxxix),[3] it seems that it is unlawful to lay ambushes for one's enemies.

Obj. 3. *Further,* It is written (Matt. 7. 12): *Whatsoever you would that men should do to you, do you also to them,* and we ought to observe this in all our dealings with our neighbour. Now our enemy is our neighbour. Therefore, since no man wishes ambushes or deceptions to be prepared for himself, it seems that no one ought to carry on war by laying ambushes.

On the contrary, Augustine says (*QQ. in Heptateuch., qu.* x, *super Jos.*):[1] "Provided the war be just, it is no concern of justice whether it be carried on openly or by ambushes," and he proves this by the authority of the Lord, Who commanded Joshua to lay ambushes for the city of Hai (Jos. 8. 2).

I answer that, The object of laying ambushes is in order to deceive the enemy. Now a man may be deceived by another's word or deed in two ways. First, through being told something false, or through the breaking of a promise, and this is always unlawful. No one ought to deceive the enemy in this way, for there are certain rights of war and convenants, which ought to be observed even among enemies, as Ambrose states (*De Offic.* i, 29).[2]

Secondly, a man may be deceived by what we say or do, because we do not declare our purpose or meaning to him. Now we are not always bound to do this, since even in the Sacred Doctrine many things have to be concealed, especially from unbelievers, lest they deride it, according to Matt. 7. 6: *Give not that which is holy, to dogs.* Therefore much more ought the plan of campaign to be hidden from the enemy. For this reason among other things that a soldier has to learn is the art of concealing his purpose lest it come to the enemy's knowledge, as stated in the Book on *Strategy* by Frontinus.[3] Concealment of this kind is what is meant by an ambush which may be lawfully employed in a just war. Nor can these ambushes be properly called deceptions, nor are they contrary to justice or to a well-ordered will. For a man would have an inordinate will if he were unwilling that others should hide from him. This suffices for the *Replies to the Objections.*

ARTICLE 4. *Whether It is Lawful To Fight on Holy Days?*

We proceed thus to the Fourth Article: It seems unlawful to fight on holy days.

Objection 1. For holy days are instituted that we may give our time to the things of God. Hence they are included in the keeping of the Sabbath prescribed Exod. 20. 8, for Sabbath is interpreted rest. But wars are full of unrest. Therefore by no means is it lawful to fight on holy days.

Obj. 2. Further, Certain persons are reproached (Isa. 58. 3) because on fast-days they exacted what was owing to them, were guilty of strife, and of striking with their fists. Much more, therefore, is it unlawful to fight on holy days.

Obj. 3. Further, No inordinate deed should be done to avoid temporal harm. But fighting on a holy day seems in itself to be an inordinate deed. Therefore no one should fight on a holy day even through the need of avoiding temporal harm.

On the contrary, It is written (I Machab. 2. 41): *The Jews rightly determined . . . saying: Whosoever shall come up against us to fight on the Sabbath-day, we will fight against him.*

I answer that, The observance of holy days is no hindrance to those things which are ordered to man's safety, even that of his body. Hence Our Lord argued with the Jews, saying (John 7. 23): *Are you angry at Me because I have healed the whole man on the Sabbath-day?* Hence physicians may lawfully attend to their patients on holy days. Yet much more reason

11

is there for safeguarding the common weal (by which many are saved from being slain, and innumerable evils both temporal and spiritual prevented), than the bodily safety of an individual. Therefore, for the purpose of safeguarding the common weal of the faithful, it is lawful to carry on a war on holy days, provided there be need for doing so; because it would be to tempt God, if notwithstanding such a need, one were to choose to refrain from fighting. However, as soon as the need ceases, it is no longer lawful to fight on a holy day, for the reasons given. And this suffices for the *Replies to the Objections.*

With only slight exaggeration, Hugo Grotius often is referred to as the "father of international law." Fruin called him a "man of all-embracing learning." Caught up in the religious disputes of his native Holland, Grotius was arrested in 1618 and sentenced to life imprisonment in the castle of Loevestein. With the aid of his wife, he arranged to be hidden in a chest and carried out of the prison. He fled to Paris where Louis XIII granted him a small pension, and there he wrote his most famous work, *On the Law of War and Peace*. Published in over a hundred editions and translations, this has had world-wide and continuing influence.

THE LAW OF WAR AND PEACE

1. The municipal law of Rome and of other states has been treated by many, who have undertaken to elucidate it by means of commentaries or to reduce it to a convenient digest. That body of law, however, which is concerned with the mutual relations among states or rulers of states, whether derived from nature, or established by divine ordinances, or having its origin in custom and tacit agreement, few have touched upon. Up to the present time no one has treated it in a comprehensive and systematic manner; yet the welfare of mankind demands that this task be accomplished.

2. Cicero justly characterized as of surpassing worth a knowledge of treaties of alliance, conventions, and understandings of peoples, kings and foreign nations—a knowledge, in short, of the whole law of war and peace. And to this knowledge Euripides gives the preference over an understanding of things divine and human, for he represents Theoclymenus as being thus addressed: [For Balbus, vi. 15.]

> For you, who know the fate of men and gods, [Helena,
> What is, what shall be, shameful would it be 928 f.]
> To know not what is just.

3. Such a work is all the more necessary because in our day, as in former times, there is no lack of men who view this branch of law with contempt as having no reality outside of an empty name. On the lips of men quite generally is the saving of Euphemus, which Thucydides quotes,[1] that in the case of a king or imperial

---

[1] The words are in Book VI [VI. lxxxv]. The same thought is found in Book V [V. lxxxix], where the Athenians, who at the time of speaking were very powerful, thus address the Melians: "According to human standards those arrangements are accounted

city nothing is unjust which is expedient. Of like implication is the statement that for those whom fortune favors might makes right, and that the administration of a state cannot be carried on without injustice.

Furthermore, the controversies which arise between peoples or kings generally have Mars as their arbiter. That war is irreconcilable with all law is a view held not alone by the ignorant populace; expressions are often let slip by well-informed and thoughtful men which lend countenance to such a view. Nothing is more common than the assertion of antagonism between law and arms.

[In Gellius, xx. 10.] Thus Ennius says:

> Not on grounds of right is battle joined,
> But rather with the sword do men
> Seek to enforce their claims.

[*Art of Poetry*, 122.] Horace, too, describes the savage temper of Achilles in this wise:

> Laws, he declares, were not for him ordained;
> By dint of arms he claims all for himself.

[Lucan, I. 225.] Another poet depicts another military leader as commencing war with the words:

> Here peace and violated laws I leave behind.

[Plutarch, *Fort. of Alex.*, 330 E.] [*Apoth.*, 202 D; *Marius*, xxviii= 421 E.] Antigonus when advanced in years ridiculed a man who brought to him a treatise on justice when he was engaged in besieging cities that did not belong to him. Marius declared that the din of arms made it impossible for him to hear the voice of the laws.[2] Even Pompey, whose ex-

---

just which are settled when the necessity on both sides is equal; as tor the rest, the more powerful do all they can, the more weak endure."

  ² In Plutarch Lysander displaying his sword says [*Apothegms, Lysander*, iii=190 E]: "He who is master of this is in the best position to discuss questions relating to boundaries between countries."

  In the same author Caesar declares [*Caesar*, xxxv=725 B]: "The time for arms is not the time for laws."

pression of countenance was so mild, dared to say: "When I am in arms, am I to think of laws?" [3]

4. Among Christian writers a similar thought finds frequent expression. A single quotation from Tertullian may serve in place of many: "Deception, harshness, and injustice are the regular business of battles." They who so think will no doubt wish to confront us with this passage in Comedy:

[*An Answer to the Jews,* vii.]

[Terence *Eunuch,* I. i. 16 ff.]

> These things uncertain should you, by reason's aid,
> Try to make certain, no more would you gain
> Than if you tried by reason to go mad.

5. Since our discussion concerning law will have been undertaken in vain if there is no law, in order to open the way for a favorable reception of our work and at the same time to fortify it against attacks, this very serious error must be briefly refuted. In order that we may not be obliged to deal with a crowd of opponents, let us assign to them a pleader. And whom should we choose in preference to Carneades? For he had attained to so perfect a mastery of the peculiar tenet of his Academy that he was able to devote the power of his eloquence to the service of falsehood not less readily than to that of truth.

Carneades, then, having undertaken to hold a brief against justice, in particular against that phase of justice with which we are concerned, was able to muster no argument stronger than this, that, for reasons of expediency,

---

Similarly Seneca, *On Benefits,* IV. xxxviii [IV. xxxvii]: "At times, especially in time of war, kings make many grants with their eyes shut. One just man cannot satisfy so many passionate desires of men in arms; no one can at the same time act the part of a good man and good commander."

[3] This viewpoint of Pompey in relation to the Mamertines Plutarch expresses thus [*Pompey,* x=623 D]: "Will you not stop quoting laws to us who are girt with swords?" Curtius says in Book IX [IX. iv. 7]: "Even to such a degree does war reverse the laws of nature."

men imposed upon themselves laws, which vary according to customs, and among the same peoples often undergo changes as times change; moreover, that there is no law of nature, because all creatures, men as well as animals, are impelled by nature toward ends advantageous to themselves; that, consequently, there is no justice, or, if such there be, it is supreme folly, since one does violence to his own interests if he consults the advantage of others.

[Horace, *Satires*, I. iii. 113.] 6. What the philosopher here says, and the poet reaffirms in verse,

And just from unjust Nature cannot know,

must not for one moment be admitted. Man is, to be sure, an animal, but an animal of a superior kind, much farther removed from all other animals than the different kinds of animals are from one another; evidence on this point may be found in the many traits peculiar to the human species. But among the traits characteristic of man is an impelling desire for society, that is, for the social life —not of any and every sort, but peaceful, and organized according to the measure of his intelligence, with those who are of his own kind; this social trend the Stoics called "sociableness."[4] Stated as a universal truth, therefore, the assertion that every animal is impelled by nature to seek only its own good cannot be conceded.

7. Some of the other animals, in fact, do in a way restrain the appetency for that which is good for them-

---

[4] Chrysostom, *On Romans*, Homily XXXI [Homily V. i, on chap. i, verse 31]: "We men have by nature a kind of fellowship with men; why not, when even wild beasts in their relation to one another have something similar?"

See also the same author, *On Ephesians*, chap. i [Homily I], where he explains that the seeds of virtue have been implanted in us by nature. The emperor Marcus Aurelius, a philosopher of parts, said [V. xvi]: "It was long ago made clear that we were born for fellowship. Is it not evident that the lower exist for the sake of the higher, and the higher for one another's sake?"

selves alone, to the advantage now of their offspring, now of other animals of the same species.[5] This aspect

[5] There is an old proverb, "Dogs do not eat the flesh of dogs." Says Juvenal [*Sat.* xv. 163, 159]:

> Tigress with ravening tigress keeps the peace;
> The wild beast spares its spotted kin.

There is a fine passage of Philo, in his commentary on the Fifth Commandment, which he who will may read in Greek. As it is somewhat long, I shall here quote it only once and in Latin [Philo, *On the Ten Commandments*, xxiii, in English as follows]: "Men, be ye at least imitators of dumb brutes. They, trained through kindness, know how to repay in turn. Dogs defend our homes; they even suffer death for their masters, if danger has suddenly come upon them. It is said that shepherd dogs go in advance of their flocks, fighting till death, if need be, that they may protect the shepherds from hurt. Of things disgraceful is not the most disgraceful this, that in return of kindness man should be outdone by a dog, the gentlest creature by the most fierce?

"But if we fail to draw our proper lesson from the things of earth, let us pass to the realm of winged creatures that make voyage through the air, that from them we may learn our duty. Aged storks, unable to fly, stay in their nests. Their offspring fly, so to say, over all lands and seas, seeking sustenance in all places for their parents; these, in consideration of their age, deservedly enjoy quiet, abundance, even comforts. And the younger storks console themselves for the irksomeness of their voyaging with the consciousness of their discharge of filial duty and the expectation of similar treatment on the part of their offspring, when they too have grown old. Thus they pay back, at the time when needed, the debt they owe, returning what they have received; for from others they cannot obtain sustenance either at the begining of life, when they are small, or, when they have become old, at life's end. From no other teacher than nature herself have they learned to care for the aged, just as they themselves were cared for when they were young.

"Should not they who do not take care of their parents have reason to hide themselves for very shame when they hear this—they that neglect those whom alone, or above all others, they ought to help, especially when by so doing they are not really called upon to give, but merely to return what they owe? Children have as their own nothing to which their parents do not possess a prior claim; their parents have either given them what they have, or have furnished to them the means of acquisition."

of their behavior has its origin, we believe, in some extrinsic intelligent principle, because with regard to other actions, which involve no more difficulty than those referred to, a like degree of intelligence is not manifest in them. The same thing must be said of children. In children, even before their training has begun, some disposition to do good to others appears, as Plutarch sagely observed; thus sympathy for others comes out spontaneously at that age. The mature man in fact has knowledge which prompts him to similar actions under similar conditions,[6] together with an impelling desire for society, for the gratification of which he alone among animals possesses a special instrument, speech. He has also been endowed with the faculty of knowing and acting in accordance with general principles. Whatever accords with that faculty is not common to all animals, but peculiar to the nature of man.

[*Consolation*, 608 D.]

8. This maintenance of the social order,[7] which we

In regard to the extraordinary care of doves for their young, see Porphyry, *On Abstaining from Animal Food,* Book III; concerning the regard of the parrot-fish and lizard-fish for their kind, see Cassiodorus, [*Variae,*] XI. xl.

[6] Marcus Aurelius, Book IX [IX. xlii]: "Man was born to benefit others"; also [IX. ix]: "It would be easier to find a thing of earth out of relation with the earth than a human being wholly cut off from human kind." The same author in Book X [X. ii]: "That which has the use of reason necessarily also craves civic life."

Nicetas of Chonae [*On Isaac Angelus*, III. ix]: "Nature has ingrained in us, and implanted in our souls, a feeling for our kin." Add what Augustine says, *On Christian Doctrine*, III, xiv.

[7] Seneca, *On Benefits,* Book IV, chap. xviii: "That the warm feeling of a kindly heart is in itself desirable you may know from this, that ingratitude is something which in itself men ought to flee from, since nothing so dismembers and destroys the harmonious union of the human race as does this fault. Upon what other resource, pray tell, can we rely for safety, than mutual aid through reciprocal services? This alone it is, this interchange of kindnesses, which makes our life well equipped, and well fortified against sudden attacks.

have roughly sketched, and which is consonant with human intelligence, is the source of law properly so called. To this sphere of law belong the abstaining from that which is another's,[8] the restoration to another of anything of his which we may have, together with any gain which we may have received from it; the obligation to fulfill promises, the making good of a loss incurred through our fault, and the inflicting of penalties upon men according to their deserts.

9. From this signification of the word "law" there has flowed another and more extended meaning. Since over other animals man has the advantage of possessing not only a strong bent toward social life, of which we have spoken, but also a power of discrimination which enables him to decide what things are agreeable or harmful (as to both things present and things to come), and

---

"Imagine ourselves as isolated individuals, what are we? The prey, the victims of brute beasts—blood most cheap, and easiest to ravage; for to all other animals strength sufficient for their own protection has been given. The beasts that are born to wander and to pass segregate lives are provided with weapons; man is girt round about with weakness. Him no strength of claws or teeth makes formidable to others. To man [deity] gave two resources, reason and society; exposed as he was to danger from all other creatures, these resources rendered him the most powerful of all. Thus he who in isolation could not be the equal of any creature, is become the master of the world.

"It was society which gave to man dominion over all other living creatures; man, born for the land, society transferred to a sovereignty of a different nature, bidding him exercise dominion over the sea also. Society has checked the violence of disease, has provided succor for old age, has given comfort against sorrows. It makes us brave because it can be invoked against Fortune. Take this away and you will destroy the sense of oneness in the human race, by which life is sustained. It is, in fact, taken away, if you shall cause that an ungrateful heart is not to be avoided on its own account."

[8] Porphyry, *On Abstaining from Animal Food*, Book III [III. xxvi]: "Justice consists in the abstaining from what belongs to others, and in doing no harm to those who do no harm."

what can lead to either alternative, in such things it is meet for the nature of man, within the limitations of human intelligence, to follow the direction of a well-tempered judgment, being neither led astray by fear or the allurement of immediate pleasure, nor carried away by rash impulse. Whatever is clearly at variance with such judgment is understood to be contrary also to the law of nature, that is, to the nature of man.

10. To this exercise of judgment belongs moreover the rational allotment [9] to each man, or to each social group, of those things which are properly theirs, in such a way as to give the preference now to him who is more wise over the less wise, now to a kinsman rather than to a stranger, now to a poor man rather than to a man of means, as the conduct of each or the nature of the thing suggests. Long ago the view came to be held by many that this discriminating allotment is a part of law, properly and strictly so called; nevertheless law, properly defined, has a far different nature, because its essence lies in leaving to another that which belongs to him, or in fulfilling our obligations to him.

11. What we have been saying would have a degree of validity even if we should concede that which cannot be conceded without the utmost wickedness, that there is no God, or that the affairs of men are of no concern to him. The very opposite of this view has been implanted in us partly by reason, partly by unbroken tradition, and confirmed by many proofs as well as by miracles attested by all ages. Hence it follows that we must without exception render obedience to God as our Creator, to whom we owe all that we are and have, especially since in manifold ways he has shown himself supremely good and supremely powerful, so that to those who obey him he is able to give supremely great rewards, even rewards that are eternal, since he himself is eternal. We

[9] Ambrose treats this subject in his first book *On Duties* [I. xxx].

ought, moreover, to believe that he has willed to give rewards, and all the more should we cherish such a belief if he has so promised in plain words; that he has done this, we Christians believe, convinced by the indubitable assurance of testimonies.

12. Herein, then, is another source of law besides the source in nature, that is, the free will of God,[10] to which beyond all cavil our reason tells us we must render obedience. But the law of nature of which we have spoken, comprising alike that which relates to the social life of man and that which is so called in a larger sense, proceeding as it does from the essential traits implanted in man, can nevertheless rightly be attributed to God [11] because of his having willed that such traits exist in us. In this sense, too, Chrysippus and the Stoics used to say that the origin of law should be sought in no other source than Jupiter [12] himself; and from the name Jupiter the Latin word for law *(ius)* was probably derived.

13. There is an additional consideration in that, by means of the laws which he has given, God has made those fundamental traits more manifest, even to those who possess feebler reasoning powers; and he has forbidden us to yield to impulses drawing us in opposite

[10] Hence, in the judgment of Marcus Aurelius, Book IX [IX. i]: "He who commits injustice is guilty of impiety."

[11] Chrysostom, *On First Corinthians,* xi. 3 [Homily XXVI, iii]: "When I say nature I mean God, for He is the creator of nature." Chrysippus in his third book *On the Gods* [Plutarch, *On the Contradictions of the Stoics,* ix=Morals, 1035 C]: "No other beginning or origin of justice can be found than in Jupiter and common nature; from that source must the beginning be traced when men undertake to treat of good and evil."

[12] Unless perhaps it would be more true to say that the Latin word for "right," *ius,* is derived, by process of cutting down, from the word for "command," *iussum,* forming *ius,* genitive *iusis,* just as the word for "bone," *os,* was shortened from *ossum; iusis* afterward becoming *iuris,* as *Papirii* was formed from *Papisii,* in regard to which see Cicero, *Letters,* Book IX. xxi [*Ad Fam.* IX. xxi. 2].

directions—affecting now our own interest, now the interest of others—in an effort to control more effectively our more violent impulses and to restrain them within proper limits.

14. But sacred history, besides enjoining rules of conduct, in no slight degree reinforces man's inclination toward sociableness by teaching that all men are sprung from the same first parents. In this sense we can rightly [*Dig.* I. i. 3.] affirm also that which Florentinus asserted from another point of view, that a blood relationship has been established among us by nature; consequently it is wrong for a man to set a snare for a fellow man. Among mankind generally one's parents are as it were divinities,[13] and to them is owed an obedience which, if not unlimited, is nevertheless of an altogether special kind.

15. Again, since it is a rule of the law of nature to abide by pacts (for it was necessary that among men there be some method of obligating themselves one to another, and no other natural method can be imagined), out of this source the bodies of municipal law have arisen. For those who had associated themselves with some group, or had subjected themselves to a man or to men, had either expressly promised, or from the nature of the transaction must be understood impliedly to have promised, that they would conform to that which should have been determined, in the one case by the majority, in the other by those upon whom authority had been conferred.

16. What is said, therefore, in accordance with the view not only of Carneades but also of others, that

13 Hierocles, in his commentary on the *Golden Verse* [rather *How parents should be treated*, quoted by Stobaeus, *Anthology*, tit. lxxix. 53], calls parents "gods upon earth"; Philo, *On the Ten Commandments* [chap. xxiii], "Visible gods, who imitate the Unbegotten God in giving life." Next after the relationship between God and man comes the relationship between parent and child; Jerome, *Letters*, xcii [cxvii. 2]. Parents are the likenesses of gods; Plato, *Laws*, Book XI [XI. ii]. Honor is due to parents as to gods; Aristotle, *Nicomachean Ethics*, Book IX, chap. ii.

Expediency is, as it were, the mother
Of what is just and fair,[14]

is not true, if we wish to speak accurately. For the very
nature of man, which even if we had no lack of anything would lead us into the mutual relations of society,
is the mother of the law of nature. But the mother of
municipal law is that obligation which arises from
mutual consent; and since this obligation derives its
force from the law of nature, nature may be considered,
so to say, the great-grandmother of municipal law.

The law of nature nevertheless has the reinforcement
of expediency; for the author of nature willed that as
individuals we should be weak, and should lack many
things needed in order to live properly, to the end
that we might be the more constrained to cultivate the
social life. But expediency afforded an opportunity also
for municipal law, since that kind of association of
which we have spoken, and subjection to authority, have
their roots in expediency. From this it follows that those
who prescribe laws for others in so doing are accustomed
to have or ought to have some advantage in view.

17. But just as the laws of each state have in view
the advantage of that state, so by mutual consent it has
become possible that certain laws should originate as
between all states, or a great many states; and it is apparent that the laws thus originating had in view the advantage, not of particular states, but of the great society
of states. And this is what is called the law of nations,
whenever we distinguish that term from the law of
nature.

This division of law Carneades passed over altogether.

14 In regard to this passage Acron, or some other ancient inter-
preter of Horace [Sat. I, iii. 98]: "The poet is writing in opposition
to the teachings of the Stoics. He wishes to show that justice does
not have its origin in nature but is born of expediency." For the
opposite view see Augustine's argument, On Christian Doctrine,
Book III, chap. xiv.

For he divided all law into the law of nature and the law of particular countries. Nevertheless if undertaking to treat of the body of law which is maintained between states—for he added a statement in regard to war and things acquired by means of war—he would surely have been obliged to make mention of this law.

18. Wrongly, moreover, does Carneades ridicule justice as folly. For since, by his own admission, the national who in his own country obeys its laws is not foolish, even though, out of regard for that law he may be obliged to forego certain things advantageous for himself, so that nation is not foolish which does not press its own advantage to the point of disregarding the laws common to nations. The reason in either case is the same. For just as the national who violates the law of his country in order to obtain an immediate advantage [15] breaks down that by which the advantage of himself and his posterity are for all future time assured, so the state which transgresses the laws of nature and of nations cuts away also the bulwarks which safeguard its own future peace. Even if no advantage were to be contemplated from the keeping of the law, it would be a mark of wisdom, not of folly, to allow ourselves to be drawn toward that to which we feel that our nature leads.

19. Wherefore, in general, it is by no means true that

[Horace, Satires, I. iii. III.]

> You must confess that laws were framed
> From fear of the unjust,[16]

[15] This comparison Marcus Aurelius pertinently uses in Book IX [IX. xxiii]: "Every act of thine that has no relation, direct or indirect, to the common interest, rends thy life and does not suffer it to be one; such an act is not less productive of disintegration than he is who creates a dissension among a people." The same author, Book XI [XI. viii]: "A man cut off from a single fellow-man cannot but be considered as out of fellowship with the whole human race." In effect, as the same Antoninus says [VI. liv]: "What is advantageous to the swarm is advantageous to the bee."

[16] As Ovid says [*Metamorphoses,* VIII. 59]:
> Strong is the cause when arms the
> cause maintain.

a thought which in Plato someone explains thus, that laws were invented from fear of receiving injury, and that men are constrained by a kind of force to cultivate justice. For that relates only to the institutions and laws which have been devised to facilitate the enforcement of right, as when many persons in themselves weak, in order that they might not be overwhelmed by the more powerful, leagued themselves together to establish tribunals and by combined force to maintain these, that as a united whole they might prevail against those with whom as individuals they could not cope. [*Republic*, II. ii; *Gorgias*, xxxviii.]

And in this sense we may readily admit also the truth of the saying that right is that which is acceptable to the stronger, so that we may understand that law fails of its outward effect unless it has a sanction behind it. In this way Solon accomplished very great results, as he himself used to declare, [Plutarch, *Solon*, xv.]

> By joining force and law together,
> Under a like bond.

20. Nevertheless law, even though without a sanction, is not entirely void of effect. For justice brings peace of conscience, while injustice causes torment and anguish, such as Plato describes, in the breasts of tyrants. Justice is approved, and injustice condemned, by the common agreement of good men. But, most important of all, in God injustice finds an enemy, justice a protector. He reserves his judgments for the life after this, yet in such a way that he often causes their effects to become manifest even in this life, as history teaches by numerous examples. [*Gorgias* lxxx.]

21. Many hold, in fact, that the standard of justice which they insist upon in the case of individuals within the state is inapplicable to a nation or the ruler of a nation. The reason for the error lies in this, first of all, that in respect to law they have in view nothing except the advantage which accrues from it, such advantage

being apparent in the case of citizens who, taken singly, are powerless to protect themselves. But great states, since they seem to contain in themselves all things required for the adequate protection of life, seem not to have need of that virtue which looks toward the outside, and is called justice.

22. But, not to repeat what I have said, that law is not founded on expediency alone, there is no state so powerful that it may not at some time need the help of others outside itself, either for purposes of trade, or even to ward off the forces of many foreign nations united against it. In consequence we see that even the most powerful peoples and sovereigns seek alliances, which are quite devoid of significance according to the point of view of those who confine law within the boundaries of states. Most true is the saying that all things are uncertain the moment men depart from law.

23. If no association of men can be maintained without law, as Aristotle showed by his remarkable illustration drawn from brigands,[17] surely also that association

[Stobaeus, x. 50.]

[17] Chrysostom, *On Ephesians,* chap. iv [Homily IX, iii]: "But how does it happen, someone will say, that brigands live on terms of peace? And when? Tell me, I pray. This happens, in fact, when they are not acting as brigands; for if, in dividing up their loot, they did not observe the precepts of justice and make an equitable apportionment, you would see them engaged in strife and battles among themselves."

Plutarch [*Pyrrhus,* ix=388 A] quotes the saying of Pyrrhus, that he would leave his kingdom to that one of his children who should have the sharpest sword, declaring that this has the same implication as the verse of Euripides in the *Phoenician Maidens* [line 68]:

That they with gory steel the house divide.

He adds, moreover, the noble sentiment: "So inimical to the social order, and ruthless, is the determination to possess more than is one's own!"

Cicero, *Letters,* XI. xvi [*Ad Fam.* IX. xvi. 3]: "All things are uncertain when one departs from law." Polybius, Book IV [IV. xxix. 4]: "This above all other causes breaks up the private organizations of criminals and thieves, that they cease to deal fairly with one another; in fine, that good faith among them has perished."

which binds together the human race, or binds many nations together, has need of law; this was perceived by him who said that shameful deeds ought not to be committed even for the sake of one's country. Aristotle takes sharply to task [18] those who, while unwilling to allow anyone to exercise authority over themselves except in accordance with law, yet are quite indifferent as to whether foreigners are treated according to law or not. [Cicero, *On Duties,* I. xlv. 159.] [*Politics,* VII. ii.]

24. That same Pompey whom I just now quoted for the opposite view, corrected the statement which a king of Sparta had made, that that state is the most fortunate whose boundaries are fixed by spear and sword; he declared that that state is truly fortunate which has justice for its boundary line. On this point he might have invoked the authority of another king of Sparta who gave the preference to justice over bravery in war,[19] using this argument, that bravery ought to be directed by a kind of justice, but if all men were just they would have no need for bravery in war.

Bravery itself the Stoics defined as virtue fighting on behalf of equity. Themistius in his address to Valens argues with eloquence that kings who measure up to the rule of wisdom make account not only of the nation [x=p. 132 BC.]

18 Plutarch, *Agesilaus* [xxxvii=617 D]: "In their conception of honor the Lacedaemonians assign the first place to the advantage of their country; they neither know nor learn any other kind of right than that which they think will advance the interests of Sparta."

In regard to the same Lacedaemonians the Athenians declared, in Thucydides, Book V [V. cv]: "In relations with one another and according to their conception of civil rights they are most strict in their practice of virtue. But with respect to others, though many considerations bearing upon the subject might be brought forward, he will state the fact in a word who will say that in their view what is agreeable is honorable, what is advantageous is just."

19 Hearing that the king of the Persians was called great, Agesilaus remarked: "Wherein is he greater than I, if he is not more just?" The saying is quoted by Plutarch [*Apothegms, Agesilaus,* lxiii= *Morals,* 213 C].

which has been committed to them, but of the whole human race, and that they are, as he himself says, not "friends of the Macedonians" alone, or "friends of the Romans," [20] but "friends of mankind." The name of Minos [21] became odious to future ages for no other reason than this, that he limited his fair dealing to the boundaries of his realm.

25. Least of all should that be admitted which some people imagine, that in war all laws are in abeyance. On the contrary war ought not to be undertaken except for the enforcement of rights; when once undertaken, it should be carried on only within the bounds of law and good faith. Demosthenes well said that war is directed against those who cannot be held in check by judicial processes. For judgments are efficacious against those who feel that they are too weak to resist; against those who are equally strong, or think that they are, wars are undertaken. But in order that wars may be justified, they must be carried on with not less scrupulousness than judicial processes are wont to be.

[On the Affairs in the Chersonese, viii. 29.]

26. Let the laws be silent, then, in the midst of arms, but only the laws of the state, those that the courts are concerned with, that are adapted only to a state of peace; not those other laws, which are of perpetual validity and suited to all times. It was exceedingly well said by Dio of Prusa, that between enemies written laws, that is, laws of particular states, are not in force, but that unwritten

[Orations, lxxvi.]

20 Marcus Aurelius exceedingly well remarks [VI. xliv]: "As Antoninus, my city and country are Rome; as a man, the world." Porphyry, *On Abstaining from Animal Food,* Book III [III. xxvii]: "He who is guided by reason keeps himself blameless in relation to his fellow citizens, likewise also in relation to strangers and men in general; the more submissive to reason, the more godlike a man is."

21 In regard to Minos there is a verse of an ancient poet:
Under the yoke of Minos all the
island groaned.
On this point see Cyril, *Against Julian,* Book VI.

laws [22] are in force, that is, those which nature prescribes, or the agreement of nations has established. This is set forth by that ancient formula of the Romans: "I think that those things ought to be sought by means of a war that is blameless and righteous." [Livy, I. xxxii. 12.]

The ancient Romans, as Varro noted, were slow in undertaking war, and permitted themselves no license in that matter, because they held the view that a war ought not to be waged except when free from reproach. Camillus said that wars should be carried on justly no less than bravely; Scipio Africanus, that the Roman people commenced and ended wars justly. In another passage you may read: "War has its laws no less than peace." Still another writer admires Fabricius as a great man who maintained his probity in war—a thing most difficult —and believed that even in relation to an enemy there is such a thing as wrongdoing. [In Nonius, XII.] [Livy, V. xxvii. 6; XXX. xvi. 9.] [V. xxvii. 6.] [Seneca, Letters, cxx. 6.]

27. The historians in many a passage reveal how great in war is the influence of the consciousness that one has justice on his side; [23] they often attribute victory chiefly

[22] Thus King Alphonse, being asked whether he owed a greater debt to books or to arms, said that from books he had learned both the practice and laws of arms. Plutarch [Camillus, x=134 B]: "Among good men certain laws even of war are recognized, and a victory ought not to be striven for in such a way as not to spurn an advantage arising from wicked and impious actions."

[23] Pompey well says in Appian [Civil Wars, II. viii. 51]: "We ought to trust in the gods and in the cause of a war which has been undertaken with the honorable and just purpose of defending the institutions of our country." In the same author Cassius [Civil Wars, IV. xii. 97]: "In wars the greatest hope lies in the justice of the cause." Josephus, Antiquities of the Jews, Book XV [XV. v. 3]: "God is with those who have right on their side." Procopius has a number of passages of similar import. One is in the speech of Belisarius, after he had started on his expedition to Africa [Vandalic War, I. xii, 21]: "Bravery is not going to give the victory, unless it has justice as a fellow-soldier." Another is in the speech of the same general before the battle not far from Carthage [I. xii. 19]. A third is in the address of the Lombards to the Herulians, where the following words, as corrected by me, are

to this cause. Hence the proverbs that a soldier's strength is broken or increased by his cause; that he who has taken up arms unjustly rarely comes back in safety; that hope is the comrade of a good cause; and others of the same purport.

No one ought to be disturbed, furthermore, by the successful outcome of unjust enterprises. For it is enough that the fairness of the cause exerts a certain influence, even a strong influence upon actions, although the effect of that influence, as happens in human affairs, is often nullified by the interference of other causes. Even for winning friendships, of which for many reasons nations as well as individuals have need, a reputation for having undertaken war not rashly nor unjustly, and of having waged it in a manner above reproach, is exceedingly efficacious. No one readily allies himself with those in

---

found [*Gothic War*, II. xiv]: "We call to witness God, the slightest manifestation of whose power is equal to all human strength. He, as may well be believed, making account of the causes of war, will give to each side the outcome of battle which each deserves." This saying was soon afterward confirmed by a wonderful occurrence.

In the same author Totila thus addresses the Goths [*Gothic War*, III, viii]: "It cannot, it cannot happen, I say, that they who resort to violence and injustice can win renown in fighting; but as the life of each is, such the fortune of war that falls to his lot." Soon after the taking of Rome Totila made another speech bearing on the same point [*Gothic War*, III. xxi].

Agathias, Book II [*Histories*, II. i]: "Injustice and forgetfulness of God are to be shunned always, and are harmful, above all, in war and in time of battle." This statement he elsewhere proves by the notable illustrations of Darius, Xerxes, and the Athenians in Sicily [*Histories*, II. x]. See also the speech of Crispinus to the people of Aquileia, in Herodian, Book VIII [*Histories*, VIII. iii. 5, 6].

In Thucydides, Book VII [VII. xviii], we find the Lacedaemonians reckoning the disasters which they had suffered in Pylus and elsewhere as due to themselves, because they had refused a settlement by arbitration which had been offered them. But as afterward the Athenians, having committed many wicked deeds, refused arbitration, a hope of greater success in their operations revived in the Lacedaemonians.

whom he believes that there is only a slight regard for law, for the right, and for good faith.

28. Fully convinced, by the considerations which I have advanced, that there is a common law among nations, which is valid alike for war and in war, I have had many and weighty reasons for undertaking to write upon this subject. Throughout the Christian world I observed a lack of restraint in relation to war, such as even barbarous races should be ashamed of; I observed that men rush to arms for slight causes, or no cause at all, and that when arms have once been taken up there is no longer any respect for law, divine or human; it is as if, in accordance with a general decree, frenzy had openly been let loose for the committing of all crimes.

29. Confronted with such utter ruthlessness, many men who are the very furthest from being bad men, have come to the point of forbidding all use of arms to the Christian,[24] whose rule of conduct above everything else comprises the duty of loving all men. To this opinion sometimes John Ferus and my fellow countryman Erasmus seem to incline, men who have the utmost devotion to peace in both Church and State; but their purpose, as I take it, is, when things have gone in one direction, to force them in the opposite direction, as we are accustomed to do, that they may come back to a true middle ground. But the very effort of pressing too hard in the opposite direction is often so far from being helpful that it does harm, because in such arguments the detection of what is extreme is easy, and results in weakening the influence of other statements which are well within the bounds of truth. For both extremes therefore a remedy must be found, that men may not believe either that nothing is allowable, or that everything is.

30. At the same time through devotion to study in

[Johann Wild]

[24] Tertullian, *On the Resurrection of the Flesh* [chap. xvi]: "The sword which has become bloodstained honorably in war, and has thus been employed in man-killing of a better sort."

private life I have wished—as the only course now open to me, undeservedly forced out from my native land, which had been graced by so many of my labors—to contribute somewhat to the philosophy of the law, which previously, in public service, I practiced with the utmost degree of probity of which I was capable. Many heretofore have purposed to give to this subject a well-ordered presentation; no one has succeeded. And in fact such a result cannot be accomplished unless—a point which until now has not been sufficiently kept in view—those elements which come from positive law are properly separated from those which arise from nature. For the principles of the law of nature, since they are always the same, can easily be brought into a systematic form; but the elements of positive law, since they often undergo change and are different in different places, are outside the domain of systematic treatment, just as other notions of particular things are.

31. If now those who have consecrated themselves to true justice should undertake to treat the parts of the natural and unchangeable philosophy of law, after having removed all that has its origin in the free will of man; if one, for example, should treat legislation, another taxation, another the administration of justice, another the determination of motives, another the proving of facts, then by assembling all these parts a body of jurisprudence could be made up.

32. What procedure we think should be followed we have shown by deed rather than by words in this work, which treats by far the noblest part of jurisprudence.

33. In the first book, having by way of introduction spoken of the origin of law, we have examined the general question, whether there is any such thing as a just war; then, in order to determine the differences between public war and private war, we found it necessary to explain the nature of sovereignty—what nations, what kings possess complete sovereignty; who possesses sovereignty

only in part, who with right of alienation, who otherwise; then it was necessary to speak also concerning the duty of subjects to their superiors.

34. The second book, having for its object to set forth all the causes from which war can arise, undertakes to explain fully what things are held in common, what may be owned in severalty; what rights persons have over persons, what obligation arises from ownership; what is the rule governing royal successions; what right is established by a pact or a contract; what is the force of treaties of alliance; what of an oath private or public, and how it is necessary to interpret these; what is due in reparation for damage done; in what the inviolability of ambassadors consists; what law controls the burial of the dead, and what is the nature of punishments.

35. The third book has for its subject, first, what is permissible in war. Having distinguished that which is done with impunity, or even that which among foreign peoples is defended as lawful, from that which actually is free from fault, it proceeds to the different kinds of peace, and all compacts relating to war.

36. The undertaking seemed to me all the more worth while because, as I have said, no one has dealt with the subject matter as a whole, and those who have treated portions of it have done so in a way to leave much to the labors of others. Of the ancient philosophers nothing in this field remains, either of the Greeks among whom Aristotle had composed a book with the title *Rights of War,* or, what was especially to be desired, of those who gave their allegiance to the young Christianity. Even the books of the ancient Romans on fetial law have transmitted to us nothing of themselves except the title. Those who have made collections of the cases which are called "cases of conscience" have merely written chapters on war, promises, oaths, and reprisals, just as on other subjects.

37. I have seen also special books on the law of war,

some by theologians, as Franciscus de Victoria, Henry of Gorkum, William Matthaei; [25] others by doctors of law, as John Lupus, Franciscus Arias, Giovanni da Legnano, Martinus Laudensis. All of these, however, have said next to nothing upon a most fertile subject; most of them have done their work without system, and in such a way as to intermingle and utterly confuse what belongs to the law of nature, to divine law, to the law of nations, to civil law, and to the body of law which is found in the canons.

38. What all these writers especially lacked, the illumination of history, the very learned Faur undertook to supply in some chapters of his *Semestria,* but in a manner limited by the scope of his own work, and only through the citation of authorities. The same thing was attempted on a larger scale, and by referring a great number of examples to some general statements, by Balthazar Ayala, and still more fully, by Alberico Gentili. Knowing that others can derive profit from Gentili's painstaking work, as I acknowledge that I have, I leave it to his readers to pass judgment on the shortcomings of his work as regards method of exposition, arrangement of matter, delimitation of inquiries, and distinctions between the various kinds of law. This only I shall say, that in treating controversial questions it is his frequent practice to base his conclusions on a few examples, which are not in all cases worthy of approval, or even to follow the opinions of modern jurists, formulated in arguments of which not a few were accommodated to the special interests of clients, not to the nature of that which is equitable and upright.

The causes which determine the characterization of a war as lawful or unlawful Ayala did not touch upon. Gentili outlined certain general classes, in the manner which seemed to him best, but he did not so much as

25 To these add the work of Joannes de Carthagena, published at Rome in 1609.

refer to many topics which have come up in notable and frequent controversies.

39. We have taken all pains that nothing of this sort escape us; and we have also indicated the sources from which conclusions are drawn, whence it would be an easy matter to verify them, even if any point has been omitted by us. It remains to explain briefly with what helps, and with what care, I have attacked this task.

First of all, I have made it my concern to refer the proofs of things touching the law of nature to certain fundamental conceptions which are beyond question, so that no one can deny them without doing violence to himself. For the principles of that law, if only you pay strict heed to them, are in themselves manifest and clear, almost as evident as are those things which we perceive by the external senses; and the senses do not err if the organs of perception are properly formed and if the other conditions requisite to perception are present. Thus in his *Phoenician Maidens* Euripides represents Poly- [494-6] nices, whose cause he makes out to have been manifestly just, as speaking thus:

> Mother, these words, that I have uttered, are not
> Inwrapped with indirection, but, firmly based
> On rules of justice and of good, are plain
> Alike to simple and to wise.[26]

The poet adds immediately a judgment of the chorus, made up of women, and barbarian women at that, approving these words.

40. In order to prove the existence of this law of nature, I have, furthermore, availed myself of the testi-

---

[26] The same Euripides represents Hermione as saying to Andromache [*Andromache*, 243]:
> Not under laws barbaric do men live
> In this our city;
and Andromache as answering [*ibid.*, 244]:
> What there is base, here too not blameless is.

mony of philosophers,[27] historians, poets; finally also of orators. Not that confidence is to be reposed in them without discrimination, for they were accustomed to serve the interests of their sect, their subject, or their cause. But when many at different times and in different places affirm the same thing as certain, that ought to be referred to a universal cause; and this cause, in the lines of inquiry which we are following, must be either a correct conclusion drawn from the principles of nature, or common consent. The former points to the law of nature, the latter to the law of nations.

The distinction between these kinds of law is not to be drawn from the testimonies themselves (for writers everywhere confuse the terms law of nature and law of nations), but from the character of the matter. For whatever cannot be deduced from certain principles by a sure process of reasoning, and yet is clearly observed everywhere, must have its origin in the free will of man.

41. These two kinds of law, therefore, I have always particularly sought to distinguish from each other and from municipal law. Furthermore, in the law of nations I have distinguished between that which is truly and in all respects law, and that which produces merely a kind of outward effect simulating that primitive law, as, for example, the prohibition to resist by force, or even the duty of defense in any place by public force, in order to secure some advantage, or for the avoidance of serious disadvantages. How necessary it is, in many cases, to observe this distinction, will become apparent in the course of our work.

With not less pains we have separated those things which are strictly and properly legal, out of which the obligation of restitution arises, from those things which

27 Why should not one avail himself of the testimony of the philosophers, when Alexander Severus constantly read Cicero *On the Commonwealth* and *On Duties?* [Lampridius, *Alexander Severus,* xxx. 2.]

37

are called legal because any other classification of them conflicts with some other stated rule of right reason. In regard to this distinction of law we have already said something above.

42. Among the philosophers Aristotle deservedly holds the foremost place, whether you take into account his order of treatment, or the subtlety of his distinctions, or the weight of his reasons. Would that this pre-eminence had not, for some centuries back, been turned into a tyranny, so that truth, to whom Aristotle devoted faithful service, was by no instrumentality more repressed than by Aristotle's name!

For my part, both here and elsewhere I avail myself of the liberty of the early Christians, who had sworn allegiance to the sect of no one of the philosophers, not because they were in agreement with those who said that nothing can be known—than which nothing is more foolish—but because they thought that there was no philosophic sect whose vision had compassed all truth, and none which had not perceived some aspect of truth. Thus they believed that to gather up into a whole the truth which was scattered among the different philosophers [28] and dispersed among the sects, was in reality

[28] The words are those of Lactantius, *Divine Institutes,* Book VI, chap. ix [VII. vii. 4].

Justin, *First Apology* [*Second Apology,* chap. xiii]: "Not because the teachings of Plato are altogether different from the teachings of Christ, but because they do not completely harmonize, as the teachings of others do not—for example, those of the Stoics, the poets, and the writers of history. For each one of these spoke rightly in part, in accordance with the reason which had been implanted in him, perceiving what was consistent therewith."

Tertullian [*On the Soul,* xx]: "Seneca often on our side"; but the same writer also warns us [*An Answer to the Jews,* ix] that the entire body of spiritual teachings was to be found in no man save Christ alone.

Augustine, *Letters,* ccii. [xci. 3]: "The rules of conduct which Cicero and other philosophers recommend are being taught and learned in the churches that are increasing all over the world."

to establish a body of teaching truly Christian.

43. Among other things—to mention in passing a point not foreign to my subject—it seems to me that not without reason some of the Platonists and early Christians [29] departed from the teachings of Aristotle in this, that he considered the very nature of virtue as a mean in passions and actions. That principle, once adopted, led him to unite distinct virtues, as generosity and frugality, into one; to assign to truth extremes between which, on any fair premise, there is no possible co-ordination, boastfulness, and dissimulation; and to apply the designation of vice to certain things which either do not exist, or are not in themselves vices, such as contempt for pleasure and for honor, and freedom from anger against men.

44. That this basic principle, when broadly stated, is unsound, becomes clear even from the case of justice. For, being unable to find in passions and acts resulting therefrom the too much and the too little opposed to that virtue, Aristotle sought each extreme in the things themselves with which justice is concerned. Now in the first place this is simply to leap from one class of things over into another class, a fault which he rightly censures in others; then, for a person to accept less than belongs to him may in fact under unusual conditions constitute a fault, in view of that which, according to the circumstances, he owes to himself and to those dependent on him; but in any case the act cannot be at variance with

---

On this point, if time is available, consult the same Augustine in regard to the Platonists, who, he says, with changes in regard to a few matters can be Christians; *Letters,* lvi [cxviii. 21]; *On the True Religion,* chap. iii, and *Confessions,* Book VII, chap. ix, and Book VIII, chap. ii.

29 Lactantius treats this subject at length in the *Institutes,* VI. xv, xvi, xvii. Says Cassiodorus [Peter of Blois, *On Friendship,* chap. *Quod affectus sine consensu non multum prosit vel obsit*]: "It is advantageous or harmful to be moved not by feelings, but in accordance with feelings."

39

justice, the essence of which lies in abstaining from that which belongs to another.

By equally faulty reasoning Aristotle tries to make out that adultery committed in a burst of passion, or a murder due to anger, is not properly an injustice. Whereas, nevertheless, injustice has no other essential quality than the unlawful seizure of that which belongs to another; and it does not matter whether injustice arises from avarice, from lust, from anger, or from ill-advised compassion, or from an overmastering desire to achieve eminence, out of which instances of the gravest injustice constantly arise. For to disparage such incitements, with the sole purpose in view that human society may not receive injury, is in truth the concern of justice.

45. To return to the point whence I started, the truth is that some virtues do tend to keep passions under control, but that is not because such control is a proper and essential characteristic of every virtue. Rather it is because right reason, which virtue everywhere follows, in some things prescribes the pursuing of a middle course,[30] in others stimulates to the utmost degree. We cannot, for example, worship God too much, for superstition errs not by worshiping God too much, but by worshiping in a perverse way. Neither can we too much seek after the blessings that shall abide forever, nor fear too much the everlasting evils, nor have too great hatred for sin.

With truth therefore was it said by Aulus Gellius, [IV. ix. 14.] that there are some things of which the extent is limited

---

[30] Agathias, Book V, in a speech of Belisarius [*Histories*, V. xviii]: "Of the emotions of the soul those ought in every case to be seized in which there is found, pure and unmixed, an impulse in harmony with the requirements of duty and worthy to be chosen. Those emotions, however, which have a trend and inclination toward evil, are not to be utilized in all cases, but only so far as they contribute to our advantage. That good judgment is a blessing pure and unmixed no one would deny. In anger the element of energy is praiseworthy, but what exceeds the proper limit is to be avoided, as involving disadvantage."

by no boundaries—the greater, the more ample they are, the more excellent. Lactantius, having discussed the passions at great length, says:

[*Divine Institutes,* VI. xvi. 7.] "The method of wisdom consists in controlling not the passions, but their causes, since they are stirred from without. And putting a check upon the passions themselves ought not to be the chief concern, because they may be feeble in the greatest crime, and very violent without leading to crime."

Our purpose is to make much account of Aristotle, but reserving in regard to him the same liberty which he, in his devotion to truth, allowed himself with respect to his teachers.

46. History in relation to our subject is useful in two ways: it supplies both illustrations and judgments. The illustrations have greater weight in proportion as they are taken from better times and better peoples. Thus we have preferred ancient examples, Greek and Roman, to the rest. And judgments are not to be slighted, especially when they are in agreement with one another; for by such statements the existence of the law of nature, as we have said, is in a measure proved, and by no other means, in fact, is it possible to establish the law of nations.

47. The views of poets and of orators do not have so great weight, and we make frequent use of them not so much for the purpose of gaining acceptance by that means for our argument, as of adding from their words some embellishment to that which we wished to say.

48. I frequently appeal to the authority of the books which men inspired by God have either written or approved, nevertheless with a distinction between the Old Testament and the New. There are some who urge that the Old Testament sets forth the law of nature. Without doubt they are in error, for many of its rules come from the free will of God. And yet this is never in conflict with the true law of nature; and up to this point the

Old Testament can be used as a source of the law of nature, provided we carefully distinguish between the law of God, which God sometimes executes through men, and the law of men in their relations with one another.

This error we have, so far as possible, avoided, and also another opposed to it, which supposes that after the coming of the New Testament the Old Testament in this respect was no longer of use. We believe the contrary, partly for the reasons which we have already given, partly because the character of the New Testament is such that in its teachings respecting the moral virtues it enjoins the same as the Old Testament or even enjoins greater precepts. In this way we see that the early Christian writers used the witnesses of the Old Testament.

49. The Hebrew writers,[31] moreover, most of all those who have thoroughly understood the speech and customs of their people, are able to contribute not a little to our understanding of the thought of the books which belong to the Old Testament.

50. The New Testament I use in order to explain—and this cannot be learned from any other source—what is permissible to Christians. This, however, contrary to the practice of most men, I have distinguished from the law of nature, considering it as certain that in that most holy law a greater degree of moral perfection is enjoined upon us than the law of nature, alone and by itself, would require. And nevertheless I have not omitted to note the things that are recommended to us rather than enjoined, that we may know that, while the turning aside from what has been enjoined is wrong and involves the risk of punishment, a striving for the highest excellence implies a noble purpose and will not fail of its reward.

51. The authentic synodical canons are collections embodying the general principles of divine law as applied

31 This was perceived by Cassian [Cassiodorus] as shown by his *Institute of Holy Writ* [Preface].

to cases which come up. They either show what the divine law enjoins, or urge us to that which God would fain persuade. And this truly is the mission of the Christian Church, to transmit those things which were transmitted to it by God, and in the way in which they were transmitted.

Furthermore, customs which were current or were considered praiseworthy among the early Christians and those who rose to the measure of so great a name, deservedly have the force of canons.

Next after these comes the authority of those who, each in his own time, have been distinguished among Christians for their piety and learning, and have not been charged with any serious error. For what these declare with great positiveness, and as if definitely ascertained, ought to have no slight weight for the interpretation of passages in Holy Writ which seem obscure. Their authority is the greater the more there are of them in agreement, and as we approach nearer to the times of pristine purity, when neither desire for domination nor any conspiracy of interests had as yet been able to corrupt the primitive truth.

52. The Schoolmen, who succeeded these writers, often show how strong they are in natural ability. But their lot was cast in an unhappy age, which was ignorant of the liberal arts; wherefore it is less to be wondered at if among many things worthy of praise there are also some things which we should receive with indulgence. Nevertheless, when the Schoolmen agree on a point of morals, it rarely happens that they are wrong, since they are especially keen in seeing what may be open to criticism in the statements of others. And yet in the very ardor of their defense of themselves against opposing views, they furnish a praiseworthy example of moderation; they contend with one another by means of arguments, not, in accordance with the practice which has

lately begun to disgrace the calling of letters, with personal abuse, base offspring of a spirit lacking self-mastery.

53. Of those who profess knowledge of the Roman law there are three classes.

The first consists of those whose work appears in the Pandects, the Codes of Theodosius and Justinian, and the Imperial Constitutions called Novellae.

To the second class belong the successors of Irnerius, that is Accursius, Bartolus, and so many other names of those who long ruled the bar.

The third class comprises those who have combined the study of classical literature with that of law.

To the first class I attribute great weight. For they frequently give the very best reasons in order to establish what belongs to the law of nature, and they often furnish evidence in favor of this law and of the law of nations. Nevertheless they, no less than the others, often confuse these terms, frequently calling that the law of nations which is only the law of certain peoples, and that, too, not as established by assent, but perchance taken over through imitation of others or by pure accident. But those provisions which really belong to the law of nations they often treat, without distinction or discrimination, along with those which belong to the Roman law, as may be seen by reference to the title *On Captives and Postliminy*. We have therefore endeavored to distinguish these two types from each other.

54. The second class, paying no heed to the divine law or to ancient history, sought to adjust all controversies of kings and peoples by application of the laws of the Romans, with occasional use of the canons. But in the case of these men also the unfortunate condition of their times was frequently a handicap which prevented their complete understanding of those laws, though, for the rest, they were skillful enough in tracing out the

nature of that which is fair and good. The result is that while they are often very successful in establishing the basis of law, they are at the same time bad interpreters of existing law. But they are to be listened to with the utmost attention when they bear witness to the existence of the usage which constitutes the law of nations in our day.

55. The masters of the third class, who confine themselves within the limits of the Roman law and deal either not at all, or only slightly, with the common law of nations, are of hardly any use in relation to our subject. They combine the subtlety of the Schoolmen with a knowledge of laws and of canons, and in fact two of them, the Spaniards Covarruvias and Vásquez, did not refrain from treating the controversies of peoples and kings, the latter with great freedom, the former with more restraint and not without precision of judgment.

The French have tried rather to introduce history into their study of laws. Among them Bodin and Hotman have gained a great name, the former by an extensive treatise, the latter by separate questions. Their statements and lines of reasoning will frequently supply us with material in searching out the truth.

56. In my work as a whole I have, above all else, aimed at three things: to make the reasons for my conclusions as evident as possible; to set forth in a definite order the matters which needed to be treated; and to distinguish clearly between things which seemed to be the same and were not.

57. I have refrained from discussing topics which belong to another subject, such as those that teach what may be advantageous in practice. For such topics have their own special field, that of politics, which Aristotle rightly treats by itself, without introducing extraneous matter into it. Bodin, on the contrary, mixed up politics with the body of law with which we are concerned. In

some places nevertheless I have made mention of that which is expedient, but only in passing, and in order to distinguish it more clearly from what is lawful.

58. If anyone thinks that I have had in view any controversies of our own times, either those that have arisen or those which can be foreseen as likely to arise, he will do me an injustice. With all truthfulness I aver that, just as mathematicians treat their figures as abstracted from bodies, so in treating law I have withdrawn my mind from every particular fact.

59. As regards manner of expression, I wished not to disgust the reader, whose interests I continually had in mind, by adding prolixity of words to the multiplicity of matters needing to be treated. I have therefore followed, so far as I could, a mode of speaking at the same time concise and suitable for exposition, in order that those who deal with public affairs may have, as it were, in a single view both the kinds of controversies which are wont to arise and the principles by reference to which they may be decided. These points being known, it will be easy to adapt one's argument to the matter at issue, and expand it at one's pleasure.

60. I have now and then quoted the very words of ancient writers, where they seemed to carry weight or to have unusual charm of expression. This I have occasionally done even in the case of Greek writers, but as a rule only when the passage was brief, or such that I dared not hope that I could bring out the beauty of it in a Latin version. Nevertheless in all cases I have added a Latin translation for the convenience of those who have not learned Greek.[32]

61. I beg and adjure all those into whose hands this work shall come, that they assume toward me the same liberty which I have assumed in passing upon the opin-

[32] [The English translation, of course, follows Grotius' Latin version, which sometimes differs from the original Greek.]

ions and writings of others. They who shall find me in error will not be more quick to advise me than I to avail myself of their advice.

And now if anything has here been said by me inconsistent with piety, with good morals, with Holy Writ, with the concord of the Christian Church, or with any aspect of truth, let it be as if unsaid.

Emeric de Vattel of Neuchatel, Switzerland, drawing to some extent on the works of such pioneers as Grotius, Puffendorf, and the Baron de Wolf, published the first edition of his *Law of Nations* in 1758. It had an almost immediate and widespread impact. It is probably the most cited work on international law in the United States as well as in Great Britain. The editor of an 1833 English edition, upon which the following excerpts are based, stated, "Everyone who has attentively read this work will admit that he has acquired a knowledge of superior sentiments, and more important information than he ever derived from any other work."

THE

LAW OF NATIONS.

PRELIMINARIES.

IDEA AND GENERAL PRINCIPLES OF THE LAW OF NATIONS.

§ 1. NATIONS or states are bodies politic, societies of men united together for the purpose of promoting their mutual safety and advantage by the joint efforts of their combined strength.

§ 2. Such a society has her affairs and her interests ; she deliberates and takes resolutions in common ; thus becoming a moral person, who possesses an understanding and a will peculiar to herself, and is susceptible of *obligations* and *rights*.

§ 3. To establish on a solid foundation the *obligations* and *rights* of *nations*, is the design of this work.

The *Law of Nations is the science which teaches the rights subsist-*

49

ing between nations or states, and the obligations correspondent to those rights (1) (*a*).

---

(1) The Law of Nations modifies the intercourse of independent commonwealths in *peace*, and prescribes limits to their hostilities in *war*. It prescribes, that in peace nations should do each other *as much good*, and in time of war *as little harm* as may be possible without injuring their own proper real interests. The law of nations, in short, establish that principle and rule of conduct which should prevent the *strongest* nation from abusing its power, and induce it to act justly and generously towards other states, upon the broad principle, that true happiness, whether of a single individual or of several, can only result from each adopting conduct influenced by a sincere desire to increase the general welfare of all mankind. (*Post*, § 13, 14; Mackintosh, Dis. 3, 4; Montesc. de l'Esprit des Lois liv. 1, c. 3; and see 1 Bla. Com. 34 to 44; 4 Bla. Com. 66, 67.) In cases of doubt arising upon what is the Law of Nations, it is now an admitted rule amongst all European nations, that our common religion, *Christianity*, pointing out the principles of *natural justice should* be equally appealed to and observed by all as an unfailing rule of construction. (2 Ward's Law of Nations, pp. 11, 339, 340). The difficulty is, that there is *no general modern international code* framed by the consent of the European powers, so desirable to be fixed, especially at this period, when harmony happily appears to subsist, and most of the nations of Europe have, by recent experience, become practically convinced of the advantages that would result from the establishment of fixed *general rules*, so as to reconcile the frequent discordancy of the decisions of their various prize tribunals and upon other contests. The statesmen of the higher powers of Europe would immortalize themselves by introducing such a code, and no period of history for the purpose has been so favorable and opportune. See Atcheson's Report of the case of *Havelock* v. *Rockwood*, Preface i.)

The law of nations is adopted in Great Britain in its full and most liberal extent by the common law, and is held to be part of the law of the land; and all statutes relating to foreign affairs should be framed with reference to that rule. (4 Bla. Com 67). But still there is no general code; and to the regret that none has been introduced,

may be also added, the want of an *international court or tribunal*, to decide upon and enforce the law of nations when disputed; and consequently, although when states are temperately inclined to ascertain and be governed by the *law of nations*, there will be little doubt upon the decision, or of the adoption of measures the most just; yet, if a state will not listen to the immutable principles of *reason*, upon the basis of which the *imperfect* law of nations is founded, then the only remedy is to appeal to arms; and hence frequently the just cause of war, which, if there were a fixed code, with a proper tribunal to construe it, would in general be prevented.

The *sources* from whence are to be gathered information—*what is the positive Law of Nations generally and permanently binding upon all independent states?* are acknowledged to be of three descriptions : *First, the long and ordinary* PRACTICE *of nations*, which affords evidence of a general custom, tacitly agreed to be observed until expressly abrogated. *Secondly*, the RECITALS of what is acknowledged to have been the law or practice of nations, and which recitals will frequently be found in modern treaties. *Thirdly*, the WRITINGS of *eminent authors*, who have long, as it were by a concurrence of testimony and opinion, declared what is the existing international jurisprudence.

Thus Lord *Mansfield*, in *Triquet* v. *Bath*, (3 Burr. Rep. 1481), stated as the declaration of Lord *Talbot*, that the law of nations is to be collected from the *practice of different nations*, (and see *per* Sir *William Scott* in *Flad* v. *Oyen*, 1 Rob. Rep. 115, *post*, lxiii. n. (7),) and the authority of *writers*, such as Grotius, Barbeyrac, Binkershoek, Wiquefort, &c., there being no English writer of eminence upon the subject; and English elementary writers of high authority have also acknowledged that such *foreign* authors are authorities to ascertain the law of nations. (Comyn's Digest, tit. " Ambassador," B.; Viner's Ab. " Merchant," A. 1; and 3 Bla. Com. 273). To these are to be added, Puffendorf, Wolf, Seldon, Valin, Clerac, Pothier, Barlamaque, Emerigon, Roccus, Casegis, Loecenius, Santurna, Maline, Molloy, and above all, the present work of *Vattel;* to which may be added some modern works of great

---

N. B. The notes numbered as 1, 2, 3, 4, &c and in general concluding with C., are by the present editor.

(*a*) ⟨ See 1 Kent's Com. Am. Law, Lecture 1st. ⟩

In this treatise it will appear, in what manner *States*, as such, *ought* to regulate all their actions. We shall examine the *Obligations* of

ability, but not yet acknowledged to be such high *general* authority as the former, viz. Ward's and Marten's Law of Nations, and the recent valuable French publication, Cours de Droit Public Interne et externé, par le Commandeur Silvestre Pinheiro Ferreira, Ministre D'Etat au Paris, A. D. 1830, which embraces the French modern view of the law of nations, upon most of the subjects discussed in Vattel and some others. It was from the more ancient of these several authors, and other similar resources, that Lord Mansfield framed the celebrated letter of the Duke of Newcastle to the King of Prussia's Secretary, which is considered a standard authority upon the law of nations, as far as respects the then disputed right to search for and seize enemies' property on board neutral ships in certain cases in time of war; see Holiday's Life of Lord Mansfield, vol. ii. p. 424, &c., and Collectanea Juridica, 1 Vol. 129; see also *Viveash* v. *Becker*, 3 Maule & Selwyn, 284, in which Lord Ellenborough quotes several of the above authors, to ascertain the law of nations upon the privilege of consuls).

Upon some *parts* of the law of nations, especially that relative to *maritime affairs*, there are *ancient codes*, which either originated in authority, or were afterwards acknowledged to have become such; but still those codes in the present state of commercial intercourse are imperfect. Of those are the *Rhodian Laws*, being one of the earliest systems of marine law, but which was superseded by the collection intitled *Consolato del Mare*, Grotius, Book 3, ch. 1, s. 5, n. 6. Next in order are the *Laws of Oleron*, promulgated about the 13th century. Another system of international law was framed by the deputies of the *Hanseatic League* in 1597, and which was confirmed with additions in 1614, and has obtained much consideration in the maritime jurisprudence of nations. (See remarks on that code, 2 Ward's Law of nations, 276 to 290.) But the most complete and comprehensive system of the *marine* law of nations is the celebrated *Ordinance of Marine* of Lewis XIV., published in 1681, and which, coupled with the commentary of Valin, Lord Mansfield always treated as of the highest authority. (See 1 Marshal on Insurance, Prelim. Dis. 18.)

In modern times, in order to prevent any dispute upon the existence or application of the general law of nations, either pending peace, or at or after the subsequently breaking out of war between two or more independent states, it has become the prac-

tice to enter into *express treaties*, carefully providing for every contingency, and especially modifying and softening the injurious consequences of sudden war upon the commercial and other intercourse between the two states, and sometimes even wholly changing the character of war or of alienage, and even enabling a foreign alien enemy during war to retain his interest in land in the opponent country. (See an illustrating instanee in *Sutton* v. *Sutton*, 1 Russ. & My. Rep. 663.) In these cases, the treaty between the two contracting states, either alters or expressly *declares* the law of nations and binds each. But still questions upon the *general* law of nations will frequently arise, and it will then become necessary to recur to the other evidence of what is the law of nations, viz. the previous ordinary and general or particular practice, or the opinion of the authors before alluded to.

In the latter part of the last, and in the present century, a great accession of learning, information, and authority upon the law of nations has been afforded by the valuable decisions of Sir W. Scott (afterwards Lord Stowell), and of Sir J. Nicholl in the Court of Admiralty and Prize Court, and by several decisions in our Courts of Law and Equity. The known learning and scrupulous justice evinced in those decisions, have commanded the respect, the admiration and adoption, of all the European states, and of that modern, enlightened and energetic nation, America. To these may be added, Chalmer's Collection of Opinions, which contain great learning upon many subjects of the public affairs of nations. These have been fully published since Vattel wrote; and the editor has attempted to improve this edition, by occasionally referring in the notes to the reports and work alluded to. The editor has also in his Treatise on Commercial Law, and in a Summary of the Law of Nations, endeavoured to take a modern and more extended view of some of those branches of the law of nations, principally as it affects foreign commerce, and of the decisions and works subsequent to the publication of Vattel.

If the *perfect general rights* or *law* of nations be violated, then it appears to be conceded, that such violation may be the actual and avowed ground of a *just* war; and it is even laid down that it is the duty of every nation to chastise the nation guilty of the aggression. (Vattel, *post*, Book I. chap. xxiii. § 283, p. 126; Book II. chap. ii. § 24, p. 144; § 65, 66, 67, p. 160, 161.

a people, as well towards themselves as towards other nations; and by that means we shall discover the *Rights* which result from those obligations. For, the *right* being nothing more than the power of doing what is morally possible, that is to say, what is proper and consistent with *duty*,—it is evident that *right* is derived from *duty*, or passive obligation,—the obligation we lie under to act in such or such manner. It is therefore *necessary that a Nation should acquire a knowledge of the *obligations* incumbent on her, in order that she may not only avoid all violation of her *duty*, but also be able distinctly to ascertain her *rights*, or what she may lawfully require from other nations.

§ 4. Nations being composed of men naturally free and independent, and who, before the establishment of civil societies, lived together in the state of nature,—*Nations*, or sovereign states, are to be considered as so many free persons living together in the state of nature.

It is a settled point with writers on the *natural* law, that all men

---

Unhappily especially in modern times, we have found that the law of nations has sometimes been set at naught by over-powerful states, adhering (to use the words of an English monarch) rather to *Cannon Law* than stepping to inquire whether the law of nature and of justice had not become, and been declared in that instance, part of the law of nations. It may therefore be asked, of what utility is the law of nations, since it is of such imperfect and inefficient obligation? The answer is, that all nations, although for a time astounded and surprised by the unexpected aggression of an oppressive and ambitious conqueror, will yet ultimately feel, and endeavor to give effect to, the true law of nations, lest, by suffering its continued violations, they may individually be sacrificed; and consequently, as in the instance alluded to, they will ultimately coalesce and associate in one common cause, to humiliate and overcome the proud invador of all just rights and principles. It is therefore of the highest importance to collect all the principles and rules, which, in cases of doubt, must ever be consulted, at least by statesmen, in endeavoring to settle differences between differing states; and no authority stands higher in this respect than Vattel.

There is no *permanent and general international court*, and it will be found, that in general the sovereign, or government of each state, who has the power of declaring war and peace, has also, as an incident, the sole power of deciding upon questions of booty, capture, prize, and hostile seizure, though sometimes that power is delegated, as in Great Britain, as respects maritime seizures, by commission to the judge of the Admiralty Court, with

an appeal from his decision to the Privy Council. In these cases no other municipal court has cognizance in case of any hostile seizure. *Elphinston* v. *Bedreechund*, Knapp's Rep. 316 to 361; and *Hill* v. *Reardon*, 2 Russ. Rep. 608, and further, *post*, p. 392. So there is no general international court in which a treaty can be directly enforced, although, collaterally, its meaning may be discussed in a municipal court; therefore, no bill to enforce a treaty can be sustained in equity. *Nabob of Carnatic* v. *East India Company*, 2 Ves. jun. 56; and *Hill* v. *Reardon*, 2 Sim. & Stu. 437; 2 Russ. Rep. 608.

Sometimes, however, especially in modern times, *treaties*, confirmed by temporary statutes in each country, appoint a *temporary international court*, with limited powers to decide upon certain claims, and to be satisfied out of an appointed public fund. Thus, in the treaty of peace between Great Britain and France, and by the 59 G. 3, c. 31, certain commissioners were appointed to carry into effect the conventions for liquidating the claims of British subjects on the French government, with an appeal to the Privy Council. In these cases the appointed jurisdiction is exclusive, and no other municipal court has any power as regards the adjustment of the claims between the two subjects of each country; though, as between private individuals, if any claimant stand in the situation of an agent or trustee, then, in a court of equity, he may be compelled to act as a trustee of the sum awarded to him. *Hill* v. *Reardon*, Jac. Rep. 84; 2 Russ. Rep. 608 to 633, over-ruling the Vice-Chancellor's decision in 2 Sim. & Stu. 437.—C.

---

inherit from *nature* a perfect *liberty* and *independence*, of which they cannot be deprived without their own consent. In a State, the individual citizens do not enjoy them *fully* and absolutely, because they have made a *partial* surrender of them to the sovereign. But the body of the nation, the State, remains absolutely free and independent with respect to all other men, and all *other* Nations, as long as it has not voluntarily submitted to them.

§ 5. As men are subject to the laws of nature,—and as their union in civil society cannot have exempted them from the obligation to observe those laws, since by that union they do not cease to be men,—the the entire nation, whose common will is but the result of the united wills of the citizens, remains subject to the *laws of nature*, and is bound to respect them in all her proceedings. And since *right* arises from obligation, as we have just observed (§ 3), the nation possesses also the same rights which nature has conferred upon men in order to enable them to perform their duties.

§ 6. We must therefore apply to nations the rules of the law of nature, in order to discover what their obligations are, and what their rights: consequently, the *law of Nations* is originally no other than the *law of Nature applied* to Nations. But as the application of a rule cannot be just and reasonable unless it be made in a manner suitable to the subject, we are not to imagine that the law of nations is precisely and in every case the same as the law of nature, with the difference only of the subjects to which it is applied, so as to allow of our substituting nations for individuals. A state or civil society is a subject very different from an individual of the human race ; from which circumstance, pursuant to the law of nature itself, there result in many cases, very different obligations and rights ; since the same general rule, applied to two subjects, cannot produce exactly the same* decisions, when the subjects are different ; and a particular rule which is perfectly just with respect to one subject, is not applicable to another subject of a quite different nature. There are many cases, therefore, in which the *law of Nature* does not decide between state and state in the same manner as it would between man and man. We must therefore know how to accommodate the application of it to different subjects ; and it is the art of thus applying it with a precision founded on right reason, that renders the *law of Nations* a distinct science(2).

---

(2) M. de Vattel then proceeds to state the different heads of international law, which has been variously subdivided by other writers. The clearest division is under *two* principal heads—*First*, the *natural* law of nations ; and *secondly*, the *positive*. The former is that of God and our conscience, and consequently immutable, and ought to be the basis of the positive laws of nations. The *positive* is threefold ; *First*, the *universal voluntary law or uniform practice* of nations in general; *secondly*, the *customary* law ; and *thirdly*, the *conventional law* or *treaties*. (See 1 Chitty's Commercial Law, 25 to 47.)—C.

The following note of a former editor is deservedly retained.

The study of the science of the law of nations presupposes an acquaintance with the ordinary law of nature, of which human individuals are the objects. Nevertheless, for the sake of those who have not systematically studied that law, it will not be amiss to give in this place a general idea of it. The natural law is the *science of the laws of nature*, of those laws which

§ 7. *We call that the *Necessary law of Nations* which consists in the application of the law of nature to *Nations*. It is *Necessary* because nations are *absolutely* bound to observe it. This law contains the precepts prescribed by the *law of nature* to *States*, on whom that law is not less obligatory than on individuals, since states are composed of men, their resolutions are taken by men, and the law of nature is binding on all men, under whatever relation they act. This is the law which Grotius, and those who follow him, call the *Internal law of Nations*, on account of its being obligatory on nations in point of *conscience*(3). Several writers term it the *Natural law of Nations*.

§ 8. Since therefore the necessary law of nations consists in the application of the law of nature to states,—which law is immutable, as being founded on the nature of things, and particularly on the nature of man,—it follows, that the *Necessary* law of nations is *immutable*.

§ 9. Whence, as this law is immutable, and the obligations that arise from it necessary and indispensable, nations can neither make any

nature imposes on mankind, or to which they are subject by the very circumstance of their being men; a science, whose first principle is this axiom of incontestable truth—"The great end of every being endowed with intellect and sentiment, is happiness." It is by the desire alone of that happiness, that we can bind a creature possessed of the faculty of thought, and form the ties of that obligation which shall make him submit to any rule. Now, by studying the nature of things, and that of man in particular, we may thence deduce the rules which man must follow in order to attain his great end,—to obtain the most perfect happiness of which he is susceptible. We call those rules the natural laws, or the laws of nature. They are certain, they are sacred, and obligatory on every man possessed of reason, independently of every other consideration than that of his nature, and even though we should suppose him totally ignorant of the existence of a God. But the sublime consideration of an eternal, necessary, infinite Being, the author of the universe, adds the most lively energy to the law of nature, and carries it to the highest degree of perfection. That necessary Being necessarily unites in himself all perfection: he is therefore superlatively good, and displays his goodness by forming creatures susceptible of happiness. It is then his wish that his creatures should be as happy as is consistent with their nature; consequently, it is his will that they should, in their whole conduct, follow the rules which that same nature lays down for them, as the most certain road to happiness. Thus the will of the Creator perfectly coincides with the simple indications of nature ; and those two sources produc-

ing the same law, unite in forming the same obligation. The whole reverts to the first great end of man, which is happiness. It was to conduct him to that great end that the laws of nature were ordained : it is from the desire of happiness that his obligation to observe those laws arises. There is, therefore, no man,—whatever may be his ideas respecting the origin of the universe,—even if he had the misfortune to be an atheist,—who is not bound to obey the laws of nature They are necessary to the general happiness of mankind; and whoever should reject them, whoever should openly despise them, would by such conduct alone declare himself an enemy to the human race, and deserve to be treated as such. Now, one of the first truths which the study of man reveals to us, and which is a necessary consequence of his nature, is, that in a state of lonely separation from the rest of his species, he cannot attain his great end—happiness : and the reason is, that he was intended to live in society with his fellow-creatures. Nature, herself, therefore, has established that society, whose great end is the common advantage of all its members; and the means of attaining that end constitute the rules that each individual is bound to observe in his whole conduct. Such are the natural laws of human society. Having thus given a general idea of them, which is sufficient for any intelligent reader, and is developed at large in several valuable works, let us return to the particular object of this treatise—Note ed. A. D. 1797.

(3) See this position illustrated, Mackintosh, Dis. 7; 1 Chitty's Commercial Law, 28, and n. (4), *post*, lx—C.

changes in it by their conventions, dispense with it in their own conduct, nor reciprocally release each other from the observance of it.

This is the principle by which we may distinguish *lawful* conventions or treaties from those that are not lawful, and innocent and rational customs from those that are unjust or censurable.

There are things, *just in themselves*, and allowed by the necessary law of nations, on which states may naturally agree with each other, and which they may consecrate and enforce by their *manners and customs. There are others of an *indifferent nature*, respecting which, it rests at the option of nations to make in their treaties whatever agreements they please, or to introduce whatever custom or practice they think proper. But every treaty, every custom, which contravenes the injunctions or prohibitions of the *Necessary* law of nations, is unlawful. It will appear, however, in the sequel, that it is only by the *Internal* law, by the law of *Conscience*, such conventions or treaties are always condemned as unlawful, and that, for reasons which shall be given in their proper place, they are nevertheless often valid by the external law. Nations being free and independent, though the conduct of one of them be illegal and condemnable by the laws of conscience, the others are bound to acquiesce in it, when it does not infringe upon *their* perfect rights. The liberty of that nation would not remain entire, if the others were to arrogate to themselves the right of inspecting and regulating *her* actions; an assumption on their part, that would be contrary to the law of nature, which declares every nation free and independent of all the others.

§ 10. Man is so formed by nature, that he cannot supply all his own wants, but necessarily stands in need of the intercourse and assistance of his fellow-creatures, whether for his immediate preservation, or for the sake of perfecting his nature, and enjoying such a life as is suitable to a rational being. This is sufficiently proved by experience. We have instances of persons, who, having grown up to manhood among the bears of the forest, enjoyed not the use of speech or of reason, but were, like the brute beasts, possessed only of sensitive faculties. We see moreover that nature has refused to bestow on men the same strength and natural weapons of defence with which she has furnished other animals—having, in lieu of those advantages, endowed mankind with the faculties of speech and reason, or at least a capability of acquiring them by an intercourse with their fellow-creatures. Speech enables them to communicate with each other, to give each other mutual assistance, to perfect their reason and knowledge; and having thus become intelligent, they find a thousand methods of preserving themselves, and supplying their wants. Each individual, moreover, is intimately conscious that he can neither live happily nor improve his nature without the intercourse and assistance of others. Since, therefore, nature has thus formed mankind, it is a convincing proof of *her intention that they should communicate with, and mutually aid and assist each other.

Hence is deduced the establishment of natural society among men. *The general law of that society is, that each individual should do for the others every thing which their necessities require, and which he can perform without neglecting the duty that he owes to himself* (4): a law which all men must observe in order to live in a manner consonant to their nature, and conformable to the views of their common creator,—a law which our own safety, our happiness, our dearest interests, ought to render sacred to every one of us. Such is the general obligation that binds us to the observance of our duties: let us fulfill them with care, if we would wisely endeavor to promote our own advantage(5).

It is easy to conceive what exalted felicity the world would enjoy, were all men willing to observe the rule that we have just laid down. On the contrary, if each man wholly and immediately directs all his thoughts to his own *interest*, if he does nothing for the sake of other men, the whole human race together will be immersed in the deepest wretchedness. Let us therefore endeavor to promote the happiness of mankind: all mankind, in return, will endeavor to promote ours, and thus we shall establish our felicity on the most solid foundations.

§ 11. The *universal society* of the human race being an institution of nature herself, that is to say, a necessary consequence of the nature of man,—all men, in whatever stations they are placed, *are bound to cultivate it, and to discharge its duties*. They cannot liberate themselves from the obligation by any convention, by any private association. When, therefore, they unite in civil society for the purpose of forming a separate state or nation, they may indeed enter into particular engagements towards those with whom they associate themselves; but they remain still bound to the performance of *their duties towards the rest of mankind*. All the difference consists in this, that having

---

(4) *Ante*, lvii. n.(2), *post* lx. n. (4).

(5) See the same position, *post*, § 13, and *post*, chap. ii. § 2 and 88. The *natural*, or primary law, is that of God and our conscience, the law which injoins us to do good to our neighbour, whether in literal strictness he may have a *perfect* right to demand such treatment from us or not. This is a law that *ought* to be as strong in obligation as the most distinct and positive rule, though it may not always be capable of the same precise definition, nor consequently may allow the same *remedies* to *enforce* its observance. As an *individual* is bound by the law of nature to deal honorably and truly with other individuals, whether the precise acts required of him be or be not such as their own municipal law will enforce; just so a *state*, in its relations with other states, is bound to conduct herself in the spirit of justice, benevolence, and good faith, even though there be no positive rules of international law, by the letter of which she may be actually tied down. The same rules of morality which hold together men in families, and which

form families into a commonwealth, also link together several commonwealths as members of the great society of mankind. Commonwealths, as well as private men, are liable to injury, and capable of benefit from each other; it is therefore their duty to reverence, to practise, and to enforce, those rules of justice which control and restrain injury, which regulate and augment benefit, which preserve civilized states in a tolerable condition of security from wrong, and which, if they could be generally obeyed, would establish, and permanently maintain, the well being of the universal commonwealth of the human race. (See Observations in 1 Chitty's Commercial Law, 28; Mackintosh, Disc. 7; Peake's Rep. 116; 2 Hen. Blac. 259; and see *ante*, § 7; and see extract from Mr. Pitt's celebrated speech on concluding the commercial treaty between Great Britain and France in A. D. 1786, and in which he powerfully refuted the doctrine of *national and hereditary antipathy* between England and France, *post*, book ii. § 21, p. 144.)—C.

agreed to act in common, and having resigned their rights and submitted their will to the body of the society, in every thing that concerns their common welfare, it thenceforward belongs to that body, that state, and its rulers, to *fulfil the duties of humanity towards strangers, in every thing that no longer depends on the liberty of individuals; and it is the state more particularly that is to perform those duties towards other states. We have already seen, (§ 5), that men united in society remain subject to the obligations imposed upon them by human nature. That society, considered as a moral person, since possessed of an understanding, volition, and strength peculiar to itself, *is therefore obliged to live on the same terms with other societies or states, as individual man was obliged, before those establishments, to live with other men*, that is to say, according to the laws of the natural society established among the human race, with the difference only of such exceptions as may arise from the different nature of the subjects.

§ 12. Since the object of the natural society established between all mankind is—that they should lend each other mutual assistance, in order to attain perfection themselves, and to render their condition as perfect as possible,—and since nations, considered as so many free persons living together in a state of nature, are bound to cultivate human society with each other,—the object of the great society established by nature *between all nations* is also the interchange of *mutual assistance* for their own improvement and that of their condition.

§ 13. The first general law that we discover in the very object of the society of nations, is that *each individual nation is bound to contribute every thing in her power to the happiness and perfection of all the others.*

§ 14. But the duties that we owe to ourselves being unquestionably paramount to those we owe to others,—a nation owes herself in the first instance, and in preference to all other nations, to do every thing she can to promote her own happiness and perfection. (I say, every thing she *can*, not only in a *physical* but in a *moral* sense,—that is, every thing that she can do *lawfully and consistently with justice and honor*.) When, therefore, she cannot contribute to the welfare of another nation without doing an essential injury to herself, her obligation *ceases on that particular occasion, and she is considered as lying under a disability to perform the office in question(6).

---

(6) Puffendorf, B. iii. c. 3, s. 6. p. 29, writes clearly and decidedly on this important subject; he observes "The law of humanity does not seem to oblige us to grant passage to any other goods, except such as are absolutely necessary for the support of their life to whom they are thus conveyed."—C.

*Xenophon points out the true reason of this first of all duties, and establishes its necessity, in the following words. "If we see a man who is uniformly eager to pursue his own private advantage, without regard to the rules of honor or the duties of friendship, why should we in any emergency think of sparing him? *Note edit A. D. 1797. See modern authorities in support of that position, ante, lv. n.(1), lx. n.(5); Book ii. chap. ii. § 21, p. 144, post.—C.

§ 15. *Nations being free and independent of each other, in the same manner as men are naturally free and independent, the *second* general law of their society is, *that each nation should be left in the peaceable enjoyment of that liberty which she inherits from nature.* The natural society of nations cannot subsist, unless the natural rights of each be duly respected. No nation is willing to renounce her liberty ; she will rather break off all commerce with those states that should attempt to infringe upon it.

§ 16. As a consequence of that liberty and independence, it exclusively belongs to each nation to form her own judgment of what her conscience prescribes to her,—of what she can or cannot do,—of what it is proper or improper for her to do: and of course it rests solely with her to examine and determine *whether she can perform any office for another nation without neglecting the duty which she owes to herself.* In all cases, therefore, in which a nation has the *right* of judging what her duty requires, no other nation can compel her to act in such particular manner : for any attempt at such compulsion would be an infringement on the liberty of nations. We have no right to use constraint against a free person except in those cases where such person is *bound to perform* some particular thing for us, and for some particular reason which does not depend on his judgment,—in those cases, in short, where we have a *perfect* right against him.

§ 17. In order perfectly to understand this, it is necessary to observe, that the obligation, and the right which corresponds to or is derived from it, are distinguished into *external* and *internal.* The obligation is *internal,* as it binds the *conscience,* and is deduced from the rules of our duty ; it is *external,* as it is considered relatively to other men, and produces some right between them. The internal obligation is always the same in its nature, though it varies in degree ; but the external obligation is divided into *perfect* and *imperfect ;* and the right that results from it is also *perfect* or *imperfect.* The *perfect right* is that which is accompanied by the *right of compelling* those who refuse to fulfil the correspondent obligation ; the *imperfect* right is unaccompanied by that right of compulsion. *The *perfect obligation* is that which gives to the opposite party the *right of compulsion ;* the *imperfect* gives him only a right *to ask.*

It is now easy to conceive why the right is always imperfect, when the correspondent obligation depends on the judgment of the party in whose breast it exists ; for if, in such a case, we had a right to compel him, he would no longer enjoy the freedom of determination respecting the conduct he is to pursue in order to obey the dictates of his own conscience. Our obligation is always imperfect with respect to other people, while we possess the liberty of judging how we are to act ; and we retain that liberty on all occasions where we ought to be free.

§ 18. Since men are naturally equal, and a perfect equality prevails in their rights and obligations, as equally proceeding from nature— Nations composed of men, and considered as so many free persons living together in the state of nature, are naturally equal, and inherit from nature the same obligations and rights. Power or weakness does not in this respect produce any difference. A dwarf is as much a man as a giant; a small republic is no less a sovereign state than the most powerful kingdom.

§ 19. By a necessary consequence of that equality, whatever is lawful for one nation, is equally lawful for any other; and whatever is unjustifiable in the one, is equally so in the other.

§ 20. A nation then is mistress of her own actions so long as they do not affect the proper and perfect rights of any other nation—so long as she is only *internally* bound, and does not lie under any *external* and *perfect* obligation. If she makes an ill use of her liberty, she is guilty of a breach of duty; but other nations are bound to acquiesce in her conduct, since they have no right to dictate to her.

§ 21. Since nations are *free, independent*, and *equal*—and since each possesses *the right of judging*, according to the dictates of her conscience, what conduct she is to pursue in order to fulfill her duties; the effect of the whole is, to produce, at least externally and in the eyes of mankind, a perfect equality of rights between nations, in the administration of their affairs and the pursuit of their pretensions, without regard to the intrinsic justice of their conduct, of which others have no right to form a definitive judgment; so that whatever may be done by any one nation, may be done by any other; *and they ought, in human society, to be considered as possessing equal rights.

Each nation in fact maintains that she has justice on her side in every dispute that happens to arise; and it does not belong to either of the parties interested, or to nations, to pronounce a judgment on the contested question. The party who is in the wrong is guilty of a crime against her own *conscience;* but as there exists a possibility that she may perhaps have justice on her side, we cannot accuse her of violating the laws of society.

It is therefore necessary, on many occasions, that nations should suffer certain things to be done, though in their own nature unjust and condemnable; because they cannot oppose them by open force, without violating the liberty of some particular state, and destroying the foundations of their natural society. And since they are bound to cultivate that society, it is of course presumed that all nations have consented to the principle we have just established. The rules that are deduced from it, constitute what Monsieur Wolf calls " *the voluntary law of nations ;*" and there is no reason why we should not use the same term, although we thought it necessary to deviate from that great man in our manner of establishing the foundation of that law (7).

---

(7) The *natural primary* or *internal* law of nations which is thus binding in conscience, and immutable, it must be admitted, is *mere theory*, until it has been assented to by a state as binding on her: but, besides that law of conscience, which, until so assented to, is *imperfect*, there is what is termed the *positive* or *secondary* law of nations, and which is *threefold; first*, the *universal voluntary law*, or those rules which are considered to have become law, by the *uniform practice* of nations *in general*, and by the manifest utility of the rules themselves ;— *secondly*, the *customary* law, or that which,

§ 22. The laws of natural society are of such importance to the safety of all the states, that, if the custom once prevailed of trampling them under foot, no nation could flatter herself with the hope of preserving her national existence, and enjoying domestic tranquillity, however attentive to pursue every measure dictated by the most consummate prudence, justice, and moderation[*]. Now all men and all states have a perfect right to those things that are necessary for their preservation, since that right corresponds to an indispensable obligation. All nations have therefore a right to resort to forcible means for the purpose of repressing any one particular nation who openly violates the laws of the society which Nature has established between them, or who directly attacks the welfare and safety of that society.

§ 23. But care must be taken not to extend that right to the prejudice of the liberty of nations. They are free and independent, but bound to observe the laws of that society which Nature has established between them; and so far bound, that, when any of them violate those laws, the others have a right to repress her. The conduct of each nation, therefore, is no farther subject to the control of the others, than as the interests of natural society are concerned. The general and common right of nations over the conduct of any sovereign state is only commensurate to the object of that society which exists between them.

§ 24. The several *engagements* into which nations may enter, produce a new kind of law of nations, called *Conventional* or *of Treaties*. As it is evident that a *treaty* binds none but the contracting parties, the conventional law of nations is not a universal but a particular law. All that can be done on this subject in a treatise on the Law of *Nations*,

---

from motives of convenience, has by tacit but implied *agreement* prevailed, not generally indeed among all nations, nor with so paramount utility as to become a portion of *universal voluntary* law, but enough to have acquired a *prescriptive* obligation among certain states, so situated as to be mutually benefitted by it, as the customary law prevailing amongst different nations in the Whale Fishery, and illustrated by the decision in *Fennings* v. *Lord Grenville*, 1 Taunt. Rep. 241, 248, upon the division of the profits arising from a whale when killed by the crews of several boats; and *thirdly*, the *conventional law*, or that which is *agreed* between particular states by *express treaties*, a law binding only upon the parties amongst whom such treaties are in force. See 1 Chitty's Commercial Law, 28, 29, and see *post*, § 27, p. 66.

In the case of the ship, *Flad Oyen*, 1 Rob. Rep. 115, Sir *William Scott* observed, "A great part of the law of nations stands on the *usage and practice of nations, and on no other foundation*; it is introduced, indeed, by general principles, but it travels with those general principles only to a certain *extent*; and if it stops there, you are

not at liberty to go farther and to say, that mere general speculations would bear you out in a further progress; thus, for instance, on mere general principles, it is lawful to destroy your enemy, and mere general principles make no great difference as to the manner by which this is to be effected; but the conventional law of mankind, which is evidenced in their *practice*, does make a distinction, and allows some and prohibits other modes of destruction; and a belligerent is bound to confine himself to those modes which the *common practice* of mankind has employed, and to relinquish "those which the same *practice* has not brought within the ordinary exercise of war, however sanctioned by its principles and purposes;" so it has ever been the *practice* of nations to bring vessels captured by them into their own ports, and to condemn them as prize in *their own* Admiralty Courts; and therefore a sentence of condemnation in a *neutral* country would be illegal and void. *Ibid.*—C.

[*] Etenim si hæc pertubare omnia et permiscere volumus, totam vitam periculosam, insidiosam, infestamque reddemus. Cicero in Verr. ii. 15.

is to lay down those general rules which nations are bound to observe with respect to their *treaties*. A minute detail of the various agreements made between particular nations ; and of the rights and obligations thence resulting, is matter of fact, and belongs to the province of history.

§ 25. Certain maxims and *customs*, consecrated by long use, and observed by nations in their mutual intercourse with each other as a kind of law, form the *Customary law of Nations*, or the *Custom of Nations*(8). This law is founded on a *tacit* consent, or, if you please, on a tacit convention of the nations that observe it towards each other. Whence it appears that it is not obligatory except on those nations who have adopted it, and that it is not universal, any more than the *conventional law*. The same remark, therefore, is equally applicable to this *customary law*, viz. that a minute detail of its particulars does not belong to a systematic treatise on the law of nations, but that we must content ourselves with giving a general theory of it ; that is to say, the rules which are to be observed in it, as well with a view to its effects, as to its substance ; and with respect to the latter, those rules will serve to distinguish lawful and innocent customs from those that are unjust and unlawful.

§ 26. When a custom or usage is *generally*, established, either between all the civilized nations in the world, or only between those of a certain continent, as of Europe, for example, or between those who have a more frequent intercourse with each other ; if that custom is in its own nature indifferent, and much more, if it be useful and reasonable, it becomes obligatory on all the nations in question, who are considered as having given their consent to it, and are bound to observe it towards each other, *as long as they have not expressly* declared their resolution of not observing it in future(9). But if that custom contains any thing unjust or unlawful, it is not obligatory ; on the contrary, every nation is bound to relinquish it, since nothing can oblige or authorize her to violate the law of nature.

§ 27. These *three* kinds of law of nations, the *Voluntary*, the *Conventional*, and the *Customary*, together constitute the *Positive Law of Nations*(10). For they all proceed from the will of Nations ; the *Voluntary* from their *presumed* consent, the *Conventional* from an *express* consent, and the *Customary* from *tacit* consent ; and as there can be no other mode of deducing any law from the will of nations, there are only these three kinds of *Positive law of Nations*.

We shall be careful to distinguish them from the *Natural* or *Necessary* law of nations, without, however, treating of them separately. But after having, under each individual head of our subject, established what

---

(8) From the authorities cited in *Benest v. Pipon*, Knapp's Rep. 67, it seems, that most nations agree, that twenty years' uninterrupted usage (for *twenty years* is evidence as well of *public* and *general customs* or practices as of *private* rights,) is sufficient to sustain the same.—C.

(9) As to this position, see further, Mar-

ten's L. N. 356, and *Fennings* v. *Lord Grenville*, 1 Taunton's Rep. 248. There must be a reasonable notification, in point of time, of the intention not to be bound by the customary law. *Ibid.* and 1 Chitty's Criminal Law, 29, 35, 92.—C.

(10) See Division of Laws of Nations, *ante*, lvii. n.(2).—C.

the *necessary* law prescribes, we shall immediately add how and why the decisions of that law must be modified by the *Voluntary* law; or (which amounts to the same thing in other terms) we shall explain how, in consequence of the liberty of nations, and pursuant to the *rules* of their natural society, the *external* law which they are to observe towards each other, differs in certain instances from the maxims of the *Internal* law, which nevertheless always remain obligatory in point of conscience. As to the rights introduced by *Treaties* or by *Custom*, there is no room to apprehend that any one will confound them with the *Natural* law of nations. They form that species of law of nations which authors have distinguished by the name of *Arbitrary*.

§ 28. To furnish the reader beforehand with a general direction respecting the distinction between the *Necessary* and the *Voluntary* law, let us here observe, that, as the *Necessary* law is always obligatory on the *conscience*, a nation ought never to lose sight of it in deliberating on the line of conduct she is to pursue in order to fulfill her duty; but when there is question of examining what she may demand of other states, she must consult the *Voluntary* law, whose maxims are devoted to the safety and advantage of the universal society of mankind.

BOOK I.

OF NATIONS CONSIDERED IN THEMSELVES.

CHAP. I.

OF NATIONS OR SOVEREIGN STATES(10).

§ 1. A NATION or a state is, as has been said at the beginning of this work, a body politic, or a society of men united together for the purpose of promoting their mutual safety and advantage by their combined strength.

From the very design that induces a number of men to form a society which has its common interests, and which is to act in concert, it is necessary that there should be established a *Public Authority*, to order and direct what is to be done by each in relation to the end of the association. This political authority is the *Sovereignty;* and he or they who are invested with it are the *Sovereign*(10).

§ 2. It is evident, that, by the very act of the civil or political association, each citizen subjects himself to the authority of the entire body, in every thing that relates to the common welfare. The authority of all over each member, therefore, essentially belongs to the body politic, or state ; but the exercise of that authority may be placed in different hands, according as the society may have ordained.

---

(10) The student desirous of enlarging his knowledge upon this subject, should read Locke on government; De Lolme on Constitution; 1 Bla. Com. 47 ; Sedgwick's Commentaries thereon; and Chitty Junior's Prerogatives of the Crown as regards Sovereignty and different Governments; and see Cours De Droit Public Interne et Externe, Paris, A. D. 1830.—C.

§ 3. If the body of the nation keep in *its own hands* the empire, *or the right to command, it is a *Popular* government, a *Democracy*; if it intrust it to a *certain number of citizens*, to a senate, it establishes an *Aristocratic* republic; finally, if it confide the government to a *single person*, the state becomes a *Monarchy*(11).

These three kinds of government may be variously combined and modified. We shall not here enter into the particulars; this subject belonging to the *public universal law:* *for the object of the present work, it is sufficient to establish the general principles necessary for the decision of those disputes that may arise between nations.

§ 4. Every nation that governs itself, under what form soever, without dependence on any foreign power, is a *Sovereign State.* Its rights are naturally the same as those of any other state. Such are the moral persons who live together in a natural society, subject to the law of nations. To give a nation a right to make an immediate figure in this grand society, it is sufficient that it be really sovereign and independent, that is, that it govern itself by its own authority and laws.

§ 5. We ought, therefore, to account as sovereign states those which have united themselves to another more powerful, by an *unequal alliance*, in which, as Aristotle says, to the more powerful, is given more honor, and to the weaker, more assistance.

The conditions of those unequal alliances may be infinitely varied. But whatever they are, provided the inferior ally reserve to itself the sovereignty, or the right of governing its own body, it ought to be considered as an independent state, that keeps up an intercourse with others under the authority of the law of nations.

§ 6. Consequently a weak state, which, in order to provide for its safety, places itself under the protection of a more powerful one, and *engages, in return, to perform several offices equivalent to that protection, without however divesting itself of the right of government and sovereignty,—that state, I say, does not, on this account, cease to rank

---

(11) See the advantages and disadvantages of each of those forms of government shortly considered. 1 Bla. Com. 49, 50.—C.

*Nor shall we examine which of those different kinds of government is the best. It will be sufficient to say in general, that the monarchial form appears preferable to every other, provided the power of the sovereign be limited, and not absolute,—qui [*principatus*] tum demum regius est, si intra modestiæ et mediocritatis fines se contineat, excessu potestatis, quam imprudentes in dies augere satagunt, minuitur. penitusque corrumpitur. Nos stulti, majoris potentiæ specie decepti, dilabimur in contrarium, non satis considerantes eam denum tutam esse potentiam quæ viribus modum imponit. The maxim has both truth and wisdom on its side. The author here quotes the saying of Theopompus, king of Sparta, who, returning to his house amidst the acclamations of the people, after the establishment of the Ephori—"You will leave to your children (said his wife) an authority diminished through your fault." "True," replied the king: "I shall leave them a smaller portion of it; but it will rest upon a firmer basis." The Lacedæmonians, during a certain period, had two chiefs to whom they very improperly gave the title of kings. They were magistrates, who possessed a very limited power, and whom it was not unusual to cite before the tribunal of justice,—to arrest,—to condemn to death.—Sweden acts with less impropriety in continuing to bestow on her chief the title of king, although she has circumscribed his power within very narrow bounds. He shares not his authority with a colleague,—he is hereditary,—and the state has, from time immemorial, borne the title of a kingdom.—Edit. A. D. 1797.

among the sovereigns who acknowledge no other law than that of nations (12).

§ 7. There occurs no greater difficulty with respect to *tributary* states; for though the payment of tribute to a foreign power does in some degree diminish the dignity of those states, from its being a confession of their weakness,—yet it suffers their sovereignty to subsist entire. The custom of paying tribute was formerly very common,—the weaker by that means purchasing of their more powerful neighbor an exemption from oppression, or at that price securing his protection, without ceasing to be sovereigns.

§ 8. The Germanic nations introduced another custom—that of requiring homage from a state either vanquished, or too weak to make resistance. Sometimes even, a prince has given sovereignties in fee, and sovereigns have voluntarily rendered themselves feudatories to others.

When the homage leaves independency and sovereign authority in the administration of the state, and only means certain duties to the lord of the fee, or even a mere honorary acknowledgment, it does not prevent the state or the feudatory prince being strictly sovereign. The king of Naples pays homage for his kingdom to the pope, and is nevertheless reckoned among the principal sovereigns of Europe.

§ 9. Two sovereign states may also be subject to the same prince, without any dependence on each other, and each may retain all its rights as a free and sovereign state. The king of Prussia is sovereign prince of Neufchatel in Switzerland, without that principality being in any manner united to his other dominions; so that the people of Neufchatel, in virtue of their franchises, may serve a foreign power at war with the king of Prussia, provided that the war be not on account of that principality.

§ 10. Finally, sovereign and independent states may unite themselves together by a perpetual confederacy, without ceasing to be, each individually, a perfect state. They will together constitute a federal republic: their joint deliberations will not impair the sovereignty of each member, though they may, in certain respects, put some restraint on the exercise of it, in virtue of voluntary engagements. A person does not cease to be free and independent, when he is obliged to fulfill engagements which he has voluntarily contracted.

Such were formerly the cities of Greece; such are *at present* the Seven United Provinces of the Netherlands (13), and such the members of the Helvetic body.

---

(12) This and other rules respecting smaller states sometimes form the subject of consideration even in the Municipal Courts. In case of a revolted colony, or part of a parent or principal state, no subject of another state can legally make a contract with it or assist the same without leave of his own government, before its separate independence has been recognised by his own government. *Jones* v. *Garcia del Rio*, 1 Turn. & Russ. 297; *Thompson* v. *Powles*, 2 Sim. Rep. 202; *Yrissari* v. *Clement*, 2 Car & P. 223; 11 B. Moore, 308; 3 Bing. 432; and *post.*—C.

(13) Of course, the words "*at present*" refer only to the time when Vattel wrote, and it is unnecessary to mention otherwise than thus cursorily the notorious recent changes.—C.

§ 11. But a people that has passed under the dominion of another is no longer a state, and can no longer avail itself directly of the law of nations. Such were the nations and kingdoms which the Romans rendered subject to their empire; the generality even of those whom they honored with the name of friends and allies no longer formed real states. Within themselves, they were *governed by their own laws and magistrates; but without, they were in every thing obliged to follow the orders of Rome; they dared not of themselves either to make war or contract alliances; and could not treat with nations.

§ 12. The law of nations is the law of sovereigns; free and independent states are moral persons, whose rights and obligations we are to establish in this treatise.

CHAP. II.

GENERAL PRINCIPLES OF THE DUTIES OF A NATION TOWARDS ITSELF.

§ 13. IF the rights of a nation spring from its obligations, it is principally from those that relate to itself. It will further appear, that its duties towards others depend very much on its duties towards itself, as the former are to be regulated and measured by the latter. As we are then to treat of the obligations and rights of nations,—an attention to order requires that we should begin by establishing what each nation owes to itself.

The general and fundamental rule of our duties towards ourselves is, that every moral being ought to live in a manner conformable to his nature, *naturæ convenienter vivere* (14). A nation is a being determined

---

(14) If to particularize may be allowed, we may instance Great Britain. Comparatively, with regard to dimensions, it would be but an insignificant state; but, with regard to its insular situation and excellent ports, and its proximity to Europe, and above all the singularly manly, brave, and adventurous character of its natives, it has been capable of acquiring and has acquired powers far beyond its diminutive extent. These being established, it becomes the duty of such a state, and of those exercising the powers of government, to cultivate and improve these natural advantages; and in that view the ancient exclusive navigation system, constituting England the carrier of Europe and the world, were highly laudable; and it is to be hoped that a return of the system, injudiciously abandoned, will ere long take place.—C.

by its essential attributes, that has its own nature, and can act in conformity to it. There are then actions of a nation as such, wherein it is concerned in its national character, and which are either suitable or opposite to what constitutes it a nation ; so that it is not a matter of indifference whether it performs some of those actions, and omits others. In this respect, the Law of Nature prescribes it certain duties. We shall see, in this first book, what conduct a nation ought to observe, in order that it may not be wanting to itself. But we shall first sketch out a general idea of this subject.

§ 14. He who no longer exists can have no duties to perform: and a moral being is charged with obligations to himself, only with a view to his perfection and happiness : for *to preserve and to perfect his own nature*, is the sum of all his duties to himself.

The *preservation* of a nation consists in the duration of the political association by which it is formed. If a period is put to this association, the nation or state no longer subsists, though the individuals that compose it still exist.

The *perfection* of a nation is found in what renders it capable of obtaining the end of civil society ; and a nation is in a perfect state, when nothing necessary is wanting to arrive at that end. We know that the perfection of a thing consists, generally, in the perfect agreement of all its constitutent parts to tend to the same end. A nation being a multitude of men united together in civil society—if in that multitude all conspire to attain the end proposed in forming a civil society, the nation is perfect ; and it is more or less so, according as it approaches more or less to that *perfect agreement. In the same manner its external state will be more or less perfect, according as it concurs with the interior perfection of the nation.

§ 15. The *end* or *object* of civil society is to procure for the citizens whatever they stand in need of for the necessities, the conveniences, the accommodation of life, and, in general, whatever constitutes happiness, —with the peaceful possession of property, a method of obtaining justice with security, and, finally, a mutual defence against all external violence.

It is now easy to form a just idea of the perfection of a state or nation :—every thing in it must conspire to promote the ends we have pointed out.

§ 16. In the act of association, by virtue of which a multitude of men form together a state or nation, each individual has entered into engagements with all, to promote the general welfare ; and all have entered into engagements with each individual, to facilitate for him the means of supplying his necessities, and to protect and defend him. It is manifest that these reciprocal engagements can no otherwise be fulfilled than by maintaining the political association. The entire nation is then obliged to maintain that association ; and as their preservation depends on its continuance, it thence follows that every nation is obliged to perform the duty of self-preservation.

This obligation, so natural to each individual of God's creation, is not derived to nations immediately from nature, but from the agreement by which civil society is formed : it is therefore not absolute, but conditional,—that is to say, it supposes a human act, to wit, the 'social compact. And as compacts may be dissolved by common consent of the parties— if the individuals that compose a nation should unanimously agree to break the link that binds them, it would be lawful for them to do so, and thus to destroy the state or nation ; but they would doubtless incur a degree of guilt, if they took this step without just and weighty reasons ; for civil societies are approved by the Law of Nature, which recommends them to mankind, as the true means of supplying all their wants, and of effectually advancing towards their own perfection. Moreover, civil society is so useful, nay so necessary to all citizens, that it may well be considered as morally impossible for them to consent unanimously to break it without necessity. But what citizens may or ought to do— what the majority of them may resolve in certain cases of necessity or of pressing exigency—are questions that will be treated of elsewhere : they cannot be solidly determined without some principles which we have not yet established. For the present, it is sufficient to have proved, that, in general, as long as the political society subsists, the whole nation is obliged to endeavor to maintain it.

§ 17. If a nation is obliged to preserve itself, it is no less obliged carefully to preserve all its members. The nation owes this to itself, since the loss even of one of its members weakens it, and is injurious to its preservation. It owes this also to the members in particular, in consequence of the very act of association ; for those who compose a nation are united for their defence and common advantage ; and none can justly be deprived of this union, and of *the advantages he expects to derive from it, while he on his side fulfills the conditions(15).

The body of a nation cannot then abandon a province, a town, or even a single individual who is a part of it, unless compelled to it by necessity, or indispensably obliged to it by the strongest reasons founded on the public safety(16).

§ 18. Since then a nation is obliged to preserve itself, it has a right to everything necessary for its preservation. For the Law of Nature gives us a right to everything, without which we cannot fulfill our obligation ; otherwise it would oblige us to do impossibilities, or rather would contradict itself in prescribing us a duty, and at the same time debarring us of the only means of fulfilling it. It will doubtless be here understood, that those means ought not to be unjust in themselves, or such as are absolutely forbidden by the Law of Nature. As it is impossible that it should ever permit the use of such means,—if on a particular occasion no other present themselves for fulfilling a general obligation, the obliga-

---

(15) This principle is in every respect recognised and acted upon by our municipal law. It is in respect of, and as a due return for, the *protection* every natural born subject is entitled to, and actually does, by law, receive from the instant of his birth, that all the obligations of allegiance attach upon him, and from which he cannot by any act of his own emancipate himself. This is the principle upon which is founded the rule "*Nemo protest exuere patriam.*" *Calvin's* case, 7 Coke, 25; Co. Lit. 129. a.; and see an interesting application of that rule in *Macdonald's* case, Foster's Crown Law, 59.—C

(16) In tracing the consequences of this rule, we shall hereafter perceive how important is the rul eitself.—C.

tion must, in that particular instance, be looked on as impossible, and consequently void.

§ 19. By an evident consequence from what has been said, a nation ought carefully to avoid. as much as is possible, whatever might cause its destruction, or that of the state, which is the same thing.

§ 20. A nation or state has a right to every thing that can help to ward off imminent danger, and to keep at a distance whatever is capable of causing its ruin; and that from the very same reasons that establish its right to the things necessary to its preservation (17).

§ 21. The second general duty of a nation towards itself is to labor at its own perfection and that of its state. It is this double perfection that renders a nation capable of attaining the end of civil society: it would be absurd to unite in society, and yet not endeavor to promote the end of that union.

Here the entire body of a nation, and each individual citizen, are bound by a double obligation, the one immediately proceeding from nature, and the other resulting from their reciprocal engagements. Nature lays an obligation upon each man to labor after his own perfection; and in so doing, he labors after that of civil society, which could not fail to be very flourishing, were it composed of none but good citizens. But the individual finding in a well-regulated society the most powerful succors to enable him to fulfill the task which Nature imposes upon him in relation to himself, for becoming better, and consequently more happy— he is doubtless obliged to contribute all in his power to render that society more perfect.

All the citizens who form a political society reciprocally engage to *advance the common welfare, and as far as possible to promote the advantage of each member. Since then the perfection of the society is what enables it to secure equally the happiness of the body and that of the members, the grand object of the engagements and duties of a citizen is to aim at this perfection. This is more particularly the duty of the body collective in all their common deliberations, and in every thing they do as a body (18).

§ 22. A nation therefore ought to prevent, and carefully to avoid, whatever may hinder its perfection and that of the state, or retard the progress either of the one or the other (19).

§ 23. We may then conclude, as we have done above in regard to the preservation of a state (§ 18), that a nation has a right to every thing without which it cannot attain the perfection of the members and of the

---

(17) *Salus populi suprema est lex.* Upon this principle it has been established, that, for national defence in war, it is legal to pull down or injure the property of any private individual. See *Governors, &c.* v. *Meredith*, 4 Term Rep. 796–7 —C.

(18) In a highly intelligent and cultivated society, like England, this principle is exemplified in an extraordinary degree; for in the legislative assembly, members of parliament, without any private interest excepting the approbation of their countrymen, almost destroy themselves by exertion in discussing the improvement of existing regulations; and this indeed even to excess as regards long speeches, sometimes even counteracting their own laudable endeavors.—C.

(19) See Book I. chap. xxiii. § 283, as to the duty of all nations to prevent the violation of the law of nations.—C.

state, or prevent and repeal whatever is contrary to this double perfection.

§ 24. On this subject, the English furnish us an example highly worthy of attention. That illustrious nation distinguishes itself in a glorious manner by its application to every thing that can render the state more flourishing. An admirable constitution there places every citizen in a situation that enables him to contribute to this great end, and everywhere diffuses that spirit of genuine patriotism which zealously exerts itself for the public welfare. We there see private citizens form considerable enterprises, in order to promote the glory and welfare of the nation. And while a bad prince would find his hands tied up, a wise and moderate king finds the most powerful aids to give success to his glorious designs. The nobles and the representatives of the people form a link of confidence between the monarch and the nation, and, concurring with him in every thing that tends to promote the public welfare, partly ease him of the burden of government, give stability to his power, and procure him an obedience the most perfect, as it is voluntary. Every good citizen sees that the strength of the state is really the advantage of all, and not that of a single person(20). Happy constitution! which they did not suddenly obtain : it has cost rivers of blood; but they have not purchased it too dear. May luxury, that pest so fatal to the manly and patriotic virtues, that minister of corruption so dangerous to liberty, never overthrow a monument that does so much honor to human nature—a monument capable of teaching kings how glorious it is to rule over a free people!

There is another nation illustrious by its bravery and its victories. Its numerous and valiant nobility, its extensive and fertile, dominions, might render it respectable throughout all Europe, and in a short time it might be in a most flourishing situation, but its constitution opposes this ; and such is its attachment to that constitution, that there is no room to expect a proper remedy will ever be applied. In vain might a magnanimous 'king, raised by his virtues above the pursuits of ambition and injustice, form the most salutary designs for promoting the happiness of his people ;—in vain might those designs be approved by the more sensible part, by the majority of the nation ;—a single deputy, obstinate, or corrupted by a foreign power, might put a stop to all, and disconcert the wisest and most necessary measures. From an excessive jealousy of its liberty, that nation has taken such precautions as must necessarily place it out of the power of the king to make any attempts on the liberties of the public. But is it not evident that those precautions exceed the end proposed,—that they tie the hands of the most just and wise prince, and deprive him of the means of securing the public freedom

---

(20) This is indeed a flattering compliment from Vattel, a foreigner : but certainly it is just : for although, as a commercial nation, it might be supposed that each individual principally labors for his own individual gain; yet when we refer to the spirited employment of capital in building national bridges, canals, rail-roads, &c. not yielding even 2l. per cent., it must be admitted that great public spirit for national good very generally prevails.—C.

against the enterprizes of foreign powers, and of rendering the nation rich and happy ? Is it not evident that the nation has deprived itself of the power of acting, and that its counsels are exposed to the caprice or treachery of a single member ?

§ 25. We shall conclude this chapter, with observing, that a nation ought *to know itself* (21). Without this knowledge it cannot make any successful endeavors after its own perfection. It ought to have a just idea of its state, to enable it to take the most proper measures ; it ought to know the progress it has already made, and what further advances it has still to make,—what advantages it possesses, and what defects it labors under, in order to preserve the former, and correct the latter. Without this knowledge a nation will act at random, and often take the most improper measures. It will think it acts with great wisdom in imitating the conduct of nations that are reputed wise and skillful,—not perceiving that such or such regulation, such or such practice, though salutary to one state, is often pernicious to another. Every thing ought to be conducted according to its nature. Nations cannot be well governed without such regulations as are suitable to their respective characters ; and in order to do this, their characters ought to be known.

CHAP. III.

OF THE CONSTITUTION OF A STATE, AND THE DUTIES AND RIGHTS OF THE NATION IN THIS RESPECT.

WE were unable to avoid, in the first chapter, anticipating something of the subject of this.

§ 26. We have seen already that every political society must necessarily establish a public authority to regulate their common affairs,—to prescribe to each individual the conduct he ought to observe with a view to the public welfare, and to possess the means of procuring obedience.

---

(21) This is one of the soundest and most important principles that can be advanced, whether it refers to individuals or to nations, and is essential even to the attainment of the rudiments of true wisdom. Every moral and wise man should enlarge on this principle, and amongst others study that excellent, but too little known work, Mason on Self Knowledge.

CHAP. III.

OF THE JUST CAUSES OF WAR (141).

§ 24. WHOEVER entertains a true idea of war,—whoever considers its terrible effects, its destructive and unhappy consequences, will readily agree that it should never be undertaken without the most cogent raesons. Humanity revolts against a sovereign, who, without necessity or without very powerful reasons, lavishes the blood of his most faithful subjects, and exposes his people to the calamities of war, when he has it in his power to maintain them in the enjoyment of an honorable and salutary peace. And if to this imprudence, this want of love for his people, he moreover adds injustice towards those he attacks,—of how great a crime, or rather, of what a frightful series of crimes, does he not become guilty! Responsible for all the misfortunes which he draws down on his own subjects, he is moreover loaded with the guilt of all those which he inflicts on an innocent nation. The slaughter of men, the pillage of cities, the devastation of provinces,—such is the black catalogue of his enormities. He is responsible to God, and accountable to human nature, for every individual that is killed, for every hut that is burned down. The violences, the crimes, the disorders of every kind, attendant on the tumult and licentiousness of war, pollute his conscience, and are set down to his account, as he is the original author of them all. Unquestionable truths! alarming ideas! which ought to affect the rulers of nations, and, in all their military enterprises, inspire them with a degree of circumspection proportionate to the importance of the subject!

§ 25. Were men always reasonable, they would terminate their contests by the arms of reason only: natural justice and equity would be

---

(141) See further, as to what are, or are not, just causes for rescinding a treaty of peace, and which seem also to be here applicable, *post*, B. 4, ch. 4, § 44, 45, p. 449.

their rule, or their judge. Force is a wretched and melancholy expedient against those who spurn at justice, and refuse to listen to the remonstrances of reason : but, in short, it becomes necessary *to adopt that mode, when every other proves ineffectual. It is only in extremities that a just and wise nation, or a good prince, has recourse to it, as we have shewn in the concluding chapter of the second book. The reasons which may determine him to take such a step are of two classes. Those of the one class shew that he has a right to make war,—that he has just grounds for undertaking it :—these are called *justificatory revsons*. The cthers, founded on fitness and ultility, determine whether it be expedient for the sovereign to undertake a war,—these are called *motives*.

§ 26. The right of employing force, or making war, belongs to nations no farther than is necessary for their own defence, and for the maintenance of their rights (§ 3). Now, if any one attacks a nation, or violates her perfect rights, he does her an injury. Then, and not till then, that nation has a right to repel the aggressor, and reduce him to reason. Further, she has a right to prevent the intended injury, when she sees herself threatened with it (Book II. § 50). Let us then say in general, that the foundation, or cause of every just war is injury, either already done or threatened. The justificatory reasons for war shew that an injury has been received, or so far threatened as to authorize a prevention of it by arms. It is evident, however, that here the question regards the principal in the war, and not those who join in it as auxiliaries. When, therefore, we would judge whether a war be just, we must consider whether he who undertakes it has in fact received an injury, or whether he be really threatened with one. And, in order to determine what is to be considered as an injury, we must be acquainted with a nation's *rights*, properly so called,—that is to say, her *perfect rights*. These are of various kinds, and very numerous, but may all be referred to the general heads of which we have already treated, and shall further treat in the course of this work. Whatever strikes at these rights is an injury, and a just cause of war.

§ 27. The immediate consequence of the premises is, that if a nation takes up arms when she has received no injury, nor is threatened with any, she undertakes an unjust war. Those alone, to whom an injury is done or intended, have a right to make war.

§ 28. From the same principle we shall likewise deduce the just and lawful object of every war, which is, to *avenge or prevent injury*. To *avenge* signifies here to prosecute the reparation of an injury, if it be of a nature to be repaired,—or, if the evil be irreparable, to obtain a just satisfaction,—and also to punish the offender, if requisite, with a view of providing for our future safety. The right to security authorizes us to do all this (Book II. §§ 49—52). We may therefore distinctly point out, as objects of a lawful war, the three following :—1. To recover what belongs, or is due to us. 2. To provide for our future safety by punishing the aggressor or offender. 3. To defend ourselves, or to protect ourselves from *injury, by repelling unjust violence. The two first are the objects of an offensive, the third that of a defensive war. Camillus, when on the point of attacking the Gauls, concisely set forth to his soldiers all the subjects on which war can be grounded justified— *omnia, quæ defendi, repetique et ulcisci fus sit* †.

§ 29. As the nation, or her ruler, ought, in every undertaking, not only to respect justice, but also to keep in view the advantage of the state, it is necessary that proper and commendable motives should concur with the justificatory reasons, to induce a determination to embark in a war. These reasons shew that the sovereign has a right to take up arms, that he has a just cause to do so. The proper motives shew, that in the present case it is advisable and expedient to make use of his right. These latter relate to prudence, as the justificatory reasons come under the head of justice.

§ 30. I call *proper and commendable motives* those derived from the good of the state, from the safety and common advantage of the citizens. They are inseparable from the justificatory reasons,—a breach of justice being never truly advantageous. Though an unjust war may for a time enrich a state, and extend her frontiers, it renders her odious to other nations, and exposes her to the danger of being crushed by them. Besides, do opulence and extent of dominion always constitute the happiness of states? Amidst the multitude of examples which might here be quoted, let us confine our view to that of the Romans. The Roman republic ruined herself by her triumphs, by the excess of her conquests and power. Rome, when mistress of the world, but enslaved by tyrants and oppressed by a military government, had reason to deplore the success of her arms, and to look back with regret on those happy times when her power did not extend beyond the bounds of Italy, or even when her dominion was almost confined within the circuit of her walls.

Vicious motives are those which have not for their object the good of the state, and which, instead of being drawn from that pure source, are suggested by the violence of the passions. Such are the arrogant desire of command, the ostentation of power, the thirst of riches, the avidity of conquest, hatred, and revenge.

§ 31. The whole right of the nation, and consequently of the sovereign, is derived from the welfare of the state; and by this rule it is to be measured. The obligation to promote and maintain the true welfare of the society or state gives the nation a right to take up arms against him who threatens or attacks that valuable enjoyment. But if a nation, on an injury done to her, is induced to take *up arms, not by the necessity of procuring a just reparation, but by a vicious motive, she abuses her right. The viciousness of the motive tarnishes the lustre of her arms, which might otherwise have shown as the cause of justice :—the war is not undertaken for the lawful cause which the nation had to engage in it: that cause is now no more than a pretext. As to the sovereign in particular, the ruler of the nation—what right has he to expose the safety of the state, with the lives and fortunes of the citizens, to gratify his passions? It is only for the good of the nation that the supreme power is intrusted to him; and it is with that view that he ought to exert it: that is the object prescribed to him even in his least important measures; and shall he undertake the most important and the most dangerous, from

---

† Livy, lib. v. cap. 49.

74

motives foreign or contrary to that great end ?   Yet nothing is more common than such a destructive inversion of views; and it is remarkable, that, on this account, the judicious Polybius gives the name of *Causes* † to the motives on which war is undertaken,—and of *pretexts* ‡ to the justificatory reasons alleged in defence of it.   Thus, he informs us that the cause of the war which Greece undertook against the Persians was the experience she had had of their weakness, and that the pretext alleged by Philip, or by Alexander after him, was, the desire of avenging the injuries which the Greeks had so often suffered, and of providing for their future safety.

§ 32. Let us, however, entertain a better opinion of nations and their rulers.   There are just causes of war, real justificatory reasons; and why should there not be sovereigns who sincerely consider them as their warrant, when they have besides reasonable motives for taking up arms?   We shall therefore give the name of *pretexts* to those reasons alleged as justificatory, but which are so only in appearance, or which are even absolutely destitute of all foundation.   The name of pretexts may likewise be applied to reasons which are, in themselves, true and well-founded, but, not being of sufficient importance for undertaking a war, are made use of only to cover ambitious views or some other vicious motive.   Such was the complaint of the czar Peter I. that sufficient honors had not been paid him on his passage through Riga.   His other reasons for declaring war against Sweden I here omit.

Pretexts are at least a homage which unjust men pay to justice.   He who screens himself with them shews that he still retains some sense of shame.   He does not openly trample on what is the most sacred in human society: he tactily acknowledges that a flagrant injustice merits the indignation of all mankind.

§ 33. Whoever, without justificatory reasons undertakes a war merely from motives of advantage, acts without any right, and his war is unjust.   And he, who, having in reality just grounds for taking up arms, is nevertheless soley actuated by interested views in resorting to hostilities, cannot indeed be charged with injustice, but he betrays a vicious disposition: his conduct is reprehensible, and sullied by the badness of his motives.   War is so dreadful a scourge, that nothing less than manifest justice, joined to a kind of necessity, can authorize it, render it commendable, or at least exempt it from reproach.

§ 34. *Nations that are always ready to take up arms on any prospect of advantage are lawless robbers: but those who seem to delight in the ravages of war, who spread it on all sides, without reasons or pretexts, and even without any other motive than their own ferocity, are monsters, unworthy the name of men.   They should be considered as enemies to the human race, in the same manner as, in civil society, professed assassins and incendiaries are guilty, not only towards the particular victims of their nefarious deeds, but also towards the state, which therefore proclaims them public enemies.   All nations have a right to join in a confederacy for the purpose of punishing and even exterminating those savage nations.   Such were several German tribes mentioned by Tacitus,

---

† *Αηιαι.* Hisior. lib. iii. cap. 6.   ‡ *Προφασεις.*

—such those barbarians who destroyed the Roman empire : nor was it till long after their conversion to Christianity that this ferocity wore off. Such have been the Turks and other Tartars,—Genghis-khan, Timur-Bec or Tamerlane, who like Attila, were scourges employed by the wrath of heaven, and who made war only for the pleasure of making it. Such are, in polished ages and among the most civilized nations, those supposed heroes, whose supreme delight is a battle, and who make war from inclination purely, and not from love to their country.

§ 35. Defensive war is just when made against an unjust aggressor. This requires no proof. Self-defence against unjust violence is not only the right, but the duty of a nation, and one of her most sacred duties. But if the enemy who wages offensive war has justice on his side, we have no right to make forcible opposition; and the defensive war then becomes unjust: for that enemy only exerts his lawful right:—he took up arms only to obtain justice which was refused to him; and it is an act of injustice to resist any one in the exertion of his right.

§ 36. All that remains to be done in such a case is to offer the invader a just satisfaction. If he will not be content with this, a nation gains one great advantage,—that of having turned the balance of justice on her own side ; and his hostilities now becoming unjust, as having no longer any foundation, may very justly be opposed.

The Samnites, instigated by the ambition of their chiefs, had ravaged the lands of the allies of Rome. When they became sensible of their misconduct, they offered full reparation for the damages, with every reasonable satisfaction : but all their submissions could not appease the Romans; whereupon Caius Pontius, general of the Samnites, said to his men, " Since the Romans are absolutely determined on war, necessity justifies it on our side ; an appeal to arms becomes lawful on the part of those who are deprived of every other resource."—*Justum est Bellum, quibus necessarium ; et pia arma, quibus nulla nisi in armis relinquitur spes.* †

§ 37. In order to estimate the justice of an offensive war, the nature of the subject for which a nation takes up arms must be first considered. We should be thoroughly assured of our right before we proceed to assert it in so dreadful a manner. If, therefore, the question relates to a thing which is evidently just, as the recovery of our property, the assertion of a clear and incontestible right, or the attainment of just satisfaction for a manifest injury, and if we cannot obtain justice otherwise than by force of arms, offensive war becomes lawful. Two things are therefore necessary to render it just :—1, some right which is to be asserted,—that is to say, that we be authorized to demand something of another nation :—2, that we be unable to obtain it otherwise than by force of arms. Necessity alone warrants the use of force. It is a dangerous and terrible resource. Nature, the common parent of mankind, allows of it only in cases of the last extremity, and when all other means fail. It is doing wrong to a nation, to make use of violence against her, before we know whether she be disposed to do us justice, or to refuse it.

---

† Livy, Lib. ix. init.

76

Those who, without trying pacific measures, run to arms on every trifling occasion, sufficiently shew that justificatory reasons are, in their mouths, mere pretexts : they eagerly seize the opportunity of indulging their passions and gratifying their ambition under some color of right.

§ 38. In a doubtful cause, where the rights are uncertain, obscure, and disputable, all that can be reasonably required is, that the question be discussed (Book II. § 331), and that, if it be impossible fully to clear it up, the contest be terminated by an equitable compromise. If therefore one of the parties should refuse to accede to such conciliatory measures, the other is justifiable in taking up arms to compel him to an accommodation. And we must observe, that war does not decide the question : victory only compels the vanquished to subscribe to the treaty which terminates the difference. It is an error, no less absurd than pernicious, to say that war is to decide the controversies between those who acknowledge no superior judge,—as is the case with nations. Victory usually favors the cause of strength and prudence, rather than that of right and justice. It would be a bad rule of decision ; but it is an effectual mode of compelling him who refuses to accede to such measures as are consonant to justice ; and it becomes just in the hands of a prince who uses it seasonably, and for a lawful cause.

§ 39. War cannot be just on both sides. One party claims a right ; the other disputes it :—the one complains of an injury : the other denies having done it. They may be considered as two individuals disputing on the truth of a proposition ; and it is impossible that two contrary sentiments should be true at the same time.

§ 40. It may however happen that both the contending parties are candid and sincere in their intentions ; and, in a doubtful cause, it is still uncertain which side is in the right. Wherefore, since nations are equal and independent (Book II. § 36, and Prelim. §§ 18, 19,) *and cannot claim a right of judgment over each other, it follows, that, in every case susceptible of doubt, the arms of the two parties at war are to be accounted equally lawful, at least as to external effects, and until the decision of the cause. But neither does that circumstance deprive other nations of the liberty of forming their own judgment on the case, in order to determine how they are to act, and to assist that party who shall appear to have right on his side,—nor does that effect of the independence of nations operate in exculpation of the author of an unjust war, who certainly incurs a high degree of guilt. But if he acts in consequence of invincible ignorance or error, the injustice of his arms is not imputable to him.

§ 41. When offensive war has for its object the punishment of a nation, it ought, like every other war, to be founded on right and necessity. 1. On right :—an injury must have been actually received. Injury alone being a just cause of war (§ 26), the reparation of it may be lawfully prosecuted : or if in its nature it be irreparable (the only case in which we are allowed to punish), we are authorized to provide for our own safety, and even for that of all other nations, by inflicting on the offender a punishment capable of correcting him, and serving as an example to others. 2. A war of this kind must have necessity to justify it : that is to say, that, to be lawful, it must be the only remaining mode to obtain a just satisfaction; which implies a reasonable security for the time to come. If that complete satisfaction be offered, or if it may be obtained without a war, the injury is done away, and the right to security no longer authorizes us to seek vengeance for it.—(See Book II. §§ 49, 52).

The nation in fault is bound to submit to a punishment which she has deserved, and to suffer it by way of atonement: but she is not obliged to give herself up to the discretion of an incensed enemy. Therefore, when attacked, she ought to make a tender of satisfaction, and ask what penalty is required; and if no explicit answer be given, or the adversary attempts to impose a disproportionate penalty, she then acquires a right to resist, and her defence becomes lawful.

On the whole, however, it is evident that the offended party alone has a right to punish independent persons. We shall not here repeat what we have said elsewhere (Book II. § 7) of the dangerous mistake, or extravagant pretensions of those who assume a right of punishing an independent nation for faults which do not concern them,—who, madly setting themselves up as defenders of the cause of God, take upon them to punish the moral depravity, or irreligion, of a people not committed to their superintendency.

§ 42. Here a very celebrated question, and of the highest importance, presents itself. It is asked, whether the aggrandisement of a neighboring power, by whom a nation fears she may one day be crushed, be a sufficient reason for making war against him,—whether she be justifiable in taking up arms to oppose his aggrandisement, or to weaken him, with the sole view of securing herself from those dangers which the weaker states have almost always reason to apprehend from an overgrown power. To the majority of politicians this question is no problem: it is more difficult *of solution to those who wish to see justice and prudence ever inseparably united.

On the one hand, a state that increases her power by all the arts of good government, does no more than what is commendable—she fulfills her duties towards herself, without violating those which she owes to other nations. The sovereign, who, by inheritance, by free election, or by any other just and honorable means, enlarges his dominions by the addition of new provinces or entire kingdoms, only makes use of his right, without injuring any person. How then should it be lawful to attack a state which, for its aggrandisement, makes use only of lawful means? We must either have actually suffered an injury or be visibly threatened with one, before we are authorized to take up arms, or have just grounds for making war (§§ 26, 27). On the other hand, it is but too well known, from sad and uniform experience, that predominating powers seldom fail to molest their neighbors, to oppress them, and even totally subjugate them, whenever an opportunity occurs, and they can do it with impunity. Europe was on the point of falling into servitude for want of a timely opposition to the growing fortune of Charles V. Is the danger to be waited for? Is the storm, which might be dispersed at its rising, to be permitted to increase? Are we to allow of the aggrandisement of a neighbor, and quietly wait till he makes his preparations to enslave us? Will it be a time to defend ourselves when we are deprived of the means?— Prudence is a duty incumbent on all men, and most pointedly so on the heads of nations, as being commissioned to watch over the safety of a whole people. Let us endeavor to solve this momentous question, agreeably to the sacred principles of the law of nature and of nations. We shall find that they do not lead to weak scruples, and that it is an invariable truth that justice is inseparable from sound policy.

§ 43. And first, let us observe, that prudence, which is, no doubt, a virtue highly necessary in sovereigns, can never recommend the use of unlawful means for the attainment of a just and laudable end. Let not the safety of the people, that supreme law of the state, be alleged here in objection ; for the very safety of the people itself, and the common safety of nations, prohibit the use of means which are repugnant to justice and probity. Why are certain means unlawful ? If we closely consider the point, if we trace it to its first principles, we shall see that it is purely because the introduction of them would be pernicious to human society, and productive of fatal consequences to all nations. See particularly what we have said concerning the observance of justice (Book II. Chap. V.) For the interest, therefore, and even the safety of nations, we ought to hold it as a sacred maxim, that the end does not sanctify the means. And since war is not justifiable *on any other ground than that of avenging an injury received, or preserving ourselves from one with which we are threatened (§ 26), it is a sacred principle of the law of nations, that an increase of power cannot, alone and of itself, give any one a right to take up arms in order to oppose it.

§ 44. No injury has been received from that power (so the question supposes) ; we must, therefore, have good grounds to think ourselves threatened by him, before he can lawfully have recourse to arms. Now, power alone does not threaten an injury :—it must be accompanied by the will. It is, indeed, very unfortunate for mankind, that the will and inclination to oppress may be almost always supposed, where there is a power of oppressing with impunity. But these two things are not necessarily inseparable : and the only right which we derive from the circumstance of their being generally or frequently united, is, that of taking the first appearances for a sufficient indication. When once a state has given proofs of injustice, rapacity, pride, ambition, or an imperious thirst of rule, she becomes an object of suspicion to her neighbors, whose duty it is to stand on their guard against her. They may come upon her at the moment when she is on the point of acquiring a formidable accession of power,—may demand securities,—and, if she hesitates to give them, may prevent her designs by force of arms. The interests of nations are, in point of importance, widely different from those of individuals : the sovereign must not be remiss in his attention to them, nor suffer his generosity and greatness of soul to supersede his suspicions. A nation that has a neighbor at once powerful and ambitious, has her all at stake. As men are under a necessity of regulating their conduct in most cases by probabilities, those probabilities claim their attention in proportion to the importance of the subject : and (to make use of a geometrical expression) their right to obviate a danger is in a compound ratio of the degree of probability and the greatness of the evil threatened. If the evil in question be of a supportable nature,—if it be only some slight loss, matters are not to be precipitated : there is no great danger in delaying our opposition to it, till there be a certainty of our being threatened. But if the safety of the state lies at stake, our precaution and foresight cannot be extended too far. Must we delay to avert our ruin till it becomes inevitable ? If the appearances are so easily credited, it is the fault of that neighbor, who has betrayed his ambition by several indications. If Charles the Second, King of Spain, instead of settling the succession on the Duke of Anjou, had appointed for his heir Louis XVI. himself,—to have tamely suffered the union of the monarchy of Spain, with that of France, would, according to all rules of human foresight, have been nothing less than delivering up all Europe to servitude, or at least reducing it to the most critical and precarious situation. But then, if two independent nations think fit to unite, so as afterwards to form one joint empire, have they not a right to *do it ? And who is authorized to oppose them ? I answer, they have a right to form such a union, provided the views by which they are actuated be not prejudicial to other states. Now, if each of the two nations in question be, separately and without assistance, able to govern and support herself, and to defend herself from insult and oppression, it may be reasonably presumed that the object of their coalition is to domineer over their neighbors. And, on occasions where it is impossible or too dangerous to wait for an absolute certainty, we may justly act on a reasonable presumption. If a stranger levels a musket at me in the middle of a forest, I am not yet certain that he intends to kill me : but shall I, in order to be convinced of his design, allow him time to fire ? What reasonable casuist will deny me the right to anticipate him. But presumption becomes nearly equivalent to certainty, if the prince who is on the point of rising to an enormous power has already given proofs of imperious pride and insatiable ambition. In the preceding supposition, who could have advised the powers of Europe to suffer such a formidable accession to the power of Louis the Fourteenth ? Too certain of the use he would have made of it, they would have joined in opposing it : and in this their safety warranted them. To say that they should have allowed him time to establish his domain over Spain, and consolidate the union of the two monarchies,—and that, for fear of doing him an injury, they should have quietly waited till he crushed them all,—would not this be, in fact, depriving mankind of the right to regulate their conduct by the dictates of prudence, and to act on the ground of probability ? Would it not be robbing them of the liberty to provide for their own safety, as long as they have not mathematical demonstration of its being in danger ? It would have been in vain to have preached such a doctrine. The principal sovereigns of Europe. habituated, by the administration of Louvois, to dread the views and power of Louis XIV. carried their mistrust so far, that they would not even suffer a prince of the house of France to sit on the throne of Spain, though invited to it by the nation, whose approbation had sanctioned the will of her former sovereign. He ascended it, however, notwithstanding the efforts of those who so strongly dreaded his elevation ; and it has since appeared that their policy was too suspicious.

§ 45. It is still easier to prove, that, should that formidable power betray an unjust and ambitious disposition, by doing the least injustice to another, all nations may avail themselves of the occasion, and, by joining the injured party, thus form a coalition of strength, in order to humble that ambitious potentate, and disable him from so easily oppressing his neighbors, or keeping them in continual awe and fear. For an injury gives us a right to provide for our future safety, by depriving the unjust aggressor of the means of injuring us; and it is lawful and even praiseworthy to assist those who are oppressed, or unjustly attacked.

Enough has been said on this subject, to set the minds of politicians at ease, and to relieve them from all apprehension that a *strict and punctilious observance of justice in this particular would pave the way to slavery. It is perhaps wholly unprecedented that a state should receive any remarkable accession of power, without giving other states just causes of complaint. Let the other nations be watchful and alert in repressing that growing power, and they will have nothing to fear. The emperor Charles V. laid hold on the pretext of religion, in order to oppress the princes of the empire, and subject them to his absolute authority. If, by following up his victory over the elector of Saxony, he had accomplished that vast design, the liberties of all Europe would have been endangered. It was therefore with good reason that France assisted the protestants of Germany:—the care of her own safety authorised and urged her to the measure. When the same prince seized on the duchy of Milan, the sovereigns of Europe ought to have assisted France in contending with him for the possession of it, and to have taken advantage of the circumstance, in order to reduce his power within just bounds. Had they prudently availed themselves of the just causes which he soon gave them to form a league against him, they would have saved themselves the subsequent anxieties for their tottering liberty.

§ 46. But, suppose that powerful state, by the justice and circumspection of her conduct, affords us no room to take exception to her proceedings, are we to view her progress with an eye of indifference? Are we to remain quiet spectators of the rapid increase of her power, and imprudently expose ourselves to such designs as it may inspire her with?— No, beyond all doubt. In a matter of so high importance, imprudent supineness would be unpardonable. The example of the Romans is a good lesson for all sovereigns. Had the potentates of those times concerted together to keep a watchful eye on the enterprises of Rome, and to check her incroachments, they would not have successively fallen into servitude. But force of arms is not the only expedient by which we may guard against a formidable power. There are other means, of a gentler nature, and which are at all times lawful. The most effectual is a confederacy of the less powerful sovereigns, who, by this coalition of strength, become able to hold the balance against that potentate whose power excites their alarms. Let them be firm and faithful in their alliance; and their union will prove the safety of each.

They may also mutually favor each other, to the exclusion of him whom they fear; and by reciprocally allowing various advantages to the subjects of the allies, especially in trade, and refusing them to those of that dangerous potentate, they will augment their own strength, and diminish his, without affording him any just cause of complaint, since every one is at liberty to grant favors and indulgences at his own pleasure.

§ 47. *Europe forms a political system, an integral body, closely connected by the relations and different interests of the nations inhabiting this part of the world. It is not, as formerly, a confused heap of detached pieces, each of which thought herself very little concerned in the fate of the others, and seldom regarded things which did not immediately concern her. The continual attention of sovereigns to every occurrence, the constant residence of ministers, and the perpetual negotiations, make of modern Europe a kind of republic, of which the members— each independent, but all linked together by the ties of common interest —unite for the maintenance of order and liberty. Hence arose that famous scheme of the political balance, or the equilibrium of power; by which is understood such a disposition of things, as that no one potentate be able absolutely to predominate, and prescribe laws to the others.

§ 48. The surest means of preserving that equilibrium would be, that no power should be much superior to the others, that all, or at least the greater part, should be nearly equal in force. Such a project has been attributed to Henry the Fourth† : but it would have been impossible to carry it into execution without injustice and violence? Besides, suppose such equality once established, how could it always be maintained by lawful means? Commerce, industry, military pre-eminence, would soon put an end to it. The right of inheritance, vesting even in women and their descendants,—a rule, which it was so absurd to establish in the case of sovereignties, but which nevertheless is established,—would completely overturn the whole system.

It is a more simple, an easier, and a more equitable plan, to have recourse to the method just mentioned, of forming confederacies in order to oppose the more powerful potentate, and prevent him from giving law to his neighbors. Such is the mode at present pursued by the sovereigns of Europe. They consider the two principal powers, which on that very account are naturally rivals, as destined to be checks on each other ; and they unite with the weaker, like so many weights thrown into the lighter scale, in order to keep it in equilibrium with the other. The house of Austria has long been the preponderating power : at present France is so in her turn. England, whose opulence and formidable fleets have a powerful influence, without alarming any state on the score of its liberty, because that nation seems cured of the rage of conquest,—England, I say, has the glory of holding the political balance. She is attentive to preserve it in equilibrium :—a system of policy, which is in itself highly just and wise, and will ever entitle her to praise, as long as she continues to pursue it only by means of alliances, confederacies, and other methods equally lawful.

§ 49. Confederacies would be a sure mode of preserving the equilibrium, and thus maintaining the liberty of nations, did all princes thoroughly understand their true interests, and make the welfare of the

---

† Of France.

state serve as the rule in all their proceedings. Great potentates, how-ever, are but too successful in gaining over partisans and *allies, who blindly adopt all their views. Dazzled by the glare of a present advan-tage, seduced by their avarice, deceived by faithless ministers,—how many princes become the tools of a power which will one day swallow up either themselves or their successors! The safest plan, therefore, is to seize the first favorable opportunity, when we can, consistently with justice, weaken that potentate who destroys the equilibrium (§ 45)—or to employ every honorable means to prevent his acquiring too formida-ble a degree of power. For that purpose, all the other nations should be particularly attentive not to suffer him to aggrandise himself by arms: and this they may at all times do with justice. For, if this prince makes an unjust war, every one has a right to succor the oppressed party. If he makes a just war, the neutral nations may interfere as mediators for an accommodation,—they may induce the weaker state to propose reasonable terms and offer a fair satisfaction, and may save her from fall-ing under the yoke of a conqueror. On the offer of equitable conditions to the prince who wages even the most justifiable war, he has all that he can demand. The justice of his cause, as we shall soon see, never gives him a right to subjugate his enemy, unless when that extremity became necessary to his own safety, or when he has no other mode of obtaining indemnification for the injury he has received. Now, that is not the case here, as the interposing nations can by no other means procure him a just indemnification, and an assurance of safety.

In fine, there cannot exist a doubt, that, if that formidable potentate certainly entertain designs of oppression and conquest,—if he betray his views by his preparations and other proceedings,—the other states have a right to anticipate him: and if the fate of war declares in their favor, they are justifiable in taking advantage of this happy opportunity to weaken and reduce a power too contrary to the equilibrium, and dan-gerous to the common liberty.

This right of nations is still more evident against a sovereign, who, from an habitual propensity to take up arms without reasons, or even so much as plausible pretexts, is continually disturbing the public tranquillity.

§ 50. This leads us to a particular question, nearly allied to the pre-ceding. When a neighbor, in the midst of a profound peace erects fortresses on our frontier, equips a fleet, augments his troops, assembles a powerful army, fills his magazines,—in a word, when he makes prep-arations for war,—are we allowed to attack him, with a view to prevent the danger with which we think ourselves threatened? The answer greatly depends on the manners and character of that neighbor. We must inquire into the reasons of those preparations, and bring him to an explanation:—such is the mode of proceeding in Europe: and if his sincerity be justly suspected, securities may be required of him. His refusal, in this case, would furnish ample indication of sinister designs, and a sufficient reason to justify us in anticipating them. But if that *sovereign has never betrayed any symptoms of baseness and perfidy, and especially, if at that time there is no dispute subsisting between him and us, why should we not quietly rest on his word, only taking such precautions as prudence renders indispensible? We ought not, without sufficient cause, to presume him capable of exposing himself to infamy by adding perfidy to violence. As long as he has not rendered his sincerity questionable, we have no right to require any other security from him.

It is true, however, that if a sovereign continues to keep up a powerful army in profound peace, his neighbors must not suffer their vigilance to be entirely lulled to sleep by his bare word ; and prudence requires that they should keep themselves on their guard. However certain they may be of the good faith of that prince, unforeseen differences may intervene ; and shall they leave him the advantage of being provided, at that juncture, with a numerous and well-disciplined army, while they themselves will have only new levies to oppose it ? Unquestionably no. This would be leaving themselves almost wholly at his discretion. They are, therefore, under the necessity of following his example, and keeping, as he does, a numerous army on foot : and what a burden is this to a state ! Formerly, and without going any farther back than the last century, it was pretty generally made an article in every treaty of peace, that the billigerent powers should disarm on both sides,—that they should disband their troops. If, in a time of profound peace, a prince was disposed to keep up any considerable number of forces, his neighbors took their measures accordingly, formed leagues against him, and obliged him to disarm. Why has not that salutary custom been preserved ? The constant maintenance of numerous armies deprives the soil of its cultivators, checks the progress of population, and can only serve to destroy the liberties of the nation by whom they are maintained. Happy England ! whose situation exempts it from any considerable charge in supporting the instruments of despotism. Happy Switzerland ! if, continuing carfully to exercise her militia, she keeps herself in a condition to repel any foreign enemies, without feeding a host of idle soldiers, who might one day crush the liberties of the people, and even bid defiance to the lawful authority of the sovereign. Of this the Roman legions furnish a signal instance. This happy method of a free republic,—the custom of training up all her citizens to the art of war,—renders the state respectable abroad, and saves it from a very pernicious defect at home. It would have been everywhere imitated, had the public good been every where the only object in view.

Sufficient has now been said on the general principles for estimating the justice of a war. Those who are thoroughly acquainted with the principles, and have just ideas of the various rights of nations, will easily apply the rules to particular cases.

§ 103. *NEUTRAL nations are those who, in time of war, do not take any part in the contest, but remain common friends to both parties, without favoring the arms of the one to the prejudice of the other. Here we are to consider the obligations and rights flowing from neutrality.

§ 104. In order rightly to understand this question, we must avoid confounding what may lawfully be done by the nation that is free from all engagements, with what she may do if she expects to be treated as perfectly neutral in a war. As long as a neutral nation wishes securely to enjoy the advantages of her neutrality, she must in all things shew *a strict impartiality towards the belligerent powers:* for, should she favor one of the parties to the prejudice of the other, she cannot complain of being treated by him as an adherent and confederate of his enemy. Her neutrality would be fraudulent neutrality, of which no nation will consent to be the dupe. It is sometimes suffered to pass unnoticed, merely for want of ability to resent it: we choose to connive at it, rather than excite a more powerful opposition against us. But the present question is, to determine what may lawfully be done, not what prudence may dictate according to circumstances. Let us therefore examine, in what consists that impartiality which a neutral nation ought to observe.

It solely relates to *war*, and includes two articles,—1. To give *no assistance* when there is no obligation to give it,—nor voluntary to furnish troops, arms, ammunition, or any thing of direct use in war. I do not say, " to give assistance equally," but " to give no assistance :" for it would be absurd that a state should at one and the same time assist two nations at war with each other ; and besides it would be impossible to do it with equality. The same things, the like number of troops, the like quantity of arms, of stores, &c., furnished in different circumstances, are no longer equivalent succors. 2. In whatever does not relate to war, a neutral and impartial nation must not refuse to one of the parties, on account of his present quarrel, what she grants to the other. This does not deprive her of the liberty to make the advantage of the state still serve as her rule of conduct in her negotiations, her friendly connections, and her commerce. When this reason induces her to give preferences in things which are ever at the free disposal of the possessor, she only makes use of her right, and is not chargeable with partiality. But to refuse any of those things to one *of the parties purely because he is at war with the other, and because she wishes to favor the latter, would be departing from the line of strict neutrality.

§ 105. I have said that a neutral state ought to give no assistance to either of the parties, when " under no obligation to give it." This restriction is necessary. We have already seen, that when a sovereign furnishes the moderate succor due in virtue of a former defensive alliance, he does not become an associate in the war (§ 101). He may, therefore, fulfill his engagement, and yet observe a strict neutrality. Of this Europe affords frequent instances.

---

upon neutrals, and neutrality, will be found collected in 1 Chitty's Commercial Law, 43 — 64, 383,—490; Id. Index, tit. *Neutrals,* and in Chitty's L. Nat. 14, 34—54, 153; and Id. Index, tit. *Neutrals.*—C.

§ 106 When a war breaks out between two nations, all other states that are not bound by treaties, are free to remain neuter ; and, if either of the belligerent powers attempted to force them to a junction with him, he would do them an injury, inasmuch as he would be guilty of an infringement on their independency in a very essential point. To themselves alone it belongs to determine whether any reason exists to induce them to join in the contest: and there are two points which claim their consideration : 1. The justice of the cause. If that be evident, injustice is not to be countenanced : on the contrary, it is generous and praiseworthy to succor oppressed innocence, when we possess the ability. If the case be dubious, the other nations may suspend their judgment, and not engage in a foreign quarrel. 2. When convinced which party has justice on his side, they have still to consider whether it be for the advantage of the state to concern themselves in this affair, and to embark in the war.

§ 107. A nation making war, or preparing to make it, often proposes a treaty of neutrality to a state of which she entertains suspicions. It is prudent to learn betimes what she has to expect, and not run the risk of a neighbor's suddenly joining with the enemy in the heat of the war. In every case, where neutrality is allowable, it is also lawful to bind ourselves to it by treaty.

Sometimes even necessity renders this justifiable. Thus, although it be the duty of all nations to assist oppressed innocence (Book II. § 4), yet, if an unjust conqueror, ready to invade his neighbor's possessions, makes me an offer of neutrality when he is able to crush me, what can I do better than to accept it ? I yield to necessity ; and my inability discharges me from a natural obligation. The same inability would even excuse me from a perfect obligation contracted by an alliance. The enemy of my ally threatens me with a vast superiority of force : my fate is in his hand : he requires me to renounce the liberty of furnishing any assistance against him. Necessity, and the care of my own safety, absolves me from my engagements. Thus, it was that Louis the Fourteenth compelled Victor Amadeus, duke of Savoy, to quit the party of the allies. But, then the necessity must be very urgent. It is only the cowardly, or the perfidious, who avail themselves of the slightest grounds of alarm, to violate their promises and desert their duty. *In the late war, the King of Poland, elector of Saxony, and the king of Sardinia, firmly held out against the unfortunate course of events, and, to their great honor, could not be brought to treat without the concurrence of their allies.

§ 108. Another reason renders these treaties of neutrality useful, and even necessary. A nation that wishes to secure her own peace, when the flames of war are kindling in her neighborhood, cannot more successfully attain that object than by concluding treaties with both parties, expressly agreeing what each may do or require in virtue of the neutrality. This is a sure mode to preserve herself in peace, and to obviate all disputes and cavils.

§ 109. Without such treaties it is to be feared that disputes will often arise respecting what neutrality does or does not allow. This subject presents many questions which authors have discussed with great heat, and which have given rise to the most dangerous quarrels between nations. Yet the law of nature, and of nations, has its invariable principles, and affords rules on this head, as well as on the others. Some things also have grown into custom among civilized nations, and are to be conformed to by those who would not incur the reproach of unjustly breaking the peace†. As to the rules of the natural law of nations, they result from a just combination of the laws of war, with the liberty, the safety, the advantages, the commerce, and the other rights of neutral nations. It is on this principle that we shall lay down the following rules :—

§ 110. First, no act on the part of a nation, which falls within the exercise of her rights, and is done solely with a view to her own good, without partiality, without a design of favoring one power to the prejudice of another,—no act of that kind, I say, can in general be considered as contrary to neutrality ; nor does it become such, except on particular occasions, when it cannot take place without injury to one of the parties, who has then a particular right to oppose it. Thus, the besieger has a right to prohibit access to the place besieged (see § 117 in the sequel). Except in cases of this nature, shall the quarrels of others deprive me of the free exercise of my rights in the pursuit of measures which I judge advantageous to my people ? Therefore, when it is the custom of a nation, for the purpose of employing and training her subjects, to permit levies of troops in favor of a particular power to whom she thinks proper to intrust them,—the enemy of that power cannot look upon such permissions as acts of hostility, unless they are given with a view to the invasion of his territories or the support *of an odious and evidently unjust cause. He cannot even demand, as matter of right, that the like favor be granted to him,—because that nation may have reasons for refusing him, which do not hold good with regard to his adversary ; and it belongs to that nation alone to judge of what best suits her circumstances. The Switzers, as we have already observed, grant levies of troops to whom they please ; and no power has hitherto thought fit to quarrel with them on that head. It must, however, be owned, that, if those levies were considerable, and constituted the principal strength of my enemy, while, without any substantial reason being alleged, I were absolutely refused all levies whatever,—I should have just cause to consider that nation as leagued with my enemy ; and, in this case, the care of my own safety would authorize me to treat her as such.

The case is the same with respect to money which a nation may have been accustomed to lend out at interest. If the sovereign, or his subjects, lend money to my enemy on that footing, and refuse it to me because they have not the same confidence in me, this is no breach of neutrality. They lodge their property where they think it safest. If such preference be not founded on good reasons, I may impute it to ill-will against me, or to a predilection for my enemy. Yet if I should make it a pretence for declaring war, both the true principles of the law

---

† The following is an instance :— " It was determined by the Dutch, that on a vessel's entering a neutral port, after having taken any of the enemies of her nation prisoners on the high seas, she should be obliged to set those prisoners at liberty, because they were then fallen into the power of a nation that was in neutrality with the belligerent parties. —The same rule had been observed by England in the war between Spain and the United Provinces."

of nations, and the general custom happily established in Europe, would join in condemning me. While it appears that this nation lends out her money purely for the sake of gaining an interest upon it, she is at liberty to dispose of it according to her own discretion ; and I have no right to complain.

But if the loan were evidently granted for the purpose of enabling an enemy to attack me, this would be concurring in the war against me.

If the troops, above alluded to, were furnished to my enemy by the state herself, and at her own expense, or the money in like manner lent by the state, without interest, it would no longer be a doubtful question whether such assistance were incompatible with neutrality.

Further, it may be affirmed on the same principles, that if a nation trades in arms, timber for ship-building, vessels, and warlike stores,—I cannot take it amiss that she sells such things to my enemy, provided she does not refuse to sell them to me also at a reasonable price. She carries on her trade without any design to injure me ; and by continuing it in the same manner as if I were not engaged in war, she gives me no just cause of complaint.

§ 111. In what I have said above, it is supposed that my enemy goes himself to a neutral country to make his purchases. Let us now discuss another case,—*that of neutral nations resorting to my enemy's country for commercial purposes.* It is certain, that, as they have no part in my quarrel, they are under no obligation to renounce their commerce for the sake of avoiding to supply my *enemy with the means of carrying on the war against me. Should they affect to refuse selling me a single article, while at the same time they take pains to convey an abundant supply to my enemy, with an evident intention to favor him, such partial conduct would exclude them from the neutrality they enjoyed. But if they only continue their *customary trade,* they do not thereby declare themselves against any interest; they only exercise a right which they are under no obligation of sacraficing to me(152).

On the other hand, whenever I am at war with a nation, both my safety and welfare prompt me to deprive her, as far as possible, of every thing which may enable her to resist or injure me. In this instance, the law of necessity exerts its full force. If that law warrants me, on occasion, to seize what belongs to other people, will not likewise warrant me to intercept every thing belonging to *war,* which neutral nations are carrying to my enemy? Even if I should, by taking such measures, render all those neutral nations my enemies, I had better run that hazard, than suffer him who is actually at war with me thus freely to receive supplies, and collect additional strength to oppose me. It is, therefore, very proper, and perfectly conformable to the law of nations (which disapproves of multiplying the *causes of war*), not to consider those seizures of the goods of neutral nations as acts of hostility.

---

(152) It must be a continuance only of such *customary* trade. See Horne on Captures, 215—233; *De Tastet* v. *Taylor,* 4 Taunt. 238; *Bell* v. *Reid,* 1 Maule & Selw. 727; and an able speech of Lord Erskine, 8th March, 1808, upon the orders in Council; 10 Cobbett's Parl. Dep. 935. It has even been holden that a British-born subject, while domiciled in a neutral country, may legally trade from that country with a state at war with this country. *Bell* v. *Reid,* 1 Maule & Selwyn. 727.—C.

When I have notified to them my declaration of war against such or such a nation, if they will afterwards expose themselves: to risk in supplying her with such things which serve to carry on war, they will have no reason to complain if their goods fall into my possession: and I, on the other hand, do not declare war against them for having attempted to convey such goods. They suffer, indeed, by a war in which they have no concern; but they suffer accidentally. I do not oppose their right: I only exert my own; and if our rights clash with and reciprocally injure each other, that circumstance is the effect of inevitable necessity. Such collisions daily happen in war. When, in pursuance of my rights, I exhaust a country from which you derive your subsistence,—when I besiege a city with which you carried on a profitable trade, I doubtless injure you; I subject you to losses and inconveniences; but it is without any design of hurting you. I only make use of my rights, and consequently do you no injustice.

But that limits may be set to these inconveniences, and that the commerce of neutral nations may subsist in as great a degree of freedom as is consistent with the laws of war, there are certain rules to be observed, on which Europe seems to be generally agreed.

§ 112. The first is, carefully to distinguish ordinary goods which have no relation to war, from those that are peculiarly subservient to it. *Neutral nations should enjoy perfect liberty to trade in the former:* *the belligerent powers cannot with any reason refuse it, or prevent the importation of such goods into the enemy's country:* the care of their own safety, the necessity of self defence, does not authorize them to do it, since those things will not render the enemy more formidable. *An attempt to interrupt or put a stop to this trade would be a violation of the rights of neutral nations, a flagrant injury to them;*—necessity, as we have above observed, being the only reason which can authorize any restraint on their trade and navigation to the ports of the enemy. England and the United Provinces having agreed, in the treaty at Whitehall, signed on the 22d of August, 1689, to notify to all states not at war with France, that they would attack every ship bound to or coming from any port of that kingdom, and that they before-hand declared every such ship to be a lawful prize,—Sweden and Denmark, from whom some ships had been taken, entered into a counter-treaty on the 17th of March, 1693, for the purpose of maintaining their rights and procuring just satisfaction. And the two maritime powers, being convinced that the complaints of the two crowns were well founded, did them justice†.

Commodities particularly *useful* in war, and the importation of which to an enemy is prohibited, are *called contraband goods.* Such are *arms, ammunition, timber for ship-building, every kind of naval stores, horses,* —and even provisions, in certain junctures, when we have hopes of reducing the enemy by famine‡(153).

---

† See other instances in Grotius, de Jure Belli et Pacis, lib. iii. cap. i. § 5, not. 6.
‡ The Pensionary De Witt, in a letter of January 14, 1654, acknowledges that it would be contrary to the law of nations to prevent neutrals from carrying *corn* to an enemy's country; but he says that we may lawfully prevent them from supplying the enemy with *cordage, and other materials for the rigging and equipment of ships of war.*
In 1597, queen Elizabeth would not allow

§ 113. But, in order to hinder the transportation of *contraband* goods to an enemy, are we only to stop and seize them, paying the value to the owner,—or have we a right to confiscate them? Barely to stop those goods would in general prove an ineffectual mode, especially at sea, where there is no possibility of entirely cutting off all access to the enemy's harbors. Recourse is therefore had to the expedient of confiscating all contraband goods that we can seize on, in order that the fear of loss may operate as a check on the avidity of gain, and deter the merchants of neutral countries from supplying the enemy with such commodities. And, indeed, it is an object of such high importance to a nation at war to prevent, as far as possible, the enemy being supplied with such articles as will add to his strength and render him more dangerous, that necessity and the care of her own welfare and safety authorize her to take effectual methods for that purpose, and to declare that *all commodities of that nature, destined for the enemy, shall be considered as lawful prize. On this account she notifies to the neutral states her declaration of war (§ 63); whereupon the latter usually gives orders to their subjects to refrain from all contraband commerce with the nations at war, declaring, that if they are captured in carrying on such trade, the sovereign will not protect them. This rule is the point where the general custom of Europe seems at present fixed, after a number of variations, as will appear from the note of Grotius, which we have just quoted, and particularly from the ordinances of the kings of France, in the year 1543 and 1584, which only allow the French to seize contraband goods, and to keep them on paying the value. The modern usage is certainly the most agreeable to the mutual duties of nations, and the best calculated to reconcile their respective rights. The nation at war is highly interested in depriving the enemy of all foreign assistance; and this circumstance gives her a right to consider all those, if not absolutely as enemies, at least as people that feel very little scruple to injure her, who carry to her enemy the articles of which he stands in need for the support of the war; she, therefore, punishes them by the confiscation of their goods. Should their sovereign undertake to protect them, such conduct would be tantamount to his furnishing the enemy with those succors himself: a measure which were undoubtedly inconsistent with neutrality. When a nation, without any other motive than the prospect

---

the Poles and Danes to furnish Spain with provisions, much less with arms, alleging that, "according to the rules of war, it is lawful to reduce an enemy even by famine, with the view of obliging him to sue for peace." The United Provinces, finding it necessary to observe a greater degree of circumspection, did not prevent neutral nations from carrying on any kind of commerce with Spain. It is true, indeed, that, while their own subjects sold both arms and provisions to the Spaniards, they could not with propriety have attempted to forbid neutral nations to carry on a similar trade. (Grotius, Hist. of the Disturbances in the Low Countries, book vi.) Nevertheless, in 1646, the United

Provinces published an edict prohibiting their own subjects in general, and even neutral nations, to carry either provisions, or any other merchandise; to Spain, because the Spaniards, "after having, under the appearance of commerce, allured foreign vessels to their ports, detained them, and made use of them, as ships of war." And for this reason, the same edict declared that "the confederates, when blockading up their enemies' ports, would seize upon every vessel they saw steering towards those places."—Ibid. book xv. p. 572.—Ed. A. D. 1797.

(153) What are *contraband goods*, see 1 Chitty's Comml. L. 444—449; and Chitty's L. Nat. 119—128.—C.

of gain, is employed in strengthening my enemy, and regardless of the irreparable evil which she may thereby entail upon me†, she is certainly not my friend, and gives me a right to consider and treat her as an associate of my enemy. In order, therefore, to avoid perpetual subjects of complaint and rupture, it has, in perfect conformity to sound principles, been agreed that the belligerent powers may seize and confiscate all contraband goods which neutral persons shall attempt to carry to their enemy, without any complaint from the sovereign of those merchants ; as, on the other hand, the power at war does not impute to the neutral sovereigns these practices of their subjects. Care is even taken to settle every particular of this kind in treaties of commerce and navigation.

§ 114. We cannot prevent the conveyance of contraband good, without *searching neutral vessels* that we meet at sea : we have *therefore* a right to *search them*. Some powerful nations have indeed, *at different times, refused to submit to this search. "After the peace of Vervins, Queen Elizabeth, continuing the war against Spain, requested permission of the king of France to cause all French ships bound for Spain to be searched, in order to discover whether they secretly carried any military stores to that country : but this was refused as an injury to trade, and a favorable occasion for pillage.‡" *At present, a neutral ship refusing to be searched, would from that preceeding alone be condemned as a lawful prize*(154). But, to avoid inconveniences, oppression, and every other abuse, the manner of the search is settled in the treaties of navigation and commerce. It is the established custom at present to give full credit to the certificates, bills of landing, &c. produced by the master of the ship, unless any fraud appear in them, or there be good reasons for suspecting it(155).

---

† In our time, the king of Spain prohibited all Hamburgh ships from entering his harbors, because that city had engaged to furnish the Algerines with military stores ; and thus he obliged the Hamburghers to cancel their treaty with the Barbarians.—Ed. A. D. 1797.

‡ Grotius, ubi supra.

(154) As to *the right of visiting and searching neutral ships,* see the celebrated letter of the Duke of Newcastle to the Prussian Secretary, A. D. 1752 ; 1 Collect. Jurid. 138 ; and Halliday's Life of Lord Mansfield ; Elements of General History, vol. iii. p. 222; Marshall on Insurance, book i. ch. 8, sect. 5; *Garrels* v. *Kensington*, 8 Term. Rep. 235; Lord Erskine's Speech upon Orders in Council, 8 March, 1808 ; 10 Cobbett's Parl. Deb. 955 ; Baring upon Orders in council, p. 102. Clearly at this day the right of search exists practically as well as theoretically. The right of search, and of the consequence of resistance, and of the papers and documents that ought to be found on board the neutral vessels, are most clearly established by the best modern decisions ; see *Barker* v. *Blakes*, 9 East, Rep. 283, and numerous other cases, collected in 1 Chitty's Commercial Law, 482—489 ; Chitty's L. Nat. 190—199. The inter-national law upon the subject will be found admirably summed up by Sir Wm. Scott, in his judgment in the case of the *Maria*, 1 Rob. Rep. 346, and 1 Edward's Rep. 208, confirming the authority of Vattel, and on which he thus concludes : "I stand with confidence upon all fair principles of reason,—upon the distinct authority of Vattel and upon the institutes of other great maritime countries, as well as those of our own country, when I venture to lay it down that, by the law of nations, as now understood, a deliberate and continued resistance of search, on the part of a neutral vessel, to a lawful cruiser, is followed by the legal consequences of confiscation." And see *Dispatch*, 3 Rob. Rep. 278 ; *Elsabe*, 4 Rob. Rep. 408 ; *Pennsylvania*, 1 Acton's Rep. 33 ; *Saint Juan Baptista*, 5 Rob. Rep. 33 ; *Maria*, 1 Rob. Rep. 340 ; *Mentor*, 1 Edward, 268 ; *Catherina Elizabeth*, 5 Rob. Rep. 232. See the modern French view of the right of visitation and search. Cours de Droits Public tom. i. p. 84. Paris : A. D. 1830—D.

(155) As to papers and documents that ought to be on board, see 1 Chitty's Com.

§ 115. If we find an enemy's effects on board a neutral ship, we seize them by the rights of war(156): but we are naturally bound to pay the freight to the master of the vessel, who is not to suffer by such seizure†(157).

The *effects of neutrals, found in an enemy's ships*, are to be restored to the owners, against whom there is no right of confiscation ; but without any allowance for detainer, decay, &c. (158). The loss sustained by the neutrals on this occasion is an accident to which they exposed themselves by embarking their property in an enemy's ship ; and the captor, in exercising the rights of war, is not responsible for the accidents which may thence result, any more than if his cannon kills a neutral passenger who happens unfortunately to be on board an enemy's vessel(159).

§ 117. Hitherto we have considered the commerce of neutral nations with the territories of the enemy in general. There is a particular case in which the rights of war extend still farther. All commerce with a besieged town is absolutely prohibited. If I lay siege to a place, or even *simply blockade* it, I have a right to hinder any one from entering, and to treat as an enemy whoever attempts to enter the place, or carry any thing to the besieged, without my leave ; for he opposes my undertaking, and may contribute to the miscarriage of it, and thus involve me in all the misfortunes of an unsuccessful war. King Demetrius hanged up *the master and pilot of a vessel carrying provisions to Athens at a time when he was on the point of reducing that city by famine‡. In the long and bloody war carried on by the United Provinces against Spain for the recovery of their liberties, they would not suffer the English to carry goods to Dunkirk, before which the Dutch fleet lay.§

---

mercial Law, 487—489, and Chitty's L. Nat. 196—199, and authorities there collected. The owner of the neutral vessel has no remedy for loss of voyage, or other injury occasioned by the reasonable exercise of the right of search, (*infra* note) but he may in sure against the risk ; *Barker* v. *Blakes*, 9 East, 283.—C.

(156) Particular states have relaxed the rigour of this rule, and, by express treaty, granted immunity, by establishing a maxim, " Free ships, free goods ;" see instances, 5 Rob. Rep. 52 ; 6 Rob. Rep. 24, 41.— 358.—C.

† " I have obtained," said the ambassador Boreel, in a letter to the Grand Pensionary De Witt, " the abrogation of that pretended French law, that *enemy's property involves in confiscation the property of friends ;* so that, if henceforward any effects belonging to the enemies of France be found in a free Dutch vessel, those effects alone shall be liable to confiscation ; and the vessel shall be released, together with all the other property on board. But I find it impossible to obtain the object of the twenty-fourth article of my instructions, which says, that *the immunity of the vessel shall extend to the cargo, even if enemies' property.*" De Witt's Letters and Negociations, vol. i. p. 80.—Such a law as the latter would be more natural than the former.—Edit. A. D. 1797.

(157) But in these cases, the freight to be paid is not necessarily to be measured by the terms of the charter-party, 1 Molloy, 1—18 ; —and *Twilling Ruit*, 5 Rob. Rep 82.—C.

(158) 1 Chitty's Commercial Law, 440 ; Grotius, b. iii. c. vi. § v ; Marshall on Insurance, b. i. c. viii. § v. The loss of voyage and damage may be insured against ; *Barker* v. *Blakes*, 9 East Rep. 283.—C.

(159) As to violation of blockade in general, see the modern decisions, 1 Chitty's Commercial Law, 449 and 460.—492 ; Chitty's L. Nat. 129—144, and 259 ; and see as to the distinction between a *military* and *Commercial* blockade, and their effect ; 1 Acton's Rep. 128. On a question of violation of Blockade, Sir *W. Scott* said, " Three things must be proved—1st, the existence of an actual blockade ; 2ndly, the knowledge of the party supposed to have offended ; and 3dly, some act of violation, either by going in or coming out with a cargo laden after the commencement of blockade." In case of *Betsy*, 1 Rob. Rep. 92, and *Nancy*, 1 Acton's Rep. 59.—C.

‡ Plutarch, in Demetrio.

§ Grotius, ubi supra.

§ 118. A neutral nation preserves, towards both the belligerent powers, the several relations which nature has instituted between nations. She ought to show herself ready to render them every office of humanity reciprocally due from one nation to another : she ought in every thing not directly relating to war, to give them all the assistance in her power, and of which they may stand in need. Such assistance, however, must be given with impartiality ; that is to say, she must not refuse any thing to one of the parties on account of his being at war with the other (§ 104). But this is no reason why a neutral state, under particular connections of friendship and good neighborhood with one of the belligerent powers, may not, in every thing that is unconnected with war, grant him all those preferences which are due to friends : much less does she afford any grounds of exception to her conduct, if, in commerce, for instance, she continues to allow him such indulgences as have been stipulated in her treaties with him. She ought, therefore, as far as the public welfare will permit, equally to allow the subjects of both parties to visit her territories on business, and there to purchase provisions, horses, and, in general, every thing they stand in need of,—unless she has, by a treaty of neutrality promised to refuse to both parties such articles as are used in war. Amidst all the wars which disturb Europe, the Switzers preserve their territories in a state of neutrality. Every nation indiscriminately is allowed free access for the purchase of provisions, if the country has a surplus, and for that of horses, ammunition, and arms.

§ 119. An innocent passage is due to all nations with whom a state is at peace (Book II. § 123) ; and this duty extends to troops as well as to individuals. But it rests with the sovereign of the country to judge whether the passage be innocent ; and it is very difficult for that of an army to be entirely so. In the late wars of Italy, the territories of the republic of Venice, and those of the pope, sustained very great damage by the passage of armies, and often became the theatre of the war.

§ 120. Since, therefore, the passage of troops, and especially that of a whole army, is by no means a matter of indifference, he who desires to march his troops through a neutral country, must apply for the sovereign's permission. To enter his territory without his consent, is a violation of his rights of sovereignty and supreme dominion, by virtue of which, that country is not to be disposed of for any use whatever, without his express or tacit permission. Now, a tacit permission for the entrance of a body of troops is not to be presumed, since their entrance may be productive of the most serious consequences.

§ 121. If the neutral sovereign has good reasons for refusing a passage, he is not obliged to grant it,—the passage in that case being no longer innocent.

§ 122. In all doubtful cases, we must submit to the judgment of the proprietor respecting the innocence of the use we desire to make of things belonging to another (Book II. §§ 128, 130), and must acquiesce in his refusal, even though we think it unjust. If the refusal be evidently unjust,—if the use, and, in the case now before us, the passage be unquestionably innocent,—a nation may do herself justice, and take by force what is unjustly denied to her. But we have already observed that it is very difficult for the passage of an army to be absolutely innocent, and much more so for the innocence to be very evident. So various are the evils it may occasion, and the dangers that may attend it,—so complicated are they in their nature, and so numerous are the circumstances with which they are connected,—that. to foresee and provide for every thing, is next to impossible. Besides self-interest has so powerful an influence on the judgments of men, that if he who requires the passage is to be the judge of its innocence, he will admit none of the reasons brought against it; and thus a door is opened to continual quarrels and hostilities. The tranquillity, therefore, and the common safety of nations, require that each should be mistress of her own territory, and at liberty to refuse every foreign army an entrance, when she has not departed from her natural liberties in that respect, by treaties. From this rule, however, let us except those very uncommon cases which admit of the most evident demonstration that the passage required is wholly unattended with inconvenience or danger. If on such an occasion, a passage be forced, he who forces it will not be so much blamed as the nation that has indiscreetly subjected herself to this violence. Another case, which carries its own exception on the very face of it, and admits not of the smallest doubt, is that of extreme necessity. Urgent and absolute necessity suspends all the rights of property (Book II. §§ 119, 123): and if the proprietor be not under the same pressure of necessity as you, it is allowable for you, even against his will, to make use of what belongs to him. When, therefore, an army find themselves exposed to imminent destruction, or unable to return to their own country, unless they pass through neutral territories, they have a right to pass in spite of the sovereign, and to force their way, sword in hand. But they ought first to request a passage, to offer securities, and pay for whatever damages they may occasion. Such was the mode pursued by the Greeks on their return from Asia, under the conduct of Agesilaus†.

*Extreme necessity may even authorise the temporary seizure of a neutral town, and the putting a garrison therein, with a view to cover ourselves from the enemy, or to prevent the execution of his designs against that town, when the sovereign is not able to defend it. But when the danger is over, we must immediately restore the place, and pay all the charges, inconveniences, and damages, which we have occasioned by seizing it.

§ 123. When a passage is not of absolute necessity, the bare danger which attends the admission of a powerful army into our territory, may authorise us to refuse them permission to enter. We may have reason to apprehend that they will be tempted to take possession of the country, or at least to act as masters while they are in it, and to live at discretion. Let it not be said with Grotius‡, that he who requires the passage is not to be deprived of his right on account of our unjust fears. A probable fear, founded on good reasons, gives us a right to avoid whatever may realise it; and the conduct of nations affords but too just grounds for the fear in question. Besides, the right of passage is not a perfect right, unless in a case of urgent necessity, or when we have the most perfect evidence that the passage is innocent.

† Plutarch's Life of Agesilaus   ‡ Book ii. chap. ii. § 13, note 5.

Thucydides,   HISTORY OF THE PELOPONNESIAN WAR
(Books I-II) (Trans. by Benjamin Jowett)

1. What distinction does Thucydides draw between the
    immediate and the remote causes of the Peloponne-
    sian War or what he calls "the real though unavowed
    cause"?

2. How did the alliances which led to the beginning
    and spread of the Peloponnesian War compare with
    those alliances which led to the beginning and
    spread of World War I?

3. Compare and contrast the statement by Pericles of
    Athens on appeasement with that of Archidamus of
    Lacedaemon (Sparta).

4. Contrast Pericles' strategy of war with that of
    Archidamus.

5. State the bases of citizen morale which Pericles
    presented in his funeral oration.

6. Why did the Athenians turn against the advice of
    Pericles?

        Arguments of opposing leaders are so impartially
and so convincingly given that one hardly would guess
that the author of *The Peloponnesian War* (431-404 B.C.)
was himself an active participant as an Athenian general. The first great historian to write objectively
on the basis of carefully considered evidence including
the testimony of others as well as his own observations,
Thucydides began writing his history as the war began.
He sensed that this would be the climactic struggle of
the Greek city states. In 1835, Macaulay wrote, "He
(Thucydides) is the greatest historian that ever lived."
And a year later, "I am still of the same mind." Earlier, Rousseau had written, "To my mind Thucydides is the
true model of historians." Sir Richard Livingstone has
noted, "It is part of a liberal education to know the

greatest things in the world, and Thucydides, is probably the greatest of historians." And further, "Great
history is rarer than great poetry or great novels.
Many ingredients are necessary for its making - knowledge ... truth ... imagination. Knowledge is difficult; learning and imaginative power are not often combined; rarest of all is a love of truth strong enough
to dominate passion and prejudice and to see things as
they are. Thucydides had all three, and their union
makes him the greatest of historians."

Thucydides' observations on the causes of war, on
appeasement, alliances, morality, and expediency in
war, and over-commitment efforts are as relevant as to-
day's headlines. Gore Vidal, contemporary American
novelist, playwright, and essayist, has expressed the
opinion that Thucydides should be required reading for
all Americans.

HISTORY OF
THE PELOPONNESIAN WAR

———＊＊———

BOOK I

THUCYDIDES, an Athenian, wrote the history of the war in which the Peloponnesians and the Athenians fought against one another. He began to write when they first took up arms, believing that it would be great and memorable above any previous war. For he argued that both states were then at the full height of their military power, and he *Greatness of the war.* saw the rest of the Hellenes either siding or intending to side with one or other of them. No movement ever stirred Hellas more deeply than this; it was shared by many of the Barbarians, and might be said even to affect the world at large. The character of the events which preceded, whether immediately or in more remote antiquity, owing to the lapse of time cannot be made out with certainty. But, judging from the evidence which I am able to trust after most careful enquiry[a], I should imagine that former ages were not great either in their wars or in anything else.

ı ı ı ı ı

23　The greatest achievement of former times was the *Length of the war, which was attended by all sorts of calamities, ordinary and extraordinary. Among the latter might be enumerated earthquakes, eclipses, droughts, and lastly, the plague.* Persian War; yet even this was speedily decided in two battles by sea and two by land. But the Peloponnesian War was a protracted struggle, and attended by calamities such as Hellas had never known within a like period of time. Never were so many cities captured and depopulated—some by Barbarians, others by Hellenes themselves fighting against one another; and several of them after their capture were repeopled by strangers. Never were exile and slaughter more frequent, whether in the war or brought about by civil strife. And traditions which had often been current before, but rarely verified by fact, were now no longer doubted. For there were earthquakes unparalleled in their extent and fury, and eclipses of the sun more numerous than are recorded to have happened in any former age; there were also in some places great droughts causing famines, and lastly the plague which did immense harm and destroyed numbers of the people. All these calamities fell upon Hellas simultaneously with the war, which began when the Athenians and Peloponnesians violated the thirty years' truce concluded by them after the recapture of Euboea[a]. Why they broke it and what were the grounds of quarrel I will first set forth, that in time to come no man may be at a loss to know what was the origin of this great war. The real though unavowed cause I believe to have been the growth of the Athenian power, which terrified the Lacedaemonians and forced them into war; but the reasons publicly alleged on either side were as follows.

The city of Epidamnus is situated on the right hand as 24. you sail up the Ionian Gulf. The neighbouring inhabitants are the Taulantians, a barbarian tribe of the Illyrian race. The place was colonised by the *The story of Epidamnus. Civil strife and war with the barbarians.* Corcyraeans, but under the leadership of a Corinthian, Phalius, son of Eratocleides, who was of the lineage of Heracles; he was invited, according to ancient custom, from the mother city, and Corinthians and other Dorians joined in the colony. In process of time Epidamnus became great and populous, but there followed a long period of civil commotion, and the city is said to have been brought low in a war against the neighbouring

---

[a] Cp. i. 115, 146.

barbarians, and to have lost her ancient power. At last, shortly before the Peloponnesian War, the notables were B.C. 435 or overthrown and driven out by the people ; the exiles went 434. Ol. 86, 2 or over to the barbarians, and, uniting with them, plundered 3. the remaining inhabitants both by sea and land. These,

The prayer of the finding themselves hard pressed, sent *Epidamnians for help* an embassy to the mother-city Corcyra, *is rejected by their* begging the Corcyraeans not to leave *mother-city Corcyra.* them to their fate, but to reconcile them to the exiles and settle the war with the barbarians. The ambassadors came, and sitting as suppliants in the temple of Herè preferred their request ; but the Corcyraeans would not listen to them, and they returned without 25 success. The Epidamnians, finding that they had no hope of assistance from Corcyra, knew not what to do, and sending to Delphi enquired of the God whether they should deliver up the city to their original founders, the Corinthians, and endeavour to obtain aid from them. The God replied that they should, and bade them place them-

They place them- selves under the leadership of the *selves under the pro-* Corinthians. So the Epidamnians *tection of Corinth.* went to Corinth, and informing the Corinthians of the answer which the oracle had given, delivered up the city to them. They reminded them that the original leader of the colony was a citizen of Corinth ; and implored the Corinthians to come and help them, and not leave them to their fate. The Corinthians took up their cause, partly in vindication of their own rights (for they considered that Epidamnus belonged to them quite as much as to the Corcyraeans), partly too because they hated the Corcyraeans, who were their own colony but slighted them. In their common festivals they would not allow them the customary privileges of founders, and at their sacrifices denied to a Corinthian the right of receiving first the lock of hair cut from the head of the victim, an honour usually granted by colonies to a representative of the mother-country. In fact they despised the Corinthians,

for they were more than a match for them in military
strength, and as rich as any state then existing in Hellas.
They would often boast that on the sea they were very far
superior to them, and would appropriate to themselves the
naval renown of the Phaeacians, who were the ancient
inhabitants of the island. Such feelings led them more
and more to strengthen their navy, which was by no means
despicable; for they had a hundred and twenty triremes
when the war broke out.

Irritated by these causes of offence, the Corinthians 26
were too happy to assist Epidamnus; *The Corinthians send*
accordingly they invited any one who *troops and colonists to*
was willing to settle there, and for the *Epidamnus. The Cor-*
protection of the colonists despatched *cyraeans demand their*
with them Ambracian and Leucadian *dismissal; on being re-*
troops and a force of their own. All *fused they besiege the*
city.
these they sent by land as far as Apollonia, which is a
colony of theirs, fearing that if they went by sea the Corcyraeans might oppose their passage. Great was the rage
of the Corcyraeans when they discovered that the settlers
and the troops had entered Epidamnus and that the colony
had been given up to the Corinthians. They immediately
set sail with five and twenty ships, followed by a second
fleet, and in insulting terms bade the Epidamnians receive
the exiled oligarchs, who had gone to Corcyra and implored
the Corcyraeans to restore them, appealing to the tie of
kindred and pointing to the sepulchres of their common
ancestors[a]. They also bade them send away the troops
and the new settlers. But the Epidamnians would not
listen to their demands. Whereupon the Corcyraeans
attacked them with forty ships. They were accompanied
by the exiles whom they were to restore, and had the
assistance of the native Illyrian troops. They sat down
before the city, and made proclamation that any Epidam-
nian who chose, and the foreigners, might depart in

---

[a] Cp. iii. 58 med., 59 init.

C 2

100

safety, but that all who remained would be treated as enemies. This had no effect, and the Corcyraeans proceeded to invest the city, which is built upon an isthmus.

27   When the news reached the Corinthians that Epidamnus

The Corinthians pre- was besieged, they equipped an army
pare for war and pro- and proclaimed that a colony was to be
claim a colony to Epi- sent thither; all who wished might go
damnus. Megara and and enjoy equal rights of citizenship;
other friendly cities fur-
nish ships. but any one who was unwilling to sail

at once might remain at Corinth, and, if he made a deposit of fifty Corinthian drachmae, might still have a share in the colony[a]. Many sailed, and many deposited the money. The Corinthians also sent and requested the Megarians to assist them with a convoy in case the Corcyraeans should intercept the colonists on their voyage. The Megarians accordingly provided eight ships, and the Cephallenians of Palè four; the Epidaurians, of whom they made a similar request, five; the Hermionians one; the Troezenians two; the Leucadians ten; and the Ambraciots eight. Of the Thebans and Phliasians they begged money, and of the Eleans money, and ships without crews. On their own account they equipped thirty ships and three thousand hoplites.

28   When the Corcyraeans heard of their preparations they

The Corcyraeans pro- came to Corinth, taking with them Lace-
pose arbitration, offering daemonian and Sicyonian envoys, and
until a decision be given summoned the Corinthians to withdraw
to withdraw their troops
if the Corinthians with- the troops and the colonists, telling
draw theirs, or to allow them that they had nothing to do with
both to remain at Epi- Epidamnus. If they made any claim
damnus by agreement.
to it, the Corcyraeans expressed them-

selves willing to refer the cause for arbitration to such Peloponnesian states as both parties should agree upon, and their decision was to be final; or, they were willing

---

[a] The sum would amount to £2 15s. 4d., or to £1 2s. 6d., according to the two systems of reckoning discussed in the note on iii. 70, q.v.

to leave the matter in the hands of the Delphian oracle. But they deprecated war, and declared that, if war there must be, they would be compelled by the Corinthians in self-defence to discard their present friends and seek others whom they would rather not, for help they must have. The Corinthians replied that if the Corcyraeans would withdraw the ships and the barbarian troops they would consider the matter, but that it would not do for them to be litigating while Epidamnus and the colonists were in a state of siege. The Corcyraeans rejoined that they would consent to this proposal if the Corinthians on their part would withdraw their forces from Epidamnus: ᵃ or again, they were willing that both parties should remainᵃ on the spot, and that a truce should be made until the decision was given.

The Corinthians turned a deaf ear to all these overtures, 29 and, when their vessels were manned and their allies had arrived, they sent a herald before them to declare war, and set sail for Epidamnus with seventy-five ships and two thousand hoplites, intending to give battle to the Corcy-raeans. Their fleet was commanded *The Corinthians refuse, and declare war. Sailing towards Epidamnus they are met and attacked by the Corcyraeans and completely defeated. On the same day Epidamnus surrenders.* by Aristeus the son of Pellichus, Callicrates the son of Callias, and Timanor the son of Timanthes; the land forces by Archetimus the son of Eurytimus, and Isarchidas the son of Isarchus. When they arrived at Actium in the territory of Anactorium, at the mouth of the Ambracian gulf, where the temple of Apollo stands, the Corcyraeans sent a herald to meet them in a small boat forbidding them to come on. Meanwhile their crews got on board; they had previously put their fleet in repair, and strengthened the old ships with cross-timbers, so as to make them serviceable. The herald brought back no message of peace

---

ᵃ Or, 'or again, they would agree to arbitration on the condition that both parties should remain' etc.

from the Corinthians. The Corcyraean ships, numbering eighty (for forty out of the hundred and twenty were engaged in the blockade of Epidamnus), were now fully manned; these sailed out against the Corinthians and, forming line, fought and won a complete victory over them, and destroyed fifteen of their ships. On the very same day the forces besieging Epidamnus succeeded in compelling the city to capitulate, the terms being that the Corinthians until their fate was determined should be imprisoned and the strangers sold.

30   After the sea-fight the Corcyraeans raised a trophy on

The Corcyraeans, having command of the sea, plunder the allies of Corinth.

Leucimnè, a promontory of Corcyra, and put to death all their prisoners with the exception of the Corinthians, whom they kept in chains. The defeated Corinthians and their allies then returned home, and the Corcyraeans (who were now masters of the Ionian sea), sailing to Leucas, a Corinthian colony, devastated the country. They also burnt Cyllenè, where the Eleans had their docks, because they had supplied the Corinthians with money and ships. And, during the greater part of the summer after the battle, they retained the command of the sea and sailed about plundering the allies of the Corinthians. But, before the season was over, the Corinthians, perceiving that their allies were suffering, sent

At length the Corinthians form a camp to protect them.

out a fleet and took up a position at Actium and near the promontory of Cheimerium in Thesprotia, that they might protect Leucas and other friendly places. The Corcyraeans with their fleet and army stationed themselves on the opposite coast at Leucimnè. Neither party attacked the other, but during the remainder of the summer they maintained their respective stations, and at the approach of winter returned home.

31   For the whole year after the battle and for a year after

B.C. 435, 434. Ol. 86, 2, 3.

that, the Corinthians, exasperated by the war with Corcyra, were busy in building ships. They took the utmost pains to create a great navy: rowers were collected from the Peloponnesus and from the rest of Hellas by the attraction of pay. The Corcyraeans were alarmed at the report of their preparations. They reflected that they had not enrolled themselves in the league either of the *The Corinthians prepare to renew the war, and the Corcyraeans in alarm send an embassy to Athens, whither they are followed by Corinthian envoys.* Athenians or of the Lacedaemonians, and that allies in Hellas they had none. They determined to go to Athens, join the Athenian alliance, and get what help they could from them. The Corinthians, hearing of their intentions, also sent ambassadors to Athens, fearing lest the combination of the Athenian and Corcyraean navies might prevent them from bringing the war to a satisfactory termination. Accordingly an assembly was held at which both parties B.C. 433. came forward to plead their respective causes; and first Ol. 86, 4. the Corcyraeans spoke as follows:—

'Men of Athens, those who, like ourselves, come to 32 others who are not their allies and to *Speech of the Corcy-* whom they have never rendered any *raeans.* considerable service and ask help of them, are bound to show, in the first place, that the granting of their request is expedient, or at any rate not inexpedient, and, secondly, that their gratitude will be lasting. If they fulfil neither requirement they have no right to complain of a refusal. Now the Corcyraeans, when they sent us hither to ask for an alliance, were confident that they could establish to your satisfaction both these points. But, unfortunately, we have had a practice alike inconsistent with the request which we are about to make and contrary to our own interest at the present moment:—Inconsistent; for hitherto we have never, if we could avoid it, been the allies of others, and now we come and ask you to enter into an alliance with us:—Contrary to our interest; for through this practice we find ourselves isolated in our war with the Corinthians. The policy of not making alliances lest they should endanger us at another's bidding, instead of being wisdom, as we once fancied, has now unmistakably proved

Our neutrality was a mistake, and has left us isolated at the mercy of the Corinthians and their allies. to be weakness and folly. True, in the last naval engagement we repelled the Corinthians single-handed. But now they are on the point of attacking us with a much greater force which they have drawn together from the Peloponnesus and from all Hellas. We know that we are too weak to resist them unaided, and may expect the worst if we fall into their hands. We are therefore compelled to ask assistance of you and of all the world ; and you must not be hard upon us if now, renouncing our indolent neutrality which was an error but not a crime, we dare to be inconsistent.

33   'To you at this moment the request which we are making

We ask the aid of Athens, who will thus assist the oppressed, and gain our undying affection. She should not reject the offer of the Corcyraean navy. offers a glorious opportunity. In the first place, you will assist the oppressed and not the oppressors ; secondly, you will admit us to your alliance at a time when our dearest interests are at stake, and will lay up a treasure of gratitude in our memories which will have the most abiding of all records. Lastly, we have a navy greater than any but your own. Reflect ; what good fortune can be more extraordinary, what more annoying to your enemies than the voluntary accession of a power for whose alliance you would have given any amount of money and could never have been too thankful ? This power now places herself at your disposal ; you are to incur no danger and no expense, and she brings you a good name in the world, gratitude from those who seek your aid, and an increase of your own strength. Few have ever had all these advantages offered them at once ; equally few when they come asking an alliance are able to give in the way of security and honour as much as they hope to receive.

'And if any one thinks that the war in which our services may be needed will never arrive, he is mistaken. He does not see that the Lacedaemonians, fearing the growth

of your empire, are eager to take up arms, and that the
Corinthians, who are your enemies,
are all-powerful with them. They   *For war is imminent.*
begin with us, but they will go on to you, that we may
not stand united against them in the bond of a common
enmity; they will not miss the chance of weakening us
or strengthening themselves.   And it is our business to
strike first, we offering and you accepting our alliance,
and to forestall their designs instead of waiting to counter-
act them.

'If they say that we are their colony and that therefore 34
you have no right to receive us, they   *True, we are a colony*
should be made to understand that all   *of the Corinthians, but*
colonies honour their mother-city when *that is no reason why*
                                         we should be wronged
she treats them well, but are estranged *by them.*
from her by injustice.   For colonists are not meant to be
the servants but the equals of those who remain at home.
And the injustice of their conduct to us is manifest: for
we proposed an arbitration in the matter of Epidamnus,
but they insisted on prosecuting their quarrel by arms and
would not hear of a legal trial [a].   When you see how they
treat us who are their own kinsmen, take warning: if they
try deception, do not be misled by them; and if they make
a direct request of you, refuse.   For he passes through
life most securely who has least reason to reproach himself with complaisance to his enemies.

'But again, you will not break the treaty with the Lace- 35
daemonians [b] by receiving us: for we   *Reasons why the*
are not allies either of you or of   *Athenians should re-*
                                     ceive the Corcyraeans
them.   What says the treaty?—"Any *into alliance. They will*
Hellenic city which is the ally of no *not break the treaty.*
one may join whichever league it pleases."

---

[a] Cp. i. 29 init.   [b] Cp. i. 115 init.

* * * * *

'Think of these things; let the younger be informed 42
of them by their elders, and resolve all of you to render B.C. 433
like for like. Do not say to yourselves that this is just, Ol. 86, 4.
but that in the event of war something else is expedient;
for the true path of expediency is the path of right. The
war with which the Corcyraeans would frighten you into
doing wrong is distant, and may never come; is it worth
while to be so carried away by the prospect of it, that
you bring upon yourselves the hatred of the Corinthians
which is both near and certain? Would you not be wiser
in seeking to mitigate the ill-feeling which your treatment
of the Megarians has already inspired[a]? The later kindness done in season, though small in comparison, may
cancel a greater previous offence. And   *To do no wrong is*
do not be attracted by their offer of a *better than a great naval*
great naval alliance; for to do no wrong *alliance.*
to a neighbour is a surer source of strength than to gain
a perilous advantage under the influence of a momentary
illusion.

'We are now ourselves in the same situation in which 43
you were, when we declared at Sparta that every one so
placed should be allowed to chastise his own allies; and
we claim to receive the same measure at your hands. You
were profited by our vote, and we ought not to be injured
by yours. Pay what you owe, knowing that this is our
time of need, in which a man's best friend is he who does
him a service, he who opposes him, his worst enemy. Do
not receive these Corcyraeans into alliance in despite of
us, and do not support them in injustice. In acting thus you
will act rightly, and will consult your own true interests.'

---

[a] Cp. i. 67 fin.

Such were the words of the Corinthians.

44   The Athenians heard both sides, and they held two

The Athenians after some hesitation enter into a defensive alliance with Corcyra. assemblies; in the first of them they were more influenced by the words of the Corinthians, but in the second they changed their minds and inclined towards the Corcyraeans. They would not go so far as to make an alliance both offensive and defensive with them;

B.C. 433. Ol. 87. for then, if the Corcyraeans had required them to join in an expedition against Corinth, the treaty with the Peloponnesians would have been broken. But they concluded a defensive league, by which the two states promised to aid each other if an attack were made on the territory or on the allies of either. For they knew that in any case the war with Peloponnesus was inevitable, and they had no mind to let Corcyra and her navy fall into the

Motives of the Athenians. hands of the Corinthians. Their plan was to embroil them more and more with one another, and then, when the war came, the Corinthians and the other naval powers would be weaker. They also considered that Corcyra was conveniently situated for the coast voyage to Italy and Sicily.

45   Under the influence of these feelings, they received the

They send ten ships to Corcyra, giving them orders to act on the defensive. Corcyraeans into alliance; the Corinthians departed; and the Athenians now despatched to Corcyra ten ships commanded by Lacedaemonius the son of Cimon, Diotimus the son of Strombichus, and Proteas the son of Epicles. The commanders received orders not to engage with the Corinthians unless they sailed against Corcyra or to any place belonging to the Corcyraeans, and attempted to land there, in which case they were to resist them to the utmost. These orders were intended to prevent a breach of the treaty[a].

---

[a] Cp. i. 40 init.

66 Such were the causes of ill-feeling which at this time existed between the Athenians and Peloponnesians: the Corinthians complaining that the Athenians were blockading their colony of Potidaea, and a Corinthian and Peloponnesian garrison in it; the Athenians rejoining that a member of the Peloponnesian confederacy had excited to revolt a state which was an ally and tributary of theirs, and that they had now openly joined the Potidaeans, and were fighting on their side. The Peloponnesian war, however, had not yet broken out; the peace still continued; for thus far the Corinthians had acted alone.

67 But now, seeing Potidaea besieged, they bestirred themselves in earnest. Corinthian troops *Excitement of the* were shut up within the walls, and *Corinthians. Assembly at Sparta. Grievances* they were afraid of losing the town; *of the Aeginetans and* *Megarians.* so without delay they invited the allies to meet at Sparta. There they inveighed against the Athenians, whom they affirmed to have broken the treaty and to be wronging the Peloponnese. The Aeginetans did not venture to send envoys openly, but secretly they acted with the Corinthians, and were among the chief instigators of the war, declaring that they had been robbed of the independence which the treaty guaranteed them. The Lacedaemonians themselves then ᵃproceeded to summon any of the allies who had similar chargesᵃ

---

* Or, adopting the inferior reading τῶν ξυμμάχων τε καὶ εἴ τις: 'proceeded to summon any of their own allies, and any one else, who had similar charges,' etc.

to bring against the Athenians, and calling their own
ordinary assembly told them to speak.   Several of them
came forward and stated their wrongs.   The Megarians
alleged, among other grounds of complaint, that they were
excluded from all harbours within the Athenian dominion
and from the Athenian market, contrary to the treaty.
The Corinthians waited until the other allies had stirred
up the Lacedaemonians ; at length they came forward,
and, last of all, spoke as follows :—

'The spirit of trust, Lacedaemonians, which animates 68
your own political and social life, *The Corinthians com-*
ᵃ makes you distrust others who, like *plain of the delays of*
ourselves, have something unpleasant *the Lacedaemonians,*
to say ᵃ, and this temper of mind, though favourable to
moderation, too often leaves you in ignorance of what
is going on outside your own country.   Time after time
we have warned you of the mischief which the Athenians
would do to us, but instead of taking our words to heart,
you chose to suspect that we only spoke from interested
motives.   And this is the reason why you have brought
the allies to Sparta too late, not before but after the injury
has been inflicted, and when they are smarting under the
sense of it.   Which of them all has a better right to speak
than ourselves, who have the heaviest accusations to make,
outraged as we are by the Athenians, and neglected by
you ?   If the crimes which they are committing against
Hellas were being done in a corner, then you might be
ignorant, and we should have to inform you of them : but
now, what need of many words ?   Some of us, as you see,
have been already enslaved ; they are at this moment
intriguing against others, notably against allies of ours ;
and long ago they had made all their preparations in the
prospect of war.   Else why did they seduce from her
allegiance Corcyra, which they still hold in defiance of

ᵃ Or, 'makes you distrustful of us when we bring a charge against
others.'

us, and why are they blockading Potidaea, the latter a most advantageous post for the command of the Thracian peninsula, the former a great naval power which might have assisted the Peloponnesians?

69   'And the blame of all this rests on you; for you *who have enslaved* originally allowed them to fortify their *Hellas by not prevent-* city after the Persian War[a], and after-*ing her enslavement.* wards to build their Long Walls[b]; and to this hour you have gone on defrauding of liberty their unfortunate subjects, and are now beginning to take it away from your own allies. For the true enslaver of a people is he who can put an end to their slavery but has no care about it; and all the more, if he be reputed the champion of liberty in Hellas.—And so we have met at last, but with what difficulty! and even now we have no definite object. By this time we ought to have been considering, not whether we are wronged, but how we are to be revenged. The aggressor is not now threatening, but advancing; he has made up his mind, while we are resolved about nothing. And we know too well how by slow degrees and with stealthy steps the Athenians encroach upon their neighbours. While they think that you are too dull to observe them, they are more careful, but, when they know that you wilfully overlook their aggressions, they will strike and not spare. Of all Hellenes, Lacedaemonians, you are the only people who never do anything: on the approach of an enemy you are content to defend yourselves against him, not by acts, but by intentions, and seek to overthrow him, not in the infancy but in the fulness of his strength. How came you to be considered safe? That reputation of yours was never justified by facts. We all know that the Persian made his way from the ends of the earth against Peloponnesus before you encountered him in a worthy manner; and now you are blind to the doings of the Athenians, who

---

[a] Cp. i. 90 92.   [b] Cp. i. 107.

are not at a distance as he was, but close at hand. Instead
of attacking your enemy, you wait to be attacked, and take
the chances of a struggle which has been deferred until
his power is doubled. And you know that the Barbarian
miscarried chiefly through his own errors; and that we
have oftener been delivered from these very Athenians
by blunders of their own, than by any aid from you.
Some have already been ruined by the hopes which you
inspired in them; for so entirely did they trust you that
they took no precautions themselves. These things we
say in no accusing or hostile spirit—let that be understood—but by way of expostulation. For men expostulate
with erring friends, they bring accusation against enemies
who have done them a wrong.

'And surely we have a right to find fault with our 70
neighbours, if any one ever had. There   *Contrast of the Athe-*
are important interests at stake to   *nian   and   Spartan*
which, as far as we can see, you are   *characters.*
insensible. And you have never considered what manner
of men are these Athenians[a] with whom you will have
to fight, and how utterly unlike yourselves. They are
revolutionary, equally quick in the conception and in the
execution of every new plan; while you are conservative—
careful only to keep what you have, originating nothing,
and not acting even when action is most urgent. They
are bold beyond their strength; they run risks which
prudence would condemn; and in the midst of misfortune
they are full of hope. Whereas it is your nature, though
strong, to act feebly; when your plans are most prudent,
to distrust them; and when calamities come upon you, to
think that you will never be delivered from them. They
are impetuous, and you are dilatory; they are always
abroad, and you are always at home. For they hope to
gain something by leaving their homes; but you are afraid

---

[a] For descriptions of Athenian character, cp. ii. 37 ff.; iii. 38; 42, 43;
vi. 76; 87.

that any new enterprise may imperil what you have
already. When conquerors, they pursue their victory
to the utmost; when defeated, they fall back the least.
Their bodies they devote to their country as though they
belonged to other men; their true self is their mind,
which is most truly their own when employed in her
service. When they do not carry out an intention which
they have formed, they seem to themselves to have
sustained a personal bereavement; when an enterprise
succeeds, they have gained a mere instalment of what is
to come; but if they fail, they at once conceive new hopes
and so fill up the void. With them alone to hope is to
have, for they lose not a moment in the execution of an
idea. This is the lifelong task, full of danger and toil,
which they are always imposing upon themselves. None
enjoy their good things less, because they are always
seeking for more. To do their duty is their only holiday,
and they deem the quiet of inaction to be as disagreeable
as the most tiresome business. If a man should say of
them, in a word, that they were born neither to have
peace themselves nor to allow peace to other men, he
would simply speak the truth.

71　　'In the face of such an enemy, Lacedaemonians, you

The Lacedaemonians persist in doing nothing. You do not
must lay aside their see that peace is best secured by those
policy of inaction. who use their strength justly, but whose
attitude shows that they have no intention of submitting
to wrong. Justice with you seems to consist in giving no
annoyance to others and [a] in defending yourselves only
against positive injury[a]. But this policy would hardly be
successful, even if your neighbours were like yourselves;
and in the present case, as we pointed out just now, your
ways compared with theirs are old-fashioned. And, as in
the arts, so also in politics, the new must always prevail
over the old. In settled times the traditions of govern-

---

[a] Or, 'in running no risk even in self-defence.'

ment should be observed : but when circumstances are
changing and men are compelled to meet them, much
originality is required.   The Athenians have had a wider
experience, and therefore the administration of their state
unlike yours has been greatly reformed.   But here let
your procrastination end ; send an army at once into
Attica and assist your allies, especially the Potidaeans,
to whom your word is pledged ᵃ.   Do not betray friends
and kindred into the hands of their worst enemies ; or
drive us in despair to seek the alliance of others ; in
taking such a course we should be doing nothing wrong
either before the Gods who are the witnesses of our oaths,
or before men whose eyes are upon us.   For the true
breakers of treaties ᵇ are not those who, when forsaken,
turn to others, but those who forsake allies whom they
have sworn to defend.   We will remain your friends if
you choose to bestir yourselves ; for we should be guilty
of an impiety if we deserted you without cause ; and we
shall not easily find allies equally congenial to us.   Take
heed then : you have inherited from your fathers the
leadership of Peloponnesus ; see that her greatness suffers
no diminution at your hands.'

Thus spoke the Corinthians.   Now there happened to 72
be staying at Lacedaemon an Athenian   *Some Athenian en-*
embassy which had come on other   *voys who happen to be*
business, and when the envoys heard   *at Sparta desire to ad-*
what the Corinthians had said, they   *dress the assembly.*
felt bound to go before the Lacedaemonian assembly, not
with the view of answering the accusations brought against
them by the cities, but they wanted to put the whole
question before the Lacedaemonians, and make them
understand that they should take time to deliberate and
not be rash.   They also desired to set forth the greatness
of their city, reminding the elder men of what they knew,
and informing the younger of what lay beyond their

ᵃ Cp. i. 58 med.   ᵇ Cp. i. 123 fin.

experience. They thought that their words would sway the Lacedaemonians in the direction of peace. So they came and said that, if they might be allowed, they too would like to address the people. The Lacedaemonians invited them to come forward, and they spoke as follows:—

73 'We were not sent here to argue with your allies, but on a special mission; observing, however, that no small outcry has arisen against us, we have come forward, not to answer the accusations which they bring (for you are not judges before whom either we or they have to plead), but to prevent you from lending too ready an ear to their bad advice and so deciding wrongly about a very serious question. We propose also, in reply to the wider charges which are raised against us, to show that what we have acquired we hold rightfully and that our city is not to be despised.

'Of the ancient deeds handed down by tradition and *They recall the memory of their services in the Persian War.* which no eye of any one who hears us ever saw, why should we speak? But of the Persian War, and other events which you yourselves remember, speak we must, ᵃ although we have brought them forward so often that the repetition of them is disagreeable to us ᵃ. When we faced those perils we did so for the common benefit: in the solid good you shared, and of the glory, whatever good there may be in that, we would not be wholly deprived. Our words are not designed to deprecate hostility, but to set forth in evidence the character of the city with which, unless you are very careful, you will soon be involved in war. We tell you that we, first and alone, dared to engage with the Barbarian at Marathon, and that when he came again, being too weak to defend ourselves by land, we and our whole people embarked on shipboard and shared with the other Hellenes in the victory of

---

ᵃ Or, 'although it may be disagreeable to you to hear what we are always bringing forward.'

115

Salamis. Thereby he was prevented from sailing to the Peloponnesus and ravaging city after city; for against so mighty a fleet how could you have helped one another? He himself is the best witness of our words; for when he was once defeated at sea, he felt that his power was gone and quickly retreated with the greater part of his army.

'The event proved undeniably that the fate of Hellas 74 depended on her navy. And the three chief elements of success were contributed by us; namely, the greatest number of ships, the ablest general, the most devoted patriotism. The ships in all numbered four hundred[a], and of these, our own contingent amounted to nearly two-thirds. To the influence of Themistocles our general it was chiefly due that we fought in the strait, which was confessedly our salvation; and for this service you yourselves honoured him above any stranger who ever visited you. Thirdly, we displayed the most extraordinary courage and devotion; there was no one to help us by land; for up to our frontier those who lay in the enemy's path were already slaves; so we determined to leave our city and sacrifice our homes. Even in that extremity we did not choose to desert the cause of the allies who still resisted, or by dispersing ourselves to become useless to them; but we embarked and fought, taking no offence at your failure to assist us sooner. We maintain then that we rendered you a service at least as great as you rendered us. The cities from which you came to help us were still inhabited and you might hope to return to them; your concern was for yourselves and not for us; at any rate you remained at a distance while we had anything to lose. But we went forth from a city which was no more, and fought for one of which there was small hope; and yet we saved ourselves, and bore our part in saving you. If, in order to preserve our land, like other states, we had gone over to the Persians at first, or afterwards had not ventured

---

[a] Reading with the great majority of MSS. τετρακοσίας.

E 2

to embark because our ruin was already complete, it would have been useless for you with your weak navy to fight at sea, but everything would have gone quietly just as the Persian desired.

75 'Considering, Lacedaemonians, the energy and sagacity

Why should they be hated for having saved Hellas? Their empire was not a usurpation, but the growth of circumstances.

which we then displayed, do we deserve to be so bitterly hated by the other Hellenes merely because we have an empire? That empire was not acquired by force; but you would not stay and make an end of the Barbarian, and the allies came of their own accord and asked us to be their leaders. The subsequent development of our power was originally forced upon us by circumstances; fear was our first motive; afterwards honour, and then interest stepped in. And when we had incurred the hatred of most of our allies; when some of them had already revolted and been subjugated, and you were no longer the friends to us which you once had been, but suspicious and ill-disposed, how could we without great risk relax our hold? For the cities as fast as they fell away from us would have gone over to you. And no man is to be reproached who seizes every possible advantage when the danger is so great.

76 'At all events, Lacedaemonians, we may retort that you,

The Lacedaemonians would have been worse than they were.

in the exercise of your supremacy, manage the cities of Peloponnesus to suit your own views; and that if you, and not we, had persevered in the command of the allies long enough to be hated, you would have been quite as intolerable to them as we are, and would have been compelled, for the sake of your own safety, to rule with a strong hand. An empire was offered to us: can you wonder that, acting as human nature always will, we accepted it and refused to give it up again, constrained by three all-powerful motives, honour, fear, interest? We are not the first who have aspired to rule; the world has ever held that the weaker must be kept down by the stronger. And

B.C. 432.
Ol. 87.

we think that we are worthy of power ; and there was
a time when you thought so too ; but now, when you mean
expediency you talk about justice.   Did justice ever deter
any one from taking by force whatever he could ?   Men
who indulge the natural ambition of empire deserve credit
if they **are in** any degree more careful of justice than they
need be.   How moderate we are would speedily appear if
others took our place ; indeed our very moderation, which
should be our glory, has been unjustly converted into
a reproach.

‘ For because in our suits with our allies, regulated by 77
treaty, we do not even stand upon our
rights, but have instituted the practice
of deciding them at Athens and by
Athenian [a] law, we are supposed to be
litigious.   None of our opponents ob-

*They were thought to
be litigious, because they
allowed their subjects a
law other than the law
of the stronger.*

serve why others, who exercise dominion elsewhere and
are less moderate than we are in their dealings with their
subjects, escape this reproach.   Why is it ?   Because men
who practise violence have no longer any need of law.
But we are in the habit of meeting our allies on terms of
equality, and, therefore, if through some legal decision of
ours, or exercise of our imperial power, contrary to their
own ideas of right, they suffer ever so little, they are not
grateful for our moderation in leaving them so much, but
are far more offended at their trifling loss than if we had
from the first plundered them in the face of day, laying
aside all thought of law.   For then they would themselves
have admitted that the weaker must give way to the
stronger.   Mankind resent injustice more than violence,
because the one seems to be an unfair advantage taken by
an equal, the other is the irresistible force of a superior.
They were patient under the yoke of the Persian, who
inflicted on them far more grievous
wrongs ; but now our dominion is
odious in their eyes.   And no wonder :

*The ruler of the day
is always unpopular.*

the ruler of the day is always detested by his subjects.   And

---

[a] (?) by impartial law.

should your empire supplant ours, may not you lose the good-will which you owe to the fear of us? Lose it you certainly will, if you mean again to exhibit the temper of which you gave a specimen when, for a short time, you led the confederacy against the Persian. For the institutions under which you live are incompatible with those of foreign states; and further, when any of you goes abroad, he respects neither these nor any other Hellenic customs [a].

78   'Do not then be hasty in deciding a question which is

The Lacedaemonians should not go to war at the instigation of others, but submit to arbitration.

serious; and do not, by listening to representations and complaints which concern others, bring trouble upon yourselves. Realise, while there is time, the inscrutable nature of war; and how when protracted it generally ends in becoming a mere matter of chance, over which neither of us can have any control, the event being equally unknown and equally hazardous to both. The misfortune is that in their hurry to go to war, men begin with blows, and when a reverse comes upon them, then have recourse to words. But neither you, nor we, have as yet committed this mistake; and therefore while both of us can still choose the prudent part, we tell you not to break the peace or violate your oaths. Let our differences be determined by arbitration, according to the treaty. If you refuse we call to witness the Gods, by whom your oaths were sworn, that you are the authors of the war; and we will do our best to strike in return.'

79   When the Lacedaemonians had heard the charges brought by the allies against the Athenians, and their rejoinder, they ordered everybody but themselves to withdraw, and deliberated alone. The majority were agreed that there was now a clear case against the Athenians, and that they must fight at once. But Archidamus their

---

[a] For the misconduct of Spartan officers abroad, cp. i. 95; 130; iii. 32; 93 fin.; viii. 84 init. Contrast Brasidas, iv. 81.

king, who was held to be both an able and a prudent man, came forward and spoke as follows:—

'At my age, Lacedaemonians, I have had experience of 80 many wars, and I see several of you who are as old as I am, and who will *We are no match for* not, as men too often do, desire war *the Athenians.* because they have never known it, or in the belief that it is either a good or a safe thing. Any one who calmly reflects will find that the war about which you are now deliberating is likely to be a very great one. When we encounter our neighbours in the Peloponnese, their mode of fighting is like ours, and they are all within a short march. But when we have to do with men whose country is a long way off, and who are most skilful seamen and thoroughly provided with the means of war,—having wealth, private and public, ships, horses, infantry, and a population larger than is to be found in any single Hellenic territory, not to speak of the numerous allies who pay them tribute,—is this a people against whom we can lightly take up arms or plunge into a contest unprepared? To what do we trust? To our navy? There we are inferior; and to exercise and train ourselves until we are a match for them, will take time. To our money? Nay, but in that we are weaker still; we have none in a common treasury, and we are never willing to contribute out of our private means.

'Perhaps some one may be encouraged by the superior 81 equipment and numbers of our infantry, *We have more hop-* which will enable us regularly to in- *lites, but their empire* vade and ravage their lands. But their *extends to distant coun-* empire extends to distant countries, *tries, by which their navy* and they will be able to introduce *ravage their land is use-* supplies by sea. Or, again, we may *less.* try to stir up revolts among their allies. But these are mostly islanders, and we shall have to employ a fleet in their defence, as well as in our own. How then shall we carry on the war? For if we can neither defeat them at sea, nor deprive them of the revenues by which their navy is maintained, we shall get the worst of it. And having gone so far, we shall no longer be able even to make peace with honour, especially if we are believed to have begun the quarrel. We must not for one moment flatter ourselves that if we do but ravage their country the war will be at an end. Nay, I fear that we shall bequeath it to our children; for the Athenians with their high spirit will never barter their liberty to save their land, or be terrified like novices at the sight of war.

82 'Not that I would have you shut your eyes to their

Do not take up arms yet.

designs and abstain from unmasking them, or tamely suffer them to injure our allies. But do not take up arms yet. Let us first send and remonstrate with them: we need not let them know positively whether we intend to go to war or not. In the meantime our own preparations may be going forward; we may seek for allies wherever we can find them, whether in Hellas or among the Barbarians, who will supply our deficiencies in ships and money. Those who, like ourselves, are exposed to Athenian intrigue cannot be blamed if in self-defence they seek the aid not of Hellenes only, but of Barbarians. And we must develope our own resources to the utmost. If they listen to our ambassadors, well and good; but, if not, in two or three years' time we shall be in a stronger position, should we then determine to attack them. Perhaps too when they begin to see that we are getting ready, ᵃand that our words are to be interpreted by our actionsᵃ, they may be more likely to yield; for their fields will be still untouched and their goods undespoiled, and it will be in their power to save them by their decision. Think of their land simply in the light of a hostage, all the more valuable in proportion as it is better cultivated; you should spare it as long as you can, and not by reducing them to despair

---

ᵃ Or, 'and that our words too sound a note of war.'

make their resistance more obstinate. For if we allow ourselves to be stung into premature action by the reproaches of our allies, and waste their country before we are ready, we shall only involve Peloponnesus in more and more difficulty and disgrace. Charges brought by cities or persons against one another can be satisfactorily arranged; but when a great confederacy, in order to satisfy private grudges, undertakes a war of which no man can foresee the issue, it is not easy to terminate it with honour.

And let no one think that there is any want of courage 83 in cities so numerous hesitating to attack a single one. The allies of the Athenians are not less numerous; they pay them tribute too; and war is not an affair of arms, but of money which gives to arms their use, and which is needed above all things when a continental is fighting against a maritime power: let us find money first, and then we may safely allow our minds to be excited by the speeches of our allies. We, on whom the future responsibility, whether for good or evil, will chiefly fall, should calmly reflect on the consequences which may follow.

There is no cowardice in hesitation; we are fighting not against Athens, but against the great Athenian empire.

'Do not be ashamed of the slowness and procrastination 84 with which they are so fond of charging you; if you begin the war in haste, you will end it at your leisure, because you took up arms without sufficient preparation. Remember that we have always been citizens of a free and most illustrious state, and that for us the policy which they condemn may well be the truest good sense and discretion. It is a policy which has saved us from growing insolent in prosperity or giving way under adversity, like other men. We are not stimulated by the allurements of flattery into dangerous courses of which we disapprove; nor are we goaded by offensive charges into compliance with any man's wishes. Our habits of discipline

Too much haste, too little speed. Our discretion and discipline are the secret of our greatness. We must not undervalue our enemies, and we must not rely on fortune.

make us both brave and wise; brave, because the spirit of loyalty quickens the sense of honour, and the sense of honour inspires courage ; wise, because we are not so highly educated that we have learned to despise the laws, and are too severely trained and of too loyal a spirit to disobey them. We have not acquired that useless over-intelligence which makes a man an excellent critic of an enemy's plans, but paralyses him in the moment of action. We think that the wits of our enemies are as good as our own, and that the element of fortune cannot be forecast in words. Let us assume that they have common prudence, and let our preparations be, not words, but deeds [a]. Our hopes ought not to rest on the probability of their making mistakes, but on our own caution and foresight. We should remember that one man is much the same as another, and that he is best who is trained in the severest school.

85 'These are principles which our fathers have handed
We can afford to wait, down to us, and we maintain to our
and should try arbitra- lasting benefit ; we must not lose sight
tion first. of them, and when many lives and
much wealth, many cities and a great name are at stake, we must not be hasty, or make up our minds in a few short hours ; we must take time. We can afford to wait, when others cannot, because we are strong. And now, send to the Athenians and remonstrate with them about Potidaea first, and also about the other wrongs of which your allies complain. They say that they are willing to have the matter tried ; and against one who offers to submit to justice you must not proceed as against a criminal until his cause has been heard. In the meantime prepare for war. This decision will be the best for yourselves and the most formidable to your enemies.'

Thus spoke Archidamus. Last of all, Sthenelaidas, at that time one of the Ephors, came forward and addressed the Lacedaemonians as follows :—

---

[a] Reading παρασκευαζώμεθα.

'I do not know what the long speeches of the Athenians **86**
mean.   They have been loud in their   *We must stand by*
own praise, but they do not pretend to   *our allies.*
say that they are dealing honestly with our allies and with
the Peloponnesus.   If they behaved well in the Persian
War and are now behaving badly to us they ought to be
punished twice over, because they were once good men
and have become bad.   But we are the same now as we
were then, and we shall not do our duty if we allow our
allies to be ill-used, and put off helping them, 'for they
cannot put off their troubles.   Others may have money and
ships and horses, but we have brave allies and we must
not betray them to the Athenians.   If they were suffering
in word only, by words and legal processes their wrongs
might be redressed ; but now there is not a moment to be
lost, and we must help them with all our might.   Let no
one tell us that we should take time to think when we are
suffering injustice.   Nay, we reply, those who mean to do
injustice should take a long time to think.   Wherefore,
Lacedaemonians, prepare for war as the honour of Sparta
demands.   Withstand the advancing power of Athens.
Do not let us betray our allies, but, with the Gods on our
side, let us attack the evil-doer.'

When Sthenelaidas had thus spoken he, being Ephor, **87**
himself put the question to the Lace-   *The Lacedaemonians,*
daemonian assembly.   Their custom is   *influenced chiefly by the*
to signify their decision by cries and not *fear of the Athenians,*
by voting.   But he professed himself   *resolve to go to war.*
unable to tell on which side was the louder cry, and wishing to call forth a demonstration which might encourage the
warlike spirit, he said, 'Whoever of you, Lacedaemonians,
thinks that the treaty has been broken and that the Athenians are in the wrong, let him rise and go yonder' (pointing
to a particular spot), 'and those who think otherwise to the
other side.'   So the assembly rose and divided, and it was
determined by a large majority that the treaty had been
broken.   The Lacedaemonians then recalled the allies and

124

told them that in their judgment the Athenians were guilty, but that they wished to hold a general assembly of the allies and take a vote from them all ; then the war, if they approved of it, might be undertaken by common consent. Having accomplished their purpose, the allies returned home ; and the Athenian envoys, when their errand was done, returned likewise. Thirteen years of the thirty years' peace which was concluded after the recovery of Euboea had elapsed and the fourteenth year had begun when the Lacedaemonian assembly decided that the treaty had been broken.

B.C. 445.
Ol. 83, 4.

88   In arriving at this decision and resolving to go to war, the Lacedaemonians were influenced, not so much by the speeches of their allies, as by the fear of the Athenians and of their increasing power[a]. For they saw the greater part of Hellas already subject to them.

118   Not long afterwards occurred the affairs of Corcyra
The history is re- and Potidaea, which have been already
sumed from chap. 88. narrated, and the various other circum-
The Lacedaemonians, stances which led to the Peloponnesian
having decided to go to
war, obtain the sanction War. Fifty years elapsed between the
of the Delphian oracle. retreat of Xerxes and the beginning of
the war; during these years took place all those operations of the Hellenes against one another and against the
Barbarian which I have been describing. The Athenians
acquired a firmer hold over their empire and the city itself
became a great power. The Lacedaemonians saw what
was going on, but during most of the time they remained
inactive and hardly attempted to interfere. They had
never been of a temper prompt to take the field unless
they were compelled; and they were in some degree em-
barrassed by wars near home. But the Athenians were
growing too great to be ignored and were laying hands on
their allies. They could now bear it no longer: they
made up their minds that they must put out all their
strength and overthrow the Athenian power by force of
arms. And therefore they commenced the Peloponnesian
War. They had already voted in their own assembly that
the treaty had been broken and that the Athenians were
guilty[a]; they now sent to Delphi and asked the God if it
would be for their advantage to make war. He is reported
to have answered that, if they did their best, they would
be conquerors, and that he himself, invited or uninvited,
would take their part.

119   So they again summoned the allies, intending to put to
Activity of the Corin- them the question of war or peace.
thians in pressing on When their representatives arrived, an
the war. assembly was held; and the allies said
what they had to say, most of them complaining of the

---

[a] But cp. vii. 18 med.

Athenians and demanding that the war should proceed. B.C. 432.
The Corinthians had already gone the round of the Ol. 87.
cities and entreated them privately to vote for war; they
were afraid that they would be too late to save Potidaea.
At the assembly they came forward last of all and spoke
as follows:—

'Fellow allies, we can no longer find fault with the 120
Lacedaemonians; they have them- *No more fault to be*
selves resolved upon war and have *found with the Lacedae-*
monians. The Athe-
brought us hither to confirm their de- *nians are dangerous to*
cision. And they have done well; for *all alike. Men should be*
the leaders of a confederacy, while they *willing to fight, though*
they should be equally
do not neglect the interests of their *ready to cease from*
own state, should look to the general *fighting.*
weal: as they are first in honour, they should be first in
the fulfilment of their duties. Now those among us who
have ever had dealings with the Athenians, do not require
to be warned against them; but such as live inland and
not on any maritime highway should clearly understand
that, if they do not protect the sea-board, they will find it
more difficult to carry their produce to the sea, or to
receive in return the goods which the sea gives to the land.
They should not lend a careless ear to our words, for they
nearly concern them; they should remember that, if they
desert the cities on the sea-shore, the danger may some
day reach them, and that they are consulting for their own
interests quite as much as for ours. And therefore let no
one hesitate to accept war in exchange for peace. Wise
men refuse to move until they are wronged, but brave men
as soon as they are wronged go to war, and when there is
a good opportunity make peace again. They are not
intoxicated by military success; but neither will they
tolerate injustice from a love of peace and ease. For he
whom pleasure makes a coward will quickly lose, if he
continues inactive, the delights of ease which he is so unwilling to renounce; and he whose arrogance is stimulated
by victory does not see how hollow is the confidence which

elates him. Many schemes which were ill-advised have
succeeded through the still greater folly which possessed
the enemy, and yet more, which seemed to be wisely contrived, have ended in foul disaster. The execution of an
enterprise is never equal[a] to the conception of it in the
confident mind of its promoter; for men are safe while
they are forming plans, but, when the time of action comes,
then they lose their presence of mind and fail.

121 'We, however, do not make war upon the Athenians in

We are superior to a spirit of vain-glory, but from a sense
the Athenians in num- of wrong; there is ample justification,
bers, in military skill, and when we obtain redress, we will
in unanimity, and our put up the sword. For every reason
fleet will soon be on a we are likely to succeed.   First, be-
level with theirs.
cause we are superior in numbers and in military skill;
secondly, because we all obey as one man the orders given
to us.   They are doubtless strong at sea, but we too will
provide a navy, for which the means can be supplied
partly by contributions from each state, partly out of the
funds at Delphi and Olympia.   A loan will be granted to
us, and by the offer of higher pay we can draw away
their foreign sailors.   The Athenian power consists of
mercenaries, and not of their own citizens; but our soldiers
are not mercenaries, and therefore cannot so be bought,
for we are strong in men if poor in money.   Let them be
beaten in a single naval engagement and they are probably
conquered at once; but suppose they hold out, we shall
then have more time in which to practise at sea.   As soon
as we have brought our skill up to the level of theirs our
courage will surely give us the victory.   For that is a natural
gift which they cannot learn, but their superior skill is a
thing acquired, [b] which we must attain by practice [b].

'And the money which is required for the war, we will

But we must find provide by a contribution.   What!
money. shall their allies never fail in paying
the tribute which is to enslave them, and shall we refuse

---

[a] Reading ὅμοια.   [b] Or, 'which we must overcome by practice.'

to give freely in order to save ourselves and be avenged on
our enemies, or rather to prevent the money which we
refused to give from being taken from us by them and used
to our destruction?

'These are some of the means by which the war may 122
be carried on; but there are others. We   *By gaining over their*
may induce their allies to revolt,—a   *allies, we may cut off*
sure mode of cutting off the revenues   *their resources.*
in which the strength of Athens consists; or we may
plant a fort in their country; and there are many
expedients which will hereafter suggest themselves.
For war, least of all things, conforms to prescribed
rules; it strikes out a path for itself when the moment
comes. And therefore he who has his temper under
control in warfare is safer far, but he who gets into
a passion is, through his own fault, liable to the greater
fall.

'If this were merely a quarrel between one of us and
our neighbours about a boundary line   *If we quietly submit*
it would not matter; but reflect: the   *we shall deserve to be*
truth is that the Athenians are a match   *slaves.*
for us all, and much more than a match for any single city.
And if we allow ourselves to be divided or are not united
against them heart and soul—the whole confederacy and
every nation and city in it—they will easily overpower us.
It may seem a hard saying, but you may be sure that
defeat means nothing but downright slavery, and the bare
mention of such a possibility is a disgrace to the Peloponnese:—shall so many states suffer at the hands of one?
Men will say, some that we deserve our fate, others that
we are too cowardly to resist: and we shall seem
a degenerate race. For our fathers were the liberators
of Hellas, but we cannot secure even our own liberty; and
while we make a point of overthrowing the rule of
a single man in this or that city, we allow a city which
is a tyrant to be set up in the midst of us. Are we
not open to one of three most serious charges—folly,

VOL. I.   G

129

cowardice, or carelessness? [a] For you certainly do not escape such imputations by wrapping yourselves in that contemptuous wisdom which has so often [a] brought men to ruin, as in the end to be pronounced contemptible folly.

123 'But why should we dwell reproachfully upon the past, except in the interest of the present?

In going to war you have the God and the feeling of Hellas on your side, and you will not break the treaty.

We should rather, looking to the future, devote our energies to the task which we have immediately in hand. By labour to win virtue,—that is the lesson which we [b] have learnt from our fathers, and which you ought not to unlearn, because you chance to have some trifling advantage over them in wealth and power; for men should not lose in the time of their wealth what was gained by them in their time of want. There are many reasons why you may advance with confidence. The God has spoken and has promised to take our part himself. All Hellas will fight at our side, from motives either of fear or of interest. And you will not break the treaty,—the God in bidding you go to war pronounces it to have been already broken,—but you will avenge the violation of it. For those who attack others, not those who defend themselves, are the real violators of treaties [c].

124 'On every ground you will be right in going to war:

We cannot go on as we are. War is the way to peace; but peace may be the way to war.

it is our united advice; [d] and if you believe community of interests to be the surest ground of strength both to states and individuals, send speedy aid [d] to the Potidaeans, who are Dorians and now besieged by Ionians (for times have changed), and recover the

---

[a] Or, 'For we cannot suppose that, having avoided these errors, you have wrapped yourselves in that contemptuous wisdom, which has so often ' etc.

[b] Reading ἡμῖν.   [c] Cp. i. 71 fin.

[d] Reading ταῦτά: or, with all the MSS. retaining ταῦτα: 'And as it is most certain that the policy which we recommend is for our advantage both as states and individuals, send speedy aid ' etc.

liberties which the rest of the allies have lost. We cannot go on as we are: for some of us are already suffering, and if it is known that we have met, but do not dare to defend ourselves, others will soon share their fate. Acknowledging then, allies, that there is no alternative, and that we are advising you for the best, vote for war; and be not afraid of the immediate danger, but fix your thoughts on the durable peace which will follow. For by war peace is assured, but to remain at peace when you should be going to war may be often very dangerous. The tyrant city which has been set up in Hellas is a standing menace to all alike; she rules over some of us already, and would fain rule over others. Let us attack and subdue her, that we may ourselves live safely for the future and deliver the Hellenes whom she has enslaved.'

Such were the words of the Corinthians.

ı ı ı ı ı

At last Pericles the son of Xanthippus, who was the first man of his day at Athens, and the greatest orator and statesman, came forward and advised as follows:—

'Athenians, I say, as I always have said, that we must 140 never yield to the Peloponnesians, *I still give you my* although I know that men are per- *old advice, — Do not* suaded to go to war in one temper of *yield to the Pelopon-* mind, and act when the time comes in *nesians.* another, and that their resolutions change with the changes of fortune. But I see that I must give you the same or nearly the same advice which I gave before, and I call upon those whom my words may convince to maintain our united determination, even if we should not escape disaster; or else, if our sagacity be justified by success, to claim no share of the credit ᵃ.

B.C. 432.
Ol. 87. The movement of events is often as wayward and in-comprehensible as the course of human thought; and this is why we ascribe to chance whatever belies our calculation.

'For some time past the designs of the Lacedaemonians

The demands of the Lacedaemonians may seem trifling, but submission to them will only provoke fresh demands and implies the loss of our independence.

have been clear enough, and they are still clearer now. Our agreement says that when differences arise, the two parties shall refer them to arbitration, and in the mean time both are to retain what they have. But for arbitration they never ask; and when it is offered by us, they refuse it[a]. They want to redress their grievances by arms and not by argument; and now they come to us, using the language, no longer of expostulation, but of command. They tell us to quit Potidaea, to leave Aegina independent, and to rescind the decree respecting the Megarians. These last ambassadors go further still, and announce that we must give the Hellenes independence. I would have none of you imagine that he will be fighting for a small matter if we refuse to annul the Megarian decree, of which they make so much, telling us that its revocation would prevent the war. You should have no lingering uneasiness about this; you are not really going to war for a trifle. For in the seeming trifle is involved the trial and confirmation of your whole purpose. If you yield to them in a small matter, they will think that you are afraid, and will immediately dictate some more oppressive condition; but if you are firm, you will prove to them that they must treat you as their equals.

141 Wherefore make up your minds once for all, either to give way while you are still unharmed, or, if we are going to war, as in my judgment is best, then on no plea small or great to give way at all; we will not condescend to possess our own in fear. Any claim, the smallest as well

---

[a] Cp. i. 78.

as the greatest, imposed on a neighbour and an equal B.C. 432. Ol. 87. when there has been no legal award, can mean nothing but slavery.

'That our resources are equal to theirs, and that we shall be as strong in the war, I will now prove to you in detail. The Peloponnesians cultivate their own lands, and they have no wealth either public or private. Nor have they any experience of long wars in countries beyond the sea;

Unless you mean to give way now, you must determine never to give way at all. Nor need you fear the result; for you have many advantages over the Peloponnesians; they are poor and till their own land, they are unaccustomed to great wars, and divided in race.

their poverty prevents them from fighting, except in person against each other, and that for a short time only. Such men cannot be often manning fleets or sending out armies. They would be at a distance from their own properties, upon which they must nevertheless draw, and they will be kept off the sea by us. Now wars are supported out of accumulated wealth, and not out of forced contributions. And men who cultivate their own lands are more ready to serve with their persons than with their property[a]; they do not despair of their lives, but they soon grow anxious lest their money should all be spent, especially if the war in which they are engaged is protracted beyond their calculation, as may well be the case. In a single pitched battle the Peloponnesians and their allies are a match for all Hellas, but they are not able to maintain a war against a power different in kind from their own[b]; they have no regular general assembly, and therefore cannot execute their plans with speed and decision. The confederacy is made up of many races; all the representatives have equal votes, and press their several interests. There follows the usual result, that nothing is ever done properly. For some are all anxiety to be revenged on an enemy, while others only want to get off with as little loss as possible. The members of such

---

[a] Cp. i. 121 med.   [b] Cp. viii. 96 fin.

B.C. 432.
Ol. 87.

a confederacy are slow to meet, and when they do meet, they give little time to the consideration of any common interest, and a great deal to schemes which further the interest of their particular state. Every one fancies that his own neglect will do no harm, but that it is somebody else's business to keep a look-out for him, and this idea, cherished alike by each, is the secret ruin of all.

142 'Their greatest difficulty will be want of money, which they can only provide slowly; delay will thus occur, and war waits for no man. Further, no fortified place which they can raise against us[a] is to be feared any more than their navy. As to the first, even in time of peace it would be hard for them to build a city able to compete with Athens; and how much more so when they are in an enemy's country, and our walls will be a menace to them quite as much as theirs to us! Or, again, if they simply raise a fort in our territory, they may do mischief to some part of our lands by sallies, and the slaves may desert to them; but that will not prevent us from sailing to the Peloponnese and there raising forts against them, and defending ourselves there by the help of our navy, which is our strong arm. For we have gained more experience of fighting on land from warfare at sea than they of naval affairs from warfare on land. And they will not easily acquire the art of seamanship[b]; even you yourselves, who have been practising ever since the Persian War, are not yet perfect. How can they, who are not sailors, but tillers of the soil, do much? They will not even be permitted to practise, because a large fleet will constantly be lying in wait for them. If they were watched by a few ships only, they might run the risk, trusting to their numbers and forgetting their inexperience; but if they are kept off the sea by our superior strength, their

They cannot do you any real harm by building a rival city or fortified posts in Attica; nor can they, mere landsmen as they are, rival you at sea.

---

[a] Cp. i. 122 init.   [b] Cp. i. 121 med.

want of practice will make them unskilful, and their want B.C. 432.
of skill timid. Maritime skill is like skill of other kinds, Ol. 87.
not a thing to be cultivated by the way or at chance times ;
it is jealous of any other pursuit which distracts the mind
for an instant from itself.

'Suppose, again, that they lay hands on the treasures 143
at Olympia and Delphi, and tempt our

Our foreign sailors will not be tempted by offers of high pay, and if they are, we can do without them.

mercenary sailors with the offer of
higher pay[a], there might be serious
danger, if we and our metics[b] embarking alone were not still a match for
them. But we are a match for them : and, best of all, our
pilots are taken from our own citizens, while no sailors
are to be found so good or so numerous as ours in all the
rest of Hellas. None of our mercenaries will choose to
fight on their side for the sake of a few days' high pay,
when he will not only be an exile, but will incur greater
danger, and will have less hope of victory.

'Such I conceive to be the prospects of the Peloponnesians. But we ourselves are free

We must guard the city and the sea, and not mind about our houses and lands in the country.

from the defects which I have noted
in them ; and we have great advantages. If they attack our country by
land, we shall attack theirs by sea ; and
the devastation, even of part of Peloponnesus, will be
a very different thing from that of all Attica. For they, if
they want fresh territory, must take it by arms, whereas
we have abundance of land both in the islands and on the
continent ; such is the power which the empire of the sea
gives. Reflect, if we were islanders, who would be more
invulnerable ? Let us imagine that we are, and acting in
that spirit let us give up land and houses, but keep a watch
over the city and the sea. We should not under any
irritation at the loss of our property give battle to the
Peloponnesians, who far outnumber us. If we conquer,

---

[a] Cp. i. 121 init.   [b] Cp. iii. 16 init.

H 2

B.C. 432.   we shall have to fight over again with as many more ; and
Ol. 87.   if we fail, besides the defeat, our confederacy, which is
our strength, will be lost to us ; for our allies will rise in
revolt when we are no longer capable of making war
upon them.   Mourn not for houses and lands, but for
men ; men may gain these, but these will not gain men.
If I thought that you would listen to me, I would say to
you, "Go yourselves and destroy them, and thereby prove
to the Peloponnesians that none of these things will move
you."

144   'I have many other reasons for believing that you will

Let our answer be: conquer, but you must not be extending
We will grant inde- your empire while you are at war, or
pendence to our allies, run into unnecessary dangers. I am
if the Lacedaemonians more afraid of our own mistakes than of
will allow their subjects more afraid of our own mistakes than of
to choose their own our enemies' designs. But of all this I
form of government. will speak again when the time of action
comes ; for the present, let us send the ambassadors away,
giving them this answer : "That we will not exclude the
Megarians from our markets and harbours, if the Lacedaemonians will cease to expel foreigners, whether ourselves
or our allies, from Sparta ; for the treaty no more forbids
the one than the other. That we will concede independence to the cities, if they were independent when we
made the treaty, and as soon as the Lacedaemonians allow
their allied states a true independence, not for the interest
of Lacedaemon, but everywhere for their own. Also that

We do not want war, we are willing to offer arbitration ac-
but offer arbitration. cording to the treaty. And that we do
Still peace is hopeless;
and we must prepare not want to begin a war, but intend to
for war in a spirit defend ourselves if attacked." This
worthy of our fathers. answer will be just, and befits the dignity
of the city. We must be aware however that war will
come ; and the more willing we are to accept the situation,
the less ready will our enemies be to lay hands upon us.
Remember that where dangers are greatest, there the
greatest honours are to be won by men and states. Our

fathers, when they withstood the Persian, had no such B.C. 432.
power as we have; what little they had they forsook: Ol. 87.
not by good fortune but by wisdom, and not by power but
by courage, they drove the Barbarian away and raised us
to our present height of greatness.   We must be worthy
of them, and resist our enemies to the utmost, that we
may hand down our empire unimpaired to posterity.'

Such were the words of Pericles.   The Athenians, 145
approving, voted as he told them, and   *The Athenians adopt*
on his motion answered the Lacedae-   *Pericles' advice.*
monians in detail as he had suggested, and on the whole
question to the effect 'that they would do nothing upon
compulsion, but were ready to settle their differences by
arbitration upon fair terms according to the treaty.'   So
the ambassadors went home and came no more.

These were the causes of offence alleged on either side 146
before the war began.   The quarrel   *War, though not*
arose immediately out of the affair of   *formally proclaimed, is*
Epidamnus and Corcyra.   But, al-   *imminent.*
though the contest was imminent, the contending parties
still kept up intercourse and visited each other, without
a herald, but not with entire confidence.   For the situation
was really an abrogation of the treaty, and might at any
time lead to war.

BOOK II

B.C. 431.
Ol. 87, 2.

1 AND now the war between the Athenians and Peloponnesians and the allies of both *Outbreak of the war.* actually began. Henceforward the struggle was uninterrupted, and they communicated with one another only by heralds. The narrative is arranged according to summers and winters and follows the order of events.

＊　＊　＊　＊　＊

On neither side were there any mean thoughts; they **8** were both full of enthusiasm: and no *Excitement and en-* wonder, for all men are energetic when *thusiasm in Hellas.* they are making a beginning. At that time the youth of Peloponnesus and the youth of Athens were numerous; they had never seen war, and were therefore very willing to take up arms. All Hellas was excited by the coming conflict between her two chief cities. Many were the prophecies circulated and many the oracles chanted by diviners, not only in the cities about to engage in the struggle, but throughout Hellas. Quite recently the island of Delos had been shaken by an earthquake for the first time within the memory of the Hellenes; this was interpreted and generally believed to be a sign of coming events. And everything of the sort which occurred was curiously noted.

The feeling of mankind was strongly on the side of **9** the Lacedaemonians; for they professed *Universal hatred and* to be the liberators of Hellas. Cities *fear of the Athenians.* and individuals were eager to assist them to the utmost, both by word and deed; and where a man could not hope

---

a Taking βεβαίως with εἰ σφίσι φίλια ταῦτα εἴη.

B.C. 431.
Ol. 87, 2. to be present, there it seemed to him that all things were at a stand. For the general indignation against the Athenians was intense ; some were longing to be delivered from them, others fearful of falling under their sway.

Such was the temper which animated the Hellenes, and *List of the allies on* such were the preparations made by *either side.* the two powers for the war. Their respective allies were as follows:—The Lacedaemonian confederacy included all the Peloponnesians with the exception of the Argives and the Achaeans—they were both neutral; only the Achaeans of Pellene took part with the Lacedaemonians at first; afterwards all the Achaeans joined them[a]. Beyond the borders of the Peloponnese, the Megarians, Phocians, Locrians, Boeotians, Ambraciots, Leucadians, and Anactorians were their allies. Of these the Corinthians, Megarians, Sicyonians, Pellenians, Eleans, Ambraciots, and Leucadians provided a navy, the Boeotians, Phocians, and Locrians furnished cavalry, the other states only infantry. The allies of the Athenians were Chios, Lesbos, Plataea, the Messenians of Naupactus, the greater part of Acarnania, Corcyra, Zacynthus, and cities in many other countries which were their tributaries. There was the maritime region of Caria, the adjacent Dorian peoples, Ionia, the Hellespont, the Thracian coast, the islands that lie to the east within the line of Peloponnesus and Crete, including all the Cyclades with the exception of Melos and Thera. Chios, Lesbos, and Corcyra furnished a navy ; the rest, land forces and money. Thus much concerning the two confederacies, and the character of their respective forces.

10 Immediately after the affair at Plataea the Lacedae-*The Lacedaemonians* monians sent round word to their *summon their allies to* Peloponnesian and other allies, bidding *meet at the Isthmus.* them equip troops and provide all things necessary for a foreign expedition, with the object

---

[a] Cp. v. 82 init.

of invading Attica. The various states made their pre- B.C. 431.
parations as fast as they could, and at the appointed time, Ol. 87, 2.
with contingents numbering two-thirds of the forces of
each, met at the Isthmus. When the whole army was
assembled, Archidamus, the king of the Lacedaemonians,
and the leader of the expedition, called together the
generals of the different states and their chief officers
and most distinguished men, and   *Speech of Archida-*
spoke as follows:—   *mus.*

'Men of Peloponnesus, and you, allies, many are the 11
expeditions which our fathers made   *We have had great*
both within and without the Pelo-   *experience in war, and*
ponnese, and the veterans among our- *our army was never*
                                      finer. But we must
selves are experienced in war; and   *beware of haste, and*
yet we never went forth with a greater *not hold our enemy too*
army than this. But then we should   *cheap.*
remember that, whatever may be our numbers or our
valour, we are going against a most powerful city. And
we are bound to show ourselves worthy of our fathers,
and not wanting to our own reputation. For all Hellas
is stirred by our enterprise, and her eyes are fixed upon
us: she is friendly and would have us succeed because
she hates the Athenians. Now although some among
you, surveying this great host, may think that there is
very little risk of the enemy meeting us in the field, we
ought not on that account to advance heedlessly; but the
general and the soldier of every state should be always
expecting that his own division of the army will be the
one first in danger. War is carried on in the dark;
attacks are generally sudden and furious, and often the
smaller army, animated by a proper fear, has been more
than a match for a larger force which, disdaining their
opponent, were taken unprepared by him. When invading
an enemy's country, men should always be confident in
spirit, but they should fear too, and take measures of precaution; and thus they will be at once most valorous
in attack and impregnable in defence.

'And the city which we are attacking is not so utterly *For they are tho-* powerless against an invader, but is in *roughly prepared, and* the best possible state of preparation, *the least likely of all men to sit idly by while* and for this reason our enemies may *we waste their lands.* be quite expected to meet us in the field. Even if they have no such intention beforehand, yet as soon as they see us in Attica, wasting and destroying their property, they will certainly change their mind. For all men are angry when they not only suffer but see, and some strange form of calamity strikes full upon the eye; the less they reflect the more ready they are to fight; above all men the Athenians, who claim imperial power, and are more disposed to invade and waste their neighbour's land than to look on while their own is being wasted. Remembering how great this city is which you are attacking, and what a fame you will bring on your ancestors and yourselves for good or evil according to the result, follow whithersoever you are led; maintain discipline and caution above all things, and be on the alert to obey the word of command. It is both the noblest and the safest thing for a great army to be visibly animated by one spirit.'

▪　▪　▪　▪　▪

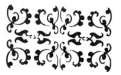

While the Peloponnesians were gathering at the Isthmus, **13** and were still on their way, but before *Pericles, suspecting* they entered Attica, Pericles the son of *that Archidamus will* Xanthippus, who was one of the ten *spare his lands, either* Athenian generals, knowing that the *from friendship, or to* invasion was inevitable, and suspecting *prejudice him with the* that Archidamus in wasting the country *Athenians, promises to* might very likely spare his lands, either *give them to the public* *if they are uninjured by* *the enemy.* out of courtesy and because he happened to be his friend, or by the order of the Lacedaemonian authorities (who had already attempted to raise a prejudice against him [a] when they demanded the expulsion of the polluted family, and might take this further means of injuring him in the eyes of the Athenians), openly declared in the assembly that Archidamus was his friend, but was not so to the injury of the state, and that supposing the enemy did not destroy his lands and buildings like the rest, he would make a present of them to the public; and he desired that the Athenians would have no suspicion of him on that account. As to the general situation, he repeated his previous advice; they must prepare for war and bring their property from the country into the city; they must defend their walls but not go out to battle; they should also equip for service the fleet in which lay their strength. Their allies B.C. 431. should be kept well in hand, for their power depended on Ol. 87, 2. the revenues which they derived from them; military successes were generally gained by a wise policy and command of money.

▪   ▪   ▪   ▪   ▪

In this first invasion Archidamus is said to have lingered about Acharnae with his army ready *where they linger, in the* for battle, instead of descending into *hope that the Athenians* the plain [b], in the hope that the Athe- *will come out to fight.* nians, who were now flourishing in youth and numbers and provided for war as they had never been before, would perhaps meet them in the field rather than allow their lands to be ravaged.

, ı ı ı ı

The Acharnians, who in their own estimation were no small part of the Athenian state, seeing their land ravaged, strongly in-sisted that they should go out and fight. The excitement in the city was universal ; the people were furious with Pericles, and, forgetting all his previous warnings, they abused him for not leading them to battle, as their general should, and laid all their miseries to his charge.

22 But he, seeing that they were overcome by the irritation of the moment and inclined to evil counsels, and con-fident that he was right in refusing to go out, would not summon an assembly or meeting of any kind, lest, coming together more in anger than in pru- *He refuses to comply* dence, they might take some false step. *with their wishes.* He maintained a strict watch over the city, and sought to calm the irritation as far as he could. Meanwhile he sent out horsemen from time to time to prevent flying parties finding their way into the fields near the city and doing mischief.

ı ı ı ı ı

When the Peloponnesians found that the Athenians did **23** not come out to meet them, they moved their army from Acharnae, and ravaged *The Athenians send* *one hundred ships to* some of the townships which lie be- *cruise round Pelopon-* tween Mount Parnes and Mount *nesus. The enemy re-* Brilessus. While they were still in *tire from Attica.* the country, the Athenians sent the fleet of a hundred ships which they had been equipping on an expedition round the Peloponnese. These ships carried on board a thousand hoplites and four hundred archers ; they were under the command of Carcinus the son of Xenotimus, Proteas the son of Epicles, and Socrates the son of Antigenes. After the departure of the fleet the Peloponnesians remained in Attica as long as their provisions lasted, and then, taking a new route, retired through Boeotia. In passing by Oropus they wasted the country called Peiraïkè [a], inhabited by the Oropians, who are subjects of the Athenians. On their return to Peloponnesus the troops dispersed to their several cities.

ı ' ı ı '

25 The Athenian forces, which had lately been dispatched
Proceedings of the to Peloponnesus in the hundred vessels,
Athenian fleet. and were assisted by the Corcyraeans
with fifty ships and by some of the allies from the same region, did considerable damage on the Peloponnesian coast.

ı ' ı ı '

In accordance with an old 34
national custom, the funeral of those   *The Athenians cele-*
who first fell in this war was celebrated *brate the funeral of their*
by the Athenians at the public charge.   *citizens who had died*
The ceremony is as follows : Three   *in the war.*
days before the celebration they erect a tent in which the bones of the dead are laid out, and every one brings to his own dead any offering which he pleases. At the time of the funeral the bones are placed in chests of cypress wood, which are conveyed on hearses ; there is one chest for each tribe. They also carry a single empty litter decked with a pall for all whose bodies are missing, and cannot be recovered after the battle. The procession is accompanied by any one who chooses, whether citizen or stranger, and the female relatives of the deceased are present at the place of interment and make lamentation. The public sepulchre is situated in the most beautiful spot outside the walls ; there they always bury those who fall in war ; only after the battle of Marathon the dead, in recognition of their pre-eminent valour, were interred on the field. When the remains have been laid in the earth, some man of known ability and high reputation, chosen by the city, delivers a suitable oration over them ; after which the people depart. Such is the manner of interment ; and

the ceremony was repeated from time to time throughout the war. Over those who were the first buried Pericles was chosen to speak. At the fitting moment he advanced from the sepulchre to a lofty stage, which had been erected in order that he might be heard as far as possible by the multitude, and spoke as follows:—

(FUNERAL SPEECH.)

35 'Most of those who have spoken here before me *The law which enjoins this oration has been often praised. But I should prefer to praise the brave by deeds only, not to imperil their reputation on the skill of an orator. Still, our ancestors approved the practice, and I must obey.* have commended the lawgiver who added this oration to our other funeral customs; it seemed to them a worthy thing that such an honour should be given at their burial to the dead who have fallen on the field of battle. But I should have preferred that, when men's deeds have been brave, they should be honoured in deed only, and with such an honour as this public funeral, which you are now witnessing. Then the reputation of many would not have been imperilled on the eloquence or want of eloquence of one, and their virtues believed or not as he spoke well or ill. For it is difficult to say neither too little nor too much; and even moderation is apt not to give the impression of truthfulness. The friend of the dead who knows the facts is likely to think that the words of the speaker fall short of his knowledge and of his wishes; another who is not so well informed, when he hears of anything which surpasses his own powers, will be envious and will suspect exaggeration. Mankind are tolerant of the praises of others so long as each hearer thinks that he can do as well or nearly as well himself, but, when the speaker rises above him, jealousy is aroused and he begins to be incredulous. However, since our ancestors have set the seal of their approval upon the practice, I must obey, and to the utmost of my power shall endeavour to satisfy the wishes and beliefs of all who hear me,

'I will speak first of our ancestors, for it is right and 36
seemly that now, when we are lament-   *I will first commemo-*
ing the dead, a tribute should be paid   *rate our predecessors,*
to their memory. There has never   *who gave us freedom*
been a time when they did not inhabit   *and empire. And be-*
this land, which by their valour they   *fore praising the dead,*
I will describe how
have handed down from generation to   *Athens has won her*
generation, and we have received from   *greatness.*
them a free state. But if they were worthy of praise, still
more were our fathers, who added to their inheritance,
and after many a struggle transmitted to us their sons this
great empire. And we ourselves assembled here to-day,
who are still most of us in the vigour of life, have carried
the work of improvement further, and have richly endowed
our city with all things, so that she is sufficient for herself
both in peace and war. Of the military exploits by which
our various possessions were acquired, or of the energy
with which we or our fathers drove back the tide of war,
Hellenic or Barbarian, I will not speak; for the tale would
be long and is familiar to you. But before I praise the
dead, I should like to point out by what principles of
action we rose [a] to power, and under what institutions and
through what manner of life our empire became great.
For I conceive that such thoughts are not unsuited to the
occasion, and that this numerous assembly of citizens and
strangers may profitably listen to them.

'Our form of government does not enter into rivalry 37
with the institutions of others. We   *Our government is*
do not copy our neighbours, but are   *a democracy, but we*
honour men of merit,
an example to them. It is true that   *whether rich or poor.*
we are called a democracy, for the   *Our public life is free*
administration is in the hands of the   *from exclusiveness, our*
many and not of the few. But while   *private from suspicion;*
yet we revere alike the
the law secures equal justice to all   *injunctions of law and*
alike in their private disputes, the   *custom.*
claim of excellence is also recognised; and when a

---
[a] Reading ἤλθομεν.

146

citizen is in any way distinguished, he is preferred to the public service, not as a matter of privilege, but as the reward of merit. Neither is poverty a bar, but a man may benefit his country whatever be the obscurity of his condition. There is no exclusiveness in our public life, and in our private intercourse we are not suspicious of one another, nor angry with our neighbour if he does what he likes; we do not put on sour looks at him which, though harmless, are not pleasant. While we are thus unconstrained in our private intercourse, a spirit of reverence pervades our public acts; we are prevented from doing wrong by respect for the authorities and for the laws, having an especial regard to those which are ordained for the protection of the injured as well as to those unwritten laws which bring upon the transgressor of them the reprobation of the general sentiment.

38   'And we have not forgotten to provide for our weary *We find relaxation in* spirits many relaxations from toil; we *our amusements, and* have regular games and sacrifices *in our homes; and the* throughout the year; our homes are *whole world contributes* beautiful and elegant; and the delight *to our enjoyment.* which we daily feel in all these things helps to banish melancholy. Because of the greatness of our city the fruits of the whole earth flow in upon us; so that we enjoy the goods of other countries as freely as of our own.

39   'Then, again, our military training is in many respects *In war we singly are* superior to that of our adversaries. *a match for the Pelopon-* Our city is thrown open to the world, *nesians united; though* and we never expel a foreigner or *we have no secrets and* prevent him from seeing or learning *undergo no laborious* anything of which the secret if revealed *training.* to an enemy might profit him. We rely not upon management or trickery, but upon our own hearts and hands. And in the matter of education, whereas they from early youth are always undergoing laborious exercises which are to make them brave, we live at ease, and yet are equally

ready to face ᵃ the perils which they face ᵃ. And here is
the proof. The Lacedaemonians come into Attica not by
themselves, but with their whole confederacy following;
we go alone into a neighbour's country; and although our
opponents are fighting for their homes and we on a foreign
soil, we have seldom any difficulty in overcoming them.
Our enemies have never yet felt our united strength; the
care of a navy divides our attention, and on land we are
obliged to send our own citizens everywhere. But they, if
they meet and defeat a part of our army, are as proud as
if they had routed us all, and when defeated they pretend
to have been vanquished by us all.

' If then we prefer to meet danger with a light heart but
without laborious training, and with *We are not enervated*
a courage which is gained by habit and *by culture, or vulgarised*
not enforced by law, are we not greatly *by wealth. We are all*
interested in public
the gainers? Since we do not antici- *affairs, believing that*
pate the pain, although, when the hour *nothing is lost by free*
comes, we can be as brave as those *discussion. Our good-*
ness to others springs
who never allow themselves to rest; *not from interest, but*
and thus too our city is equally ad- *from the generous con-*
mirable in peace and in war. For we *fidence of freedom.*   40
are lovers of the beautiful, yet simple in our tastes, and
we cultivate the mind without loss of manliness. Wealth
we employ, not for talk and ostentation, but when there is
a real use for it. To avow poverty with us is no disgrace;
the true disgrace is in doing nothing to avoid it. An
Athenian citizen does not neglect the state because he
takes care of his own household; and even those of us
who are engaged in business have a very fair idea of
politics. We alone regard a man who takes no interest
in public affairs, not as a harmless, but as a useless
character; and if few of us are originators, we are all
sound judges of a policy. The great impediment to action

ᵃ Or, 'perils such as our strength can bear;' or 'perils which are
enough to daunt us.'

VOL. I.   K

is, in our opinion, not discussion, but the want of that knowledge which is gained by discussion preparatory to action. For we have a peculiar power of thinking before we act and of acting too, whereas other men are courageous from ignorance but hesitate upon reflection. And they are surely to be esteemed the bravest spirits who, having the clearest sense both of the pains and pleasures of life, do not on that account shrink from danger. In doing good, again, we are unlike others; we make our friends by conferring, not by receiving favours. Now he who confers a favour is the firmer friend, because he would fain by kindness keep alive the memory of an obligation; but the recipient is colder in his feelings, because he knows that in requiting another's generosity he will not be winning gratitude but only paying a debt. We alone do good to our neighbours not upon a calculation of interest, but in the confidence of freedom and in a frank

41 *In fine, Athens is the school of Hellas. She alone in the hour of trial rises above her reputation. Her citizens need no poet to sing their praises: for every land bears witness to their valour.*

and fearless spirit. To sum up: I say that Athens is the school of Hellas, and that the individual Athenian in his own person seems to have the power of adapting himself to the most varied forms of action with the utmost versatility and grace. This is no passing and idle word, but truth and fact; and the assertion is verified by the position to which these qualities have raised the state. For in the hour of trial Athens alone among her contemporaries is superior to the report of her. No enemy who comes against her is indignant at the reverses which he sustains at the hands of such a city; no subject complains that his masters are unworthy of him. And we shall assuredly not be without witnesses; there are mighty monuments of our power which will make us the wonder of this and of succeeding ages; we shall not need the praises of Homer or of any other panegyrist whose poetry may please for the moment [a],

---

[a] Cp. i. 10 med., and 21.

although his representation of the facts will not bear the light of day. For we have compelled every land and every sea to open a path for our valour, and have everywhere planted eternal memorials of our friendship and of our enmity. Such is the city for whose sake these men nobly fought and died; they could not bear the thought that she might be taken from them; and every one of us who survive should gladly toil on her behalf.

'I have dwelt upon the greatness of Athens because **42** I want to show you that we are con- *The praise of the city* tending for a higher prize than those *is the praise of these* who enjoy none of these privileges, and *men, for they made her* to establish by manifest proof the merit *rich and poor alike,* of these men whom I am now com- *preferred death to dis-* memorating. Their loftiest praise has *honour.* been already spoken. For in magnifying the city I have magnified them, and men like them whose virtues made her glorious. And of how few Hellenes can it be said as of them, that their deeds when weighed in the balance have been found equal to their fame! Methinks that a death such as theirs has been gives the true measure of a man's worth; it may be the first revelation of his virtues, but is at any rate their final seal. For even those who come short in other ways may justly plead the valour with which they have fought for their country; they have blotted out the evil with the good, and have benefited the state more by their public services than they have injured her by their private actions. None of these men were enervated by wealth or hesitated to resign the pleasures of life; none of them put off the evil day in the hope, natural to poverty, that a man, though poor, may one day become rich. But, deeming that the punishment of their enemies was sweeter than any of these things, and that they could fall in no nobler cause, they determined at the hazard of their lives to be honourably avenged, and to leave the rest. They resigned to hope their unknown chance of happiness; but in the face of death they resolved to rely upon them-

K 2

150

selves alone. And when the moment came they were minded to resist and suffer, rather than to fly and save their lives; they ran away from the word of dishonour, but on the battle-field their feet stood fast, and [a] in an instant, at the height of their fortune, they passed away from the scene, not of their fear, but of their glory [a].

43   'Such was the end of these men; they were worthy of Athens, and the living need not desire

Contemplate and love Athens, and you will know how to value them. They were united in their deaths, but their glory is separate and single. Their sepulchre is the remembrance of them in the hearts of men. Follow their example without fear: it is the prosperous, not the unfortunate, who should be reckless.

to have a more heroic spirit, although they may pray for a less fatal issue. The value of such a spirit is not to be expressed in words. Any one can discourse to you for ever about the advantages of a brave defence, which you know already. But instead of listening to him I would have you day by day fix your eyes upon the greatness of Athens, until you become filled with the love of her; and when you are impressed by the spectacle of her glory, reflect that this empire has been acquired by men who knew their duty and had the courage to do it, who in the hour of conflict had the fear of dishonour always present to them, and who, if ever they failed in an enterprise, would not allow their virtues to be lost to their country, but freely gave their lives to her as the fairest offering which they could present at her feast. The sacrifice which they collectively made was individually repaid to them; for they received again each one for himself a praise which grows not old, and the noblest of all sepulchres—I speak not of that in which their remains are laid, but of that in which their glory survives, and is proclaimed always and on every

---

[a] Or, taking τύχης with καιροῦ: 'while for a moment they were in the hands of fortune, at the height, not of terror but of glory, they passed away.'

fitting occasion both in word and deed. For the whole earth is the sepulchre of famous men; not only are they commemorated by columns and inscriptions in their own country, but in foreign lands there dwells also an unwritten memorial of them, graven not on stone but in the hearts of men. Make them your examples, and, esteeming courage to be freedom and freedom to be happiness, do not weigh too nicely the perils of war. The unfortunate who has no hope of a change for the better has less reason to throw away his life than the prosperous who, if he survive, is always liable to a change for the worse, and to whom any accidental fall makes the most serious difference. To a man of spirit, cowardice and disaster coming together are far more bitter than death striking him unperceived at a time when he is full of courage and animated by the general hope.

'Wherefore I do not now commiserate the parents of the dead who stand here; I would rather comfort them. You know that your life has been passed amid manifold vicissitudes; and that they may be deemed fortunate who have gained most honour, whether an honourable death like theirs, or an honourable sorrow like yours, and whose days have been so ordered that the term of their happiness is likewise the term of their life. I know how hard it is to make you feel this, when the good fortune of others will too often remind you of the gladness which once lightened your hearts. And sorrow is felt at the want of those blessings, not which a man never knew, but which were a part of his life before they were taken from him. Some of you are of an age at which they may hope to have other children, and they ought to bear their sorrow better; not only will the children who may hereafter be born make them forget their own lost ones, but the city

The parents of the dead are to be comforted rather than pitied. Some of them may yet have children who will lighten their sorrow and serve the state; while others should remember how large their share of happiness has been, and be consoled by the glory of those who are gone.

will be doubly a gainer. She will not be left desolate, and she will be safer. For a man's counsel cannot have equal weight or worth, when he alone has no children to risk in the general danger. To those of you who have passed their prime, I say: "Congratulate yourselves that you have been happy during the greater part of your days; remember that your life of sorrow will not last long, and be comforted by the glory of those who are gone. For the love of honour alone is ever young, and not riches, as some say, but honour is the delight of men when they are old and useless."

Such was the order of the funeral celebrated in this 47 winter, with the end of which ended *Second invasion of* the first year of the Peloponnesian *Attica; outbreak of the* B.C. 430. Ol. 87, 3. War. As soon as summer returned, *plague,* the Peloponnesian army, comprising as before two-thirds of the force of each confederate state, under the command of the Lacedaemonian king Archidamus, the son of Zeuxidamus, invaded Attica, where they established themselves and ravaged the country. They had not been there many days when the plague broke out at Athens for the first time. A similar disorder is said to have previously smitten many places, particularly Lemnos, but there is no record of such a pestilence occurring elsewhere, or of so great a destruction of human life. For a while physicians, in ignorance of the nature of the disease, sought to apply remedies; but it was in vain, and they themselves were among the first victims, because they oftenest came into contact with it. No human art was of any avail, and as to supplications in temples, enquiries of oracles, and the like, they were utterly useless, and at last men were overpowered by the calamity and gave them all up.

The disease is said to have begun south of Egypt in 48 Aethiopia; thence it descended into *which commenced in* Egypt and Libya, and after spreading *Aethiopia. The origin and causes of it are un-* over the greater part of the Persian *known, but I shall con-* empire, suddenly fell upon Athens. It *fine myself to the facts.* first attacked the inhabitants of the *I was myself a sufferer.* Piraeus, and it was supposed that the Peloponnesians had poisoned the cisterns, no conduits having as yet been made there. It afterwards reached the upper city, and then the mortality became far greater. As to its probable origin or the causes which might or could have produced such a disturbance of nature, every man, whether a physician or not, will give his own opinion. But I shall describe its actual course, and the symptoms by which any one who knows them beforehand may recognise the disorder should it ever reappear. For I was myself attacked, and witnessed the sufferings of others.

49 The season was admitted to have been remarkably free
The characteristics of from ordinary sickness; and if any-
the disease. body was already ill of any other
disease, it was absorbed in this. Many who were in perfect health, all in a moment, and without any apparent reason, were seized with violent heats in the head and with redness and inflammation of the eyes. Internally the throat and the tongue were quickly suffused with blood, and the breath became unnatural and fetid. There followed sneezing and hoarseness; in a short time the disorder, accompanied by a violent cough, reached the chest; then fastening lower down, it would move the stomach and bring on all the vomits of bile to which physicians have ever given names; and they were very distressing. An ineffectual retching producing violent convulsions attacked most of the sufferers; [a] some as soon as the previous symptoms had abated, others not until long afterwards[a]. The body externally was not so very hot to the touch, nor yet pale; it was of a livid colour inclining to red, and breaking out in pustules and ulcers. But the internal fever was intense; the sufferers could not bear to have on them even the finest linen garment; they insisted on being naked, and there was nothing which they longed for more eagerly than to throw themselves into cold water. And many of those who had no one to look after them actually plunged into the cisterns, for they were tormented by unceasing thirst, which was not in the least assuaged whether they drank little or much. They could not sleep; a restless-ness which was intolerable never left them. While the disease was at its height the body, instead of wasting away,

---

[a] Or, taking λωφήσαντα with σπασμόν : 'these convulsions in some cases soon abated, in others not until long afterwards.'

held out amid these sufferings in a marvellous manner, and either they died on the seventh or ninth day, not of weakness, for their strength was not exhausted, but of internal fever, which was the end of most; or, if they survived, then the disease descended into the bowels and there produced violent ulceration; severe diarrhoea at the same time set in, and at a later stage caused exhaustion, which finally with few exceptions carried them off. For the disorder which had originally settled in the head passed gradually through the whole body, and, if a person got over the worst, would often seize the extremities and leave its mark, attacking the privy parts and the fingers and the toes; and some escaped with the loss of these, some with the loss of their eyes. Some again had no sooner recovered than they were seized with a forgetfulness of all things and knew neither themselves nor their friends.

The general character of the malady no words can 50 describe, and the fury with which it *Even the animals and* fastened upon each sufferer was too *birds of prey refused to* much for human nature to endure. *touch the corpses.* There was one circumstance in particular which distinguished it from ordinary diseases. The birds and animals which feed on human flesh, although so many bodies were lying unburied, either never came near them, or died if they touched them. This was proved by a remarkable disappearance of the birds of prey, which were not to be seen either about the bodies or anywhere else; while in the case of the dogs the result was even more obvious, because they live with man.

    ı ı ı ı ı

59   After the second Peloponnesian invasion, now that

The Athenians sue Attica had been once more ravaged,
for peace and are re- and the war and the plague together
jected. They turn upon lay heavy upon the Athenians, a change
Pericles. His defence. came over their spirit.   They blamed
Pericles because he had persuaded them to go to war,
declaring that he was the author of their troubles; and
they were anxious to come to terms with the Lacedaemonians.   Accordingly envoys were despatched to Sparta,
but they met with no success.   And now, being completely
at their wits' end, they turned upon Pericles.   He saw

---

^a Cp. i. 64 med.   ^b Cp. i. 59, 61 init.

that they were exasperated by their misery and were
behaving just as he had always anticipated that they would.
And so, being still general, he called an assembly, wanting
to encourage them and to convert their angry feelings into
a gentler and more hopeful mood. At this assembly he
came forward and spoke as follows :—

'I was expecting this outburst of indignation ; the 60
causes of it are not unknown to me. *Your anger is incon-*
And I have summoned an assembly *siderate and unmanly;*
that I may remind you of your resolu- *you forget that the for-*
tunes of the individual
tions and reprove you for your incon- *depend on those of the*
siderate anger against me, and want *state. If you believed*
of fortitude in misfortune. In my *that I was wise, loyal,*
disinterested, when you
judgment it would be better for in- *consented to the war,*
dividuals themselves that the citizens *why should you attack*
should suffer and the state flourish *me now ?*
than that the citizens should flourish and the state suffer.
A private man, however successful in his own dealings, if
his country perish is involved in her destruction ; but if he
be an unprosperous citizen of a prosperous city he is much
more likely to recover. Seeing then that states can bear
the misfortunes of individuals, but individuals cannot bear
the misfortunes of the state, let us all stand by our country
and not do what you are doing now, who because you are
stunned by your private calamities are letting go the hope
of saving the state, and condemning not only me who
advised, but yourselves who consented to, the war. Yet
I with whom you are so angry venture to say of myself,
that I am as capable as any one of devising and explaining
a sound policy ; and that I am a lover of my country, and
incorruptible. Now a man may have a policy which he
cannot clearly expound, and then he might as well have
none at all ; or he may possess both ability and eloquence,
but if he is disloyal to his country he cannot, like a true
man, speak in her interest ; or again he may be unable to
resist a bribe, and then all his other good qualities will be
sold for money. If, when you determined to go to war,

you believed me to have somewhat more of the statesman in me than others, it is not fair that I should now be charged with anything like crime.

61 'I allow that for men who are in prosperity and free to
I am not changed, choose it is great folly to make war.
but you are changed by But when they must either submit and
misfortune. Such a at once surrender independence, or
change is unbecoming strike and be free, then he who shuns
the citizens of Athens: and not he who meets the danger is
you should forget your and not he who meets the danger is
sorrows, and think only deserving of blame. For my own part,
of the public good. I am the same man and stand where
I did. But you are changed; for you have been driven by misfortune to recall the consent which you gave when you were yet unhurt, and to think that my advice was wrong because your own characters are weak. The pain is present and comes home to each of you, but the good is as yet unrealised by any one; and your minds have not the strength to persevere in your resolution, now that a great reverse has overtaken you unawares. Anything which is sudden and unexpected and utterly beyond calculation, such a disaster for instance as this plague coming upon other misfortunes, enthralls the spirit of a man. Nevertheless, being the citizens of a great city and educated in a temper of greatness, you should not succumb to calamities however overwhelming, or darken the lustre of your fame. For if men hate the presumption of those who claim a reputation to which they have no right, they equally condemn the faint-heartedness of those who fall below the glory which is their own. You should lose the sense of your private sorrows and cling to the deliverance of the state.

62 'As to your sufferings in the war, if you fear that they may be very great and after all fruitless, I have shown you already over and over again that such a fear is groundless. If you are still unsatisfied I will indicate [a] one element of

---

[a] Or, taking ὑπάρχον ὑμῖν absolutely: 'a consideration which, however obvious, appears to have escaped you.' Or, again, taking μεγέθους

your superiority which appears to have escaped you *,
although it nearly touches your imperial
greatness. I too have never mentioned
it before, nor would I now, because the
claim may seem too arrogant, if I did
not see that you are unreasonably depressed. You think that your empire
is confined to your allies, but I say that
of the two divisions of the world accessible to man, the land and the sea, there
is one of which you are absolute masters,
and have, or may have, the dominion to
any extent which you please. Neither
the great King nor any nation on earth can hinder
a navy like yours from penetrating whithersoever you
choose to sail. When we reflect on this great power,
houses and lands, of which the loss seems so dreadful
to you, are as nothing. We ought not to be troubled
about them or to think much of them in comparison;
they are only the garden of the house, the superfluous
ornament of wealth; and you may be sure that if we
cling to our freedom and preserve that, we shall soon
enough recover all the rest. But, if we are the servants
of others, we shall be sure to lose not only freedom, but
all that freedom gives. And where your ancestors doubly
succeeded, you will doubly fail. For their empire was
not inherited by them from others but won by the labour
of their hands, and by them preserved and bequeathed to
us. And to be robbed of what you have is a greater
disgrace than to attempt a conquest and fail. Meet your
enemies therefore not only with spirit but with disdain.
A coward or a fortunate fool may brag and vaunt, but he
only is capable of disdain whose conviction that he is

Do you fear that your sufferings will be fruitless? I tell you that you are absolute masters of the sea, which is half the world. What are your possessions in comparison with freedom? Keep that, and you will soon regain the rest. Meet your enemies with disdain, as having a rational conviction of your superiority.

πέρι with ἐνθυμηθῆναι: 'one element of your superiority which nearly
touches your empire, but of which you never seem to have considered
the importance.'

VOL. I.   L stronger than his enemy rests, like our own, on grounds of reason. Courage fighting in a fair field is fortified by the intelligence which looks down upon an enemy; an intelligence relying, not on hope, which is the strength of helplessness, but on that surer foresight which is given by reason and observation of facts.

63 'Once more, you are bound to maintain the imperial dignity of your city in which you all take pride; for you should not covet the glory unless you will endure the toil. And do not imagine that you are fighting about a simple issue, freedom or slavery; you have an empire to lose, and there is the danger to which the hatred of your imperial rule has exposed you. Neither can you resign your power, if, at this crisis, any timorous or inactive spirit is for thus playing the honest man. For by this time your empire has become a tyranny which in the opinion of mankind may have been unjustly gained, but which cannot be safely surrendered. The men of whom I was speaking, if they could find followers, would soon ruin a city, and if they were to go and found a state of their own, would equally ruin that. For inaction is secure only, when arrayed by the side of activity; nor is it expedient or safe for a sovereign, but only for a subject state, to be a servant.

Your empire is at stake, and it is too late to resign it; for you have already incurred the hatred of mankind.

64 'You must not be led away by the advice of such citizens as these, nor be angry with me; for the resolution in favour of war was your own as much as mine. What if the enemy has come and done what he was certain to do when you refused to yield? What too if the plague followed? That was an unexpected blow, but we might have foreseen all the rest. I am well aware that your hatred of me is aggravated by it. But how unjustly, unless to me you also ascribe the credit of any extraordinary

Nothing has happened, except the plague, but what we all anticipated when we agreed on war. Do not lose the spirit which has made Athens great and, even though she fall, will render her glorious for all time.

161

success which may befall you[a]! The visitations of heaven should be borne with resignation, the sufferings inflicted by an enemy with manliness. This has always been the spirit of Athens, and should not die out in you. Know that our city has the greatest name in all the world because she has never yielded to misfortunes, but has sacrificed more lives and endured severer hardships in war than any other; wherefore also she has the greatest power of any state up to this day; and the memory of her glory will always survive. Even if we should be compelled at last to abate somewhat of our greatness (for all things have their times of growth and decay), yet will the recollection live, that, of all Hellenes, we ruled over the greatest number of Hellenic subjects; that we withstood our enemies, whether single or united, in the most terrible wars, and that we were the inhabitants of a city endowed with every sort of wealth and greatness. The indolent may indeed find fault, but [b]the man of action[b] will seek to rival us, and he who is less fortunate will envy us. To be hateful and offensive has ever been at the time the fate of those who have aspired to empire. But he judges well who accepts unpopularity in a great cause. Hatred does not last long, and, besides the immediate splendour of great actions, the renown of them endures for ever in men's memories. Looking forward to such future glory and present avoidance of dishonour, make an effort now and secure both. Let no herald be sent to the Lacedaemonians, and do not let them know that you are depressed by your sufferings. For those are the greatest states and the greatest men, who, when misfortunes come, are the least depressed in spirit and the most resolute in action.'

By these and similar words Pericles endeavoured to 65 appease the anger of the Athenians against himself, and

---

[a] Cp. i. 140 init.

[b] Or, taking καὶ αὐτὸς with βουλόμενος: 'he who is ambitious like ourselves.'

L 2

to divert their minds from their terrible situation. In the conduct of public affairs they took his advice, and sent no more embassies to Sparta; they were again eager to prosecute the war. Yet in private they felt their sufferings keenly; the common people had been deprived even of the little which they possessed, while the upper class had lost fair estates in the country with all their houses and rich furniture. Worst of all, instead of enjoying peace, they were now at war. The popular indignation was not pacified until they had fined Pericles; but, soon afterwards, with the usual fickleness of a multitude, they elected him general and committed all their affairs to his charge. Their private sorrows were beginning to be less acutely

The Athenians follow Pericles' advice, but are not appeased until they have fined him. He soon regains their esteem, and takes the lead of affairs. After his death his wisdom was even better appreciated than during his life. His advice about the war was sound if the Athenians would only have followed it. But they were continually embarking on rash enterprises, and the city was distracted by the struggles of rival demagogues, whereas Pericles had been their natural leader.

felt, and for a time of public need they thought that there was no man like him. During the peace while he was at the head of affairs he ruled with prudence; under his guidance Athens was safe, and reached the height of her greatness in his time. When the war began he showed that here too he had formed a true estimate of the Athenian power. He survived the commencement of hostilities two years and six months; and, after his death, his foresight was even better appreciated than during his life. For he had told the Athenians that if they would be patient and would attend to their navy, and not seek to enlarge their dominion while the war was going on, nor imperil the existence of the city, they would be victorious; but they did all that he told them not to do, and in matters which seemingly had nothing to do with the war, from motives of private ambition and private interest they adopted a policy which had disastrous effects in respect both of themselves and of their allies; their measures,

[a] had they been successful, **would only have brought** [a] honour and profit to individuals, and, when unsuccessful, crippled the city in the conduct of the war. The reason of the difference was that he, deriving authority from his capacity and acknowledged worth, being also a man of transparent integrity, was able to control the multitude in a free spirit; he led them rather than was led by them; for, not seeking power by dishonest arts, he had no need to say pleasant things, but, on the strength of his own high character, could venture to oppose and even to anger them. When he saw them unseasonably elated and arrogant, his words humbled and awed them; and, when they were depressed by groundless fears, he sought to reanimate their confidence. Thus Athens, though still in name a democracy, was in fact ruled by her greatest citizen. But his successors were more on an equality with one another, and, each one struggling to be first himself, they were ready to sacrifice the whole conduct of affairs to the whims of the people. Such weakness in a great and imperial city led to many errors, of which the greatest was the Sicilian expedition; not that the Athenians miscalculated their enemy's power, but they themselves, instead of consulting for the interests of the expedition which they had sent out, were occupied in intriguing against one another for the leadership of the democracy [b], and not only hampered the operations of the army, but became embroiled, for the first time, at home. And yet after they had lost in the Sicilian expedition the greater part of their fleet and army, and were now distracted by revolution, still they held out three years not only against their former enemies, but against the Sicilians who had combined with them, and against most of their own allies who had risen in revolt. Even when Cyrus the son of the King joined

Even after the Sicilian disaster they held out against their old enemies and many new ones, and were at last only ruined by themselves. So that Pericles was quite right after all.

---

[a] Or, 'while they continued to succeed, only brought.'   [b] Cp. vi. 28.

in the war and supplied the Peloponnesian fleet with
money, they continued to resist, and were at last overthrown, not by their enemies, but by themselves and their
own internal dissensions. So that at the time Pericles
was more than justified in the conviction at which his
foresight had arrived, that the Athenians would win an
easy victory over the unaided forces of the Peloponnesians.

3

Thucydides,   HISTORY OF THE PELOPONNESIAN WAR
              (Books III, IV, VI, VII)
              (Trans. by Richard Crowley;
               Ed. by Richard Livingstone)

1. Compare the involvement of the United States in
    Viet-Nam with the Athenian expedition to Sicily.

2. Analyze the arguments for and against a policy of
    expediency rather than one based on morality as in
    the Athenian approach to the revolt of Mythilene
    and in their attitude toward the Melians.

3. Why did the Athenians turn down the Spartan over-
    tures for a peace during the battle of Pylos? What
    were the consequences?

4. Compare the position of Cuba today with that of
    Melos. Would you recommend that the United States
    adopt the Athenian attitude in similar circumstances?
    Explain your reasons.

    In his appraisal of Thucydides, Macaulay included
this statement: "I assure you that there is no prose
composition in the world which I place so high as the
seventh book of Thucydides. It is the *ne plus ultra*
of human art."

THE HISTORY OF
THE PELOPONNESIAN WAR

Debate at Athens on the treatment of a revolted ally.

36. Upon the arrival of the Mitylenaean prisoners the Athenians at once put Salaethus to death, although he offered, among other things, to procure the withdrawal of the Peloponnesians from Plataea, which was still under siege; and after deliberating as to what they should do with the rest, determined in the fury of the moment to put to death not only the prisoners at Athens, but the whole adult male population of Mitylene, and to make slaves of the women and children. It was remarked that Mitylene had revolted without being, like the rest, subjected to the empire; and what especially enraged the Athenians was the fact of the Peloponnesian fleet having ventured over to Ionia to her support; this was held to prove a long-meditated rebellion. They accordingly sent a galley to communicate the decree to Paches, ordering him to lose no time in dispatching the Mitylenians. The morrow brought repentance with it, and reflexion on the horrid cruelty of a decree which condemned a whole city to the fate merited only by the guilty. This was no sooner perceived by the Mitylenian ambassadors at Athens, and their Athenian supporters, than they moved the authorities to put the question again to the vote; this they the more easily consented to do, as they themselves plainly saw that most of the citizens wished someone to give them an opportunity for reconsidering the matter. An assembly was therefore at once called, and after much expression of opinion upon both sides, Cleon, son of Cleaenetus (who had carried the former

motion to put the Mitylenians to death), the most violent man at Athens, and at that time by far the most powerful with the democracy, came forward again and spoke as follows:—

37. 'I have often before now realized that a democracy is incapable of empire, and never more so than by your present change of mind over Mitylene. Fears or plots are unknown to you in your daily relations with each other, and you feel just the same with regard to your allies, and never reflect that the mistakes into which you may be led by listening to their appeals, or by giving way to your own compassion, are full of danger to yourselves, and bring you no thanks for your weakness from your allies; you forget entirely that your empire is a despotism and your subjects disaffected conspirators, whose obedience is ensured not by your suicidal concessions, but by the superiority which your own strength, not their loyalty, gives. The most alarming feature in the case is the constant change of measures with which we appear to be

threatened, and our seeming ignorance of the fact that bad laws which are never changed are better for a city than good ones that have no authority; that steadiness without education is more helpful than cleverness without character; and that ordinary men usually manage public affairs better than their more gifted fellows. The latter are always wanting to appear wiser than the laws, and to overrule every proposition brought forward, thinking that they can find no more important field for their intelligence, and by such behaviour too often ruin their country; while those who mistrust their own cleverness are content to be less learned than the laws, and less able to pick holes in the speech of a good speaker; impartial judges rather than competing disputants, they are generally more successful. That is the type to which we should conform, and not be led on by cleverness and intellectual rivalry to advise your people against our real views.

38. 'For myself, I adhere to my former opinion, and wonder at those who have proposed to reopen the case of the Mitylenians, and who are so causing a delay which is all in favour of the guilty, by making the sufferer proceed against the offender with the edge of his anger blunted; where vengeance follows most closely upon the wrong, it best equals it and most amply requites it. I wonder also who will be the man who will maintain the contrary, and will pretend to show that the crimes of the Mitylenians are of service to us, and our misfortunes injurious to the allies. Such a man must plainly either have such confidence in his rhetoric as to attempt to prove that what is universally admitted is still an open question, or he must have been bribed to try to delude us by elaborate sophisms. In such disputes the state gives the rewards to others, and takes the dangers for herself. The persons to blame are you who are so foolish as to institute these debates; you go to see an oration as you would to see a sight, take your facts on hearsay, judge of the practicability of a project by the wit of

its advocates, and trust for the truth about past events not to your eyes but to your ears—to some clever critic's words; the easy victims of newfangled arguments, unwilling to follow approved conclusions; slaves to the paradox of the moment, despisers of the normal; the first wish of each of you is that he could speak himself, the next to rival those who can speak by seeming to be abreast of their ideas by applauding every hit almost before it is made, and by being as quick in catching an argument as you are slow in foreseeing its consequences; asking, if I may so say, for something different from the conditions under which we live, and yet comprehending inadequately those very conditions; very slaves to the pleasure of the ear, and more like the audience of a rhetorician than the council of a city.

39. 'To save you from this, I proceed to show that no one state has ever injured you as much as Mitylene. I can make allowance for those who revolt because they cannot bear our empire, or who have been forced to do so by the enemy. But for those who possessed an island with fortifications; who could fear our enemies only by sea, and there had their own force of galleys to protect them; who were independent and held in the highest honour by you—to act as these have done, this is not revolt—revolt implies oppression; it is deliberate and wanton aggression; an attempt to ruin us by siding with our bitterest enemies; a worse offence than a war undertaken on their own account in the acquisition of power. The fate of their neighbours who had already rebelled and had been subdued was no lesson to them; their own prosperity could not dissuade them from affronting danger; blindly confident in the future, and full of hopes beyond their power though not beyond their ambition, they declared war and made their decision to prefer might to right. Their attack was prompted not by ill-treatment but by a prospect of impunity. The truth is that great good fortune coming suddenly and unexpectedly tends to

make a people insolent: in most cases it is safer for mankind to have success in reason than out of reason; and it is easier for them to stave off adversity than to preserve prosperity. Our mistake has been to distinguish the Mitylenians as we have done; had they been long ago treated like the rest, they never would have so far forgotten themselves; for human nature is as surely made arrogant by consideration, as it is awed by firmness. Let them now therefore be punished as their crime requires, and do not absolve the people while you condemn the aristocracy. This is certain, that all attacked you without distinction, although they might have come over to us, and been now again in possession of their city. But no, they thought it safer to throw in their lot with their aristocrats and so joined their rebellion! Consider therefore! if you inflict the same punishment on allies who are compelled by the enemy to rebel and on those who desert you by their own choice, which of them, think you, is there that will not revolt upon the slightest pretext; when the reward of success is freedom, and the penalty of failure nothing so very terrible? We meanwhile shall have to risk our money and our lives against one state after another; if successful we shall recover a ruined town from which we can no longer draw the revenue upon which our strength depends; if unsuccessful, we shall have an enemy the more upon our hands, and shall spend in war with our own allies the time that might be employed in combating our existing foes.

40. 'No hope, therefore, that rhetoric may instil or money purchase, of the mercy due to human infirmity must be held out to the Mitylenians. Their offence was not involuntary, but of malice and deliberate; and mercy is only for unwilling offenders. I therefore now as before persist against your reversing your first decision, or giving way to the three failings most fatal to empire—pity, sentiment, and indulgence.[1]

[1] Note this philosophy of empire.

Compassion is due to those who can reciprocate the feeling, not to those who will never pity us, but are our natural and necessary foes: the orators who charm us with sentiment may find other less important arenas for their talents, and avoid one where the city pays a heavy penalty for a momentary pleasure, while they receive fine acknowledgements for their fine phrases; indulgence should be kept for those who will be our friends in future, not for men who will remain just what they were, and as much our enemies as before. To sum up shortly, I say that if you follow my advice you will do what is just towards the Mitylenians, and at the same time expedient; while by a different decision you will not oblige them so much as pass sentence upon yourselves. If they were right in rebelling, you must be wrong in ruling. But if, right or wrong, you determine to rule, you must carry out your principle and punish the Mitylenians as your interest requires; or else you must give up your empire and cultivate honesty without danger. Make up your minds, therefore, punish them as they would have punished you, do not let the victims who escaped the plot be more insensible than the conspirators who hatched it; reflect what they would have done if victorious over you, especially as they were the aggressors. It is they who wrong their neighbour without a cause, that pursue their victim to the death, on account of the danger which they foresee in letting their enemy survive; for a man who has been gratuitously injured is more dangerous, if he escape, than an ordinary enemy. Do not be traitors to yourselves, but recall as nearly as possible your feelings in the moment of crisis and the supreme importance which you then attached to their reduction, and now pay them back in their turn; do not turn soft-hearted at the sight of their distress or forget the peril that once hung over you. Punish them as they deserve, and teach your other allies by a striking example that the penalty of rebellion is death. Let them once understand this and you will not have so often to neglect your enemies while you are fighting with your own allies.'

41. So spoke Cleon. After him Diodotus, son of Eucrates, who had also in the previous assembly spoken most strongly against putting the Mitylenians to death, came forward and said:

42. 'I do not blame the persons who have reopened the case of the Mitylenians, nor do I approve the protests which we have heard against important questions being frequently debated. I think the two things most opposed to good counsel are haste and passion; haste usually goes hand in hand with folly, passion with coarseness and narrowness of mind. As for the argument that speech ought not to be the exponent of action, the man who uses it must be either senseless or interested: senseless if he believes it possible to treat of the uncertain future through any other medium; interested if, wishing to carry a disgraceful measure and doubting his ability to speak well in a bad cause, he thinks to frighten opponents and hearers by well-aimed calumny. What is still more intolerable is to accuse a speaker of making a display in order to be paid for it. If ignorance only were imputed, an unsuccessful speaker might retire with a reputation for honesty, if not for wisdom; the charge of dishonesty makes him suspected, if successful, and thought, if defeated, not only a fool but a rogue. The city is no gainer by such a system, since fear deprives it of its advisers; although in truth, if our speakers are to make such assertions, it would be better for the country if they could not speak at all, as we should then make fewer blunders. The good citizen ought to triumph not by frightening his opponents but by beating them fairly in argument; and a wise city, without over-distinguishing its best advisers, will nevertheless not deprive them of their due, and far from punishing an unlucky counsellor will not even regard him as disgraced.   In this way successful orators will be least tempted to sacrifice their convictions to popularity, in the hope of still higher honours, and unsuccessful speakers to resort to the same popular arts in order to win over the crowd.

43. 'This is not our way; and, besides, the moment that a man is suspected of giving advice, however good, from corrupt motives, we feel such a grudge against him for the gain which after all we are not certain he will receive, that we deprive the city of certain benefit.   Plain good advice has thus come to be no less suspected than bad; and the advocate of the most monstrous measures is not more obliged to use deceit to gain the people, than the best counsellor is to lie in order to be believed.   The city and the city only, owing to these refinements, can never be served openly and without disguise; he who does serve it openly is always suspected of serving himself in some secret way in return.   Still, considering the magnitude of the interests involved, and the position of affairs, we orators must make it our business to look a little further than you who judge offhand; especially as we, your advisers, are responsible, while you, our audience, are not so.   For if those who gave the advice, and those who took it, suffered equally, you would judge more calmly; as it is, you visit the disasters into which the whim of the moment may have led you, upon the single person of your adviser, not upon yourselves, his numerous companions in error.

44. 'However, I have not come forward either to oppose or to accuse in the matter of Mitylene; indeed, the question before us as sensible men is not their guilt, but our interests.   Though I prove them ever so guilty, I shall not, therefore, advise their death,

unless it be expedient; nor though they should have claims to indulgence, shall I recommend it, unless it be clearly for the good of the country.[1] I consider that we are deliberating for the future more than for the present; and where Cleon is so positive as to the useful deterrent effects that will follow from making rebellion capital, I, who consider the interests of the future quite as much as he, as positively maintain the contrary. And I ask you not to reject my useful considerations for his specious ones: his speech may have the attraction of seeming the more just in your present temper against Mitylene; but we are not in a court of justice, but in a political assembly; and the question is not justice, but how to make the Mitylenians useful to Athens.

45. 'Of course communities have enacted the penalty of death for many offences far lighter than this: still hope leads men to venture, and no one ever yet put himself in peril without the inward conviction that he would succeed in his design. Again, did ever city rebel unless it believed that it possessed either in itself or in its alliances resources adequate to the enterprise? All, states and individuals, are alike prone to err, and there is no law that will prevent them; or why should men have exhausted the list of punishments in search of enactments to protect them from evildoers? It is probable that in early times the penalties for the greatest offences were less severe, and that, as these were disregarded, the penalty of death has been by degrees generally arrived at; and this too is similarly disregarded. Either then some more terrible means of terror must be discovered, or it must be owned that this restraint is useless, and that as long as poverty gives men the courage of necessity, or plenty fills them with the ambition which belongs to insolence and pride, and the other conditions of life remain each under the thraldom of some fatal and master passion, so long will the impulse never be wanting to drive men into danger. Hope

[1] A view even more cynical than Cleon's.

also and cupidity, the one leading and the other following, the one conceiving the attempt, the other suggesting that fortune will help, cause the widest ruin, and, although invisible agents, are far stronger than visible dangers. Fortune, too, powerfully helps the delusion, and by the unexpected aid that she sometimes lends tempts men to venture with inferior means; and this is especially true with communities, because the stakes played for are the highest, freedom or empire, and, when all are acting together, each man irrationally magnifies his own capacity. In fine, it is impossible to prevent, and only great simplicity can hope to prevent, human nature doing what it has once set its mind upon, by force of law or by any other deterrent force whatsoever.

46. 'We must not, therefore, commit ourselves to a false policy through a belief in the efficacy of the punishment of death, or exclude rebels from the hope of repentance and an early atonement of their error. Consider a moment! At present, if a city that has already revolted sees that it cannot succeed, it will come to terms while it is still able to afford an indemnity, and pay tribute afterwards. In the other case, what city think you would not prepare better than it does now, and hold out to the last against its besiegers, if it is all one whether it surrenders late or soon? And how can it be otherwise than hurtful to us to be put to the expense of a siege, because surrender is out of the question; and if we take the city, to receive a ruined town from which we can no longer draw the revenue which forms our real strength against the enemy?[1] We must not sit as strict judges of the offenders to our own prejudice, but rather see how by moderate punishment we may be enabled to benefit in future by the revenue-producing powers of our dependencies; and we must make up our minds to look for our protection not to legal

[1] Diodotus here, using Cleon's words, puts a point that he has made in a different light and draws an opposite conclusion from it.

terrors but to careful administration. At present we do exactly the opposite. When a free community, held in subjection by force, rises, as is only natural, and asserts its independence, it is no sooner reduced than we fancy ourselves obliged to punish it severely; although the right course with freemen is not to punish them rigorously when they do rise, but rigorously to watch them before they rise, and to prevent their ever entertaining the idea, and, the insurrection suppressed, to make as few responsible for it as possible.

47. 'Only consider what a blunder you would commit in doing as Cleon recommends. As things are at present, in all the cities the democracy is your friend, and either does not revolt with the oligarchy, or, if forced to do so, becomes at once the enemy of the insurgents; so that in the war with the hostile city you have the masses on your side. But if you butcher the people of Mitylene, who had nothing to do with the revolt, and who, as soon as they got arms, of their own motion surrendered the town, you will commit the crime of killing your benefactors; and you will play directly into the hands of the upper classes, who, when they induce their cities to rise, will immediately have the people on their side, through your having announced in advance the same punishment for those who are guilty and for those who are not. Even if they were guilty, you ought to seem not to notice it, in order to avoid alienating the only class still friendly to us. In short, I consider it far more useful for the preservation of our empire voluntarily to put up with injustice, than to put to death, however justly, those whom it is our interest to keep alive. As for Cleon's idea that in punishment the claims of justice and expediency can both be satisfied, facts do not confirm the possibility of such a combination.

48. 'Confess, therefore, that this is the wisest course, and without conceding too much either to pity or to indulgence, by neither of which motives do I any more than Cleon wish you to be influenced, upon the

plain merits of the case before you, be persuaded by me to try calmly those of the Mitylenians whom Paches sent off as guilty, and to leave the rest undisturbed. This is at once best for the future, and most formidable to your enemies at the present moment; good policy against an adversary is superior to the senseless attacks of mere force.'

49. So spoke Diodotus. These opinions most nearly represented the two opposing policies, and the Athenians, notwithstanding their change of feeling, now proceeded to a division, in which the show of hands was almost equal, although the motion of Diodotus carried the day. Another galley was at once sent off in haste, for fear that the first might reach Lesbos in the interval, and the city be found destroyed; the first ship had about a day and a night's start. Wine and barley-cakes were provided for the vessel by the Mitylenian ambassadors, and great promises made if they arrived in time; this caused the men to use such energy upon the voyage that they took their meals of barley-cakes kneaded with oil and wine as they rowed, and only slept by turns while the others were at the oar. Luckily they met with no contrary wind, and the first ship making no haste upon so horrid an errand, while the second pressed on in the manner described, the first arrived so little before them, that Paches had only just had time to read the decree, and to prepare to execute the sentence, when the second put into port and prevented the massacre. The danger of Mitylene had indeed been great.

50. The persons whom Paches had sent off as the prime movers in the rebellion were upon Cleon's motion put to death by the Athenians, to the number of rather more than a thousand. The Athenians also demolished the walls of the Mitylenians, and took possession of their ships. Afterwards tribute was not imposed upon the Lesbians; but all their land, except that of the Methymnians, was divided into three thousand allotments, three hundred of which

were reserved as sacred for the gods, and the rest
assigned by lot to Athenian shareholders, who were
sent out to the island. The Lesbians agreed with
these to pay a rent of two minae [1] a year for each
allotment, and cultivated the land themselves. The
Athenians also took possession of the towns on the
continent belonging to the Mitylenians, which thus
became for the future subject to Athens. So ended
the revolt of Lesbos.

　　　ɪ　　ɪ　　ɪ　　ɪ　　ɪ

82.   Such was the pitch of savagery reached by the
revolution; and it made the greater impression
because it was the first of such incidents. Later,
practically the whole Greek world was affected; there
was a struggle everywhere between the leaders of the
democratic and oligarchic parties, the former wishing
to secure the support of Athens, the latter that of
Lacedaemon. In peace there would have been
neither the desire nor the excuse for appealing to
them, but the war gave both sides, if they wished for
a revolution, a ready chance to invoke outside help
in order to injure their opponents and to gain power.
Revolution brought on the cities of Greece many
calamities, such as exist and always will exist till
human nature changes, varying in intensity and
character with changing circumstances. In peace and
prosperity states and individuals are governed by
higher ideals because they are not involved in necessities beyond their control, but war deprives them of
their easy existence and is a rough teacher that brings
most men's dispositions down to the level of their
circumstances. So civil war broke out in the cities,
and the later revolutionaries, with previous examples
before their eyes, devised new ideas which went far
beyond earlier ones, so elaborate were their enterprises, so novel their revenges. Words changed
their ordinary meanings and were construed in new
senses. Reckless daring passed for the courage of a
loyal partisan, far-sighted hesitation was the excuse

of a coward, moderation was the pretext of the unmanly, the power to see all sides of a question was complete inability to act. Impulsive rashness was held the mark of a man, caution in conspiracy was a specious excuse for avoiding action. A violent attitude was always to be trusted, its opponents were suspect. To succeed in a plot was shrewd, it was still more clever to divine one: but if you devised a policy that made such success or suspicion needless, you were breaking up your party and showing fear of your opponents. In fine, men were applauded if they forestalled an injury or instigated one that had not been conceived. Ties of party were closer than those of blood, because a partisan was readier to take risks without asking why; for the basis of party association was not an advantage consistent with the laws of the state but a self-interest which ignored them, and the seal of their mutual good faith was complicity in crime and not the divine law. If a stronger opponent made a fair proposal, it was met with active precautions and not in a generous spirit. Revenge was more prized than self-preservation. An agreement sworn to by either party, when they could do nothing else, was binding as long as both were powerless, but the first side to pluck up courage, when they saw an opening and an undefended point, took more pleasure in revenge on a confiding enemy than if they had achieved it by an open attack; apart from considerations of security, a success won by treachery was a victory in a battle of wits. Villainy is sooner called clever than simplicity good, and men in general are proud of cleverness and ashamed of simplicity.

The cause of all these evils was love of power due to ambition and greed, which led to the rivalries from which party spirit sprung. The leaders of both sides used specious phrases, championing a moderate aristocracy or political equality for the masses. They professed to study public interests but made them their prize, and in the struggle to get the better of each other by any means committed terrible excesses and went to still greater extremes in revenge. Neither justice nor the needs of the state restrained them, their only limit was the caprice of the hour, and they were prepared to satisfy a momentary rivalry by the unjust condemnation of an opponent or by a forcible seizure of power. Religion meant nothing to either party, but the use of fair phrases to achieve a criminal end was highly respected. The moderates were destroyed by both parties, either because they declined to co-operate or because their survival was resented.

83. So civil war gave birth to every kind of iniquity in the Greek world. Simplicity, the chief ingredient in a noble nature, was ridiculed and disappeared, and society was divided into rival camps in which no man trusted his fellow. There was no reconciling force—no promise binding, no oath that inspired awe. Each party in its day of power despairing of security was more concerned to save itself from ruin than to trust others. Inferior minds were as a rule the more successful; aware of their own defects and of the intelligence of their opponents, to whom they felt themselves inferior in debate, and by whose versatility of intrigue they were afraid of being surprised, they struck boldly and at once. Their enemies despised them, were confident of detecting their plots and thought it needless to effect by violence what they could achieve by their brains, and so were taken off their guard and destroyed.[1]

84. It was in Corcyra that most of these crimes were first perpetrated: the reprisals taken by subjects when their hour came on rulers who had governed them oppressively; the unjust designs of those who wished to escape from a life of poverty and who were stung by passion and covetous of their neighbours' wealth; the savage and pitiless excesses of those with whom greed was not a motive, but who were carried

[1] Many critics, chiefly on external grounds, reject the following chapter as spurious, but its power and insight are worthy of Thucydides.

away by undisciplined rage in the struggle with their equals.

In the chaos of city life under these conditions human nature, always rebellious against the law and now its master, was delighted to display its uncontrolled passions, its superiority to justice, its hostility to all above itself; for vengeance would not have been set above religion, or gain above justice, had it not been for the fatal power of envy. But in their revenges men are reckless of the future and do not hesitate to annul those common laws of humanity on which everyone relies in the hour of misfortune for his own hope of deliverance; they forget that in their own need they will look for them in vain.

85. While the revolutionary passions thus for the first time displayed themselves in the factions of Corcyra, Eurymedon and the Athenian fleet sailed away; after this some five hundred Corcyraean exiles, who had succeeded in escaping, took some forts on the mainland, and becoming masters of the Corcyraean territory over the water made this their base to plunder their countrymen in the island, and did so much damage as to cause a severe famine in the town. They also sent envoys to Lacedaemon and Corinth to negotiate their restoration; but meeting with no success, afterwards got together boats and mercenaries and crossed over to the island; there were about six hundred of them, and burning their boats, so as to have no hope except in becoming masters of the country, they went up to Mount Istone, and fortifying themselves there, began to harass those in the city and obtained command of the country.

ı ı ı ı ı

13. After continuing their attacks during that day and most of the next, the Peloponnesians desisted, and the day after sent some of their ships to Asine [1] for timber to make engines, hoping by their aid, in spite of its height, to take the wall opposite the harbour, where the landing was easiest. At this moment the Athenian fleet from Zacynthus arrived, now numbering fifty sail, having been reinforced by some of the ships on guard at Naupactus and by four Chian vessels. Seeing the coast and the island both crowded with heavy infantry, and the hostile ships in harbour showing no signs of sailing out, at a loss where to anchor, they sailed for the moment to the desert island of Prote, not far off, where they passed the night. The next day they got under way in readiness to engage in the open sea if the enemy chose to put out to meet them, and determined in the event of his not doing so to sail in and attack him. The Lacedaemonians did not put out to sea, and having omitted to close the entrances, as they had intended, remained quiet on shore, engaged in manning their ships and getting ready, in the case of anyone sailing in, to fight in the harbour, which is fairly large.

14. Seeing this, the Athenians advanced against them by each entrance, and falling on the enemy's fleet, most of which was by this time afloat and in line, at once put it to flight, and giving chase, as far as the

[1] About thirty miles away.

short distance allowed, disabled a good many vessels, and took five, one with its crew on board; they dashed in at the rest that had taken refuge on shore, and disabled some that were still being manned, before they could put out; others whose crews had fled they lashed to their own ships and towed off empty. At this sight the Lacedaemonians, maddened by a disaster which cut off their men on the island, rushed to the rescue, and going into the sea with their heavy armour, laid hold of the ships and tried to drag them back, each man thinking that success depended on his individual exertions. Great was the mêlée, and quite in contradiction to the naval tactics usual to the two combatants; the Lacedaemonians in their excitement and dismay were actually engaged in a sea-fight on land, while the victorious Athenians, in their eagerness to push their success as far as possible, were carrying on a land-fight from their ships. After great exertions and numerous wounds on both sides they separated, the Lacedaemonians saving their empty ships, except those first taken; and both parties returning to their camp, the Athenians set up a trophy, gave back the dead, secured the wrecks, and at once began to cruise round and jealously watch the island, with its intercepted garrison, while the Peloponnesians on the mainland, whose contingents had now all come up, stayed where they were before Pylos.

15. When the news of what had happened at Pylos reached Sparta, the disaster was thought so serious that the Lacedaemonians resolved that the authorities should go down to the camp, and decide the best course of action on the spot. There seeing that it was impossible to help their men, and not wishing to risk their being reduced by hunger or overpowered by numbers, they determined, with the consent of the Athenian generals, to conclude an armistice at Pylos and send envoys to Athens to obtain a convention, and to endeavour to get back their men as quickly as possible.

16. The generals accepted their offers and an armistice was concluded upon the terms following [1]:—

That the Lacedaemonians should bring to Pylos and surrender to the Athenians the ships that had fought in the late engagement, and all vessels of war in Laconia, and should make no attack on the fortification either by land or by sea.

That the Athenians should allow the Lacedaemonians on the mainland to send to the men in the island a certain fixed quantity of corn ready kneaded, that is to say, two quarts of barley meal, one pint of wine, and a piece of meat for each man, and half the same quantity for a servant.

That this allowance should be sent in under the eyes of the Athenians, and that no boat should sail to the island except openly.

That the Athenians should continue to guard the island as before, without however landing upon it, and should refrain from attacking the Peloponnesian troops either by land or by sea.

That if either party should infringe any of these terms in the slightest particular, the armistice should be at once void.

That the armistice should hold good until the return of the Lacedaemonian envoys from Athens—the Athenians sending them thither in a galley and bringing them back again—and upon the arrival of the envoys should be at an end, and the ships be restored by the Athenians in the same state as they received them.

Such were the terms of the armistice; sixty ships were surrendered, and the envoys sent off. Arrived at Athens they spoke as follows:—

17. 'Athenians, the Lacedaemonians sent us to try

[1] The terms 'reflect the anxiety and depression of the Spartans'.

to find some way of making an arrangement about our men on the island, that shall be at once satisfactory to your interests, and as consistent with our dignity as circumstances permit in our misfortune. We can venture to speak at some length without any departure from the habit of our country. Men of few words where many are not wanted,[1] we can be less brief when there is a matter of importance to be illustrated and an end to be served by its illustration. Meanwhile we beg you to take what we may say, not in a hostile spirit, nor as if we thought you ignorant and wished to lecture you, but rather as a suggestion on the best course to be taken, addressed to intelligent critics. You can now, if you choose, employ your present success to advantage, so as to keep what you have got and gain honour and reputation besides, and you can avoid the mistake of those who meet with an extraordinary piece of good fortune, and are led on by hope to grasp continually at something further, because they have had an unexpected success. Those who have known most vicissitudes of good and bad have also justly least faith in their prosperity; and experience has not been wanting to teach your city and ours this lesson.

18. 'You have only to look at our present misfortune to be convinced of this. What Greek power stood higher than we did? And yet we are come to you, although we used to think ourselves more able to grant what we are now here to ask. Nevertheless, we have not been brought to this by any decay in our power, or through having our heads turned by aggrandizement; no, our resources are what they have always been, and our error has been an error of judgement, to which all are equally liable. Accordingly the prosperity which your city now enjoys, and the accession that it has lately received, must not make you fancy that fortune will be always with you. Sensible men are prudent enough to treat their gains

[1] We owe the word 'laconic' to the traditional brevity of Spartan speech.

as precarious, just as they would also keep a clear head in adversity, and think that war, so far from staying within the limit to which a combatant may wish to confine it, will run the course that its chances prescribe; and so, not being elated by confidence in military success, they are less likely to come to grief, and most ready to make peace, if they can, while their fortune lasts. This, Athenians, you have a good opportunity to do now with us, and so to escape the possible disasters which may follow upon your refusal, and the consequent imputation of having owed to accident even your present advantages, when you might have left behind you a reputation for power and wisdom which nothing could endanger.

19. 'The Lacedaemonians accordingly invite you to make a treaty and to end the war, and offer peace and alliance and the most friendly and intimate relations in every way and on every occasion between us, and in return ask for the men on Sphacteria, thinking it better for both parties not to stand out to the end, on the chance of some favourable accident enabling the men to force their way out, or of their being compelled to succumb under the pressure of blockade. Indeed if great enmities are ever to be really settled, we think it will be, not by the system of revenge and military success, and by forcing an opponent to swear to a treaty to his disadvantage, but when the more fortunate combatant waives these his privileges, is guided by gentler feelings, conquers his rival in generosity, and accords peace on more moderate conditions than were expected. From that moment, instead of the debt of revenge which violence must entail, his adversary owes a debt of generosity to be paid in kind, and is inclined by honour to stand to his agreement. Men oftener act in this manner towards their greatest enemies than in less important quarrels; they are also by nature as glad to give way to those who first yield to them, as they are apt to be provoked by arrogance to risks condemned by their own judgement.

20. 'To apply this to ourselves: if peace was ever desirable for both parties, it is surely so at the present moment, before any irreparable incident intervenes, which forces us to hate you eternally, personally as well as politically, and you to miss the advantages that we now offer you. While the issue is still in doubt, and you have reputation and our friendship in prospect, and we a reasonable settlement of our difficulties without disgrace, let us be reconciled, and for ourselves choose peace instead of war, and grant the rest of Greece a remission from their sufferings, for which be sure they will think they have chiefly you to thank. The war that they labour under they know not which began, but the peace that concludes it depends on your decision and will by their gratitude be laid to your door. By such a decision you can become firm friends with the Lacedaemonians at their own invitation, which you do not force from them, but oblige them by accepting. Consider the advantages that are likely to follow from this friendship: when Attica and Sparta are at one, the rest of Greece, be sure, which is less powerful than we, will show us the greatest deference.'

21. So spoke the Lacedaemonians; their idea was that the Athenians, already anxious for a truce and only kept back by the opposition of Sparta, would joyfully accept a peace freely offered, and give back the men. The Athenians, however, having the men on the island, thought that the treaty would be ready for them whenever they chose to make it, and grasped at something further. Foremost to encourage them in this policy was Cleon, son of Cleaenetus, a popular leader of the time and very powerful with the masses, who persuaded them to answer that: First, the men in the island must surrender themselves and their arms and be brought to Athens. Next, the Lacedaemonians must restore Nisaea, Pegae, Troezen, and Achaea, all places acquired not by arms, but by the previous convention,[1] under which they had been

[1] In 445 B.C.

ceded by Athens herself at a moment of disaster, when a truce was more necessary to her than at present. This done they might take back their men, and make a truce for as long as both parties might agree.

22. To this answer the envoys made no reply, but asked that commissioners might be chosen with whom they might confer on each point, and quietly talk the matter over and try to come to some agreement. Hereupon Cleon violently attacked them, saying that he knew from the first that they had no honest intentions, and that it was clear enough now by their refusing to speak before the people, and wanting to confer in secret with a committee of two or three.[1] No! if they meant anything honest let them say it out before all. The Lacedaemonians, however, seeing that, whatever concessions they might be prepared to make in their misfortune, it was impossible for them to speak before the multitude and lose credit with their allies for a negotiation which might after all miscarry, and on the other hand, that the Athenians would never grant what they asked upon moderate terms, returned from Athens without having effected anything.

Further events at Pylos.

23. Their arrival at once put an end to the armistice at Pylos, and the Lacedaemonians asked back their ships according to the convention. The Athenians, however, alleged an attack on the fort in contravention of the truce, and other grievances seemingly not worth mentioning, and refused to give them back, insisting upon the clause by which the slightest infringement made the armistice void. The Lacedaemonians, after denying the contravention and protesting against their bad faith over the ships, went away and earnestly addressed themselves to the war. Hostilities were now carried on at Pylos upon both

[1] Cleon's denunciation of 'secret diplomacy' was both specious and disastrous.

sides with vigour. The Athenians cruised round the island all day with two ships going different ways; and by night, except on the seaward side in windy weather, anchored round it with their whole fleet, which had been reinforced by twenty ships from Athens come to help in the blockade, and now numbered seventy sail; the Peloponnesians remained encamped on the mainland, making attacks on the fort, and on the look-out for any opportunity which might offer itself for the deliverance of their men.

ı ı ı ı ı

84. The next summer the Athenians made an expedition against the isle of Melos. The Melians are a colony of Lacedaemon that would not submit to the Athenians like the other islanders, and at first remained neutral and took no part in the struggle, but afterwards, upon the Athenians using violence and plundering their territory, assumed an attitude of open hostility. The Athenian generals encamped in their territory with their army, and before doing any harm to their land sent envoys to negotiate. These the Melians did not bring before the people, but told them to state the object of their mission to the magistrates and the council; the Athenian envoys then said:

85. *Athenians.*—'As we are not to speak to the people, for fear that if we made a single speech without interruption we might deceive them with attractive arguments to which there was no chance of replying —we realize that this is the meaning of our being brought before your ruling body—we suggest that you who sit here should make security doubly sure. Let us have no long speeches from you either, but deal separately with each point, and take up at once any statement of which you disapprove, and criticize it.'

86. *Melians.*—'We have no objection to your reasonable suggestion that we should put our respective points of view quietly to each other, but the military preparations which you have already made seem

inconsistent with it. We see that you have come to be yourselves the judges of the debate, and that its natural conclusion for us will be slavery if you convince us, and war if we get the better of the argument and therefore refuse to submit.'

87. *Athenians.*—'If you have met us in order to make surmises about the future, or for any other purpose than to look existing facts in the face and to discuss the safety of your city on this basis, we will break off the conversations; otherwise, we are ready to speak.'

88. *Melians.*—'In our position it is natural and excusable to explore many ideas and arguments. But the problem that has brought us here is our security, so, if you think fit, let the discussion follow the line you propose.'

89. *Athenians.*—'Then we will not make a long and unconvincing speech, full of fine phrases, to prove that our victory over Persia justifies our empire, or that we are now attacking you because you have wronged us, and we ask you not to expect to convince us by saying that you have not injured us, or that, though a colony of Lacedaemon, you did not join her. Let each of us say what we really think and reach a practical agreement. You know and we know, as practical men, that the question of justice arises only between parties equal in strength, and that the strong do what they can, and the weak submit.'

90. *Melians.*—'As you ignore justice and have made self-interest the basis of discussion, we must take the same ground, and we say that in our opinion it is in your interest to maintain a principle which is for the good of all—that anyone in danger should have just and equitable treatment and any advantage, even if not strictly his due, which he can secure by persuasion. This is your interest as much as ours, for your fall would involve you in a crushing punishment that would be a lesson to the world.'

91. *Athenians.*—'We have no apprehensions about the fate of our empire, if it did fall; those who rule other

peoples, like the Lacedaemonians, are not formidable to a defeated enemy. Nor is it the Lacedaemonians with whom we are now contending: the danger is from subjects who of themselves may attack and conquer their rulers. But leave that danger to us to face. At the moment we shall prove that we have come in the interest of our empire and that in what we shall say we are seeking the safety of your state; for we wish you to become our subjects with least trouble to ourselves, and we would like you to survive in our interests as well as your own.'

92. *Melians.*—'It may be your interest to be our masters: how can it be ours to be your slaves?'

93. *Athenians.*—'By submitting you would avoid a terrible fate, and we should gain by not destroying you.'

94. *Melians.*—'Would you not agree to an arrangement under which we should keep out of the war, and be your friends instead of your enemies, but neutral?'

95. *Athenians.*—'No: your hostility injures us less than your friendship. That, to our subjects, is an illustration of our weakness, while your hatred exhibits our power.'

96. *Melians.*—'Is this the construction which your subjects put on it? Do they not distinguish between states in which you have no concern, and peoples who are most of them your colonies, and some conquered rebels?'

97. *Athenians.*—'They think that one nation has as good rights as another, but that some survive because they are strong and we are afraid to attack them. So, apart from the addition to our empire, your subjection would give us security: the fact that you are islanders (and weaker than others) makes it the more important that you should not get the better of the mistress of the sea.'

98. *Melians.*—'But do you see no safety in our neutrality? You debar us from the plea of justice and press us to submit to your interests, so we must expound our own, and try to convince you, if the

two happen to coincide. Will you not make enemies of all neutral Powers when they see your conduct and reflect that some day you will attack them? Will not your action strengthen your existing opponents, and induce those who would otherwise never be your enemies to become so against their will?'

99. *Athenians.*—'No. The mainland states, secure in their freedom, will be slow to take defensive measures against us, and we do not consider them so formidable as independent island powers like yourselves, or subjects already smarting under our yoke. These are most likely to take a thoughtless step and bring themselves and us into obvious danger.'

100. *Melians.*—'Surely then, if you are ready to risk so much to maintain your empire, and the enslaved peoples so much to escape from it, it would be criminal cowardice in us, who are still free, not to take any and every measure before submitting to slavery?'

101. *Athenians.*—'No, if you reflect calmly: for this is not a competition in heroism between equals, where your honour is at stake, but a question of self-preservation, to save you from a struggle with a far stronger Power.'

102. *Melians.*—'Still, we know that in war fortune is more impartial than the disproportion in numbers might lead one to expect. If we submit at once, our position is desperate; if we fight, there is still a hope that we shall stand secure.'

103. *Athenians.*—'Hope encourages men to take risks; men in a strong position may follow her without ruin, if not without loss. But when they stake all that they have to the last coin (for she is a spendthrift), she reveals her real self in the hour of failure, and when her nature is known she leaves them without means of self-protection. You are weak, your future hangs on a turn of the scales; avoid the mistake most men make, who might save themselves by human means, and then, when visible hopes desert them, in their extremity turn to the invisible—prophecies and

oracles and all those things which delude men with hopes, to their destruction.'

104.   *Melians.*—'We too, you can be sure, realize the difficulty of struggling against your power and against Fortune if she is not impartial.   Still we trust that Heaven will not allow us to be worsted by Fortune, for in this quarrel we are right and you are wrong.   Besides, we expect the support of Lacedaemon to supply the deficiencies in our strength, for she is bound to help us as her kinsmen, if for no other reason, and from a sense of honour.   So our confidence is not entirely unreasonable.'

105.   *Athenians.*—'As for divine favour, we think that we can count on it as much as you, for neither our claims nor our actions are inconsistent with what men believe about Heaven or desire for themselves. We believe that Heaven, and we know that men, by a natural law, always rule where they are stronger.   We did not make that law nor were we the first to act on it; we found it existing, and it will exist for ever, after we are gone; and we know that you and anyone else as strong as we are would do as we do.   As to your expectations from Lacedaemon and your belief that she will help you from a sense of honour, we congratulate you on your innocence but we do not admire your folly.   So far as they themselves and their national traditions are concerned, the Lacedaemonians are a highly virtuous people; as for their behaviour to others, much might be said, but we can put it shortly by saying that, most obviously of all people we know, they identify their interests with justice and the pleasantest course with honour.   Such principles do not favour your present irrational hopes of deliverance.' [1]

106.   *Melians.*—'That is the chief reason why we have confidence in them now; in their own interest they will not wish to betray their own colonists and so help their enemies and destroy the confidence that their friends in Greece feel in them.'

[1] Sparta did not help Melos.

107. *Athenians.*—'Apparently you do not realize that safety and self-interest go together, while the path of justice and honour is dangerous; and danger is a risk which the Lacedaemonians are little inclined to run.'

108. *Melians.*—'Our view is that they would be more likely to run a risk in our case, and would regard it as less hazardous, because our nearness to Peloponnese makes it easier for them to act and our kinship gives them more confidence in us than in others.'

109. *Athenians.*—'Yes, but an intending ally looks not to the good will of those who invoke his aid but to marked superiority of real power, and of none is this truer than of the Lacedaemonians. They mistrust their own resources and attack their neighbours only when they have numerous allies, so it is not likely that, while we are masters of the sea, they would cross it to an island.'

110. *Melians.*—'They might send others. The sea of Crete [1] is large, and this will make it more difficult for its masters to capture hostile ships than for these to elude them safely. If they failed by sea, they would attack your country and those of your allies whom Brasidas did not reach; and then you will have to fight not against a country in which you have no concern, but for your own country and your allies' lands.'

111. *Athenians.*—'Here experience may teach you like others, and you will learn that Athens has never abandoned a siege from fear of another foe. You said that you proposed to discuss the safety of your city, but we observe that in all your speeches you have never said a word on which any reasonable expectation of it could be founded. Your strength lies in deferred hopes; in comparison with the forces now arrayed against you, your resources are too small for any hope of success. You will show a great want of judgement if you do not come to a more reasonable decision after we have withdrawn. Surely you will

[1] The part of the Aegean between Melos and Crete.

not fall back on the idea of honour, which has been the ruin of so many when danger and disgrace were staring them in the face. How often, when men have seen the fate to which they were tending, have they been enslaved by a phrase and drawn by the power of this seductive word to fall of their own free will into irreparable disaster, bringing on themselves by their folly a greater dishonour than fortune could inflict! If you are wise, you will avoid that fate. The greatest of cities makes you a fair offer, to keep your own land and become her tributary ally: there is no dishonour in that. The choice between war and safety is given you; do not obstinately take the worse alternative. The most successful people are those who stand up to their equals, behave properly to their superiors, and treat their inferiors fairly. Think it over when we withdraw, and reflect once and again that you have only one country, and that its prosperity or ruin depends on one decision.'

112. The Athenians now withdrew from the conference; and the Melians, left to themselves, came to a decision corresponding with what they had maintained in the discussion, and answered, 'Our resolution, Athenians, is unaltered. We will not in a moment deprive of freedom a city that has existed for seven hundred years; we put our trust in the fortune by which the gods have preserved it until now, and in the help of men, that is, of the Lacedaemonians; and so we will try and save ourselves. Meanwhile we invite you to allow us to be friends to you and foes to neither party, and to retire from our country after making such a treaty as shall seem fit to us both.'

113. Such was the answer of the Melians. The Athenians broke up the conference saying, 'To judge from your decision, you are unique in regarding the future as more certain than the present and in allowing your wishes to convert the unseen into reality; and as you have staked most on, and trusted most in, the Lacedaemonians, your fortune, and your hopes, so will you be most completely deceived.'

114.   The Athenian envoys now returned to the army; and as the Melians showed no signs of yielding the generals at once began hostilities, and drew a line of circumvallation round the Melians, dividing the work among the different states.   Subsequently the Athenians returned with most of their army, leaving behind them a certain number of their own citizens and of the allies to keep guard by land and sea.   The force thus left stayed on and besieged the place.

115.   Meanwhile the Athenians at Pylos took so much plunder from the Lacedaemonians that the latter, although they still refrained from breaking off the treaty and going to war with Athens, proclaimed that any of their people that chose might plunder the Athenians.   The Corinthians also commenced hostilities with the Athenians for private quarrels of their own; but the rest of the Peloponnesians stayed quiet. Meanwhile the Melians in a night attack took the part of the Athenian lines opposite the market, killed some of its garrison, and brought in corn and as many useful stores as they could.   Then, retiring, they remained inactive, while the Athenians took measures to keep better guard in future.

117.   Summer was now over.   The next winter the Lacedaemonians intended to invade the Argive territory, but on arriving at the frontier found the sacrifices for crossing unfavourable, and went back again.   This intention of theirs made the Argives suspicious of certain of their fellow-citizens, some of whom they arrested; others, however, escaped them. About the same time the Melians again took another part of the Athenian lines which were but feebly garrisoned.   In consequence reinforcements were sent from Athens, and the siege was now pressed vigorously; there was some treachery in the town, and the Melians surrendered at discretion to the Athenians, who put to death all the grown men whom they took, and sold the women and children for slaves; subsequently they sent out five hundred settlers and colonized the island.

BOOK VI

1. The same winter the Athenians resolved to sail again to Sicily, with a greater armament than that under Laches and Eurymedon, and, if possible, to conquer the island; most of them were ignorant of its size and of the number of its inhabitants, Greek and foreign, and of the fact that they were undertaking a war not much inferior to that against the Peloponnesians. For the voyage round Sicily in a merchantman is not far short of eight days; and yet, large as the island is, only two miles of sea separate it from the mainland.

8. Early in the spring of the following year the Athenian envoys arrived from Sicily, and the Egestaeans with them, bringing sixty talents of uncoined silver, as a month's pay for sixty ships, which they were to ask to have sent them. The Athenians held an assembly, and after hearing from the Egestaeans

198

and their envoys a report, as attractive as it was untrue, upon the state of affairs generally, and in particular of the large amount of money reported to be in the temples and the treasury, voted to send sixty ships to Sicily, under the command of Alcibiades, Nicias, and Lamachus, who were appointed with full powers; they were to help the Egestaeans against the Selinuntines; if successful, to restore Leontini[1]; and to arrange Sicilian affairs generally as they thought best for the interests of Athens. Five days after this a second assembly was held, to consider the speediest means of equipping the ships, and to vote whatever else might be required by the generals for the expedition; and Nicias, who had been chosen to the command against his will, and who thought that the state was not well advised, but upon a slight and specious pretext was aspiring to the great task of conquering the whole of Sicily, came forward in the hope of diverting the Athenians from the enterprise, and gave them the following advice:—

9. 'This assembly was convened to consider the preparations to be made for sailing to Sicily, but I think that we have still the question to examine, whether it is desirable to send out a fleet at all, and that we ought not to give so little consideration to a matter of such moment, or let ourselves be persuaded by foreigners into undertaking a war with which we have nothing to do. Individually I gain in honour by such a course, and fear as little as other men for my person—not that I think a man need be any the worse citizen for taking some thought for his person and property; on the contrary, such a

[1] Conquered by Syracuse.

man would for his own interests wish his country to prosper. Still, I have never spoken against my convictions to gain honour, and I shall not begin to do so now, but shall say what I think best. I might advise your keeping what you have got and not risking what is actually yours for advantages which are dubious in themselves, and which you may or may not attain; but any words of mine would be impotent in view of your temperament.[1] I will, therefore, content myself with showing that your enthusiasm is out of season, and your ambition not easy of accomplishment.

10. 'I affirm, then, that you leave many enemies behind you here, to go to Sicily and bring more back with you. You imagine, perhaps, that the treaty which you have made can be trusted; it will continue to exist nominally as long as you keep quiet—for nominal it has become, owing to the practices of certain men here [2] and at Sparta—but in the event of a serious reverse in any quarter it would not delay our enemies a moment in attacking us. For it was an agreement forced upon them by disaster and less honourable to them than to us; and, further, in this very agreement there are many still disputed points. Again, some of the most powerful states have never yet accepted the arrangement at all. Some of these are at open war with us; others (as the Lacedae-monians do not yet move) are restrained by truces renewed every ten days, and it is only too probable that if they found our power divided, as we are hurrying to divide it, they would attack us vigorously with the Siceliots,[3] whose alliance they would have in the past valued as they would that of few others. We ought, therefore, to consider these points, and not to think of running risks with a country placed so critically, or of grasping at another empire before

[1] See the portrait of the Athenian temperament, p. 57.
[2] As Alcibiades.
[3] The Siceliots are the Greek settlers in Sicily, as opposed to the Sicels, the native inhabitants.

we have secured the one we have already; for in
fact the Thracian Chalcidians have been all these years
in revolt from us without being yet subdued, and
others on the continents yield us but a doubtful
obedience. The Egestaeans, our allies, have been
wronged, and we run to help them, but the rebels who
have so long wronged us still remain unpunished.

11. 'Yet these, if brought under, might be kept
under; while the Sicilians, even if conquered, are too
far off and too numerous to be ruled without difficulty.
It is folly to attack men who could not be kept under
even if conquered, while failure would leave us in a
very different position from that which we occupied
before the enterprise. The Siceliots, again, to take
them as they are at present, in the event of a Syracusan
conquest (the favourite bugbear of the Egestaeans),
would to my thinking be even less dangerous to us
than before. At present individual states might
possibly come here for love of Lacedaemon; if they
were united under Syracuse, one empire would
scarcely attack another; for after joining the Peloponnesians to overthrow ours, they could only
expect to see the same hands overthrow their own in
the same way. The Greeks in Sicily would fear us
most if we never went there at all, and next to this,
if after displaying our power we went away again as
soon as possible. Men, as we know, respect most
what is most remote and least liable to have its
reputation put to the test; at the least reverse they
would at once begin to look down upon us, and
would join our enemies here against us. You have
yourselves experienced this with regard to the Lacedaemonians and their allies, whom your unexpected
success, as compared with what you feared at first,
has made you suddenly despise, tempting you further
to aspire to the conquest of Sicily. Instead, however,
of being elated by the misfortunes of your adversaries,
you ought to think of breaking their spirit before
giving yourselves up to confidence, and to understand
that the one thought awakened in the Lacedaemonians

by their disgrace is how they may even now, if possible, overthrow us and repair their dishonour; for military reputation is their oldest and chiefest study. Our struggle, therefore, if we are wise, will not be for foreigners like the Egestaeans in Sicily, but how to defend ourselves most effectually against the oligarchical machinations of Lacedaemon.

12. 'We should also remember that we are but now enjoying some respite from a great pestilence and from war, to the no small benefit of our estates and persons, and that it is right to employ these at home on our own behalf, instead of using them on behalf of these exiles whose interest it is to lie as finely as they can, who do nothing themselves but talk and leave the danger to others, and who if they succeed will show no proper gratitude, and if they fail will drag down their friends with them. If anyone here,[1] overjoyed at being chosen to command, urges you to make the expedition, merely for ends of his own—especially if he is still over young to command—who seeks to be admired for his stud of horses, and on account of its heavy expenses hopes for some profit from his appointment, do not allow such a person to maintain his private splendour at his country's risk, but remember that such persons injure the public fortune while they squander their own, and that this is a matter of importance, and not for a young man to decide or hastily to take in hand.

13. 'I see men of this type now sitting here at the side of that individual and summoned to his aid, and I am alarmed: I, in my turn, summon any older man that may have such a person sitting next him, not to let himself be shamed into fear of being thought a coward if he does not vote for war, but, remembering how rarely success is got by wishing and how often by forethought, to leave to them the mad dream of conquest, and as a true lover of his country, now threatened by the greatest danger in its history, to hold up his hand on the other side; to vote that the

---

[1] Alcibiades is meant.

Siceliots be left to enjoy their own possessions and to settle their own quarrels; that the Egestaeans be told to end by themselves with the Selinuntines the war which they began without consulting the Athenians; and that for the future we do not enter into alliance, as we have been used to do,[1] with people whom we must help in their need, and who can never help us in ours.

14. 'And you, Prytanis,[2] if you think it your duty to care for the commonwealth, and if you wish to show yourself a good citizen, put the question to the vote, and take a second time the opinions of the Athenians. If you are afraid to move the question again, consider that in the presence of so many witnesses you cannot incur blame for breaking the law, that you will be the physician of your misguided city, and that the virtue of men in office is briefly this, to do their country as much good as they can, or in any case no harm that they can avoid.'

15. So spoke Nicias. Most of the Athenians who came forward spoke in favour of the expedition, and of not annulling what had been voted, although some spoke on the other side. By far the warmest advocate of the expedition was, however, Alcibiades, who wished to thwart Nicias both as his political opponent and also because of the attack he had made upon him in his speech, and who was, besides, exceedingly ambitious of a command by which he hoped to reduce Sicily and Carthage,[3] and personally to gain in wealth and reputation by means of his successes. The position he held among the citizens led him to indulge his tastes beyond his real means, both in keeping horses and in the rest of his expenditure; and this later on had not a little to do with the ruin of the Athenian state. Alarmed at the greatness of his licence in his own life and habits, and of the ambition which he showed in all things that he undertook,

[1] No doubt he has Corcyra in mind.
[2] The presiding officer.
[3] Note Athenian imperial ambitions.

the mass of the people set him down as a pretender to absolute power, and became his enemies; and although publicly his conduct of the war was as good as could be desired, individually his habits gave offence to everyone, and caused them to commit affairs to other hands, and thus before long to ruin the city. Meanwhile he now came forward and gave the following advice to the Athenians:—

16. 'Athenians, I have a better right to command than others—I must begin with this as Nicias has attacked me—and at the same time I believe myself to be worthy of it. The things for which I am abused bring fame to my ancestors and to myself, and to the country profit besides. The Greeks, after expecting to see our city ruined by the war, concluded it to be even greater than it really is, because of the magnificence with which I represented it at the Olympic games, when I sent into the lists seven chariots, a number never before entered by any private person, and won the first prize, and was second and fourth, and took care to have everything else in a style worthy of my victory. Custom regards such displays as honourable, and they cannot be made without leaving behind them an impression of power. Again, any splendour that I have exhibited at home in providing choruses,[1] or otherwise, is naturally envied by my fellow-citizens, but foreigners regard it as a sign of strength. Folly has its uses when a man at his own cost benefits his city as well as himself. There is no injustice in a man who is proud of himself being on a level by himself. The unfortunate do not go shares in their misfortunes. We do not expect to be saluted when we are down in the world; and on the same principle why should anyone complain when the more fortunate treat him with disdain? Let him treat his

[1] Private persons paid for the chorus and their trainer in dramatic and other performances.

inferiors as equals before he claims like treatment himself. What I know is that persons like myself, and all others that have attained to any distinction, may in their lifetime be unpopular with their fellow-men and especially with their equals, but posterity loves to claim connexion with them even when there is no ground for the claim, and their country treats them not as strangers or sinners but as national heroes of which it is proud. Such are my ambitions, and however I am abused for them in private, the question is whether anyone manages public affairs better than I do. I united the most powerful states of Peloponnese, without great danger or expense to you, and compelled the Lacedaemonians to stake their all upon the issue of a single day at Mantinea [1]; and although victorious in the battle they have never since fully recovered confidence.

17. 'Thus did my youth and so-called monstrous folly find fit arguments to deal with the power of the Peloponnesians, and by its ardour win their confidence and prevail. And do not be afraid of my youth now, but while I am still in its flower, and Nicias enjoys the reputation of success, avail yourselves to the utmost of the services of us both. Do not rescind your resolution to sail to Sicily, on the ground that you would be going to attack a great Power. The cities in Sicily are peopled by motley rabbles, and easily change their institutions and adopt new ones; and consequently the inhabitants have no real feeling of patriotism; the individual is not armed and the land has no regular defences; every man thinks that either by fair words or by party strife he can obtain something at the public expense, and then in the event of a catastrophe settle in some other country, and makes his preparations accordingly. From a mob like this you need not look for either unanimity in counsel or concert in action; they will probably one by one come in as they get a fair offer, especially if

[1] See p. 261. This is Alcibiades' way of describing a disastrous Athenian defeat.

they are torn by civil strife as we are told. Further, the Siceliots have not so many heavy infantry as they boast; just as the states of Greece greatly over-estimated their numbers, and have hardly had an adequate force of heavy infantry throughout this war. The states in Sicily, therefore, from all that I can hear, will be found as I say; and I have not pointed out all our advantages, for we shall have the help of many foreign peoples, who from their hatred of the Syracusans will join us in attacking them; nor will the mainland powers hinder us, if you judge rightly. Our fathers with these very adversaries, which it is said we shall now leave behind us when we sail, and Persia as their enemy as well, were able to win the empire, solely by their superiority at sea. The Peloponnesians had never so little hope against us as at present; and let them be ever so sanguine, although strong enough to invade our country even if we stay at home, they can never hurt us with their navy, as we leave one of our own behind us that is a match for them.

18. 'In this state of things what reason can we give to ourselves for holding back, or what excuse can we offer to our allies in Sicily for not helping them? They are our allies, and we are bound to assist them, without objecting that they have not assisted us. We did not take them into alliance to have their help in Greece, but that they might so annoy our enemies in Sicily as to prevent them from coming over here and attacking us. It is thus that empire has been won, both by us and by all others that have held it, by a constant readiness to support all, whether foreigners or Greeks, that ask for help; if all were to keep quiet, or to pick and choose whom they ought to assist, we should make but few new conquests, and should imperil those we have already won. Men do not rest content with parrying the attacks of a superior, but often strike the first blow to prevent the attack being made. And we cannot fix the exact point at which our empire shall stop; we have reached a

position in which we must not be content with re-taining but must scheme to extend it, for, if we cease to rule others, we are in danger of being ruled our-selves. You cannot look at inaction from the same point of view as others, unless you are prepared to change your habits and make them like theirs.

'Be convinced then that we shall augment our power at home by this adventure abroad, and let us make the expedition, and so humble the pride of the Peloponnesians by sailing off to Sicily, and letting them see how indifferent we are to the peace that we are now enjoying; at the same time we shall either become masters, as we very easily may, of the whole of Greece through the accession of the Greeks in Sicily, or in any case ruin the Syracusans, to the no small advantage of ourselves and our allies. Our navy will enable us safely to stay, if successful, or to withdraw, as we shall be superior at sea to all the Siceliots put together. Do not let the do-nothing policy which Nicias advocates, or his setting of the young against the old, turn you from your purpose, but in the good old fashion by which our fathers, old and young together, by their united counsels brought our affairs to their present height, do you endeavour still to advance them; reflect that neither youth nor old age can do anything the one without the other, but that humble, average, and first-rate abilities are strongest when united, and that, by sinking into inaction, the city, like everything else, will wear itself out, and its skill in everything decay; while each fresh struggle will give it fresh experience, and make it more used to defend itself not in word but in deed. In short, my conviction is that a city naturally active could no choose a quicker way to ruin itself than by suddenly adopting a policy of inactivity, and that the safest rule of life is to take one's character and institutions for better and for worse, and to live up to them as closely as one can.'

＊　＊　＊　＊　＊

BOOK VII

*The arrival of reinforcements under Demosthenes and
its sequel.*

42. In the meantime, while the Syracusans were
preparing for a second attack by sea and land,
Demosthenes and Eurymedon arrived with the
reinforcements from Athens, consisting of about
seventy-three ships, including foreigners; nearly five
thousand heavy infantry, Athenian and allied; a large
number of javelin-men, Greek and foreign, slingers
and archers, and everything else upon a corresponding
scale. The Syracusans and their allies were for the
moment considerably dismayed at the idea that there
was to be no term or end to their dangers; in spite
of the fortification of Decelea, they saw a new army
arrive nearly equal to the former, and the power of
Athens visibly great in every field of the war. On
the other hand, the first Athenian armament regained
a certain confidence in the midst of its misfortunes.
Demosthenes, seeing how matters stood, felt that he
could not drag on and fare as Nicias had done, who
by wintering in Catana instead of at once attacking
Syracuse had allowed the terror of his first arrival
to evaporate in contempt, and had given time to
Gylippus to arrive with a force from Peloponnese,
which the Syracusans would never have sent for if
he had attacked immediately; for they fancied that
they were a match for him by themselves, and would
not have discovered their inferiority until they were
already invested, and even if they sent for help they
would no longer have been equally able to profit by

208

its arrival.   Reflecting on this, and aware that it was
on the first day after his arrival that he like Nicias
was most formidable to the enemy, Demosthenes
determined to lose no time in drawing the utmost
profit from the consternation at the moment inspired
by his army; and seeing that the counterwall of the
Syracusans, which hindered the Athenians from
investing them, was a single one, and that if he
mastered the way up to Epipolae, and the camp there,
he would find no difficulty in taking it, as no one
would even wait for his attack, made all haste to
attempt the enterprise.   It seemed the shortest way
of ending the war; he would either succeed and take
Syracuse, or would take the expedition home, instead
of frittering away the lives of the Athenians engaged
in it and the resources of the country at large.

43.   First therefore the Athenians went out and laid
waste the lands of the Syracusans about the Anapus
and, as at first, carried all before them, by land and
by sea; the Syracusans made no attempt to oppose
them upon either element, except with their cavalry
and javelin-men from the Olympieum.   Next Demosthenes resolved to attempt the counterwall first by
siege-engines.   As, however, those that he brought
up were burnt by the enemy fighting from the wall,
and the rest of his forces repulsed after attacking at
many different points, he determined not to delay,
and having obtained the consent of Nicias and his
fellow-commanders proceeded to put in execution
his plan of attacking Epipolae.   As by day it seemed
impossible to climb the heights and approach unobserved, he ordered provisions for five days, took
all the masons and carpenters, and other things, such
as arrows, and everything else necessary for the work
of fortification if successful; in the early hours of
the night he set out with Eurymedon and Menander
and the whole army for Epipolae; Nicias was left
behind in the lines.   Mounting by the hill of Euryalus
(where the earlier attack had been made), unobserved
by the enemy's guards, they went up to the fort which

the Syracusans had there, took it, and killed part of the garrison. The greater number, however, escaped at once and gave the alarm to the camps, of which there were three upon Epipolae, defended by outworks, one of the Syracusans, one of the other Siceliots, and one of the allies; and also to the six hundred Syracusans forming the original garrison for this part of Epipolae. These at once advanced against the assailants, and fell in with Demosthenes and the Athenians, but were routed by them after a sharp struggle, the victors immediately pushing on, eager to achieve the objects of the attack without giving time for their ardour to cool; meanwhile others had already begun taking the counterwall of the Syracusans, which was abandoned by its garrison, and pulling down the battlements. The Syracusans and the allies, and Gylippus with the troops under his command, advanced to the rescue from the outworks, but they were dismayed by the unexpected audacity of a night attack, and were at first compelled to retreat. The Athenians, flushed with their victory, were advancing in some disorder, wishing as quickly as possible to break through the force of the enemy not yet engaged, without relaxing their attack or giving them time to rally, when the Boeotians made the first stand, attacked, routed, and put them to flight.

44. The Athenians now fell into great disorder and perplexity, so that it was not easy to get from one side or the other the details of what happened.[1] By day the combatants have a clearer notion, though even then by no means of all that takes place, no one knowing much of anything except in his own immediate neighbourhood; but in a night engagement (and this was the only one that occurred between large forces during the war) how could anyone know anything for certain? Although there was a bright moon they saw each other only as men do by moon-light; they could distinguish the outline of figures,

[1] We have a glimpse here of the care with which Thucydides collected his facts.

but could not tell for certain whether they were friends or enemies. Both had great numbers of heavy infantry moving about in a small space. Some of the Athenians were already defeated, while others were fresh troops coming up for their first attack. A large part of their remaining forces either had only just climbed the hill, or were still ascending, so that they did not know which way to march. The rout threw the whole front into confusion, and the noise made it difficult to distinguish anything. The victorious Syracusans and allies cheered each other on with loud cries, by night the only possible means of communication, and met the onset of all who came against them; while the Athenians were looking for one another, taking all in front of them for enemies, even although they might be some of their now flying friends; they kept demanding the watchword, their only means of recognition, and not only caused great confusion among themselves by asking all at once, but also revealed it to the enemy, whose own they did not so readily discover, as the Syracusans were victorious and not scattered, and so recognized each other more easily. The result was that if the Athenians fell in with a weaker party of the enemy it escaped them because it knew their watchword; while if they themselves failed to answer they were put to the sword. Most disastrous of all was the singing of the Paean [1]; each side used the same and it led to confusion; for when it was raised by the Argive, Corinthian, or other Dorian allies of Athens it alarmed the Athenians as much as the enemy. So, after being once thrown into disorder, they ended by coming into collision with each other in many parts of the field, friends with friends, and citizens with citizens, and not only terrified one another, but even came to blows and could only be parted with difficulty. In the pursuit many lost their lives by throwing themselves over the cliffs; for the path down from Epipolae was narrow. Many who

[1] A battle-song used by Dorians.

reached the plain safely, especially those who belonged to the first expedition, escaped through their better knowledge of the ground, but some of the new-comers lost their way, wandered over the country, and were cut off in the morning by the Syracusan cavalry, and killed.

45. The next day the Syracusans set up two trophies, one upon Epipolae where the ascent had been made, and the other on the spot where the first check was given by the Boeotians; and the Athenians took back their dead under truce. A great many of the Athenians and allies were killed, although more arms were taken than could be accounted for by the number of the dead, as some of those who were obliged to leap down from the cliffs without their shields escaped with their lives.

46. After such an unexpected stroke of good fortune the Syracusans recovered their old confidence, and sent Sicanus with fifteen ships to Agrigentum where there was a revolution, to induce if possible the city to join them; while Gylippus again went by land to collect reinforcements elsewhere in Sicily; he now hoped to take the Athenian lines by storm, after the result of the battle on Epipolae.

47. In the meantime the Athenian generals held a council of war upon the disaster and the general demoralization of the army. They saw that their attempts had failed and that their men were weary of remaining; disease was rife among them owing to its being the sickly season of the year, and to the marshy and unhealthy site of the camp; and their position seemed desperate. Accordingly, Demosthenes was of opinion that they ought not to stay any longer; his original idea had been to risk the attempt upon Epipolae; now that this had failed, he voted for going away without loss of time, while the sea might yet be crossed, and their late reinforcement gave them at all events naval superiority. He also

said that it would be more in the interest of Athens to carry on the war against those who were building fortifications [1] in Attica than against the Syracusans, whom there was little chance of conquering; nor was it right to squander large sums of money uselessly by going on with the siege.

48. This was the opinion of Demosthenes. Nicias agreed that their position was bad, but was unwilling to admit their weakness, or to have it reported to the enemy that the Athenians in full council were openly voting for retreat; in that case they would be much less likely to withdraw unobserved when they wanted. Further, his private information still gave him reason to hope that the enemy would soon be worse off than themselves, if the Athenians persevered in the siege; they would exhaust the Syracusan finances, especially with the more extensive command of the sea now given them by their present fleet. Besides this, there was a party in Syracuse who wished to betray the city to the Athenians, and kept sending him messages and telling him not to raise the siege. Accordingly, knowing this and really waiting because he hesitated between the two courses and wished to see his way more clearly, in his public speech on this occasion he refused to withdraw the army, saying he was sure the Athenians would never approve of their returning without authorization from home. If they did, they would have to give an account to persons who, unlike themselves, had not seen the position with their own eyes and who would judge it from the statements of hostile critics, and would simply be guided by the calumnies of the first clever speaker; while many, indeed most, of the soldiers on the spot, who now so loudly proclaimed the danger of their position, when they reached Athens would proclaim the opposite just as loudly, and would say that their generals had been bribed to betray them and return. He himself, knowing the Athenian temper, would rather take his chance and die, if die he must, a soldier's

[1] At Decelea.

death at the hand of the enemy, sooner than perish
under a dishonourable charge and by an unjust
sentence at the hands of the Athenians.[1] Besides,
after all, the Syracusans were in a worse case than
themselves. What with paying mercenaries, spending
upon fortified posts, and now for a full year maintaining a large navy, they were already at a loss and
would soon be at a standstill: they had already spent
two thousand talents and incurred heavy debts
besides, and could not lose ever so small a fraction of
their present force, through not paying it, without
ruin to their cause; for they depended more upon
mercenaries than upon soldiers obliged to serve, like
their own. He therefore said that they ought to stay
and carry on the siege, and not go away defeated by
the finances of an enemy who was poorer than they
were.

49. Nicias spoke positively because he had exact
information of the financial distress at Syracuse, and
also because of the strength of the Athenian party
there which kept sending him messages not to raise
the siege; besides which he had more confidence
than before in his fleet, and felt sure at least of its
success. Demosthenes, however, would not hear
for a moment of continuing the siege, but said that
if they could not withdraw the army without a decree
from Athens, and if they were obliged to stay on,
they ought to remove to Thapsus or Catana, where
their land forces would have a wide extent of country
to overrun, and could live by plundering, and so
injuring the enemy; while the fleet, instead of a
narrow space which was all in the enemy's favour,
would have the open sea to fight in, where their
science would be of use, and they could retreat or
advance without being confined or circumscribed
either when they put out or put in. In any case he
was altogether opposed to their staying on where they
were, and insisted on removing at once, as quickly

[1] This political cowardice of Nicias cost Athens her
empire.

and with as little delay as possible; and in this judgement Eurymedon agreed. Nicias however still objecting, a certain diffidence and hesitation came over them, with a suspicion that Nicias might have some further information to make him so positive.

50. While the Athenians lingered on in this way without moving from where they were, Gylippus and Sicanus arrived at Syracuse. Sicanus had failed to gain Agrigentum, where the party friendly to the Syracusans had been driven out; but Gylippus was accompanied not only by a large number of troops raised in Sicily, but by the heavy infantry sent off in the spring from Peloponnese in the merchantmen, who had arrived at Selinus from Libya. They had been carried to Libya by a storm. There they obtained two warships and pilots from Cyrene, and on their coasting voyage helped the Euesperitae [1] to defeat the Libyans who were besieging them. They then sailed on to Neapolis, a Carthaginian trading post, and the nearest point to Sicily, from which it is only two days' and a night's voyage, crossed over and came to Selinus. Immediately upon their arrival the Syracusans prepared to attack the Athenians again by land and sea. The Athenian generals seeing a fresh army come to the aid of the enemy, and their own circumstances far from improving, becoming daily worse, and above all distressed by the illness among the soldiers, now began to regret not having removed before. Nicias no longer offered the same opposition, except by urging that there should be no open voting, so they gave orders as secretly as possible for all to be prepared to sail out from the camp at a given signal. All was at last ready, and they were on the point of leaving, when an eclipse of the moon,

---

[1] In the territory of Cyrene.

which was then at the full, took place. Most of the
Athenians, deeply impressed by this occurrence,[1] now
urged the generals to wait; and Nicias, who was
over-addicted to divination and that kind of thing,
refused from that moment even to discuss the question
of departure, until they had waited the twenty-seven
days prescribed by the soothsayers.

51. The besiegers were thus condemned to stay
where they were. The Syracusans got wind of what
had happened, and became more eager than ever to
press the Athenians, who had now themselves admitted
their own inferiority by sea and land—otherwise they
would never have planned to sail away. Besides the
Syracusans did not wish them to settle in any other
part of Sicily, where they would be more difficult to
deal with, but desired to force them to fight at sea as
quickly as possible, in a position favourable to themselves. Accordingly they manned their ships and
practised for as many days as they thought sufficient.
When the moment arrived they assaulted the Athenian
lines, and upon a small force of heavy infantry and
horse sallying out against them by certain gates, cut
off some of the former and routed and pursued them
to their lines; the entrance was narrow, and the
Athenians lost seventy horses and some few of the
heavy infantry.

52. Drawing off their troops for this day, on the
next the Syracusans went out with a fleet of seventy-six
sail, and at the same time advanced with their land
forces against the lines. The Athenians put out to
meet them with eighty-six ships, came to close
quarters and engaged. The Syracusans and their
allies first defeated the Athenian centre, and then
caught Eurymedon, the commander of the right
wing, who was extending his line towards the land

[1] Even before Anaxagoras (fl. 460 B.C.) the true
explanation of eclipses was known. But science had not
affected superstition.

in order to surround the enemy, in the hollow and recess of the harbour, killed him and destroyed his ships; they then chased the whole Athenian fleet before them and drove them ashore.

53. Gylippus, seeing the enemy's fleet defeated and carried ashore beyond their stockades and camp, ran down to the causeway[1] with some of his troops, in order to cut off the men as they landed and make it easier for the Syracusans to tow off the vessels from a shore held by their friends. The Etruscans who guarded this point for the Athenians, seeing the Syracusans come on in disorder, advanced against them and attacked and routed their van, hurling it into the marsh of Lysimeleia. Afterwards the Syracusan and allied troops arrived in greater numbers, and the Athenians, alarmed for their ships, came up to the rescue, engaged them, and defeated and pursued them to some distance, killing a few of their heavy infantry. They succeeded in rescuing most of their ships and brought them within their lines; eighteen, however, were taken by the Syracusans and their allies, and the crews killed. The rest the enemy tried to burn by means of an old merchantman which they filled with faggots and pine-wood, set on fire and let drift down the wind, which blew full on the Athenians. The Athenians, however, anxious about their ships, contrived to put it out, and checking the flames and the nearer approach of the merchantman, escaped the danger.

54. After this the Syracusans set up a trophy for the sea-fight and for their victory over the Athenian infantry near the lines, where they took the horses; and the Athenians for the rout of the foot driven by the Etruscans into the marsh, and for their own success with the rest of the army.

55. The Syracusans had now gained a decisive victory at sea, where until now they had feared the

[1] Running along the edge of the harbour from the marsh. The Athenian ships had been driven ashore south-east of their camp.

reinforcement brought by Demosthenes, and deep, in consequence, was the despondency of the Athenians, and great their disappointment, and greater still their regret for having come on the expedition. The Sicilian cities were the only ones that they had yet encountered, similar to their own in character, under democracies like themselves, which had ships and cavalry, and were of considerable size. They had been unable to divide and bring them over by holding out the prospect of changes in their governments, or to crush them by their great superiority in force. They had failed at almost every point, and were already in great difficulties when their defeat at sea, where defeat could never have been expected, made their position far worse.

56. Meanwhile the Syracusans immediately began to sail freely round the harbour, and determined to close its mouth, so that the Athenians could not steal out in future, even if they wished. Their aim now was not merely to save themselves but to prevent their enemy escaping; they thought rightly that they were now much the stronger, and that to conquer the Athenians and their allies by land and sea would win them great glory in Greece. The rest of the Greeks would thus immediately be either freed or released from apprehension, as the remaining forces of Athens would be henceforth unable to sustain the war that would be waged against her; while Syracuse would be regarded as the author of this deliverance, and would be held in high admiration both by the contemporary world and by posterity. Nor were these the only considerations that gave dignity to the struggle. They would conquer not only the Athenians but also their numerous allies. They would have fought side by side with Sparta and Corinth and shared their leadership; they would have offered their city to stand in the van of danger, and been in a great measure the pioneers of naval success.

Indeed, there were never so many peoples assembled

before a single city, if we except the grand total gathered together in this war under Athens and Lacedaemon.[1]

59. It was not surprising, therefore, if the Syracusans and their allies thought that it would win them great glory if they could follow up their recent victory in the sea-fight by the capture of the whole Athenian armada. They began at once to close the Great Harbour by means of boats, merchant vessels, and warships moored broadside across its mouth, which is nearly a mile wide, and made every preparation in case the Athenians again ventured to fight at sea. All their ideas were on a grand scale.

60. The Athenians, seeing them closing the harbour and informed of their further designs, called a council of war. The generals and higher officers met and discussed the difficulties of the situation; the most serious was that they no longer had provisions for immediate use (in the belief that they were leaving Syracuse, they had notified Catana to send none); and they would not have any in future unless they could command the sea. They therefore determined to evacuate their upper lines, to enclose with a cross-wall and garrison a small space close to the ships, only just sufficient to hold their stores and sick, and manning all the ships, seaworthy or not, with every man that could be spared from the rest of their land forces, to fight it out at sea, and if victorious to go to Catana, if not, to burn their vessels, form in close order, and retreat by land for the nearest friendly place they could reach, Greek or foreign. This was no sooner settled than done: they gradually evacuated the upper lines and manned all their vessels, embarking all who were of age to be of any use. They thus succeeded in manning about one hundred and ten ships in all; they put on board a number of archers and javelin-men taken from the Acarnanians and from

[1] Thucydides then gives a detailed list of the allies on both sides.

the other foreigners, and made such other arrangements as their difficult position and their plan allowed. All was now nearly ready, and Nicias, who saw that his men were disheartened by their unprecedented and decided defeat at sea, and by the shortage of food, was eager to fight it out as soon as possible, and calling them all together addressed them as follows:—

61. 'Soldiers of Athens and of the allies, we have all an equal interest in the coming struggle, in which life and country are at stake for us quite as much as they can be for the enemy; if our fleet wins the day, each can see his native city again, wherever that city may be. You must not lose heart, or be like raw recruits who are defeated in their first battle and ever afterwards are full of timid forebodings of a similar disaster. You, Athenians, have fought in many wars; you, allies, have been our constant companions in arms: remember the surprises of war, and with the hope that fortune will not be always against us, prepare to fight again in a way worthy of this great army, which you see.

62. 'After discussion with the navigating officers [1] we have taken such measures as our means allow against the crowding of vessels in such a narrow harbour, and against the force upon the decks of the enemy, from which we suffered before. A number of archers and javelin-men will be embarked, and a number of troops that we should not have employed in an action in the open sea, where our science would be crippled by the weight of the vessels; but now, when we are compelled to fight a land battle by sea, all this will be useful. We have also thought of the changes in construction necessary to meet theirs; and against the thickness of their bows, which did us the greatest mischief, we have provided grappling-irons, which

[1] Lit. helmsmen.

will prevent an assailant backing water after charging, if the soldiers on deck here do their duty; we are absolutely compelled to fight a land battle from the fleet, and our best plan is neither to back water, nor to let the enemy do so, especially as the shore, except so much of it as may be held by our troops, is hostile ground.

63. 'Remember this and fight on as long as you can, and do not let yourselves be driven ashore, but once alongside make up your minds not to part company until you have swept the heavy infantry from the enemy's deck. I say this more for the heavy infantry than for the seamen, as it is mainly the business of the men on deck; and our land forces are even now on the whole the strongest. The sailors I advise, yes, and implore, not to be too much daunted by their misfortunes, now that we have our decks better armed and a greater number of vessels. Some of you, though not Athenians, have long been so regarded; think how pleasant that privilege is and how well worth keeping: you are honoured in Greece because you spoke our language and adopted our ways; you shared equally with us in the advantages of our empire, and even more in the respect of its subject peoples and in security against wrong. You, therefore, with whom alone we freely share our empire, we now justly require not to betray that empire in its extremity, and in scorn of Corinthians, whom you have often conquered, and of Siceliots, none of whom so much as presumed to stand against us when our navy was in its prime, we ask you to repel them, and to show that even in sickness and disaster your skill is more than a match for the fortune and vigour of any enemy.

64. 'Once more I appeal to the Athenians among you: I want to remind you that there are no more ships like these in the dockyards at home and no men fit for service. If the battle ends in anything but victory our enemies here will immediately sail against Athens, and our countrymen left there will be unable to repel

their present enemies, reinforced by these new allies. You here will fall at once into the hands of the Syracusans—I need not remind you of the intentions with which you attacked them—and your countrymen at home will fall into those of the Lacedaemonians. Their fate and ours hangs upon this single battle— now, if ever, stand firm, and remember, each and all, that you who are now going on board are the army and navy of the Athenians, and all that is left of the state and the great name of Athens; if any man has any superiority in skill and courage, now is the time for him to show it in her defence, and thus serve himself and save all.'

65. After this address Nicias at once gave orders to man the ships. Meanwhile Gylippus and the Syracusans could perceive by the preparations which they saw going on that the Athenians meant to fight at sea. They had also notice of the grappling-irons, against which they specially provided by stretching hides over the prows and much of the upper part of their vessels, in order that the irons when thrown might slip off without taking hold. All being now ready, the generals and Gylippus addressed them in the following terms:—

66. 'Syracusans and allies, the glorious character of our past achievements and the no less glorious results at issue in the coming battle are, we think, understood by most of you, or you would never have thrown yourselves with such ardour into the struggle; and if anyone does not realize them as he should, we will enlighten him. The Athenians came to this country first to conquer Sicily, and after that, if successful, Peloponnese and the rest of the Greeks. They had already the greatest empire ever known in Greece, either in the past or to-day. Here for the first time they found in you men who faced their navy which made them masters everywhere; you have already defeated them in the previous sea-fights, and will in all likelihood defeat them again now. When men are once checked in what they consider their special

excellence, their whole opinion of themselves suffers more than if they had not at first believed in their superiority, and the unexpected shock to their pride causes them to give way more than their real strength warrants; this is probably now the case with the Athenians.

67. 'With us it is different. The original estimate of ourselves which gave us courage in the days of our unskilfulness has been strengthened, while the conviction superadded to it that we must be the best seamen of the time, if we have conquered the best, has given a double measure of hope to every man among us; and generally where there is the greatest hope there is also the greatest ardour for action. The means to combat us which they have tried to find in copying our armaments are familiar to our warfare, and will be met by proper provisions. It will be a novelty for them to have numbers of heavy infantry on the decks, and numbers of javelin-men—Acarnanians and the rest—landsmen put into a ship, who in a cramped position will not find means of discharging their darts. Will they not make the ships unsteady, and, having to use unaccustomed tactics, fall into confusion themselves? They will gain nothing by the number of their ships—I say this to those of you who may be alarmed by having to fight against odds—as a quantity of ships in a confined space will only be slower in executing the movements required, and fall easy victims to our preparations. Let me tell you what I believe on good authority to be the plain truth; their extreme sufferings and the embarrassments of their position have made them desperate; they have no confidence in their force, but wish to try their fortune in the only way they can, and either to force their passage and sail out, or failing this to retreat by land, as it is impossible for them to be worse off than they are.

68. 'Such is the disorder of our bitter enemies; their fortune has already capitulated: let us attack them fiercely, convinced that nothing is more legitimate

than to sate the whole wrath of one's soul in punishing
the aggressor, and nothing more sweet, as the proverb
says, than the vengeance upon an enemy, which it
will now be ours to take.   They are enemies, mortal
enemies, as you all know; they came here to enslave
our country, and if successful they would have inflicted
the worst sufferings on our men, and the worst in-
dignities on our women and children, and the worst
shame on our whole state.   None should therefore
relent or think it gain if they go away without further
danger to us.   That is all they can do, even if they
win, while if we succeed, as we may expect, in punishing them, and in handing down to all Sicily her
ancient freedom strengthened and confirmed, we shall
have achieved no mean triumph.   And the rarest
dangers are those in which failure brings little loss
and success the greatest advantage.'

69.   After this address to their soldiers, the Syracusan
generals and Gylippus saw that the Athenians were
manning their ships, and immediately proceeded to
man their own also.   Meanwhile Nicias, appalled by
the position, realizing the greatness and the nearness
of the danger now that they were on the point of
putting out from shore, and thinking, as men do
think in great crises, that when all has been done
they have still something left to do, and when all
has been said that they have not yet said enough,
again called on the captains one by one. He addressed
each by his father's name and by his own, and by
that of his tribe, and adjured them not to belie their
own personal renown, or to obscure the hereditary
virtues for which their ancestors were illustrious: he
reminded them of their country, the freest of the free,
and of the unfettered liberty allowed in it to all to
live as they pleased; and added other arguments such
as men use at such a crisis, and which, with little
alteration, are made to serve on all occasions alike—
appeals to wives, children, and national gods—without
caring whether they seem commonplaces, reiterating
them in the belief that they will be of use in the con-

sternation of the moment.[1] After exhorting them, not, he felt, as he would, but as he could, Nicias withdrew and led the troops to the sea, and ranged them in as long a line as he was able, in order to help as far as possible in sustaining the courage of the men afloat; while Demosthenes, Menander, and Euthydemus, who took the command on board, put out from their own camp and sailed straight to the barrier across the mouth of the harbour and to the passage left open, in the attempt to force their way out.

70. The Syracusans and their allies had already put out with about the same number of ships as before; one detachment guarded the entrance of the harbour, the rest were disposed all round it, so as to attack the Athenians on all sides at once; while the land forces held themselves in readiness at the points at which the vessels might put in to the shore. The Syracusan fleet was commanded by Sicanus and Agatharchus, who had each a wing of the whole force, with Pythen and the Corinthians in the centre. When the Athenians came up to the barrier, the first shock of their charge overpowered the ships stationed there, and they tried to undo the fastenings; after this, as the Syracusans and allies bore down upon them from all quarters, the action spread from the barrier over the whole harbour, and was more obstinately disputed than any preceding. On either side the rowers showed great zeal in bringing up their vessels at the boatswains' orders, and the pilots great skill in manœuvring, rivalling each other's efforts; once the

[1] 'Thucydides is a gentleman whose truth I never appreciated so thoroughly before. He tells how the officers encouraged their men up to the last moment, always remembering another word of counsel, yet feeling that however much they said it would still be inadequate. Just the same with us now. We've all lectured our platoons, but something still keeps turning up.' (Letter from the Front in the last War.)

ships were alongside, the soldiers on board did their best not to let the service on deck be inferior; in short, every man strove to prove himself the first in his particular department. As many ships were engaged in a small compass (never had fleets so large —there were almost 200 vessels—fought in so narrow a space), the regular attacks with the beak were few, for there was no opportunity to back water or break the line [1]; while the collisions caused by one ship chancing to run foul of another, either in avoiding or attacking a third, were more frequent. So long as a vessel was coming up to the charge the men on the decks rained darts and arrows and stones upon her; but once alongside, the heavy infantry tried to board each other's vessel, and fought hand to hand. In many places it happened, owing to want of room, that a vessel was charging an enemy on one side and being charged herself on another, and that two, or sometimes more, ships had unavoidably got entangled round one, and the pilots had to make plans of attack and defence against several adversaries coming from different quarters; while the huge din caused by the number of ships crashing together not only spread terror, but made the orders of the boatswains inaudible. The boatswains on either side in the discharge of their duty and in the heat of the conflict shouted incessantly orders and appeals to their men; the Athenians they urged to force the passage, and now if ever to show their mettle and make sure of a safe return to their country; to the Syracusans and their allies they cried that it would be glorious to prevent the escape of the enemy, and to win a victory which would bring glory to their country. The generals, on either side, if they saw any vessel in any part of the battle backing ashore without being forced to do so, called out to the captain by name and asked him—the Athenians, whether they were retreating because they thought that they would be more at home on a bitterly hostile shore than on that sea

which had cost them so much labour to win; the
Syracusans, whether they were flying from the flying
Athenians, whom they well knew to be eager to
escape by any possible means.

71. Meanwhile the two armies on shore, while
victory hung in the balance, were a prey to the most
agonizing and conflicting emotions; the Sicilians
thirsting to add to the glory that they had already won,
while the invaders feared to find themselves in even
worse plight than before. The last hope of the
Athenians lay in their fleet, their fear for the outcome
was like nothing they had ever felt; while their view of
the struggle was necessarily as chequered as the battle
itself. Close to the scene of action, and not all looking at the same point at once, some saw their friends
victorious and took courage, and fell to calling upon
heaven not to deprive them of salvation, while others,
who had their eyes turned upon the losers, wept and
cried aloud, and, although spectators, were more
overcome than the actual combatants. Others, again,
were gazing at some spot where the battle was evenly
disputed; as the strife was protracted without decision, their swaying bodies reflected the agitation of
their minds, and they suffered the worst agony of all,
ever just within reach of safety or just on the point
of destruction. In short, in that one Athenian army,
as long as the sea-fight remained doubtful, there was
every sound to be heard at once, shrieks, cheers, '*We
win*,' '*We lose*,' and all the other sounds wrung from
a great host in desperate peril; with the men in the
fleet it was nearly the same; until at last the Syracusans and their allies, after the battle had lasted a
long while, put the Athenians to flight, and with
much shouting and cheering chased them in open
rout to the shore. The naval force fell back in
confusion to the shore, except those who were taken
afloat, and rushed from their ships to their camp;
while the army, no more with divided feelings, but
carried away by one impulse, ran down with a
universal cry of dismay, some to help the ships, others

to guard what was left of their wall, while the majority began to consider how they should save themselves. Their panic was as great as any of their disasters. They now suffered very nearly what they had inflicted at Pylos; then the Lacedaemonians, besides losing their fleet, lost also the men who had crossed over to Sphacteria; so now the Athenians had no hope of escaping by land, without the help of some extraordinary accident.

72. The sea-fight had been severe, and many ships and lives had been lost on both sides; the victorious Syracusans and their allies now picked up their wrecks and dead, and sailed off to the city and set up a trophy, while the Athenians, overwhelmed by their disaster, never even thought of asking leave to take up their dead or wrecks, but wished to retreat that very night. Demosthenes, however, went to Nicias and gave it as his opinion that they should man the ships they had left and make another effort to force their passage out next morning; saying that they had still left more ships fit for service than the enemy, the Athenians having about sixty remaining as against less than fifty of their opponents. Nicias was quite of his mind; but when they wished to man the vessels, the sailors, who were so utterly overcome by their defeat as no longer to believe in the possibility of success, refused to go on board.

73. They all now made up their minds to retreat by land. Meanwhile the Syracusan Hermocrates, who suspected their intention, and was impressed by the danger of allowing a force of that magnitude to retire by land, establish itself in some other part of Sicily, and from thence renew the war, went and stated his views to the authorities, and pointed out to them that they ought not to let the enemy get away by night, but that all the Syracusans and their allies should at once march out, block the roads, and seize and guard the passes. The authorities were entirely of his

opinion, and thought that it ought to be done, but on the other hand felt sure that the people, who had given themselves over to rejoicing and were taking their ease after a great battle at sea, would not be easily brought to obey; besides, they were celebrating a festival, a sacrifice to Heracles, and most of them in their rapture at the victory had fallen to drinking, and would probably consent to anything sooner than to take up their arms and march out at that moment. For these reasons the magistrates thought the proposal impracticable; and Hermocrates, finding himself unable to do anything further with them, had recourse to the following stratagem of his own. What he feared was that the Athenians might quietly get the start of them by passing the most difficult places during the night; so, as soon as it was dusk, he sent some friends of his own to the camp with some horsemen. They rode up within earshot and, pretending to be well-wishers of the Athenians, called out to some of the men, and told them to tell Nicias (who had in fact some correspondents who informed him of what went on inside the town) not to lead off the army by night as the Syracusans were guarding the roads, but to make his preparations at his leisure and to retreat by day. After saying this they went off; and their hearers informed the Athenian generals, who put off going for that night on the strength of this message, not doubting its sincerity.

74. Having abandoned the idea of an immediate start, they now determined to stay the following day also, to give time to the soldiers to pack up as best they could the most useful things, and, abandoning everything else, to start only with the bare necessaries of life. Meanwhile the Syracusans and Gylippus marched out and blocked up the roads through the country by which the Athenians were likely to pass, and guarded the fords of the streams and rivers, posting themselves at the best points to receive and stop the retreating army; while their fleet sailed up to the beach and towed off the ships of the Athenians.

Some few were burned by the Athenians themselves
as they had intended; the rest the Syracusans lashed
to their own at their leisure, as they had been thrown
up on shore, and towed to the town; no one tried to
stop them.

75.   As soon as Nicias and Demosthenes thought
their preparations adequate the army began to move on,
the second day after the sea-fight. It was a lamentable
scene; not merely were they retreating after having
lost all their ships, their great hopes gone, and themselves and the state in peril; but, as they left the camp,
they saw sights melancholy both to eye and mind.
The dead lay unburied, and when a man recognized
a friend among them he shuddered with grief and
horror; while the living whom they were leaving
behind, wounded or sick, were more distressing to
the survivors than the dead, and more to be pitied
than those who had fallen.   Their prayers and groans
drove their friends to distraction, as they implored to
be taken, appealing loudly to each individual comrade
or relative whom they could see, hanging upon the
necks of their departing tent-fellows, following as far
as they could, and when their strength failed calling
again and again upon heaven, and shrieking aloud as
they were left behind.   The whole army was in tears,
and so distracted that they found it difficult to start,
even though they were leaving a hostile country,
where they had already suffered evils too great for
tears and in the unknown future before them feared
to suffer more.   Dejection and self-condemnation
were general.   Indeed they could only be compared
to a starved-out town, and that no small one, escaping;
the whole multitude upon the march were not less
than forty thousand men.   All carried anything they
could which might be of use, and the heavy infantry
and cavalry, contrary to their habit while under arms,
carried their own food, in some cases for want of
servants, in others through not trusting them; they
had long been deserting and now did so in greater
numbers than ever.   Yet even so they did not carry

enough, as there was no food left in the camp. The disgrace and the universal suffering were somewhat mitigated by being shared by many, but even so seemed difficult to bear, especially when they contrasted the splendour and glory of their setting out with the humiliation in which it had ended. For this was by far the greatest reverse that ever befell a Greek army. They had come to enslave others, and were leaving in fear of being enslaved themselves: they had sailed out with prayer and paeans, and now started to go back with omens directly contrary; they were travelling by land instead of by sea, and trusting not in their fleet but in their infantry. Nevertheless the greatness of the danger hanging over their heads made all this appear tolerable.

76. Nicias, seeing the army dejected and greatly altered, passed along the ranks and encouraged and comforted them as far as the circumstances allowed, raising his voice higher and higher as he went from one company to another in his eager anxiety that his words might reach as many as possible and be a help:

77. 'Athenians and allies, even in our present position we must still hope on, for men have been saved from worse straits; and you must not condemn yourselves too severely either because of your disasters or because of your present undeserved sufferings. I myself am no stronger than any of you—indeed you see how I am reduced by my illness—and I have been, I think, as fortunate as anyone in my private life and otherwise, but am now exposed to the same danger as the meanest among you; and yet I have led a religious life and I have been just and blameless in my relations with men. I have, therefore, still a strong hope for the future, and our misfortunes do not terrify me as much as they might. Indeed we may hope that they will be lightened: our enemies have had good fortune enough; and if any of the gods was offended at our expedition, we have been already amply punished. Others before us have attacked their neighbours and have done what men will do without suffering more

than they could bear; and we may now fairly expect to find the gods more kind, for we have become fitter objects for their pity than their jealousy. And then look at yourselves, mark the numbers and efficacy of the heavy infantry marching in your ranks, and do not give way too much to despondency, but reflect that you yourselves at once constitute a city wherever you settle, and that there is no other in Sicily that could easily resist your attack, or expel you when once established. The safety and order of the march is for yourselves to look to; let the one thought of each man be that the spot on which he may be forced to fight must be conquered and held as his country and stronghold. Meanwhile we shall hasten on our way night and day alike, as our provisions are scanty; and if we can reach some friendly place of the Sicels, whom fear of the Syracusans still keeps true to us, you may forthwith consider yourselves safe. A message has been sent on to them with directions to meet us with supplies of food. To sum up, be convinced, soldiers, that you must be brave, as there is no refuge near for cowardice, and that, if you now escape from the enemy, you may all see again what your hearts desire, while those of you who are Athenians will raise up again the great power of the state, fallen though it be. Men make the city, and not walls or ships without men in them.'

78. As he made this address Nicias went along the ranks, and brought back to their place any troops that he saw straggling out of the line; while Demosthenes did as much for his part of the army, addressing them in very similar words. The army marched in a hollow square, the division under Nicias leading, and that of Demosthenes following, the heavy infantry outside and the baggage-carriers and the bulk of the army in the middle. When they arrived at the ford of the river Anapus they there found a body of the Syracusans and allies drawn up, and routing these, made good their passage and pushed on, harassed by the charges of the Syracusan horse and by the missiles of their

light troops. On that day they advanced about four miles and a half, halting for the night upon a hill. On the next they started early, got on about two miles further, and descended into a place in the plain and there encamped, in order to obtain food from the houses, as the place was inhabited, and to carry on with them water from thence, as for many furlongs in front, in the direction in which they were going, it was not plentiful. The Syracusans meanwhile went on and fortified the pass in front, where there was a steep hill with a rocky ravine on each side of it, called the Acraean cliff. The next day the Athenians advanced, but were hampered by large forces of the enemy, cavalry and javelin-men, who rode alongside and shot at them; after fighting for a long while, they finally retired to the same camp, where they were less well off for provisions, as the cavalry made it impossible for them to leave their position.

79. Early next morning they started afresh and forced their way to the hill, which had been fortified, where they found before them the enemy's infantry drawn up many shields deep, to defend the fortification, in a narrow pass. The Athenians assaulted the work, but were greeted by a storm of missiles from the hill, which told with the greater effect through its steepness, and unable to force the passage retreated again and rested. Meanwhile there was thunder and rain, as often happens towards autumn; this still further disheartened the Athenians, who thought that it was all ominous of their ruin. While they were resting Gylippus and the Syracusans sent a part of their army to throw up works in their rear on the way by which they had advanced; however, the Athenians immediately sent some of their men and prevented them; after this they retreated with their whole army towards the plain and halted for the night. When they advanced the next day the Syracusans surrounded and attacked them on every side, and disabled many of them, falling back if the Athenians advanced and coming on if they retired, and in particular assaulting their rear, in the

hope of routing them in detail, and thus striking a panic into the whole army. For a long while the Athenians persevered in this fashion, but after advancing for four or five furlongs halted to rest in the plain, the Syracusans also withdrawing to their own camp.

80. During the night Nicias and Demosthenes, seeing the wretched condition of their troops, now in want of every kind of necessary, and numbers of them disabled in the numerous attacks of the enemy, determined to light as many fires as possible, and to lead off the army by another route towards the sea, in the opposite direction to that guarded by the Syracusans. All this route led not to Catana but to the other side of Sicily, towards Camarina, Gela, and the other Greek and foreign towns in that quarter. So they lit a number of fires and set out by night. All armies, and most of all large ones, are liable to alarms, especially when they are marching by night through an enemy's country and with the enemy near; the Athenians fell into one of these panics, and the leading division, under Nicias, kept together and got on a good way in front, but that of Demosthenes, comprising rather more than half the army, got separated and marched on in some disorder. By morning, however, they reached the sea, and getting into the Helorine Road pushed on to reach the river Cacyparis, and to follow the stream up through the interior, where they hoped to be met by the Sicels for whom they had sent. Arrived at the river, they found there a Syracusan party engaged in barring the passage of the ford with a wall and a palisade, and forcing this guard crossed the river, and went on to another called the Erineus, following the advice of their guides.

81. Meanwhile, when day came and the Syracusans and allies found that the Athenians were gone, most of them accused Gylippus of having let them escape on purpose, and hastily pursuing by the road which the enemy had taken, and which they had no difficulty in finding, overtook them about dinner-time. They

first came up with the troops under Demosthenes, who were behind and marching somewhat slowly and in disorder, owing to the night-panic mentioned above. They at once attacked and engaged them, the Syracusan horse surrounding them with more ease now that they were separated from the rest, and hemming them in on one spot. The division of Nicias was five or six miles on in front, as he led them more rapidly, thinking that under the circumstances their safety lay in retreating as fast as possible, and fighting only when forced to do so. On the other hand, Demosthenes was harassed more incessantly, as his post in the rear left him the first exposed to the attacks of the enemy; and now, finding that the Syracusans were in pursuit, he omitted to push on, in order to form his men for battle, and so delayed until he was surrounded by his pursuers. He and his men now found themselves in the greatest confusion; they were huddled into an enclosure with a wall all round it, a road on both sides, and a large number of olive-trees, and they were shot at from every side. The Syracusans had with good reason adopted this method of attack in preference to fighting at close quarters, as to risk a struggle with desperate men was now more for the advantage of the Athenians than for their own; besides, their success had become so certain that they began to spare themselves a little in order not to be cut off in the moment of victory, thinking too that, as it was, they would be able in this way to conquer and capture the enemy.

82. After plying the Athenians and allies all day long from every side with missiles, they at length saw that they were worn out with their wounds and other sufferings; and Gylippus and the Syracusans and their allies made a proclamation, offering their liberty to any of the islanders who chose to come over to them; a few cities accepted the offer. Afterwards a capitulation was agreed upon for the remaining force of Demosthenes: to lay down their arms on condition that no one was to be put to death either by violence

or imprisonment or want of the necessaries of life.
Upon this they surrendered to the number of six
thousand, gave up all the money in their possession,
which filled the hollows of four shields, and were
immediately taken by the Syracusans to the town.

83.   Meanwhile Nicias with his division arrived that
day at the river Erineus, crossed over and posted his
army upon high ground on the far side.   The next day
the Syracusans overtook him and told him that the
troops under Demosthenes had surrendered, and invited him to follow their example.   Incredulous of the
fact, Nicias asked for a truce to send a horseman to see,
and upon the return of the messenger, with the news
that they had surrendered, sent a herald to Gylippus and
the Syracusans, saying that he was ready to agree with
them on behalf of the Athenians to repay whatever
money the Syracusans had spent upon the war if they
would let his army go; he offered until the money was
paid to give Athenians as hostages, one for every
talent.   The Syracusans and Gylippus rejected this
proposal, and attacked this division as they had the
other, standing all round and hurling missiles at them
until the evening.   Food and necessaries were as
miserably wanting to the troops of Nicias as they had
been to their comrades; nevertheless they watched
for the quiet of the night to resume their march.   But
as they were taking up their arms the Syracusans
detected it and raised their paean, and the Athenians,
finding that they were discovered, laid them down
again, except about three hundred men who forced
their way through the guards and went on during the
night as best they could.

84.   As soon as it was day Nicias put his army in
motion, pressed, as before, by the Syracusans and their
allies, pelted from every side by their missiles, and
struck down by their javelins.   The Athenians pushed
on for the Assinarus, harassed by the attacks made upon
them from every side by a large force of cavalry and
other arms, fancying that they would breathe more
freely if once across the river, and driven on by their

distress and craving for water. Once there they rushed in, and all order was at an end, each man wanting to cross first, and the attacks of the enemy making it difficult to cross at all; forced to huddle together, they trampled and fell on each other, some dying immediately pierced by javelins, others getting entangled in the baggage, and being carried down by the stream. Meanwhile the opposite bank, which was steep, was lined by the Syracusans, who showered missiles down upon the Athenians, most of them drinking greedily and crowded together in disorder in the deep bed of the river. The Peloponnesians came down and butchered them, especially those in the water, which was fouled, but they went on drinking just the same, mud and all, bloody as it was, most even fighting to have it.

85. At last, when the dead lay heaped one upon another in the stream, and part of the army had been destroyed at the river, and the few that escaped cut off by the cavalry, Nicias surrendered himself to Gylippus, whom he trusted more than the Syracusans, and told him and the Lacedaemonians to do what they liked with him, but to stop the slaughter of his men. Gylippus then immediately gave orders to make prisoners, and the rest were brought together alive, except a large number secreted by the soldiery; a party was sent in pursuit of the three hundred who had got through the guard during the night, and who were now taken with the rest. The number collected as public prisoners was not great; but very many were privately concealed, and all Sicily was filled with them, no convention having been made in their case as for those taken with Demosthenes. Besides this, a large portion were killed outright; the carnage was very great, as great as any in this Sicilian war. Many too had fallen in the numerous other engagements upon the march. Nevertheless many escaped, some at the moment, others served as slaves, and then ran away subsequently. These found refuge at Catana.

The fate of the prisoners.

86. The Syracusans and their allies now mustered and took up the spoils and as many prisoners as they could, and went back to the city. The rest of their Athenian and allied captives were deposited in the quarries, which seemed the safest place to keep them; But Nicias and Demosthenes were killed, against the will of Gylippus, who thought that it would be the crown of his triumph if he could take the enemy's generals to Lacedaemon. One of them, as it happened, Demosthenes, was one of her greatest enemies, on account of his achievement at Sphacteria and Pylos; while the other, Nicias, was for the same reasons one of her greatest friends, owing to his exertions to procure the release of the prisoners by persuading the Athenians to make peace. For these reasons the Lacedaemonians felt kindly towards him; and it was in this that Nicias himself mainly confided when he surrendered to Gylippus. But some of the Syracusans who had been in correspondence with him were afraid, it was said, of his being put to the torture and troubling their success by his revelations; others, especially the Corinthians, of his escaping, as he was rich, by bribery, and living to do them further mischief; and these persuaded the allies and put him to death. This or the like was the cause of the death of a man who, of all the Greeks in my time, least deserved such a fate, for he had lived in the practice of every virtue.

87. The prisoners in the quarries were at first hardly treated by the Syracusans. Crowded in a narrow hole, without any roof to cover them, the heat of the sun and the stifling closeness of the air tormented them during the day, and then the nights, which came on autumnal and chilly, made them ill by the violence of the change; they had to do everything in the same place for want of room, the bodies of those who died of their wounds or from the variation in the temperature, or similar causes, were left heaped together one upon another, and there were intolerable smells; hunger and thirst tormented them, each man during eight months having only half a pint of water and a pint of corn given him daily. In short, no single suffering to be apprehended by men thrust into such a place was spared them. For some seventy days they lived in this way all together; then all, except the Athenians and any Siceliots or Italiots who had joined in the expedition, were sold. The total number of prisoners taken it would be difficult to state exactly, but it could not have been less than seven thousand.

This was the greatest event in the war, or, in my opinion, in Greek history; at once most glorious to the victors, and most calamitous to the conquered. They were beaten at all points and altogether; their sufferings in every way were great. They were totally destroyed—their fleet, their army, everything—and few out of many returned home. So ended the Sicilian expedition.[1]

---

[1] The total numbers have been estimated at between 45,000 and 50,000. Many of these were not Athenians, but it was a crushing disaster for a country whose total male citizen population over the age of eighteen did not exceed 60,000.

Dante Alighieri,   DE MONARCHIA
                  (Trans. by Herbert W. Schneider)
Niccolo Machiavelli,   THE PRINCE
                  (Trans. by N. H. Thomson)

1.   Why does Dante consider Universal Peace to be essential? What is his view on the best means to achieve World Peace?

2.   What is Machiavelli's advice on attempting to avoid a probable war?

3.   How would you define "Machiavellianism" based on your reading of *The Prince*?

4.   What does Machiavelli consider to be the duty of a leader in preparing and maintaining armed forces?

5.   According to Machiavelli, is it better for a leader to be feared or loved? Explain. How important is it for the leader to have integrity?

      Although best known for his *Divine Comedy*, and holding a place in the development of the Italian language comparable to that of Shakespeare for English, Dante Alighieri also was concerned about peace. In *De Monarchia*, written in Latin, and first published about 1312, he offered as a means for world peace the example of the Roman Empire. After a printing in Basel in 1559, the book was placed on the Index of forbidden books.

DE MONARCHIA

ON WORLD-GOVERNMENT

BOOK ONE

THAT MANKIND NEEDS UNITY
AND PEACE

1

*The knowledge of a single temporal government over man-
kind is most important and least explored.*

All men whose higher nature has endowed them with a love
of truth obviously have the greatest interest in working for posterity, so that in return for the patrimony provided for them
by their predecessors' labors they may make provision for the
patrimony of future generations. Certainly a man who has received public instruction would be far from performing his
duty if he showed no concern for the public weal, for he would
not be a "tree by the streams of waters, bearing his fruit in due
season," but rather an erosive whirlpool always sucking in and
never returning what it devours. Therefore, as I have often reminded myself of these things and wish not to be charged with
burying my talent, I endeavor not only to grow in public use-
fulness but also to bear fruit by publishing truths that have not
been attempted by others. For what fruit is there in proving
once more a theorem in Euclid, or in trying to show man his
true happiness, which Aristotle has already shown, or in defending old age as Cicero did? Fruitless and positively tiresome are
such superfluous "works."

Among the truths that remain hidden, though useful, the
knowledge of the temporal government of the world is most
useful and most unknown, but since this knowledge is not directly gainful it has been neglected by all. I therefore propose

to drag it from its hiding place, in order that my alertness may be useful to the world and may bring me the glory of being the first to win this great prize. It is a difficult task I attempt and beyond my powers, but I rely not on my own ability; I trust in that giver of light who gives abundantly to all and reproaches none.

2

Since this theory is a practical science, its first principle is the goal of human civilization, which must be one and the same for all particular civilizations.

First, we must see what is meant by the temporal government of the world, both its kind and its aim. By the temporal government of the world or universal empire we mean a single government over all men in time, that is, over and in all things which can be measured by time. On this subject there are three chief questions to be examined: first, we must ask and inquire whether such a government is necessary for the good of the world; secondly, whether the Roman people has a right to assume such an office; and thirdly, whether the authority of this government comes directly from God or through some servant or vicar of God.

Since any truth which is not itself a principle is demonstrated as following from the truth of some principle, it is necessary in any inquiry to make clear from what principle the certainty of the subordinate propositions may be analytically derived. And since this treatise is an inquiry, we must first of all look for the principle on whose validity the derived propositions rest.

Now it is important to remember that there are some things entirely beyond our control, about which we can reason but do nothing, such as mathematics, physics, and theology, and there are others within our control not only for reasoning but for practice. In the latter case, action is not for the sake of thought, but thought for the sake of action, since in such matters the aim is action. Since our present concern is with politics, with the very source and principle of all right politics, and since all political matters are in our control, it is clear that our present concern is not aimed primarily at thought but at action. And furthermore, since in matters of action the final goal is the principle and cause of all, for by it the agent is first moved, it follows that any reasons for actions directed to this goal must be themselves derived from it. For example, the way to cut wood for building a house is different from the way to cut wood for a ship. Whatever, then, is the universal goal of human civilization, if there be such a goal, will serve as a first principle and will make sufficiently clear all the derivative propositions that follow. Now it would be foolish to admit that one civilization may have one goal, and another, another, and not to admit one goal for all.

3

This goal is proved to be the realization of man's ability to grow in intelligence.

Accordingly, we must now see what the whole of human civilization aims at; with this aim before us more than half our work is done, as the Philosopher says in his *Nicomachean Ethics.* And as evidence for what we seek we ought to note that just as nature makes the thumb for one purpose, the whole hand for another, the arm for still another, and the whole man for a purpose different from all these, so an individual man has one purpose, a family another, a neighborhood another, a city another, a state another, and finally there is another for all of mankind, established by the Eternal God's art, which is nature. This goal it is that we are now seeking as the guiding principle of our inquiry. We should know, in this connection, that God and nature make nothing in vain, and that whatever is produced serves some function. For the intention of any act of creation, if it is really creative, is not merely to produce the existence of something but to produce the proper functioning of that existence. Hence a proper functioning does not exist for the sake of the being which functions, but rather the being exists for the sake of its function. There is therefore some proper function for the whole of mankind as an organized multitude which can not be achieved by any single man, or family, or neighborhood, or city, or state. What that may be would be plain if we could see what the basic capacity of the whole of humanity is. Now I would say that no capacity which several different species have in common can be the basic power of any one of them. For in that case the basic capacity, which characterizes a species, would be the same for several species, which is impossible. Accordingly, man's basic power is not mere being, for he shares being with the elements; nor is it to be compounded, for this is found in minerals, too; nor is it to be alive, for so are plants; nor is it to be sensitive, for other animals share this power; but it is to be sensitive to intellectual growth, for this trait is not found in beings either above or below man. For though there are angelic beings that share intellect with man, they do not have intellectual growth, since their very being is to be intellect and nothing else and hence they are intellectual continuously, otherwise they would not be changeless. Therefore, it is clear that man's basic capacity is to have a potentiality or power for being intellectual. And since this power can not be completely actualized in a single man or in any of the particular communities of men above mentioned, there must be a multitude in mankind through whom this whole power can be actualized; just as there must be a multitude of created beings to manifest adequately the whole power of prime matter, otherwise there would have to be a power distinct from prime matter, which is impossible. With this judgment Averroes agrees in his commentary on *De anima*. This intellectual power of which I am speaking is directed not only toward universals or species, but also by a sort of extension toward particulars. Hence it is commonly said that the speculative intellect becomes practical by extension, and acquires thus the aims of action and production. I distinguish between matters of action which are governed by political prudence, and matters of production which are governed by the arts; but all of them are extensions of theoretical intellect, which is the best function for which the Primal Goodness brought mankind into being. Now we have already thrown light on that saying in the *Politics* —that the intellectually vigorous naturally govern others.

4

The best means toward this end is universal peace.

I have now made clear enough that the proper work of mankind taken as a whole is to exercise continually its entire capacity for intellectual growth, first, in theoretical matters, and, secondarily, as an extension of theory, in practice. And since the part is a sample of the whole, and since individual men find that they grow in prudence and wisdom when they can sit quietly, it is evident that mankind, too, is most free and easy to carry on its work when it enjoys the quiet and tranquillity of peace. Man's work is almost divine ("Thou hast made him a little lower than the angels"), and it is clear that of all the things that have been ordained for our happiness, the greatest is universal peace. Hence there rang out to the shepherds from on high the good news, not of riches, nor pleasures, nor honors, nor long life, nor health, nor strength, nor beauty, but peace. For the heavenly host proclaimed "glory to God in the highest and on earth peace to men of good will." Hence, too, "Peace be with you" was the salutation of Him who is the Salvation of men; for it was fitting that the Supreme Saviour should give voice to the supreme salutation. His disciples took care to make this salutation customary, and so did Paul in his salutations, as must be evident to all.

What I have now said makes clear what is that better, that best way, by following which mankind may achieve its proper work, and consequently it is also clear what way we must directly take to attain that final goal set for all our work, which is universal peace. Let this, then, be our principle underlying all our subsequent arguments, as I said, and let it serve as a standard set before us by which to test the truth of whatever we shall try to prove.

5

To achieve this state of universal well-being a single world-government is necessary.

There are three chief questions, as I said in the beginning, which must be raised and discussed concerning the temporal government of the world, more commonly called empire, and these three I propose, as I said, to take up in order. And so the first question is, whether a single temporal world-government is necessary for the world's well-being. There exists no weight of argument or of authority against this necessity and there are very strong and clear arguments for it. The first argument, which enjoys the authority of the Philosopher, is in his *Politics*, where this venerable authority states that whenever several things are united into one thing, one of them must regulate and rule, the others must be regulated and ruled. This seems credible not only on the strength of the glorious name of its author, but also for inductive reasons. Consider, for example, an individual man; we see this truth exhibited in him, for while all his energies are directed toward happiness, he could not attain it did not his intellectual power rule and guide the others. Or consider a household whose aim it is to prepare the members of the family to live well; one alone must regulate and rule, whom we call father of the family, or else there is someone who takes his place. So says our Philosopher: "Every home is ruled by the eldest." It is his duty, as Homer says, to govern all and give laws to others. Hence the proverbial curse: "May you have an equal in your home!" Or consider a neighborhood whose aim is to provide mutual aid in persons and things. Someone must govern the others, either someone appointed by the others or some outstanding member whom the others consent to follow, otherwise the community will not only fail to furnish the mutual aid for which it exists, but, as sometimes happens when several strive for pre-eminence, the whole neighborhood is destroyed. Likewise a city, whose aim is to live well and self-sufficiently, must have a single government, whether the city have a just or corrupt constitution. Otherwise not only does civil life fail to reach its goal, but the city ceases to be what it was. Or take finally a state or kingdom, whose aim is the same as that of a city, save that it takes more responsibility for peace—there must be a single government which both rules and governs; otherwise the end of the state is lost sight of, or the state itself falls to pieces, according to the infallible truth: "Every kingdom directed against itself shall be laid waste." If, therefore, these things are true among individuals and particular communities which have a unified goal, what we proposed above must be true. Since it appears that the whole of mankind is ordained to one end, as we proved above, it should therefore have a single rule and government, and this power should be called the Monarch or Emperor. And thus it is plain that for the well-being of the world there must be a single world-rule or empire.

6

Since any particular institution needs unity of direction, mankind as a whole must also need it.

Whatever relation a part bears to its whole, the structure of that part must bear to the total structure. But a part is related to the whole as to its end or greatest good. Hence we must conclude that the goodness of the partial structure cannot exceed the goodness of the total structure, rather the contrary. Now since there is a double structure among things—namely, the structure which relates part to part, and the structure which relates parts to a whole that is not itself a part, as in any army soldiers are related to each other and also to their commander —it follows the structure which makes a unity out of parts is better than the other structure, for it *is* what the other aims at. Therefore the relations among parts exist for the sake of the unifying structure, not vice versa. Hence, if the form of this structure is found among the partial associations of men, much more should it be found in the society of men as a totality, on the strength of the preceding syllogism, since the total structure or its form is the greater good. But, as we have seen sufficiently clearly in the preceding chapter, this unifying structure is found in all parts of human society; therefore it is found or should be found in mankind as a whole; and as those societies that are partial in a state and the state itself, as we saw, should be composed of a structure unified by a governor or government, so there must be a single world-ruler or world-government.[1]

7

Human government is but a part of that single world-admin-istration which has its unity in God.

Furthermore, human society is a totality in relation to its parts, but is itself a part of another totality. For it is the totality of particular states and peoples, as we have seen, but it is obviously a mere part of the whole universe. Therefore, as through it the lower parts of human society are well-ordered, so it, too, should fit into the order of the universe as a whole. But its parts are well-ordered only on the basis of a single principle (this follows from all we have said), and hence it too must be well-ordered on the basis of a single principle, namely, through its governor, God, who is the absolute world-government. Hence we conclude that a single world-government is necessary for the well-being of the world.

8

Man is by nature in God's likeness and therefore should, like God, be one.

Things are at their best when they go according to the intention of their original mover, who is God. And this is self-evident to all except those who deny that the divine goodness achieves

1 The term "prince" and cognate terms are used by writers in the classical tradition as a technical term for sovereign government and may be translated impersonally.

the highest perfection. In the intention of God every creature exists to represent the divine likeness in so far as its nature makes this possible. According to what is said: "Let us make man after our image and likeness." Though we cannot speak of the divine "image" as being in things lower than man, we can speak of anything as being in His "likeness," since the whole universe is nothing but a kind of imprint of the divine goodness. Therefore, mankind exists at its best when it resembles God as much as it can. But mankind resembles God most when it is most unified, for the true ground of unity exists in Him alone, as is written: "Hear, O Israel, the Lord thy God is one." But mankind is then most one when it is unified into a single whole; which is possible only when it submits wholly to a single government, as is self-evident. Therefore mankind in submitting to a single government most resembles God and most nearly exists according to the divine intention, which is the same as enjoying well-being, as was proved at the beginning of this chapter.

9

The heavens are ruled by a single mover, God, and man is at his best when he follows the pattern of the heavens and the heavenly father.

So also a person is a good or perfect child when he follows, as far as nature permits, in the footsteps of a perfect father. But mankind is the son of heaven, which is most perfect in all its works; for "man is generated of man and sun," according to the author of *The Physics*.[2] Hence mankind is best when it follows in the footsteps of heaven as far as its nature permits. And as the whole heaven is governed in all its parts, motions, and movers by a single motion, the *primum mobile,* and by a single mover, God, as is very evident to a philosophizing reason if it syllogizes truly, it follows that mankind is then at its best when in all its movers and movements it is governed by a single mover or government and by a single motion or law. Thus it seems

[2] II. 2, 11.

necessary that for the well-being of the world there be world-government, that is, a single power, called Empire. This reasoning inspired Boethius when he said:

> O happy race of men,
> If like heaven your hearts
> Were ruled by love! [3]

10

Human governments are imperfect as long as they are not subordinate to a supreme tribunal.

Wherever there can be contention, there judgment should exist; otherwise things would exist imperfectly, without their own means of adjustment or correction, which is impossible, since in things necessary God or Nature is not defective. Between any two governments, neither of which is in any way subordinate to the other, contention can arise either through their own fault or that of their subjects. This is evident. Therefore there should be judication between them. And since neither can know the affairs of the other, not being subordinated (for among equals there is no authority), there must be a third and wider power which can rule both within its own jurisdiction. This third power is either the world-government or it is not. If it is, we have reached our conclusion; if it is not, it must in turn have its equal outside its jurisdiction, and then it will need a third party as judge, and so *ad infinitum,* which is impossible. So we must arrive at a first and supreme judge for whom all contentions are judiciable either directly or indirectly; and this will be our world-governor or emperor. Therefore, world-government is necessary for the world. The Philosopher saw this argument when he said, "Things hate to be in disorder, but a plurality of authorities is disorder; therefore, authority is single." [4]

[3] *On the Consolation of Philosophy* II.8.
[4] Quoted in Aristotle's *Metaphysics* XI.10 from Homer's *Iliad* II.204.

11

The world-government is apt to be least greedy and most just.

Moreover, the world is best ordered when justice is its greatest power. Thus Virgil, seeking to praise an age which seemed to be arising in his day, sang in his *Bucolics*:

Iam redit et Virgo, redeunt Saturnia regna.[5]

By "Virgo" he meant justice, sometimes called "the starry." By "Saturnia regna" he meant the best ages, sometimes called "the golden." Justice has greatest power under a unitary government; therefore the best order of the world demands world-government or empire. The minor premise will become evident if we recall that justice is by its nature a kind of rightness or straight rule without deviation, and therefore, like whiteness, justice in the abstract is not susceptible of degrees. For certain forms are of this kind, entering into various compounds but each being in itself single and invariable, as the author of the *Book of the Six Principles* [6] rightly says. However, when they are qualified by "more or less," they owe this qualification to the things with which they are mixed and which contain a mixture of qualities more or less incompatible. Hence wherever justice exists with the least mixture of what is incompatible with it, either in *disposition* or in *action,* there justice is most powerful. And then what the Philosopher says can truly be said of her: "She is fairer than the morning or the evening star." [7] For then she resembles Phoebe in the glow and calm of dawn facing her brother [Phoebus Apollo]. As to its *disposition,* justice is often obscured by volition, for when the will is not entirely freed of greed before justice is introduced, its justice lacks the brightness of purity, for it is mixed, however slightly, with something foreign to it; hence it is well that those be condemned

[5] "At last the Virgin and the Saturnian Kingdoms are returning."
[6] Gilbertus Porretanus.
[7] *Ethics* V. I.

who try to influence the sentiments of a judge. And as to its *action,* justice suffers from the limitations of human ability; for since justice is a virtue affecting others, how can a person act justly when he lacks the ability of giving to each his due? Whence it follows that the more powerful a just man is, the more adequate can justice be in its action.

And so, on the basis of this proposition, we may argue as follows: justice is most powerful in the world when it resides in the most willing and able being; the only being of this nature is the world-governor. Therefore, justice is the most powerful in the world when it resides solely in the world-governor. This compound syllogism is in the second figure necessarily negative, thus:

$$
\begin{array}{lll}
\text{All B is A} & & \text{All B is A} \\
\text{Only C is A} & \quad\text{or}\quad & \text{No non-C is A} \\
\text{Only C is B} & & \text{No non-C is B}
\end{array}
$$

The major premise is evident from the foregoing. The minor is justified as follows: first, respecting *volition,* then, respecting *ability.* As evidence for the first we must note that greed is the extreme opposite of justice, as Aristotle says in the Fifth Book of his *Nicomachean Ethics.* Take away greed completely and nothing opposed to justice remains in the will. Hence the opinion of the Philosopher that whatever can be decided by law should not be left to a judge, is based on the fear of greed, which readily twists the minds of men. Now where there is nothing left to desire, greed is impossible, for passions cannot exist when their objects are destroyed. But a universal ruler has nothing that he still desires, for his jurisdiction is bounded only by the ocean, which is true of no other ruler whose realm is bounded by those of others, as, for example, the King of Castile's is bounded by the King of Aragon's. Hence it follows that the world-ruler is the purest among mortal wills in which justice may reside. Moreover, as greed, however slight, obscures the habits of justice, so charity or joy in righteousness refines and enlightens it. Whoever, therefore, is most disposed to find joy in righteousness can give to justice the greatest pre-eminence. Such is the world-ruler, and if he exist, justice is or can be most powerful. That righteous joy does what I have claimed for it can be proved as follows: greed ignores man himself and seeks other things, but charity ignores all other things and seeks God and man, and consequently man's good. And since of all human goods the greatest is to live in peace, as we said above, and since justice is its chief and most powerful promoter, charity is the chief promoter of justice—the greater charity, the more justice. And that of all men the world-ruler should most enjoy righteousness can be made clear thus: if we love a thing, we love it more the closer it is to us; but men are closer to the world-ruler than to other rulers; therefore he loves them most or should love them most. The major premise is evident to anyone who considers the nature of being passive and being active; the minor follows from the fact that men are close to other rulers only in part, but to the world-ruler totally. Also, men approach other rulers through the ruler of all, not *vice versa*, and thus all men are the primary and immediate objects of concern for the world-ruler, whereas other rulers care for them only through him from whose supreme care their own is derived. Besides, the more universal a cause is, the more genuinely it is a cause, for lower causes operate through the higher, as is explained in the book *De causis*, and the more a cause is a cause, the more it loves its effect, since such a love makes a cause what it is. Therefore, since the world-ruler is among mortals the most universal cause of well-being, other rulers being so through him, as I have explained, it follows that he has the greatest love for human welfare.

Secondly, concerning the *ability* [rather than the will] to do justice, who could doubt such an ability in the world-ruler, if he understands the meaning of the term? For since he governs all, he can have no enemies. The minor premise is now evident enough, and the conclusion seems certain—namely, that the world needs for its well-being a universal government.

12

Human freedom consists in being ruled by reason and in living for the goal of mankind. Such freedom is possible only under world-government.

Mankind is at its best when it is most free. This will be clear if we grasp the principle of liberty. We must realize that the basic principle of our freedom is freedom to choose, which saying many have on their lips but few in their minds. For they go only so far as to say freedom of choice is freedom of will in judging. This is true, but they do not understand its import. They talk as our logicians do, who for their exercises in logic constantly use certain propositions, such as "A triangle has three angles equal to two right angles." And so I must explain that judgment lies between apprehension and appetition; for, first a thing is apprehended, then, being apprehended, is judged to be good or bad, and lastly, being judged, is either sought or rejected. Therefore, if the judgment completely dominates the appetite and is in no way prejudiced by appetite, it is free; but if the appetite somehow antecedes the judgment and influences it, the judgment can not be free, since it does not move itself, but is led captive by another. For this reason, the lower animals can not have free judgment, since their appetites always get ahead of their judgments. This also explains why intellectual beings whose wills are immutable and those spirits who have departed this life in grace do not lose their freedom of judgment, though their wills are fixed, but retain and exercise it perfectly.

If we grasp this principle, we can again appreciate why this liberty, the principle of all our liberty, is God's greatest gift to human nature (as I said in the "Paradiso"),[8] for in this life it makes us happy as men, and in another it makes us happy as gods. If all this is true, who can deny that mankind lives best when it makes the most use of this principle?

[8] This is probably a gloss. See Preface, p. x.

But to live under a world-ruler is to be most free. To understand this, we must know that to be free means to exist for one's own sake, not for another's, as the Philosopher puts it in his *De simpliciter ente*.[9] For whatever exists for the sake of another is under a necessity derived from that for which it exists, as a road is necessarily determined by its goal. Now it is only under the reign of a world-ruler that mankind exists for itself and not for another, since then only is there a check on perverted forms of government such as democracies, oligarchies, and tyrannies, which carry mankind into slavery, as anyone can see who runs down the list of them all, whereas those only govern who are kings, aristocrats (called "the best"), and champions of the people's liberty. Hence the world-ruler, who has the greatest love for men, as I have explained, desires that all men be made good, which is impossible among perverted politicians. Thus the Philosopher says in his *Politics* that "under a perverted form of government a good man is a bad citizen, while under a right form a good man and a good citizen are identical." In this way right forms of government aim at liberty, that is, men live for their own sake. For citizens do not live for their representatives nor peoples for their kings, but, on the contrary, representatives exist for citizens and kings for peoples. As a social order is established not for the sake of the laws, but the laws for its sake, so they who live according to law are ordered not for the sake of the legislator but rather he for them. This is the way the Philosopher puts it in his books on this subject that have come down to us. Hence it is clear that though in matters of policy representatives and kings are the rulers of others, in matters of aims they are the servants of others, and most of all the world-ruler, who should be regarded as the servant of all. Hence we must be well aware that world-government is itself governed by a pre-established end in establishing its laws. Therefore mankind lives best when it lives under a single ruler; and it follows that a single world-government is necessary for the world's well-being.

[9] *Metaphysics* I.

13

The universal government is most apt to be reasonable.

Another argument: Whoever is himself best disposed to rule can best dispose others. For in any action what is primarily intended by the agent, either because his nature demands it or because he does it purposely, is to make manifest his own image; hence an agent is delighted when he is thus active, for as all things desire their own being, and as an agent in acting unfolds his own being, a state of delight naturally arises, for a thing desired always brings delight. An agent acts, therefore, only because he already is the kind of thing which what he acts on is supposed to become. On this subject the Philosopher says in *De simpliciter ente*: "Whatever is changed from potentiality into act is changed by something which actually exists in the form to which it is changed; if an agent tried to act otherwise, he would act in vain." And thus we can overcome the error of those who speak well but do ill and who nevertheless believe that they can improve the life and ways of others; they forget that Jacob's hands were more persuasive than his words, even though his words were true and his hands false. Hence the Philosopher says in his *Nicomachean Ethics*: "In matters of passion and action, words are less persuasive than deeds." Hence also heaven spoke to David when he sinned, saying: "Wherefore dost thou tell of my righteousness?"—as much as to say: "Your speech is in vain when you are not as you speak." From all this we gather that whoever wishes to order others well should himself be well-ordered. But it is the world-ruler alone who is best constituted for ruling. The proof is as follows: A thing is most easily and perfectly adapted to a given course of action when it contains in itself few obstacles to this action. Thus those who have never heard of philosophizing truly are more easily and perfectly taught the habit [of it] than those who heard of it long ago and are full of false opinions. On this subject Galen well says: "It takes such persons double time to acquire science." Now since the world-ruler can have no occasion for greed, or at least has much less than other mortals, as we explained above, and since this does not apply to other rulers, and since greed is itself the great corrupter of judgment and impediment to justice, it follows that the world-ruler is wholly or to the greatest possible degree well-constituted for ruling, since he above all others can let judgment and justice hold sway. These are the two chief qualities that legislators and administrators of law should have, as that most holy king testified when he asked God to give him what a king and a king's son should have: "God give thy judgment to the king, and thy justice to the king's son." Therefore, our minor premise is sound, in which we say that the world-ruler alone has the best qualifications for ruling. Therefore, the world-ruler can best govern others. Hence it follows that for the best state of the world a world-government is necessary.

14

The universal government can best guide particular governments by establishing the laws which lead all men in common toward peace.

It is better that what can be done by one should be done by one, not by many. The demonstration of this proposition is: Let *A* be able to do something; let *A* and *B* be several who could also do it. Now if *A* can do what *A* and *B* do, *B* is useless, for his addition makes no difference to what *A* alone did. Such useless additions are superfluous and otiose, displeasing to God and Nature, and whatever is displeasing to God and Nature is evil (which is self-evident); it follows not only that it is better that one rather than many should do this work, but that it is good for one to do it and evil for several to do it.

Another proof: A thing is said to be better the nearer it is to the best. Now the end for which a deed is done is the standard of its goodness. But when it is done by one it is nearer the end. Therefore, it is better so. To prove that when it is done by one, it is nearer the end, let *C* be the end, let *A* be the deed of one, and let *A* and *B* be the deed of several. It is clear that the way from *A* direct to *C* is shorter than via *B*. Now mankind can be ruled by a single supreme ruler or world-governor. In this connection it should be clearly understood that not every little regulation for every city could come directly from the world-government, for even municipal regulations are sometimes defective and need amendment, as the Philosopher makes clear in his praise of equity in the *Nicomachean Ethics*. Thus nations, states, and cities have their own internal concerns which require special laws. For law is a rule to guide our lives. The Scythians must rule their lives in one way, living as they do beyond the seventh clime, suffering great inequalities of days and nights and being harried by an almost intolerable, freezing cold, whereas the Garamantes must do otherwise, living below the equinoctial circle, where daylight and dark of night are always balanced, and where the excessive heat makes clothes unendurable. World-government, on the other hand, must be understood in the sense that it governs mankind on the basis of what all have in common and that by a common law it leads all toward peace. This common norm or law should be received by local governments in the same way that practical intelligence in action receives its major premises from the speculative intellect. To these it adds its own particular minor premises and then draws particular conclusions for the sake of its action. These basic norms not only can come from a single source, but must do so in order to avoid confusion among universal principles. Moses himself followed this pattern in the law which he composed, for, having chosen the chiefs of the several tribes, he left them the lesser judgments, reserving to himself alone the higher and more general. These common norms were then used by the tribal chiefs according to their special needs. Therefore, it is better for mankind to be governed by one, not by many; and hence by a single governor, the world-ruler; and if it is better, it is pleasing to God, since He always wills the better. And when there are only two alternatives—the better is also the best, and is consequently not only pleasing to God, but the choice of "one" rather than "many" is what most pleases Him. Hence it follows that mankind lives best under a single government, and therefore that such a government is necessary for the well-being of the world.

15

Unity is basic to both "being" and "good."

Now I must explain that "being," "unity," and "good" have an order of precedence in the fifth sense of "precedence," namely, priority. For by its nature being is prior to unity and unity prior to the good, because whatever is in the fullest sense a being is most unified, and when most unified it is most good. Hence the less a thing has complete being, the less unity it has, and consequently it is less good. For this reason it is true in all matters whatsoever that the most unified is the best; so the Philosopher maintains in *De simpliciter ente*. Thus we see that at the root of what it means to be good is being one; and the root of what it means to be evil is being many. For this reason, as is explained in *De simpliciter ente*, Pythagoras in his system of relations places unity on the side of good and plurality on the side of evil. Thus we can see what sin is: it is to scorn unity and hence to proceed toward plurality. The Psalmist saw this very well when he said: "They are multiplied in the fruit of corn and wine and oil." It is therefore certain that whatever is good is good because it is unified. And since concord is essentially a good, it is clear that at its root there must be some kind of unity; what this root is will become evident if we examine the nature and ground of concord. Now concord is a uniform movement of many wills; in this definition we see that the uniform movement is due to the union of wills, and that this union is the root and very being of concord. For example, we would say that a number of clods of earth would all agree in falling toward the center and that they fell "in concord," if they did so voluntarily, and similarly flames would agree in rising to the circumference. So we speak of a number of men as being in concord when in moving together toward a single goal their wills are formally united, that is, the form of unity is in their wills, just as the quality of gravity is formally in the clods, and levity in the flames. For the ability to will is a kind of power, but the form of the will is the idea of an apprehended good. This form, like any other form (such as soul or number) is in itself a unity, but is multiplied in the various things with which it is compounded.

With this in mind we can now proceed to our argument in behalf of our proposition, as follows: All concord depends on a unity in wills; the best state of mankind is a kind of concord, for as a man is in excellent health when he enjoys concord in soul and body, and similarly a family, city, or state, so mankind as a whole. Therefore the well-being of mankind depends on the unity of its wills. But this is possible only if there is a single, dominant will which directs all others toward unity, for the wills of mortals need direction because they are subject to the captivating delights of youth (so teaches the Philosopher at the end of his *Nicomachean Ethics*). And this will can not be if there be not a single governor of all whose will can be dominant and directive for all others. Now, if all the above arguments are true, and they are, it is necessary for the best state of mankind that there be in the world a single governor, and consequently world-government is necessary for the well-being of the world.

16

The incarnation of Christ during the Augustan Empire when there prevailed a maximum of world peace bears witness that these principles are divine, and the miseries which have overtaken man since he departed from that golden age likewise bear witness.

Memorable experience confirms the above rational arguments. I refer to the state of things among mortals at the time when the Son of God took on human form for man's salvation, a state of things which He either awaited or arranged according to his will. For if we recall all the ages and conditions of men since the fall of our first parent, when the whole course of our wanderings began, we shall find that not until the time of Divus Augustus was there a complete and single world-government which pacified the world. That in his time mankind enjoyed the blessing of universal peace and tranquillity is the testimony of all historians, of the illustrious poets, and even of the evangelist of Christ's gentleness [St. Luke]; and lastly this happiest of ages was called by Paul the "fullness of time." Truly the time was full and all things temporal so ordered that for every service toward our happiness there was a servant.

But the condition of the world since the day when the nail of greed tore that seamless garment is something we can all read about, if only we did not have to see it, too! O race of men, how many storms and misfortunes must thou endure, and how many shipwrecks, because thou, beast of many heads, strugglest in many directions! Thou art sick at heart and sick in mind, both theoretical and practical! No irrefutable arguments appeal to thy theoretical reason, and no amount of experience to thy practical intelligence, and even thine emotions are not moved by the sweet, divine persuasiveness which sounds to thee from the trumpet of the Holy Spirit: "Behold how good and how pleasant it is for brethren to dwell together in unity. Why have the nations raged, and the people devised vain things? The kings of the earth stood up and the princes met together against the Lord, and against his Christ. Let us break their bonds asunder: and let us cast away their yoke from us." [10]

10 Psalm 2:1-3.

During a time of imprisonment and torture in 1513, Niccolo Machiavelli wrote *The Prince* and dedicated it to Lorenzo the Magnificent in an effort to ingratiate himself with the ruling Medici family of Florence. It earned for its author such opprobrium that his first name became identified with the devil as "Old Nick," and his last name gave us the term "machiavellian."(To describe unscrupulous cunning in the conduct of affairs of state.) But he emphasized that he wrote of conditions as they were, not as they should be.

The Prince

CHAPTER XII

How Many Different Kinds of Soldiers There Are, and of Mercenaries

HAVING spoken particularly of all the various kinds of Princedom whereof at the outset I proposed to treat, considered in some measure what are the causes of their strength and weakness, and pointed out the methods by which men commonly seek to acquire them, it now remains that I should discourse generally concerning the means for attack and defence of which each of these different kinds of Princedom may make use.

I have already said that a Prince must lay solid foundations, since otherwise he will inevitably be destroyed. Now the main foundations of all States, whether new, old, or mixed, are good laws and good arms. But since you cannot have the former without the latter, and where you have the latter, are likely to have the former, I shall here omit all discussion on the subject of laws, and speak only of arms.

I say then that the arms wherewith a Prince defends his State are either his own subjects, or they are mercenaries, or they are auxiliaries, or they are partly one and partly another. Mercenaries and auxiliaries are at once useless and dangerous, and he who holds his State by means of mercenary troops can never be solidly or securely seated. For such troops are disunited, ambitious, insubordinate, treacherous, insolent among friends, cowardly before foes, and without fear of God or faith with man. Whenever they are attacked defeat follows; so that in peace you are plundered by them, in war by your enemies. And this because they have no tie or motive to keep them in the field beyond their paltry pay, in return for which it would be too much to expect them to give their lives. They are ready enough, therefore, to be your soldiers while you are at peace, but when war is declared they make off and disappear. I ought to have little difficulty in getting this believed, for the present ruin of Italy is due to no other cause than her having for many years trusted to mercenaries, who though heretofore they may have helped the fortunes of some one man, and made a show of strength when matched with one another, have always revealed themselves in their true colours so soon as foreign enemies appeared. Hence it was that Charles of France was suffered to conquer Italy *with chalk;* and he who said our sins were the cause, said truly, though it was not the sins he meant, but those which I have noticed. And as these were the sins of Princes, they it is who have paid the penalty.

But I desire to demonstrate still more clearly the untoward character of these forces. Captains of mercenaries are either able men or they are not. If they are, you cannot trust them, since they will always seek their own aggrandizement, either by overthrowing you who are their master, or by the overthrow of others contrary to your desire. On the other hand, if your captain be not an able man the chances are you will be ruined. And if it be said that whoever has arms in his hands will act in the same way whether he be a mercenary or no, I answer that when arms have to be employed by a Prince or a Republic, the Prince ought to go in person to take command as captain, the Republic should send one of her citizens, and if he prove incapable should change him, but if he prove capable should by the force of the laws confine him within proper bounds. And we see from experience that both Princes and Republics when they depend on their own arms have the greatest success, whereas from employing mercenaries nothing but loss results. Moreover, a

Republic trusting to her own forces, is with greater difficulty than one which relies on foreign arms brought to yield obedience to a single citizen. Rome and Sparta remained for ages armed and free. The Swiss are at once the best armed and the freest people in the world.

Of mercenary arms in ancient times we have an example in the Carthaginians, who at the close of their first war with Rome, were well-nigh ruined by their hired troops, although these were commanded by Carthaginian citizens. So too, when, on the death of Epaminondas, the Thebans made Philip of Macedon captain of their army, after gaining a victory for them, he deprived them of their liberty. The Milanese, in like manner, when Duke Filippo died, took Francesco Sforza into their pay to conduct the war against the Venetians. But he, after defeating the enemy at Caravaggio, combined with them to overthrow the Milanese, his masters. His father too while in the pay of Giovanna, Queen of Naples, suddenly left her without troops, obliging her, in order to save her kingdom, to throw herself into the arms of the King of Aragon.

And if it be said that in times past the Venetians and the Florentines have extended their dominions by means of these arms, and that their captains have served them faithfully, without seeking to make themselves their masters, I answer that in this respect the Florentines have been fortunate, because among those valiant captains who might have given them cause for fear, some have not been victorious, some have had rivals, and some have turned their ambition in other directions.

Among those not victorious, was Giovanni Acuto, whose fidelity, since he was unsuccessful, was not put to the proof: but any one may see, that had he been victorious the Florentines must have been entirely in his hands. The Sforzas, again, had constant rivals in the Bracceschi, so that the one following was a check upon the other; moreover, the ambition of Francesco was directed against Milan, while that of Braccio was directed against the Church and the kingdom of Naples. Let us turn, however, to what took place lately. The Florentines chose for their captain Paolo Vitelli, a most prudent commander, who had raised himself from privacy to the highest renown in arms. Had he been successful in reducing Pisa, none can deny that the Florentines would have been completely in his power, for they would have been ruined had he gone over to their enemies, while if they retained him they must have submitted to his will.

Again, as to the Venetians, if we consider the growth of their power, it will be seen that they conducted their affairs with glory and safety so long as their subjects of all ranks, gentle and simple alike, valiantly bore arms in their wars; as they did before they directed their enterprises landwards. But when they took to making war by land, they forsook those methods in which they excelled and were content to follow the customs of Italy.

At first, indeed, in extending their possessions on the mainland, having as yet but little territory and being held in high repute, they had not much to fear from their captains; but when their territories increased, which they did under Carmagnola, they were taught their mistake. For as they had found him a most valiant and skilful leader when, under his command, they defeated the Duke of Milan, and, on the other hand, saw him slack in carrying on the war, they made up their minds that no further victories were to be had under him; and because, through fear of losing what they had gained, they could not discharge him, to secure themselves against him they were forced to put him to death. After him they have had for captains, Bartolommeo of Bergamo, Roberto of San Severino, the Count of Pitigliano, and the like, under whom their danger has not been from victories, but from defeats; as, for instance, at Vaila, where they lost in a single day what it had taken the efforts of eight hundred years to acquire. For the gains resulting from mercenary arms are slow, and late, and inconsiderable, but the losses sudden and astounding.

And since these examples have led me back to Italy, which for many years past has been defended by mercenary arms, I desire to go somewhat deeper into the matter, in order that the causes which led to the adoption of these arms being seen, they may the more readily be corrected. You are to understand, then, that when in these later times the Imperial control began to be rejected by Italy, and the temporal power of the Pope to be more thought of, Italy suddenly split up into a number of separate States. For many of the larger cities took up arms against their nobles, who, with the favour of the Emperor, had before kept them in subjection, and were supported by the Church with a view to add to her temporal authority: while in many others of these cities, private citizens became rulers. Hence Italy, having passed almost entirely into the hands of the Church and of certain Republics, the former made up of priests, the latter of citizens unfamiliar with arms, began to take foreigners into her pay.

The first who gave reputation to this service was Alberigo of Conio in Romagna, from whose school of warlike training descended, among others, Braccio and Sforza, who in their time were the arbiters of Italy; after whom came all those others who down to the present hour have held similar commands, and to whose merits we owe it that our country has been overrun by Charles, plundered by Louis, wasted by Ferdinand, and insulted by the Swiss.

The first object of these mercenaries was to bring foot soldiers into disrepute, in order to enhance the merit of their own followers; and this they did, because lacking territory of their own and depending on their profession for their support, a few foot soldiers gave them no importance, while for a large number they were unable to provide. For these reasons they had recourse to horsemen, a less retinue of whom was thought to confer distinction, and could be more easily maintained. And the matter went to such a length, that in an army of twenty thousand men, not two thousand foot soldiers were to be found. Moreover, they spared no endeavour to relieve themselves and their men from fatigue and danger, not killing one another in battle, but making prisoners who were afterwards released without ransom. They would attack no town by night; those in towns would make no sortie by night against a besieging army. Their camps were without rampart or trench. They had no winter campaigns. All which arrangements were sanctioned by their military rules, contrived by them, as I have said already, to escape fatigue and danger; but the result of which has been to bring Italy into servitude and contempt.

CHAPTER XIII

Of Auxiliary, Mixed, and National Arms

THE second sort of unprofitable arms are auxiliaries, by whom I mean, troops brought to help and protect you by a potentate whom you summon to your aid; as when in recent times, Pope Julius II observing the pitiful behaviour of his mercenaries at the enterprise of Ferrara, betook himself to auxiliaries, and arranged with Ferdinand of Spain to be supplied with horse and foot soldiers.

Auxiliaries may be excellent and useful soldiers for themselves, but are always hurtful to him who calls them in; for if they are defeated, he is undone, if victorious, he becomes their prisoner. Ancient histories abound with instances of this, but I shall not pass from the example of Pope Julius, which is still fresh in men's minds. It was the height of rashness for him, in his eagerness to gain Ferrara, to throw himself without reserve into the arms of a stranger. Nevertheless, his good fortune came to his rescue, and he had not to reap the fruits of his ill-considered conduct. For after his auxiliaries were defeated at Ravenna, the Swiss suddenly descended and, to their own surprise and that of every one else, swept the victors out of the country, so that, he neither remained a prisoner with his enemies, they being put to flight, nor with his auxiliaries, because victory was won by other arms than theirs. The Florentines, being wholly without soldiers of their own, brought ten thousand French men-at-arms to the siege of Pisa, thereby incurring greater peril than at any previous time of trouble. To protect himself from his neighbours, the Emperor of Constantinople summoned ten thousand Turkish soldiers into Greece, who, when the war was over, refused to leave, and this was the beginning of the servitude of Greece to the Infidel.

Let him, therefore, who would deprive himself of every chance of success, have recourse to auxiliaries, these being far more dangerous than mercenary arms, bringing ruin with them ready made. For they are united, and wholly under the control of their own officers; whereas, before mercenaries, even after gaining a victory, can do you hurt, longer time and better opportunities are needed; because, as they are made up of separate companies, raised and paid by you, he whom you place in command cannot at once acquire such authority over them as will be injurious to you. In short, with mercenaries your greatest danger is from their inertness and cowardice, with auxiliaries from their valour. Wise Princes, therefore, have always eschewed these arms, and trusted rather to their own, and have preferred defeat with the latter to victory with the former, counting that as no true victory which is gained by foreign aid.

I shall never hesitate to cite the example of Cesare Borgia and his actions. He entered Romagna with a force of auxiliaries, all of them French men-at-arms, with whom he took Imola and Forli. But it appearing to him afterwards that these troops were not to be trusted, he had recourse to mercenaries from whom he thought there would be less danger, and took the Orsini and Vitelli into his pay. But finding these likewise while under his command to be fickle, false, and treacherous, he got rid of them, and fell back on troops of his own raising. And we may readily discern the difference between these various kinds of arms, by observing the different degrees of reputation in which the Duke stood while he depended upon the French alone, when he took the Orsini and Vitelli into his pay, and when he fell back on his own troops and his own resources; for we find his reputation always increasing, and that he was never so well thought of as when every one perceived him to be sole master of his own forces.

I am unwilling to leave these examples, drawn from what has taken place in Italy and in recent times; and yet I must not omit to notice the case of Hiero of Syracuse, who is one of those whom I have already named. He, as I have before related, being made captain of their armies by the Syracusans, saw at once that a force of mercenary soldiers, supplied by men resembling our Italian *condottieri,* was not serviceable; and as he would not retain and could not disband them, he caused them all to be cut to pieces, and afterwards made war with native soldiers only, without other aid.

And here I would call to mind a passage in the Old Testament as bearing on this point. When David offered himself to Saul to go forth and fight Goliath the Philistine champion, Saul to encourage him armed him with his own armour, which David, so soon as he had put it on, rejected, saying that with these untried arms he could not prevail, and that he chose rather to meet his enemy with only his sling and his sword. In a word, the armour of others is too wide, or too strait for us; it falls off us, or it weighs us down.

Charles VII, the father of Louis XI, who by his good fortune and valour freed France from the English, saw this necessity of strengthening himself with a national army, and drew up ordinances regulating the service both of men-at-arms and of foot soldiers throughout his kingdom. But afterwards his son, King Louis, did away with the national infantry, and began to hire Swiss mercenaries. Which blunder having been followed by subsequent Princes, has been the cause, as the result shows, of the dangers into which the kingdom of France has fallen; for, by enhancing the reputation of the Swiss, the whole of the national troops of France have been deteriorated. For from their infantry being done away with, their men-at-arms are made wholly dependent on foreign assistance, and being accustomed to co-operate with the Swiss, have grown to think they can do nothing without them. Hence the French are no match for the Swiss, and without them cannot succeed against others.

The armies of France, then, are mixed, being partly national and partly mercenary. Armies thus composed are far superior to mere mercenaries or mere auxiliaries, but far inferior to forces purely national. And this example is in itself conclusive, for the realm of France would be invincible if the military ordinances of Charles VII had been retained and extended. But from want of foresight men make changes which relishing well at first do not betray their hidden venom, as I have already observed respecting hectic fever. Nevertheless, the ruler is not truly wise who cannot discern evils before they develop themselves, and this is a faculty given to few.

If we look for the causes which first led to the overthrow of the Roman Empire, they will be found to have had their source in the employment of Gothic mercenaries, for from that hour the strength of the Romans began to wane and all the virtue which went from them passed to the Goths. And, to be brief, I say that without national arms no Princedom is safe, but on the contrary is wholly dependent on Fortune, being without the strength that could defend it in adversity. And it has always been the deliberate opinion of the wise, that nothing is so infirm and fleeting as a reputation for power not founded upon a national army, by which I mean one composed of subjects, citizens, and dependents, all others being mercenary or auxiliary.

The methods to be followed for organizing a national army may readily be ascertained, if the rules above laid down by me, and by which I abide, be well considered, and attention be given to the manner in which Philip, father of Alexander the Great, and many other Princes and Republics have armed and disposed their forces.

CHAPTER XIV

Of the Duty of a Prince In Respect of Military Affairs

A PRINCE, therefore, should have no care or thought but for war, and for the regulations and training it requires, and should apply himself exclusively to this as his peculiar province; for war is the sole art looked for in one who rules, and is of such efficacy that it not merely maintains those who are born Princes, but often enables men to rise to that eminence from a private station; while, on the other hand, we often see that when Princes devote themselves rather to pleasure than to arms, they lose their dominions. And as neglect of this art is the prime cause of such calamities, so to be a proficient in it is the surest way to acquire power. Francesco Sforza, from his renown in arms, rose from privacy to be Duke of Milan, while his descendants, seeking to avoid the hardships and fatigues of military life, from being Princes fell back into privacy. For among other causes of misfortune which your not being armed brings upon you, it makes you despised, and this is one of those reproaches against which, as shall presently be explained, a Prince ought most carefully to guard.

Between an armed and an unarmed man no proportion holds, and it is contrary to reason to expect that the armed man should voluntarily submit to him who is unarmed, or that the unarmed man should stand secure among armed retainers. For with contempt on one side, and distrust on the other, it is impossible that men should work well together. Wherefore, as has already been said, a Prince who is ignorant of military affairs, besides other disadvantages, can neither be respected by his soldiers, nor can he trust them. A Prince, therefore, ought never to allow his attention to be diverted from warlike pursuits, and should occupy himself with them even more in peace than in war. This he can do in two ways, by practice or by study.

As to the practice, he ought, besides keeping his soldiers well trained and disciplined, to be constantly engaged in the chase, that he may inure his body to hardships and fatigue, and gain at the same time a knowledge of places, by observing how the mountains slope, the valleys open, and the plains spread; acquainting himself with the characters of rivers and marshes, and giving the greatest attention to this subject. Such knowledge is useful to him in two ways; for first, he learns thereby to know his own country, and to understand better how it may be defended; and next, from his familiar acquaintance with its localities, he readily comprehends the character of other districts when obliged to observe them for the first time. For the hills, valleys, plains, rivers, and marshes of Tuscany, for example, have a certain resemblance to those elsewhere; so that from a knowledge of the natural features of that province, similar knowledge in respect of other provinces may readily be gained. The Prince who is wanting in this kind of knowledge, is wanting in the first qualification of a good captain, for by it he is taught how to surprise an enemy, how to choose an encampment, how to lead his army on a march, how to array it for battle, and how to post it to the best advantage for a siege.

Among the commendations which Philopoemon, Prince of the Achaians, has received from historians is this—that in times of peace he was always thinking of methods of warfare, so that when walking in the country with his friends he would often stop and talk with them on the subject. 'If the enemy,' he would say, 'were posted on that hill, and we found ourselves here with our army, which of us would have the better position? How could we most safely and in the best order advance to meet them? If we had to retreat, what direction should we take? If they retired, how should we pursue?' In this way he put to his friends, as he went along, all the contingencies that can befall an army. He listened to their opinions, stated his own, and supported them with reasons; and from his being constantly occupied with such meditations, it resulted, that when in actual command no complication could ever present itself with which he was not prepared to deal.

As to the mental training of which we have spoken, a Prince should read histories, and in these should note the actions of great men, observe how they conducted themselves in their wars, and examine the causes of their victories and defeats, so as to avoid the latter and imitate them in the former. And above all, he should, as many great men of past ages have done, assume for his models those persons who before his time have been renowned and celebrated, whose deeds and achievements he should constantly keep in mind, as it is related that Alexander the Great sought to resemble Achilles, Cæsar Alexander, and Scipio Cyrus. And any one who reads the life of this last-named hero, written by Xenophon, recognizes afterwards in the life of Scipio, how much this imitation was the source of his glory, and how nearly in his chastity, affability, kindliness, and generosity, he conformed to the character of Cyrus as Xenophon describes it.

A wise Prince, therefore, should pursue such methods as these, never resting idle in times of peace, but strenuously seeking to turn them to account, so that he may derive strength from them in the hour of danger, and find himself ready should Fortune turn against him, to resist her blows.

CHAPTER XV

Of the Qualities In Respect of Which Men, and Most of All Princes, Are Praised or Blamed

It now remains for us to consider what ought to be the conduct and bearing of a Prince in relation to his subjects and friends. And since I know that many have written on this subject, I fear it may be thought presumptuous in me to write of it also; the more so, because in my treatment of it, I depart from the views that others have taken.

But since it is my object to write what shall be useful to whosoever understands it, it seems to me better to follow the real truth of things than an imaginary view of them. For many Republics and

Princedoms have been imagined that were never seen or known to exist in reality. And the manner in which we live, and that in which we ought to live, are things so wide asunder, that he who quits the one to betake himself to the other is more likely to destroy than to save himself; since any one who would act up to a perfect standard of goodness in everything, must be ruined among so many who are not good. It is essential, therefore, for a Prince who desires to maintain his position, to have learned how to be other than good, and to use or not to use his goodness as necessity requires.

Laying aside, therefore, all fanciful notions concerning a Prince, and considering those only that are true, I say that all men when they are spoken of, and Princes more than others from their being set so high, are characterized by some one of those qualities which attach either praise or blame. Thus one is accounted liberal, another miserly (which word I use, rather than *avaricious,* to denote the man who is too sparing of what is his own, *avarice* being the disposition to take wrongfully what is another's); one is generous, another greedy; one cruel, another tender-hearted; one is faithless, another true to his word; one effeminate and cowardly, another high-spirited and courageous; one is courteous, another haughty; one impure, another chaste; one simple, another crafty; one firm, another facile; one grave, another frivolous; one devout, another unbelieving; and the like. Every one, I know, will admit that it would be most laudable for a Prince to be endowed with all of the above qualities that are reckoned good; but since it is impossible for him to possess or constantly practise them all, the conditions of human nature not allowing it, he must be discreet enough to know how to avoid the infamy of those vices that would deprive him of his government, and, if possible, be on his guard also against those which might not deprive him of it; though if he cannot wholly restrain himself, he may with less scruple indulge in the latter. He need never hesitate, however, to incur the reproach of those vices without which his authority can hardly be preserved; for if he well consider the whole matter, he will find that there may be a line of conduct having the appearance of virtue, to follow which would be his ruin, and that there may be another course having the appearance of vice, by following which his safety and well-being are secured.

CHAPTER XVI

OF LIBERALITY AND MISERLINESS

BEGINNING, then, with the first of the qualities above noticed, I say that it may be a good thing to be reputed liberal, but, nevertheless, that liberality without the reputation of it is hurtful; because, though it be worthily and rightly used, still if it be not known, you escape not the reproach of its opposite vice. Hence, to have credit for liberality with the world at large, you must neglect no circumstance of sumptuous display; the result being, that a Prince of a liberal disposition will consume his whole substance in things of this sort, and, after all, be obliged, if he would maintain his reputation for liberality, to burden his subjects with extraordinary taxes, and to resort to confiscations and all the other shifts whereby money is raised. But in this way he becomes hateful to his subjects, and growing impoverished is held in little esteem by any. So that in the end, having by his liberality offended many and obliged few, he is worse off than when he began, and is exposed to all his original dangers. Recognizing this, and endeavouring to retrace his steps, he at once incurs the infamy of miserliness.

A Prince, therefore, since he cannot without injury to himself practise the virtue of liberality so that it may be known, will not, if he be wise, greatly concern himself though he be called miserly. Because in time he will come to be regarded as more and more liberal, when it is seen that through his parsimony his revenues are sufficient; that he is able to defend himself against any who make war on him; that he can engage in enterprises against others without burdening his subjects; and thus exercise liberality towards all from whom he does not take, whose number is infinite, while he is miserly in respect of those only to whom he does not give, whose number is few.

In our own days we have seen no Princes accomplish great results save those who have been accounted miserly. All others have been ruined. Pope Julius II, after availing himself of his reputation for liberality to arrive at the Papacy, made no effort to preserve that reputation when making war on the King of France, but carried on all his numerous campaigns without levying from his subjects a single extraordinary tax, providing for the increased expenditure out of his long-continued savings. Had the present King of Spain been accounted liberal, he never could have engaged or succeeded in so many enterprises.

A Prince, therefore, if he is enabled thereby to forbear from plundering his subjects, to defend himself, to escape poverty and contempt, and the necessity of becoming rapacious, ought to care little though he incur the reproach of miserliness, for this is one of those vices which enable him to reign.

And should any object that Cæsar by his liberality rose to power, and that many others have been advanced to the highest dignities from their having been liberal and so reputed, I reply, 'Either you are already a Prince or you seek to become one; in the former case liberality is hurtful, in the latter it is very necessary that you be thought liberal; Cæsar was one of those who sought the sovereignty of Rome; but if after obtaining it he had lived on without retrenching his expenditure, he must have ruined the Empire.' And if it be further urged that many Princes reputed to have been most liberal have achieved great things with their armies, I answer that a Prince spends either what belongs to himself and his subjects, or what belongs to others; and that in the former case he ought to be sparing, but in the latter ought not to refrain from any kind of liberality. Because for a Prince who leads his armies in person and maintains them by plunder, pillage, and forced contributions, dealing as he does with the property of others this liberality is necessary, since otherwise he would not be followed by his soldiers. Of what does not belong to you or to your subjects you should, therefore, be a lavish giver, as were Cyrus, Cæsar, and Alexander; for to be liberal with the property of others does not take from your reputation, but adds to it. What injures you is to give away what is your own. And there is no quality so self-destructive as liberality; for while you practise it you lose the means whereby it can be practised, and become poor and despised, or else, to avoid poverty, you become rapacious and hated. For liberality leads to one or other of these two results, against which, beyond all others, a Prince should guard.

Wherefore it is wiser to put up with the name of being miserly, which breeds ignominy, but without hate, than to be obliged, from the desire to be reckoned liberal, to incur the reproach of rapacity, which breeds hate as well as ignominy.

CHAPTER XVII

Of Cruelty and Clemency, and Whether It Is Better To Be Loved or Feared

Passing to the other qualities above referred to, I say that every Prince should desire to be accounted merciful and not cruel. Nevertheless, he should be on his guard against the abuse of this quality of mercy. Cesare Borgia was reputed cruel, yet his cruelty restored Romagna, united it, and brought it to order and obedience; so that if we look at things in their true light, it will be seen that he was in reality far more merciful than the people of Florence, who, to avoid the imputation of cruelty, suffered Pistoja to be torn to pieces by factions.

A Prince should therefore disregard the reproach of being thought cruel where it enables him to keep his subjects united and obedient. For he who quells disorder by a very few signal examples will in the end be more merciful than he who from too great leniency permits things to take their course and so to result in rapine and bloodshed; for these hurt the whole State, whereas the severities of the Prince injure individuals only.

And for a new Prince, of all others, it is impossible to escape a name for cruelty, since new States are full of dangers. Wherefore Virgil, by the mouth of Dido, excuses the harshness of her reign on the plea that it was new, saying:—

'A fate unkind, and newness in my reign
Compel me thus to guard a wide domain.'

Nevertheless, the new Prince should not be too ready of belief, nor too easily set in motion; nor should he himself be the first to raise alarms; but should so temper prudence with kindliness that too great confidence in others shall not throw him off his guard, nor groundless distrust render him insupportable.

And here comes in the question whether it is better to be loved rather than feared, or feared rather than loved. It might perhaps be answered that we should wish to be both; but since love and fear can hardly exist together, if we must choose between them, it is far safer to be feared than loved. For of men it may generally be affirmed that they are thankless, fickle, false, studious to avoid danger, greedy of gain, devoted to you while you are able to confer benefits upon them, and ready, as I said before, while danger is distant, to shed their blood, and sacrifice their property, their lives, and their children for you; but in the hour of need they turn against you. The Prince, therefore, who without otherwise securing himself builds wholly on their professions is undone. For the friendships which we buy with a price, and do not gain by greatness and nobility of character, though they be fairly earned are not made good, but fail us when we have occasion to use them.

Moreover, men are less careful how they offend him who makes himself loved than him who makes himself feared. For love is held by the tie of obligation, which, because men are a sorry breed, is broken on every whisper of private interest; but fear is bound by the apprehension of punishment which never relaxes its grasp.

Nevertheless a Prince should inspire fear in such a fashion that if he do not win love he may escape hate. For a man may very well be feared and yet not hated, and this will be the case so long as he does not meddle with the property or with the women of his citizens and subjects. And if constrained to put any to death, he should do so only when there is manifest cause or reasonable justification. But, above all, he must abstain from the property of others. For men will sooner forget the death of their father than the loss of their patrimony. Moreover, pretexts for confiscation are never to seek, and he who has once begun to live by rapine always finds reasons for taking what is not his; whereas reasons for shedding blood are fewer, and sooner exhausted.

But when a Prince is with his army, and has many soldiers under his command, he must needs disregard the reproach of cruelty, for without such a reputation in its Captain, no army can be held together or kept under any kind of control. Among other things remarkable in Hannibal this has been noted, that having a very great army, made up of men of many different nations and brought to fight in a foreign country, no dissension ever arose among the soldiers themselves, nor any mutiny against their leader, either in his good or in his evil fortunes. This we can only ascribe to the transcendent cruelty, which, joined with numberless great qualities, rendered him at once venerable and terrible in the eyes of his soldiers; for without this reputation for cruelty these other virtues would not have produced the like results.

Unreflecting writers, indeed, while they praise his achievements, have condemned the chief cause of them; but that his other merits would not by themselves have been so efficacious we may see from the case of Scipio, one of the greatest Captains, not of his own time only but of all times of which we have record, whose armies rose against him in Spain from no other cause than his too great leniency in allowing them a freedom inconsistent with military strictness. With which weakness Fabius Maximus taxed him in the Senate House, calling him the corrupter of the Roman soldiery. Again, when the Locrians were shamefully outraged by one of his lieutenants, he neither avenged them, nor punished the insolence of his officer; and this from the natural easiness of his disposition. So that it was said in the Senate by one who sought to excuse him, that there were many who knew better how to refrain from doing wrong themselves than how to correct the wrong-doing of others. This temper, however, must in time have marred the name and fame even of Scipio, had he continued in it, and retained his command. But living as he did under the control of the Senate, this hurtful quality was not merely disguised, but came to be regarded as a glory.

Returning to the question of being loved or feared, I sum up by saying, that since his being loved depends upon his subjects, while his being feared depends upon himself, a wise Prince should build on what is his own, and not on what rests with others. Only, as I have said, he must do his utmost to escape hatred.

CHAPTER XVIII

How Princes Should Keep Faith

Every one understands how praiseworthy it is in a Prince to keep faith, and to live uprightly and not craftily. Nevertheless, we see from what has taken place in our own days that Princes who have set little store by their word, but have known how to overreach men by their cunning, have accomplished great things, and in the end got the better of those who trusted to honest dealing.

Be it known, then, that there are two ways of contending, one in accordance with the laws, the other by force; the first of which is proper to men, the second to beasts. But since the first method is often ineffectual, it becomes necessary to resort to the second. A Prince should, therefore, understand how to use well both the man and the beast. And this lesson has been covertly taught by the ancient writers, who relate how Achilles and many others of these old Princes were given over to be brought up and trained by Chiron the Centaur; since the only meaning of their having for instructor one who was half man and half beast is, that it is necessary for a Prince to know how to use both natures, and that the one without the other has no stability.

But since a Prince should know how to use the beast's nature wisely, he ought of beasts to choose both the lion and the fox; for the lion cannot guard himself from the toils, nor the fox from wolves. He must therefore be a fox to discern toils, and a lion to drive off wolves.

To rely wholly on the lion is unwise; and for this reason a prudent Prince neither can nor ought to keep his word when to keep it is hurtful to him and the causes which led him to pledge it are removed. If all men were good, this would not be good advice, but since they are dishonest and do not keep faith with you, you, in return, need not keep faith with them; and no prince was ever at a loss for plausible reasons to cloak a breach of faith. Of this numberless recent instances could be given, and it might be shown how many solemn treaties and engagements have been rendered inoperative and idle through want of faith in Princes, and that he who was best known to play the fox has had the best success.

It is necessary, indeed, to put a good colour on this nature, and to be skilful in simulating and dissembling. But men are so simple, and governed so absolutely by their present needs, that he who wishes to deceive will never fail in finding willing dupes. One recent example I will not omit. Pope Alexander VI had no care or thought but how to deceive, and always found material to work on. No man ever had a more effective manner of asseverating, or made promises with more solemn protestations, or observed them less. And yet, because he understood this side of human nature, his frauds always succeeded.

It is not essential, then, that a Prince should have all the good qualities which I have enumerated above, but it is most essential that he should seem to have them; I will even venture to affirm that if he has and invariably practises them all, they are hurtful, whereas the appearance of having them is useful. Thus, it is well to seem merciful, faithful, humane, religious, and upright, and also to be so; but the mind should remain so balanced that were it needful not to be so, you should be able and know how to change to the contrary.

And you are to understand that a Prince, and most of all a new Prince, cannot observe all those rules of conduct in respect whereof men are accounted good, being often forced, in order to preserve his Princedom, to act in opposition to good faith, charity, humanity, and religion. He must therefore keep his mind ready to shift as the winds and tides of Fortune turn, and, as I have already said, he ought not to quit good courses if he can help it, but should know how to follow evil courses if he must.

A Prince should therefore be very careful that nothing ever escapes his lips which is not replete with the five qualities above named, so that to see and hear him, one would think him the embodiment of mercy, good faith, integrity, humanity, and religion. And there is no virtue which it is more necessary for him to seem to possess than this last; because men in general judge rather by the eye than by the hand, for every one can see but few can touch. Every one sees what you seem, but few know what you are, and these few dare not oppose themselves to the opinion of the many who have the majesty of the State to back them up.

Moreover, in the actions of all men, and most of all of Princes, where there is no tribunal to which we can appeal, we look to results. Wherefore if a Prince succeeds in establishing and maintaining his authority, the means will always be judged honourable and be approved by every one. For the vulgar are always taken by appearances and by results, and the world is made up of the vulgar, the few only finding room when the many have no longer ground to stand on.

A certain Prince of our own days, whose name it is as well not to mention, is always preaching peace and good faith, although the mortal enemy of both; and both, had he practised them as he preaches them, would, oftener than once, have lost him his kingdom and authority.

CHAPTER XIX

That a Prince Should Seek To Escape Contempt and Hatred

Having now spoken of the chief of the qualities above referred to, the rest I shall dispose of briefly with these general remarks, that a Prince, as has already in part been said, should consider how he may avoid such courses as would make him hated or despised; and that whenever he succeeds in keeping clear of these, he has performed his part, and runs no risk though he incur other infamies.

A Prince, as I have said before, sooner becomes hated by being rapacious and by interfering with the property and with the women of his subjects, than in any other way. From these, therefore, he should abstain. For so long as neither their property nor their honour is touched, the mass of mankind live contentedly, and the Prince has only to cope with the ambition of a few, which can in many ways and easily be kept within bounds.

A Prince is despised when he is seen to be fickle, frivolous, effeminate, pusillanimous, or irresolute, against which defects he ought therefore most carefully to guard, striving so to bear himself that greatness, courage, wisdom, and strength may appear in all his actions. In his private dealings with his subjects his decisions should be irrevocable, and his reputation such that no one would dream of overreaching or cajoling him.

The Prince who inspires such an opinion of himself is greatly esteemed, and against one who is greatly esteemed conspiracy is difficult; nor, when he is known to be an excellent Prince and held in reverence by his subjects, will it be easy to attack him. For a Prince is exposed to two dangers, from within in respect of his subjects, from without in respect of foreign powers. Against the latter he will defend himself with good arms and good allies, and if he have good arms he will always have good allies; and when things are settled abroad, they will always be settled at home, unless disturbed by conspiracies; and even should there be hostility from without, if he has taken those measures, and has lived in the way I have recommended, and if he never abandons hope, he will withstand every attack; as I have said was done by Nabis the Spartan.

As regards his own subjects, when affairs are quiet abroad, he has to fear they may engage in secret plots; against which a Prince best secures himself when he escapes being hated or despised, and keeps on good terms with his people; and this, as I have already shown at length, it is essential he should do. Not to be hated or despised by the body of his subjects, is one of the surest safeguards that a Prince can have against conspiracy. For he who conspires always reckons on pleasing the people by putting the Prince to death; but when he sees that instead of pleasing he will offend them, he cannot summon courage to carry out his design. For the difficulties that attend conspirators are infinite, and we know from experience that while there have been many conspiracies, few of them have succeeded.

He who conspires cannot do so alone, nor can he assume as his companions any save those whom he believes to be discontented; but so soon as you impart your design to a discontented man, you supply him with the means of removing his discontent, since by betraying you he can procure for himself every advantage; so that seeing on the one hand certain gain, and on the other a doubtful and dangerous risk, he must either be a rare friend to you, or the mortal enemy of his Prince, if he keep your secret.

To put the matter shortly, I say that on the side of the conspirator there are distrust, jealousy, and dread of punishment to deter him, while on the side of the Prince there are the laws, the majesty of the throne, the protection of friends and of the government to defend him; to which if the general good-will of the people be added, it is hardly possible that any should be rash enough to conspire. For while in ordinary cases, the conspirator has ground for fear only before the execution of his villainy, in this case he has also cause to fear after the crime has been perpetrated, since he has the people for his enemy, and is thus cut off from every hope of shelter.

Of this, endless instances might be given, but I shall content myself with one that happened within the recollection of our fathers. Messer Annibale Bentivoglio, Lord of Bologna and grandfather of the present Messer Annibale, was conspired against and murdered by the Canneschi, leaving behind none belonging to him save Messer Giovanni, then an infant in arms. Immediately upon the murder, the people rose and put all the Canneschi to death. This resulted from the general goodwill with which the House of the Bentivogli was then regarded in Bologna; which feeling was so strong, that when upon the death of Messer Annibale no one was left who could govern the State, there being reason to believe that a descendant of the family (who up to that time had been thought to be the son of a smith), was living in Florence, the citizens of Bologna came there for him, and entrusted him with the government of their city; which he retained until Messer Giovanni was old enough to govern.

To be brief, a Prince has little to fear from conspiracies when his subjects are well disposed towards him; but when they are hostile and hold him in detestation, he has then reason to fear everything and every one. And well ordered States and wise Princes have provided with extreme care that the nobility shall not be driven to desperation, and that the commons shall be kept satisfied and contented; for this is one of the most important matters that a Prince has to look to.

Among the well ordered and governed Kingdoms of our day is that of France, wherein we find an infinite number of wise institutions, upon which depend the freedom and the security of the King, and of which the most important are the Parliament and its authority. For he who gave its constitution to this Realm, knowing the ambition and arrogance of the nobles, and judging it necessary to bridle and restrain them, and on the other hand knowing the hatred, originating in fear, entertained against them by the commons, and desiring that they should be safe, was unwilling that the responsibility for this should rest on the King; and to relieve him of the ill-will which he might incur with the nobles by favouring the commons, or with the commons by favouring the nobles, appointed a third party to be arbitrator, who without committing the King, might depress the nobles and uphold the commons. Nor could there be any better, wiser, or surer safeguard for the King and the Kingdom. And hence we may draw another notable lesson, namely, that Princes should devolve on others those matters that entail responsibility, and reserve to themselves those that relate to grace and favour. And again I say that a Prince should esteem the great, but must not make himself odious to the people.

To some it may perhaps appear, that if the lives and deaths of many of the Roman Emperors be considered, they offer examples opposed to the views expressed by me; since we find that some among them who had always lived good lives, and shown themselves possessed of great qualities, were nevertheless deposed and even put to death by their subjects who had conspired against them.

In answer to such objections, I shall examine the characters of several Emperors, and show that the causes of their downfall were in no way different from those which I have indicated. In doing this I shall submit for consideration such matters only as must strike every one who reads the history of these times; and it will be enough for my purpose to take those Emperors who reigned from the time of Marcus the Philosopher to the time of Maximinus, who were, inclusively, Marcus, Commodus his son, Pertinax, Julianus, Severus, Caracalla his son, Macrinus, Heliogabalus, Alexander, and Maximinus.

In the first place, then, we have to note that while in other Princedoms the Prince has only to contend with the ambition of the nobles and the insubordination of the people, the Roman Emperors had a further difficulty to encounter in the cruelty and rapacity of their soldiers, which were so distracting as to cause the ruin of many of these Princes. For it was hardly possible for them to satisfy both the soldiers and the people; the latter loving peace and therefore preferring sober Princes, while the former preferred a Prince of a warlike spirit, however harsh, haughty, or rapacious; being willing that he should exercise these qualities against the people, as the means of procuring for themselves double pay, and indulging their greed and cruelty.

Whence it followed that those Emperors who had not inherited or won for themselves such authority as enabled them to keep both people and soldiers in check, were always ruined. The most of them, and those especially who came to the Empire new and without experience, seeing the difficulty of dealing with these conflicting humours, set themselves to satisfy the soldiers, and made little account of offending the people. And for them this was a necessary course to take; for as Princes cannot escape being hated by some, they should, in the first place, endeavour not to be hated by a class; failing in which, they must do all they can to escape the hatred of that class which is the stronger. Wherefore those Emperors who, by reason of their newness, stood in need of extraordinary support, sided with the soldiery rather than with the people; a course which turned out advantageous or otherwise, according as the Prince knew, or did not know, how to maintain his authority over them.

From the causes indicated it resulted that Marcus, Pertinax, and Alexander, being Princes of a temperate disposition, lovers of justice, enemies of cruelty, gentle, and kindly, had all, save Marcus, an unhappy end. Marcus alone lived and died honoured in the highest degree; and this because he had succeeded to the Empire by right of inheritance, and not through the favour either of the soldiery or of the people; and also because, being endowed with many virtues which made him revered, he kept, while he lived, both factions within bounds, and was never either hated or despised.

But Pertinax was chosen Emperor against the will of the soldiery, who being accustomed to a licentious life under Commodus, could not tolerate the stricter discipline to which his successor sought to bring them back. And having thus made himself hated, and being at the same time despised by reason of his advanced age, he was ruined at the very outset of his reign.

And here it is to be noted that hatred is incurred as well on account of good actions as of bad; for which reason, as I have already said, a Prince who would maintain his authority is often compelled to be other than good. For when the class, be it the people, the soldiers, or the nobles, on whom you judge it necessary to rely for your support, is corrupt, you must needs adapt yourself to its humours, and satisfy these, in which case virtuous conduct will only prejudice you.

Let us now come to Alexander, who was so just a ruler that among the praises ascribed to him it is recorded, that, during the fourteen years he held the Empire, no man was ever put to death by him without trial. Nevertheless, being accounted effeminate, and thought to be governed by his mother, he fell into contempt, and the army conspiring against him, slew him.

When we turn to consider the characters of Commodus, Severus, and Caracalla, we find them all to have been most cruel and rapacious Princes, who to satisfy the soldiery, scrupled not to inflict every kind of wrong upon the people. And all of them, except Severus, came to a bad end. But in Severus there was such strength of character, that, keeping the soldiers his friends, he was able, although he oppressed the people, to reign on prosperously to the last; because his great qualities made him so admirable in the eyes both of the people and the soldiers, that the former remained in a manner amazed and awestruck, while the latter were respectful and contented.

And because his actions, for one who was a new Prince, were thus remarkable, I will point out shortly how well he understood to play the part both of the lion and of the fox, each of which natures, as I have observed before, a Prince should know how to assume.

Knowing the indolent disposition of the Emperor Julianus, Severus persuaded the army which he commanded in Illyria that it was their duty to go to Rome to avenge the death of Pertinax, who had been slain by the Pretorian guards. Under this pretext, and without disclosing his design on the Empire, he put his army in march, and reached Italy before it was known that he had set out. On his arrival in Rome, the Senate, through fear, elected him Emperor and put Julianus to death. After taking this first step, two obstacles still remained to his becoming sole master of the Empire; one in Asia, where Niger who commanded the armies of the East had caused himself to be proclaimed Emperor; the other in the West, where Albinus, who also aspired to the Empire, was in command. And as Severus judged it dangerous to declare open war against both, he resolved to proceed against Niger by arms, and against Albinus by artifice. To the latter, accordingly, he wrote, that having been chosen Emperor by the Senate, he desired to share the dignity with him; that he therefore sent him the title of Caesar, and in accordance with a resolution of the Senate assumed him as his colleague. All which statements Albinus accepted as true. But so soon as Severus had defeated and slain Niger, and restored tranquillity in the East, returning to Rome he complained in the Senate that Albinus, all unmindful of the favours he had received from him, had treacherously sought to destroy him; for which cause he was compelled to go and punish his ingratitude. Whereupon he set forth to seek Albinus in Gaul, where he at once deprived him of his dignities and his life.

Whoever, therefore, examines carefully the actions of this Emperor, will find in him all the fierceness of the lion and all the craft of the fox, and will note how he was feared and respected by the people, yet not hated by the army, and will not be surprised that though a new man, he was able to maintain his hold of so great an Empire. For the splendour of his reputation always shielded him from the odium which the people might otherwise have conceived against him by reason of his cruelty and rapacity.

Caracalla, his son, was likewise a man of great parts, endowed with qualities that made him admirable in the sight of the people, and endeared him to the army, being of a warlike spirit, most patient of fatigue, and contemning all luxury in food and every other effeminacy. Nevertheless, his ferocity and cruelty were so extravagant and unheard of (he having put to death a vast number of the inhabitants of Rome at different times, and the whole of those of Alexandria at a stroke), that he came to be detested by all the world, and so feared even by those whom he had about him, that at the last he was slain by a centurion in the midst of his army.

And here let it be noted that deaths like this which are the result of a deliberate and fixed resolve, cannot be escaped by Princes, since any one who disregards his own life can effect them. A Prince, however, needs the less to fear them as they are seldom attempted. The only precaution he can take is to avoid doing grave wrong to any of those who serve him, or whom he has near him as officers of his Court, a precaution which Caracalla neglected in putting to a shameful death the brother of this centurion, and in using daily threats against the man himself, whom he nevertheless retained as one of his bodyguard. This, as the event showed, was a rash and fatal course.

We come next to Commodus, who, as he took the Empire by hereditary right, ought to have held it with much ease. For being the son of Marcus, he had only to follow in his father's footsteps to content both the people and the soldiery. But being of a cruel and brutal nature, to sate his rapacity at the expense of the people, he sought support from the army, and indulged it in every kind of excess. On the other hand, by an utter disregard of his dignity, in frequently descending into the arena to fight with gladiators, and by other base acts wholly unworthy of the Imperial station, he became contemptible in the eyes of the soldiery; and being on the one hand hated, on the other despised, was at last conspired against and murdered.

The character of Maximinus remains to be touched upon. He was of a very warlike disposition, and on the death of Alexander, of whom we have already spoken, was chosen Emperor by the army who had been displeased with the effeminacy of that Prince. But this dignity he did not long enjoy, since two causes concurred to render him at once odious and contemptible; the one the baseness of his origin, he having at one time herded sheep in Thrace, a fact well known to all, and which led all to look on him with disdain; the other that on being proclaimed Emperor, delaying to repair to Rome and enter on possession of the Imperial throne, he incurred the reputation of excessive cruelty by reason of the many atrocities perpetrated by his prefects in Rome and other parts of the Empire. The result was that the whole world, stirred at once with scorn of his mean birth and with the hatred which the dread of his ferocity inspired, combined against him, Africa leading the way, the Senate and people of Rome and the whole of Italy following. In which conspiracy his own army joined. For they, being engaged in the siege of Aquileja and finding difficulty in reducing it, disgusted with his cruelty, and less afraid of him when they saw so many against him, put him to death.

I need say nothing of Heliogabalus, Macrinus, or Julianus, all of whom being utterly despicable, came to a speedy downfall, but shall conclude these remarks by observing, that the Princes of our own days are less troubled with the difficulty of having to make constant efforts to keep their soldiers in good humour. For though they must treat them with some indulgence, the need for doing so is soon over, since none of these Princes possesses a standing army which, like the armies of the Roman Empire, has strengthened with the growth of his government and the administration of his State. And if it was then necessary to satisfy the soldiers rather than the people, because the soldiers were more powerful than the people, now it is more necessary for all Princes, except the Turk and the Soldan, to satisfy the people rather than the soldiery, since the former are more powerful than the latter.

I except the Turk because he has always about him some twelve thousand foot soldiers and fifteen thousand horse, on whom depend the security and strength of his kingdom, and with whom he must needs keep on good terms, all regard for the people being subordinate. The government of the Soldan is similar, so that he too being wholly in the hands of his soldiers, must keep well with them without regard to the people.

And here you are to note that the State of the Soldan, while it is unlike all other Princedoms, resembles the Christian Pontificate in this, that it can neither be classed as new, nor as hereditary. For the sons of a Soldan who dies do not succeed to the kingdom as his heirs, but he who is elected to the post by those who have authority to make such elections. And this being the ancient and established order of things, the Princedom cannot be accounted new, since none of the difficulties that attend new Princedoms are found in it. For although the Prince be new, the institutions of the State are old, and are so contrived that the elected Prince is accepted as though he were an hereditary Sovereign.

But returning to the matter in hand, I say that whoever reflects on the above reasoning will see that either hatred or contempt was the ruin of the Emperors whom I have named; and will also understand how it happened that some taking one way and some the opposite, one only by each of these roads came to a happy, and all the rest to an unhappy end. Because for Pertinax and Alexander, they being new Princes, it was useless and hurtful to try to imitate Marcus, who was an hereditary Prince; and similarly for Caracalla, Commodus, and Maximinus it was a fatal error to imitate Severus, since they lacked the qualities that would have enabled them to tread in his footsteps.

In short, a Prince new to the Princedom cannot imitate the actions of Marcus, nor is it necessary that he should imitate all those of Severus; but he should borrow from Severus those parts of his conduct which are needed to serve as a foundation for his government, and from Marcus those suited to maintain it, and render it glorious when once established.

CHAPTER XX

Whether Fortresses, and Certain Other Expedients to Which Princes Often Have Recourse, are Profitable or Hurtful

To govern more securely some Princes have disarmed their subjects, others have kept the towns subject to them divided by factions; some have fostered hostility against themselves, others have sought to gain over those who at the beginning of their reign were looked on with suspicion; some have built fortresses, others have dismantled and destroyed them; and though no definite judgment can be pronounced respecting any of these methods, without regard to the special circumstances of the State to which it is proposed to apply them, I shall nevertheless speak of them in as comprehensive a way as the nature of the subject will admit.

It has never chanced that any new Prince has disarmed his subjects. On the contrary, when he has found them unarmed he has always armed them. For the arms thus provided become yours, those whom you suspected grow faithful, while those who were faithful at the first, continue so, and from your subjects become your partisans. And though all your subjects cannot be armed, yet if those of them whom you arm be treated with marked favour, you can deal more securely with the rest. For the difference which those whom you supply with arms perceive in their treatment, will bind them to you, while the others will excuse you, recognizing that those who incur greater risk and responsibility merit greater rewards. But by disarming, you at once give offence, since you show your subjects that you distrust them, either as doubting their courage, or as doubting their fidelity, each of which imputations begets hatred against you. Moreover, as you cannot maintain yourself without arms you must have recourse to mercenary troops. What these are I have already shown, but even if they were good, they could never avail to defend you, at once against powerful enemies abroad and against subjects whom you distrust. Wherefore, as I have said already, new Princes in new Princedoms have always provided for their being armed; and of instances of this History is full.

But when a Prince acquires a new State, which thus becomes joined on like a limb to his old possessions, he must disarm its inhabitants, except such of them as have taken part with him while he was acquiring it; and even these, as time and occasion serve, he should seek to render soft and effeminate; and he must so manage matters that all the arms of the new State shall be in the hands of his own soldiers who have served under him in his ancient dominions.

Our forefathers, even such among them as were esteemed wise, were wont to say that 'Pistoja was to be held by feuds, and Pisa by fortresses,' and on this principle used to promote dissensions in various subject towns with a view to retain them with less effort. At a time when Italy was in some measure in equilibrium, this may have been a prudent course to follow; but at the present day it seems impossible to recommend it as a general rule of policy. For I do not believe that divisions purposely caused can ever lead to good; on the contrary, when an enemy approaches, divided cities are lost at once, for the weaker faction will always side with the invader, and the other will not be able to stand alone.

The Venetians, influenced as I believe by the reasons above mentioned, fostered the factions of Guelf and Ghibelline in the cities subject to them; and though they did not suffer blood to be shed, fomented their feuds, in order that the citizens having their minds occupied with these disputes might not conspire against them. But this, as we know, did not turn out to their advantage, for after their defeat at Vaila, one of the two factions, suddenly taking courage, deprived them of the whole of their territory.

Moreover methods like these argue weakness in a Prince, for under a strong government such divisions would never be permitted, since they are profitable only in time of peace as an expedient whereby subjects may be more easily managed; but when war breaks out their insufficiency is demonstrated.

Doubtless, Princes become great by vanquishing difficulties and opposition, and Fortune, on that account, when she desires to aggrandize a new Prince, who has more need than an hereditary Prince to win reputation, causes enemies to spring up, and urges them on to attack him, to the end that he may have opportunities to overcome them, and make his ascent by the very ladder which they have planted. For which reason, many are of the opinion that a wise Prince, when he has the occasion, ought dexterously to promote hostility to himself in certain quarters, in order that his greatness may be enhanced by crushing it.

Princes, and new Princes especially, have found greater fidelity and helpfulness in those whom, at the beginning of their reign, they have held in suspicion, than in those who at the outset have enjoyed their confidence; and Pandolfo Petrucci, Lord of Siena, governed his State by the instrumentality of those whom he had at one time distrusted, in preference to all others. But on this point it is impossible to lay down any general rule, since the course to be followed varies with the circumstances. This only I will say, that those men who at the beginning of a reign have been hostile, if of a sort requiring support to maintain them, may always be won over by the Prince with much ease, and are the more bound to serve him faithfully because they know that they have to efface by their conduct the unfavourable impression he had formed of them; and in this way a Prince always obtains better help from them, than from those who serving him in too complete security neglect his affairs.

And since the subject suggests it, I must not fail to remind the Prince who acquires a new State through the favour of its inhabitants, to weigh well what were the causes which led those who favoured him to do so; and if it be seen that they have acted not from any natural affection for him, but merely out of discontent with the former government, that he will find the greatest difficulty in keeping them his friends, since it will be impossible for him to content them. Carefully considering the cause of this, with the aid of examples taken from times ancient and modern, he will perceive that it is far easier to secure the friendship of those who being satisfied with things as they stood, were for that very reason his enemies, than of those who sided with him and aided him in his usurpation only because they were discontented.

It has been customary for Princes, with a view to hold their dominions more securely, to build fortresses which might serve as a curb and restraint on such as have designs against them, and as a safe refuge against a first onset. I approve this custom, because it has been followed from the earliest times. Nevertheless, in our own days, Messer Niccolo Vitelli thought it prudent to dismantle two fortresses in Città di Castello in order to secure that town: and Guido Ubaldo, Duke of Urbino, on returning to his dominions, whence he had been driven by Cesare Borgia, razed to their foundations the fortresses throughout the Dukedom, judging that if these were removed, it would not again be so easily lost. A like course was followed by the Bentivogli on their return to Bologna.

Fortresses, therefore, are useful or no, according to circumstances, and if in one way they benefit, in another they injure you. We may state the case thus: the Prince who is more afraid of his subjects than of strangers ought to build fortresses, while he who is more afraid of strangers than of his subjects, should leave them alone. The citadel built by Francesco Sforza in Milan, has been, and will hereafter prove to be, more dangerous to the House of Sforza than any other disorder of that State. So that, on the whole, the best fortress you can have, is in not being hated by your subjects. If they hate you no fortress will save you; for when once the people take up arms, foreigners are never wanting to assist them.

Within our own time it does not appear that fortresses have been of service to any Prince, unless to the Countess of Forli after her husband Count Girolamo was murdered; for by this means she was able to escape the first onset of the insurgents, and awaiting succour from Milan, to recover her State; the circumstances of the times not allowing any foreigner to lend assistance to the people. But afterwards, when she was attacked by Cesare Borgia, and the people, out of hostility to her, took part with the invader, her fortresses were of little avail. So that, both on this and on the former occasion, it would have been safer for her to have had no fortresses, than to have had her subjects for enemies.

All which considerations taken into account, I shall applaud him who builds fortresses, and him who does not; but I shall blame him who, trusting in them, reckons it a light thing to be held in hatred by his people.

CHAPTER XXI

How a Prince Should Bear Himself So As to Acquire Reputation

Nothing makes a Prince so well thought of as to undertake great enterprises and give striking proofs of his capacity.

Among the Princes of our time Ferdinand of Aragon, the present King of Spain, may almost be accounted a new Prince, since from one of the weakest he has become, for fame and glory, the foremost King in Christendom. And if you consider his achievements you will find them all great and some extraordinary.

In the beginning of his reign he made war on Granada, which enterprise was the foundation of his power. At first he carried on the war leisurely, without fear of interruption, and kept the attention and thoughts of the Barons of Castile so completely occupied with it, that they had no time to think of changes at home. Meanwhile he insensibly acquired reputation among them and authority over them. With the money of the Church and of his subjects he was able to maintain his armies, and during the prolonged contest to lay the foundations of that military discipline which afterwards made him so famous. Moreover, to enable him to engage in still greater undertakings, always covering himself with the cloak of religion, he had recourse to what may be called *pious cruelty,* in driving out and clearing his Kingdom of the Moors; than which exploit none could be more wonderful or uncommon. Using the same pretext he made war on Africa, invaded Italy, and finally attacked France; and being thus constantly busied in planning and executing vast designs, he kept the minds of his subjects in suspense and admiration, and occupied with the results of his actions, which arose one out of another in such close succession as left neither time nor opportunity to oppose them.

Again, it greatly profits a Prince in conducting the internal government of his State, to follow striking methods, such as are recorded of Messer Bernabo of Milan, whenever the remarkable actions of any one in civil life, whether for good or for evil, afford him occasion; and to choose such ways of rewarding and punishing as cannot fail to be much spoken of. But above all, he should strive by all his actions to inspire a sense of his greatness and goodness.

A Prince is likewise esteemed who is a stanch friend and a thorough foe, that is to say, who without reserve openly declares for one against another, this being always a more advantageous course than to stand neutral. For supposing two of your powerful neighbours come to blows, it must either be that you have, or have not, reason to fear the one who comes off victorious. In either case it will always be well for you to declare yourself, and join in frankly with one side or other. For should you fail to do so you are certain, in the former of the cases put, to become the prey of the victor to the satisfaction and delight of the vanquished, and no reason or circumstance that you may plead will avail to shield or shelter you; for the victor dislikes doubtful friends, and such as will not help him at a pinch; and the vanquished will have nothing to say to you, since you would not share his fortunes sword in hand.

When Antiochus, at the instance of the Aetolians, passed into Greece in order to drive out the Romans, he sent envoys to the Achaians, who were friendly to the Romans, exhorting them to stand neutral. The Romans, on the other hand, urged them to take up arms on their behalf. The matter coming to be discussed in the Council of the Achaians, the legate of Antiochus again urged neutrality, whereupon the Roman envoy answered—'Nothing can be less to your advantage than the course which has been recommended as the best and most useful for your State, namely, to refrain from taking any part in our war, for by standing aloof you will gain neither favour nor fame, but remain the prize of the victor.' And it will always happen that he who is not your friend will invite you to neutrality, while he who is your friend will call on you to declare yourself openly in arms. Irresolute Princes, to escape immediate danger, commonly follow the neutral path, in most instances to their destruction. But when you pronounce valiantly in favour of one side or other, if he to whom you give your adherence conquers, although he be powerful and you are at his mercy, still he is under obligations to you, and has become your friend; and none are so lost to shame as to destroy with manifest ingratitude, one who has helped them. Besides which, victories are never so complete that the victor can afford to disregard all considerations whatsoever, more especially considerations of justice. On the other hand, if he with whom you take part should lose, you will always be favourably regarded by him; while he can he will aid you, and you become his companion in a cause which may recover.

In the second case, namely, when both combatants are of such limited strength that whichever wins you have no cause to fear, it is all the more prudent for you to take a side, for you will then be ruining the one with the help of the other, who were he wise would endeavour to save him. If he whom you help conquers, he remains in your power, and with your aid he cannot but conquer.

And here let it be noted that a Prince should be careful never to join with one stronger than himself in attacking others, unless, as already said, he be driven to it by necessity. For if he whom you join prevails, you are at his mercy; and Princes, so far as in them lies, should avoid placing themselves at the mercy of others. The Venetians, although they might have declined the alliance, joined with France against the Duke of Milan, which brought about their ruin. But when an alliance cannot be avoided, as was the case with the Florentines when the Pope and Spain together led their armies to attack Lombardy, a Prince, for the reasons given, must take a side. Nor let it be supposed that any State can choose for itself a perfectly safe line of policy. On the contrary, it must reckon on every course which it may take being doubtful; for it happens in all human affairs that we never seek to escape one mischief without falling into another. Prudence therefore consists in knowing how to distinguish degrees of disadvantage, and in accepting a less evil as a good.

Again, a Prince should show himself a patron of merit, and should honour those who excel in every art. He ought accordingly to encourage his subjects by enabling them to pursue their callings, whether mercantile, agricultural, or any other, in security, so that this man shall not be deterred from beautifying his possessions from the apprehension that they may be taken from him, or that other refrain from opening a trade through fear of taxes; and he should provide rewards for those who desire so to employ themselves, and for all who are disposed in any way to add to the greatness of his City or State.

He ought, moreover, at suitable seasons of the year to entertain the people with festivals and shows. And because all cities are divided into guilds and companies, he should show attention to these societies, and sometimes take part in their meetings; offering an example of courtesy and munificence, but always maintaining the dignity of his station, which must under no circumstances be compromised.

Sun Tzu, THE ART OF WAR (Trans. by Samuel B. Griffith)

Karl von Clausewitz, ON WAR (Trans. by J. J. Graham)

Alfred Thayer Mahan, THE INFLUENCE OF SEA POWER UPON HISTORY 1660-1783

1. Explain the five factors upon which Sun Tzu says military victory depends.

2. Compare and contrast the views of Sun Tzu and Clausewitz concerning the object of war.

3. What are the main points in Sun Tzu's strategy and tactics?

4. How does Clausewitz define war?

5. How does Clausewitz differentiate between war in theory, or in the abstract, from war in practice, in the "real world"?

6. What does Clausewitz mean by the statement, "War is never an isolated act"?

7. What is the object of a war?

8. What is the relation between war and policy?

9. Which is stronger in war, the offense or the defense? Explain.

10. What distinctions does Mahan draw between naval strategy and naval tactics?

11. What role does he see for sea power in the United States?

12. According to Mahan's reasoning, what would be some of the major strategic waterways of the world?

13. What is Mahan's criticism of what he refers to as the *guerre de course?*

14. What is the essence of Mahan's strategic doctrine?
    What are the implications of this for current U.S.
    defense policy and for the military budget?

    As the British military historian and analyst, B.
H. Liddell Hart, has noted, "Sun Tzu's essays on 'The
Art of War' form the earliest known treatises on the
subject... Among all the military thinkers of the past,
only Clausewitz is comparable." Written about 500 B.C.,
The Art of War remains a fresh and clear commentary on
war in any age.

THE ART OF WAR

I

ESTIMATES[1]

SUN TZU said:

1. War is a matter of vital importance to the State; the province of life or death; the road to survival or ruin.[2] It is mandatory that it be thoroughly studied.

> *Li Ch'üan*: 'Weapons are tools of ill omen.' War is a grave matter; one is apprehensive lest men embark upon it without due reflection.

2. Therefore, appraise it in terms of the five fundamental factors and make comparisons of the seven elements later named.[3] So you may assess its essentials.

3. The first of these factors is moral influence; the second, weather; the third, terrain; the fourth, command; and the fifth, doctrine.[4]

> *Chang Yü*: The systematic order above is perfectly clear. When troops are raised to chastise transgressors, the temple council first considers the adequacy of the rulers' benevolence

---

[1] The title means 'reckoning', 'plans', or 'calculations'. In the Seven Military Classics edition the title is 'Preliminary Calculations'. The subject first discussed is the process we define as an Estimate (or Appreciation) of the Situation.

[2] Or 'for [the field of battle] is the place of life and death [and war] the road to survival or ruin'.

[3] Sun Hsing-yen follows the *T'ung T'ien* here and drops the character *shih* (事): 'matters', 'factors', or 'affairs'. Without it the verse does not make much sense.

[4] Here *Tao* (道) is translated 'moral influence'. It is usually rendered as 'The Way', or 'The Right Way'. Here it refers to the morality of government; specifically to that of the sovereign. If the sovereign governs justly, benevolently, and righteously, he follows the Right Path or the Right Way, and thus exerts a superior degree of moral influence. The character *fa* (法), here rendered 'doctrine', has as a primary meaning 'law' or 'method'. In the title of the work it is translated 'Art'. But in v. 8 Sun Tzu makes it clear that here he is talking about what we call doctrine.

and the confidence of their peoples; next, the appropriateness of nature's seasons, and finally the difficulties of the topography. After thorough deliberation of these three matters a general is appointed to launch the attack.[1] After troops have crossed the borders, responsibility for laws and orders devolves upon the general.

4. By moral influence I mean that which causes the people to be in harmony with their leaders, so that they will accompany them in life and unto death without fear of mortal peril.[2]

Chang Yü: When one treats people with benevolence, justice, and righteousness, and reposes confidence in them, the army will be united in mind and all will be happy to serve their leaders. The Book of Changes says: 'In happiness at overcoming difficulties, people forget the danger of death.'

5. By weather I mean the interaction of natural forces; the effects of winter's cold and summer's heat and the conduct of military operations in accordance with the seasons.[3]

6. By terrain I mean distances, whether the ground is traversed with ease or difficulty, whether it is open or constricted, and the chances of life or death.

Mei Yao-ch'en: . . . When employing troops it is essential to know beforehand the conditions of the terrain. Knowing the distances, one can make use of an indirect or a direct plan. If he knows the degree of ease or difficulty of traversing the ground he can estimate the advantages of using infantry or cavalry. If he knows where the ground is constricted and

---

[1] There are precise terms in Chinese which cannot be uniformly rendered by our word 'attack'. Chang Yü here uses a phrase which literally means 'to chastise criminals', an expression applied to attack of rebels. Other characters have such precise meanings as 'to attack by stealth', 'to attack suddenly', 'to suppress the rebellious', 'to reduce to submission', &c.

[2] Or 'Moral influence is that which causes the people to be in accord with their superiors. . . .' Ts'ao Ts'ao says the people are guided in the right way (of conduct) by 'instructing' them.

[3] It is clear that the character *t'ien* (天) (Heaven) is used in this verse in the sense of 'weather', as it is today.

where open he can calculate the size of force appropriate. If he knows where he will give battle he knows when to concentrate or divide his forces.[1]

7. By command I mean the general's qualities of wisdom, sincerity, humanity, courage, and strictness.

Li Ch'üan: These five are the virtues of the general. Hence the army refers to him as 'The Respected One'.

Tu Mu:. . . . If wise, a commander is able to recognize changing circumstances and to act expediently. If sincere, his men will have no doubt of the certainty of rewards and punishments. If humane, he loves mankind, sympathizes with others, and appreciates their industry and toil. If courageous, he gains victory by seizing opportunity without hesitation. If strict, his troops are disciplined because they are in awe of him and are afraid of punishment.

Shen Pao-hsu . . . said: 'If a general is not courageous he will be unable to conquer doubts or to create great plans.'

8. By doctrine I mean organization, control, assignment of appropriate ranks to officers, regulation of supply routes, and the provision of principal items used by the army.

9. There is no general who has not heard of these five matters. Those who master them win; those who do not are defeated.

10. Therefore in laying plans compare the following elements, appraising them with the utmost care.

11. If you say which ruler possesses moral influence, which commander is the more able, which army obtains the advantages of nature and the terrain, in which regulations and instructions are better carried out, which troops are the stronger;[2]

Chang Yü: Chariots strong, horses fast, troops valiant, weapons sharp—so that when they hear the drums beat the

---

[1] 'Knowing the ground of life and death . . .' is here rendered 'If he knows where he will give battle'.

[2] In this and the following two verses the seven elements referred to in v. 2 are named.

attack they are happy, and when they hear the gongs sound the retirement they are enraged. He who is like this is strong.

12. Which has the better trained officers and men;

Tu Yu: ... Therefore Master Wang said: 'If officers are unaccustomed to rigorous drilling they will be worried and hesitant in battle; if generals are not thoroughly trained they will inwardly quail when they face the enemy.'

13. And which administers rewards and punishments in a more enlightened manner;

Tu Mu: Neither should be excessive.

14. I will be able to forecast which side will be victorious and which defeated.

15. If a general who heeds my strategy is employed he is certain to win. Retain him! When one who refuses to listen to my strategy is employed, he is certain to be defeated. Dismiss him!

16. Having paid heed to the advantages of my plans, the general must create situations which will contribute to their accomplishment.[1] By 'situations' I mean that he should act expediently in accordance with what is advantageous and so control the balance.

17. All warfare is based on deception.

18. Therefore, when capable, feign incapacity; when active, inactivity.

19. When near, make it appear that you are far away; when far away, that you are near.

20. Offer the enemy a bait to lure him; feign disorder and strike him.

Tu Mu: The Chao general Li Mu released herds of cattle

---

[1] Emending *i* (以) to *i* (㠯). The commentators do not agree on an interpretation of this verse.

with their shepherds; when the Hsiung Nu had advanced a short distance he feigned a retirement, leaving behind several thousand men as if abandoning them. When the Khan heard this news he was delighted, and at the head of a strong force marched to the place. Li Mu put most of his troops into formations on the right and left wings, made a horning attack, crushed the Huns and slaughtered over one hundred thousand of their horsemen.[1]

21. When he concentrates, prepare against him; where he is strong, avoid him.

22. Anger his general and confuse him.

Li Ch'uan: If the general is choleric his authority can easily be upset. His character is not firm.

Chang Yü: If the enemy general is obstinate and prone to anger, insult and enrage him, so that he will be irritated and confused, and without a plan will recklessly advance against you.

23. Pretend inferiority and encourage his arrogance.

Tu Mu: Toward the end of the Ch'in dynasty, Mo Tun of the Hsiung Nu first established his power. The Eastern Hu were strong and sent ambassadors to parley. They said: 'We wish to obtain T'ou Ma's thousand-*li* horse.' Mo Tun consulted his advisers, who all exclaimed: 'The thousand-*li* horse! The most precious thing in this country! Do not give them that!' Mo Tun replied: 'Why begrudge a horse to a neighbour?' So he sent the horse.[2]

Shortly after, the Eastern Hu sent envoys who said: 'We wish one of the Khan's princesses.' Mo Tun asked advice of his ministers who all angrily said: 'The Eastern Hu are unrighteous! Now they even ask for a princess! We implore

---

[1] The Hsiung Nu were nomads who caused the Chinese trouble for centuries. The Great Wall was constructed to protect China from their incursions.

[2] Mo Tun, or T'ou Ma or T'ouman, was the first leader to unite the Hsiung Nu. The thousand-*li* horse was a stallion reputedly able to travel a thousand *li* (about three hundred miles) without grass or water. The term indicates a horse of exceptional quality, undoubtedly reserved for breeding.

you to attack them!' Mo Tun said: 'How can one begrudge his neighbour a young woman?' So he gave the woman.

A short time later, the Eastern Hu returned and said: 'You have a thousand *li* of unused land which we want.' Mo Tun consulted his advisers. Some said it would be reasonable to cede the land, others that it would not. Mo Tun was enraged and said: 'Land is the foundation of the State. How could one give it away?' All those who had advised doing so were beheaded.

Mo Tun then sprang on his horse, ordered that all who remained behind were to be beheaded, and made a surprise attack on the Eastern Hu. The Eastern Hu were contemptuous of him and had made no preparations. When he attacked he annihilated them. MoTun then turned westward and attacked the Yueh Ti. To the south he annexed Lou Fan . . . and invaded Yen. He completely recovered the ancestral lands of the Hsiung Nu previously conquered by the Ch'in general Meng T'ien.[1]

Ch'en Hao: Give the enemy young boys and women to infatuate him, and jades and silks to excite his ambitions.

24. Keep him under a strain and wear him down.

Li Ch'üan: When the enemy is at ease, tire him.

Tu Mu: . . . Toward the end of the Later Han, after Ts'ao Ts'ao had defeated Liu Pei, Pei fled to Yuan Shao, who then led out his troops intending to engage Ts'ao Ts'ao. T'ien Fang, one of Yuan Shao's staff officers, said: 'Ts'ao Ts'ao is expert at employing troops; one cannot go against him heedlessly. Nothing is better than to protract things and keep him at a distance. You, General, should fortify along the mountains and rivers and hold the four prefectures. Externally, make alliances with powerful leaders; internally, pursue an agro-military policy.[2] Later, select crack troops

---

[1] Meng T'ien subdued the border nomads during the Ch'in, and began the construction of the Great Wall. It is said that he invented the writing-brush. This is probably not correct, but he may have improved the existing brush in some way.

[2] This refers to agricultural military colonies in remote areas in which soldiers

and form them into extraordinary units. Taking advantage of spots where he is unprepared, make repeated sorties and disturb the country south of the river. When he comes to aid the right, attack his left; when he goes to succour the left, attack the right; exhaust him by causing him continually to run about. . . . Now if you reject this victorious strategy and decide instead to risk all on one battle, it will be too late for regrets.' Yuan Shao did not follow this advice and therefore was defeated.[1]

25. When he is united, divide him.

Chang Yü: Sometimes drive a wedge between a sovereign and his ministers; on other occasions separate his allies from him. Make them mutually suspicious so that they drift apart. Then you can plot against them.

26. Attack where he is unprepared; sally out when he does not expect you.

Ho Yen-hsi: . . . Li Ching of the T'ang proposed ten plans to be used against Hsiao Hsieh, and the entire responsibility of commanding the armies was entrusted to him. In the eighth month he collected his forces at K'uei Chou.[2]

As it was the season of the autumn floods the waters of the Yangtze were overflowing and the roads by the three gorges were perilous, Hsiao Hsieh thought it certain that Li Ching would not advance against him. Consequently he made no preparations.

In the ninth month Li Ching took command of the troops and addressed them as follows: 'What is of the greatest importance in war is extraordinary speed; one cannot afford

---

and their families were settled. A portion of the time was spent cultivating the land, the remainder in drilling, training, and fighting when necessary. The Russians used this policy in colonizing Siberia. And it is in effect now in Chinese borderlands.

[1] During the period known as 'The Three Kingdoms', Wei in the north and west, Shu in the south-west, and Wu in the Yangtze valley contested for empire.

[2] K'uei Chou is in Ssu Ch'uan.

to neglect opportunity. Now we are concentrated and Hsiao Hsieh does not yet know of it. Taking advantage of the fact that the river is in flood, we will appear unexpectedly under the walls of his capital. As is said: 'When the thunder-clap comes, there is no time to cover the ears.' Even if he should discover us, he cannot on the spur of the moment devise a plan to counter us, and surely we can capture him.'

He advanced to I Ling and Hsiao Hsieh began to be afraid and summoned reinforcements from south of the river, but these were unable to arrive in time. Li Ching laid siege to the city and Hsieh surrendered.

'To sally forth where he does not expect you' means as when, toward its close, the Wei dynasty sent Generals Chung Hui and Teng Ai to attack Shu.[1]. . . In winter, in the tenth month, Ai left Yin P'ing and marched through uninhabited country for over seven hundred *li*, chiselling roads through the mountains and building suspension bridges. The mountains were high, the valleys deep, and this task was extremely difficult and dangerous. Also, the army, about to run out of provisions, was on the verge of perishing. Teng Ai wrapped himself in felt carpets and rolled down the steep mountain slopes; generals and officers clambered up by grasping limbs of trees. Scaling the precipices like strings of fish, the army advanced.

Teng Ai appeared first at Chiang Yu in Shu, and Ma Mou, the general charged with its defence, surrendered. Teng Ai beheaded Chu-ko Chan, who resisted at Mien-chu, and marched on Ch'eng Tu. The King of Shu, Liu Shan, surrendered.

27. These are the strategist's keys to victory. It is not possible to discuss them beforehand.

Mei Yao-ch'en: When confronted by the enemy respond to changing circumstances and devise expedients. How can these be discussed beforehand?

---

[1] This campaign was conducted *c.* A.D. 255.

28. Now if the estimates made in the temple before hostilities indicate victory it is because calculations show one's strength to be superior to that of his enemy; if they indicate defeat, it is because calculations show that one is inferior. With many calculations, one can win; with few one cannot. How much less chance of victory has one who makes none at all! By this means I examine the situation and the outcome will be clearly apparent.[1]

[1] A confusing verse difficult to render into English. In the preliminary calculations some sort of counting devices were used. The operative character represents such a device, possibly a primitive abacus. We do not know how the various 'factors' and 'elements' named were weighted, but obviously the process of comparison of relative strengths was a rational one. It appears also that two separate calculations were made, the first on a national level, the second on a strategic level. In the former the five basic elements named in v. 3 were compared; we may suppose that if the results of this were favourable the military experts compared strengths, training, equity in administering rewards and' punishments, and so on (the seven factors).

Karl von Clausewitz wrote his great treatise *On War* during a twelve year period from 1818 to 1830 when he, as a major general in the Prussian Army, served as director of the War Academy in Berlin. His military theories are based largely upon his own experiences and observations of the campaigns of Napoleon. Clausewitz died in 1831 without a chance to complete the revision of the manuscript which he had intended. His wife, with the assistance of friends, edited and published it. Its influence has been world-wide. Actually, some of the ideas attributed to Clausewitz are the result of misinterpretation by overly zealous followers.

ON WAR

BOOK I

ON THE NATURE OF WAR

CHAPTER I

WHAT IS WAR?

I. INTRODUCTION.

WE propose to consider first the single elements of our subject, then each branch or part, and, last of all, the whole, in all its relations—therefore to advance from the simple to the complex. But it is necessary for us to commence with a glance at the nature of the whole, because it is particularly necessary that in the consideration of any of the parts their relation to the whole should be kept constantly in view.

2. DEFINITION.

We shall not enter into any of the abstruse definitions of War used by publicists. We shall keep to the element of the thing itself, to a duel. War is nothing but a duel on an extensive scale. If we would conceive as a unit the countless number of duels which make up a War, we shall do so best by supposing to ourselves two wrestlers. Each strives by physical force to compel the other to submit to his will : each endeavours to throw his adversary, and thus render him incapable of further resistance.

War therefore is an act of violence intended to compel our opponent to fulfil our will.

Violence arms itself with the inventions of Art and Science in order to contend against violence. Self-imposed restrictions, almost imperceptible and hardly worth mentioning, termed usages of International Law, accompany it without essentially impairing its power. Violence, that is to say, physical force (for there is no moral force without the conception of States and Law), is therefore the *means ;* the compulsory submission of the enemy to our will is the ultimate *object.* In order to attain this object fully, the enemy must be disarmed, and disarmament becomes therefore the immediate object of hostilities in theory. It takes the place of the final object, and puts it aside as something we can eliminate from our calculations.

3. UTMOST USE OF FORCE.

Now, philanthropists may easily imagine there is a skilful method of disarming and overcoming an enemy without causing great bloodshed, and that this is the proper tendency of the Art of War. However plausible this may appear, still it is an error which must be extirpated ; for in such dangerous things as War, the errors which proceed from a spirit of benevolence are the worst. As the use of physical power to the utmost extent by no means excludes the co-operation of the intelligence, it follows that he who uses force unsparingly, without reference to the bloodshed involved, must obtain a superiority if his adversary uses less vigour in its application. The former then dictates the law to the latter, and both proceed to extremities to which the only limitations are those imposed by the amount of counteracting force on each side.

This is the way in which the matter must be viewed

and it is to no purpose, it is even against one's own interest, to turn away from the consideration of the real nature of the affair because the horror of its elements excites repugnance.

If the Wars of civilised people are less cruel and destrucsive than those of savages, the difference arises from the social condition both of States in themselves and in their relations to each other. Out of this social condition and its relations War arises, and by it War is subjected to conditions, is controlled and modified. But these things do not belong to War itself ; they are only given conditions ; and to introduce into the philosophy of War itself a principle of moderation would be an absurdity.

Two motives lead men to War : instinctive hostility and hostile intention. In our definition of War, we have chosen as its characteristic the latter of these elements, because it is the most general. It is impossible to conceive the passion of hatred of the wildest description, bordering on mere instinct, without combining with it the idea of a hostile intention. On the other hand, hostile intentions may often exist without being accompanied by any, or at all events by any extreme, hostility of feeling. Amongst savages views emanating from the feelings, amongst civilised nations those emanating from the understanding, have the predominance ; but this difference arises from attendant circumstances, existing institutions, &c., and, therefore, is not to be found necessarily in all cases, although it prevails in the majority. In short, even the most civilised nations may burn with passionate hatred of each other.

We may see from this what a fallacy it would be to refer the War of a civilised nation entirely to an intelligent act on the part of the Government, and to imagine it as continually freeing itself more and more from all feeling of passion in such a way that at last the physical masses of combatants would no longer be required ; in reality, their mere relations would suffice—a kind of algebraic action.

Theory was beginning to drift in this direction until the facts of the last War * taught it better. If War is an *act* of force, it belongs necessarily also to the feelings. If it does not originate in the feelings, it *reacts*, more or less, upon them, and the extent of this reaction depends not on the degree of civilisation, but upon the importance and duration of the interests involved.

Therefore, if we find civilised nations do not put their prisoners to death, do not devastate towns and countries, this is because their intelligence exercises greater influence on their mode of carrying on War, and has taught them more effectual means of applying force than these rude acts of mere instinct.   The invention of gunpowder, the constant progress of improvements in the construction of firearms, are sufficient proofs that the tendency to destroy the adversary which lies at the bottom of the conception of War is in no way changed or modified through the progress of civilisation.

We therefore repeat our proposition, that War is an act of violence pushed to its utmost bounds ; as one side dictates the law to the other, there arises a sort of reciprocal action, which logically must lead to an extreme.   This is the first reciprocal action, and the first extreme with which we meet (*first reciprocal action*).

4. THE AIM IS TO DISARM THE ENEMY.

We have already said that the aim of all action in War is to disarm the enemy, and we shall now show that this, theoretically at least, is indispensable.

* Clauswitz alludes here to the " Wars of Liberation," 1813, 14, 15.

If our opponent is to be made to comply with our will, we must place him in a situation which is more oppressive to him than the sacrifice which we demand ; but the disadvantages of this position must naturally not be of a transitory nature, at least in appearance, otherwise the enemy, instead of yielding, will hold out, in the prospect of a change for the better. Every change in this position which is produced by a continuation of the War should therefore be a change for the worse. The worst condition in which a belligerent can be placed is that of being completely disarmed. If, therefore, the enemy is to be reduced to submission by an act of War, he must either be positively disarmed or placed in such a position that he is threatened with it. From this it follows that the disarming or overthrow of the enemy, whichever we call it, must always be the aim of Warfare. Now War is always the shock of two hostile bodies in collision, not the action of a living power upon an inanimate mass, because an absolute state of endurance would not be making War ; therefore, what we have just said as to the aim of action in War applies to both parties. Here, then, is another case of reciprocal action. As long as the enemy is not defeated, he may defeat me ; then I shall be no longer my own master ; he will dictate the law to me as I did to him. This is the second reciprocal action, and leads to a second extreme (*second reciprocal action*).

5. UTMOST EXERTION OF POWERS.

If we desire to defeat the enemy, we must proportion our efforts to his powers of resistance. This is expressed by the product of two factors which cannot be separated, namely, *the sum of available means* and *the strength of the Will*. The sum of the available means may be estimated in a measure, as it depends (although not entirely) upon numbers ; but the strength of volition is more difficult to determine, and can only be estimated to a certain extent by the strength of the motives. Granted we have obtained in this way an approximation to the strength of the power to be contended with, we can then take a review of our own means, and either increase them so as to obtain a preponderance, or, in case we have not the resources to effect this, then do our best by increasing our means as far as possible. But the adversary does the same ; therefore, there is a new mutual enhancement, which, in pure conception, must create a fresh effort towards an extreme. This is the third case of reciprocal action, and a third extreme with which we meet (*third reciprocal action*).

6. MODIFICATION IN THE REALITY.

Thus reasoning in the abstract, the mind cannot stop short of an extreme,because it has to deal with an extreme, with a conflict of forces left to themselves, and obeying no other but their own inner laws. If we should seek to deduce from the pure conception of War an absolute point for the aim which we shall propose and for the means which we shall apply, this constant reciprocal action would involve us in extremes, which would be nothing but a play of ideas produced by an almost invisible train of logical subtleties. If, adhering closely to the absolute, we try to avoid all difficulties by a stroke of the pen, and insist with logical strictness that in every case the extreme must be the object, and the utmost effort must be exerted in that direction, such a stroke of the pen would be a mere paper law, not by any means adapted to the real world.

Even supposing this extreme tension of forces was an

absolute which could easily be ascertained, still we must admit that the human mind would hardly submit itself to this kind of logical chimera. There would be in many cases an unnecessary waste of power, which would be in opposition to other principles of statecraft ; an effort of Will would be required disproportioned to the proposed object, which therefore it would be impossible to realise, for the human will does not derive its impulse from logical subtleties.

But everything takes a different shape when we pass from abstractions to reality. In the former, everything must be subject to optimism, and we must imagine the one side as well as the other striving after perfection and even attaining it. Will this ever take place in reality ? It will if,

(1) War becomes a completely isolated act, which arises suddenly, and is in no way connected with the previous history of the combatant States.

(2) If it is limited to a single solution, or to several simultaneous solutions.

(3) If it contains within itself the solution perfect and complete, free from any reaction upon it, through a calculation beforehand of the political situation which will follow from it.

7. WAR IS NEVER AN ISOLATED ACT.

With regard to the first point, neither of the two opponents is an abstract person to the other, not even as regards that factor in the sum of resistance which does not depend on objective things, viz., the Will. This Will is not an entirely unknown quantity ; it indicates what it will be to-morrow by what it is to-day. War does not spring up quite suddenly, it does not spread to the full in a moment ; each of the two opponents can, therefore, form an opinion of the other, in a great measure, from what he is and what he does, instead of judging of him according to what he, strictly speaking, should be or should do. But, now, man with his incomplete organisation is always below the line of absolute perfection, and thus these deficiencies, having an influence on both sides, become a modifying principle.

8. WAR DOES NOT CONSIST OF A SINGLE INSTANTANEOUS BLOW.

The second point gives rise to the following considerations :—

If War ended in a single solution, or a number of simultaneous ones, then naturally all the preparations for the same would have a tendency to the extreme, for an omission could not in any way be repaired ; the utmost, then, that the world of reality could furnish as a guide for us would be the preparations of the enemy, as far as they are known to us ; all the rest would fall into the domain of the abstract. But if the result is made up from several successive acts, then naturally that which precedes with all its phases may be taken as a measure for that which will follow, and in this manner the world of reality again takes the place of the abstract, and thus modifies the effort towards the extreme.

Yet every War would necessarily resolve itself into a single solution, or a sum of simultaneous results, if all the means required for the struggle were raised at once, or could be at once raised ; for as one adverse result necessarily diminishes the means, then if all the means have been applied in the first, a second cannot properly be supposed. All hostile acts which might follow would belong essentially to the first, and form in reality only its duration.

But we have already seen that even in the preparation for War the real world steps into the place of mere abstract conception—a material standard into the place of the hypotheses of an extreme : that therefore in that way both parties, by the influence of the mutual reaction, remain below the line of extreme effort, and therefore all forces are not at once brought forward.

It lies also in the nature of these forces and their application that they cannot all be brought into activity at the same time. These forces are *the armies actually on foot, the country*, with its superficial extent and its population, *and the allies*.

In point of fact, the country, with its superficial area and the population, besides being the source of all military force, constitutes in itself an integral part of the efficient quantities in War, providing either the theatre of war or exercising a considerable influence on the same.

Now, it is possible to bring all the movable military forces of a country into operation at once, but not all fortresses, rivers, mountains, people, &c.—in short, not the whole country, unless it is so small that it may be completely embraced by the first act of the War. Further, the co-operation of allies does not depend on the Will of the belligerents ; and from the nature of the political relations of states to each other, this co-operation is frequently not afforded until after the War has commenced, or it may be increased to restore the balance of power.

That this part of the means of resistance, which cannot at once be brought into activity, in many cases, is a much greater part of the whole than might at first be supposed, and that it often restores the balance of power, seriously affected by the great force of the first decision, will be more fully shown hereafter. Here it is sufficient to show that a complete concentration of all available means in a moment of time is contradictory to the nature of War.

Now this, in itself, furnishes no ground for relaxing our efforts to accumulate strength to gain the first result, because an unfavourable issue is always a disadvantage to which no one would purposely expose himself, and also because the first decision, although not the only one, still will have the more influence on subsequent events, the greater it is in itself.

But the possibility of gaining a later result causes men to take refuge in that expectation, owing to the repugnance in the human mind to making excessive efforts; and therefore forces are not concentrated and measures are not taken for the first decision with that energy which would otherwise be used. Whatever one belligerent omits from weakness, becomes to the other a real objective ground for limiting his own efforts, and thus again, through this reciprocal action, extreme tendencies are brought down to efforts on a limited scale.

9. THE RESULT IN WAR IS NEVER ABSOLUTE.

Lastly, even the final decision of a whole War is not always to be regarded as absolute. The conquered State often sees in it only a passing evil, which may be repaired in after times by means of political combinations. How much this must modify the degree of tension, and the vigour of the efforts made, is evident in itself.

10. THE PROBABILITIES OF REAL LIFE TAKE THE PLACE OF THE CONCEPTIONS OF THE EXTREME AND THE ABSOLUTE.

In this manner, the whole act of War is removed from the rigorous law of forces exerted to the utmost. If the extreme is no longer to be apprehended, and no longer to be sought for, it is left to the judgment to determine the limits for the efforts to be made in place of it, and this can only be done on the data furnished by the facts of the real world by the *laws of probability*. Once the belligerents are no longer mere conceptions, but individual States and Governments, once the War is no longer an ideal, but a definite substantial procedure, then the reality will furnish the data to compute the unknown quantities which are required to be found.

From the character, the measures, the situation of the adversary, and the relations with which he is surrounded, each side will draw conclusions by the law of probability as to the designs of the other, and act accordingly.

II. THE POLITICAL OBJECT NOW REAPPEARS.

Here the question which we had laid aside forces itself again into consideration (*see* No. 2), viz., *the political object of the War*. The law of the extreme, the view to disarm the adversary, to overthrow him, has hitherto to a certain extent usurped the place of this end or object. Just as this law loses its force, the political object must again come forward. If the whole consideration is a calculation of probability based on definite persons and relations, then the political object, being the original motive, must be an essential factor in the product. The smaller the sacrifice we demand from our opponent, the smaller, it may be expected, will be the means of resistance which he will employ ; but the smaller his preparation, the smaller will ours require to be. Further, the smaller our political object, the less value shall we set upon it, and the more easily shall we be induced to give it up altogether.

Thus, therefore, the political object, as the original motive of the War, will be the standard for determining both the aim of the military force and also the amount of effort to be made. This it cannot be in itself, but it is so in relation to both the belligerent States, because we are concerned with realities, not with mere abstractions. One and the same political object may produce totally different effects upon different people, or even upon the same people at different times ; we can, therefore, only admit the political object as the measure, by considering it in its effects upon those masses which it is to move, and consequently the nature of those masses also comes into consideration. It is easy to see that thus the result may be very different according as these masses are animated with a spirit which will infuse vigour into the action or otherwise. It is quite possible for such a state of feeling to exist between two States that a very trifling political motive for War may produce an effect quite disproportionate—in fact, a perfect explosion.

This applies to the efforts which the political object will call forth in the two States, and to the aim which the military action shall prescribe for itself. At times it may itself be that aim, as, for example, the conquest of a province. At other times the political object itself is not suitable for the aim of military action ; then such a one must be chosen as will be an equivalent for it, and stand in its place as regards the conclusion of peace. But also, in this, due attention to the peculiar character of the States concerned is always supposed. There are circumstances in which the equivalent must be much greater than the political object, in order to secure the latter. The political object will be so much the more the standard of aim and effort, and have more influence in itself, the more the masses are indifferent, the less that any mutual feeling of hostility prevails in the two States from other causes, and therefore there are cases where the political object almost alone will be decisive.

If the aim of the military action is an equivalent for the political object, that action will in general diminish as the political object diminishes, and in a greater degree the more the political object dominates. Thus it is explained how, without any contradiction in itself, there may be Wars of all degrees of importance and energy, from a War of extermination down to the mere use of an army of observation. This, however, leads to a question of another kind which we have hereafter to develop and answer.

12. A SUSPENSION IN THE ACTION OF WAR UNEXPLAINED BY ANYTHING SAID AS YET.

However insignificant the political claims mutually advanced, however weak the means put forth, however small the aim to which military action is directed, can this action be suspended even for a moment ? This is a question which penetrates deeply into the nature of the subject.

Every transaction requires for its accomplishment a certain time which we call its duration. This may be longer or shorter, according as the person acting throws more or less despatch into his movements.

About this more or less we shall not trouble ourselves here. Each person acts in his own fashion ; but the slow person does not protract the thing because he wishes to spend more time about it, but because by his nature he requires more time, and if he made more haste would not do the thing so well. This time, therefore, depends on subjective causes, and belongs to the length, so called, of the action.

If we allow now to every action in War this, its length, then we must assume, at first sight at least, that any expenditure of time beyond this length, that is, every suspension of hostile action, appears an absurdity ; with respect to this it must not be forgotten that we now speak not of the progress of one or other of the two opponents, but of the general progress of the whole action of the War.

13. THERE IS ONLY ONE CAUSE WHICH CAN SUSPEND THE ACTION, AND THIS SEEMS TO BE ONLY POSSIBLE ON ONE SIDE IN ANY CASE.

If two parties have armed themselves for strife, then a feeling of animosity must have moved them to it ; as long now as they continue armed, that is, do not come to terms of peace, this feeling must exist ; and it can only be brought to a standstill by either side by one single motive alone, which is, *that he waits for a more favourable moment for action.* Now, at first sight, it appears that this motive can never exist except on one side, because it, *eo ipso*, must be prejudicial to the other. If the one has an interest in acting, then the other must have an interest in waiting.

A complete equilibrium of forces can never produce a suspension of action, for during this suspension he who has the positive object (that is, the assailant) must continue progressing ; for if we should imagine an equilibrium in this way, that he who has the positive object, therefore the strongest motive, can at the same time only command the lesser means, so that the equation is made up by the product of the motive and the power, then we must say, if no alteration in this condition of equilibrium is to be expected, the two parties must make peace ; but if an alteration is to be expected, then it can only be favourable to one side, and therefore the other has a manifest interest to act without delay. We see that the conception of an equilibrium cannot explain a suspension of arms, but that it ends in the question of the *expectation of a more favourable moment.*

Let us suppose, therefore, that one of two States has a positive object, as, for instance, the conquest of one of the enemy's provinces—which is to be utilised in the settlement of peace. After this conquest, his political object is accomplished, the necessity for action ceases, and for him a pause ensues. If the adversary is also contented with this solution, he will make peace ; if not, he must act. Now, if we suppose that in four weeks he will be in a better condition to act, then he has sufficient grounds for putting off the time of action.

But from that moment the logical course for the enemy appears to be to act that he may not give the conquered party *the desired* time. Of course, in this mode of reasoning a complete insight into the state of circumstances on both sides is supposed.

14. THUS A CONTINUANCE OF ACTION WILL ENSUE WHICH WILL ADVANCE TOWARDS A CLIMAX.

If this unbroken continuity of hostile operations really existed, the effect would be that everything would again be driven towards the extreme ; for, irrespective of the effect of such incessant activity in inflaming the feelings, and infusing into the whole a greater degree of passion, a greater elementary force, there would also follow from this continuance of action a stricter continuity, a closer connection between cause and effect, and thus every single action would become of more importance, and consequently more replete with danger.

But we know that the course of action in War has seldom or never this unbroken continuity, and that there have been many Wars in which action occupied by far the smallest portion of time employed, the whole of the rest being consumed in inaction. It is impossible that this should be always an anomaly ; suspension of action in War must therefore be possible, that is no contradiction in itself. We now proceed to show how this is.

15. HERE, THEREFORE, THE PRINCIPLE OF POLARITY IS BROUGHT INTO REQUISITION.

As we have supposed the interests of one Commander to be always antagonistic to those of the other, we have assumed a true *polarity*. We reserve a fuller explanation of this for another chapter, merely making the following observation on it at present.

The principle of polarity is only valid when it can be conceived in one and the same thing, where the positive and its opposite the negative completely destroy each other. In a battle both sides strive to conquer; that is true polarity, for the victory of the one side destroys that of the other. But when we speak of two different things which have a common relation external to themselves, then it is not the things but their relations which have the polarity.

16. ATTACK AND DEFENCE ARE THINGS DIFFERING IN KIND AND OF UNEQUAL FORCE. POLARITY IS, THEREFORE, NOT APPLICABLE TO THEM.

If there was only one form of War, to wit, the attack of the enemy, therefore no defence; or, in other words, if the attack was distinguished from the defence merely by the positive motive, which the one has and the other has not, but the methods of each were precisely one and the same: then in this sort of fight every advantage gained on the one side would be a corresponding disadvantage on the other, and true polarity would exist.

But action in War is divided into two forms, attack and defence, which, as we shall hereafter explain more particularly, are very different and of unequal strength. Polarity therefore lies in that to which both bear a relation, in the decision, but not in the attack or defence itself.

If the one Commander wishes the solution put off, the other must wish to hasten it, but only by the same form of action. If it is A's interest not to attack his enemy at present, but four weeks hence, then it is B's interest to be attacked, not four weeks hence, but at the present moment. This is the direct antagonism of interests, but it by no means follows that it would be for B's interest to attack A at once. That is plainly something totally different.

17. THE EFFECT OF POLARITY IS OFTEN DESTROYED BY THE SUPERIORITY OF THE DEFENCE OVER THE ATTACK, AND THUS THE SUSPENSION OF ACTION IN WAR IS EXPLAINED.

If the form of defence is stronger than that of offence, as we shall hereafter show, the question arises, Is the advantage of a deferred decision as great on the one side as the advantage of the defensive form on the other ? If it is not, then it cannot by its counter-weight over-balance the latter, and thus influence the progress of the action of the War. We see, therefore, that the impulsive force existing in the polarity of interests may be lost in the difference between the strength of the offensive and the defensive, and thereby become ineffectual.

If, therefore, that side for which the present is favourable, is too weak to be able to dispense with the advantage of the defensive, he must put up with the unfavourable prospects which the future holds out ; for it may still be better to fight a defensive battle in the unpromising future than to assume the offensive or make peace at present. Now, being convinced that the superiority of the defensive * (rightly understood) is very great, and much greater than may appear at first sight, we conceive that the

* It must be remembered that all this antedates by some years the introduction of long-range weapons.

greater number of those periods of inaction which occur in war are thus explained without involving any contradiction. The weaker the motives to action are, the more will those motives be absorbed and neutralised by this difference between attack and defence, the more frequently, therefore, will action in warfare be stopped, as indeed experience teaches.

18. A SECOND GROUND CONSISTS IN THE IMPERFECT KNOWLEDGE OF CIRCUMSTANCES.

But there is still another cause which may stop action in War, viz., an incomplete view of the situation. Each Commander can only fully know his own position ; that of his opponent can only be known to him by reports, which are uncertain ; he may, therefore, form a wrong judgment with respect to it upon data of this description, and, in consequence of that error, he may suppose that the power of taking the initiative rests with his adversary when it lies really with himself. This want of perfect insight might certainly just as often occasion an untimely action as untimely inaction, and hence it would in itself no more contribute to delay than to accelerate action in War. Still, it must always be regarded as one of the natural causes which may bring action in War to a standstill without involving a contradiction. But if we reflect how much more we are inclined and induced to estimate the power of our opponents too high than too low, because it lies in human nature to do so, we shall admit that our imperfect insight into facts in general must contribute very much to delay action in War, and to modify the application of the principles pending our conduct.

The possibility of a standstill brings into the action of War a new modification, inasmuch as it dilutes that action with the element of time, checks the influence or sense of danger in its course, and increases the means of

reinstating a lost balance of force. The greater the
tension of feelings from which the War springs, the greater
therefore the energy with which it is carried on, so much
the shorter will be the periods of inaction ; on the other
hand, the weaker the principle of warlike activity, the
longer will be these periods : for powerful motives increase
the force of the will, and this, as we know, is always a
factor in the product of force.

19. FREQUENT PERIODS OF INACTION IN WAR REMOVE
    IT FURTHER FROM THE ABSOLUTE, AND MAKE IT
    STILL MORE A CALCULATION OF PROBABILITIES.

But the slower the action proceeds in War, the more
frequent and longer the periods of inaction, so much the
more easily can an error be repaired ; therefore, so much
the bolder a General will be in his calculations, so much
the more readily will he keep them below the line of
the absolute, and build everything upon probabilities and
conjecture. Thus, according as the course of the War is
more or less slow, more or less time will be allowed for
that which the nature of a concrete case particularly
requires, calculation of probability based on given
circumstances.

20. THEREFORE, THE ELEMENT OF CHANCE ONLY IS
    WANTING TO MAKE OF WAR A GAME, AND IN THAT
    ELEMENT IT IS LEAST OF ALL DEFICIENT.

We see from the foregoing how much the objective
nature of War makes it a calculation of probabilities ;
now there is only one single element still wanting to make
it a game, and that element it certainly is not without :
it is chance. There is no human affair which stands
so constantly and so generally in close connection with
chance as War. But together with chance, the accidental,

and along with it good luck, occupy a great place in War.

21. WAR IS A GAME BOTH OBJECTIVELY AND SUBJECTIVELY.

If we now take a look at the *subjective nature* of War, that is to say, at those conditions under which it is carried on, it will appear to us still more like a game. Primarily the element in which the operations of War are carried on is danger ; but which of all the moral qualities is the first in danger ? *Courage.* Now certainly courage is quite compatible with prudent calculation, but still they are things of quite a different kind, essentially different qualities of the mind ; on the other hand, daring reliance on good fortune, boldness, rashness, are only expressions of courage, and all these propensities of the mind look for the fortuitous (or accidental), because it is their element.

We see, therefore, how, from the commencement, the absolute, the mathematical as it is called, nowhere finds any sure basis in the calculations in the Art of War ; and that from the outset there is a play of possibilities, probabilities, good and bad luck, which spreads about with all the coarse and fine threads of its web, and makes War of all branches of human activity the most like a gambling game.

22. HOW THIS ACCORDS BEST WITH THE HUMAN MIND IN GENERAL.

Although our intellect always feels itself urged towards clearness and certainty, still our mind often feels itself attracted by uncertainty. Instead of threading its way with the understanding along the narrow path of philosophical investigations and logical conclusions, in order, almost unconscious of itself, to arrive in spaces where it feels itself a stranger, and where it seems to part from all well-known objects, it prefers· to remain with the imagination in the realms of chance and luck. Instead of living yonder on poor necessity, it revels here in the wealth of possibilities ; animated thereby, courage then takes wings to itself, and daring and danger make the element into which it launches itself as a fearless swimmer plunges into the stream.

Shall theory leave it here, and move on, self-satisfied with absolute conclusions and rules ? Then it is of no practical use. Theory must also take into account the human element ; it must accord a place to courage, to boldness, even to rashness. The Art of War has to deal with living and with moral forces, the consequence of which is that it can never attain the absolute and positive. There is therefore everywhere a margin for the accidental, and just as much in the greatest things as in the smallest. As there is room for this accidental on the one hand, so on the other there must be courage and self-reliance in proportion to the room available. If these qualities are forthcoming in a high degree, the margin left may like-wise be great. Courage and self-reliance are, therefore, principles quite essential to War ; consequently, theory must only set up such rules as allow ample scope for all degrees and varieties of these necessary and noblest of military virtues. In daring there may still be wisdom, and prudence as well, only they are estimated by a different standard of value.

23. WAR IS ALWAYS A SERIOUS MEANS FOR A SERIOUS OBJECT. ITS MORE PARTICULAR DEFINITION.

Such is War ; such the Commander who conducts it ; such the theory which rules it. But War is no pastime ; no mere passion for venturing and winning ; no work of a free enthusiasm : it is a serious means for a serious object. All that appearance which it wears from the varying hues of fortune, all that it assimilates into itself of the oscillations of passion, of courage, of imagination, of enthusiasm, are only particular properties of this means.

The War of a community—of whole Nations, and particularly of civilised Nations—always starts from a political condition, and is called forth by a political motive. It is, therefore, a political act. Now if it was a perfect, unrestrained, and absolute expression of force, as we had to deduce it from its mere conception, then the moment it is called forth by policy it would step into the place of policy, and as something quite independent of it would set it aside, and only follow its own laws, just as a mine at the moment of explosion cannot be guided into any other direction than that which has been given to it by preparatory arrangements. This is how the thing has really been viewed hitherto, whenever a want of harmony between policy and the conduct of a War has led to theoretical distinctions of the kind. But it is not so, and the idea is radically false. War in the real world, as we have already seen, is not an extreme thing which expends itself at one single discharge ; it is the operation of powers which do not develop themselves completely in the same manner and in the same measure, but which at one time expand sufficiently to overcome the resistance opposed by inertia or friction, while at another they are too weak to produce an effect ; it is therefore, in a certain measure, a pulsation of violent force more or less vehement, consequently making its discharges and exhausting its powers more or less quickly—in other words, conducting more or less quickly to the aim, but always lasting long enough to admit of influence being exerted on it in its course, so as to give it this or that direction, in short, to be subject to the will of a guiding intelligence. Now, if we reflect that War has its root in a politial object, then naturally this original motive which called it into existence should also continue the first and highest consideration in its conduct. Still, the political object is no despotic lawgiver on that account ; it must accommodate itself to the nature of the means, and though changes in these means may involve modification in the political objective, the latter always retains a prior right to consideration. Policy, therefore, is interwoven with the whole action of War, and must exercise a continuous influence upon it, as far as the nature of the forces liberated by it will permit.

24. WAR IS A MERE CONTINUATION OF POLICY BY OTHER MEANS.

We see, therefore, that War is not merely a political act, but also a real political instrument, a continuation of political commerce, a carrying out of the same by other means. All beyond this which is strictly peculiar to War relates merely to the peculiar nature of the means which it uses. That the tendencies and views of policy shall not be incompatible with these means, the Art of War in general and the Commander in each particular case may demand, and this claim is truly not a trifling one. But however powerfully this may react on political views in particular cases, still it must always be regarded as only a modification of them ; for the political view is the object, War is the means, and the means must always include the object in our conception.

25. DIVERSITY IN THE NATURE OF WARS.

The greater and the more powerful the motives of a War, the more it affects the whole existence of a people. The more violent the excitement which precedes the War, by so much the nearer will the War approach to its abstract form, so much the more will it be directed to the destruction of the enemy, so much the nearer will the military and political ends coincide, so much the more purely military and less political the War appears to be ; but the weaker the motives and the tensions, so much the less will the natural direction of the military element— that is, force—be coincident with the direction which the political element indicates ; so much the more must, therefore, the War become diverted from its natural direction, the political object diverge from the aim of an ideal War, and the War appear to become political.

But, that the reader may not form any false conceptions, we must here observe that by this natural tendency of War we only mean the philosophical, the strictly logical, and by no means the tendency of forces actually engaged in conflict, by which would be supposed to be included all the emotions and passions of the combatants. No doubt in some cases these also might be excited to such a degree as to be with difficulty restrained and confined to the political road ; but in most cases such a contradiction will not arise, because by the existence of such strenuous exertions a great plan in harmony therewith would be implied. If the plan is directed only upon a small object, then the impulses of feeling amongst the masses will be also so weak that these masses will require to be stimulated rather than repressed.

26. THEY MAY ALL BE REGARDED AS POLITICAL ACTS.

Returning now to the main subject, although it is true that in one kind of War the political element seems almost to disappear, whilst in another kind it occupies a very prominent place, we may still affirm that the one is as political as the other ; for if we regard the State policy as the intelligence of the personified State, then amongst all the constellations in the political sky whose movements it has to compute, those must be included which arise when the nature of its relations imposes the necessity of a great War. It is only if we understand by policy not a true appreciation of affairs in general, but the conventional conception of a cautious, subtle, also dishonest craftiness, averse from violence, that the latter kind of War may belong more to policy than the first.

27. INFLUENCE OF THIS VIEW ON THE RIGHT UNDERSTANDING OF MILITARY HISTORY, AND ON THE FOUNDATIONS OF THEORY.

We see, therefore, in the first place, that under all circumstances War is to be regarded not as an independent thing, but as a political instrument ; and it is only by taking this point of view that we can avoid finding ourselves in opposition to all military history. This is the only means of unlocking the great book and making it intelligible. Secondly, this view shows us how Wars must differ in character according to the nature of the motives and circumstances from which they proceed.

Now, the first, the grandest, and most decisive act of judgment which the Statesman and General exercises is rightly to understand in this respect the War in which he engages, not to take it for something, or to wish to make of it something, which by the nature of its relations it is impossible for it to be. This is, therefore, the first, the most comprehensive, of all strategical questions. We shall enter into this more fully in treating of the plan of a War.

For the present we content ourselves with having brought the subject up to this point, and having thereby fixed the chief point of view from which War and its theory are to be studied.

28. RESULT FOR THEORY.

War is, therefore, not only chameleon-like in character, because it changes its colour in some degree in each particular case, but it is also, as a whole, in relation to the predominant tendencies which are in it, a wonderful trinity, composed of the original violence of its elements, hatred and animosity, which may be looked upon as blind instinct ; of the play of probabilities and chance, which make it a free activity of the soul ; and of the subordinate nature of a political instrument, by which it belongs purely to the reason.

The first of these three phases concerns more the people ; the second, more the General and his Army ; the third, more the Government. The passions which break forth in War must already have a latent existence in the peoples. The range which the display of courage and talents shall get in the realm of probabilities and of chance depends on the particular characteristics of the General and his Army, but the political objects belong to the Government alone.

These three tendencies, which appear like so many different law-givers, are deeply rooted in the nature of the subject, and at the same time variable in degree. A theory which would leave any one of them out of account, or set up any arbitrary relation between them, would immediately become involved in such a contradiction with the reality, that it might be regarded as destroyed at once by that alone.

The problem is, therefore, that theory shall keep itself poised in a manner between these three tendencies, as between three points of attraction.

The way in which alone this difficult problem can be solved we shall examine in the book on the " Theory of War." In every case the conception of War, as here defined, will be the first ray of light which shows us the true foundation of theory, and which first separates the great masses and allows us to distinguish them from one another.

CHAPTER II

END AND MEANS IN WAR

HAVING in the foregoing chapter ascertained the complicated and variable nature of War, we shall now occupy ourselves in examining into the influence which this nature has upon the end and means in War.

If we ask, first of all, for the object upon which the whole effort of War is to be directed, in order that it may suffice for the attainment of the political object, we shall find that it is just as variable as are the political object and the particular circumstances of the War.

If, in the next place, we keep once more to the pure conception of War, then we must say that the political object properly lies out of its province, for if War is an act of violence to compel the enemy to fulfil our will, then in every case all depends on our overthrowing the enemy, that is, disarming him, and on that alone. This object, developed from abstract conceptions, but which is also the one aimed at in a great many cases in reality, we shall, in the first place, examine in this reality.

In connection with the plan of a campaign we shall hereafter examine more closely into the meaning of disarming a nation, but here we must at once draw a distinction between three things, which, as three general objects, comprise everything else within them. They are the *military power, the country,* and *the will of the enemy.*

The *military power* must be destroyed, that is, reduced to such a state as not to be able to prosecute the War. This is the sense in which we wish to be understood hereafter, whenever we use the expression " destruction of the enemy's military power."

The *country* must be conquered, for out of the country a new military force may be formed.

But even when both these things are done, still the War, that is, the hostile feeling and action of hostile agencies, cannot be considered as at an end as long as the *will* of the enemy is not subdued also ; that is, its Government and its Allies must be forced into signing a peace, or the people into submission ; for whilst we are in full occupation of the country, the War may break out afresh, either in the interior or through assistance given by Allies. No doubt, this may also take place after a peace, but that shows nothing more than that every War does not carry in itself the elements for a complete decision and final settlement.

But even if this is the case, still with the conclusion of peace a number of sparks are always extinguished which would have smouldered on quietly, and the excitement of the passions abates, because all those whose minds are disposed to peace, of which in all nations and under all circumstances there is always a great number, turn themselves away completely from the road to resistance. Whatever may take place subsequently, we must always look upon the object as attained, and the business of War as ended, by a peace.

As protection of the country is the primary object for which the military force exists, therefore the natural order is, that first of all this force should be destroyed, then the country subdued ; and through the effect of these two results, as well as the position we then hold, the enemy should be forced to make peace. Generally the destruction of the enemy's force is done by degrees, and in just the same measure the conquest of the country follows immediately. The two likewise usually react upon each other, because the loss of provinces occasions a diminution of military force. But this order is by no means necessary, and on that account it also does not always take place. The enemy's Army, before it is sensibly weakened, may retreat to the opposite side of the country, or even quite outside of it. In this case, therefore, the greater part or the whole of the country is conquered.

But this object of War in the abstract, this final means of attaining the political object in which all others are combined, the *disarming the enemy*, is rarely attained in practice and is not a condition necessary to peace. Therefore it can in no wise be set up in theory as a law. There are innumerable instances of treaties in which peace has been settled before either party could be looked upon as disarmed ; indeed, even before the balance of power had undergone any sensible alteration. Nay, further, if we look at the case in the concrete, then we must say that in a whole class of cases, the idea of a complete defeat of the enemy would be a mere imaginative flight, especially when the enemy is considerably superior.

The reason why the object deduced from the conception of War is not adapted in general to real War lies in the difference between the two, which is discussed in the preceding chapter. If it was as pure theory gives it, then a War between two States of very unequal military strength would appear an absurdity ; therefore impossible. At most, the inequality between the physical forces might be such that it could be balanced by the moral forces, and that would not go far with our present social condition in Europe. Therefore, if we have seen Wars take place between States of very unequal power, that has been the case because there is a wide difference between War in reality and its original conception.

There are two considerations which as motives may practically take the place of inability to continue the contest. The first is the improbability, the second is the excessive price, of success.

According to what we have seen in the foregoing chapter, War must always set itself free from the strict law of logical

necessity, and seek aid from the calculation of probabilities ; and as this is so much the more the case, the more
the War has a bias that way, from the circumstances
out of which it has arisen—the smaller its motives are,
and the excitement it has raised—so it is also conceivable
how out of this calculation of probabilities even motives
to peace may arise. War does not, therefore, always
require to be fought out until one party is overthrown ;
and we may suppose that, when the motives and passions
are slight, a weak probability will suffice to move that
side to which it is unfavourable to give way. Now, were
the other side convinced of this beforehand, it is natural
that he would strive for this probability only, instead of
first wasting time and effort in the attempt to achieve
the total destruction of the enemy's Army.

Still more general in its influence on the resolution to
peace is the consideration of the expenditure of force
already made, and further required. As War is no act
of blind passion, but is dominated by the political
object, therefore the value of that object determines
the measure of the sacrifices by which it is to be purchased.
This will be the case, not only as regards extent, but also
as regards duration. As soon, therefore, as the required
outlay becomes so great that the political object is no
longer equal in value, the object must be given up, and
peace will be the result.

We see, therefore, that in Wars where one side cannot
completely disarm the other, the motives to peace on
both sides will rise or fall on each side according to the
probability of future success and the required outlay.
If these motives were equally strong on both sides, they
would meet in the centre of their political difference.
Where they are strong on one side, they might be weak on
the other. If their amount is only sufficient, peace will
follow, but naturally to the advantage of that side which

has the weakest motive for its conclusion. We purposely pass over here the difference which the *positive* and *negative* character of the political end must necessarily produce practically ; for although that is, as we shall hereafter show, of the highest importance, still we are obliged to keep here to a more general point of view, because the original political views in the course of the War change very much, and at last may become totally different, *just because they are determined by results and probable events.*

Now comes the question how to influence the probability of success. In the first place, naturally by the same means which we use when the object is the subjugation of the enemy, by the destruction of his military force and the conquest of his provinces ; but these two means are not exactly of the same import here as they would be in reference to that object. If we attack the enemy's Army, it is a very different thing whether we intend to follow up the first blow with a succession of others, until the whole force is destroyed, or whether we mean to content ourselves with a victory to shake the enemy's feeling of security, to convince him of our superiority, and to instil into him a feeling of apprehension about the future. If this is our object, we only go so far in the destruction of his forces as is sufficient. In like manner, the conquest of the enemy's provinces is quite a different measure if the object is not the destruction of the enemy's Army. In the latter case the destruction of the Army is the real effectual action, and the taking of the provinces only a consequence of it ; to take them before the Army had been defeated would always be looked upon only as a necessary evil. On the other hand, if our views are not directed upon the complete destruction of the enemy's force, and if we are sure that the enemy does not seek but fears to bring matters to a bloody decision, the taking possession of a weak or defenceless province is an advantage in itself, and if this advantage is of sufficient importance to make the enemy apprehensive about the general result, then it may also be regarded as a shorter road to peace.

But now we come upon a peculiar means of influencing the probability of the result without destroying the enemy's Army, namely, upon the expeditions which have a direct connection with political views. If there are any enterprises which are particularly likely to break up the enemy's alliances or make them inoperative, to gain new alliances for ourselves, to raise political powers in our own favour, &c. &c., then it is easy to conceive how much these may increase the probability of success, and become a shorter way towards our object than the routing of the enemy's forces.

The second question is how to act upon the enemy's expenditure in strength, that is, to raise the price of success.

The enemy's outlay in strength lies in the *wear and tear* of his forces, consequently in the *destruction* of them on our part, and in the *loss* of *provinces*, consequently the *conquest* of them by us.

Here, again, on account of the various significations of these means, so likewise it will be found that neither of them will be identical in its signification in all cases if the objects are different. The smallness in general of this difference must not cause us perplexity, for in reality the weakest motives, the finest shades of difference, often decide in favour of this or that method of applying force. Our only business here is to show that, certain conditions being supposed, the possibility of attaining our purpose in different ways is no contradiction, absurdity, nor even error.

Besides these two means, there are three other peculiar

ways of directly increasing the waste of the enemy's force. The first is *invasion*, that is *the occupation of the enemy's territory, not with a view to keeping it,* but in order to levy contributions upon it, or to devastate it.

The immediate object here is neither the conquest of the enemy's territory nor the defeat of his armed force, but merely to *do him damage in a general way.* The second way is to select for the object of our enterprises those points at which we can do the enemy most harm. Nothing is easier to conceive than two different directions in which our force may be employed, the first of which is to be preferred if our object is to defeat the enemy's Army, while the other is more advantageous if the defeat of the enemy is out of the question. According to the usual mode of speaking, we should say that the first is primarily military, the other more political. But if we take our view from the highest point, both are equally military, and neither the one nor the other can be eligible unless it suits the circumstances of the case. The third, by far the most important, from the great number of cases which it embraces, is the *wearing out* of the enemy. We choose this expression not only to explain our meaning in few words, but because it represents the thing exactly, and is not so figurative as may at first appear. The idea of wearing out in a struggle amounts in practice to *a gradual exhaustion of the physical powers and of the will by the long continuance of exertion.*

Now, if we want to overcome the enemy by the durati n of the contest, we must content ourselves with as small objects as possible, for it is in the nature of the thing that a great end requires a greater expenditure of force than a small one ; but the smallest object that we can propose to ourselves is simple passive resistance, that is a combat without any positive view. In this way, therefore, our means attain their greatest relative value, and therefore the result is best secured. How far now can this negative mode of proceeding be carried ? Plainly not to absolute passivity, for mere endurance would not be fighting ; and the defensive is an activity by which so much of the enemy's power must be destroyed that he must give up his object. That alone is what we aim at in each single act, and therein consists the negative nature of our object.

No doubt this negative object in its single act is not so effective as the positive object in the same direction would be, supposing it successful ; but there is this difference in its favour, that it succeeds more easily than the positive, and therefore it holds out greater certainty of success ; what is wanting in the efficacy of its single act must be gained through time, that is, through the duration of the contest, and therefore this negative intention, which constitutes the principle of the pure defensive, is also the natural means of overcoming the enemy by the duration of the combat, that is of wearing him out.

Here lies the origin of that difference of *Offensive* and *Defensive*, the influence of which prevails throughout the whole province of War. We cannot at present pursue this subject further than to observe that from this negative intention are to be deduced all the advantages and all the stronger forms of combat which are on the side of the *Defensive*, and in which that philosophical-dynamic law which exists between the greatness and the certainty of success is realised. We shall resume the consideration of all this hereafter.

If then the negative purpose, that is the concentration of all the means into a state of pure resistance, affords a superiority in the contest, and if this advantage is sufficient to *balance* whatever superiority in numbers the adversary may have, then the mere *duration* of the contest

will suffice gradually to bring the loss of force on the part
of the adversary to a point at which the political object
can no longer be an equivalent, a point at which, therefore,
he must give up the contest. We see then that this class
of means, the wearing out of the enemy, includes the great
number of cases in which the weaker resists the stronger.

Frederick the Great, during the Seven Years' War,
was never strong enough to overthrow the Austrian
monarchy ; and if he had tried to do so after the fashion
of Charles the Twelfth, he would inevitably have had to
succumb himself. But after his skilful application of the
system of husbanding his resources had shown the powers
allied against him, through a seven years' struggle. that the
actual expenditure of strength far exceeded what they
had at first anticipated, they made peace.

We see then that there are many ways to one's object
in War ; that the complete subjugation of the enemy is
not essential in every case ; that the destruction of the
enemy's military force, the conquest of the enemy's provinces, the mere occupation of them, the mere invasion of
them—enterprises which are aimed directly at political
objects—lastly, a passive expectation of the enemy's
blow, are all means which, each in itself, may be used
to force the enemy's will according as the peculiar
circumstances of the case lead us to expect more from
the one or the other. We could still add to these a
whole category of shorter methods of gaining the end,
which might be called arguments *ad hominem*. What
branch of human affairs is there in which these sparks
of individual spirit have not made their appearance,
surmounting all formal considerations ? And least of all
can they fail to appear in War, where the personal character
of the combatants plays such an important part, both in
the cabinet and in the field. We limit ourselves to pointing this out, as it would be pedantry to attempt to reduce

such influences into classes. Including these, we may say that the number of possible ways of reaching the object rises to infinity.

To avoid under-estimating these different short roads to one's purpose, either estimating them only as rare exceptions, or holding the difference which they cause in the conduct of War as insignificant, we must bear in mind the diversity of political objects which may cause a War— measure at a glance the distance which there is between a death struggle for political existence and a War which a forced or tottering alliance makes a matter of disagreeable duty. Between the two innumerable gradations occur in practice. If we reject one of these gradations in theory, we might with equal right reject the whole, which would be tantamount to shutting the real world completely out of sight.

These are the circumstances in general connected with the aim which we have to pursue in War ; let us now turn to the means.

There is only one single means, it is the *Fight*. However diversified this may be in form, however widely it may differ from a rough vent of hatred and animosity in a hand-to-hand encounter, whatever number of things may introduce themselves which are not actual fighting, still it is always implied in the conception of War that all the effects manifested have their roots in the combat.

That this must always be so in the greatest diversity and complication of the reality is proved in a very simple manner. All that takes place in War takes place through armed forces, but where the forces of War, *i.e.*, armed men, are applied, there the idea of fighting must of necessity be at the foundation.

All, therefore, that relates to forces of War—all that is connected with their creation, maintenance, and application—belongs to military activity.

Creation and maintenance are obviously only the means, whilst application is the object.

The contest in War is not a contest of individual against individual, but an organised whole, consisting of manifold parts; in this great whole we may distinguish units of two kinds, the one determined by the subject, the other by the object. In an Army the mass of combatants ranges itself always into an order of new units, which again form members of a higher order. The combat of each of these members forms, therefore, also a more or less distinct unit. Further, the motive of the fight; therefore its object forms its unit.

Now, to each of these units which we distinguish in the contest we attach the name of combat.

If the idea of combat lies at the foundation of every application of armed power, then also the application of armed force in general is nothing more than the determining and arranging a certain number of combats.

Every activity in War, therefore, necessarily relates to the combat either directly or indirectly. The soldier is levied, clothed, armed, exercised, he sleeps, eats, drinks, and marches, all *merely to fight at the right time and place.*

If, therefore, all the threads of military activity terminate in the combat, we shall grasp them all when we settle the order of the combats. Only from this order and its execution proceed the effects, never directly from the conditions preceding them. Now, in the combat all the action is directed to the *destruction* of the enemy, or rather of *his fighting powers,* for this lies in the conception of combat. The destruction of the enemy's fighting power is, therefore, always the means to attain the object of the combat.

This object may likewise be the mere destruction of the enemy's armed force; but that is not by any means necessary, and it may be something quite different.

347

Whenever, for instance, as we have shown, the defeat of the enemy is not the only means to attain the political object, whenever there are other objects which may be pursued as the aim in a War, then it follows of itself that such other objects may become the object of particular acts of Warfare, and therefore also the object of combats.

But even those combats which, as subordinate acts, are in the strict sense devoted to the destruction of the enemy's fighting force need not have that destruction itself as their first object.

If we think of the manifold parts of a great armed force, of the number of circumstances which come into activity when it is employed, then it is clear that the combat of such a force must also require a manifold organisation, a subordinating of parts and formation. There may and must naturally arise for particular parts a number of objects which are not themselves the destruction of the enemy's armed force, and which, while they certainly contribute to increase that destruction, do so only in an indirect manner. If a battalion is ordered to drive the enemy from a rising ground, or a bridge, &c., then properly the occupation of any such locality is the real object, the destruction of the enemy's armed force which takes place only the means or secondary matter. If the enemy can be driven away merely by a demonstration, the object is attained all the same ; but this hill or bridge is, in point of fact, only required as a means of increasing the gross amount of loss inflicted on the enemy's armed force. If this is the case on the field of battle, much more must it be so on the whole theatre of war, where not only one Army is opposed to another, but one State, one Nation, one whole country to another. Here the number of possible relations, and consequently possible combinations, is much greater, the diversity of measures increased, and by the gradation of objects, each subordinate to another the first means employed is further apart from the ultimate object.

It is therefore for many reasons possible that the object of a combat is not the destruction of the enemy's force, that is, of the force immediately opposed to us, but that this only appears as a means. But in all such cases it is no longer a question of complete destruction, for the combat is here nothing else but a measure of strength—has in itself no value except only that of the present result, that is, of its decision.

But a measuring of strength may be effected in cases where the opposing sides are very unequal by a mere comparative estimate. In such cases no fighting will take place, and the weaker will immediately give way.

If the object of a combat is not always the destruction of the enemy's forces therein engaged—and if its object can often be attained as well without the combat taking place at all, by merely making a resolve to fight, and by the circumstances to which this resolution gives rise— then that explains how a whole campaign may be carried on with great activity without the actual combat playing any notable part in it.

That this may be so military history proves by a hundred examples. How many of those cases can be justified, that is, without involving a contradiction, and whether some of the celebrities who rose out of them would stand criticism, we shall leave undecided, for all we have to do with the matter is to show the possibility of such a course of events in War.

We have only one means in War—the battle , but this means, by the infinite variety of paths in which it may be applied, leads us into all the different ways which the multiplicity of objects allows of, so that we seem to have gained nothing ; but that is not the case, for from this unity of means proceeds a thread which assists the study of the subject, as it runs through the whole web of military activity and holds it together.

But we have considered the destruction of the enemy's force as one of the objects which may be pursued in War, and left undecided what relative importance should be given to it amongst other objects. In certain cases it will depend on circumstances, and as a general question we have left its value undetermined. We are once more brought back upon it, and we shall be able to get an insight into the value which must necessarily be accorded to it.

The combat is the single activity in War ; in the combat the destruction of the enemy opposed to us is the means to the end ; it is so even when the combat does not actually take place, because in that case there lies at the root of the decision the supposition at all events that this destruction is to be regarded as beyond doubt. It follows, therefore, that the destruction of the enemy's military force is the foundation-stone of all action in War, the great support of all combinations, which rest upon it like the arch on its abutments. All action, therefore, takes place on the supposition that if the solution by force of arms which lies at its foundation should be realised, it will be a favourable one. The decision by arms is, for all operations in War, great and small, what cash payment is in bill transactions. However remote from each other these relations, however seldom the realisation may take place, still it can never entirely fail to occur.

If the decision by arms lies at the foundation of all combinations, then it follows that the enemy can defeat each of them by gaining a victory on the field, not merely in the one on which our combination directly depends, but also in any other encounter, if it is only important enough ; for every important decision by arms —that is, destruction of the enemy's forces—reacts upon all preceding it, because, like a liquid element, they tend to bring themselves to a level.

Thus, the destruction of the enemy's armed force appears, therefore, always as the superior and more effectual means, to which all others must give way.

It is, however, only when there is a supposed equality in all other conditions that we can ascribe to the destruction of the enemy's armed force the greater efficacy. It would, therefore, be a great mistake to draw the conclusion that a blind dash must always gain the victory over skill and caution. An unskilful attack would lead to the destruction of our own and not of the enemy's force, and therefore is not what is here meant. The superior efficacy belongs not to the *means* but to the *end*, and we are only comparing the effect of one realised purpose with the other.

If we speak of the destruction of the enemy's armed force, we must expressly point out that nothing obliges us to confine this idea to the mere physical force ; on the contrary, the moral is necessarily implied as well, because both in fact are interwoven with each other, even in the most minute details, and therefore cannot be separated. But it is just in connection with the inevitable effect which has been referred to, of a great act of destruction (a great victory) upon all other decisions by arms, that this moral element is most fluid, if we may use that expression, and therefore distributes itself the most easily through all the parts.

Against the far superior worth which the destruction of the enemy's armed force has over all other means stands the expense and risk of this means, and it is only to avoid these that any other means are taken. That these must be costly stands to reason, for the waste of our own military forces must, *ceteris paribus*, always be greater the more our aim is directed upon the destruction of the enemy's power.

The danger lies in this, that the greater efficacy which we seek recoils on ourselves, and therefore has worse consequences in case we fail of success.

Other methods are, therefore, less costly when they succeed, less dangerous when they fail ; but in this is necessarily lodged the condition that they are only opposed to similar ones, that is, that the enemy acts on the same principle ; for if the enemy should choose the way of a great decision by arms, *our means must on that account be changed against our will, in order to correspond with his*. Then all depends on the issue of the act of destruction ; but of course it is evident that, *ceteris paribus*, in this act we must be at a disadvantage in all respects because our views and our means had been directed in part upon other objects, which is not the case with the enemy. Two different objects of which one is not part of the other exclude each other, and therefore a force which may be applicable for the one may not serve for the other. If, therefore, one of two belligerents is determined to seek the great decision by arms, then he has a high probability of success, as soon as he is certain his opponent will not take that way, but follows a different object ; and every one who sets before himself any such other aim only does so in a reasonable manner, provided he acts on the supposition that his adversary has as little intention as he has of resorting to the great decision by arms.

But what we have here said of another direction of views and forces relates only to other *positive objects*, which we may propose to ourselves in War, besides the destruction of the enemy's force, not by any means to the pure defensive, which may be adopted with a view thereby to exhaust the enemy's forces. In the pure defensive the positive object is wanting, and therefore, while on the defensive, our forces cannot at the same time be directed on other objects ; they can only be employed to defeat the intentions of the enemy.

We have now to consider the opposite of the destruction of the enemy's armed force, that is to say, the preservation of our own. These two efforts always go together, as they mutually act and react on each other ; they are integral parts of one and the same view, and we have only to ascertain what effect is produced when one or the other has the predominance. The endeavour to destroy the enemy's force has a positive object, and leads to positive results, of which the final aim is the conquest of the enemy. The preservation of our own forces has a negative object, leads therefore to the defeat of the enemy's intentions, that is to pure resistance, of which the final aim can be nothing more than to prolong the duration of the contest, so that the enemy shall exhaust himself in it.

The effort with a positive object calls into existence the act of destruction ; the effort with the negative object awaits it.

How far this state of expectation should and may be carried we shall enter into more particularly in the theory of attack and defence, at the origin of which we again find ourselves. Here we shall content ourselves with saying that the awaiting must be no absolute endurance, and that in the action bound up with it the destruction of the enemy's armed force engaged in this conflict may be the aim just as well as anything else. It would therefore be a great error in the fundamental idea to suppose that the consequence of the negative course is that we are precluded from choosing the destruction of the enemy's military force as our object, and must prefer a bloodless solution. The advantage which the negative effort gives may certainly lead to that, but only at the risk of its not being the most advisable method, as that question is dependent on totally different conditions, resting not with ourselves but with our opponents. This other bloodless way cannot, therefore, be looked upon at all as the natural means of satisfying our great anxiety to spare our forces; on the contrary, when circumstances are not favourable, it would be the means of completely ruining them. Very many Generals have fallen into this error, and been ruined by it. The only necessary effect resulting from the superiority of the negative effort is the delay of the decision, so that the party acting takes refuge in that way, as it were, in the expectation of the decisive moment. The consequence of that is generally *the postponement of the action* as much as possible in time, and also in space, in so far as space is in connection with it. If the moment has arrived in which this can no longer be done without ruinous disadvantage, then the advantage of the negative must be considered as exhausted, and then comes forward unchanged the effort for the destruction of the enemy's force, which was kept back by a counterpoise, but never discarded.

We have seen, therefore, in the foregoing reflections, that there are many ways to the aim, that is, to the attainment of the political object; but that the only means is the combat, and that consequently everything is subject to a supreme law: which is the *decision by arms*; that where this is really demanded by one, it is a redress which cannot be refused by the other; that, therefore, a belligerent who takes any other way must make sure that his opponent will not take this means of redress, or his cause may be lost in that supreme court; hence therefore the destruction of the enemy's armed force, amongst all the objects which can be pursued in War, appears always as the one which overrules all others.

What may be achieved by combinations of another kind in War we shall only learn in the sequel, and naturally only by degrees. We content ourselves here with acknowledging in general their possibility, as something pointing to the difference between the reality and the conception, and to the influence of particular circumstances. But we could not avoid showing at once that the *bloody solution of the crisis*, the effort for the destruction of the enemy's force, is the firstborn son of War. If when political objects are unimportant, motives weak, the excitement of forces small, a cautious commander tries in all kinds of ways, without great crises and bloody solutions, to twist himself skilfully into a peace through the characteristic weaknesses of his enemy in the field and in the Cabinet, we have no right to find fault with him, if the premises on which he acts are well founded and justified by success ; still we must require him to remember that he only travels on forbidden tracks, where the God of War may surprise him ; that he ought always to keep his eye on the enemy, in order that he may not have to defend himself with a dress rapier if the enemy takes up a sharp sword.

The consequences of the nature of War, how ends and means act in it, how in the modifications of reality it deviates sometimes more, sometimes less, from its strict original conception, fluctuating backwards and forwards, yet always remaining under that strict conception as under a supreme law : all this we must retain before us, and bear constantly in mind in the consideration of each of the succeeding subjects, if we would rightly comprehend their true relations and proper importance, and not become involved incessantly in the most glaring contradictions with the reality, and at last with our own selves.

Born at West Point, the son of a professor at the
U.S. Military Academy, Alfred Thayer Mahan (1840-1914)
emerged as the foremost naval historian and strategist
of the century. Graduation from the Naval Academy,
Annapolis, began a forty-year career in the Navy.
Service as a lecturer and then as president of the
Naval War College (1884-1889) gave him an opportunity
to concentrate on his historical and strategic studies.

Margaret T. Sprout wrote of him: "No other single
person has so directly and profoundly influenced the
theory of sea power and naval strategy.   He precipitated and guided a long-pending revolution in American
naval policy, provided a theoretical foundation for
Britain's determination to remain the dominant sea
power, and gave impetus to German naval development
under William II and Admiral Tirpitz.   By direct influence and through the political power of his friends,
Theodore Roosevelt and Henry Cabot Lodge, he played a
leading role in persuading the United States to pursue
a larger destiny overseas during the opening years of
the twentieth century."

Some say that *The Influence of Sea Power upon
History 1660-1783*, published in 1890, actually precipitated the naval race between Great Britain and Germany
which was a major factor in the coming of World War I.

INFLUENCE

OF

SEA POWER UPON HISTORY.

———•———

INTRODUCTORY.

THE history of Sea Power is largely, though by no means solely, a narrative of contests between nations, of mutual rivalries, of violence frequently culminating in war. The profound influence of sea commerce upon the wealth and strength of countries was clearly seen long before the true principles which governed its growth and prosperity were detected. To secure to one's own people a disproportionate share of such benefits, every effort was made to exclude others, either by the peaceful legislative methods of monopoly or prohibitory regulations, or, when these failed, by direct violence. The clash of interests, the angry feelings roused by conflicting attempts thus to appropriate the larger share, if not the whole, of the advantages of commerce, and of distant unsettled commercial regions, led to wars. On the other hand, wars arising from other causes have been greatly modified in their conduct and issue by the control of the sea. Therefore the history of sea power, while embracing in its broad sweep all that tends to make a people great upon the sea or by the sea, is largely a military history; and it is in this aspect that it will be mainly, though not exclusively, regarded in the following pages.

A study of the military history of the past, such as this, is enjoined by great military leaders as essential to correct ideas and to the skilful conduct of war in the future. Napoleon names among the campaigns to be studied by the aspiring soldier, those of Alexander, Hannibal, and Cæsar, to whom gunpowder was unknown; and there is a substantial agreement among professional writers that, while many of the conditions of war vary from age to age with the progress of weapons, there are certain teachings in the school of history which remain constant, and being, therefore, of universal application, can be elevated to the rank of general principles. For the same reason the study of the sea history of the past will be found instructive, by its illustration of the general principles of maritime war, notwithstanding the great changes that have been brought about in naval weapons by the scientific advances of the past half century, and by the introduction of steam as the motive power.

It is doubly necessary thus to study critically the history and experience of naval warfare in the days of sailing-ships, because while these will be found to afford lessons of present application and value, steam navies have as yet made no history which can be quoted as decisive in its teaching. Of the one we have much experimental knowledge; of the other, practically none. Hence theories about the naval warfare of the future are almost wholly presumptive; and although the attempt has been made to give them a more solid basis by dwelling upon the resemblance between fleets of steamships and fleets of galleys moved by oars, which have a long and well-known history, it will be well not to be carried away by this analogy until it has been thoroughly tested. The resemblance is indeed far from superficial. The feature which the steamer and the galley have in common is the ability to move in any direction independent of the wind. Such a power makes a radical distinction between those classes of vessels and the sailing-ship; for the latter can follow only a limited number of courses when the wind blows, and must remain motionless when it fails. But while it is wise to observe things that are alike, it is also wise to look for things that differ; for when the imagination is carried away by the de-

tection of points of resemblance, — one of the most pleasing of
mental pursuits, — it is apt to be impatient of any divergence
in its new-found parallels, and so may overlook or refuse to
recognize such. Thus the galley and the steamship have in
common, though unequally developed, the important characteristic mentioned, but in at least two points they differ ; and
in an appeal to the history of the galley for lessons as to
fighting steamships, the differences as well as the likeness
must be kept steadily in view, or false deductions may be
made. The motive power of the galley when in use necessarily and rapidly declined, because human strength could
not long maintain such exhausting efforts, and consequently
tactical movements could continue but for a limited time ;[1]
and again, during the galley period offensive weapons were
not only of short range, but were almost wholly confined to
hand-to-hand encounter. These two conditions led almost
necessarily to a rush upon each other, not, however, without
some dexterous attempts to turn or double on the enemy, followed by a hand-to-hand *mêlée*. In such a rush and such a
mêlée a great consensus of respectable, even eminent, naval
opinion of the present day finds the necessary outcome of
modern naval weapons, — a kind of Donnybrook Fair, in which,
as the history of *mêlées* shows, it will be hard to know friend
from foe. Whatever may prove to be the worth of this opinion, it cannot claim an historical basis in the sole fact that
galley and steamship can move at any moment directly upon
the enemy, and carry a beak upon their prow, regardless of
the points in which galley and steamship differ. As yet this
opinion is only a presumption, upon which final judgment
may well be deferred until the trial of battle has given further light. Until that time there is room for the opposite

---

[1] Thus Hermocrates of Syracuse, advocating the policy of thwarting the
Athenian expedition against his city (B.C. 413) by going boldly to meet it, and
keeping on the flank of its line of advance, said : " As their advance must be slow,
we shall have a thousand opportunities to attack them ; but if they clear their
ships for action and in a body bear down expeditiously upon us, they must ply
hard at their oars, and *when spent with toil* we can fall upon them."

view, — that a *mêlée* between numerically equal fleets, in which skill is reduced to a minimum, is not the best that can be done with the elaborate and mighty weapons of this age. The surer of himself an admiral is, the finer the tactical development of his fleet, the better his captains, the more reluctant must he necessarily be to enter into a *mêlée* with equal forces, in which all these advantages will be thrown away, chance reign supreme, and his fleet be placed on terms of equality with an assemblage of ships which have never before acted together.[1] History has lessons as to when *mêlées* are, or are not, in order.

The galley, then, has one striking resemblance to the steamer, but differs in other important features which are not so immediately apparent and are therefore less accounted of. In the sailing-ship, on the contrary, the striking feature is the difference between it and the more modern vessel ; the points of resemblance, though existing and easy to find, are not so obvious, and therefore are less heeded. This impression is enhanced by the sense of utter weakness in the sailing-ship as compared with the steamer, owing to its dependence upon the wind ; forgetting that, as the former fought with its equals, the tactical lessons are valid. The galley was never reduced to impotence by a calm, and hence receives more respect in our day than the sailing-ship ; yet the latter displaced it and remained supreme until the utilization of steam. The powers to injure an enemy from a great distance, to manœuvre for an unlimited length of time without wearing out the men, to devote the greater part of the crew to the offensive weapons instead of to the oar, are common to the sailing vessel and the steamer, and are at least as important, tactically considered, as the power of the galley to move in a calm or against the wind.

---

[1] The writer must guard himself from appearing to advocate elaborate tactical movements issuing in barren demonstrations. He believes that a fleet seeking a decisive result must close with its enemy, but not until some advantage has been obtained for the collision, which will usually be gained by manœuvring, and will fall to the best drilled and managed fleet. In truth, barren results have as often followed upon headlong, close encounters as upon the most timid tactical trifling.

In tracing resemblances there is a tendency not only to overlook points of difference, but to exaggerate points of likeness, — to be fanciful. It may be so considered to point out that as the sailing-ship had guns of long range, with comparatively great penetrative power, and carronades, which were of shorter range but great smashing effect, so the modern steamer has its batteries of long-range guns and of torpedoes, the latter being effective only within a limited distance and then injuring by smashing, while the gun, as of old, aims at penetration. Yet these are distinctly tactical considerations, which must affect the plans of admirals and captains ; and the analogy is real, not forced. So also both the sailing-ship and the steamer contemplate direct contact with an enemy's vessel,— the former to carry her by boarding, the latter to sink her by ramming ; and to both this is the most difficult of their tasks, for to effect it the ship must be carried to a single point of the field of action, whereas projectile weapons may be used from many points of a wide area.

The relative positions of two sailing-ships, or fleets, with reference to the direction of the wind involved most important tactical questions, and were perhaps the chief care of the seamen of that age. To a superficial glance it may appear that since this has become a matter of such indifference to the steamer, no analogies to it are to be found in present conditions, and the lessons of history in this respect are valueless. A more careful consideration of the distinguishing characteristics of the lee and the weather " gage," [1] directed to their essential features and disregarding secondary details, will show that this is a mistake. The distinguishing feature of the weather-gage was that it conferred the power of giving

---

[1] A ship was said to have the weather-gage, or " the advantage of the wind," or " to be to windward," when the wind allowed her to steer for her opponent, and did not let the latter head straight for her. The extreme case was when the wind blew direct from one to the other ; but there was a large space on either side of this line to which the term " weather-gage " applied. If the lee ship be taken as the centre of a circle, there were nearly three eighths of its area in which the other might be and still keep the advantage of the wind to a greater or less degree. Lee is the opposite of weather.

or refusing battle at will, which in turn carries the usual advantage of an offensive attitude in the choice of the method of attack. This advantage was accompanied by certain drawbacks, such as irregularity introduced into the order, exposure to raking or enfilading cannonade, and the sacrifice of part or all of the artillery-fire of the assailant, — all which were incurred in approaching the enemy. The ship, or fleet, with the lee-gage could not attack; if it did not wish to retreat, its action was confined to the defensive, and to receiving battle on the enemy's terms. This disadvantage was compensated by the comparative ease of maintaining the order of battle undisturbed, and by a sustained artillery-fire to which the enemy for a time was unable to reply. Historically, these favorable and unfavorable characteristics have their counterpart and analogy in the offensive and defensive operations of all ages. The offence undertakes certain risks and disadvantages in order to reach and destroy the enemy; the defence, so long as it remains such, refuses the risks of advance, holds on to a careful, well-ordered position, and avails itself of the exposure to which the assailant submits himself. These radical differences between the weather and the lee gage were so clearly recognized, through the cloud of lesser details accompanying them, that the former was ordinarily chosen by the English, because their steady policy was to assail and destroy their enemy; whereas the French sought the lee-gage, because by so doing they were usually able to cripple the enemy as he approached, and thus evade decisive encounters and preserve their ships. The French, with rare exceptions, subordinated the action of the navy to other military considerations, grudged the money spent upon it, and therefore sought to economize their fleet by assuming a defensive position and limiting its efforts to the repelling of assaults. For this course the lee-gage, skilfully used, was admirably adapted so long as an enemy displayed more courage than conduct; but when Rodney showed an intention to use the advantage of the wind, not merely to attack, but to make a formidable concentration on a part of the enemy's line, his wary opponent, De Guichen, changed his tactics. In the first of their three actions the Frenchman took the lee-gage; but after recognizing Rodney's purpose he manœuvred for the advantage of the wind, not to attack, but to refuse action except on his own terms. The power to assume the offensive, or to refuse battle, rests no longer with the wind, but with the party which has the greater speed; which in a fleet will depend not only upon the speed of the individual ships, but also upon tneir tactical uniformity of action. Henceforth the ships which have the greatest speed will have the weather-gage.

It is not therefore a vain expectation, as many think, to look for useful lessons in the history of sailing-ships as well as in that of galleys. Both have their points of resemblance to the modern ship; both have also points of essential differ-ence, which make it impossible to cite their experiences or modes of action as tactical *precedents* to be followed. But a precedent is different from and less valuable than a principle. The former may be originally faulty, or may cease to apply through change of circumstances; the latter has its root in the essential nature of things, and, however various its application as conditions change, remains a standard to which action must conform to attain success. War has such prin-ciples; their existence is detected by the study of the past, which reveals them in successes and in failures, the same from age to age. Conditions and weapons change; but to cope with the one or successfully wield the others, respect must be had to these constant teachings of history in the tactics of the battlefield, or in those wider operations of war which are comprised under the name of strategy.

It is however in these wider operations, which embrace a whole theatre of war, and in a maritime contest may cover a large portion of the globe, that the teachings of history have a more evident and permanent value, because the conditions remain more permanent. The theatre of war may be larger or smaller, its difficulties more or less pronounced, the con-tending armies more or less great, the necessary movements

363

more or less easy, but these are simply differences of scale, of degree, not of kind. As a wilderness gives place to civilization, as means of communication multiply, as roads are opened, rivers bridged, food-resources increased, the operations of war become easier, more rapid, more extensive; but the principles to which they must be conformed remain the same. When the march on foot was replaced by carrying troops in coaches, when the latter in turn gave place to railroads, the scale of distances was increased, or, if you will, the scale of time diminished; but the principles which dictated the point at which the army should be concentrated, the direction in which it should move, the part of the enemy's position which it should assail, the protection of communications, were not altered. So, on the sea, the advance from the galley timidly creeping from port to port to the sailing-ship launching out boldly to the ends of the earth, and from the latter to the steamship of our own time, has increased the scope and the rapidity of naval operations without necessarily changing the principles which should direct them; and the speech of Hermocrates twenty-three hundred years ago, before quoted, contained a correct strategic plan, which is as applicable in its principles now as it was then. Before hostile armies or fleets are brought into con*tact* (a word which perhaps better than any other indicates the dividing line between tactics and strategy), there are a number of questions to be decided, covering the whole plan of operations throughout the theatre of war. Among these are the proper function of the navy in the war; its true objective; the point or points upon which it should be concentrated; the establishment of depots of coal and supplies; the maintenance of communications between these depots and the home base; the military value of commerce-destroying as a decisive or a secondary operation of war; the system upon which commerce-destroying can be most efficiently conducted, whether by scattered cruisers or by holding in force some vital centre through which commercial shipping must pass. All these are strategic questions, and upon all these history

has a great deal to say. There has been of late a valuable discussion in English naval circles as to the comparative merits of the policies of two great English admirals, Lord Howe and Lord St. Vincent, in the disposition of the English navy when at war with France. The question is purely strategic, and is not of mere historical interest; it is of vital importance now, and the principles upon which its decision rests are the same now as then. St. Vincent's policy saved England from invasion, and in the hands of Nelson and his brother admirals led straight up to Trafalgar.

It is then particularly in the field of naval strategy that the teachings of the past have a value which is in no degree lessened. They are there useful not only as illustrative of principles, but also as precedents, owing to the comparative permanence of the conditions. This is less obviously true as to tactics, when the fleets come into collision at the point to which strategic considerations have brought them. The unresting progress of mankind causes continual change in the weapons; and with that must come a continual change in the manner of fighting, — in the handling and disposition of troops or ships on the battlefield. Hence arises a tendency on the part of many connected with maritime matters to think that no advantage is to be gained from the study of former experiences; that time so used is wasted. This view, though natural, not only leaves wholly out of sight those broad strategic considerations which lead nations to put fleets afloat, which direct the sphere of their action, and so have modified and will continue to modify the history of the world, but is one-sided and narrow even as to tactics. The battles of the past succeeded or failed according as they were fought in conformity with the principles of war; and the seaman who carefully studies the causes of success or failure will not only detect and gradually assimilate these principles, but will also acquire increased aptitude in applying them to the tactical use of the ships and weapons of his own day. He will observe also that changes of tactics have not only taken place *after* changes in weapons. which necessarily is the case, but that the interval between such changes has been unduly long. This doubtless arises from the fact that an improvement of weapons is due to the energy of one or two men, while changes in tactics have to overcome the inertia of a conservative class; but it is a great evil. It can be remedied only by a candid recognition of each change, by careful study of the powers and limitations of the new ship or weapon, and by a consequent adaptation of the method of using it to the qualities it possesses, which will constitute its tactics. History shows that it is vain to hope that military men generally will be at the pains to do this, but that the one who does will go into battle with a great advantage, — a lesson in itself of no mean value.

We may therefore accept now the words of a French tactician, Morogues, who wrote a century and a quarter ago: "Naval tactics are based upon conditions the chief causes of which, namely the arms, may change; which in turn causes necessarily a change in the construction of ships, in the manner of handling them, and so finally in the disposition and handling of fleets." His further statement, that "it is not a science founded upon principles absolutely invariable," is more open to criticism. It would be more correct to say that the application of its principles varies as the weapons change. The application of the principles doubtless varies also in strategy from time to time, but the variation is far less; and hence the recognition of the underlying principle is easier. This statement is of sufficient importance to our subject to receive some illustrations from historical events.

The battle of the Nile, in 1798, was not only an overwhelming victory for the English over the French fleet, but had also the decisive effect of destroying the communications between France and Napoleon's army in Egypt. In the battle itself the English admiral, Nelson, gave a most brilliant example of grand tactics, if that be, as has been defined, "the art of making good combinations preliminary to battles as well as during their progress." The particular tactical combination depended upon a condition now passed away, which was the inability of the lee ships of a fleet at anchor to come to the help of the weather ones before the latter were destroyed ; but the principles which underlay the combination, namely, to choose that part of the enemy's order which can least easily be helped, and to attack it with superior forces, has not passed away. The action of Admiral Jervis at Cape St. Vincent, when with fifteen ships he won a victory over twenty-seven, was dictated by the same principle, though in this case the enemy was not at anchor, but under way. Yet men's minds are so constituted that they seem more impressed by the transiency of the conditions than by the undying principle which coped with them. In the strategic effect of Nelson's victory upon the course of the war, on the contrary, the principle involved is not only more easily recognized, but it is at once seen to be applicable to our own day. The issue of the enterprise in Egypt depended upon keeping open the communications with France. The victory of the Nile destroyed the naval force, by which alone the communications could be assured, and determined the final failure ; and it is at once seen, not only that the blow was struck in accordance with the principle of striking at the enemy's line of communication, but also that the same principle is valid now, and would be equally so in the days of the galley as of the sailing-ship or steamer.

Nevertheless, a vague feeling of contempt for the past, supposed to be obsolete, combines with natural indolence to blind men even to those permanent strategic lessons which lie close to the surface of naval history. For instance, how many look upon the battle of Trafalgar, the crown of Nelson's glory and the seal of his genius, as other than an isolated event of exceptional grandeur ? How many ask themselves the strategic question, " How did the ships come to be just there ? " How many realize it to be the final act in a great strategic drama, extending over a year or more, in which two of the greatest leaders that ever lived, Napoleon and Nelson, were pitted against each other ? At Trafalgar it was not Villeneuve that failed, but Napoleon that was vanquished ; not Nelson that won, but England that was saved ; and why ? Because

Napoleon's combinations failed, and Nelson's intuitions and activity kept the English fleet ever on the track of the enemy, and brought it up in time at the decisive moment.[1] The tactics at Trafalgar, while open to criticism in detail, were in their main features conformable to the principles of war, and their audacity was justified as well by the urgency of the case as by the results ; but the great lessons of efficiency in preparation, of activity and energy in execution, and of thought and insight on the part of the English leader during the previous months, are strategic lessons, and as such they still remain good.

In these two cases events were worked out to their natural and decisive end. A third may be cited, in which, as no such definite end was reached, an opinion as to what should have been done may be open to dispute. In the war of the American Revolution, France and Spain became allies against England in 1779. The united fleets thrice appeared in the English Channel, once to the number of sixty-six sail of the line, driving the English fleet to seek refuge in its ports because far inferior in numbers. Now, the great aim of Spain was to recover Gibraltar and Jamaica ; and to the former end immense efforts both by land and sea were put forth by the allies against that nearly impregnable fortress. They were fruitless. The question suggested — and it is purely one of naval strategy — is this : Would not Gibraltar have been more surely recovered by controlling the English Channel, attacking the British fleet even in its harbors, and threatening England with annihilation of commerce and invasion at home, than by far greater efforts directed against a distant and very strong outpost of her empire ? The English people, from long immunity, were particularly sensitive to fears of invasion, and their great confidence in their fleets, if rudely shaken, would have left them proportionately disheartened. However decided, the question as a point of strategy is fair ; and it is proposed in another form by a French officer of the period, who favored directing the great effort on a West India island

[1] See note at end of Introductory Chapter, page 28.

which might be exchanged against Gibraltar. It is not, however, likely that England would have given up the key of the Mediterranean for any other foreign possession, though she might have yielded it to save her firesides and her capital. Napoleon once said that he would reconquer Pondicherry on the banks of the Vistula. Could he have controlled the English Channel, as the allied fleet did for a moment in 1779, can it be doubted that he would have conquered Gibraltar on the shores of England?

To impress more strongly the truth that history both suggests strategic study and illustrates the principles of war by the facts which it transmits, two more instances will be taken, which are more remote in time than the period specially considered in this work. How did it happen that, in two great contests between the powers of the East and of the West in the Mediterranean, in one of which the empire of the known world was at stake, the opposing fleets met on spots so near each other as Actium and Lepanto? Was this a mere coincidence, or was it due to conditions that recurred, and may recur again?[1] If the latter, it is worth while to study out the reason; for if there should again arise a great eastern power of the sea like that of Antony or of Turkey, the strategic questions would be similar. At present, indeed, it seems that the centre of sea power, resting mainly with England and France, is overwhelmingly in the West; but should any chance add to the control of the Black Sea basin, which Russia now has, the possession of the entrance to the Mediterranean, the existing strategic conditions affecting sea power would all be modified. Now, were the West arrayed against the East, England and France would go at once unopposed to the Levant, as they did in 1854, and as England alone went in 1878; in case of the change suggested, the East, as twice before, would meet the West half-way.

At a very conspicuous and momentous period of the world's history, Sea Power had a strategic bearing and weight which

---

[1] The battle of Navarino (1827) between Turkey and the Western Powers was fought in this neighborhood.

has received scant recognition. There cannot now be had the full knowledge necessary for tracing in detail its influence upon the issue of the second Punic War; but the indications which remain are sufficient to warrant the assertion that it was a determining factor. An accurate judgment upon this point cannot be formed by mastering only such facts of the particular contest as have been clearly transmitted, for as usual the naval transactions have been slightingly passed over; there is needed also familiarity with the details of general naval history in order to draw, from slight indications, correct inferences based upon a knowledge of what has been possible at periods whose history is well known. The control of the sea, however real, does not imply that an enemy's single ships or small squadrons cannot steal out of port, cannot cross more or less frequented tracts of ocean, make harassing descents upon unprotected points of a long coast-line, enter blockaded harbors. On the contrary, history has shown that such evasions are always possible, to some extent, to the weaker party, however great the inequality of naval strength. It is not therefore inconsistent with the general control of the sea, or of a decisive part of it, by the Roman fleets, that the Carthaginian admiral Bomilcar in the fourth year of the war, after the stunning defeat of Cannæ, landed four thousand men and a body of elephants in south Italy; nor that in the seventh year, flying from the Roman fleet off Syracuse, he again appeared at Tarentum, then in Hannibal's hands; nor that Hannibal sent despatch vessels to Carthage; nor even that, at last, he withdrew in safety to Africa with his wasted army. None of these things prove that the government in Carthage could, if it wished, have sent Hannibal the constant support which, as a matter of fact, he did not receive; but they do tend to create a natural impression that such help could have been given. Therefore the statement, that the Roman preponderance at sea had a decisive effect upon the course of the war, needs to be made good by an examination of ascertained facts. Thus the kind and degree of its influence may be fairly estimated.

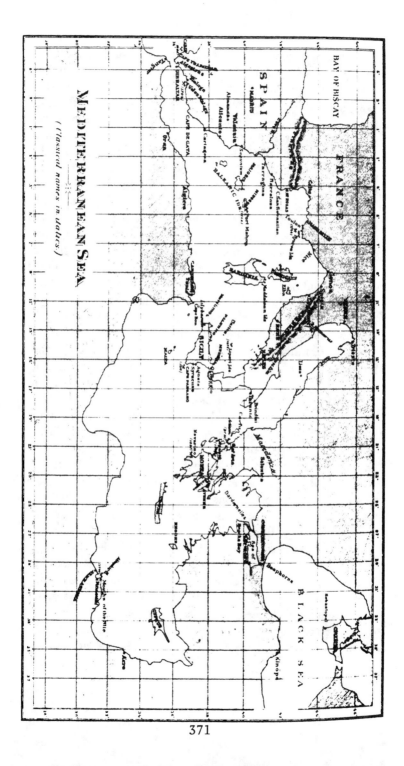

At the beginning of the war, Mommsen says, Rome controlled the seas. To whatever cause, or combination of causes, it be attributed, this essentially non-maritime state had in the first Punic War established over its sea-faring rival a naval supremacy, which still lasted. In the second war there was no naval battle of importance, — a circumstance which in itself, and still more in connection with other well-ascertained facts, indicates a superiority analogous to that which at other epochs has been marked by the same feature.

As Hannibal left no memoirs, the motives are unknown which determined him to the perilous and almost ruinous march through Gaul and across the Alps. It is certain, however, that his fleet on the coast of Spain was not strong enough to contend with that of Rome. Had it been, he might still have followed the road he actually did, for reasons that weighed with him; but had he gone by the sea, he would not have lost thirty-three thousand out of the sixty thousand veteran soldiers with whom he started.

While Hannibal was making this dangerous march, the Romans were sending to Spain, under the two elder Scipios, one part of their fleet, carrying a consular army. This made the voyage without serious loss, and the army established itself successfully north of the Ebro, on Hannibal's line of communications. At the same time another squadron, with an army commanded by the other consul, was sent to Sicily. The two together numbered two hundred and twenty ships. On its station each met and defeated a Carthaginian squadron with an ease which may be inferred from the slight mention made of the actions, and which indicates the actual superiority of the Roman fleet.

After the second year the war assumed the following shape: Hannibal, having entered Italy by the north, after a series of successes had passed southward around Rome and fixed himself in southern Italy, living off the country, — a condition which tended to alienate the people, and was especially precarious when in contact with the mighty political and military system of control which Rome had there established. It was therefore from the first urgently necessary that he should establish, between himself and some reliable base, that stream of supplies and reinforcements which in terms of modern war is called " communications." There were three friendly regions which might, each or all, serve as such a base, — Carthage itself, Macedonia, and Spain. With the first two, communication could be had only by sea. From Spain, where his firmest support was found, he could be reached by both land and sea, unless an enemy barred the passage ; but the sea route was the shorter and easier.

In the first years of the war, Rome, by her sea power, controlled absolutely the basin between Italy, Sicily, and Spain, known as the Tyrrhenian and Sardinian Seas. The seacoast from the Ebro to the Tiber was mostly friendly to her. In the fourth year, after the battle of Cannæ, Syracuse forsook the Roman alliance, the revolt spread through Sicily, and Macedonia also entered into an offensive league with Hannibal. These changes extended the necessary operations of the Roman fleet, and taxed its strength. What disposition was made of it, and how did it thereafter influence the struggle ?

The indications are clear that Rome at no time ceased to control the Tyrrhenian Sea, for her squadrons passed unmolested from Italy to Spain. On the Spanish coast also she had full sway till the younger Scipio saw fit to lay up the fleet. In the Adriatic, a squadron and naval station were established at Brindisi to check Macedonia, which performed their task so well that not a soldier of the phalanxes ever set foot in Italy. " The want of a war fleet," says Mommsen, " paralyzed Philip in all his movements." Here the effect of Sea Power is not even a matter of inference.

In Sicily, the struggle centred about Syracuse. The fleets of Carthage and Rome met there, but the superiority evidently lay with the latter ; for though the Carthaginians at times succeeded in throwing supplies into the city, they avoided meeting the Roman fleet in battle. With Lilybæum, Palermo, and Messina in its hands, the latter was well based in the north coast of the island. Access by the south was left open to the Carthaginians, and they were thus able to maintain the insurrection.

Putting these facts together, it is a reasonable inference, and supported by the whole tenor of the history, that the Roman sea power controlled the sea north of a line drawn from Tarragona in Spain to Lilybæum (the modern Marsala), at the west end of Sicily, thence round by the north side of the island through the straits of Messina down to Syracuse, and from there to Brindisi in the Adriatic. This control lasted, unshaken, throughout the war. It did not exclude maritime raids, large or small, such as have been spoken of; but it did forbid the sustained and secure communications of which Hannibal was in deadly need.

On the other hand, it seems equally plain that for the first ten years of the war the Roman fleet was not strong enough for sustained operations in the sea between Sicily and Carthage, nor indeed much to the south of the line indicated. When Hannibal started, he assigned such ships as he had to maintaining the communications between Spain and Africa, which the Romans did not then attempt to disturb.

The Roman sea power, therefore, threw Macedonia wholly out of the war. It did not keep Carthage from maintaining a useful and most harassing diversion in Sicily; but it did prevent her sending troops, when they would have been most useful, to her great general in Italy. How was it as to Spain?

Spain was the region upon which the father of Hannibal and Hannibal himself had based their intended invasion of Italy. For eighteen years before this began they had occupied the country, extending and consolidating their power, both political and military, with rare sagacity. They had raised, and trained in local wars, a large and now veteran army. Upon his own departure, Hannibal intrusted the government to his younger brother, Hasdrubal, who preserved toward him to the end a loyalty and devotion which he had no reason to hope from the faction-cursed mother-city in Africa.

At the time of his starting, the Carthaginian power in

Spain was secured from Cadiz to the river Ebro. The region between this river and the Pyrenees was inhabited by tribes friendly to the Romans, but unable, in the absence of the latter, to oppose a successful resistance to Hannibal. He put them down, leaving eleven thousand soldiers under Hanno to keep military possession of the country, lest the Romans should establish themselves there, and thus disturb his communications with his base.

Cnæus Scipio, however, arrived on the spot by sea the same year with twenty thousand men, defeated Hanno, and occupied both the coast and interior north of the Ebro. The Romans thus held ground by which they entirely closed the road between Hannibal and reinforcements from Hasdrubal, and whence they could attack the Carthaginian power in Spain; while their own communications with Italy, being by water, were secured by their naval supremacy. They made a naval base at Tarragona, confronting that of Hasdrubal at Cartagena, and then invaded the Carthaginian dominions. The war in Spain went on under the elder Scipios, seemingly a side issue, with varying fortune for seven years; at the end of which time Hasdrubal inflicted upon them a crushing defeat, the two brothers were killed, and the Carthaginians nearly succeeded in breaking through to the Pyrenees with reinforcements for Hannibal. The attempt, however, was checked for the moment; and before it could be renewed, the fall of Capua released twelve thousand veteran Romans, who were sent to Spain under Claudius Nero, a man of exceptional ability, to whom was due later the most decisive military movement made by any Roman general during the Second Punic War. This seasonable reinforcement, which again assured the shaken grip on Hasdrubal's line of march, came by sea, — a way which, though most rapid and easy, was closed to the Carthaginians by the Roman navy.

Two years later the younger Publius Scipio, celebrated afterward as Africanus, received the command in Spain, and captured Cartagena by a combined military and naval attack;

after which he took the most extraordinary step of breaking up his fleet and transferring the seamen to the army. Not contented to act merely as the "containing"[1] force against Hasdrubal by closing the passes of the Pyrenees, Scipio pushed forward into southern Spain, and fought a severe but indecisive battle on the Guadalquivir; after which Hasdrubal slipped away from him, hurried north, crossed the Pyrenees at their extreme west, and pressed on to Italy, where Hannibal's position was daily growing weaker, the natural waste of his army not being replaced.

The war had lasted ten years, when Hasdrubal, having met little loss on the way, entered Italy at the north. The troops he brought, could they be safely united with those under the command of the unrivalled Hannibal, might give a decisive turn to the war, for Rome herself was nearly exhausted ; the iron links which bound her own colonies and the allied States to her were strained to the utmost, and some had already snapped. But the military position of the two brothers was also perilous in the extreme. One being at the river Metaurus, the other in Apulia, two hundred miles apart, each was confronted by a superior enemy, and both these Roman armies were between their separated opponents. This false situation, as well as the long delay of Hasdrubal's coming, was due to the Roman control of the sea, which throughout the war limited the mutual support of the Carthaginian brothers to the route through Gaul. At the very time that Hasdrubal was making his long and dangerous circuit by land, Scipio had sent eleven thousand men from Spain by sea to reinforce the army opposed to him. The upshot was that messengers from Hasdrubal to Hannibal, having to pass over so wide a belt of hostile country, fell into the hands of Claudius Nero, commanding the southern Roman army, who thus learned the route which Hasdrubal intended to take. Nero correctly appreciated the situation, and, escaping the vigilance

[1] A "containing" force is one to which, in a military combination, is assigned the duty of stopping, or delaying the advance of a portion of the enemy, while the main effort of the army or armies is being exerted in a different quarter.

of Hannibal, made a rapid march with eight thousand of his best troops to join the forces in the north. The junction being effected, the two consuls fell upon Hasdrubal in overwhelming numbers and destroyed his army ; the Carthaginian leader himself falling in the battle. Hannibal's first news of the disaster was by the head of his brother being thrown into his camp. He is said to have exclaimed that Rome would now be mistress of the world ; and the battle of Metaurus is generally accepted as decisive of the struggle between the two States.

The military situation which finally resulted in the battle of the Metaurus and the triumph of Rome may be summed up as follows : To overthrow Rome it was necessary to attack her in Italy at the heart of her power, and shatter the strongly linked confederacy of which she was the head. This was the objective. To reach it, the Carthaginians needed a solid base of operations and a secure line of communications. The former was established in Spain by the genius of the great Barca family ; the latter was never achieved. There were two lines possible, — the one direct by sea, the other circuitous through Gaul. The first was blocked by the Roman sea power, the second imperilled and finally intercepted through the occupation of northern Spain by the Roman army. This occupation was made possible through the control of the sea, which the Carthaginians never endangered. With respect to Hannibal and his base, therefore, Rome occupied two central positions, Rome itself and northern Spain, joined by an easy interior line of communications, the sea ; by which mutual support was continually given.

Had the Mediterranean been a level desert of land, in which the Romans held strong mountain ranges in Corsica and Sardinia, fortified posts at Tarragona, Lilybæum, and Messina, the Italian coast-line nearly to Genoa, and allied fortresses in Marseilles and other points ; had they also possessed an armed force capable by its character of traversing that desert at will, but in which their opponents were very inferior and therefore compelled to a great circuit in order to concentrate their troops, the military situation would have been at once recognized, and no words would have been too strong to express the value and effect of that peculiar force. It would have been perceived, also, that the enemy's force of the same kind might, however inferior in strength, make an inroad, or raid, upon the territory thus held, might burn a village or waste a few miles of borderland, might even cut off a convoy at times, without, in a military sense, endangering the communications. Such predatory operations have been carried on in all ages by the weaker maritime belligerent, but they by no means warrant the inference, irreconcilable with the known facts, " that neither Rome nor Carthage could be said to have undisputed mastery of the sea," because " Roman fleets sometimes visited the coasts of Africa, and Carthaginian fleets in the same way appeared off the coast of Italy." In the case under consideration, the navy played the part of such a force upon the supposed desert; but as it acts on an element strange to most writers, as its members have been from time immemorial a strange race apart, without prophets of their own, neither themselves nor their calling understood, its immense determining influence upon the history of that era, and consequently upon the history of the world, has been overlooked. If the preceding argument is sound, it is as defective to omit sea power from the list of principal factors in the result, as it would be absurd to claim for it an exclusive influence.

Instances such as have been cited, drawn from widely separated periods of time, both before and after that specially treated in this work, serve to illustrate the intrinsic interest of the subject, and the character of the lessons which history has to teach. As before observed, these come more often under the head of strategy than of tactics; they bear rather upon the conduct of campaigns than of battles, and hence are fraught with more lasting value. To quote a great authority in this connection, Jomini says: " Happening to be in Paris near the end of 1851, a distinguished person did me the honor to ask my opinion as to whether recent improvements in fire

378

arms would cause any great modifications in the way of mak· ing war. I replied that they would probably have an influence upon the details of tactics, but that in great strategic operations and the grand combinations of battles, victory would, now as ever, result from the application of the principles which had led to the success of great generals in all ages ; of Alexander and Cæsar, as well as of Frederick and Napoleon." This study has become more than ever important now to navies, because of the great and steady power of movement possessed by the mod· ern steamer. The best-planned schemes might fail through stress of weather in the days of the galley and the sailing-ship; but this difficulty has almost disappeared. The principles which should direct great naval combinations have been applicable to all ages, and are deducible from history ; but the power to carry them out with little regard to the weather is a recent gain.

The definitions usually given of the word "strategy" con- fine it to military combinations embracing one or more fields of operations, either wholly distinct or mutually dependent, but always regarded as actual or immediate scenes of war. How- ever this may be on shore, a recent French author is quite right in pointing out that such a definition is too narrow for naval strategy. "This," he says, "differs from military strategy in that it is as necessary in peace as in war. Indeed, in peace it may gain its most decisive victories by occupying in a country, either by purchase or treaty, excellent positions which would perhaps hardly be got by war. It learns to profit by all opportunities of settling on some chosen point of a coast, and to render definitive an occupation which at first was only transient." A generation that has seen England within ten years occupy successively Cyprus and Egypt, under terms and conditions on their face transient, but which have not yet led to the abandonment of the positions taken, can readily agree with this remark ; which indeed receives con· stant illustration from the quiet persistency witn which all the great sea powers are seeking position after position, less noted and less noteworthy than Cyprus and Egypt, in the different seas to which their people and their ships penetrate.

" Naval strategy has indeed for its end to found, support, and increase, as well in peace as in war, the sea power of a country ; " and therefore its study has an interest and value for all citizens of a free country, but especially for those who are charged with its foreign and military relations.

The general conditions that either are essential to or powerfully affect the greatness of a nation upon the sea will now be examined ; after which a more particular consideration of the various maritime nations of Europe at the middle of the seventeenth century, where the historical survey begins, will serve at once to illustrate and give precision to the conclusions upon the general subject.

Note. — The brilliancy of Nelson's fame, dimming as it does that of all his contemporaries, and the implicit trust felt by England in him as the one man able to save her from the schemes of Napoleon, should not of course obscure the fact that only one portion of the field was, or could be, occupied by him. Napoleon's aim, in the campaign which ended at Trafalgar, was to unite in the West Indies the French fleets of Brest, Toulon, and Rochefort, together with a strong body of Spanish ships, thus forming an overwhelming force which he intended should return together to the English Channel and cover the crossing of the French army. He naturally expected that, with England's interests scattered all over the world, confusion and distraction would arise from ignorance of the destination of the French squadrons, and the English navy be drawn away from his objective point. The portion of the field committed to Nelson was the Mediterranean, where he watched the great arsenal of Toulon and the highways alike to the East and to the Atlantic. This was inferior in consequence to no other, and assumed additional importance in the eyes of Nelson from his conviction that the former attempts on Egypt would be renewed. Owing to this persuasion he took at first a false step, which delayed his pursuit of the Toulon fleet when it sailed under the command of Villeneuve ; and the latter was further favored by a long continuance of fair winds, while the English had head winds. But while all this is true, while the failure of Napoleon's combinations must be attributed to the tenacious grip of the English blockade off Brest, *as well as* to Nelson's energetic pursuit of the Toulon fleet when it escaped to the West Indies and again on its hasty return to Europe, the latter is fairly entitled to the eminent distinction which history has accorded it, and which is asserted in the text. Nelson did not, indeed, fathom the intentions of Napoleon. This may have been owing, as some have said, to lack of insight; but it may be more simply laid to the usual disadvantage under which the defence lies before the blow has fallen, of ignorance as to the point threat. ened by the offence. It is insight enough to fasten on the key of a situation; and this Nelson rightly saw was the fleet, not the station. Consequently, his action has afforded a striking instance of how tenacity of purpose and untiring energy in execution can repair a first mistake and baffle deeply laid plans. His Mediterranean command embraced many duties and cares; but amid and dominating them all, he saw clearly the Toulon fleet as the controlling factor there, and an important factor in any naval combination of the Emperor. Hence his attention was unwaveringly fixed upon it; so much so that he called it "his fleet," a phrase which has somewhat vexed the sensibilities of French critics. This simple and accurate view of the military situation strengthened him in taking the fearless resolution and bearing the immense responsibility of abandoning his station in order to follow "his fleet." Determined thus on a pursuit the undeniable wisdom of which should not obscure the greatness of mind that undertook it, he rollowed so vigorously as to reach Cadiz on his return a week before Villeneuve entered Ferrol, despite unavoidable delays arising from false information and uncertainty as to the enemy's movements. The same untiring ardor enabled him to bring up his own ships from Cadiz to Brest in time to make the fleet there superior to Villeneuve's, had the latter persisted in his attempt to reach the neighborhood. The English, very inferior in aggregate number of vessels to the allied fleets, were by this seasonable reinforcement of eight veteran ships put into the best possible position strategically, as will be pointed out in dealing with similar conditions in the war of the American Revolution. Their forces were united in one great fleet in the Bay of Biscay, interposed between the two divisions of the enemy in Brest and Ferrol, superior in number to either singly, and with a strong probability of being able to deal with one before the other could come up. This was due to able action all round on the part of the English authorities; but above all other factors in the result stands Nelson's single-minded pursuit of "his fleet."

This interesting series of strategic movements ended on the 14th of August, when Villeneuve, in despair of reaching Brest, headed for Cadiz, where he anchored on the 20th. As soon as Napoleon heard of this, after an outburst of rage against the admiral, he at once dictated the series of movements which resulted in Ulm and Austerlitz, abandoning his purposes against England. The battle of Trafalgar, fought October 21, was therefore separated by a space of two months from the extensive movements of which it was nevertheless the outcome. Isolated from them in point of time, it was none the less the seal of Nelson's genius, affixed later to the record he had made in the near past. With equal truth is it said that England was saved at Trafalgar, though the Emperor had then given up his intended invasion; the destruction there emphasized and sealed the strategic triumph which had noiselessly foiled Napoleon's plans.

Before going on again with the general course of the history of the times, it will be well to consider for a moment the theory which worked so disastrously for England in 1667; that, namely, of maintaining a sea-war mainly by preying upon the enemy's commerce. This plan, which involves only the maintenance of a few swift cruisers and can be backed by the spirit of greed in a nation, fitting out privateers without direct expense to the State, possesses the specious attractions which economy always presents. The great injury done to the wealth and prosperity of the enemy is also undeniable; and although to some extent his merchant-ships can shelter themselves ignobly under a foreign flag while the war lasts, this *guerre de course*, as the French call it, this commerce-destroying, to use our own phrase, must, if in itself successful, greatly embarrass the foreign government and distress its people. Such a war, however, cannot stand alone; it must be *supported*, to use the military phrase; unsubstantial and evanescent in itself, it cannot reach far from its base. That base must be either home ports, or else some solid outpost of the national power, on the shore or the sea; a distant dependency or a powerful fleet. Failing such support, the cruiser can only dash out hurriedly a short distance from home, and its blows, though painful, cannot be fatal. It was not the policy of 1667, but Cromwell's powerful fleets of ships-of-the-line in

1652, that shut the Dutch merchantmen in their ports and caused the grass to grow in the streets of Amsterdam. When, instructed by the suffering of that time, the Dutch kept large fleets afloat through two exhausting wars, though their commerce suffered greatly, they bore up the burden of the strife against England and France united. Forty years later, Louis XIV. was driven, by exhaustion, to the policy adopted by Charles II. through parsimony. Then were the days of the great French privateers, Jean Bart, Forbin, Duguay-Trouin, Du Casse, and others. The regular fleets of the French navy were practically withdrawn from the ocean during the great War of the Spanish Succession (1702–1712). The French naval historian says : —

"Unable to renew the naval armaments, Louis XIV. increased the number of cruisers upon the more frequented seas, especially the Channel and the German Ocean [not far from home, it will be noticed]. In these different spots the cruisers were always in a position to intercept or hinder the movements of transports laden with troops, and of the numerous convoys carrying supplies of all kinds. In these seas, in the centre of the commercial and political world, there is always work for cruisers. Notwithstanding the difficulties they met, owing to the absence of large friendly fleets, they served advantageously the cause of the two peoples [French and Spanish]. These cruisers, in the face of the Anglo-Dutch power, needed good luck, boldness, and skill. These three conditions were not lacking to our seamen; but then, what chiefs and what captains they had!" [1]

The English historian, on the other hand, while admitting how severely the people and commerce of England suffered from the cruisers, bitterly reflecting at times upon the administration, yet refers over and over again to the increasing prosperity of the whole country, and especially of its commercial part. In the preceding war, on the contrary, from 1689 to 1697, when France sent great fleets to sea and disputed the supremacy of the ocean, how different the result! The same English writer says of that time : —

[1] Lapeyrouse-Bonfils : Hist. de la Marine Française.

" With respect to our trade it is certain that we suffered infinitely more, not merely than the French, for that was to be expected from the greater number of our merchant-ships, but than we ever did in any former war. . . . This proceeded in great measure from the vigilance of the French, who carried on the war in a piratical way. It is out of all doubt that, taking all together, our traffic suffered excessively; our merchants were many of them ruined." [1]

Macaulay says of this period : " During many months of 1693 the English trade with the Mediterranean had been interrupted almost entirely. There was no chance that a merchantman from London or Amsterdam would, if unprotected, reach the Pillars of Hercules without being boarded by a French privateer ; and the protection of armed vessels was not easily obtained." Why ? Because the vessels of England's navy were occupied watching the French navy, and this diversion of them from the cruisers and privateers constituted the support which a commerce-destroying war must have. A French historian, speaking of the same period in England (1696), says : " The state of the finances was deplorable ; money was scarce, maritime insurance thirty per cent, the Navigation Act was virtually suspended, and the English shipping reduced to the necessity of sailing under the Swedish and Danish flags." [2] Half a century later the French government was again reduced, by long neglect of the navy, to a cruising warfare. With what results ? First, the French historian says : " From June, 1756, to June, 1760, French privateers captured from the English more than twenty-five hundred merchantmen. In 1761, though France had not, so to speak, a single ship-of-the-line at sea, and though the English had taken two hundred and forty of our privateers, their comrades still took eight hundred and twelve vessels. But," he goes on to say, " the prodigious growth of the English shipping explains the number of these prizes." [3] In other words, the suffering involved to England in such numerous

[1] Campbell: Lives of the Admirals.   [2] Martin: History of France.
[3] Martin : History of France.

captures, which must have caused great individual injury and discontent, did not really prevent the growing prosperity of the State and of the community at large. The English naval historian, speaking of the same period, says: " While the commerce of France was nearly destroyed, the trading-fleet of England covered the seas. Every year her commerce was increasing; the money which the war carried out was returned by the produce of her industry. Eight thousand merchant vessels were employed by the English merchants." And again, summing up the results of the war, after stating the immense amount of specie brought into the kingdom by foreign conquests, he says : " The trade of England increased gradually every year, and such a scéne of national prosperity, while waging a long, bloody, and costly war, was never before shown by any people in the world." On the other hand, the historian of the French navy, speaking of an earlier phase of the same wars, says: " The English fleets, having nothing to resist them, swept the seas. Our privateers and single cruisers, having no fleet to keep down the abundance of their enemies, ran short careers. Twenty thousand French seamen lay in English prisons." [1] When, on the other hand, in the War of the American Revolution France resumed the policy of Colbert and of the early reign of Louis XIV., and kept large battle-fleets afloat, the same result again followed as in the days of Tourville. "For the first time," says the Annual Register, forgetting or ignorant of the experience of 1693, and remembering only the glories of the later wars, " English merchant-ships were driven to take refuge under foreign flags." [2] Finally, in quitting this part of the subject, it may be remarked that in the island of Martinique the French had a powerful distant dependency upon which to base a cruising warfare; and during the Seven Years' War, as afterward during the First Empire, it, with Guadeloupe, was the refuge of numerous privateers. "The records of the English admiralty raise the losses of the English in the West Indies during the first years of the Seven Years' War to fourteen hundred

[1] Lapeyrouse-Bonfils.   [2] Annual Reg., vol. xxvii. p 10

merchantmen taken or destroyed." The English fleet was therefore directed against the islands, both of which fell, involving a loss to the trade of France greater than all the depredations of her cruisers on the English commerce, besides breaking up the system; but in the war of 1778 the great fleets protected the islands, which were not even threatened at any time.

So far we have been viewing the effect of a purely cruising warfare, not based upon powerful squadrons, only upon that particular part of the enemy's strength against which it is theoretically directed, — upon his commerce and general wealth; upon the sinews of war. The evidence seems to show that even for its own special ends such a mode of war is inconclusive, worrying but not deadly; it might almost be said that it causes needless suffering. What, however, is the effect of this policy upon the general ends of the war, to which it is one of the means, and to which it is subsidiary? How, again, does it react upon the people that practise it? As the historical evidences will come up in detail from time to time, it need here only be summarized. The result to England in the days of Charles II. has been seen, — her coast insulted, her shipping burned almost within sight of her capital. In the War of the Spanish Succession, when the control of Spain was the military object, while the French depended upon a cruising war against commerce, the navies of England and Holland, unopposed, guarded the coasts of the peninsula, blocked the port of Toulon, forced the French succors to cross the Pyrenees, and by keeping open the sea highway, neutralized the geographical nearness of France to the seat of war. Their fleets seized Gibraltar, Barcelona, and Minorca, and cooperating with the Austrian army failed by little of reducing Toulon. In the Seven Years' War the English fleets seized, or aided in seizing, all the most valuable colonies of France and Spain, and made frequent descents on the French coast. The War of the American Revolution affords no lesson, the fleets being nearly equal. The next most striking instance to Americans is the War of 1812. Everybody knows how our

privateers swarmed over the seas, and that from the smallness of our navy the war was essentially, indeed solely, a
cruising war. Except upon the lakes, it is doubtful if more
than two of our ships at any time acted together. The injury
done to English commerce, thus unexpectedly attacked by a
distant foe which had been undervalued, may be fully conceded; but on the one hand, the American cruisers were
powerfully supported by the French fleet, which being assembled in larger or smaller bodies in the many ports under the
emperor's control from Antwerp to Venice, tied the fleets of
England to blockade duty; and on the other hand, when the
fall of the emperor released them, our coasts were insulted in
every direction, the Chesapeake entered and controlled, its
shores wasted, the Potomac ascended, and Washington burned.
The Northern frontier was kept in a state of alarm, though
there squadrons, absolutely weak but relatively strong, sustained the general defence; while in the South the Mississippi
was entered unopposed, and New Orleans barely saved. When
negotiations for peace were opened, the bearing of the English
toward the American envoys was not that of men who felt
their country to be threatened with an unbearable evil. The
late Civil War, with the cruises of the "Alabama" and
"Sumter" and their consorts, revived the tradition of commerce-destroying. In so far as this is one means to a general end, and is based upon a navy otherwise powerful, it is
well; but we need not expect to see the feats of those ships
repeated in the face of a great sea power. In the first place,
those cruises were powerfully supported by the determination
of the United States to blockade, not only the chief centres
of Southern trade, but every inlet of the coast, thus leaving
few ships available for pursuit; in the second place, had
there been ten of those cruisers where there was one, they
would not have stopped the incursion in Southern waters of
the Union fleet, which penetrated to every point accessible
from the sea; and in the third place, the undeniable injury,
direct and indirect, inflicted upon individuals and upon one
branch of the nation's industry (and how high that shipping

industry stands in the writer's estimation need not be re peated), did not in the least influence or retard the event of the war. Such injuries, unaccompanied by others, are more irritating than weakening. On the other hand, will any refuse to admit that the work of the great Union fleets powerfully modified and hastened an end which was probably inevitable in any case? As a sea power the South then occupied the place of France in the wars we have been considering, while the situation of the North resembled that of England; and, as in France, the sufferers in the Confederacy were not a class, but the government and the nation at large. It is not the taking of individual ships or convoys, be they few or many, that strikes down the money power of a nation; it is the possession of that overbearing power on the sea which drives the enemy's flag from it, or allows it to appear only as a fugitive; and which, by controlling the great common, closes the highways by which commerce moves to and from the enemy's shores. This overbearing power can only be exercised by great navies, and by them (on the broad sea) less efficiently now than in the days when the neutral flag had not its present immunity. It is not unlikely that, in the event of a war between maritime nations, an attempt may be made by the one having a great sea power and wishing to break down its enemy's commerce, to interpret the phrase "effective blockade" in the manner that best suits its interests at the time; to assert that the speed and disposal of its ships make the blockade effective at much greater distances and with fewer ships than formerly. The determination of such a question will depend, not upoh the weaker belligerent, but upon neutral 'powers; it will raise the issue between belligerent and neutral rights; and if the belligerent have a vastly overpowering navy he may carry his point, just as England, when possessing the mastery of the seas, long refused to admit the doctrine of the neutral flag covering the goods.

6

Leo Tolstoy,   WAR AND PEACE
                (Trans. by Louise & Aylmer Maude)

Halford J. Mackinder,   DEMOCRATIC IDEALS AND REALITY

1. In spite of the French success at Borodino and
    their occupation of Moscow, Napoleon's Russian
    campaign of 1812 failed. How does Tolstoy account
    for this?

2. Compare the partisan warfare in Russia in 1812 with
    that of the European countries in World War II and
    with that of Viet-Cong of the 1960s.

3. How would Tolstoy regard the application of Clause-
    witz's principles of war in analyzing Napoleon's
    campaign in 1812?

4. Why did the French not cut off Napoleon's retreat
    and destroy the French Army?

5. Define the "World Island" and the "Heartland" ac-
    cording to Mackinder.

6. What are the strategic and policy implications of
    control of the "Heartland" in our time?

        Clifton Fadiman has noted, "*War and Peace* has been
called the greatest novel ever written. These very
words have been used, to my knowledge, by E.M. Forster,
Hugh Walpole, John Galsworthy, and Compton Mackenzie;
and a similar judgment has been made by many others."

        Tolstoy himself served as an artillery officer in
the Russian Army during the Crimean War. His great
novel, based on Russian responses to Napoleon's invasion of 1812, appeared in 1865-69. The excerpt given
here is an aside from the central narrative. Tolstoy
inserts it to give his interpretation on the nature of
victory and defeat in terms of the success of the
French before Moscow and then their disaster which followed.

WAR AND PEACE

1812

BOOK FOURTEEN

*1. National character of the war. A duelist who drops his
rapier and seizes a cudgel. Guerrilla warfare.
The spirit of the army*

THE BATTLE OF BORODINÓ, with the occupation of Moscow that followed it and the flight of the French without further conflicts, is one of the most instructive phenomena in history.

All historians agree that the external activity of states and nations in their conflicts with one another is expressed in wars, and that as a direct result of greater or less success in war the political strength of states and nations increases or decreases.

Strange as may be the historical account of how some king or emperor, having quarreled with another, collects an army, fights his enemy's army, gains a victory by killing three, five, or ten thousand men, and subjugates a kingdom and an entire nation of several millions, all the facts of history (as far as we know it) confirm the truth of the statement that the greater or lesser success of one army against another is the cause, or at least an essential indication, of an increase or decrease in the strength of the nation—even though it is unintelligible why the defeat of an army—a hundredth part of a nation—should oblige that whole nation to submit. An army gains a victory, and at once the rights of the conquering nation have increased to the detriment of the defeated. An army has suffered defeat, and at once a people loses its rights in proportion to the severity of the reverse, and if its army suffers a complete defeat the nation is quite subjugated.

So according to history it has been found from the most ancient times, and so it is to our own day. All Napoleon's wars serve to confirm this rule. In proportion to the defeat of the Austrian army Austria loses its rights, and the rights and the strength of France increase. The victories of the French at Jena and Auerstädt destroy the independent existence of Prussia.

But then, in 1812, the French gain a victory near Moscow. Moscow is taken and after that, with no further battles, it is not Russia that ceases to exist, but the French army of six hundred thousand, and then Napoleonic France itself. To strain the facts to fit the rules of history: to say that the field of battle at Borodinó remained in the hands of the Russians, or that after Moscow there were other battles that destroyed Napoleon's army, is impossible.

After the French victory at Borodinó there was no general engagement nor any that were at all serious, yet the French army ceased to exist. What does this mean? If it were an example taken from the history of China, we might say that it was not an historic phenomenon (which is the historians' usual expedient when anything does not fit their standards); if the matter concerned some brief conflict in which only a small number of troops took part, we might treat it as an exception; but this event occurred before our fathers' eyes, and for them it was a question of the life or death of their fatherland, and it happened in the greatest of all known wars.

The period of the campaign of 1812 from the battle of Borodinó to the expulsion of the French proved that the winning of a battle does not produce a conquest and is not even an invariable indication of conquest; it proved that the force which decides the fate of peoples lies not in the conquerors, nor even in armies and battles, but in something else.

The French historians, describing the condition of the French army before it left Moscow, affirm that all was in order in the Grand Army, except the cavalry, the artillery, and the transport—there was no forage for the horses or the cattle. That was a misfortune no one could remedy, for the peasants of the district burned their hay rather than let the French have it.

The victory gained did not bring the usual results because the peasants Karp and Vlas (who after the French had evacuated Moscow drove in their carts to pillage the town, and in general personally failed to manifest any heroic feelings), and the whole innumerable multitude of such peasants, did not bring their hay to Moscow for the high price offered them, but burned it instead.

Let us imagine two men who have come out to fight a duel with rapiers according to all the rules of the art of fencing. The fencing has gone on for some time; suddenly one of the combatants, feeling himself wounded and understanding that the matter is no joke but concerns his life, throws down his rapier, and seizing the first cudgel that comes to hand begins to brandish it. Then let us imagine that the combatant who so sensibly employed the best and simplest means to attain his end was at the same time influenced by traditions of chivalry and, desiring to conceal the facts of the case, insisted that he had gained his victory with the rapier according to all the rules of art. One can imagine what confusion and obscurity would result from such an account of the duel.

The fencer who demanded a contest according to the rules of fencing was the French army; his opponent who threw away the rapier and snatched up the cudgel was the Russian people; those who try to explain the matter according to the rules of fencing are the historians who have described the event.

After the burning of Smolénsk a war began which did not follow any previous traditions of war. The burning of towns and villages, the retreats after battles, the blow dealt at Borodinó and the renewed retreat, the burning of Moscow, the capture of marauders, the seizure of transports, and the guerrilla war were all departures from the rules.

Napoleon felt this, and from the time he took up the correct fencing attitude in Moscow and instead of his opponent's rapier saw a cudgel raised above his head, he did not cease to complain to Kutúzov and to the Emperor Alexander that the war was being carried on contrary to all the rules—as if there were any rules for killing people. In spite of the complaints of the French as to the nonobservance of the rules, in spite of the fact that to some highly placed Russians it seemed rather disgraceful to fight with a cudgel and they wanted to assume a pose *en quarte* or *en tierce* according to all the rules, and to make an adroit thrust *en prime*, and so on—the cudgel of the people's war was lifted with all its menacing and majestic strength, and without consulting anyone's tastes or rules and regardless of anything else, it rose and fell with stupid simplicity, but consistently, and belabored the French till the whole invasion had perished.

And it is well for a people who do not—as the French did in 1813—salute according to all the rules of art, and, presenting the hilt of their rapier gracefully and politely, hand it to their magnanimous conqueror, but at the moment of trial, without asking what rules others have adopted in similar cases, simply and easily pick up the first cudgel that comes to hand and strike with it till the feeling of resentment and revenge in their soul yields to a feeling of contempt and compassion.

ONE OF THE MOST obvious and advantageous departures from the so-called laws of war is the action of scattered groups against men pressed together in a mass. Such action always occurs in wars that take on a national character. In such actions, instead of two crowds opposing each other, the men disperse, attack singly, run away when attacked by stronger forces, but again attack when opportunity offers. This was done by the guerrillas in Spain, by the mountain tribes in the Caucasus,* and by the Russians in 1812.

People have called this kind of war "guerrilla warfare" and assume that by so calling it they have explained its meaning. But such a war does not fit in under any rule and is directly opposed to a well-known rule of tactics which is accepted as infallible. That rule says that an attacker should concentrate his forces in order to be stronger than his opponent at the moment of conflict.

Guerrilla war (always successful, as history shows) directly infringes that rule.

This contradiction arises from the fact that military science assumes the strength of an army to be identical with its numbers. Military science says that the more troops the greater the strength. *Les gros bataillons ont toujours raison* [Large battalions are always victorious].

For military science to say this is like defining momentum in mechanics by reference to the mass only: stating that momenta are equal or unequal to each other simply because the masses involved are equal or unequal.

Momentum (quantity of motion) is the product of mass and velocity.

In military affairs the strength of an army is the product of its mass and some unknown x.

Military science, seeing in history innumerable instances of the fact that the size of any army does not coincide with its strength and that small detachments defeat larger ones, obscurely admits the existence of this unknown factor and tries to discover it—now in a geometric formation, now in the equipment employed, now, and most usually, in the genius of the commanders. But the assignment of these various meanings to the factor does not yield results which accord with the historic facts.

Yet it is only necessary to abandon the false view (adopted to gratify the "heroes") of the efficacy of the directions issued in wartime by commanders, in order to find this unknown quantity.

That unknown quantity is the spirit of the army, that is to say, the greater or lesser readiness to fight and face danger felt by all the men composing an army, quite independently of whether they are, or are not, fighting under the command of a genius, in two- or three-line formation, with cudgels or with rifles that repeat thirty times a minute. Men who want to fight will always put themselves in the most advantageous conditions for fighting.

* *Tolstóy in 1851-53 served in the army against the Caucasian mountain tribes and there began to obtain the military experience, subsequently enlarged by service against the Turks and especially in the defense of Sevastopol, which makes his descriptions of war in War and Peace so vivid.*—A.M.

The spirit of an army is the factor which multiplied by the mass gives the resulting force. To define and express the significance of this unknown factor—the spirit of an army—is a problem for science.

This problem is only solvable if we cease arbitrarily to substitute for the unknown x itself the conditions under which that force becomes apparent—such as the commands of the general, the equipment employed, and so on—mistaking these for the real significance of the factor, and if we recognize this unknown quantity in its entirety as being the greater or lesser desire to fight and to face danger. Only then, expressing known historic facts by equations and comparing the relative significance of this factor, can we hope to define the unknown.

Ten men, battalions, or divisions, fighting fifteen men, battalions, or divisions, conquer—that is, kill or take captive—all the others, while themselves losing four, so that on the one side four and on the other fifteen were lost. Consequently the four were equal to the fifteen, and therefore $4x = 15y$. Consequently $x/y = 15/4$. This equation does not give us the value of the unknown factor but gives us a ratio between two unknowns. And by bringing variously selected historic units (battles, campaigns, periods of war) into such equations, a series of numbers could be obtained in which certain laws should exist and might be discovered.

The tactical rule that an army should act in masses when attacking, and in smaller groups in retreat, unconsciously confirms the truth that the strength of an army depends on its spirit. To lead men forward under fire more discipline (obtainable only by movement in masses) is needed than is needed to resist attacks. But this rule which leaves out of account the spirit of the army continually proves incorrect and is in particularly striking contrast to the facts when some strong rise or fall in the spirit of the troops occurs, as in all national wars.

The French, retreating in 1812—though according to tactics they should have separated into detachments to defend themselves—congregated into a mass because the spirit of the army had so fallen that only the mass held the army together. The Russians, on the contrary, ought according to tactics to have attacked in mass, but in fact they split up into small units, because their spirit had so risen that separate individuals, without orders, dealt blows at the French without needing any compulsion to induce them to expose themselves to hardships and dangers.

2. The partisans or guerrillas. Denísov, Dólokhov, Pétya Rostóv, and Tíkhon. A French drummer boy. A visit to the enemy's camp. Attack on a French convoy. The death of Pétya

THE SO-CALLED PARTISAN WAR began with the entry of the French into Smolénsk.

Before partisan warfare had been officially recognized by the government, thousands of enemy stragglers, marauders, and foragers had been destroyed by the Cossacks and the peasants, who killed them off as instinctively as dogs worry a stray mad dog to death. Denís Davýdov, with his Russian instinct, was the first to recognize the value of this terrible cudgel which regardless of the rules of military science destroyed the French, and to him belongs the credit for taking the first step toward regularizing this method of warfare.

On August 24 Davýdov's first partisan detachment was formed and then others were recognized. The further the campaign progressed the more numerous these detachments became.

The irregulars destroyed the great army piecemeal. They gathered the fallen leaves that dropped of themselves from that withered tree—the French army—and sometimes shook that tree itself. By October, when the French were fleeing toward Smolénsk, there were hundreds of such companies, of various sizes and characters. There were some that adopted all the army methods and had infantry, artillery, staffs, and the comforts of life. Others consisted solely of Cossack cavalry. There were also small scratch groups of foot and horse, and groups of peasants and landowners that remained unknown. A sacristan commanded one party which captured several hundred prisoners in the course of a month; and there was Vasilísa, the wife of a village elder, who slew hundreds of the French.

The partisan warfare flamed up most fiercely in the latter days of October. Its first period had passed: when the partisans themselves, amazed at their own boldness, feared every minute to be surrounded and captured by the French, and hid in the forests without unsaddling, hardly daring to dismount and always expecting to be pursued. By the end of October this kind of warfare had taken definite shape: it had become clear to all what could be ventured against the French and what could not. Now only the commanders of detachments with staffs, and moving according to rules at a distance from the French, still regarded many things as impossible. The small bands that had started their activities long before and had already observed the French closely considered things possible which the commanders of the big detachments did not dare to contemplate. The Cossacks and peasants who crept in among the French now considered everything possible.

On October 22, Denísov (who was one of the irregulars) was with his group at the height of the guerrilla enthusiasm. Since early morning he and his party had been on the move. All day long he had been watching from the forest that skirted the highroad a large French convoy of cavalry baggage and Russian prisoners separated from the rest of the army, which—as was learned from spies and prisoners—was moving under a strong escort to Smolénsk. Besides Denísov and Dólokhov (who also led a small party and moved in Denísov's vicinity), the commanders of some large divisions with staffs also knew of this convoy and, as Denísov expressed it, were sharpening their teeth for it. Two of the commanders of large parties—one a Pole and the other a German—sent invitations to Denísov almost simultaneously, requesting him to join up with their divisions to attack the convoy.

"No, bwother, I have gwown mustaches myself," * said Denísov on reading these documents, and he wrote to the German that, despite his heartfelt desire to serve under so valiant and renowned a general, he had to forgo that pleasure because he was already under the command of the Polish general.[2] To the Polish general he replied to the same effect, informing him that he was already under the command of the German.

Having arranged matters thus, Denísov and Dólokhov intended, without reporting matters to the higher command, to attack and seize that convoy with their own small forces. On October 22 it was moving from the village of Mikúlino to that of Shámshevo. To the left of the road between Mikúlino and Shámshevo there were large forests, extending in some places up to the road itself though in others a mile or more back from it. Through these forests Denísov and his party rode all day, sometimes keeping well back in them and sometimes coming to the very edge, but never losing sight of the moving French. That morning, Cossacks of Denísov's party had seized and carried off into the forest two wagons loaded with cavalry saddles, which had stuck in the mud not far from Mikúlino where the forest ran close to the road. Since then, and until evening, the party had watched the movements of the French without attacking. It was necessary to let the French reach Shámshevo quietly without alarming them and then, after joining Dólokhov who was to

* Equivalent to: "I was not born yesterday."—A.M.

[2] Tolstóy borrowed this expedient, by which Denísov preserved his independent command, from an incident recorded in Davýdov's Diary of Guerrilla Operations.—A.M.

come that evening to a consultation at a watchman's hut in the forest less than a mile from Shámshevo, to surprise the French at dawn, falling like an avalanche on their heads from two sides, and rout and capture them all at one blow.

In their rear, more than a mile from Mikúlino where the forest came right up to the road, six Cossacks were posted to report if any fresh columns of French should show themselves.

Beyond Shámshevo, Dólokhov was to observe the road in the same way, to find out at what distance there were other French troops. They reckoned that the convoy had fifteen hundred men. Denísov had two hundred, and Dólokhov might have as many more, but the disparity of numbers did not deter Denísov. All that he now wanted to know was what troops these were and to learn that he had to capture a "tongue"— that is, a man from the enemy column. That morning's attack on the wagons had been made so hastily that the Frenchmen with the wagons had all been killed; only a little drummer boy had been taken alive, and as he was a straggler he could tell them nothing definite about the troops in that column.

Denísov considered it dangerous to make a second attack for fear of putting the whole column on the alert, so he sent Tíkhon Shcherbáty, a peasant of his party, to Shamshevo to try and seize at least one of the French quartermasters who had been sent on in advance.

It was a warm rainy autumn day. The sky and the horizon were both the color of muddy water. At times a sort of mist descended, and then suddenly heavy slanting rain came down.

Denísov in a felt cloak and a sheepskin cap from which the rain ran down was riding a thin thoroughbred horse with sunken sides. Like his horse, which turned its head and laid its ears back, he shrank from the driving rain and gazed anxiously before him. His thin face with its short, thick black beard looked angry.

Beside Denísov rode an esaul, Denísov's fellow worker, also in felt cloak and sheepskin cap, and riding a large sleek Don horse.

Esaul Lováyski the Third * was a tall man as straight as an arrow, pale-faced, fair-haired, with narrow light eyes and with calm self-satisfaction in his face and bearing. Though it was impossible to say in what the peculiarity of the horse and rider lay, yet at first glance at the esaul and Deni-

* What is here told was actual fact. After Davýdov's (in the novel Denísov's) first successes, Kutúzov gave him two Cossack regiments to strengthen his force. Lováyski is a familiar form of the well-known Don family name, Ilováyski. An esaul is a captain of Cossacks.—A.M.

sov one saw that the latter was wet and uncomfortable and was a man mounted on a horse, while looking at the *esaul* one saw that he was as comfortable and as much at ease as always and that he was not a man who had mounted a horse, but a man who was one with his horse, a being consequently possessed of twofold strength.

A little ahead of them walked a peasant guide, wet to the skin and wearing a gray peasant coat and a white knitted cap.

A little behind, on a poor, small, lean Kirghíz mount with an enormous tail and mane and a bleeding mouth, rode a young officer in a blue French overcoat.

Beside him rode an hussar, with a boy in a tattered French uniform and blue cap behind him on the crupper of his horse. The boy held on to the hussar with cold, red hands, and raising his eyebrows gazed about him with surprise. This was the French drummer boy captured that morning.

Behind them along the narrow, sodden, cut-up forest road came hussars in threes and fours, and then Cossacks: some in felt cloaks, some in French greatcoats, and some with horsecloths over their heads. The horses, being drenched by the rain, all looked black whether chestnut or bay. Their necks, with their wet, close-clinging manes, looked strangely thin. Steam rose from them. Clothes, saddles, reins, were all wet, slippery, and sodden, like the ground and the fallen leaves that strewed the road. The men sat huddled up trying not to stir, so as to warm the water that had trickled to their bodies and not admit the fresh cold water that was leaking in under their seats, their knees, and at the back of their necks. In the midst of the outspread line of Cossacks two wagons, drawn by French horses and by saddled Cossack horses that had been hitched on in front, rumbled over the tree stumps and branches and splashed through the water that lay in the ruts.

Denísov's horse swerved aside to avoid a pool in the track and bumped his rider's knee against a tree.

"Oh, the devil!" exclaimed Denísov angrily, and showing his teeth he struck his horse three times with his whip, splashing himself and his comrades with mud.

Denísov was out of sorts both because of the rain and also from hunger (none of them had eaten anything since morning), and yet more because he still had no news from Dólokhov and the man sent to capture a "tongue" had not returned.

"There'll hardly be another such chance to fall on a transport as today. It's too risky to attack them by oneself, and if we put it off till another day one of the big guerrilla detachments will snatch the prey from under our noses," thought Denísov, continually peering forward, hoping to see a messenger from Dólokhov.

On coming to a path in the forest along which he could see far to the right, Denísov stopped.

"There's someone coming," said he.

The esaul looked in the direction Denísov indicated.

"There are two, an officer and a Cossack. But it is not presupposable that it is the lieutenant colonel himself," said the esaul, who was fond of using words the Cossacks did not know.

The approaching riders having descended a decline were no longer visible, but they reappeared a few minutes later. In front, at a weary gallop and using his leather whip, rode an officer, disheveled and drenched, whose trousers had worked up to above his knees. Behind him, standing in the stirrups, trotted a Cossack. The officer, a very young lad with a broad rosy face and keen merry eyes, galloped up to Denísov and handed him a sodden envelope.

"From the general," said the officer. "Please excuse its not being quite dry."

Denísov, frowning, took the envelope and opened it.

"There, they kept telling us: 'It's dangerous, it's dangerous,' " said the officer, addressing the esaul while Denísov was reading the dispatch. "But Komaróv and I"—he pointed to the Cossack—"were prepared. We have each of us two pistols. . . . But what's this?" he asked, noticing the French drummer boy. "A prisoner? You've already been in action? May I speak to him?"

"Wostóv! Pétya!" exclaimed Denísov, having run through the dispatch. "Why didn't you say who you were?" and turning with a smile he held out his hand to the lad.

The officer was Pétya Rostóv.

All the way Pétya had been preparing himself to behave with Denísov as befitted a grown-up man and an officer—without hinting at their previous acquaintance. But as soon as Denísov smiled at him Pétya brightened up, blushed with pleasure, forgot the official manner he had been rehearsing, and began telling him how he had already been in a battle near Vyázma and how a certain hussar had distinguished himself there.

"Well, I am glad to see you," Denísov interrupted him, and his face again assumed its anxious expression.

"Michael Feoklítych," said he to the esaul, "this is again fwom that German, you know. He"—he indicated Pétya—"is serving under him."

And Denísov told the esaul that the dispatch just delivered was a repetition of the German general's demand that he should join forces with him for an attack on the transport.

"If we don't take it tomowwow, he'll snatch it fwom under our noses," he added.

While Denísov was talking to the esaul, Pétya—abashed by Denísov's cold tone and supposing that it was due to the condition of his trousers —furtively tried to pull them down under his greatcoat so that no one should notice it, while maintaining as martial an air as possible.

"Will there be any orders, your honor?" he asked Denísov, holding his hand at the salute and resuming the game of adjutant and general for which he had prepared himself, "or shall I remain with your honor?"

"Orders?" Denisov repeated thoughtfully. "But can you stay till to-mowwow?"

"Oh, please . . . May I stay with you?" cried Pétya.

"But, just what did the genewal tell you? To wetturn at once?" asked Dénisov.

Pétya blushed.

"He gave me no instructions. I think I could?" he returned, inquiringly.

"Well, all wight," said Denísov.

And turning to his men he directed a party to go on to the halting place arranged near the watchman's hut in the forest, and told the officer on the Kirghíz horse (who performed the duties of an adjutant) to go and find out where Dólokhov was and whether he would come that evening. Denísov himself intended going with the esaul and Pétya to the edge of the forest where it reached out to Shámshevo, to have a look at the part of the French bivouac they were to attack next day.

"Well, old fellow," said he to the peasant guide, "lead us to Shám-shevo."

Denísov, Pétya, and the esaul, accompanied by some Cossacks and the hussar who had the prisoner, rode to the left across a ravine to the edge of the forest.

THE RAIN HAD STOPPED, and only the mist was falling and drops from the trees. Denísov, the esaul, and Pétya rode silently, following the peasant in the knitted cap who, stepping lightly with outturned toes and moving noiselessly in his bast shoes over the roots and wet leaves, silently led them to the edge of the forest.

He ascended an incline, stopped, looked about him, and advanced to where the screen of trees was less dense. On reaching a large oak tree that had not yet shed its leaves, he stopped and beckoned mysteriously to them with his hand.

Denísov and Pétya rode up to him. From the spot where the peasant was standing they could see the French. Immediately beyond the forest, on a downward slope, lay a field of spring rye. To the right, beyond a steep ravine, was a small village and a landowner's house with a broken roof. In the village, in the house, in the garden, by the well, by the pond, over all the rising ground, and all along the road uphill from the bridge leading to the village, not more than five hundred yards away, crowds of men could be seen through the shimmering mist. Their un-Russian shouting at their horses which were straining uphill with the carts, and their calls to one another, could be clearly heard.

"Bwing the prisoner here," said Denísov in a low voice, not taking his eyes off the French.

A Cossack dismounted, lifted the boy down, and took him to Denísov. Pointing to the French troops, Denísov asked him what these and those of them were. The boy, thrusting his cold hands into his pockets and lifting his eyebrows, looked at Denísov in affright, but in spite of an evident desire to say all he knew gave confused answers, merely assenting to everything Denísov asked him. Denísov turned away from him frowning and addressed the esaul, conveying his own conjectures to him.

Pétya, rapidly turning his head, looked now at the drummer boy, now at Denísov, now at the esaul, and now at the French in the village and along the road, trying not to miss anything of importance.

"Whether Dólokhov comes or not, we must seize it, eh?" said Denísov with a merry sparkle in his eyes.

"It is a very suitable spot," said the esaul.

"We'll send the infantwy down by the swamps," Denísov continued. "They'll cweep up to the garden; you'll wide up fwom there with the Cossacks"—he pointed to a spot in the forest beyond the village—"and I with my hussars fwom here. And at the signal shot . . ."

"The hollow is impassable—there's a swamp there," said the esaul. "The horses would sink. We must ride round more to the left. . . ."

While they were talking in undertones the crack of a shot sounded from the low ground by the pond, a puff of white smoke appeared, then another, and the sound of hundreds of seemingly merry French voices shouting together came up from the slope. For a moment Denísov and the esaul drew back. They were so near that they thought they were the cause of the firing and shouting. But the firing and shouting did not relate to them. Down below, a man wearing something red was running through the marsh. The French were evidently firing and shouting at him.

"Why, that's our Tíkhon," said the esaul.

"So it is! It is!"

"The wascal!" said Denísov.

"He'll get away!" said the esaul, screwing up his eyes.

The man whom they called Tíkhon, having run to the stream, plunged in so that the water splashed in the air, and, having disappeared for an instant, scrambled out on all fours, all black with the wet, and ran on. The French who had been pursuing him stopped.

"Smart, that!" said the esaul.

"What a beast!" said Denísov with his former look of vexation. "What has he been doing all this time?"

"Who is he?" asked Pétya.

"He's our plastún.* I sent him to capture a 'tongue.' "

"Oh, yes," said Pétya, nodding at the first words Denísov uttered as if he understood it all, though he really did not understand anything of it.

Tíkhon Shcherbáty was one of the most indispensable men in their band. He was a peasant from Pokróvsk, near the river Gzhat. When Denísov had come to Pokróvsk at the beginning of his operations and had as usual summoned the village elder and asked him what he knew about the French, the elder, as though shielding himself, had replied, as all village elders did, that he had neither seen nor heard anything of them. But when Denísov explained that his purpose was to kill the French, and asked if no French had strayed that way, the elder replied that some "more-orderers" had really been at their village, but that Tíkhon Shcherbáty was the only man who dealt with such matters. Denísov had Tíkhon called and, having praised him for his activity, said a few words in the elder's presence about loyalty to the Tsar and the country and the hatred of the French that all sons of the fatherland should cherish.

"We don't do the French any harm," said Tíkhon, evidently frightened by Denísov's words. "We only fooled about with the lads for fun, you know! We killed a score or so of 'more-orderers,' but we did no harm else. . . ."

Next day when Denísov had left Pokróvsk, having quite forgotten about this peasant, it was reported to him that Tíkhon had attached himself to their party and asked to be allowed to remain with it. Denísov gave orders to let him do so.

Tíkhon, who at first did rough work, laying campfires, fetching water,

* Plastún—an unmounted sharpshooter among the Black Sea Cossacks. Strictly speaking, the plastúns were special detachments of Black Sea Cossacks in the wars with the Caucasian hill tribes. Their speciality was to track down the enemy among the forests of the Kubán. In the present case Denísov uses the word to indicate a man who operates as the plastúns did in the Caucasus.—A.M.

flaying dead horses, and so on, soon showed a great liking and aptitude for partisan warfare. At night he would go out for booty and always brought back French clothing and weapons, and when told to would bring in French captives also. Denísov then relieved him from drudgery and began taking him with him when he went out on expeditions and had him enrolled among the Cossacks.

Tikhon did not like riding, and always went on foot, never lagging behind the cavalry. He was armed with a musketoon (which he carried rather as a joke), a pike and an ax, which latter he used as a wolf uses its teeth, with equal ease picking fleas out of its fur or crunching thick bones. Tikhon with equal accuracy would split logs with blows at arm's length, or holding the head of the ax would cut thin little pegs or carve spoons. In Denísov's party he held a peculiar and exceptional position. When anything particularly difficult or nasty had to be done—to push a cart out of the mud with one's shoulders, pull a horse out of a swamp by its tail, skin it, slink in among the French, or walk more than thirty miles in a day —everybody pointed laughingly at Tikhon.

"It won't hurt that devil—he's as strong as a horse!" they said·of him.

Once a Frenchman Tikhon was trying to capture fired a pistol at him and shot him in the fleshy part of the back. That wound (which Tikhon treated only with internal and external applications of vodka) was the subject of the liveliest jokes by the whole detachment—jokes in which Tikhon readily joined.

"Hallo, mate! Never again? Gave you a twist?" the Cossacks would banter him. And Tikhon, purposely writhing and making faces, pretended to be angry and swore at the French with the funniest curses. The only effect of this incident on Tikhon was that after being wounded he seldom brought in prisoners.

He was the bravest and most useful man in the party. No one found more opportunities for attacking, no one captured or killed more Frenchmen, and consequently he was made the buffoon of all the Cossacks and hussars and willingly accepted that role. Now he had been sent by Denísov overnight to Shámshevo to capture a "tongue." But whether because he had not been content to take only one Frenchman or because he had slept through the night, he had crept by day into some bushes right among the French and, as Denísov had witnessed from above, had been detected by them.

AFTER TALKING for some time with the esaul about next day's attack, which now, seeing how near they were to the French, he seemed to have definitely decided on, Denísov turned his horse and rode back.

"Now, my lad, we'll go and get dwy," he said to Pétya.

As they approached the watchhouse Denísov stopped, peering into the forest. Among the trees a man with long legs and long, swinging arms, wearing a short jacket, bast shoes, and a Kazán hat, was approaching with long, light steps. He had a musketoon over his shoulder and an ax stuck in his girdle. When he espied Denísov he hastily threw something into the bushes, removed his sodden hat by its floppy brim, and approached his commander. It was Tíkhon. His wrinkled and pockmarked face and narrow little eyes beamed with self-satisfied merriment. He lifted his head high and gazed at Denísov as if repressing a laugh.

"Well, where did you disappear to?" inquired Denísov.

"Where did I disappear to? I went to get Frenchmen," answered Tíkhon boldly and hurriedly, in a husky but melodious bass voice.

"Why did you push yourself in there by daylight? You ass! Well, why haven't you taken one?"

"Oh, I took one all right," said Tíkhon.

"Where is he?"

"You see, I took him first thing at dawn," Tíkhon continued, spreading out his flat feet with outturned toes in their bast shoes. "I took him into the forest. Then I see he's no good and think I'll go and fetch a likelier one."

"You see? . . . What a wogue—it's just as I thought," said Denísov to the esaul. "Why didn't you bwing that one?"

"What was the good of bringing him?" Tíkhon interrupted hastily and angrily—"that one wouldn't have done for you. As if I don't know what sort you want!"

"What a bwute you are! . . . Well?"

"I went for another one," Tíkhon continued, "and I crept like this through the wood and lay down." (He suddenly lay down on his stomach with a supple movement to show how he had done it.) "One turned up and I grabbed him, like this." (He jumped up quickly and lightly.) "'Come along to the colonel,' I said. He starts yelling, and suddenly there were four of them. They rushed at me with their little swords. So I went for them with my ax, this way: 'What are you up to?' says I. 'Christ be with you!'" shouted Tíkhon, waving his arms with an angry scowl and throwing out his chest.

"Yes, we saw from the hill how you took to your heels through the puddles!" said the esaul, screwing up his glittering eyes.

Pétya badly wanted to laugh, but noticed that they all refrained from laughing. He turned his eyes rapidly from Tíkhon's face to the esaul's and Denísov's, unable to make out what it all meant.

"Don't play the fool!" said Denísov, coughing angrily. "Why didn't you bwing the first one?"

Tíkhon scratched his back with one hand and his head with the other, then suddenly his whole face expanded into a beaming, foolish grin, disclosing a gap where he had lost a tooth (that was why he was called Shcherbáty—the gap-toothed). Denísov smiled, and Pétya burst into a peal of merry laughter in which Tíkhon himself joined.

"Oh, but he was a regular good-for-nothing," said Tíkhon. "The clothes on him—poor stuff! How could I bring him? And so rude, your honor! Why, he says: 'I'm a general's son myself, I won't go!' he says."

"You are a bwute!" said Denísov. "I wanted to question . . ."

"But I questioned him," said Tíkhon. "He said he didn't know much. 'There are a lot of us,' he says, 'but all poor stuff—only soldiers in name,' he says. 'Shout loud at them,' he says, 'and you'll take them all,' " Tíkhon concluded, looking cheerfully and resolutely into Denísov's eyes.

"I'll give you a hundwed sharp lashes—that'll teach you to play the fool!" said Denísov severely.

"But why are you angry?" remonstrated Tíkhon, "just as if I'd never seen your Frenchmen! Only wait till it gets dark and I'll fetch you any of them you want—three if you like."

"Well, let's go," said Denísov, and rode all the way to the watchhouse in silence and frowning angrily.

Tíkhon followed behind and Pétya heard the Cossacks laughing with him and at him, about some pair of boots he had thrown into the bushes.

When the fit of laughter that had seized him at Tíkhon's words and smile had passed and Pétya realized for a moment that this Tíkhon had killed a man, he felt uneasy. He looked round at the captive drummer boy and felt a pang in his heart. But this uneasiness lasted only a moment. He felt it necessary to hold his head higher, to brace himself, and to question the esaul with an air of importance about tomorrow's undertaking, that he might not be unworthy of the company in which he found himself.

The officer who had been sent to inquire met Denísov on the way with the news that Dólokhov was soon coming and that all was well with him.

Denísov at once cheered up and, calling Pétya to him, said: "Well, tell me about yourself."

Pétya, having left his people after their departure from Moscow, joined his regiment and was soon taken as orderly by a general commanding a large guerrilla detachment. From the time he received his commission, and especially since he had joined the active army and taken part in the

BOOK FOURTEEN

battle of Vyázma, Pétya had been in a constant state of blissful excitement at being grown-up and in a perpetual ecstatic hurry not to miss any chance to do something really heroic. He was highly delighted with what he saw and experienced in the army, but at the same time it always seemed to him that the really heroic exploits were being performed just where he did not happen to be. And he was always in a hurry to get where he was not.

When on the twenty-first of October his general expressed a wish to send somebody to Denísov's detachment, Pétya begged so piteously to be sent that the general could not refuse. But when dispatching him he recalled Pétya's mad action at the battle of Vyázma, where instead of riding by the road to the place to which he had been sent, he had galloped to the advanced line under the fire of the French and had there twice fired his pistol. So now the general explicitly forbade his taking part in any action whatever of Denísov's. That was why Pétya had blushed and grown confused when Denísov asked him whether he could stay. Before they had ridden to the outskirts of the forest Pétya had considered that he must carry out his instructions strictly and return at once. But when he saw the French and saw Tíkhon and learned that there would certainly be an attack that night, he decided, with the rapidity with which young people change their views, that the general, whom he had greatly respected till then, was a rubbishy German, that Denísov was a hero, the esaul a hero, and Tíkhon a hero too, and that it would be shameful for him to leave them at a moment of difficulty.

It was already growing dusk when Denísov, Pétya, and the esaul rode up to the watchhouse. In the twilight saddled horses could be seen, and Cossacks and hussars who had rigged up rough shelters in the glade and were kindling glowing fires in a hollow of the forest where the French could not see the smoke. In the passage of the small watchhouse a Cossack with sleeves rolled up was chopping some mutton. In the room three officers of Denísov's band were converting a door into a tabletop. Pétya took off his wet clothes, gave them to be dried, and at once began helping the officers to fix up the dinner table.

In ten minutes the table was ready and a napkin spread on it. On the table were vodka, a flask of rum, white bread, roast mutton, and salt.

Sitting at table with the officers and tearing the fat savory mutton with his hands, down which the grease trickled, Pétya was in an ecstatic childish state of love for all men, and consequently of confidence that others loved him in the same way.

"So then what do you think, Vasíli Dmítrich?" said he to Denísov. "It's all right my staying a day with you?" And not waiting for a reply he answered his own question: "You see I was told to find out—well, I am finding out. . . . Only do let me into the very . . . into the chief . . . I don't want a reward. . . . But I want . . ."

Pétya clenched his teeth and looked around, throwing back his head and flourishing his arms.

"Into the vewy chief . . ." Denísov repeated with a smile.

"Only, please let me command something, so that I may really command . . ." Pétya went on. "What would it be to you? . . . Oh, you want a knife?" he said, turning to an officer who wished to cut himself a piece of mutton.

And he handed him his clasp knife. The officer admired it.

"Please keep it. I have several like it," said Pétya, blushing. "Heavens! I was quite forgetting!" he suddenly cried. "I have some raisins, fine ones; you know, seedless ones. We have a new sutler and he has such capital things. I bought ten pounds. I am used to something sweet. Would you like some? . . ." and Pétya ran out into the passage to his Cossack and brought back some bags which contained about five pounds of raisins. "Have some, gentlemen, have some!"

"You want a coffeepot, don't you?" he asked the esaul. "I bought a capital one from our sutler! He has splendid things. And he's very honest, that's the chief thing. I'll be sure to send it to you. Or perhaps your flints are giving out, or are worn out—that happens sometimes, you know. I have brought some with me, here they are"—and he showed a bag—"a hundred flints. I bought them very cheap. Please take as many as you want, or all if you like. . . ."

Then suddenly, dismayed lest he had said too much, Pétya stopped and blushed.

He tried to remember whether he had not done anything else that was foolish. And running over the events of the day he remembered the French drummer boy. "It's capital for us here, but what of him? Where have they put him? Have they fed him? Haven't they hurt his feelings?" he thought. But having caught himself saying too much about the flints, he was now afraid to speak out.

"I might ask," he thought, "but they'll say: 'He's a boy himself and so he pities the boy.' I'll show them tomorrow whether I'm a boy. Will it seem odd if I ask?" Pétya thought. "Well, never mind!" and immediately, blushing and looking anxiously at the officers to see if they appeared ironical, he said:

"May I call in that boy who was taken prisoner and give him something to eat? . . . Perhaps . . ."

"Yes, he's a poor little fellow," said Denísov, who evidently saw nothing shameful in this reminder. "Call him in. His name is Vincent Bosse. Have him fetched."

"I'll call him," said Pétya.

"Yes, yes, call him. A poor little fellow," Denísov repeated.

Pétya was standing at the door when Denísov said this. He slipped in between the officers, came close to Denísov, and said:

"Let me kiss you, dear old fellow! Oh, how fine, how splendid!"

And having kissed Denísov he ran out of the hut.

"Bosse! Vincent!" Pétya cried, stopping outside the door.

"Who do you want, sir?" asked a voice in the darkness.

Pétya replied that he wanted the French lad who had been captured that day.

"Ah, Vesénny?" said a Cossack.

Vincent, the boy's name, had already been changed by the Cossacks into Vesénny (vernal) and into Vesénya by the peasants and soldiers. In both these adaptations the reference to spring (vesná) matched the impression made by the young lad.

"He is warming himself there by the bonfire. Ho, Vesénya! Vesénya!— Vesénny!" laughing voices were heard calling to one another in the darkness.

"He's a smart lad," said an hussar standing near Pétya. "We gave him something to eat a while ago. He was awfully hungry!"

The sound of bare feet splashing through the mud was heard in the darkness, and the drummer boy came to the door.

"Ah, c'est vous [Ah, it's you]!" said Pétya. "Voulez-vous manger? N'ayez pas peur, on ne vous fera pas de mal [Do you want something to eat? Don't be afraid, they won't hurt you]," he added shyly and affectionately, touching the boy's hand. "Entrez, entrez [Come in, come in]."

"Merci, monsieur [Thank you, sir]," said the drummer boy in a trembling almost childish voice, and he began scraping his dirty feet on the threshold.

There were many things Pétya wanted to say to the drummer boy, but did not dare to. He stood irresolutely beside him in the passage. Then in the darkness he took the boy's hand and pressed it.

"Come in, come in!" he repeated in a gentle whisper. "Oh, what can I do for him?" he thought, and opening the door he let the boy pass in first.

When the boy had entered the hut, Pétya sat down at a distance from him, considering it beneath his dignity to pay attention to him. But he fingered the money in his pocket and wondered whether it would seem ridiculous to give some to the drummer boy.

The arrival of Dólokhov diverted Pétya's attention from the drummer boy, to whom Denísov had had some mutton and vodka given, and whom he had had dressed in a Russian coat so that he might be kept with their band and not sent away with the other prisoners. Pétya had heard in the army many stories of Dólokhov's extraordinary bravery and of his cruelty to the French, so from the moment he entered the hut Pétya did not take his eyes from him, but braced himself up more and more and held his head high, that he might not be unworthy even of such company. Dólokhov's appearance amazed Pétya by its simplicity.

Denísov wore a Cossack coat, had a beard, had an icon of Nicholas the Wonder-Worker on his breast, and his way of speaking and everything he did indicated his unusual position. But Dólokhov, who in Moscow had worn a Persian costume, had now the appearance of a most correct officer of the Guards. He was clean-shaven and wore a Guardsman's padded coat with an Order of St. George at his buttonhole and a plain forage cap set straight on his head. He took off his wet felt cloak in a corner of the room, and without greeting anyone went up to Denísov and began questioning him about the matter in hand. Denísov told him of the designs the large detachments had on the transport, of the message Pétya had brought, and his own replies to both generals. Then he told him all he knew of the French detachment.

"That's so. But we must know what troops they are and their numbers," said Dólokhov. "It will be necessary to go there. We can't start the affair without knowing for certain how many of them there are. I like to work accurately. Here now—wouldn't one of these gentlemen like to ride over to the French camp with me? I have brought a spare uniform."

"I, I . . . I'll go with you!" cried Pétya.

"There's no need for you to go at all," said Denísov, addressing Dólokhov, "and as for him, I won't let him go on any account."

"I like that!" exclaimed Pétya. "Why shouldn't I go?"

"Because it's useless."

"Well, you must excuse me, because . . . because . . . I shall go, and that's all. You'll take me, won't you?" he said, turning to Dólokhov.

"Why not?" Dólokhov answered absently, scrutinizing the face of the French drummer boy. "Have you had that youngster with you long?" he asked Denísov.

"He was taken today but he knows nothing. I'm keeping him with me."

"Yes, and where do you put the others?" inquired Dólokhov.

"Where? I send them away and take a weceipt for them," shouted Denísov, suddenly flushing. "And I say boldly that I have not a single man's life on my conscience. Would it be difficult for you to send thirty or thwee hundwed men to town under escort, instead of staining—I speak bluntly—staining the honor of a soldier?"

"That kind of amiable talk would be suitable from this young count of sixteen," said Dólokhov with cold irony, "but it's time for you to drop it."

"Why, I've not said anything! I only say that I'll certainly go with you," said Pétya shyly.

"But for you and me, old fellow, it's time to drop these amenities," continued Dólokhov, as if he found particular pleasure in speaking of this subject which irritated Denísov. "Now, why have you kept this lad?" he went on, swaying his head. "Because you are sorry for him! Don't we know those 'receipts' of yours? You send a hundred men away, and thirty get there. The rest either starve or get killed. So isn't it all the same not to send them?"

The esaul, screwing up his light-colored eyes, nodded approvingly.

"That's not the point. I'm not going to discuss the matter. I do not wish to take it on my conscience. You say they'll die. All wight. Only not by my fault!"

Dólokhov began laughing.

"Who has told them not to capture me these twenty times over? But if they did catch me they'd string me up to an aspen tree, and you with all your chivalry just the same." He paused. "However, we must get to work. Tell the Cossack to fetch my kit. I have two French uniforms in it. Well, are you coming with me?" he asked Pétya.

"I? Yes, yes, certainly!" cried Pétya, blushing almost to tears and glancing at Denísov.

While Dólokhov had been disputing with Denísov what should be done with prisoners, Pétya had once more felt awkward and restless; but again he had no time to grasp fully what they were talking about. "If grown-up, distinguished men think so, it must be necessary and right," thought he. "But above all Denísov must not dare to imagine that I'll obey him and that he can order me about. I will certainly go to the French camp with Dólokhov. If he can, so can I!"

And to all Denísov's persuasions, Pétya replied that he too was accustomed to do everything accurately and not just anyhow, and that he never considered personal danger.

"For you'll admit that if we don't know for sure how many of them there are . . . hundreds of lives may depend on it, while there are only two of us. Besides, I want to go very much and certainly will go, so don't hinder me," said he. "It will only make things worse. . . ."

WAR AND PEACE

HAVING PUT ON French greatcoats and shakos, Pétya and Dólokhov rode to the clearing from which Denísov had reconnoitered the French camp, and emerging from the forest in pitch darkness they descended into the hollow. On reaching the bottom, Dólokhov told the Cossacks accompanying him to await him there and rode on at a quick trot along the road to the bridge. Pétya, his heart in his mouth with excitement, rode by his side.

"If we're caught, I won't be taken alive! I have a pistol," whispered he.

"Don't talk Russian," said Dólokhov in a hurried whisper, and at that very moment they heard through the darkness the challenge: "Qui vive? [Who goes there]" and the click of a musket.

The blood rushed to Pétya's face and he grasped his pistol.

"Lanciers du 6-me [Lancers of the 6th Regiment]," replied Dólokhov, neither hastening nor slackening his horse's pace.

The black figure of a sentinel stood on the bridge.

"Mot d'ordre [Password]."

Dólokhov reined in his horse and advanced at a walk.

"Dites donc, le colonel Gérard est ici? [Tell me, is Colonel Gérard here]" he asked.

"Mot d'ordre," repeated the sentinel, barring the way and not replying.

"Quand un officier fait sa ronde, les sentinelles ne demandent pas le mot d'ordre . . . [When an officer is making his round sentinels don't ask him for the password]" cried Dólokhov suddenly flaring up and riding straight at the sentinel. "Je vous demande si le colonel est ici [I am asking you if the colonel is here]."

And without waiting for an answer from the sentinel, who had stepped aside, Dólokhov rode up the incline at a walk.

Noticing the black outline of a man crossing the road, Dólokhov stopped him and inquired where the commander and officers were. The man, a soldier with a sack over his shoulder, stopped, came close up to Dólokhov's horse, touched it with his hand, and explained simply and in a friendly way that the commander and the officers were higher up the hill to the right in the courtyard of the farm, as he called the landowner's house.

Having ridden up the road, on both sides of which French talk could be heard around the campfires, Dólokhov turned into the courtyard of the landowner's house. Having ridden in, he dismounted and approached a big blazing campfire, around which sat several men talking noisily. Something was boiling in a small cauldron at the edge of the fire and a soldier in a peaked cap and blue overcoat, lit up by the fire, was kneeling beside it stirring its contents with a ramrod.

411

"Oh, he's a hard nut to crack," said one of the officers who was sitting in the shadow at the other side of the fire.

"He'll make them get a move on, those fellows!" said another, laughing.

Both fell silent, peering out through the darkness at the sound of Dólokhov's and Pétya's steps as they advanced to the fire leading their horses.

"Bonjour, messieurs [Good day, gentlemen]!" said Dólokhov loudly and clearly.

There was a stir among the officers in the shadow beyond the fire, and one tall, long-necked officer, walking round the fire, came up to Dólokhov. "Is that you, Clément?" he asked. "Where the devil . . . ?" But, noticing his mistake, he broke off short and, with a frown, greeted Dólokhov as a stranger, asking what he could do for him.

Dólokhov said that he and his companion were trying to overtake their regiment, and addressing the company in general asked whether they knew anything of the 6th Regiment. None of them knew anything, and Pétya thought the officers were beginning to look at him and Dólokhov with hostility and suspicion. For some seconds all were silent.

"If you were counting on the evening soup, you have come too late," said a voice from behind the fire with a repressed laugh.

Dólokhov replied that they were not hungry and must push on farther that night.

He handed the horses over to the soldier who was stirring the pot and squatted down on his heels by the fire beside the officer with the long neck. That officer did not take his eyes from Dólokhov and again asked to what regiment he belonged. Dólokhov, as if he had not heard the question, did not reply, but lighting a short French pipe which he took from his pocket began asking the officer in how far the road before them was safe from Cossacks.

"Those brigands are everywhere," replied an officer from behind the fire.

Dólokhov remarked that the Cossacks were a danger only to stragglers such as his companion and himself, "but probably they would not dare to attack large detachments?" he added inquiringly. No one replied.

"Well, now he'll come away," Pétya thought every moment as he stood by the campfire listening to the talk.

But Dólokhov restarted the conversation which had dropped and began putting direct questions as to how many men there were in the battalion, how many battalions, and how many prisoners. Asking about the Russian prisoners with that detachment, Dólokhov said:

"A horrid business dragging these corpses about with one! It would be better to shoot such rabble," and burst into loud laughter, so strange

412

that Pétya thought the French would immediately detect their disguise, and involuntarily took a step back from the campfire.

No one replied a word to Dólokhov's laughter, and a French officer whom they could not see (he lay wrapped in a greatcoat) rose and whispered something to a companion. Dólokhov got up and called to the soldier who was holding their horses.

"Will they bring our horses or not?" thought Pétya, instinctively drawing nearer to Dólokhov.

The horses were brought.

"Good evening, gentlemen," said Dólokhov.

Pétya wished to say "Good night" but could not utter a word. The officers were whispering together. Dólokhov was a long time mounting his horse which would not stand still, then he rode out of the yard at a footpace. Pétya rode beside him, longing to look round to see whether or no the French were running after them, but not daring to.

Coming out onto the road Dólokhov did not ride back across the open country, but through the village. At one spot he stopped and listened. "Do you hear?" he asked. Pétya recognized the sound of Russian voices and saw the dark figures of Russian prisoners round their campfires. When they had descended to the bridge Pétya and Dólokhov rode past the sentinel, who without saying a word paced morosely up and down it, then they descended into the hollow where the Cossacks awaited them.

"Well now, good-by. Tell Denísov, 'at the first shot at daybreak,' " said Dólokhov and was about to ride away, but Pétya seized hold of him.

"Really!" he cried, "you are such a hero! Oh, how fine, how splendid! How I love you!"

"All right, all right!" said Dólokhov. But Pétya did not let go of him and Dólokhov saw through the gloom that Pétya was bending toward him and wanted to kiss him. Dólokhov kissed him, laughed, turned his horse, and vanished into the darkness.

HAVING RETURNED to the watchman's hut, Pétya found Denísov in the passage. He was awaiting Pétya's return in a state of agitation, anxiety, and self-reproach for having let him go.

"Thank God!" he exclaimed. "Yes, thank God!" he repeated, listening to Pétya's rapturous account. "But, devil take you, I haven't slept because of you! Well, thank God. Now lie down. We can still get a nap before morning."

"But . . . no," said Pétya, "I don't want to sleep yet. Besides I know myself, if I fall asleep it's finished. And then I am used to not sleeping before a battle."

He sat awhile in the hut joyfully recalling the details of his expedition and vividly picturing to himself what would happen next day. Then, noticing that Denísov was asleep, he rose and went out of doors.

It was still quite dark outside. The rain was over, but drops were still falling from the trees. Near the watchman's hut the black shapes of the Cossacks' shanties and of horses tethered together could be seen. Behind the hut the dark shapes of the two wagons with their horses beside them were discernible, and in the hollow the dying campfire gleamed red. Not all the Cossacks and hussars were asleep; here and there, amid the sounds of falling drops and the munching of the horses near by, could be heard low voices which seemed to be whispering.

Pétya came out, peered into the darkness, and went up to the wagons. Someone was snoring under them, and around them stood saddled horses munching their oats. In the dark Pétya recognized his own horse, which he called "Karabákh" * though it was of Ukrainian breed, and went up to it.

"Well, Karabákh! We'll do some service tomorrow," said he, sniffing its nostrils and kissing it.

"Why aren't you asleep, sir?" said a Cossack who was sitting under a wagon.

"No, ah . . . Likhachёv—isn't that your name? Do you know I have only just come back! We've been into the French camp."

And Pétya gave the Cossack a detailed account not only of his ride but also of his object, and why he considered it better to risk his life than to act "just anyhow."

"Well you should get some sleep now," said the Cossack.

"No, I am used to this," said Pétya. "I say, aren't the flints in your pistols worn out? I brought some with me. Don't you want any? You can have some."

The Cossack bent forward from under the wagon to get a closer look at Pétya.

"Because I am accustomed to doing everything accurately," said Pétya. "Some fellows do things just anyhow, without preparation, and then they're sorry for it afterwards. I don't like that."

"Just so," said the Cossack.

"Oh yes, another thing! Please, my dear fellow, will you sharpen my saber for me? It's got bl . . ." (Pétya feared to tell a lie, and the saber never had been sharpened.) "Can you do it?"

"Of course I can."

* Karabákh is a district in the Southern Caucasus, famous for its breed of horses.—A.M.

Likhachëv got up, rummaged in his pack, and soon Pétya heard the warlike sound of steel on whetstone. He climbed onto the wagon and sat on its edge. The Cossack was sharpening the saber under the wagon.

"I say! Are the lads asleep?" asked Pétya.

"Some are, and some aren't—like us."

"Well, and that boy?"

"Vesénny? Oh, he's thrown himself down there in the passage. Fast asleep after his fright. He was that glad!"

After that Pétya remained silent for a long time, listening to the sounds. He heard footsteps in the darkness and a black figure appeared.

"What are you sharpening?" asked a man coming up to the wagon.

"Why, this gentleman's saber."

"That's right," said the man, whom Pétya took to be an hussar. "Was the cup left here?"

"There, by the wheel!"

The hussar took the cup.

"It must be daylight soon," said he, yawning, and went away.

Pétya ought to have known that he was in a forest with Denísov's guerrilla band, less than a mile from the road, sitting on a wagon captured from the French beside which horses were tethered, that under it Likhachëv was sitting sharpening a saber for him, that the big dark blotch to the right was the watchman's hut, and the red blotch below to the left was the dying embers of a campfire, that the man who had come for the cup was an hussar who wanted a drink; but he neither knew nor wanted to know anything of all this. He was in a fairy kingdom where nothing resembled reality. The big dark blotch might really be the watchman's hut or it might be a cavern leading to the very depths of the earth. Perhaps the red spot was a fire, or it might be the eye of an enormous monster. Perhaps he was really sitting on a wagon, but it might very well be that he was not sitting on a wagon but on a terribly high tower from which, if he fell, he would have to fall for a whole day or a whole month, or go on falling and never reach the bottom. Perhaps it was just the Cossack, Likhachëv, who was sitting under the wagon, but it might be the kindest, bravest, most wonderful, most splendid man in the world, whom no one knew of. It might really have been that an hussar came for water and went back into the hollow, but perhaps he had simply vanished—disappeared altogether and dissolved into nothingness.

Nothing Pétya could have seen now would have surprised him. He was in a fairy kingdom where everything was possible.

He looked up at the sky. And the sky was a fairy realm like the earth. It was clearing, and over the tops of the trees clouds were swiftly sailing as if unveiling the stars. Sometimes it looked as if the clouds were passing, and a clear black sky appeared. Sometimes it seemed as if the black spaces were clouds. Sometimes the sky seemed to be rising high, high overhead, and then it seemed to sink so low that one could touch it with one's hand.

Pétya's eyes began to close and he swayed a little.

The trees were dripping. Quiet talking was heard. The horses neighed and jostled one another. Someone snored.

"Ozheg-zheg, Ozheg-zheg . . ." hissed the saber against the whetstone, and suddenly Pétya heard an harmonious orchestra playing some unknown, sweetly solemn hymn. Pétya was as musical as Natásha and more so than Nicholas, but had never learned music or thought about it, and so the melody that unexpectedly came to his mind seemed to him particularly fresh and attractive. The music became more and more audible. The melody grew and passed from one instrument to another. And what was played was a fugue—though Pétya had not the least conception of what a fugue is. Each instrument—now resembling a violin and now a horn, but better and clearer than violin or horn—played its own part, and before it had finished the melody merged with another instrument that began almost the same air, and then with a third and a fourth; and they all blended into one and again became separate and again blended, now into solemn church music, now into something dazzlingly brilliant and triumphant.

"Oh—why, that was in a dream!" Pétya said to himself, as he lurched forward. "It's in my ears. But perhaps it's music of my own. Well, go on, my music! Now! . . ."

He closed his eyes, and, from all sides as if from a distance, sounds fluttered, grew into harmonies, separated, blended, and again all mingled into the same sweet and solemn hymn. "Oh, this is delightful! As much as I like and as I like!" said Pétya to himself. He tried to conduct that enormous orchestra.

"Now softly, softly die away!" and the sounds obeyed him. "Now fuller, more joyful. Still more and more joyful!" And from an unknown depth rose increasingly triumphant sounds. "Now voices join in!" ordered Pétya. And at first from afar he heard men's voices and then women's. The voices grew in harmonious triumphant strength, and Pétya listened to their surpassing beauty in awe and joy.

With a solemn triumphal march there mingled a song, the drip from the trees, and the hissing of the saber, "Ozheg-zheg-zheg . . ." and again the horses jostled one another and neighed, not disturbing the choir but joining in it.

Pétya did not know how long this lasted: he enjoyed himself all the time, wondered at his enjoyment and regretted that there was no one to share it. He was awakened by Likhachëv's kindly voice.

"It's ready, your honor; you can split a Frenchman in half with it!"

Pétya woke up.

"It's getting light, it's really getting light!" he exclaimed.

The horses that had previously been invisible could now be seen to their very tails, and a watery light showed itself through the bare branches. Pétya shook himself, jumped up, took a ruble from his pocket and gave it to Likhachëv; then he flourished the saber, tested it, and sheathed it. The Cossacks were untying their horses and tightening their saddle girths.

"And here's the commander," said Likhachëv.

Denísov came out of the watchman's hut and, having called Pétya, gave orders to get ready.

THE MEN rapidly picked out their horses in the semidarkness, tightened their saddle girths, and formed companies. Denísov stood by the watchman's hut giving final orders. The infantry of the detachment passed along the road and quickly disappeared amid the trees in the mist of early dawn, hundreds of feet splashing through the mud. The esaul gave some orders to his men. Pétya held his horse by the bridle, impatiently awaiting the order to mount. His face, having been bathed in cold water, was all aglow, and his eyes were particularly brilliant. Cold shivers ran down his spine and his whole body pulsed rhythmically.

"Well, is ev'wything weady?" asked Denísov. "Bwing the horses."

The horses were brought. Denísov was angry with the Cossack because the saddle girths were too slack, reproved him, and mounted. Pétya put his foot in the stirrup. His horse by habit made as if to nip his leg, but Pétya leaped quickly into the saddle unconscious of his own weight and, turning to look at the hussars starting in the darkness behind him, rode up to Denísov.

"Vasíli Dmítrich, entrust me with some commission! Please . . . for God's sake . . . !" said he.

Denísov seemed to have forgotten Pétya's very existence. He turned to glance at him.

"I ask one thing of you," he said sternly, "to obey me and not shove you'self fo'ward anywhere."

He did not say another word to Pétya but rode in silence all the way. When they had come to the edge of the forest it was noticeably growing light over the field. Denísov talked in whispers with the esaul and the Cossacks rode past Pétya and Denísov. When they had all ridden by, Denísov touched his horse and rode down the hill. Slipping onto their haunches and sliding, the horses descended with their riders into the ravine. Pétya rode beside Denísov, the pulsation of his body constantly increasing. It was getting lighter and lighter, but the mist still hid distant objects. Having reached the valley, Denísov looked back and nodded to a Cossack beside him.

"The signal!" said he.

The Cossack raised his arm and a shot rang out. In an instant the tramp of horses galloping forward was heard, shouts came from various sides, and then more shots.

At the first sound of trampling hoofs and shouting, Pétya lashed his horse and loosening his rein galloped forward, not heeding Denísov who shouted at him. It seemed to Pétya that at the moment the shot was fired it suddenly became as bright as noon. He galloped to the bridge. Cossacks were galloping along the road in front of him. On the bridge he collided with a Cossack who had fallen behind, but he galloped on. In front of him soldiers, probably Frenchmen, were running from right to left across the road. One of them fell in the mud under his horse's feet.

Cossacks were crowding about a hut, busy with something. From the midst of that crowd terrible screams arose. Pétya galloped up, and the first thing he saw was the pale face and trembling jaw of a Frenchman, clutching the handle of a lance that had been aimed at him.

"Hurrah! . . . Lads! . . . ours!" shouted Pétya, and giving rein to his excited horse he galloped forward along the village street.

He could hear shooting ahead of him. Cossacks, hussars, and ragged Russian prisoners, who had come running from both sides of the road, were shouting something loudly and incoherently. A gallant-looking Frenchman, in a blue overcoat, capless, and with a frowning red face, had been defending himself against the hussars. When Pétya galloped up the Frenchman had already fallen. "Too late again!" flashed through Pétya's mind and he galloped on to the place from which the rapid firing could be heard. The shots came from the yard of the landowner's house he had visited the night before with Dólokhov. The French were making a stand there behind a wattle fence in a garden thickly overgrown with bushes and were firing at the Cossacks who crowded at the gateway. Through the smoke, as he approached the gate, Pétya saw Dólokhov, whose face was of a pale-greenish tint, shouting to his men. "Go round! Wait for the infantry!" he exclaimed as Pétya rode up to him.

"Wait? . . . Hurrah-ah-ah!" shouted Pétya, and without pausing a moment galloped to the place whence came the sounds of firing and where the smoke was thickest.

A volley was heard, and some bullets whistled past, while others plashed against something. The Cossacks and Dólokhov galloped after Pétya into the gateway of the courtyard.

In the dense wavering smoke some of the French threw down their arms and ran out of the bushes to meet the Cossacks, while others ran down the hill toward the pond. Pétya was galloping along the courtyard, but instead of holding the reins he waved both his arms about rapidly and strangely, slipping farther and farther to one side in his saddle. His horse, having galloped up to a campfire that was smoldering in the morning light, stopped suddenly, and Pétya fell heavily on to the wet ground. The Cossacks saw that his arms and legs jerked rapidly though his head was quite motionless. A bullet had pierced his skull.

After speaking to the senior French officer, who came out of the house with a white handkerchief tied to his sword and announced that they surrendered, Dólokhov dismounted and went up to Pétya, who lay motionless with outstretched arms.

"Done for!" he said with a frown, and went to the gate to meet Denísov who was riding toward him.

"Killed?" cried Denísov, recognizing from a distance the unmistakably lifeless attitude—very familiar to him—in which Pétya's body was lying.

"Done for!" repeated Dólokhov as if the utterance of these words afforded him pleasure, and he went quickly up to the prisoners, who were surrounded by Cossacks who had hurried up. "We won't take them!" he called out to Denísov.

Denísov did not reply; he rode up to Pétya, dismounted, and with trembling hands turned toward himself the bloodstained, mud-bespattered face which had already gone white.

"I am used to something sweet. Raisins, fine ones . . . take them all!" he recalled Pétya's words. And the Cossacks looked round in surprise at the sound, like the yelp of a dog, with which Denísov turned away, walked to the wattle fence, and seized hold of it.

Among the Russian prisoners rescued by Denísov and Dólokhov was Pierre Bezúkhov.

3. Pierre's journey among the prisoners. Karatáev. His story of the merchant. His death. Pierre rescued

DURING THE WHOLE of their march from Moscow no fresh orders had been issued by the French authorities concerning the party of prisoners among whom was Pierre. On the twenty-second of October that party was no longer with the same troops and baggage trains with which it had left Moscow. Half the wagons laden with hardtack that had traveled the first stages with them had been captured by Cossacks, the other half had gone on ahead. Not one of those dismounted cavalrymen who had marched in front of the prisoners was left; they had all disappeared. The artillery the prisoners had seen in front of them during the first days was now replaced by Marshal Junot's enormous baggage train, convoyed by Westphalians. Behind the prisoners came a cavalry baggage train.

From Vyázma onwards the French army, which had till then moved in three columns, went on as a single group. The symptoms of disorder that Pierre had noticed at their first halting place after leaving Moscow had now reached the utmost limit.

The road along which they moved was bordered on both sides by dead horses; ragged men who had fallen behind from various regiments continually changed about, now joining the moving column, now again lagging behind it.

Several times during the march false alarms had been given and the soldiers of the escort had raised their muskets, fired, and run headlong, crushing one another, but had afterwards reassembled and abused each other for their causeless panic.

These three groups traveling together—the cavalry stores, the convoy of prisoners, and Junot's baggage train—still constituted a separate and united whole, though each of the groups was rapidly melting away.

Of the artillery baggage train which had consisted of a hundred and twenty wagons, not more than sixty now remained; the rest had been captured or left behind. Some of Junot's wagons also had been captured or abandoned. Three wagons had been raided and robbed by stragglers from Davout's corps. From the talk of the Germans Pierre learned that a larger guard had been allotted to that baggage train than to the prisoners, and that one of their comrades, a German soldier, had been shot by the marshal's own order because a silver spoon belonging to the marshal had been found in his possession.

The group of prisoners had melted away most of all. Of the three hundred and thirty men who had set out from Moscow fewer than a hundred now remained. The prisoners were more burdensome to the escort than even the cavalry saddles or Junot's baggage. They understood that the saddles and Junot's spoon might be of some use, but that cold and hungry soldiers should have to stand and guard equally cold and hungry Russians who froze and lagged behind on the road (in which case the order was to shoot them) was not merely incomprehensible but revolting. And the escort, as if afraid, in the grievous condition they themselves were in, of giving way to the pity they felt for the prisoners and so rendering their own plight still worse, treated them with particular moroseness and severity.

At Dorogobúzh while the soldiers of the convoy, after locking the prisoners in a stable, had gone off to pillage their own stores, several of the soldier prisoners tunneled under the wall and ran away, but were recaptured by the French and shot.

The arrangement adopted when they started, that the officer prisoners should be kept separate from the rest, had long since been abandoned. All who could walk went together, and after the third stage Pierre had rejoined Karatáev and the gray-blue bandy-legged dog that had chosen Karatáev for its master.

On the third day after leaving Moscow Karatáev again fell ill with the fever he had suffered from in hospital in Moscow, and as he grew gradually weaker Pierre kept away from him. Pierre did not know why, but since Karatáev had begun to grow weaker it had cost him an effort to go near him. When he did so and heard the subdued moaning with which Karatáev generally lay down at the halting places, and when he smelled the odor emanating from him which was now stronger than before, Pierre moved farther away and did not think about him.

While imprisoned in the shed Pierre had learned not with his intellect but with his whole being, by life itself, that man is created for happiness, that happiness is within him, in the satisfaction of simple human needs, and that all unhappiness arises not from privation but from superfluity. And now during these last three weeks of the march he had learned still another new, consolatory truth—that nothing in this world is terrible. He had learned that as there is no condition in which man can be happy and entirely free, so there is no condition in which he need be unhappy and lack freedom. He learned that suffering and freedom have their limits and that those limits are very near together; that the person in a bed of roses with one crumpled petal suffered as keenly as he now, sleeping on the bare damp earth with one side growing chilled while the other was warming; and that when he had put on tight dancing shoes he had suffered just as he did now when he walked with bare feet that were covered with sores—his footgear having long since fallen to pieces. He discovered that when he had married his wife—of his own free will as it had seemed to him—he had been no more free than now when they locked him up at night in a stable. Of all that he himself subsequently termed his sufferings, but which at the time he scarcely felt, the worst was the state of his bare, raw, and scab-covered feet. (The horseflesh was appetizing and nourishing, the saltpeter flavor of the gunpowder they used instead of salt was even pleasant; there was no great cold, it was always warm walking in the daytime, and at night there were the campfires; the lice that devoured him warmed his body.) The one thing that was at first hard to bear was his feet.

After the second day's march Pierre, having examined his feet by the campfire, thought it would be impossible to walk on them; but when everybody got up he went along, limping, and, when he had warmed up, walked without feeling the pain, though at night his feet were more terrible to look at than before. However, he did not look at them now, but thought of other things.

Only now did Pierre realize the full strength of life in man and the saving power he has of transferring his attention from one thing to another, which is like the safety valve of a boiler that allows superfluous steam to blow off when the pressure exceeds a certain limit.

He did not see and did not hear how they shot the prisoners who lagged behind, though more than a hundred perished in that way. He did not think of Karatáev who grew weaker every day and evidently would soon have to share that fate. Still less did Pierre think about himself. The harder his position became and the more terrible the future, the more independent of that position in which he found himself were the joyful and comforting thoughts, memories, and imaginings that came to him.

AT MIDDAY on the twenty-second of October Pierre was going uphill along the muddy, slippery road, looking at his feet and at the roughness of the way. Occasionally he glanced at the familiar crowd around him and then again at his feet. The former and the latter were alike familiar and his own. The blue-gray bandy-legged dog ran merrily along the side of the road, sometimes in proof of its agility and self-satisfaction lifting one hind leg and hopping along on three, and then again going on all four and rushing to bark at the crows that sat on the carrion. The dog was merrier and sleeker than it had been in Moscow. All around lay the flesh of different animals—from men to horses—in various stages of decomposition; and as the wolves were kept off by the passing men the dog could eat all it wanted.

It had been raining since morning and had seemed as if at any moment it might cease and the sky clear, but after a short break it began raining harder than before. The saturated road no longer absorbed the water, which ran along the ruts in streams.

Pierre walked along, looking from side to side, counting his steps in threes, and reckoning them off on his fingers. Mentally addressing the rain, he repeated: "Now then, now then, go on! Pelt harder!"

It seemed to him that he was thinking of nothing, but far down and deep within him his soul was occupied with something important and comforting. This something was a most subtle spiritual deduction from a conversation with Karatáev the day before.

At their yesterday's halting place, feeling chilly by a dying campfire, Pierre had got up and gone to the next one, which was burning better. There Platón Karatáev was sitting covered up—head and all—with his greatcoat as if it were a vestment, telling the soldiers in his effective and pleasant though now feeble voice a story Pierre knew. It was already past midnight, the hour when Karatáev was usually free of his fever and particularly lively. When Pierre reached the fire and heard Platón's voice enfeebled by illness, and saw his pathetic face brightly lit up by the blaze, he felt a painful prick at his heart. His feeling of pity for this man frightened him and he wished to go away, but there was no other fire, and Pierre sat down, trying not to look at Platón.

"Well, how are you?" he asked.

"How am I? If we grumble at sickness, God won't grant us death," replied Platón, and at once resumed the story he had begun.

"And so, brother," he continued, with a smile on his pale emaciated face and a particularly happy light in his eyes, "you see, brother . . ."

Pierre had long been familiar with that story.* Karatáev had told it to him alone some half-dozen times and always with a specially joyful emotion. But well as he knew it, Pierre now listened to that tale as to something new, and the quiet rapture Karatáev evidently felt as he told it communicated itself also to Pierre. The story was of an old merchant who lived a good and God-fearing life with his family, and who went once to the Nízhni fair with a companion—a rich merchant.

Having put up at an inn they both went to sleep, and next morning his companion was found robbed and with his throat cut. A bloodstained knife was found under the old merchant's pillow. He was tried, knouted, and his nostrils having been torn off, "all in due form" as Karatáev put it, he was sent to hard labor in Siberia.

"And so, brother" (it was at this point that Pierre came up), "ten years or more passed by. The old man was living as a convict, submitting as he should and doing no wrong. Only he prayed to God for death. Well, one night the convicts were gathered just as we are, with the old man among

*The tale Karatáev tells was a particular favorite of Tolstóy's. He wrote it out much more fully under the title of God Sees the Truth but Waits (the full Russian title is God Sees the Truth But Speaks not Soon) in the volume of Twenty-Three Tales. In What Is Art? he refers to it as being in his opinion one of the two best he ever wrote, as regards its subject matter of forgiveness of injuries.—A.M.

them. And they began telling what each was suffering for, and how they had sinned against God. One told how he had taken a life, another had taken two, a third had set a house on fire, while another had simply been a vagrant and had done nothing. So they asked the old man: 'What are you being punished for, Daddy?'—'I, my dear brothers,' said he, 'am being punished for my own and other men's sins. But I have not killed anyone or taken anything that was not mine, but have only helped my poorer brothers. I was a merchant, my dear brothers, and had much property.' And he went on to tell them all about it in due order. 'I don't grieve for myself,' he says, 'God, it seems, has chastened me. Only I am sorry for my old wife and the children,' and the old man began to weep. Now it happened that in the group was the very man who had killed the other merchant. 'Where did it happen, Daddy?' he said. 'When, and in what month?' He asked all about it and his heart began to ache. So he comes up to the old man like this, and falls down at his feet! 'You are perishing because of me, Daddy,' he says. 'It's quite true, lads, that this man,' he says, 'is being tortured innocently and for nothing! I,' he says, 'did that deed, and I put the knife under your head while you were asleep. Forgive me, Daddy,' he says, 'for Christ's sake!' "

Karatáev paused, smiling joyously as he gazed into the fire, and he drew the logs together.

"And the old man said, 'God will forgive you, we are all sinners in His sight. I suffer for my own sins,' and he wept bitter tears. Well, and what do you think, dear friends?" Karatáev continued, his face brightening more and more with a rapturous smile as if what he now had to tell contained the chief charm and the whole meaning of his story: "What do you think, dear fellows? That murderer confessed to the authorities. 'I have taken six lives,' he says (he was a great sinner), 'but what I am most sorry for is this old man. Don't let him suffer because of me.' So he confessed and it was all written down and the papers sent off in due form. The place was a long way off, and while they were judging, what with one thing and another, filling in the papers all in due form—the authorities I mean—time passed. The affair reached the Tsar. After a while the Tsar's decree came: to set the merchant free and give him a compensation that had been awarded. The paper arrived and they began to look for the old man. 'Where is the old man who has been suffering innocently and in vain? A paper has come from the Tsar!' So they began looking for him," here Karatáev's lower jaw trembled, "but God had already forgiven him— he was dead! That's how it was, dear fellows!" Karatáev concluded and sat for a long time silent, gazing before him with a smile.

And Pierre's soul was dimly but joyfully filled not by the story itself but by its mysterious significance: by the rapturous joy that lit up Karatáev's face as he told it, and the mystic significance of that joy.

"À vos places [To your places]!" suddenly cried a voice.

A pleasant feeling of excitement and an expectation of something joyful and solemn was aroused among the soldiers of the convoy and the prisoners. From all sides came shouts of command, and from the left came smartly dressed cavalrymen on good horses, passing the prisoners at a trot. The expression on all faces showed the tension people feel at the approach of those in authority. The prisoners thronged together and were pushed off the road. The convoy formed up.

"The Emperor! The Emperor! The Marshal! The Duke!" and hardly had the sleek cavalry passed, before a carriage drawn by six gray horses rattled by. Pierre caught a glimpse of a man in a three-cornered hat with a tranquil look on his handsome, plump, white face. It was one of the marshals. His eye fell on Pierre's large and striking figure, and in the expression with which he frowned and looked away Pierre thought he detected sympathy and a desire to conceal that sympathy.

The general in charge of the stores galloped after the carriage with a red and frightened face, whipping up his skinny horse. Several officers formed a group and some soldiers crowded round them. Their faces all looked excited and worried.

"What did he say? What did he say?" Pierre heard them ask.

While the marshal was passing, the prisoners had huddled together in a crowd, and Pierre saw Karatáev whom he had not yet seen that morning. He sat in his short overcoat leaning against a birch tree. On his face, besides the look of joyful emotion it had worn yesterday while telling the tale of the merchant who suffered innocently, there was now an expression of quiet solemnity.

Karatáev looked at Pierre with his kindly round eyes now filled with tears, evidently wishing him to come near that he might say something to him. But Pierre was not sufficiently sure of himself. He made as if he did not notice that look and moved hastily away.

When the prisoners again went forward Pierre looked round. Karatáev was still sitting at the side of the road under the birch tree and two Frenchmen were talking over his head. Pierre did not look round again but went limping up the hill.

From behind, where Karatáev had been sitting, came the sound of a shot. Pierre heard it plainly, but at that moment he remembered that he had not yet finished reckoning up how many stages still remained to Smolénsk—a calculation he had begun before the marshal went by. And he again started reckoning. Two French soldiers ran past Pierre, one of whom carried a lowered and smoking gun. They both looked pale, and in the expression on their faces—one of them glanced timidly at Pierre— there was something resembling what he had seen on the face of the young soldier at the execution. Pierre looked at the soldier and remembered that, two days before, that man had burned his shirt while drying it at the fire and how they had laughed at him.

Behind him, where Karatáev had been sitting, the dog began to howl. "What a stupid beast! Why is it howling?" thought Pierre.

His comrades, the prisoner soldiers walking beside him, avoided looking back at the place where the shot had been fired and the dog was howling, just as Pierre did, but there was a set look on all their faces.

THE STORES, the prisoners, and the marshal's baggage train stopped at the village of Shámshevo. The men crowded together round the campfires. Pierre went up to the fire, ate some roast horseflesh, lay down with his back to the fire, and immediately fell asleep. He again slept as he had done at Mozháysk after the battle of Borodinó.

Again real events mingled with dreams and again someone, he or another, gave expression to his thoughts, and even to the same thoughts that had been expressed in his dream at Mozháysk.

"Life is everything. Life is God. Everything changes and moves and that movement is God. And while there is life there is joy in consciousness of the divine. To love life is to love God. Harder and more blessed than all else is to love this life in one's sufferings, in innocent sufferings."

"Karatáev!" came to Pierre's mind.

And suddenly he saw vividly before him a long-forgotten, kindly old man who had given him geography lessons in Switzerland. "Wait a bit," said the old man, and showed Pierre a globe. This globe was alive—a vibrating ball without fixed dimensions. Its whole surface consisted of drops closely pressed together, and all these drops moved and changed places, sometimes several of them merging into one, sometimes one dividing into many. Each drop tried to spread out and occupy as much space as possible, but others striving to do the same compressed it, sometimes destroyed it, and sometimes merged with it.

"That is life," said the old teacher.

"How simple and clear it is," thought Pierre. "How is it I did not know it before?"

"God is in the midst, and each drop tries to expand so as to reflect Him to the greatest extent. And it grows, merges, disappears from the surface, sinks to the depths, and again emerges. There now, Karatáev has spread out and disappeared. Do you understand, my child?" said the teacher. "Do you understand, damn you?" shouted a voice, and Pierre woke up.* He lifted himself and sat up. A Frenchman who had just pushed a Russian soldier away was squatting by the fire, engaged in roasting a piece of meat stuck on a ramrod. His sleeves were rolled up and his sinewy, hairy, red hands with their short fingers deftly turned the ramrod. His brown morose face with frowning brows was clearly visible by the glow of the charcoal.

"It's all the same to him," he muttered, turning quickly to a soldier who stood behind him. "Brigand! Get away!"

And twisting the ramrod he looked gloomily at Pierre, who turned away, and gazed into the darkness. A prisoner, the Russian soldier the Frenchman had pushed away, was sitting near the fire patting something with his hand. Looking more closely Pierre recognized the blue-gray dog, sitting beside the soldier, wagging its tail.

"Ah, he's come?" said Pierre. "And Plat—" he began, but did not finish.

Suddenly and simultaneously a crowd of memories awoke in his fancy —of the look Platón had given him as he sat under the tree, of the shot heard from that spot, of the dog's howl, of the guilty faces of the two Frenchmen as they ran past him, of the lowered and smoking gun, and of Karatáev's absence at this halt—and he was on the point of realizing that Karatáev had been killed, but just at that instant, he knew not why, the recollection came to his mind of a summer evening he had spent with a beautiful Polish lady on the veranda of his house in Kiev. And without linking up the events of the day or drawing a conclusion from them, Pierre closed his eyes, seeing a vision of the country in summertime mingled with memories of bathing and of the liquid, vibrating globe, and he sank into water so that it closed over his head.

Before sunrise he was awakened by shouts and loud and rapid firing. French soldiers were running past him.

"The Cossacks!" one of them shouted, and a moment later a crowd of Russians surrounded Pierre.

For a long time he could not understand what was happening to him. All around he heard his comrades sobbing with joy.

"Brothers! Dear fellows! Darlings!" old soldiers exclaimed, weeping, as they embraced Cossacks and hussars.

* As a young man Tolstóy was interested in the phenomena of dreams, and he adopted a theory that dreams, however complex and prolonged they may seem, occur at the instant of waking and are suggested by external sounds, smells, or sensations.—A.M.

The hussars and Cossacks crowded round the prisoners; one offered them clothes, another boots, and a third bread. Pierre sobbed as he sat among them and could not utter a word. He hugged the first soldier who approached him, and kissed him, weeping.

Dólokhov stood at the gate of the ruined house, letting a crowd of disarmed Frenchmen pass by. The French, excited by all that had happened, were talking loudly among themselves, but as they passed Dólokhov who gently switched his boots with his whip and watched them with cold glassy eyes that boded no good, they became silent. On the opposite side stood Dólokhov's Cossack, counting the prisoners and marking off each hundred with a chalk line on the gate.

"How many?" Dólokhov asked the Cossack.

"The second hundred," replied the Cossack.

"Filez, filez [Get along, get along]!" Dólokhov kept saying, having adopted this expression from the French, and when his eyes met those of the prisoners they flashed with a cruel light.

Denísov, bareheaded and with a gloomy face, walked behind some Cossacks who were carrying the body of Pétya Rostóv to a hole that had been dug in the garden.

4. The French retreat. Berthier's report to Napoleon. Their flight beyond Smolénsk

AFTER THE TWENTY-EIGHTH OF OCTOBER when the frosts began, the flight of the French assumed a still more tragic character, with men freezing, or roasting themselves to death at the campfires, while carriages with people dressed in furs continued to drive past, carrying away the property that had been stolen by the Emperor, kings, and dukes; but the process of the flight and disintegration of the French army went on essentially as before.

From Moscow to Vyázma the French army of seventy-three thousand men not reckoning the Guards (who did nothing during the whole war but pillage) was reduced to thirty-six thousand, though not more than five thousand had fallen in battle. From this beginning the succeeding terms of the progression could be determined mathematically. The French army melted away and perished at the same rate from Moscow to Vyázma, from Vyázma to Smolénsk, from Smolénsk to the Berëzina, and from the Berëzina to Vílna—independently of the greater or lesser intensity of the cold, the pursuit, the barring of the way, or any other particular conditions.

Beyond Vyázma the French army instead of moving in three columns huddled together into one mass, and so went on to the end. Berthier wrote to his Emperor (we know how far commanding officers allow themselves to diverge from the truth in describing the condition of an army) and this is what he said:

I deem it my duty to report to Your Majesty the condition of the various corps I have had occasion to observe during different stages of the last two or three days' march. They are almost disbanded. Scarcely a quarter of the soldiers remain with the standards of their regiments, the others go off by themselves in different directions hoping to find food and escape discipline. In general they regard Smolénsk as the place where they hope to recover. During the last few days many of the men have been seen to throw away their cartridges and their arms. In such a state of affairs, whatever your ultimate plans may be, the interest of Your Majesty's service demands that the army should be rallied at Smolénsk and should first of all be freed from ineffectives, such as dismounted cavalry, unnecessary baggage, and artillery material that is no longer in proportion to the present forces. The soldiers, who are worn out with hunger and fatigue, need supplies as well as a few days' rest. Many have died these last days on the road or at the bivouacs. This state of things is continually becoming worse and makes one fear that unless a prompt remedy is applied the troops will no longer be under control in case of an engagement.

November 9: twenty miles from Smolénsk.

After staggering into Smolénsk which seemed to them a promised land, the French, searching for food, killed one another, sacked their own stores, and when everything had been plundered fled farther.

They all went without knowing whither or why they were going. Still less did that genius, Napoleon, know it, for no one issued any orders to him. But still he and those about him retained their old habits: wrote commands, letters, reports, and orders of the day; called one another *sire*, *mon cousin, prince d'Eckmühl, roi de Naples*, and so on. But these orders and reports were only on paper, nothing in them was acted upon for they could not be carried out, and though they entitled one another Majesties, Highnesses, or Cousins, they all felt that they were miserable wretches who had done much evil for which they had now to pay. And though they pretended to be concerned about the army, each was thinking only of himself and of how to get away quickly and save himself.

THE MOVEMENTS of the Russian and French armies during the campaign from Moscow back to the Niemen were like those in a game of Russian blindman's buff, in which two players are blindfolded and one of them occasionally rings a little bell to inform the catcher of his whereabouts. First he rings his bell fearlessly, but when he gets into a tight place he runs away as quietly as he can, and often thinking to escape runs straight into his opponent's arms.

At first while they were still moving along the Kalúga road, Napoleon's armies made their presence known, but later when they reached the Smolénsk road they ran holding the clapper of their bell tight—and often thinking they were escaping ran right into the Russians.

Owing to the rapidity of the French flight and the Russian pursuit and the consequent exhaustion of the horses, the chief means of approximately ascertaining the enemy's position—by cavalry scouting—was not available. Besides, as a result of the frequent and rapid change of position by each army, even what information was obtained could not be delivered in time. If news was received one day that the enemy had been in a certain position the day before, by the third day when something could have been done, that army was already two days' march farther on and in quite another position.

One army fled and the other pursued. Beyond Smolénsk there were several different roads available for the French, and one would have thought that during their stay of four days they might have learned where the enemy was, might have arranged some more advantageous plan and undertaken something new. But after a four days' halt the mob, with no maneuvers or plans, again began running along the beaten track, neither to the right nor to the left but along the old—the worst—road, through Krásnoe and Orshá.

Expecting the enemy from behind and not in front, the French separated in their flight and spread out over a distance of twenty-four hours. In front of them all fled the Emperor, then the kings, then the dukes. The Russian army, expecting Napoleon to take the road to the right beyond the Dnieper—which was the only reasonable thing for him to do—themselves turned to the right and came out onto the highroad at Krásnoe. And here as in a game of blindman's buff the French ran into our vanguard. Seeing their enemy unexpectedly the French fell into confusion and stopped short from the sudden fright, but then they resumed their flight, abandoning their comrades who were farther behind. Then for three days separate portions of the French army—first Murat's (the vice-king's), then Davout's, and then Ney's—ran, as it were, the gauntlet of the Russian army. They abandoned one another, abandoned all their heavy baggage, their artillery, and half their men, and fled, getting past the Russians by night by making semicircles to the right.

Ney, who came last, had been busying himself blowing up the walls of Smolénsk which were in nobody's way, because despite the unfortunate plight of the French or because of it, they wished to punish the floor against which they had hurt themselves. Ney, who had had a corps of ten thousand men, reached Napoleon at Orshá with only one thousand men left, having abandoned all the rest and all his cannon, and having crossed the Dnieper at night by stealth at a wooded spot.

From Orshá they fled farther along the road to Vílna, still playing at blindman's buff with the pursuing army. At the Berëzina they again became disorganized, many were drowned and many surrendered, but those who got across the river fled farther. Their supreme chief donned a fur coat and, having seated himself in a sleigh, galloped on alone, abandoning his companions. The others who could do so drove away too, leaving those who could not to surrender or die.

THIS CAMPAIGN consisted in a flight of the French during which they did all they could to destroy themselves. From the time they turned onto the Kalúga road to the day their leader fled from the army, none of the movements of the crowd had any sense. So one might have thought that regarding this period of the campaign the historians, who attributed the actions of the mass to the will of one man, would have found it impossible to make the story of the retreat fit their theory. But no! Mountains of books have been written by the historians about this campaign, and everywhere are described Napoleon's arrangements, the maneuvers, and his profound plans which guided the army, as well as the military genius shown by his marshals.

The retreat from Málo-Yaroslávets when he had a free road into a well-supplied district and the parallel road was open to him along which Kutúzov afterwards pursued him—this unnecessary retreat along a devastated road—is explained to us as being due to profound considerations. Similarly profound considerations are given for his retreat from Smolénsk to Orshá. Then his heroism at Krásnoe is described, where he is reported to have been prepared to accept battle and take personal command, and to have walked about with a birch stick and said:

"J'ai assez fait l'empereur; il est temps de faire le général [I have acted the Emperor long enough, it is time to act the general]," but nevertheless immediately ran away again, abandoning to its fate the scattered fragments of the army he left behind.

Then we are told of the greatness of soul of the marshals, especially of Ney—a greatness of soul consisting in this: that he made his way by night around through the forest and across the Dnieper and escaped to Orshá, abandoning standards, artillery, and nine tenths of his men.

And lastly, the final departure of the great Emperor from his heroic army is presented to us by the historians as something great and characteristic of genius. Even that final running away, described in ordinary language as the lowest depth of baseness which every child is taught to be ashamed of—even that act finds justification in the historians' language.

When it is impossible to stretch the very elastic threads of historical ratiocination any farther, when actions are clearly contrary to all that humanity calls right or even just, the historians produce a saving conception of "greatness." "Greatness," it seems, excludes the standards of right and wrong. For the "great" man nothing is wrong, there is no atrocity for which a "great" man can be blamed.

"C'est grand [It is great]!" say the historians, and there no longer exists either good or evil but only "grand" and "not grand." Grand is good, not grand is bad. Grand is the characteristic, in their conception, of some special animals called "heroes." And Napoleon, escaping home in a warm fur coat and leaving to perish those who were not merely his comrades but were (in his opinion) men he had brought there, feels que c'est grand [that it is great], and his soul is tranquil.

"Du sublime [he saw something sublime in himself] au ridicule il n'y a qu'un pas [From the sublime to the ridiculous is but a step]," said he. And the whole world for fifty years has been repeating: "Sublime! Grand! Napoléon le Grand!" Du sublime au ridicule il n'y a qu'un pas.

And it occurs to no one that to admit a greatness not commensurable with the standard of right and wrong is merely to admit one's own nothingness and immeasurable meanness.

For us with the standard of good and evil given us by Christ, no human actions are incommensurable. And there is no greatness where simplicity, goodness, and truth are absent.

5. Why the French were not cut off by the Russians

WHAT RUSSIAN, reading the account of the last part of the campaign of 1812, has not experienced an uncomfortable feeling of regret, dissatisfaction, and perplexity? Who has not asked himself how it is that the French were not all captured or destroyed when our three armies surrounded them in superior numbers, when the disordered French, hungry and freezing, surrendered in crowds, and when (as the historians relate) the aim of the Russians was to stop the French, to cut them off, and capture them all?

How was it that the Russian army, which when numerically weaker than the French had given battle at Borodinó, did not achieve its purpose when it had surrounded the French on three sides and when its aim was to capture them? Can the French be so enormously superior to us that when we had surrounded them with superior forces we could not beat them? How could that happen?

History (or what is called by that name) replying to these questions says that this occurred because Kutúzov and Tormásov and Chichagóv, and this man and that man, did not execute such and such maneuvers. . . .

But why did they not execute those maneuvers? And why if they were guilty of not carrying out a prearranged plan were they not tried and punished? But even if we admitted that Kutúzov, Chichagóv, and others were the cause of the Russian failures, it is still incomprehensible why, the position of the Russian army being what it was at Krásnoe and at the Berëzina (in both cases we had superior forces), the French army with its marshals, kings, and Emperor was not captured, if that was what the Russians aimed at.

The explanation of this strange fact given by Russian military historians (to the effect that Kutúzov hindered an attack) is unfounded, for we know that he could not restrain the troops from attacking at Vyázma and Tarútino.

Why was the Russian army—which with inferior forces had withstood the enemy in full strength at Borodinó—defeated at Krásnoe and the Berëzina by the disorganized crowds of the French when it was numerically superior?

If the aim of the Russians consisted in cutting off and capturing Napoleon and his marshals—and that aim was not merely frustrated but all attempts to attain it were most shamefully baffled—then this last period of the campaign is quite rightly considered by the French to be a series of victories, and quite wrongly considered victorious by Russian historians.

The Russian military historians in so far as they submit to claims of logic must admit that conclusion, and in spite of their lyrical rhapsodies about valor, devotion, and so forth, must reluctantly admit that the French retreat from Moscow was a series of victories for Napoleon and defeats for Kutúzov.

But putting national vanity entirely aside one feels that such a conclusion involves a contradiction, since the series of French victories brought the French complete destruction, while the series of Russian defeats led to the total destruction of their enemy and the liberation of their country.

The source of this contradiction lies in the fact that the historians study-ing the events from the letters of the sovereigns and the generals, from memoirs, reports, projects, and so forth, have attributed to this last period of the war of 1812 an aim that never existed, namely that of cutting off and capturing Napoleon with his marshals and his army.

There never was or could have been such an aim, for it would have been senseless and its attainment quite impossible.

It would have been senseless, first because Napoleon's disorganized army was flying from Russia with all possible speed, that is to say, was doing just what every Russian desired. So what was the use of performing various operations on the French who were running away as fast as they possibly could?

Secondly, it would have been senseless to block the passage of men whose whole energy was directed to flight.

Thirdly, it would have been senseless to sacrifice one's own troops in order to destroy the French army, which without external interference was destroying itself at such a rate that, though its path was not blocked, it could not carry across the frontier more than it actually did in December, namely a hundredth part of the original army.

Fourthly, it would have been senseless to wish to take captive the Emperor, kings, and dukes—whose capture would have been in the highest degree embarrassing for the Russians, as the most adroit diplomatists of the time (Joseph de Maistre * and others) recognized. Still more sense-less would have been the wish to capture army corps of the French, when our own army had melted away to half before reaching Krásnoe and a whole division would have been needed to convoy the corps of prisoners, and when our men were not always getting full rations and the prisoners already taken were perishing of hunger.

All the profound plans about cutting off and capturing Napoleon and his army were like the plan of a market gardener who, when driving out of his garden a cow that had trampled down the beds he had planted, should run to the gate and hit the cow on the head. The only thing to be said in excuse of that gardener would be that he was very angry. But not even that could be said for those who drew up this project, for it was not they who had suffered from the trampled beds.

But besides the fact that cutting off Napoleon with his army would have been senseless, it was impossible.

* *Joseph de Maistre (1754-1821). This able neo-Catholic and antirevolu-tionary writer was Sardinian ambassador at Petersburg. He lived there for fifteen years, was well received, and exerted a considerable antiliberal and reactionary influence.*—A.M.

It was impossible first because—as experience shows that a three-mile movement of columns on a battlefield never coincides with the plans— the probability of Chichagóv, Kutúzov, and Wittgenstein effecting a junction on time at an appointed place was so remote as to be tantamount to impossibility, as in fact thought Kutúzov, who when he received the plan remarked that diversions planned over great distances do not yield the desired results.

Secondly it was impossible, because to paralyze the momentum with which Napoleon's army was retiring, incomparably greater forces than the Russians possessed would have been required.

Thirdly it was impossible, because the military term "to cut off" has no meaning. One can cut off a slice of bread, but not an army. To cut off an army—to bar its road—is quite impossible, for there is always plenty of room to avoid capture and there is the night when nothing can be seen, as the military scientists might convince themselves by the example of Krásnoe and of the Berëzina. It is only possible to capture prisoners if they agree to be captured, just as it is only possible to catch a swallow if it settles on one's hand. Men can only be taken prisoners if they surrender according to the rules of strategy and tactics, as the Germans did. But the French troops quite rightly did not consider that this suited them, since death by hunger and cold awaited them in flight or captivity alike.

Fourthly and chiefly it was impossible, because never since the world began has a war been fought under such conditions as those that obtained in 1812, and the Russian army in its pursuit of the French strained its strength to the utmost and could not have done more without destroying itself.

During the movement of the Russian army from Tarútino to Krásnoe it lost fifty thousand sick or stragglers, that is a number equal to the population of a large provincial town. Half the men fell out of the army without a battle.

And it is of this period of the campaign—when the army lacked boots and sheepskin coats, was short of provisions and without vodka, and was camping out at night for months in the snow with fifteen degrees of frost,* when there were only seven or eight hours of daylight and the rest was night in which the influence of discipline cannot be maintained, when men were taken into that region of death where discipline fails, not for a few hours only as in a battle, but for months, where they were every moment fighting death from hunger and cold, when half the army perished in a single month—it is of this period of the campaign that the historians tell us how Milorádovich should have made a flank march to

* *Réaumur—two degrees below zero Fahrenheit.*—A.M.

435

such and such a place, Tormásov to another place, and Chichagóv should have crossed (more than knee-deep in snow) to somewhere else, and how so-and-so "routed" and "cut off" the French and so on and so on.

The Russians, half of whom died, did all that could and should have been done to attain an end worthy of the nation, and they are not to blame because other Russians, sitting in warm rooms, proposed that they should do what was impossible.

All that strange contradiction now difficult to understand between the facts and the historical accounts only arises because the historians dealing with the matter have written the history of the beautiful words and sentiments of various generals, and not the history of the events.

To them the words of Milorádovich seem very interesting, and so do their surmises and the rewards this or that general received; but the question of those fifty thousand men who were left in hospitals and in graves does not even interest them, for it does not come within the range of their investigation.

Yet one need only discard the study of the reports and general plans and consider the movement of those hundreds of thousands of men who took a direct part in the events, and all the questions that seemed insoluble easily and simply receive an immediate and certain solution.

The aim of cutting off Napoleon and his army never existed except in the imaginations of a dozen people. It could not exist because it was senseless and unattainable.

The people had a single aim: to free their land from invasion. That aim was attained in the first place of itself, as the French ran away, and so it was only necessary not to stop their flight. Secondly it was attained by the guerrilla warfare which was destroying the French, and thirdly by the fact that a large Russian army was following the French, ready to use its strength in case their movement stopped.

The Russian army had to act like a whip to a running animal. And the experienced driver knew it was better to hold the whip raised as a menace than to strike the running animal on the head.

Halford J. Mackinder (1861-1947) was born in England and educated at Oxford where he specialized in the physical sciences at Christ Church College. Subsequently he turned to geography, and with financial assistance from the Royal Geographical Society, he led in the foundation of a school of geography at Oxford in 1899. He served as principal of the Oxford extension college at Reading, and later served as director of the London School of Economics.

Mackinder was a member of Parliament from Glasgow from 1910 to 1922. He was British High Commissioner for South Russia during the turbulent years 1919-1920.

He first presented his general concept of the "World Island" and the "Heartland" in a paper for the Royal Geographical Society in 1904. He refined and expanded upon this theme in *Democratic Ideals and Reality*, published in 1919 mainly as a warning to the statesmen who were seeking to restore the peace after World War I. It has become a classical statement of geopolitics.

Democratic Ideals and Reality

One reason why the seamen did not long ago rise to the generalization implied in the expression "World-Island," is that they could not make the round voyage of it. An ice-cap, two thousand miles across, floats on the polar sea, with one edge aground on the shoals off the north of Asia. For the common purposes of navigation, therefore, the continent is not an island. The seamen of the last four centuries have treated it as a vast promontory stretching southward from a vague north, as a mountain peak may rise out of the clouds from hidden foundations. Even in the last century, since the opening of the Suez Canal, the eastward voyage has still been round a promontory, though with the point at Singapore instead of Cape Town.

This fact and its vastness have made men think of the Continent as though it differed from other islands in more than size. We speak of its parts as Europe, Asia, and Africa in precisely the same way that we speak of the parts of the ocean as Atlantic, Pacific, and Indian. In theory even the ancient Greeks regarded it as insular, yet they spoke of it as the "World." The school children of to-day are taught of it as the "Old World," in contrast with a certain pair of peninsulas which together constitute the "New World." Seamen speak of it merely as "the Continent," the continuous land.

Let us consider for a moment the proportions and relations of this newly realized Great Island.[1] It is set as it were on the shoulder of the earth with reference to the North Pole. Measuring from Pole to Pole along the central meridian of Asia, we have first a thousand miles of ice-clad sea as far as the northern shore of Siberia, then five thousand miles of land to the southern point of India, and then seven thousand miles of sea to the Antarctic cap of ice-clad land. But measured along the meridian of the Bay of Bengal or of the Arabian Sea, Asia is only some three thousand five hundred miles across. From Paris to Vladivostok is six thousand miles, and from Paris to the Cape of Good Hope is a similar distance; but these measurements are on a globe twenty-six thousand miles round. Were it not for the ice impediment to its circumnavigation, practical seamen would long ago have spoken of the Great Island by some such name, for it is only a little more than one-fifth as large as their ocean.

The World-Island ends in points northeastward and southeastward. On a clear day you can see from the northeastern headland across Bering Strait to the beginning of the long pair of peninsulas, each measuring about one twenty-sixth of the globe, which we call the

---

[1] It would be misleading to attempt to represent the statements which follow in map form. They can only be appreciated on a globe. Therefore they are illustrated by diagrams; see Figs. 12 and 13.

Americas. Superficially there is no doubt a certain resemblance of symmetry in the Old and New Worlds;
each consists of two peninsulas, Africa and Euro-Asia
in the one case, and North and South America in the
other. But there is no real likeness between them. The
northern and northeastern shores of Africa for nearly
four thousand miles are so intimately related with the
opposite shores of Europe and Asia that the Sahara constitutes a far more effective break in social continuity
than does the Mediterranean. **In the days of air navigation which are coming, sea-power will use the water-
way of the Mediterranean and Red Seas only by the
sufferance of land-power, a new amphibious cavalry,
when the contest with sea-power is in question.**

But North and South America, slenderly connected
at Panama, are for practical purposes insular rather than
peninsular in regard to one another. South America
lies not merely to south, but also in the main to east
of North America; the two lands are in echelon, as soldiers would say, and thus the broad ocean encircles
South America, except for a minute proportion of its
outline. A like fact is true of North America with reference to Asia, for it stretches out into the ocean from
Bering Strait so that, as may be seen upon a globe,
the shortest way from Pekin to New York is across
Bering Strait, a circumstance which may some day have
importance for the traveler by railway or air. The third
of the new continents, Australia, lies a thousand miles
from the southeastern point of Asia, and measures only
one sixty-fifth of the surface of the globe.

Thus.the three so-called new continents are in point
of area merely satellites of the old continent. There is

one ocean covering nine-twelfths of the globe; there is
one continent—the World-Island—covering two-twelfths
of the globe; and there are many smaller islands, whereof North America and South America are, for effective
purposes, two, which together cover the remaining one-
twelfth. The term "New World" implies, now that we
can see the realities and not merely historic appearances,
a wrong perspective.

The truth, seen with a broad vision, is that in the
great world-promontory, extending southward to the
Cape of Good Hope, and in the North American sea-
base we have, on a vast scale, yet a third contrast of
peninsula and island to be set beside the Greek peninsula and the island of Crete, and the Latin Peninsula
and the British Island. But there is this vital difference,
that the world-promontory, when united by modern
overland communications, is in fact the World-Island,
possessed potentially of the advantages both of insu-
larity and of incomparably great resources.

Leading Americans have for some time appreciated
the fact that their country is no longer a world apart,
and President Wilson had brought his whole people
round to that view when they consented to throw themselves into the war. But North America is no longer
even a continent; in this twentieth century it is shrink-
ing to be an island. Americans used to think of their
three millions of square miles as the equivalent of all
Europe; some day, they said, there would be a United
States of Europe as sister to the United States of America. Now, though they may not all have realized it, they
must no longer think of Europe apart from Asia and
Africa. The Old World has become insular, or in other

words a unit, incomparably the largest geographical unit on our globe.

There is a remarkable parallelism between the short history of America and the longer history of England; both countries have now passed through the same succession of colonial, continental, and insular stages. The Angle and Saxon settlements along the east and south coast of Britain have often been regarded as anticipating the thirteen English colonies along the east coast of North America; what has not always been remembered is that there was a continental stage in English history to be compared with that of Lincoln in America. The wars of Alfred the Great and William the Conqueror were in no small degree between contending parts of England, with the Norsemen intervening, and England was not effectively insular until the time of Elizabeth, because not until then was she free from the hostility of Scotland, and herself united, and therefore a unit, in her relations with the neighboring continent. America is to-day a unit, for the American people have fought out their internal differences, and it is insular, because events are compelling Americans to realize that their so-called continent lies on the same globe as *the* Continent.

Picture upon the map of the world this war as it has been fought in the year 1918. It has been a war between Islanders and Continentals, there can be no doubt of that. It has been fought on the Continent, chiefly across the landward front of peninsular France; and ranged on the one side have been Britain, Canada, the United States, Brazil, Australia, New Zealand, and Japan—all insular. France and Italy are peninsular, but

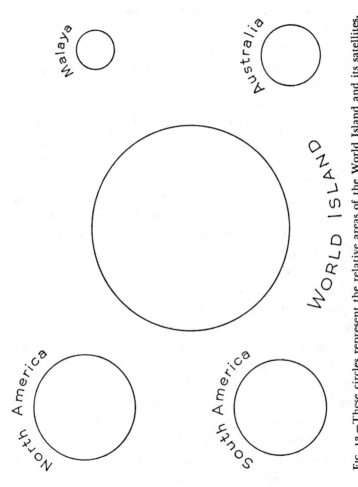

FIG. 12.—These circles represent the relative areas of the World Island and its satellites.

even with that advantage they would not have been in the war to the end had it not been for the support of the Islanders. India and China—so far as China has been in the war on the Manchurian front—may be regarded as advanced guards of British, American, and Japanese sea-power. Dutch Java is the only island of large population which is not in the Western Alliance, and even Java is not on the side of the Continentals. There can be no mistaking the significance of this unanimity of the islanders. The collapse of Russia has cleared our view of the realities, as the Russian Revolution purified the ideals for which we have been fighting.

The facts appear in the same perspective if we consider the population of the globe. **More than fourteen-sixteenths of all humanity live on the Great Continent, and nearly one-sixteenth more on the closely offset islands of Britain and Japan.** Even to-day, after four centuries of emigration, only about one-sixteenth live in the lesser continents. Nor is time likely to change these proportions materially. If the middle west of North America comes presently to support, let us say, another hundred million people, it is probable that the interior of Asia will at the same time carry two hundred millions more than now, and if the tropical part of South America should feed a hundred million more, then the tropical parts of Africa and the Indies may not improbably support two hundred millions more. The Congo forest alone, subdued to agriculture, would maintain some four hundred million souls if populated with the same density as Java, and the Javanese population is still growing. Have we any right, moreover, to assume that, given its climate and history, the interior of Asia

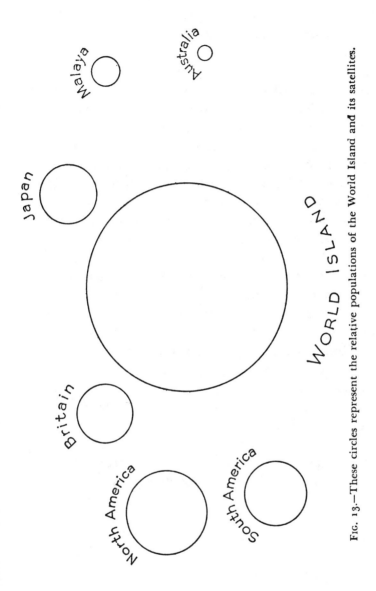

FIG. 13.—These circles represent the relative populations of the World Island and its satellites.

445

would not nourish a population as virile as that of Europe, North America, or Japan?

What if the Great Continent, the whole World-Island or a large part of it, were at some future time to become a single and united base of sea-power? Would not the other insular bases be outbuilt as regards ships and outmanned as regards seamen? Their fleets would no doubt fight with all the heroism begotten of their histories, but the end would be fated. Even in the present war, insular America has had to come to the aid of insular Britain, not because the British fleet could not have held the seas for the time being, but lest such a building and manning base were to be assured to Germany at the Peace, or rather Truce, that Britain would inevitably be outbuilt and outmanned a few years later.

The surrender of the German fleet in the Firth of Forth is a dazzling event, but in all soberness, if we would take the long view, must we not still reckon with the possibility that a large part of the Great Continent might some day be united under a single sway, and that an invincible sea-power might be based upon it? May we not have headed off that danger in this war, and yet leave by our settlement the opening for a fresh attempt in the future? Ought we not to recognize that that is the great ultimate threat to the world's liberty so far as strategy is concerned, and to provide against it in our new political system?

Let us look at the matter from the landsman's point of view.

．　　．　　．　　．　　．　　．　　．

The conclusion to which this discussion leads is that the connection between the Heartland, and especially its more open western regions of Iran, Turkestan, and Siberia, is much more intimate with Europe and Arabia than it is with China and India, or yet with the Southern Heartland of Africa. The strong natural frontiers of the Sahara Desert and the Tibetan Heights have no equivalent where the Northern Heartland merges with Arabia and Europe. The close connection of these three regions is well typified by that geographical formula into which it was attempted to crystallize just now certain essential aspects of Mesopotamian and Syrian history; the plowmen of Mesopotamia and Syria have always been exposed to descents of the horsemen from the Heartland, of the camel-men from Arabia, and of the shipmen from Europe. None the less—and indeed just because of its more transitional character—the boundary between the Heartland on the one hand, and Arabia and Europe on the other, is worth following with some care.

FIG. 24.—The Heartland, with the addition of the basins of the Black and Baltic Seas, and the uppermost (plateau) valleys of the Chinese and Indian rivers.

The long range of the Persian Mountains bends westward round the upper end of Mesopotamia and becomes the Taurus Range, which is the high southern brink of the peninsular upland of Asia Minor. The surface of Asia Minor is a patch of steppes, verging on desert in the center, where salt lakes receive some of the streams from the Taurus; but the larger rivers flow northward to the Black Sea. Beyond the break made by the Aegean Sea, we have the great basin of the Danube, also draining into the Black Sea; the head-streams of the Danube tributaries rise almost within sight of the Adriatic, but high on those Illyrian Uplands whose steep outer brink forms the mountain wall above the beautiful Dalmatian coast. That wall we name the Dinaric Alps.

Thus the Taurus and the Dinaric Alps present steep fronts to the Mediterranean and Adriatic, but send long rivers down to the Black Sea. But for the Aegean Sea, breaking through the uplands towards the Black Sea, and but for the Dardanelles, whose current races southward with the water of all the Black Sea rivers, these high, outward fronts of the Taurus and Dinaric Alps would be a single curving range, the edge of a continuous bar of land dividing the inner Black Sea from the outer Mediterranean and Adriatic. Were it not for the Dardanelles that edge would form the border of the Heartland, and the Black Sea and all its rivers would be added to the "Continental" systems of drainage. When the Dardanelles are closed by land-power to the sea-power of the Mediterranean, as they have been in the Great War, that condition of things is in effect realized so far as human movements are concerned.

The Roman emperors put their eastern capital at Constantinople (Istanbul: *ed.*), midway between the Danube and Euphrates frontiers, but Constantinople was to them more than the bridge-town from Europe into Asia. Rome, the Mediterranean Power, did not annex the northern shore of the Black Sea, and that sea, therefore, was itself a part of the frontier of the empire. The steppes were left to the Scythians, as the Turks were then called, and at most a few trading stations were dotted by the seamen along the coast of the Crimea. Thus Constantinople was the point from which Mediterranean sea-power held the middle sea-frontier, as the land-power of the Legions held the western and eastern frontiers along the rivers. Under Rome, sea-power thus advanced into the Heartland, if that term be understood, in a large, a strategical sense, as including Asia Minor and the Balkan Peninsula.

Later history is no less transparent to the underlying facts of geography, but in the inverse direction. Some of the Turks from Central Asia turned aside from the way down into Arabia, and rode over the Median and Armenian Uplands into the open steppe of Asia Minor, and there made their home, just as the Magyar Turks only a century or two earlier rode round the north of the Black Sea into the Hungarian Steppe. Under great leaders of cavalry of the Ottoman dynasty, these Turks crossed the Dardanelles, and, following the "Corridor" of the Maritza and Morava Valleys through the Balkan Mountains, achieved the conquest of Magyar Hungary itself. From the moment that the city of Constantinople fell into Turkish hands in 1453, the Black Sea was closed to the Venetian and Genoese seamen. Under Rome, the realm of the seamen had been advanced to the northern shore of the Black Sea; under the Ottoman Turks the Heartland, the realm of the horsemen, was advanced to the Dinaric Alps and the Taurus. This essential fact has been masked by the extension of

Constantinople
(Istanbul)

Fig. 25.—Showing the boundary of the Heartland when Mediterranean sea power enters the Black Sea + + + +, and when land power advances from the steppes to the Taurus and Dinaric Alps.

Turkish dominion into Arabia outside the Heartland; but it is evident again to-day when Britain has conquered Arabia for the Arabs. Within the Heartland, the Black Sea has of late been the path of strategical design eastward for our German enemy.

We defined the Heartland originally in accordance with river drainage; but does not history, as thus recounted, show that for the purposes of strategical thought it should be given a somewhat wider extension? Regarded from the point of view of human mobility, and of the different modes of mobility, it is evident that since land-power can to-day close the Black Sea, the whole basin of that sea must be regarded as of the Heartland. Only the Bavarian Danube, of very little value for navigation, may be treated as lying outside.

One more circumstance remains to be added, and we shall have before us the whole conception of the Heartland as it emerges from the facts of geography and history. The Baltic is a sea which can now be "closed" by land-power. The fact that the German fleet at Kiel was responsible for the mines and submarines which kept the Allied squadrons from entering the Baltic does not, of course, in any way vitiate the statement that the closing was by land-power; the Allied armies in France were there by virtue of sea-power, and the German sea defenses of the Baltic were there as a result of land-power. It is of prime importance in regard to any terms of peace which are to guarantee us against future war that we should recognize that under the conditions of to-day, as was admitted by responsible ministers in the House of Commons, the fleets of the islanders could no more penetrate into the Baltic than they could into the Black Sea.

The Heartland, for the purposes of strategical thinking, includes the Baltic Sea, the navigable Middle and Lower Danube, the Black Sea, Asia Minor, Armenia, Persia, Tibet, and Mongolia. Within it, therefore, were Brandenburg-Prussia and Austria-Hungary, as well as Russia—a vast triple base of man-power, which was lacking to the horse-riders of history. The Heartland is the region to which, under modern conditions, sea-power can be refused access, though the western part of it lies without the region of Arctic and Continental drainage. There is one striking physical circumstance which knits it graphically together; the whole of it, even to the brink of the Persian Mountains overlooking torrid Mesopotamia, lies under snow in the winter-time. The line indicative of an *average* freezing temperature for the whole month of January passes from the North Cape of Norway southward, just within the "Guard" of islands along the Norwegian shore, past Denmark, across mid-Germany to the Alps, and from the Alps eastward along the Balkan range. The Bay of Odessa and the Sea of Azof are frozen over annually, and also the greater part of the Baltic Sea. At mid-winter, as seen from the moon, a vast white shield would reveal the Heartland in its largest meaning.

When the Russian Cossacks first policed the steppes at the close of the Middle Ages, a great revolution was effected, for the Tartars, like the Arabs, had lacked the necessary man-power upon which to found a lasting empire, but behind the Cossacks were the Russian plowmen, who have to-day grown to be a people of a hundred millions on the fertile plains between the Black and Baltic Seas. During the nineteenth century, the Russian Czardom loomed large within the great Heartland, and seemed to threaten all the marginal lands of Asia and Europe. Towards the end of the century, however, the Germans of Prussia and Austria determined to subdue the Slavs and to exploit them for the occupation of the Heartland, through which run the land-ways into China, India, Arabia, and the African Heartland. The German military colonies of Kiauchau and East Africa were established as termini of the projected overland routes.

To-day armies have at their disposal not only the Transcontinental Railway but also the motor-car. They have, too, the aeroplane, which is of a boomerang nature, a weapon of land-power as against sea-power. Modern artillery, moreover, is very formidable against ships. In short, **a great military power in possession of the Heartland and of Arabia could take easy possession of the crossways of the world at Suez. Sea-power would have found it very difficult to hold the Canal if a fleet of submarines had been based from the beginning of the war on the Black Sea.** We have defeated the danger on this occasion, but the facts of geography remain, and offer ever-increasing strategical opportunities to land-power as against sea-power.

It is evident that **the Heartland is as real a physical fact within the World-Island as is the World-Island itself within the ocean, although its boundaries are not quite so clearly defined.** Not until about a hundred years ago, however, was there available a base of man-power sufficient to begin to threaten the liberty of the world from within this citadel of the World-Island. No mere scraps of paper, even though they be the written constitution of a League of Nations, are, under the conditions of to-day, a sufficient guarantee that the Heartland will not again become the center of a world war. Now is the time, when the nations are fluid, to consider what guarantees, based on geographical and economic realities, can be made available for the future security of mankind. With this in view, it will be worth our while to see how the storm gathered in the Heartland on the present occasion.

Fig. 26.—The World Island united, as it soon will be, by railways, and by

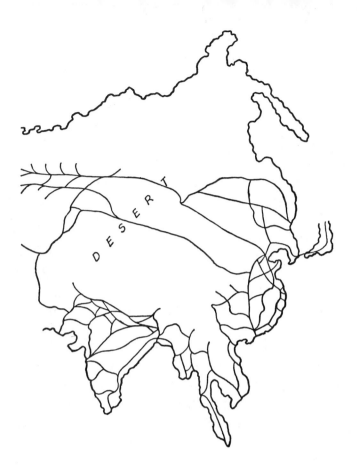

aeroplane routes, the latter for the most part parallel with the **main railways**.

Chapter Six

THE FREEDOM OF NATIONS

THE Allies have won the war. But how have we won? The process is full of warning. We were saved, in the first place, by the readiness of the British fleet, and by the decision which sent it to sea; so British communications with France were secured. That readiness and decision were the outcome of the British habit of looking to the one thing essential in the midst of many things we leave slipshod: it is the way of the capable amateur. We were saved, in the second place, by the wonderful victory of French genius on the Marne, prepared for by many years of deep thought in the great French *Ecole Militaire;* in other respects the French army was not as ready as it might have been, except in courage. We were saved in the third place by the sacrifice—it was no less—of the old British professional army at Ypres, a name that will stand in history beside Thermopylae. We were saved, in short, by exceptional genius and exceptional heroism from the results of an average refusal to foresee and prepare: eloquent testimony both to the strength and the weakness of democracy.

Then for two years the fighting was stabilized, and became a war of trenches on land and of submarines at sea, a war of attrition in which time told in favor of Britain but against Russia. In 1917 Russia cracked and then broke. Germany had conquered in the East, but postponed the utter subjection of the Slavs in order first to strike down her Western foes. West Europe had to call in the help of America, for West Europe alone would not have been able to reverse the decision in the East. Again time was needed, because America, the third of the greater democracies to go to war, was even less prepared than the other two. And time was bought by the heroism of British seamen, the sacrifice of British merchant shipping, and the endurance of the French and British soldiers against an offensive in France which all but overwhelmed them. In short, we once more pitted character and a right insight into essentials against German organization, and we just managed to win. At the eleventh hour Britain accepted the principle of the single strategical command, giving scope once more to the *École Militaire*.

But this whole record of Western and oceanic fighting, so splendid and yet so humiliating, has very little direct bearing on the international resettlement. There was no immediate quarrel between East Europe and West Europe; the time was past when France would have attacked Germany to recover Alsace and Lorraine. The war, let us never forget, began as a German effort to subdue the Slavs who were in revolt against Berlin. We all know that the murder of the Austrian (German) Archduke in Slav Bosnia was the pretext, and that the Austrian (German) ultimatum to Slav Serbia was the method of forcing the war. But it cannot be too often repeated that these events were the result of a fundamental antagonism between the Germans, who wished to be masters in East Europe, and the Slavs, who refused to submit to them. Had Germany elected to stand on the defensive on her short frontier towards France, and had she thrown her main strength against Russia, it is not improbable that the world would be nominally at peace to-day, but overshadowed by a German East Europe in command of all the Heartland. The British and American insular peoples would not have realized the strategical danger until too late.

Unless you would lay up trouble for the future, you cannot now accept any outcome of the war which does not finally dispose of the issue between German and Slav in East Europe. You must have a balance as between German and Slav, and true independence of each. You cannot afford to leave such a condition of affairs in East Europe and the Heartland, as would offer scope for ambition in the future, for you have escaped too narrowly from the recent danger.

A victorious Roman general, when he entered the city, amid all the head-turning splendor of a "Triumph," had behind him on the chariot a slave who whispered into his ear that he was mortal. When our statesmen are in conversation with the defeated enemy, some airy cherub should whisper to them from time to time this saying:

Who rules East Europe commands the Heartland:
Who rules the Heartland commands the World-Island:
Who rules the World-Island commands the World.

.   .   .   .

7

Eyre Crowe,   MEMORANDUM ON PRESENT STATE OF BRITISH
RELATIONS WITH FRANCE AND GERMANY

R. G. Hawtrey,   ECONOMIC ASPECTS OF SOVEREIGNTY

1. Compare Crowe's analysis of German intentions in
   1907 and the consequences for British policy with
   what you perceive to be current Soviet intentions
   and the consequences for United States policy.

2. On what basis does Crowe describe the historical
   foreign policy of England?

3. Explain Hawtrey's statement that "the principal
   cause of war is war itself."

4. Compare the views of Hawtrey and Crowe concerning
   the balance of power.

5. What is Hawtrey's view on arms limitations?

6. In what direction does Hawtrey see the main hope
   for maintaining peace?

It is not often that a memorandum prepared by a
civil servant for a government bureau emerges as a
classic. Sir Eyre Crowe's memorandum of 1907 on British foreign policy has done just that. This is because
it provides a clear and timeless approach in analyzing
foreign policy. It can be as useful to the U.S. Department of State in arriving at a policy vis a vis the
Soviet Union as to the British Foreign Office of an
earlier day in developing a policy toward Germany.

BRITISH RELATIONS WITH FRANCE
AND GERMANY[*]

THE general character of England's foreign policy is determined by the immutable conditions of her geographical situation on the ocean flank of Europe as an island State with vast oversea colonies and dependencies, whose existence and survival as an independent community are inseparably bound up with the possession of preponderant sea power. The tremendous influence of such preponderance has been described in the classical pages of Captain Mahan. No one now disputes it. Sea power is more potent than land power, because it is as pervading as the element in which it moves and has its being. Its formidable character makes itself felt the more directly that a maritime State is, in the literal sense of the word, the neighbour of every country accessible by sea. It would, therefore, be but natural that the power of a State supreme at sea should inspire universal jealousy and fear, and be ever exposed to the danger of being overthrown by a general combination of the world. Against such a combination no single nation could in the long run stand, least of all a small island kingdom not possessed of the military strength of a people trained to arms, and dependent for its food supply on oversea commerce. The danger can in practice only be averted — and history shows that it has been so averted — on condition that the national policy of the insular and naval State is so directed as to harmonize with the general desires and ideals common to all mankind, and more particularly that it is closely identified with the primary and vital interests of a majority, or as many as possible, of the other nations. Now, the first interest of all countries is the preservation of national independence. It follows that England, more than any other non-insular Power, has a direct and positive interest in the maintenance of the independence of nations, and therefore must be the natural enemy of any country threatening the independence of others, and the natural protector of the weaker communities.

Second only to the ideal of independence, nations have always cherished the right of free intercourse and trade in the world's markets, and in proportion as England champions the principle of the largest measure of general freedom of commerce, she undoubtedly strengthens her hold on the interested friendship of other nations, at least to the extent of making them feel less apprehensive of naval supremacy in the hands of a free trade England than they would in the face of a predominant protectionist Power. This is an aspect of the free trade question which is apt to be overlooked. It has been well said that every country, if it had the option, would, of course, prefer itself to hold the power of supremacy at sea, but that, this choice being excluded, it would rather see England hold that power than any other State.

---

[*] "Memorandum by Sir Eyre Crowe on the Present State of British Relations with France and Germany, January 1, 1907," *British Documents on the Origins of the War 1898–1914,* ed. by G. P. Gooch and H. Temperley (London: His Majesty's Stationery Office, 1928), vol. III, pp. 402–07, 414–20.

History shows that the danger threatening the independence of this or that nation has generally arisen, at least in part, out of the momentary predominance of a neighbouring State at once militarily powerful, economically efficient, and ambitious to extend its frontiers or spread its influence, the danger being directly proportionate to the degree of its power and efficiency, and to the spontaneity or "inevitableness" of its ambitions. The only check on the abuse of political predominance derived from such a position has always consisted in the opposition of an equally formidable rival, or of a combination of several countries forming leagues of defence. The equilibrium established by such a grouping of forces is technically known as the balance of power, and it has become almost an historical truism to identify England's secular policy with the maintenance of this balance by throwing her weight now in this scale and now in that, but ever on the side opposed to the political dictatorship of the strongest single State or group at a given time.

If this view of British policy is correct, the opposition into which England must inevitably be driven to any country aspiring to such a dictatorship assumes almost the form of a law of nature. . . .

For purposes of foreign policy the modern German Empire may be regarded as the heir, or descendant of Prussia. Of the history of Prussia, perhaps the most remarkable feature, next to the succession of talented Sovereigns and to the energy and love of honest work characteristic of their subjects, is the process by which on the narrow foundation of the modest Margraviate of Brandenburg there was erected, in the space of a comparatively short period, the solid fabric of a European Great Power. That process was one of systematic territorial aggrandizement achieved mainly at the point of the sword, the most important and decisive conquests being deliberately embarked upon by ambitious rulers or statesmen for the avowed object of securing for Prussia the size, the cohesion, the square miles and the population necessary to elevate her to the rank and influence of a first class State. All other countries have made their conquests, many of them much larger and more bloody. There is no question now, or in this place, of weighing or discussing their relative merits or justification. Present interest lies in fixing attention on the special circumstances which have given the growth of Prussia its peculiar stamp. It has not been a case of a King's love of conquest as such, nor of the absorption of lands regarded geographically or ethnically as an integral part of the true national domain, nor of the more or less unconscious tendency of a people to expand under the influence of an exuberant vitality, for the fuller development of national life and resources. Here was rather the case of the Sovereign of a small and weak vassal State saying: "I want my country to be independent and powerful. This it cannot be within its present frontiers and with its present population. I must have a larger territory and more inhabitants, and to this end I must organize strong military forces."

The greatest and classic exponent in modern history of the policy of setting out deliberately to turn a small State into a big one was Frederick the Great. By his sudden seizure of Silesia in times of profound peace, and by the first partition of Poland, he practically doubled his inherited dominions. By keeping up the most efficient and powerful army of his time, and by joining England in her great effort to preserve the balance of power in face of the encroachments of France, he successfully maintained the position of his country as one of the European Great Powers. Prussian policy remained inspired by the same principles under his successors. It is hardly necessary to do more than mention the second and the third partitions of Poland; the repeated attempts to annex Hanover in complicity with Napoleon; the dismemberment of Saxony, and the exchange of the Rhenish Provinces for the relinquishment of Polish lands in 1815; the annexation of Schleswig-Holstein in 1864; the definite incorporation of Hanover and Electoral Hesse and other appropriations of territory in 1866; and, finally, the reconquest of Alsace-Lorraine from France in 1871. It is not, of course, pretended that all these acquisitions stand on the same footing. They have this in common — that they were all planned for the purpose of creating a big Prussia or Germany.

With the events of 1871 the spirit of Prussia passed into the new Germany. In no other country is there a conviction so deeply rooted in the very body and soul of all classes of the population that the preservation of national rights and the realization of national ideals rest absolutely on the readiness of every citizen in the last resort to stake himself and his State on their assertion and vindication. With "blood and iron" Prussia had forged her position in the councils of the Great Powers of Europe. In due course it came to pass that, with the impetus given to every branch of national activity by the newly-won unity, and more especially by the growing development of oversea trade flowing in ever-increasing volume through the now Imperial ports of the formerly "independent" but politically insignificant Hanse Towns, the young empire found opened to its energy a whole world outside Europe, of which it had previously hardly had the opportunity to become more than dimly conscious. Sailing across the ocean in German ships, German merchants began for the first time to divine the true position of countries such as England, the United States, France, and even the Netherlands, whose political influence extends to distant seas and continents. The colonies and foreign possessions of England more especially were seen to give to that country a recognized and enviable status in a world where the name of Germany, if mentioned at all, excited no particular interest. The effect of this discovery upon the German mind was curious and instructive. Here was a vast province of human activity to which the mere title and rank of a European Great Power were not in themselves a sufficient passport. Here in a field of portentous magnitude, dwarfing altogether the proportions of European countries, others, who had been perhaps rather looked down upon as comparatively smaller folk, were at home and commanded, whilst Germany was at best received but as an honoured guest. Here was distinct inequality, with a heavy bias in favour of the maritime and colonizing Powers.

464

If, merely by way of analogy and illustration, a comparison not intended to be either literally exact or disrespectful be permitted, the action of Germany towards this country since 1890 might be likened not inappropriately to that of a professional blackmailer, whose extortions are wrung from his victims by the threat of some vague and dreadful consequences in case of a refusal. To give way to the blackmailer's menaces enriches him, but it has long been proved by uniform experience that, although this may secure for the victim temporary peace, it is certain to lead to renewed molestation and higher demands after ever-shortening periods of amicable forbearance. The blackmailer's trade is generally ruined by the first resolute stand made against his exactions and the determination rather to face all risks of a possibly disagreeable situation than to continue in the path of endless concessions. But, failing such determination, it is more than probable that the relations between the two parties will grow steadily worse.

If it be possible, in this perhaps not very flattering way, to account for the German Government's persistently aggressive demeanour towards England, and the resulting state of almost perpetual friction, notwithstanding the pretence of friendship, the generally restless, explosive, and disconcerting activity of Germany in relation to all other States would find its explanation partly in the same attitude towards them and partly in the suggested want of definite political aims and purposes. A wise German statesman would recognise the limits within which any world-policy that is not to provoke a hostile combination of all the nations in arms must confine itself. He would realize that the edifice of Pan-Germanism, with its outlying bastions in the Netherlands, in the Scandinavian countries, in Switzerland, in the German provinces of Austria, and on the Adriatic, could never be built up on any other foundation than the wreckage of the liberties of Europe. A German maritime supremacy must be acknowledged to be incompatible with the existence of the British Empire, and even if that Empire disappeared, the union of the greatest military with the greatest naval Power in one State would compel the world to combine for the riddance of such an incubus. The acquisition of colonies fit for German settlement in South America cannot be reconciled with the Monroe doctrine, which is a fundamental principle of the political faith of the United States. The creation of a German India in Asia Minor must in the end stand or fall with either a German command of the sea or a German conquest of Constantinople and the countries intervening between Germany's present southeastern frontiers and the Bosphorus. Whilst each of these grandiose schemes seems incapable of fulfilment under anything like the present conditions of the world, it looks as if Germany were playing with them all together simultaneously, and thereby wilfully concentrating in her own path all the obstacles and oppositions of a world set at defiance. That she should do this helps to prove how little of logical and consistent design and of unrelenting purpose lies behind the impetuous mobility, the bewildering surprises, and the heedless disregard of the susceptibilities of other people that have been so characteristic of recent manifestations of German policy.

If it be considered necessary to formulate and accept a theory that will fit all the ascertained facts of German foreign policy, the choice must lie between the two hypotheses here presented: —

Either Germany is definitely aiming at a general political hegemony and maritime ascendency, threatening the independence of her neighbours and ultimately the existence of England;

Or Germany, free from any such clear-cut ambition, and thinking for the present merely of using her legitimate position and influence as one of the leading Powers in the council of nations, is seeking to promote her foreign commerce, spread the benefits of German culture, extend the scope of her national energies, and create fresh German interests all over the world wherever and whenever a peaceful opportunity offers, leaving it to an uncertain future to decide whether the occurrence of great changes in the world may not some day assign to Germany a larger share of direct political action over regions not now a part of her dominions, without that violation of the established rights of other countries which would be involved in any such action under existing political conditions.

In either case Germany would clearly be wise to build as powerful a navy as she can afford.

The above alternatives seem to exhaust the possibilities of explaining the given facts. The choice offered is a narrow one, nor easy to make with any close approach to certainty. It will, however, be seen, on reflection, that there is no actual necessity for a British Government to determine definitely which of the two theories of German policy it will accept. For it is clear that the second scheme (of semi-independent evolution, not entirely unaided by statecraft) may at any stage merge into the first, or conscious-design scheme. Moreover, if ever the evolution scheme should come to be realized, the position thereby accruing to Germany would obviously constitute as formidable a menace to the rest of the world as would be presented by any deliberate conquest of a similar position by "malice aforethought."

It appears, then, that the element of danger present as a visible factor in one case, also enters, though under some disguise, into the second; and against such danger, whether actual or contingent, the same general line of conduct seems prescribed. It should not be difficult briefly to indicate that line in such a way as to command the assent of all persons competent to form a judgment in this matter.

So long as England remains faithful to the general principle of the preservation of the balance of power, her interests would not be served by Germany being reduced to the rank of a weak Power, as this might easily lead to a Franco-Russian predominance equally, if not more, formidable to the British Empire. There are no existing German rights, territorial or other, which this country could wish to see diminished. Therefore, so long as Germany's action does not overstep the line of legitimate protection of existing rights she can always count upon the sympathy and good-will, and even the moral support, of England.

Further, it would be neither just nor politic to ignore the claims to a healthy expansion which a vigorous and growing country like Germany has a natural right to assert in the field of legitimate endeavour. The frank recognition of this right has never been grudged or refused by England to any foreign country. It may be recalled that the German Empire owes such expansion as has already taken place in no small measure to England's co-operation or spirit of accommodation, and to the British principle of equal opportunity and no favour. It cannot be good policy for England to thwart such a process of development where it does not directly conflict either with British interests or with those of other nations to which England is bound by solemn treaty obligations. If Germany, within the limits imposed by these two conditions, finds the means peacefully and honourably to increase her trade and shipping, to gain coaling stations or other harbours, to acquire landing rights for cables, or to secure concessions for the employment of German capital or industries, she should never find England in her way.

Nor is it for British Governments to oppose Germany's building as large a fleet as she may consider necessary or desirable for the defence of her national interests. It is the mark'.of an independent State that it decides such matters for itself, free from any outside interference, and it would ill become England with her large fleets to dictate to another State what is good for it in matters of supreme national concern. Apart from the question of right and wrong, it may also be urged that nothing would be more likely than any attempt at such dictation, to impel Germany to persevere with her shipbuilding programmes. And also, it may be said in parenthesis, nothing is more likely to produce in Germany the impression of the practical hopelessness of a never-ending succession of costly naval programmes than the conviction, based on ocular demonstration, that for every German ship England will inevitably lay down two, so maintaining the present relative British preponderance.

It would be of real advantage if the determination not to bar Germany's legitimate and peaceful expansion, nor her schemes of naval development, were made as patent and pronounced as authoritatively as possible, provided care were taken at the same time to make it quite clear that this benevolent attitude will give way to determined opposition at the first sign of British or allied interests being adversely affected. This alone would probably do more to bring about lastingly satisfactory relations with Germany than any other course. . . .

Here, again, however, it would be wrong to suppose that any discrimination is intended to Germany's disadvantage. On the contrary, the same rule will naturally impose itself in the case of all other Powers. It may, indeed, be useful to cast back a glance on British relations with France before and after 1898. A reference to the official records will show that ever since 1882 England had met a growing number of French demands and infringements of British rights in the same spirit of ready accommodation which inspired her dealings with Germany. The not unnatural result was that every successive French Government embarked on a policy of "squeezing" England, until the crisis came in the year of Fashoda, when the stake at issue was the maintenance of the British position on the Upper Nile. The French Minister for Foreign Affairs of that day argued, like his predecessors, that England's apparent opposition was only half-hearted, and would collapse before the persistent threat of French displeasure. Nothing would persuade him England could in a question of this kind assume an attitude of unbending resistance. It was this erroneous impression, justified in the eyes of the French Cabinet by their deductions from British political practice, that brought the two countries to the verge of war. When the Fashoda chapter had ended with the just discomfiture of France, she remained for a time very sullen, and the enemies of England rejoiced, because they believed that an impassable gulf had now been fixed between the two nations. As a matter of fact, the events at Fashoda proved to be the opening of a new chapter of Anglo-French relations. These, after remaining for some years rather formal, have not since been disturbed by any disagreeable incidents. France behaved more correctly and seemed less suspicious and inconsiderate than had been her wont, and no fresh obstacle arose in the way which ultimately led to the Agreement of 1904.

Although Germany has not been exposed to such a rebuff as France encountered in 1898, the events connected with the Algeciras Conference appear to have had on the German Government the effect of an unexpected revelation, clearly showing indications of a new spirit in which England proposes to regulate her own conduct towards France on the one hand and to Germany on the other. That the result was a very serious disappointment to Germany has been made abundantly manifest by the turmoil which the signature of the Algeciras Act has created in the country, the official, semi-official, and unofficial classes vying with each other in giving expression to their astonished discontent. The time which has since elapsed has, no doubt, been short. But during that time it may be observed that our relations with Germany, if not exactly cordial, have at least been practically free from all symptoms of direct friction, and there is an impression that Germany will think twice before she now gives rise to any fresh disagreement. In this attitude she will be encouraged if she meets on England's part with unvarying courtesy and consideration in all matters of common concern, but also with a prompt and firm refusal to enter into any one-sided bargains or arrangements, and the most unbending determination to uphold British rights and interests in every part of the globe. There will be no surer or quicker way to win the respect of the German Government and of the German nation.

Writing during the period between the two world wars on the causes of war, British economist R. G. Hawtrey struck a note of deep significance. This was to point to what some have referred to as "the assumption of violence" in the international community as one of the key obstacles to a secure peace.

ECONOMIC ASPECTS OF SOVEREIGNTY

ECONOMIC CAUSES OF WAR

THE principal cause of war is war itself. War is a calamity even to the victor, and the most whole-hearted devotee of *Realpolitik* does not recommend resort to it except for some great purpose commensurate in importance with the sacrifices to be faced. What objects can possibly fulfil that condition?

There may be obligations of honour or religion against which no balance of material loss and gain can be allowed to weigh. Of such motives I shall have something to say presently.

But if the calculation has to be made not on the moral but on the material plane, it is difficult to conceive of a case under modern conditions where the gain in material welfare promised by a serious war would be an adequate equivalent for the sacrifices.

If, nevertheless, wars are made for material aims, the reason is that those aims are thought of in terms not of welfare but of economic power. Each country has its fund of prestige to employ in diplomacy. Prestige means reputation for power, and economic power is its most important component. Military skill and the military virtues also contribute to prestige, but they are not subject to the same visible and measurable fluctuations in peace-time as economic power. With given military skill and military virtues, the magnitude of the force that can be put into the field depends upon economic power.

Any country which gains an accession of resources may be presumed to gain in power and prestige. Suppose that there are two neighbouring countries, rivals to one another but sufficiently removed from rivalry with any others, and suppose that they are approximately of equal power. Let one claim some territory that has hitherto belonged to the other. If the claim is disputed, will it be worth while to fight? If the dispute is settled by war, it is very unlikely that the country which gains the disputed territory will derive material benefits from it equivalent to the sacrifices suffered. But then if the country which has hitherto possessed it agrees to give it up, it will find its own resources diminished and those of its rival increased. It will be weakened in any future dispute On a dispute arising, the same question will have to be settled as before, whether to fight or give in. If the country decides to fight, it will fight at a disadvantage in consequence of its surrender on the former occasion. If it decides to give in, it will be still further weakened on the occasion of the next dispute. Thus to yield once may be to tip the scale irretrievably against the country in the future.

In the case assumed the arguments for a peaceful settlement would be much stronger from the standpoint of the country which started the claim. The claim, however good in law and right, need never have been put forward. The country, being the equal of its rival, has nothing to fear from the peaceful settlement of future disputes. Can the claim be worth a conflict, of which the issue is *ex hypothesi* doubtful, and in which even victory is bound to be costly?

The political leaders may decide in favour of war, for they may think the future preponderance of power which victory may bring an equivalent for any sacrifice. Their view will depend partly on the nature and intensity of the rivalry between the two countries. Such preponderance is often put forward as a leading object of policy under the name of security.

If the disputed territory has not previously belonged to either country, and both claim it or both have opportunities of acquiring it, then the case for a conflict becomes stronger. Whichever country gets the disputed territory will become preponderant, and whichever fails to get it must accept a position of inferiority. In such circumstances a solution is sometimes found in compromise or partition. But that is not always possible.

When I say that the principal cause of war is war itself, I mean that the aim for which war is judged worth while is most often something which itself affects military power. Just as in military operations each side aims at getting anything which will give it a military advantage, so in diplomacy each side aims at getting anything which will enhance its power. Diplomacy is potential war. It is permeated by the struggle for power, and when potential breaks out into actual war; that is usually because irreconcilable claims have been made to some element of power, and neither side can claim such preponderance as to compel the other to give way by a mere threat.

In military operations themselves the threat of force is sufficient to obtain an object, so long as the force is overwhelming. The inferior force will not resist unless there is hope of at any rate some degree of success. Otherwise it will retreat or surrender.

Manœuvres for position will proceed without fighting, up to the stage at which substantial forces are in contact on both sides, and neither side can pursue its objectives without overcoming the resistance of the other. Then fighting will begin, and it will continue so long as neither side can establish an acknowledged superiority. If a decision is reached, that means that one side is in the position of being able to threaten the other with complete destruction, or at any rate with more injury than it is prepared to face. It is the threat that compels retreat or surrender.

In time of peace every conflict of interests is liable to bring the threat of force, and the threat may be decisive, just as it may be decisive in military operations. Fighting is but a clumsy expedient if the desired object can be obtained without it.

In war the force which has obtained a decisive victory can pick up the spoils at its leisure. Without war the decisively powerful country can despoil its weak neighbours and make itself more powerful still. Under the rule of force the strong grows stronger and the weak weaker.

If that were the only tendency at work, the end would inevitably be the hegemony of a single great power. Any equilibrium between two or more powers would be unstable; it would be liable to be upset at any moment by the encroachments of one, and, apart from the chapter of accidents, the one which gained a start would eventually prevail over all resistance.

This tendency to hegemony is a real one, but it is offset by two counteracting causes.

In the first place *distance* is a big factor in all military operations. Power is local. A country which has become powerful enough to overawe all its near neighbours, may yet be unable to impose its will upon a distant country, no more powerful than they, which is out of reach of a successful attack. The economic effort required to maintain a given force grows rapidly greater as the distance of the force from its base is increased. Or in other words the amount of force that can be maintained by a given amount of economic power grows rapidly less as the distance increases. The hegemony of the great power will only be effective within the distance at which it can make its threat of force effective.

Secondly, there is the more fundamental principle of the balance of power. If one country among a group gains in power relatively to the others and threatens to predominate, the others can save themselves by uniting in an alliance or federation against it. It is to the interest of each of the weaker to make some sacrifice, if need be, to bring this about, and therefore any pre-existing disputes among them need not prevent their association together. It may be indeed that one or several of the weaklings will prefer to make common cause with the strong power on condition of sharing the spoils. But this is not likely to be attractive, for afterwards the strong power will be free to impose its will on its own allies, and under the international anarchy no treaty or agreement can eventually prevent it from doing so.

The principle of the balance of power is of wider application than to the simple formation of an alliance to withstand the threatened hegemony of one power. More generally it may be formulated to include the tendency of rivals to equality in reputed power. That does not mean absolute equality. Absolute equality could be no more than an abstraction, for the margin of error in calculations of power is very wide. A great part is played in war both by the imponderables and also by chance.

But a palpable inequality is clearly unstable. All those interests of the weaker party in regard to which there is rivalry exist on sufferance. There is a tendency towards a new equilibrium in which the stronger will have worked its will upon the weaker. But in this new equilibrium there will not necessarily be either the unchallenged hegemony of a single power, or a balance between one strong power and an association of weaker ones. There may be a system of several powers or groups of powers, such that there is no such palpable inequality between any one and any other as would make the system unstable.

The equilibrium, however, is precarious. It may be disturbed by a change in the relative power of the countries or by a regrouping.

Changes in relative power are always occurring. Without any extension of territory or similar overt act, the natural growth of population and wealth and the march of economic progress will bring about a greater increase of power in one country than in another. And while some countries are growing stronger in unequal degrees, others may stand still or may actually decay.

These gradual changes are full of danger. A group which is losing in relative power must look forward to a time when the balance of power will be destroyed, and it must accept a position of inferiority. It will endeavour to find the means of strengthening itself, while it can still meet its rivals on an equality. Failing other means, it will be tempted to resort to war.

The changes due to regrouping, on the other hand, are likely to come in as a corrective rather to redress the balance than to upset it further. An alliance is the natural resort of the weaker powers against the stronger. But it is not always practicable, and there is sometimes a cynical eagerness on the part of the minor powers to rush to the succour of the strongest in the hope of sharing the spoils.

A balance of power is limited and local. One country may have rivalries in half a dozen different directions and may be kept in check by a balance of power in each of them. The power which has to be balanced in regard to each is the power which the country could exert for the purpose of attaining that particular objective.

And there may be a balance among small powers concurrently with a separate balance among great, provided the small powers have no grounds of rivalry with the great.

And further, there may be links between the balance of great powers and that of small powers. The small powers are sometimes themselves the grounds of rivalry among the great, and are preserved from destruction by the balance of power among their would-be despoilers. Such complexities are well illustrated by the Balkan question before 1914.

The balance of power is not a principle that is always and in all circumstances operative. It is a tendency which makes itself felt from time to time. On occasions in the world's history it has broken down completely. The most famous instances are to be found in ancient times. The Empire of Alexander the Great within its own region and period was not troubled by any balance of power. And the Roman Empire was a still more remarkable instance.

It is among the nations of modern Europe that the principle has been best exemplified. The principle of maintaining a counterpoise to a single too great power has been illustrated again and again, more especially by the coalitions formed against the Spain of Philip II, against the France of Louis XIV or against Napoleon. On the other hand, the grouping of the great powers in the period from 1871 to 1914 illustrates the utmost complexities of the system.

A local balance of power had existed in the Germany of 1815 to 1866, a Germany which included Austria, and in which Austrian and Prussian leadership were balanced against one another. The war of 1866 destroyed the balance, and there emerged a Germany (exclusive of Austria) moving rapidly towards a close union under Prussian hegemony. Prussia had long ranked as a great power, but her federation with the other German States would bring her a great accession of power. The federation would form an aggregate equal in population to France. It would not, it is true, be her equal in wealth, but the formidable military skill shown in the war of 1866 might well make up for that.

The position of France was threatened. The statesman who at this period compared France and Prussia to two trains approaching one another at express speed on the same line of rails expressed the significance of the balance of power in the eyes of a contemporary. The war of 1870 did no more than confirm the upset of the balance. It showed that united Germany was quite as formidable as had been feared. In the twenty years that followed, the main preoccupation of German foreign policy as directed by Bismarck was to guard against a recrudescence of the French power and a war for the recovery of the lost provinces. With the steady economic growth of Germany a single-handed attempt by France became less and less likely, however thorough the French military revival might be. The problem was one of the balance of power, of alliances and combinations. Bismarck's diplomacy was directed to isolating France and reinforcing Germany by alliances.

The fall of Bismarck in 1890 was quickly followed by the collapse of his policy. The Franco-Russian alliance ended the isolation of France and at the same time Germany lost one of her contingent supports, the reinsurance treaty with Russia.

The Triple Alliance survived, and for the time being, comprising as it did the united forces of Germany, Austria-Hungary and Italy, it might be regarded as the most powerful group in Europe. Its preponderance was not so certain but that a balance might be said to exist between the two groups. The fact that the Franco-Russian combination was not strong enough for attack clearly made for peace; to that extent the Bismarck policy was still operative.

But when the Anglo-French Entente followed in 1904, the encirclement of France was at an end. A true balance of power was then established. The six great powers of Europe were divided into two groups, and no one could say which was the stronger of the two.

The very expression "Great Power" presupposes a balance of power. It is applied to any country has has attained a certain standard of strength. The Great Powers at any given time are far from being exactly equal to one another, but there is no such inequality among them as would enable any one to impose its will arbitrarily upon any other. This balance may coexist with another balance dependent on grouping; for some purposes it is the power of an individual country that counts and for others it is the power of the group. But groups, once formed, tend to become the sole basis of calculation. A group cannot afford to see one of its members weakened; it must support the members in order to maintain the balance of power. So the grouping of 1904 became confirmed and reinforced. The Concert of Europe, the consultations of the six great powers, familiar to diplomatists in the closing years of the nineteenth century, dropped out of vogue. The affairs of Europe (and therefore of a great part of the world) had to be negotiated not between the six powers acting in independence of one another, but between the two groups of three.

The strain was first felt in the Morocco question. The Anglo-French Entente had expressly conceded France a free hand in Morocco, and the objections raised by Germany naturally encountered Anglo-French solidarity. Germany had been left out in the distribution of all the most eligible colonies and openings for exploitation all over the world. Bismarck had initiated his change of policy too late. Indeed, the major openings had been offered and seized long before his day. Morocco might have supplied a modest opportunity for redressing the balance.

Such were the niceties of the balance of power in 1905 and again in 1911, that neither of the two great groups could afford to yield an inch to the other. However small the material gains and losses might be, they would be accompanied by implications in the form of gains and losses of prestige, which seemed full of danger. The Morocco crises were eventually settled by a compromise, which gave Germany compensation in the form of a rectification of colonial frontiers in West Africa.

The crucial test of the balance of power arose, as it turned out, in the Balkan Peninsula. Here there was a local balance of power between Russia and Austria-Hungary. Russia had been prevented since the Crimean War from expanding by way of annexation of territory, and Russian policy was directed towards supporting small independent States with affinities of religion and in some cases of race and language to herself. Austria-Hungary, on the other hand, looked forward to absorbing territory. After the war of 1878 she had been authorised by the Berlin Congress to "occupy and administer" the Turkish provinces of Bosnia and Herzegovina. And that might have been a final settlement, but for one insidious danger.

The danger arose from the fact that there were racial affinities between the independent Serbians, and the inhabitants both of the Turkish provinces which Austria was occupying and administering, and of the southern portions of Austria and Hungary themselves. Racial affinities had been exalted by the liberalism of the nineteenth century into a bond of adherents, the principle of nationality. That principle was incompatible with the existence of the Austro-Hungarian Empire, which contained a medley of subject races.

Serbian nationalism was looking forward to union with the Serbians still remaining under Turkish rule, and its ambitions showed clear signs of overflowing the Austro-Hungarian frontier too.

The first disturbance of equilibrium occurred in 1908, when

Austria-Hungary declared the formal annexation of Bosnia and Herzegovina. The Serbian inhabitants of the Provinces ceased to be nominally Turkish subjects and became Austro-Hungarian.

Austria-Hungary had scored a point. But there was soon to be a score on the other side. The Balkan Alliance of 1912 united in war against Turkey all the independent States of the Balkan peninsula, and freed the remaining Christian inhabitants of Turkey in Europe outside Constantinople. Serbia in particular was doubled in area and population.

But before a settlement was effected it was once again the turn of Austria-Hungary. By her influence an independent Albania was created, and Serbia was thereby cut off from access to the Adriatic. There resulted a breakdown of the Balkan Alliance and war between Bulgaria and the others.

Bulgaria was defeated, and Serbia emerged expanded and infuriated. Serbia by herself was insignificant, but Serbian nationalism threatened Austria-Hungary from within. Serbian nationalism might be followed by Czech nationalism in Bohemia and Roumanian nationalism in Transylvania.

The balance of power in Europe was threatened. Germany's principal ally might relapse through internal dissensions out of the class of great powers. The other party to the Triple Alliance, Italy, was tied to it conditionally and dubiously.

And while Germany's group was being thus loosened, the opposite group was being tightened up. Germany complained bitterly of "encirclement." She was in danger of an isolation like that in which Bismarck had aimed at keeping France. Meanwhile the Franco-German feud had never been forgotten. The danger which Bismarck had sought to guard against still existed.

As M. Poincaré has said, "The one thing which all our Governments in succession, ever since 1871, refused to do was to renounce their own private sentiments, to repudiate the two lost French provinces, to be guilty of a cowardly betrayal."[1]

The War may be attributed to the system of the balance of power. That does not mean that the war can be explained by purely economic causes. But tendencies which are ordinarily classed as political are often beneath the surface predominantly economic. That is so because of the intimate relation between wealth and power.

The Balkan question appeared to be political and not economic. But a little consideration of the map will soon show how closely bound up together the political and economic issues were.

Among all the conditions of the mobility of wealth in a country

[1] *The Origins of the War*, p. 26.

access to the sea is one of the most vital. Access to the sea means not merely the possession of a stretch of sea-coast but the possession of a suitable seaport which itself in turn has adequate communications with the interior.

Austria-Hungary possessed important seaports, Trieste and Fiume, at the head of the Adriatic, together with the Dalmatian coast along the eastern shore. If Serbian nationalism gained its aims, nearly if not quite the whole of this territory would be lost, and access to the sea cut off.[1] On the other hand, had the ambitions of Austrian Imperialists taken effect, and Serbia itself been added on to the provinces annexed in 1908, a new outlet might have been acquired down to the Ægean, with great opportunities of economic development.

Without doubt it was possibilities of that kind that made the maintenance of the independence of the Balkan States a cardinal object of Russian policy. And Russian policy itself had economic aims. These, like those of Austria-Hungary, were governed by geography. Russia had access to the sea, but so far as South Russia was concerned, it was access only to the Black Sea, and access therefore to the Mediterranean and the ocean was only to be had past Constantinople through the narrow Straits, the Bosphorus and Dardanelles.

In time of peace passage through the Straits was not interfered with, and the question was always dealt with primarily as a strategic one. By the Treaty that followed the Crimean War in 1856 the Straits had been closed to warships (other than Turkish). Russia had also agreed not to maintain a fleet in the Black Sea, but in 1871 she took advantage of the Franco-German War to denounce this part of the Treaty.[2] She was therefore in the position of having two fleets, one in the Baltic and the other in the Black Sea, which were precluded from meeting, and the Black Sea fleet was prevented from having any but purely local influence.

Nevertheless Russian ambitions in regard to the Straits were not purely strategic. Russian expansionists looked forward to the annexation of Conŝtantinople itself to Russia. The possibilities of Constantinople as an economic centre are immense, and under Turkish rule very little has been made of them. Even though it could not, consistently with Russia's policy towards the independent Balkan States, have been joined continuously to Russian territory, Constantinople in Russian hands would have opened up great

[1] Italy could (and did) put in a rival claim on grounds of nationality. But that could hardly be expected to increase the chances of the seaports remaining Austro-Hungarian.
[2] A classic illustration of the International Anarchy.

opportunities of exploitation, and would have done much to give mobility to the resources of the southern half of Russia.

Want of that essential quality has always been a source of weakness to Russia. The growth of the population, which by 1914 was estimated at nearly 150,000,000 in European Russia, looked very formidable to the rest of Europe and especially to Germany. And the natural resources of the country are great. But in the War, as several times before, it was found that the resources could not be made available, and without adequate resources the numbers could not be made effective. The shortcomings of Russia were partly due to want of leadership and to administrative inefficiency. But the want of mobility of the country's material resources was the principal cause.

Efforts had been made, since the French alliance had been concluded in 1891, to remedy the deficiency. Great amounts of French capital had been lent to Russia, and much of the money was spent on the development of the railway system. But the economic system had not progressed far from its primitive condition, and when the test came the amount of power the country could exert at the critical point was disastrously restricted by want of economic resources.

In the balance of power as it existed in Europe in 1914 the rapid economic development of Germany was as conspicuous a feature as the tardy economic development of Russia. I have already pointed out how the balance of power is always threatened by changes in the relative economic power of the countries or groups concerned.

The economic development of Germany in the generation preceding 1914 was sensational. The industrial revolution had taken effect first in England, then in France, Belgium and Switzerland. In 1870 the rate of progress, though still great, was beginning to slow down in those countries. But in Germany industrialisation was only just beginning. And Germany was an exceptionally favourable field for the industrial revolution. In regard to her material resources the annexation of Lorraine placed the richest iron ore deposits in Europe in intimate contact with coal fields which were soon to be shown to be second only to those of Great Britain. And Germany's intellectual endowments were such that she was soon to take the foremost place in the world in the technical applications of science, that is to say, in that line of progress upon which the industrial revolution mainly depended.

The economic progress that followed, accompanied as it was by a rapid increase in population, was everywhere recognised as meaning a formidable growth in power. Yet it would seem, in the light of the experience of the war, that the real increase in power surpassed even the appearance. For the war was not waged by the two groups of three between which there had been a reputed balance of power. Germany and Austria-Hungary had to face the other four, and they held their own up to 1917.

Germany indeed may be said to have underestimated her own power, at any rate in relation to Russia. People both in Germany and other countries underestimated economic power and overestimated the power of mere numbers.

On the other hand it may be said that the German fear of Russia was really a fear of future development. The industrialisation which had successively transformed England, Western Europe and Central Europe might work similar miracles in Eastern Europe. The balance of power had become momentarily and exceptionally favourable to Germany. It was likely to become more and more unfavourable through the economic growth of Russia and the political disintegration of Austria-Hungary.

It will now be clear that the distinction between political and economic causes of war is an unreal one. The political motives at work can only be expressed in terms of the economic. Every conflict is one of power, and power depends on resources. Population itself is an economic quantity; its growth and movement are governed by economic conditions.

This does not mean that what I have called the imponderables may be neglected. Military skill and military virtues may outweigh a great disparity of power. Sovereignty over great economic resources may be nullified for purposes of power by disaffection among the population, or by administrative incompetence.

But countries do not fight for the imponderables. France, when she annexed Corsica, annexed Napoleon, but nations do not seize territory for the sake of the military talent it is likely to breed.

I have dwelt at some length on the underlying motives of the War of 1914 partly because it is by reference to it that any theory as to the causation of war is sure to be first tested, and partly because nearly all the causes of quarrel that existed in Europe in the preceding years had their bearing upon the War.

But if we look back over history we find again and again the same type of conflict arising. The friction over Morocco merely reproduced the kind of friction that had repeatedly arisen over territory becoming available for domination or exploitation.

The wars of the eighteenth century were wars of colonial expansion and of the balance of power. The Balkan question began to take shape almost as soon as the Turks had retreated from before

G

Vienna. The objects of contention in the struggles of the balance of power were the economic centres, where wealth was to be found in mobile form, the cities of the Rhine Valley, of the Netherlands or of Northern Italy, or Constantinople and the marketing centres of Syria.

But it may be asked, are there not conflicts of religion, conflicts of ideas, conflicts of culture? The War of 1914 itself was precipitated by the principle of nationality. Was not the eighteenth century an exceptional interval when colonial expansion usurped the first place as an object of national ambition, and did not the nineteenth century see a reversion to wars of ideas?

The French Revolution started a world-wide movement in support of the doctrines of liberalism. The ideal of racially homogeneous self-governing states was in conflict with the feudal and monarchical regime which had come down from the past. The wars through which the break-up of the Turkish Empire and the union of Germany and Italy were brought about may be regarded as directed towards this ideal. That does not mean that the principles of nationality and self-government were everywhere successful. But it may be contended that the wars of the nineteenth century were to a great extent wars of ideas and not wars of the balance of power.

But the distinction is a false one. Ideas, whether religious, political or racial, only so far modify the position in that they supply a different principle for sifting out the adherents of a contending power.

The adherent is devoted to a religion or a political party or to a race, instead of to a country. But the conflict is none the less in terms of power, and power, including economic power, is the indispensable means of success.

It is easy to be ironical about the absurdity of converting people from one religious belief to another by force, or of compelling them to be free, as the Jacobins promised. Force may compel outward conformity, but it cannot compel inward belief.

But the wars of religion cannot be interpreted as wars of opinion. The Church was a political structure. In the Middle Ages it had more of the attributes of sovereignty than the lay States themselves.

The sovereign authority of the medieval Church was responsible not only for religious worship, but for the entire apparatus of intellectual culture and education in Europe, for the relief of the poor, and for important branches of jurisdiction, for example over the marriage law. To supply it with the means of discharging its functions it possessed vast endowments, and also certain taxing powers, which, however, were by no means allowed by the lay authorities to pass unchallenged even at the zenith of the Church's power. The Church was manned with feudal functionaries, some of whom had the same rights as lay barons over their fiefs, though these ecclesiastical fiefs were prevented by the rule of celibacy among the clergy from becoming hereditary.

The Reformation meant the disruption of this organisation. Thereby was everywhere raised the question of the future control of the vast resources by which it had been supported. If war is an industry, so also is religion. Priests have a whole-time occupation as much as soldiers, and the subsistence of the clergy has to be provided for like the subsistence of an army. At a time when the Church was coextensive with culture, the resources of the Church and the uses to which they were put were matters of the highest public concern.

When there arose a profound divergence of opinion as to how the resources of the Church should be used, what means existed for arriving at a settlement? Persuasion is no answer. Had persuasion been possible, the difficulty would not have arisen. In the Middle Ages the appeal had been to authority. The Church could itself settle and prescribe all matters of doctrine or practice through general councils. Anyone who challenged the authoritative pronouncements of the Church was a heretic.

The power of the Church to enforce its authority not only on the people generally, but even on its own functionaries, depended ultimately on consent. Resistance to authority, so long as it was exceptional and isolated, was easily overcome. The lay authorities were adherents of the Church. They were willing to use their military and police organisation to enforce its will, whether by punishing heretics at home or by undertaking crusades abroad. By ordaining a crusade the Church could declare war either against the Turks or Saracens, or against Christian princes who resisted its authority, like the Counts of Toulouse who championed the Albigensian heresy in the thirteenth century.

The early sixteenth century saw this system in decay. Abuses within the Church, doctrinal movements, new national ambitions, combined to weaken the sentiments upon which Christendom was founded. The Church had become the "sick man" of Europe in the same sense in which Turkey was so called by Nicholas I of Russia a few years before the Crimean War. It was a sovereign power with vast possessions at the mercy of stronger rivals. But while the spoils to be yielded by the break-up of Turkey were composed of provinces and States, those to be yielded by the break-up of the Church constituted in each country throughout Christendom the entire cultural inheritance of the people. Ecclesiastical fiefs, benefices, monastic foundations and endowments supplied the indispensable revenues for those branches of government which had been undertaken by the Church. Control of these sources of wealth and of the administrative organisation they supported was the real subject of dispute in the wars of religion. The great economic mechanism had to be manned, and the manner in which it was to be used would depend on the people selected to man it. The secular State could impose its will upon the ecclesiastical institutions within its borders if it chose to do so. It possessed the organised force requisite for coercion. The crucial question everywhere was whether this organised force should be in the hands of adherents of the Church or of the Reformers.

Looking back from the standpoint of modern ideas one is tempted to say that toleration would have been the right solution. But toleration by itself, even had it been recognised in the sixteenth century as a possibility, would not have been a solution. The tolerant prince would have known that he ought to allow freedom of association, of worship and of teaching to people of every faith and persuasion, but his principles would have told him nothing as to how he should deal with the existing ecclesiastical revenues and appointments. If he left the revenues untouched in the hands of the Church of Rome, he would in effect be taking the side of that Church, notwithstanding all his toleration. If he divided up the revenues, and opened the door to the appointment of Protestants to benefices, he would become an enemy of the Church and even then his principle of toleration would give him no guidance as to what principle of division to adopt.

In the sixteenth century toleration was hardly thought of. In each country in Europe the adherents of the Church and of the Reformation strove with one another for control of the sovereign authority. In many the contest was only settled by sanguinary civil wars. Those States where the Church prevailed, especially Spain, assumed the part of crusaders. Deeming themselves the champions of the Church, they tried to restore its power in the States where the adherents of the Reformation had prevailed. Thus the conflict passed from the phase of civil war to that of international war. In the course of the seventeenth century the questions at issue settled themselves. The power of the State to legislate on religious and cultural questions came to be fully recognised. This was so even in Catholic countries which used the power to maintain the functions of the Church.

Early in the wars of religion the grouping of countries began to be affected by considerations of the balance of power. French policy, for example, was detached from religious motives. The Anglo-Dutch alliance which survived into the eighteenth century was partly, it is true, a Protestant alliance, but that did not prevent it from acting with Catholic Austria.

In some respects the wars of the French Revolution may be classed as wars of ideas. Jacobinism was a new religion, spreading, like the Reformation, among adherents everywhere. But it did not give rise in countries other than France to spontaneous uprisings of its adherents to seize the reins of government. The wars were really wars of conquest, and extended the new ideas *pari passu* with French sovereignty. And as the conquests extended, the ideas evaporated, till the empire at its height represented not the adherents of any ideas at all, but the adherents of Napoleon.

It was rather in the later developments of Europe that the influence of ideas is to be seen. Liberalism became as cosmopolitan as Protestantism had been, and in international relations one aspect of it, the principle of nationality, became a dominant influence.

Liberalism taught that all should be free, and that freedom should be exercised through democratic institutions. Clearly all those who participated in the government of a democratic State ought to be adherents. There was no room in the liberal ideal for groups of malcontents or for oppressed nationalities. It was therefore implied that the State should be formed out of those people who had sufficient community of outlook to act voluntarily together, and should include no others. The requisite community of outlook could be secured if a state were formed, as nearly as might be, all of one race, like unified Italy or unified Germany. It could not be secured if the State were formed of discrepant races like Austria-Hungary or Turkey.

The principle of nationality is twofold. On its negative side it condemns the oppression of subject nationalities, and on its positive side it recommends the delimitation of states on a basis of racial homogeneity.

The condemnation of the oppression of subject nationalities is a wise maxim of statesmanship. How far it should be pushed in any particular case depends on circumstances. In general, what is wrong is to use the power of the State to enforce laws and administrative practices which are inappropriate to some racial group within the country, in respect for example of language, religion or social customs.

A democratic constitution giving representation to the racial group is not necessarily a remedy. A majority may use its power in a democratic state to oppress a minority. In order to safeguard the special interests of racial groups, either the governing authorities (whether democratic or not) must adopt a policy of tolerance, or alternatively the racial groups must be given some form of self-government, amounting either to a limited autonomy or to complete independence.

The formation of States on the basis of homogeneity of race is one method, but not the only one, of safeguarding nationalities against oppression. Thus the second or positive part of the liberal principle of nationality is not bound up with the first or negative part. It only has to be appealed to when there is a failure of tolerance on the part of the constituted authorities.

Tolerance here is to be taken in a wide sense. It includes not only abstention from any discrimination direct or indirect against the practices, customs or characteristics of racial groups, but impartiality among them in the distribution of public appointments and governmental favours. Here there is apt to be a vicious circle. Racial intolerance makes the minority disaffected, and the disaffection prevents a modification of the intolerance. It is natural, therefore, that in many cases the oppressed races seek refuge in the second part of the principle of nationality, the formation of racially homogeneous states.

But this principle is full of dangers. In the first place it presupposes that racially homogeneous populations can be marked out by local boundaries. That is not usually the case. Any practicable frontier will leave some racial minorities on either side. Secondly, the creation of a new state on a racial basis tends to intensify racial feeling, rather than to allay it. Thirdly, the constitution of new States on a racial basis will upset the balance of power, and so may cause a conflict.

Were it possible to redraw boundaries once and for all all over the world, so as to make all States racially homogeneous, this last danger would be only transitional. But racial boundaries are apt to cut right across economic. Italian and Serbian populations cut off Austria and Hungary from access to the Adriatic, Greek populations cut off Serbia and Bulgaria from access to the Ægean. A corridor is necessary to connect Poland with the Baltic.

More generally, what from an economic standpoint is a key position may have its sovereignty determined by the racial affinities of inhabitants whose presence there has no connexion with its economic potentialities, and may be cut off by a frontier from other places closely dependent upon those potentialities. Manufacturers may be cut off from supplies of materials or from markets, lines of communication may be interrupted, concessions indispensable to development may be impossible to arrange owing to divided sovereignty. The nationally homogeneous State may be too weak to maintain its independence against neighbours whose economic development its existence interferes with. A balance of power may be established, but that is precarious, and all the more so if it is maintaining a condition of things which opponents regard as intolerable.

The fact is that the principle of nationality cannot be classed as an "idea," nor wars of nationality as wars of ideas, like wars of religion. Wars of nationality have sometimes been described as conflicts of rival cultures. Where they are engaged in to prevent one race from using the machinery of government to repress the individuality of another, the claim may be allowed.

But there is no natural conflict of cultures. If one race attacks the culture of another, that is not in order to defend its own. The motive is usually the desire to obliterate differences which impair the unity and therefore the strength of the State. If the differences can be forgotten, a new generation of the racial minority may be merged in the majority and all will be loyal adherents of the State.

Wars of nationality are therefore merely a particular case of the conflict of power.

THE FUTURE

IT seems to be a law of history in modern times that after a war of the first magnitude there follows a period of peace equal to about one generation. That does not mean a period of uninterrupted peace, but one in which such wars as break out do not tend to set the world ablaze.

Such a period of peace followed the Peace of Utrecht in 1713. If the generation which intervened between the end of the Seven Years War in 1763 and the outbreak of the wars of the French Revolution in 1792, saw its tranquillity broken by the American War of Independence, it must be remembered that the European powers which intervened were not involved in campaigns on a great scale outside America.

The peace which followed 1815 was not seriously broken till the entry of France and England into the Crimean War in 1854. The period from then till 1871 saw no world war such as the Seven Years War, the Napoleonic Wars or that of 1914-18. But it was a time when countries entered upon war with a light heart. Every one of the great powers of Europe fought at least one war and several of them more than one, and the greatest war of all was fought in America against the Confederate States.

The generation of peace from 1871 to 1914 resembled previous such intervals, in being no more than relatively peaceful. The wars which marred it were not of a kind to demand the utmost efforts of a great power, and what is more, they did not spread. That was because European statesmanship for the time being was not being conducted in the spirit of Napoleon III, Palmerston or Cavour. Bismarck belonged to both periods, but the Bismarck of the second was very different from the Bismarck of the first.

In 1914 a new generation had grown up, and the old lesson had to be taught them over again. It was taught with a terrible severity—so terrible that there is hope that this time it may be the occasion of a permanent change.

The abolition of war has become a practical issue such as it has never been before. We have seen the effect of the industrial revolution applied to destruction. The effect has been such as to bear comparison with the greatest achievements in production, and yet we know that the limit is not in sight. Technical developments are even now making war more and more destructive. We are faced with the prospect that the application of science to destruction may in the end outweigh all that it has ever done or can do for production.

It is this growing destructiveness that makes the abolition of war more urgently to be desired than ever before. If the international anarchy is allowed to continue, mankind may be surprised one day by the irreparable destruction of the entire fabric of civilisation.

A sharp distinction has to be drawn between those improvements in the art of war which strengthen the defence and those which strengthen the attack. A strengthening of the defence relatively to the attack tends not only to make war less destructive when it occurs, but to make it less likely to occur. A balance of power is rendered more secure.

But the tendency is now to strengthen the attack. New means of destruction are devised against which no defence has been invented. The industrialisation of war means the close dependence of the fighting line on the entire working population of the country. The entire working population is therefore destined to be the object of attack, and it looks as if the means of exterminating them would soon be perfected.

It is not surprising that the statesmanship of the world is looking for a means of escape. Several paths are being explored.

Of the limitation of armaments, important as it is in its own field, I shall have little to say. It does not set out to be a complete solution. And whenever a war breaks out anywhere, all agreements between neutrals and the belligerents for the limitation of armaments necessarily lapse. The belligerents cannot be subject to any limitations, and the other parties to any agreements with them for limitation are consequently relieved from their obligations. And any which have agreed with these latter on a scheme of limitation are in turn relieved.

It may also be mentioned that the mere limitation of peace-time preparations for war tends actually to *prolong* a war when it does occur. Any country which is insufficiently prepared at the outset will try to act on the defensive until it can develop its full power, and that may be a matter of years. For that reason no war that England is engaged in (apart from expeditions of a local character) is ever short.

On the other hand the limitation of armaments has in one respect a very important bearing upon the economic causes of war. Peace-time preparations for war become competitive. The competition is part of the balance of power, and no country can afford to be left behind at the risk of being caught at a disadvantage. As the burden of competition in armaments becomes heavier and heavier, the countries concerned begin to question whether as a permanency it will be supportable at all. Since the only significance of the burden is as a preliminary to war, each of the countries concerned is inclined to hasten the war and get it over, rather than submit to an indefinite continuance of the strain. European armaments seemed to be working up to just such a climax in the years preceding 1914.

Yet at their worst peace-time armaments are a trifle compared to the losses and the agonies of war. The idea of escaping from the burden by having recourse to war would seem a fantastic absurdity, were it not that the appeal to force is always present at the foundation of international relations. If peace is no more than an interval between two wars, it is natural enough to shorten the interval when circumstances so suggest.

Nor is a mere calculation of loss or gain all that is involved. If the burden of peace-time armaments is felt in any country to be excessive, there is a danger of internal dissension. Opposition may be encountered to the necessary expenditure and taxation. A country which is threatened with such opposition may be tempted to plunge into war rather than run the risk of having its preparations curtailed and being placed in a position of inferiority. Here once more we see that, when calculations of welfare could not make out even a plausible case for war, calculations of power may do so.

Armaments also have an influence on the psychology of nations. If people are called upon to make efforts and sustain sacrifices for a purpose, the extent of the sacrifices itself becomes in their eyes a measure of the importance of the cause. In a perfectly rational democracy, where everyone arrived independently at a reasoned opinion on every public issue, that would not be so; the people would refuse to be biased in their views of warlike policy. But in the world as it is very little independent thought can be brought to bear. The view of the constituted authorities on matters of public policy passes unchallenged, except where a body of critics may make an organised onslaught, and the matter is brought into the political arena.

In the wide range of questions outside political controversy opinion is likely to be guided more by the acts than by the words of the authorities. Indeed, where there is no controversy, there will be no words, except perorations which no one listens to. The burden of armaments therefore expresses the national will in regard to defence, or rather, I should say, in regard to attack and defence. The limitation to defence belongs to the language of perorations.

The greater the burden of armaments in any country, the greater the importance of military power in the eyes of the people who bear the burden. That is an application of the general doctrine of sacrifice. A religion exacts sacrifices from its devotees; in their eyes the sacrifice is an expression of the depth and sincerity of their religious convictions. A lover asks for the opportunity to prove his devotion by undergoing pain, loss or danger. A patriot will offer up his possessions and his life for his country.

It is true that the sacrifice of the patriot is not in general a voluntary one. But though it is compulsory upon the individual, it is the voluntary act of the community, and, so long as the policy underlying it is unchallenged, the sacrifice is accepted as a true expression of that policy.

Thus the limitation of armaments is something more than a mere relief from an unnecessary and undesirable economic burden. It is a change in the language in which human communities organised into sovereign States speak to one another.

Nevertheless, as I have already said, the limitation of armaments does not set out to be a complete solution. Since 1918 people have been turning their thoughts more and more to the search for methods of settling the disputes which might otherwise lead to war. If such methods could once be securely established so that nations ceased to rely on force at all, the limitation of armaments would settle itself.

Of this wider problem three aspects may be distinguished, first the tribunal or agency by which the settlement of a dispute is to be pronounced; secondly, the principles on which the decision is to be based; and thirdly, the manner in which acceptance of the decision is to be enforced.

Of he first and last of these three I do not propose to say anything. I shall confine myself to considering the principles on which international differences should be settled, if the international anarchy is to be brought to an end. I may observe, however, that a satisfactory settlement of the principles would greatly facilitate the task both of those who have to pronounce a decision and of those who have to enforce it.

At the outset one is tempted to formulate the ideal as the substitution of the rule of right for the rule of force. Arbitrators in any dispute can say how much in the claims of either party is right, and, that once decided, the party which rejects any portion of the decision is clearly put in the wrong.

But nowadays the limitations of arbitration are well recognised.

8

Alistair Horne, THE PRICE OF GLORY

Peter Bowman, BEACH RED

1. What were the German and French objectives at Verdun in 1916? How do these square with Clausewitz's view of the political object of war?

2. How do you account for the willingness of the soldiers on both sides to stand up against the terrible artillery bombardments at Verdun?

3. According to Horne, what were the long range consequences for France of the Battle of Verdun? Why would not these same effects hold also for Germany?

4. What different impressions do you get concerning the nature of combat from your reading of *The Price of Glory* as compared with *Beach Red*?

In *The Price of Glory*, Alistair Horne has written a vivid, thoroughly researched, account of one of the greatest battles in history - Verdun, 1916. There, from February to December, French and German armies spent their strength in unbelievable violence. In an area three and one-half miles wide, 250,000 men were killed outright, another 100,000 disappeared, unidentifiable on the battlefield, and 300,000 were wounded by shell fragments, machine-gun and rifle bullets, and poison gas. And at the end, the armies were about where they were when it started.

Educated at Cambridge and in the United States, and a veteran of the RAF and the Coldstream Guards in World War II, Horne published this book in 1962.

THE PRICE OF GLORY

CHAPTER NINETEEN

THE TRIUMVIRATE

We have the formula.

GENERAL ROBERT NIVELLE

Douaumont! Douaumont! Ce n'est le nom d'un village, c'est le cri de détresse de la Douleur immense.—CHARLES LAQUIÈZE

O N March 24th, President Poincaré, clad in that para-military uniform of his own design that somehow contrived to make him look like an elderly chauffeur, and accompanied by Joffre and Prince Alexander of Serbia, made his first visit to Verdun since the battle began. Climbing up to a fort, he noted that Joffre had put on a lot of weight and was badly out of breath; in contrast, ' Pétain has in his eyes a nervous tic, which betrays a certain fatigue.' In fact, Pétain's ' tic' betrayed more than that. Already the battle had made a deep emotional impression upon him. As he stood on the steps of his HQ in the *Mairie* at Souilly, watching the coming and going along the *Voie Sacrée*, he had deduced as clearly as through the eyes of a combatant the full horror of the fighting before Verdun. In a passage that reveals a compassion to be found virtually nowhere else in the writings of the other great French commanders, he says:

My heart leapt as I saw our youths of twenty going into the furnace of Verdun, reflecting that with the light-heartedness of their age they would pass too rapidly from the enthusiasm of the first engagement to the lassitude provoked by suffering. . . . Jolted about in their uncomfortable trucks, or bowed by the weight of their fighting equipment, they encouraged one another to feign indifference by their songs or by their badinage. . . . But how depressing it was when they returned, whether singly as wounded or footsore stragglers, or in the ranks of companies impoverished by their losses! Their expressions, indescribably, seemed frozen by a vision of terror; their gait and their postures betrayed a total dejection; they sagged beneath the weight of horrifying memories; when I spoke to them, they could hardly reply, and even the jocular words of the old soldiers awoke no echo from their troubled minds.

492

A grim quandary had faced Pétain from the start. There is little doubt that, tactically, in accordance with his ideals of firepower on the defensive and of limiting losses, had it been left to him he would have evacuated the murderous salient on the Right Bank, abandoned Verdun, and 'bled white' the Crown Prince's army as it advanced through a series of carefully prepared lines. Soon after taking up his command he had prepared highly secret plans for just such a withdrawal, and put them under lock and key. After the war, Joffre claimed that on at least two occasions Pétain had to be prevented from evacuating the Right Bank; the claim should perhaps be taken with a judicious amount of salt, but at least it infers that the thought was never far from Pétain's mind. But, whatever he might have liked to do out of good, tactical commonsense, it was brutally apparent to him that on the first move towards evacuation he would instantly be sacked by Joffre and de Castelnau; almost certainly to be replaced by an *attaque à outrance* general with none of Pétain's concern about husbanding lives. Thus, to a very real extent, his hands were tied. Nevertheless, in compensation for fighting a battle he disliked, he was at least able to mitigate conditions firstly by placing the strictest permissible limits on French offensive action at Verdun, and partly through getting Joffre to agree to a system of rapid replacements, known as the ' *Noria* '.

Pétain, from his own combat experience augmented by what he saw daily from the *Mairie* at Souilly, had at once sensed the rapid decline in the fighting value of troops that had been too long in the line at Verdun. Under the *Noria* system, divisions were pulled out after a matter of days, before their numbers were decimated and morale was impaired, and sent to rest far from the front where they could peacefully regain their strength and assimilate replacements. In contrast, the Germans (perhaps banking on the national ability to accept horror more phlegmatically than their opponents) kept units in the line until they were literally ground to powder, constantly topping up levels with replacements fresh from the depots. The weaknesses of this system have already been commented on. By May 1st, forty French divisions had passed through Verdun, to twenty-six German. The discrepancy had two important effects upon the Germans: firstly, it tended to demoralise the men in the field, who asked themselves repeatedly ' where do the French get all these fresh men from? '; secondly, it deceived the German Intelligence into assuming that French losses were far heavier than they in fact were — thus further encouraging Knobelsdorf to continue the offensive. (To the French, it also meant that more men of that generation would have the memory of Verdun engraved upon their memory than any other First War battle.)

Back at Chantilly, Joffre was becoming increasingly restive at Pétain's conduct of the battle. Admittedly the territorial losses had been minute, but since his appointment Pétain seemed to have done nothing but surrender ground, and by the beginning of April he was still refusing to contemplate a major counter-stroke. It was strictly against the book! Moreover — with their miraculous arithmetical process, described by Pierrefeu as simply adding 'a hundred thousand or thereabouts' every fortnight — the *Deuxième Bureau* placed German casualties by April 1st at 200,000 to only 65,000 French. (Strangely enough, the magical figure of 200,000 was also the figure selected by Falkenhayn as representing French losses up to that date; as has already been noted, the true totals were in fact 81,607 Germans to 89,000 French.) Deceived by these estimates, Joffre could not believe the enemy would be able to maintain his effort much longer; goaded on by the Young Turks of G.Q.G., Pétain's tic worsened, but he stood firm. At Chantilly, it was noted that for the first time in his career as Generalissimo, the mighty Joffre found his authority thwarted. Worse still, the needs of Pétain's *Noria* were draining the reserves that Joffre had been hoarding for the great Anglo-French 'push' on the Somme that summer, upon which he had staked his all. In his Memoirs, Joffre claims that if he had yielded to all Pétain's demands for reinforcements 'the whole French Army would have been absorbed in this battle. . . . It would have meant accepting the imposition of the enemy's will.' In fact, by 'accepting' Falkenhayn's challenge at Verdun in the first place, the French High Command had obviously done just that; and, with the hand de Castelnau had dealt Pétain in February, it looked to the man on the spot as if the securing of Verdun would indeed require 'the whole French Army'.

Thus began the rift between Joffre and Pétain. Joffre was determined not to abandon the Somme offensive, determined to give it first priority in men and material; but, at the same time, he also wanted Pétain to strike an offensive attitude at Verdun. Pétain, growing ever more aggrieved at G.Q.G.'s lack of sympathy, was convinced that — if Verdun were to be held — the major French effort for 1916 must be devoted to it; eventually moving to the extreme position that the Somme should be left entirely to the British. He also left Joffre in no doubt that he thought that a break-through would not be achieved on the Somme with the means available. As a general, Pétain certainly had his limitations. He had none of the broad strategic grasp of Foch or de Castelnau; with his gaze concentrated upon his immediate front (as so often happens to field commanders), he lacked the overall vision of the war that was accessible to Joffre. All this is true. But, though Pétain may have seen Verdun as everything, what he saw there in terms of human intangibles the French Army mutinies of spring 1917 proved he saw with far greater clairvoyance than Joffre, Foch or de Castelnau.

Within a matter of weeks of Pétain's appointment, Joffre was thoroughly regretting it and already contemplating ways of removing him. But Pétain, regarded as the 'saviour of Verdun', was already the idol of France, while Joffre's own popularity — following the stories that had begun to creep out about Verdun's unpreparedness — was at its lowest ebb since the first disastrous month of the war. Those inveterate intriguers at Chantilly counselled that it would be professional suicide to sack Pétain now. Suddenly, the advent of a new star at Verdun presented Joffre with a ready-made solution.

General Robert Nivelle, 58 at the time of Verdun, came from an old military family and had a mixture of Italian and English blood. Though he afterwards chose to become a gunner, he had passed through the famous cavalry school of Saumur, and still retained all the *panache* of a French cavalryman. At the Marne, Nivelle had been a colonel in command of an artillery regiment. When the French infantry in front of him broke, Nivelle drove his field-guns through the retreating rabble and engaged von Kluck's troops at close range with such speed and precision that they too broke and ran. In October 1914, Nivelle was promoted brigadier; a divisional commander three months later, and by December 1915 he had been put in command of III Corps. Meteor-like, his orbit was swift and brilliant; also like a meteor, he was to disappear without a trace. In the rapidity of his early promotion he resembled Pétain, but no further. He was an out-and-out Grandmaisonite, and like Foch he believed that victory was purely a matter of moral force. His am-bition was as boundless as his self-confidence. When it came to casualty lists among the infantry he commanded, he combined the blind eye of an artilleryman with the unshakeable belief that so long as the end was success the means mattered not. But, in complete antithesis to both Pétain and Joffre, the supreme attribute of Nivelle — cultured, courteous, suave and eloquent — was his ability to handle the politicians. His allure seems to have been almost hypnotic. Abel Ferry, the youngest and most critical member of the parliamentary Army Commission, gives a typical description of the impact of Nivelle:

> Good impression; clear eyes which look you in the face, neat and precise thoughts, no bluff in his speech, good sense dominates everything.

Poincaré was utterly captivated; even Pierrefeu, the cynical chronicler of G.Q.G., fell at first sight, and Lloyd-George, for all his generic, instinctive distrust of generals, was seduced into endorsing the disastrous offensive that bore Nivelle's name, in 1917. With an English mother, Nivelle's perfect English may have played its part here, but it was his irradiating self-confidence that really swept people away. His square shoulders gave a potent impression of strength and audacity. His face burned with ruthless determination, and when he expressed an intent his audience was somehow made to feel that it was already *fait accompli*. It was he, not Pétain as is sometimes thought, who gave birth to the immortalised challenge at Verdun:

> *'Ils ne passeront pas!'*

But Nivelle was in reality a triumvirate. His left hand was his Chief-of-Staff, a sombre and sinister character called Major d'Alenson. Immensely tall and bony, with a cavernous face and arresting eyes:

> Always badly dressed, with untidy hair and beard, he walked about the corridors with his hand in the belt of his breeches, seeing no one, lost in thought with the air of a melancholy Quixote . . . [says Pierrefeu].

CHAPTER TWENTY

'MAY CUP'

Of all man's miseries the bitterest is this: to know so much and to have control over nothing.—HERODOTUS.

. . . I cannot too often repeat, the battle was no longer an episode that spent itself in blood and fire; it was a conditioned thing that dug itself in remorselessly week after week. . . .—ERNST JUNGER, *The Storm of Steel*

As May gave way to a torrid June at Verdun, the three-and-a-half-month-old battle entered its deadliest phase. It was not merely the purely military aspects that made it so. In all man's affairs no situation is more lethal than when an issue assumes the status of a symbol. Here all reason, all sense of value, abdicate. Verdun had by now become a transcendent symbol for both sides; worst of all, it had by now become a symbol of honour. *L'honneur de France!* That magical phrase, still capable today of rousing medieval passions, bound France inextricably to the holding of Verdun's Citadel. To the Germans, its seizure had become an equally inseparable part of national destiny. On a plane far above the mere warlords conducting operations, both nations had long been too far gone to be affected by the strategic insignificance of that Citadel. In their determination to possess this symbol, this challenge-cup of national supremacy, the two nations flailed at each other with all the stored-up rage of a thousand years of Teuton-Gaul rivalry. Paul Valéry, in his eulogy welcoming Marshal Pétain to the Academie, referred to the Battle of Verdun as a form 'of single combat . . . where you were the champion of France face to face with the Crown Prince'. As in the single combats of legend, it was more than simply the honour, it was the virility of two peoples that was at stake. Like two stags battling to the death, antlers locked, neither would nor could give until the virility of one or the other finally triumphed.

Confined to the most sublime plane, Valéry's metaphor was a noble and apt one. But, to the men actually engaged in it, a less noble form of symbolism was apparent. In the last days of peace, there had seemed to come a point where the collective will of Europe's leaders had abdicated and was usurped by some evil, superhuman

Will from Stygian regions that wrested control out of their feeble hands. Seized by this terrible force, nations were swept along at ever-mounting speed towards the abyss. And once the fighting had started, one also senses repeatedly the presence of that Evil Being, marshalling events to its own pattern; whereas in the Second World War somehow the situation never seemed entirely to escape human manipulation — perhaps because the warlords, Churchill and Roosevelt, Hitler and Stalin, were titans when contrasted with the diminutive statures of the Asquiths, the Briands, and the Bethmann-Hollwegs. So now, as the Battle of Verdun moved into June, its conduct had in fact been placed beyond the direct control of the two 'champions', Pétain and Crown Prince Wilhelm. With the ascendancy of Nivelle and Knobelsdorf, each pledged to the continuance of the battle regardless of cost, the fighting had reached a higher peak of brutality and desperation. The battle seemed to have somehow rid itself of all human direction and now continued through its own impetus. There could be no end to it, thought one German writer,

until the last German and the last French hobbled out of the trenches on crutches to exterminate each other with pocket knives or teeth and finger nails.

In the diaries and journals of the time, on both sides, mention of the vileness of the enemy becomes more and more infrequent; even the infantryman's hatred for the murderous artillery grows less pronounced. The battle itself had become the abhorred enemy. It had assumed its own existence, its own personality; and its purpose nothing less than the impartial ruin of the human race. In the summer of 1916, its chroniclers accord it with increasing regularity the personifications of 'ogre', 'monster', 'Moloch' and 'Minotaur', indicative of the creature's insatiable need for its daily ration of lives, regardless of nationality. All other emotions, such as simple, nationalist, warlike feelings, had become dwarfed in the united loathing of the incubus; at the same time it was accompanied by a sense of hopeless resignation that would leave an indelible mark on a generation of French and Germans

Abroad, beyond the general admiration for France's heroism at Verdun, there was widespread unanimity in the kind of symbol it evoked among the cartoonists. In the United States, *The Baltimore*

American printed an adaptation from Millet, with the Kaiser sowing skulls at Verdun; and a similar figurative device was employed by the *Philadelphia Inquirer*, above a caption of 'Attrition Gone Mad'.[1] In an Italian cartoon Death says to the Crown Prince, 'I am weary of work — don't send me any more victims'; a British cartoon of the period shows Death sitting on top of the world — 'The only ruler whose new conquests are undisputed.' From Germany, a grisly armed knight pours blood over the earth out of a copious 'Horn of Plenty', and in a propaganda medallion — dedicated with an ironic twist of things, to Pétain — Death is portrayed as a skeleton

The Sower

—From The Baltimore American.

As ye sow, so shall ye reap.

[1] See illustrations.

pumping blood out of the world. Looking back from the autumn of 1916, the *New York Times* summarised the diseased, *Totentanz* imagery which Verdun had sparked off with a monstrous Mars surveying three-and-a-half million crosses; 'The end of a perfect year'.

*　　*　　*

When the Chief-of-Staff of the German Third Army visited Supreme Headquarters during the French counter-attack on Douaumont, he had found the normally insusceptible Falkenhayn rubbing his hands with glee, declaring that this was 'the stupidest thing they could do'. Far from disrupting new German offensive plans

Wearing-Down Tactics

" Attrition " Gone Mad.

as Nivelle might have hoped, the French failure temporarily halted Falkenhayn's wavering and threw his full support behind Knobelsdorf. Preparations for the new assault, bearing the delectable code name of 'MAY CUP', now went ahead at top speed, with reinforcements in men and material promised by Falkenhayn. The prospects seemed rosier than they had for some time; the French line on the Right Bank had been seriously weakened by the losses suffered in the Douaumont venture;[1] there were also indications of a decline in morale. On the Left Bank, both the commanding hills of Mort Homme and Côte 304 had been taken at last, and from them German guns could place a deadly restraint on the French heavy artillery massed behind Bois Bourrus ridge. Despite all Pétain's efforts, by the end of May the Germans still had an appreciable superiority in artillery at Verdun, with 2,200 pieces against 1,777. Everywhere the French margin of retreat had become exceedingly slim. Once again the German Press was encouraged to declare bombastically:

'Assuredly we are proposing to take Verdun. . . .'

'MAY CUP', the most massive assault on the Right Bank since the initial onslaught in February, was to be launched with three army corps, I Bavarian, X Reserve, and XV Corps, attacking with a total of five divisions. The weight of the attack was nearly equal to that of February 21st, but this time it was concentrated along a front only five, instead of twelve kilometres, wide; or roughly one man for every metre of front. This time there would be no surprise, no provision for manoeuvre; the attack would punch a hole through the French lines by sheer brute force alone. Its objective was to gain 'bases of departure' for the final thrust on Verdun. These comprised, reading from west to east, the Thiaumont stronghold, the Fleury ridge and Fort Souville; but, first and foremost, Fort Vaux, the bastion on which was anchored the northeastern extremity of the French line.

It will be recalled that premature claims to the capture of Fort Vaux had brought much ridicule upon the Germans in early March. There had been subsequent vain attempts to take the fort in April and May; with Falkenhayn arriving in person to attend its delivery on the last occasion. After each failure, the German

---

[1] During the last fortnight in May, French casualties were in fact considerably higher than for any other period since the initial German onslaught, and 9 out of 17 divisions in the line had to be relieved.

infantry had been pulled back while the 420 mm. 'Big Berthas resumed the siege.

Verdun marked the final eclipse of this 'terror weapon' which had brought the Germans such cheap and unattended successes at the beginning of the war. From February onwards the 420s had kept the Verdun forts under steady bombardment from their one ton projectiles. After the fall of Douaumont, Fort Moulainville — Douaumont's 'twin' to the east of Verdun — had become their principal target. Perhaps because its concrete carapace was less efficiently cushioned than Douaumont, Moulainville had suffered the most structural damage of any Verdun fort. One (fortunately unexploded) 420 shell was discovered to have penetrated six feet of earth, ten feet of concrete and finally a wall thirty inches thick. In several places the shells burst inside the fort, with terrible effects. Casualties were high, with many simply asphyxiated by the deadly TNT gases trapped inside the fort. The Commandant at once ordered the removal of all the covers that the garrison — with typical French horror of '*courants d'air*' — had placed over the fort's ventilators; but the moment his back was turned they were replaced! The terrifying noise of the descending shell (described as like 'an express rushing over a metal viaduct'), followed by the atrocious concussion that was felt throughout the fort — to say nothing of the sheer suspense of waiting for the daily bombardment to begin — drove many of the occupants out of their wits. After one bad shelling, the Commandant, finding himself confronted with a minor mutiny by shell-shocked 'lunatics', was forced to round them up at pistol point and lock them up in a casemate. Then the fort M.O. himself went mad and ran out of the fort into the neighbouring woods, where he was later discovered sitting on a tree stump, in a state of complete amnesia. But gradually the garrison became acclimatised to the bombardment. A nineteen-year-old Sergeant noted that from an observation post on top of the fort he could see the flash of the 'Big Bertha' firing from behind the Jumelles d'Ornes, seven miles away, and that thereafter he had a whole 63 seconds to warn the fort, and take cover himself. The knowledge that the giant projectiles would not plunge down on the fort unawares seemed to ease nerves; at last, when the shelling was at its worst, the Commandant took the simple expedient of evacuating the whole garrison during the day, into trenches outside.

The Germans made a serious tactical error in concentrating the

420s on Moulainville. They had primarily been persuaded by the need to knock out its 155 mm. turret which had caused much annoyance. But in fact the fort — never in the front line — was only of secondary importance. Much more promising candidates for the undivided attention of the 'Big Berthas' would have been Forts Vaux and Souville. Though neither mounted guns, Souville was the vital nerve centre of the whole French defence on the Right Bank — as well as being its chief observatory — and its thinner protection might well have caused it to succumb. Equally an all-out bombardment might have rendered Fort Vaux uninhabitable. But two other factors had further impaired the efficacy of the 420s. By June they had all fired far more shots than the maximum allowed for by Krupp. Barrels were badly worn so that shells had a habit of 'keyholing', sometimes turning end over end in flight, which seriously reduced penetrating power. More than one gun had actually blown up, with nasty conseqences for their crews.

The immobile 420s had also suffered heavily from French counterbattery fire, in which French artillerists excelled. Minutes after the 'dud' 420 shell had embedded itself in Fort Moulainville, experts arrived to compute from its position the angle of its trajectory, and thereby pinpointed the gun that fired it. An endless battle of David and Goliath went on, the French opposing the 420 mm. giants with light, but long-barrelled pieces of 155 mm. or less. One of the high-precision naval batteries brought to Verdun specially for this purpose was commanded by Lieutenant — later Admiral — Darlan. The odds were against the Goliaths, which were exceedingly vulnerable because of their immobility, the hugeness of their ammunition stockpiles, and their short range that forced them to come perilously close to the front. One by one they were knocked out, and one vast dump containing 450,000 heavy shells in the Forest of Spincourt was sent skyhigh by the French naval gunners early in the battle. To support its attack on Fort Vaux in June, the Fifth Army possessed only four worn-out 'Big Berthas' out of the original thirteen of the previous February.

*   *   *

June 1st was a glorious summer day; it was also, in the view of the *Reichs Archives*, 'one of the very few days of German victories not clouded over by some failure'. On each previous occasion attacks on Fort Vaux had been stopped dead before even approach-

503

ing the fort by enfilading fire from the denuded slopes of la
Caillette and Fumin woods. These lay between Vaux and Douaumont and were still in French hands. With startling rapidity, the
massed storm troops of the 1st and 7th German divisions now swept
down la Caillette, across the Vaux Ravine, and up again on to the
Fumin promontory that abutted Fort Vaux; a distance of about 800-
1,000 yards. By the evening the French sector commander, General
Lebrun, was forced to admit to Nivelle the 'total disappearance' of
the units holding the lost ground. He got back the inevitable order
to counter-attack immediately. But it was already too late; with
one leap the Germans had eliminated the flanking fire that covered
the approaches to Fort Vaux. Although the German plans envisaged
no attack on the fort itself until four days later, at 6 p.m. that evening the commander of XV Corps, General von Deimling, called
his staff together and told them that the day's successes had been
so encouraging that he intended now to rush Fort Vaux with a surprise attack at 3 a.m. the very next morning. Taken aback, his
Chief-of-Staff complained that there simply was not enough time to
make preparations. But the General insisted.

The only success registered that day by the French was the maintenance of a position called R.1.[1] Bois Fumin was defended by three
concrete entrenchments running along it from Northwest to South-
east, respectively R.3, R.2 and R.1; the last lying only 400 yards
from Fort Vaux. R.3 and R.2 fell within a matter of hours, but
R.1, occupied by a company of the 101 Regiment under command of
Captain Charles Delvert, was to hold out against enormous odds for
a full week. Delvert's own account of its defence ranks among
the most realistic of the whole battle. His company had arrived
at the front just before the Douaumont attack, for which he had had
a grandstand seat. As he moved up towards Vaux, the communication trench crowded with soldiers, twilight glinting upon their helmets made him think of being

> on the ramparts of Elsinore and among sentinels being relieved
> during the night. But the sentinels here were not being relieved.

At the Regimental Command Post, chaos. The Colonel could spare
no men to provide Delvert with a guide, so for two hours his company wandered lost in the dark, among exploding shells and howling

---

[1] 'R' stands for 'Retranchement'.

wounded men who blocked what remained of the communication trenches. When he finally reached R.1, it was, he discovered, little more now than a chain of shell holes; his own Company HQ 'a niche under a slab of reinforced concrete torn up by a 380 shell'. The soil in the Bois Fumin itself 'had been so churned up by the shells that the earth had become as fluid as sand and the shell holes now resembled sand dunes'. The unit relieved by Delvert told him that fifteen of its men had been killed by their own 75s during the past four days; it was 'very encouraging'.

As soon as the German bombardment had lifted on the morning of June 1st, Delvert saw the German infantry swarm out of their trenches, 'like ants when one has kicked an antheap'. Out of range, there was nothing he could do but watch, once again, 'as if from a balcony'. Soon he could see the enemy jumping into the French front-line trenches on the Caillette slopes; 'puffs of white smoke showed us that a hand-to-hand grenade battle was taking place. Then silence returned. . . .' Then the blue-clad figures were falling back 'in disorder', down into the valley below the Bois Fumin, with shells bursting in their midst. Next, there was a thin line of the same blue-clad figures sixty to eighty strong moving in the opposite direction, without weapons. Prisoners! A short time later, coal-scuttle helmets were seen bobbing up and down in the trench immediately to Delvert's front, little more than 25 yards distant. A spirited exchange of fire — 'the kind of fighting that excites everyone' — took place. At Delvert's side a nineteen-year-old soldier collapsed with a hole in his forehead. Then suddenly there was a shout that the enemy had reached R.2, 200 yards away, on Delvert's left flank; 'a lively fusilade. They are resisting! At last!'

By 2.30 that afternoon, R.2 had been overwhelmed too. 'Almost immediately, the conquering Germans were observed beginning to dig sap-heads towards us. Now the ravine alone separates us from them. Are we going to be trapped here like mice?'

For the rest of that day Delvert's machine guns managed to keep the enemy on two sides at a respectful distance, while in the afternoon heat a nauseating plague of bloated bluebottles descended on the dead in the trench.

Friday, June 2nd. A night of anxiety and constant alerts . . . No rations reached us yesterday. Thirst is particularly troublesome. Biscuits are foul . . .

Abruptly Delvert's writing was interrupted by a violent concussion and he was covered with earth. A French 75 shell had landed in the next dugout, blowing to pieces his quartermaster-sergeant. The rest of the day passed in an exchange of rifle fire. That evening the Germans opposite made their first attack:

> I issued grenades all round, because at such close range rifles are useless.

The enemy was repulsed. Suddenly, flame and smoke billowed out behind Delvert. It must be an enemy flamethrower! 'Even the boxes of grenades began to catch fire!' (Actually, as it transpired later, Delvert's absent-minded runner, Champion, ordered to send up a red rocket appealing for an artillery barrage, had set it off between his legs and ignited the rest of the rockets.) At 10 o'clock that night an *homme soupe* arrived with five water bottles — one of which was empty — for the whole company. That meant two gallons between sixty-eight men and three officers — and it 'smelt of corpses'.

But there was worse to come for the men inside Fort Vaux.

CHAPTER TWENTY-ONE

FORT VAUX

Verdun has brought war back into honour, the sort of war
in which the individual man and personal courage are given their
full chances of values.—H. H. von Mellenthin, *The New York
Times Monthly Magazine* (June 1916)

FORT VAUX was the smallest in the whole Verdun system,
covering less than one-quarter the area of Douaumont. It had
no 155 mm. turret, only one bearing a single 75. But this had been
completely destroyed when a German 420 detonated a three-quarters
of a ton demolition charge laid there in the panic following the
fall of Douaumont. As Vaux too had had all its flanking 75s removed
by Joffre, by June 1916 it possessed no armament bigger than a
machine gun. None of these was mounted in an armoured turret.
Apart from the shattering of the 75 turret, one of the underground
corridors had been opened by a shell, and was now blocked with
sandbags; most of the outlying galleries had been damaged in some
degree, and an enormous crack ran disquietingly along the length
of the underground barracks. Otherwise the fort had withstood the
bombardment well. Less satisfactory was the work carried out (or
rather, *not* carried out) under Pétain's orders of February to rehabili-
tate the forts. No deep underground approach tunnel had been dug
(as the Germans had done at Douaumont) to link the fort with the
rear — so that it could easily be cut off. Worse still, nothing had been
done to improve the water supply, despite grave warnings. Both
these shortcomings were to have serious consequencs.

In command of the fort was Major Sylvain-Eugène Raynal, a
tough Colonial soldier from Bordeaux, aged forty-nine, to whom
promotion had not been particularly kind. Badly wounded several
times in the war already, he limped on a cane and should by rights
have been invalided out of the army. He had however managed to
persuade his seniors to send him back to the front, on fortress duty,
which was considered less arduous than the trenches. On May 24th,
the day the attempt to recapture Douaumont failed, Raynal reached
his new post at Vaux. His first impression of the fort was of soldiers
crowded together:

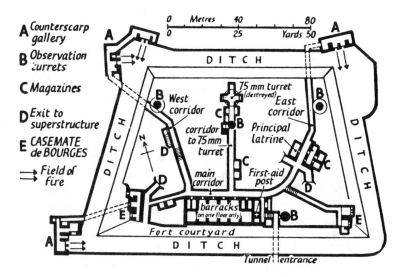

A **Counterscarp gallery**

B **Observation turrets**

C **Magazines**

D **Exit to superstructure**

E **CASEMATE de BOURGES**

⟶ **Field of fire**

in such numbers that it is extremely difficult to move, and I took a very long time to reach my command post. . . . If an attack materialised all the occupants would be captured before they could defend themselves.

Apart from its regular garrison, the fort was filled with stray stretcher-bearers, signallers and the debris of regiments that had lost contact with their units in the chaos of the German onslaught and had come to seek refuge. Raynal at once tried to chase these fugitives out, but still more arrived and soon it became impossible for troops to leave the fort. Thus when the siege began, instead of the maximum complement of 250 for which it was designed, Raynal found himself with over 600 troops in his charge, many of them wounded. In addition, Vaux's garrison numbered four carrier pigeons and a cocker-spaniel brought in by the survivors of a signal unit.

On June 1st, Raynal had watched helplessly through binoculars as the Germans advanced across the Bois de la Caillette a mile and a half away. If only he had had one 75 in the fort! Nevertheless, two machine guns set up on the superstructure, firing at extreme range, achieved miraculous results. Baffled by the mysterious, invisible weapon that was tearing holes in their ranks, the German Grenadiers kept on coming until Raynal could see a whole trench choked with grey bodies. Then the attackers disappeared out of sight into the valley.

To the northeast of Vaux, the land falls so rapidly towards the Woevre that the approaches right up to the fort wall lay in dead ground both to its guns and those of Delvert in R.1. Now that the protective flank of La Caillette and Fumin had been lost, it was abundantly clear to Raynal that nothing could stop the Germans reaching Fort Vaux the following morning. The night was spent frantically erecting sandbag barricades, with loopholes for throwing grenades through, at nine breaches in various parts of the fort. Meanwhile the German bombardment rose in a tremendous crescendo; at one period, according to Raynal, shells were falling on the small area of the fort at a rate of 1,500 to 2,000 an hour. Just before dawn on the 2nd the barrage abruptly ceased. The moment had come.

Waiting in trenches less than 150 yards below the lip of the fort were two battalions of the German 50th Division, under the special direction of Major-General Weber Pasha who had recently distinguished himself in organising the defence of the Turkish forts at Gallipoli. In a matter of seconds his men were swarming into the fort moat. At once, they came under heavy machine-gun fire from the two flanking galleries, similar to those that the Brandenburgers had found untenanted in Fort Douaumont, at the north-west and north-east corners. On these the initial fighting was focused. Crouching on the roof of the north-east gallery, German pioneers first tried unsuccessfully to knock it out by lowering bundles of hand-grenades and exploding them outside the loopholes.

The French machine-gunners continued to fire at the Germans attacking the other gallery. Then the pioneers heard below the unmistakable click followed by curses as the machine gun jammed. Quickly they hurled grenades into the gallery, dispatching the gun crew. Out leaped a courageous French officer, Raynal's second-in-command, Captain Tabourot. For a while, almost single-handed, he kept the attackers away from the entrance to the gallery by hurling hand-grenades, until — his abdomen ripped open by a German grenade — he crawled back into the interior to die. Shortly afterwards, the defenders, thirty-two men and an officer, surrendered the gallery; in it the Germans found two small cannon — minus their breech-blocks.

It was now 5 a.m., and the attackers had already taken one of Vaux's two main strongpoints. Things did not go quite so easily with the larger, double gallery at the northwest. Pioneers tried first to 'smoke out' its inmates by poking over the fort wall specially elongated tubes fitted to flamethrowers. In the initial surprise, the French machine guns stopped firing, and taking advantage of this Lieutenant Rackow of the 158th Paderborn Regiment managed to slip across the moat with about thirty men. They were the first Germans to reach the superstructure of the fort itself. But almost immediately the French machine guns were back in operation, and for several agonising hours Rackow and his small group sat isolated on the fort. In the terrible din of the Verdun bombardment their comrades only twenty yards away were unable to hear their shouts for support. The German pioneers, with considerable fortitude, now tried lowering sacks full of grenades on a rope outside the gallery, but did themselves more damage. All through the morning the struggle continued, until one after the other the French machine guns were silenced and some fifteen of the gallery's inhabitants had been wounded. Still it held out. Then at last the Germans on top of the fort discovered the sandbags with which Raynal had plugged a large breach in the corridor leading to the north-west gallery. They removed them, and began hurling grenades into the corridor. Realising what was happening, Raynal ordered the gallery to be abandoned immediately, before its defenders could be taken from the rear.

By about 4 p.m., Raynal had lost both his exterior defences, the superstructure was solidly occupied by the enemy, and the battle was about to move underground. A little like the children and the pirates in 'Peter Pan', members of the fort garrison gazed helplessly through the slits of the observation cupolas at the young Germans sprawled out on the ground just above their heads, nonchalantly smoking pipes and occasionally making insulting gestures for their consumption. Meanwhile, during the contest for the galleries, Raynal had hastened to build sandbag barricades inside the corridors leading to them from the central fort.

As soon as both galleries had been occupied, Lieutenant Rackow, who had now assumed control of all operations on the fort, ordered a party under Lieutenant Ruberg of the Pioneers to break into the fort proper along the north-east corridor. Obediently Ruberg and a handful of men set off down a dark narrow passage, similar to the one that had confronted Sergeant Kunze in Douaumont three months earlier. A long flight of steps led down under the moat and then up again, and soon Ruberg came to a steel door barring his path.

Behind it he could hear French voices whispering. Swiftly he prepared a charge out of hand-grenades (because of General von Deimling's acceleration of the attack on Vaux the Pioneers had had no time in which to prepare proper demolition charges), pulled the pin out of the last grenade and ran.

Behind the steel door was Raynal himself, inspecting a hastily erected barricade which was not entirely to his liking. From the noises made by Ruberg, he realised what was afoot and quickly ordered his men back. Just in time; for the barricade 'disintegrated in a powerful explosion.' On the other side of the door, the five-and-a-half-second grenade fuse had not given Ruberg time to get clear, and he was hurled backwards by the explosion, lacerated with splinters. The force of the blast and the wounding of their chief caused the Germans to hestitate before re-entering the deadly tunnel just long enough for Raynal to rebuild his barricade and site a machine gun behind it. For the time being the French remained masters of the corridor.

That night Raynal, with all his telephone lines to the rear already severed, sent off the first of his four pigeons bearing a report of the situation.

Early on the 3rd of June, German assault troops worked their way round to the south of the fort. Vaux was now completely cut off, even from R.1 which still maintained a tenuous link with the rest of the Second Army. The siege was on, and a curious stalemate was established with a German commander, Rackow, on top of the fort, and a French commander, Raynal, underground. All through the day the main battle continued ferociously in the two corridors leading to the heart of the fort. In each the French had built sandbag barricades several feet thick, defended by one brave grenadier. The German pioneers had meanwhile brought up more powerful explosives, so that it was only a matter of time before the French grenadier was knocked out, and his rampart demolished. But beyond was yet another barricade, from behind which a machine gun spewed death on the attackers at point-blank range, while the French were preparing yet a further series of obstacles to its rear. Yard by yard the Germans advanced, but at heavy cost.

Of all the horrors in the fighting at Verdun, it is difficult to imagine any much more appalling than the struggle that took place day after day in the underground corridors of Fort Vaux. Here the battle went on in pitch darkness, relieved only by the flash of explod-

511

ing grenades, in a shaft for the most part no more than three feet wide and five feet high, in which no grown man could stand upright. Machine-gun bullets ricochetting from wall to wall inflicted wounds as terrible as any dum-dum, and in the confined space the concussion of the grenades was almost unendurable. Repeatedly men of both sides felt themselves asphyxiating in the air polluted by TNT fumes and cement dust stirred up by the explosions. Added to it was the ever-worsening stink of the dead, rapidly decomposing in the June heat, for whom there was no means of burial inside the fort.

The two attacking German battalions had already suffered grave losses. Before being silenced, Vaux's gallery machine guns had cut swathes in the attackers, and by the evening of June 2nd the battalion of the 53rd Regiment had only one officer left unwounded. Meanwhile, Rackow and his men on the roof of the fort were being exposed to an ever-increasing intensity of French gun-fire, to which the deadly 155 in nearby Fort Moulainville now added its voice. On the night of June 3rd both battallions had to be withdrawn exhausted. But for Raynal and his six hundred there was no relief.

Out at R.1 Delvert had meanwhile successfully repulsed two more German attacks, and spent the rest of the day under heavy bombardment. He noted in his diary that he had not slept for seventy-two hours. At 10 o'clock that night, Captain Delvert was overjoyed by the arrival of a subaltern, bringing a company of reinforcements. But the company numbered only eighteen men. An hour later, another subaltern appeared, claiming to have brought up a company.

'How many men have you?' asked Delvert.

'One hundred and seventy.'

Delvert counted them. There were twenty-five.

Back at Sector Headquarters, General Lebrun had received Raynal's pigeon message, and — under heavy pressure from Nivelle — prescribed an immediate counter-attack to regain the fort. Almost hysterically, Lebrun told the wretched general commanding the 124th Division that he was, if necessary, to lead the attack in person. At dawn on the 4th, the French went in in six dense waves, actually reaching the western extremity of the fort. But fresh replacements of Düsseldorf Fusiliers were already in position, and they drove off the attackers at bayonet point.

For Raynal, June 4th was to be the grimmest day so far. It nearly proved fatal. The previous night German Pioneers had managed, with a great effort, to bring up six flame-throwers on to the fort superstructure (four having been destroyed by artillery fire en route). They would smoke Vaux's heroic garrison out like rats. At a given moment, the Germans attacking below ground were withdrawn, and the nozzles of the infernal devices were inserted into apertures and breaches in the fort exterior. (Fortunately for the garrison a detachment of Germans trying to seal hermetically the fort by filling in one of the larger breaches was dispersed by the vigilant crew of the Moulainville 155.) The first warning Raynal had was a cry of 'Gas!' from all parts of the fort. Almost immediately an asphyxiating black smoke poured into the central gallery. Down the north-west corridor fled its defenders, faces blackened and burnt, their barricades abandoned. Flickers of flame began to appear in the main body of the fort, and for a moment mass panic threatened. Then the flame-throwers ceased. Reacting quickly, and with almost superhuman courage, Lieutenant Girard darted back into the smoke-filled north-west corridor. He reached the abandoned machine gun there a second before the Germans. Wounded several times in the ensuing action, he held on until the situation was re-established; then fell unconscious from the toxic effects of the smoke. Meanwhile, Raynal had ordered the opening of all possible vents to clear the smoke, and to minimise the recurrence of such an attack.

A similar German attempt to rush the defenders in the north-east corridor had also failed, while an attack on the bunker at the south-west corner of the fort had ended in a minor French triumph. All the German Pioneers had been killed, and their flame-throwers captured. With this acquisition the garrison were able to keep the southern moat of the fort clear of the enemy. The net result of the new German effort had been dreadful burns for some fifteen members of the French garrison and the capture of twenty-five yards of the north-west corridor, with one of Raynal's three observation cupolas.

Shortly before midday Raynal dispatched his last pigeon with the message:

> We are still holding. But . . . relief is imperative. Communicate with us by Morse-blinker from Souville, which does not reply to our calls. This is my last pigeon.

Badly gassed in the recent attack, the wretched bird fluttered around half-heartedly, returning to settle on the loophole of Raynal's

Command Post. After several more failures, it was finally coaxed
into the air. It reached Verdun, was delivered of its message, then
— like Pheidippides at Marathon — fell dead. (The only one of its
species to be 'decorated' with the *Légion d'Honneur*, the noble
emissary was stuffed and sits to this day in a Paris Museum.)

Reaction to the message brought by Raynal's last pigeon was
speedy. Fort Souville, which suspected that Vaux had already succumbed and its signals were a German trick, now blinked out an
encouraging message to Raynal, and the mounting of yet another
relief attack was prepared.

Grave as had been the events of the morning, something far more
menacing transpired in the fort that afternoon. Says Raynal:

> A sergeant of the fort Quartermaster's Staff came to me, request-
> ing a word in private, and said in a choking voice: '*Mon Com-
> mandant*, there is practically no water left in the cistern.'
>
> I leaped up, I shook the sergeant, I made him repeat his words;
> 'But this is treachery!'
>
> '*Non, mon Commandant*, we have distributed only the quanti-
> ties you indicated, but the gauge was inaccurate.'
>
> The agony began. I gave the order to preserve what little re-
> mained and to make no distribution today.[1]

The three-hundred odd supernumerary troops inside the fort had
now become useless mouths that could endanger the whole garrison.
Somehow, Raynal realised, it was imperative to evacuate them. But
Vaux was encircled by the enemy. A desperate risk had to be taken.
Summoning Officer Cadet Buffet, a nineteen-year-old brought up
in an orphanage, he ordered him to scout a way out from the fort
late that night. The bulk of the escaping troops would then follow
in small, well-spaced packets.

While in the acrid darkness of the fort the garrison knew and
cared little about the weather outside, Delvert in R.1 recorded that
the 4th was a beautiful sunny Sunday. There were more German
attacks, but in the June sunshine Delvert had time to comment
lyrically on the essential beauty of the grenadiers poised to hurl their

---

[1] In fact, as a later inquiry showed, despite warnings as early as March about the
inadequacy of Vaux's water supply, nothing had been done, and the cisterns appear
to have been half-empty when Raynal assumed command. It was a piece of negligence
on a par with the failure to garrison Fort Douaumont.

missiles, '*avec le beau geste du joueur de balle*'. Unfortunately, the day was later spoilt by a new prolonged bombardment from French guns, and by maddening thirst exacerbated by the heat. That night at 9.30, Delvert ordered his company to stand by to be relieved. The men were almost too tired to rejoice. An hour and a half later a runner arrived from regimental headquarters postponing the relief, 'because of circumstances'. Mercifully, there was rain the next day, and the company put out groundsheets to catch the water. Meanwhile, in the German trenches opposite there were signs of unprecedented activity. Communication trenches were being widened, all of which could only mean a new all-out attack on R.1. Would relief come before the remnants of Delvert's heroic company were submerged?

After dark on the 5th, the awaited relief at last arrived. But the ordeal was not yet over. With no communication trench to provide cover, Delvert's company were silhouetted targets for the machine guns installed in R.2. Then followed a dreadfully accurate artillery barrage. When the company reached safety, it numbered only thirty-seven broken men; but — on German figures — it had inflicted over three hundred casualties. For another three days Delvert's successors continued the valiant defence; then R.1 fell to the Germans with 500 prisoners.

For Raynal and his men there could be neither relief nor rain-water to assuage their growing thirst. June 5th, the fourth day of the siege, had begun at dawn with a shattering explosion near the *Casemate de Bourges* on the south-west corner of the fort. A huge breach had been blown in the wall, and German Pioneers were on the spot at once with a flame-thrower. But a freak current of air blew the flame back in their faces. A grenade-thrower counter-sally, led by Lieutenant Girard, restored the situation. In the course of it, Girard was wounded again.

Through peepholes Raynal could now see the Germans, thwarted in their attacks up the corridors, digging fresh mineshafts under other parts of the fort from the outside.

It was not a pleasant sight. He flashed a message to Souville, requesting 'hit them quick with artillery'. The reply came with gratifying alacrity; there was a muffled thud, and the watching Raynal saw 'German bodies hurled into the moat. Work above us ceased at once.'

Outside the fort, the latest failure of the flame-throwers had flung the attackers into acute depression. The infernal machines, it was felt, were causing them more casualties than the besieged, and they were withdrawn. Little did the Germans realise how close the flame-throwers had come to breaking Vaux's resistance the day before; or that its water had run out. All they could see was the heavy toll exacted by the incessant French gunfire on the fort's superstructure, and the almost negligible progress being made along the under-ground corridors. The fort indeed seemed impregnable. Perhaps the men inside could hold out for another month, or a year. Finally, to make things worse, the Pioneers had received an insulting message from General von Deimling, declaring that the fort had been taken, but that a few isolated groups of French were still holding out in one or two cellars. These were to be 'mopped up' forthwith.

Later that same day, Raynal suffered two new reverses. A second after the blinker operator had completed a message to Souville a shell landed on the post, killing three men, and wounding several others, while destroying the signal equipment. In the course of the day's subterranean fighting along the north-east corridor, the enemy had taken the entrance to the last accessible latrine; an important morale factor in the already foully stinking fort. By now of the eight surviving officers under Raynal, one was gravely wounded; three had been wounded to a lesser extent (two of them at least twice), but stayed at their posts; a fourth had a bad case of fever, while Raynal himself was shivering with recurrent malaria. That evening he in-spected his men,

> crushed with fatigue, silent and gloomy. If I were to ask one more effort of them, they would have been incapable. Therefore I decided to distribute to them the last drops of water. . . .

This amounted to less than a quarter of a pint per person, for men who had not had a drop the previous twenty-four hours — and it reeked vilely of corpses. There was no question of eating any of the highly salted '*singe*' (of which there was a plentiful supply); Raynal noted that no food had passed his lips for two days. How much longer could the garrison keep up its strength? That night, rigging up an *ad hoc* blinker, Raynal signalled Fort Souville:

> Imperative be relieved and receive water tonight. I am reaching the end of my tether . . .

516

Suddenly, into this atmosphere of extreme dejection burst a mud-stained figure from another world. It was young Buffet, proudly wearing a bright new medal. The garrison crowded around him, fatigue and thirst temporarily forgotten.

He had achieved the impossible. It transpired that most of the escapers had been cut down by German machine guns, or taken prisoner, but Buffet and eight others had made it. Reaching the refuge of Fort Tavannes, he had been passed from the Brigadier to the Sector Commander, General Lebrun, and finally on to Nivelle himself, who had decorated him and told of an imminent counter-attack being prepared which would, this time, succeed. At once the nineteen-year-old Officer Cadet volunteered to creep through the German lines again to take the news back to the fort. The sergeant accompanying him was wounded and had to be abandoned on the way, but a second time Buffet got through.

Eagerly the garrison officers pressed Buffet for details of the promised relief attack. It was to begin at 2 a.m. the following morning, said Buffet, and a whole battalion would be taking part. ' I saw the faces of my officers darken,' recalls Raynal, ' and I guessed what was going on inside them, because I shared their thoughts; the operation, as conceived, seemed to be, *a priori*, inadequate.'

Shortly after midnight the fort defenders heard the characteristic scream of French 75 mm. shells. But not a single explosion. The ' softening-up' barrage was falling, quite harmlessly, well over the fort. At 2 a.m., the garrison took up positions to give support to the relief force. The barrage lifted, and anxiously the besieged searched the horizon for their deliverers. At 2.30, still no sign. Finally, towards 3 a.m., a message from the *Casemate de Bourges* reported sighting a small force, of about platoon strength, pinned down by German machine-gun fire a few yards from the fort. The observers watched in despair as the isolated French were picked off one by one and then rose from their shell-holes, hands above their heads. It was all Vaux saw of the relieving attack that Nivelle had promised Buffet. The relief force had done its best, and suffered terrible losses, with a sergeant-major taking over command of the battalion when every single officer was either killed or wounded.

Morale inside the fort fell to its lowest point. Under the strain, a young lieutenant went off his head and threatened to blow up the grenade depot. It would be impossible to hold out much longer. Raynal blinked out another message, pleading ' intervene before

complete exhaustion . . . *Vive la France!*' But there was no longer
any response from Souville, once again convinced that the fort must
have succumbed. Later that day a huge shell landing on the fort
caved in part of the vault of the central gallery, and now the threat
of being buried alive was added to that of asphyxiation and thirst.
Still the Germans could make no headway along the underground
corridors. But by evening the suffering from thirst was indescribable.
Over the past three June days each of the garrison had received a
total of one half-glass of foul water. In their despair, men tried to
lick the moisture and slime off the fort walls. As he inspected the
fort, leaning heavily on his stick, Raynal found men fainting in the
corridors, others retching violently — having drunk their own urine.
Worst of all was the plight of the ninety-odd wounded, with no drop
of water to assuage their raging fever, some atrociously burnt, and
many lying in the dark, foul lazaret without proper attention since
the beginning of June.

Fort Vaux had done its duty, Major Raynal decided. Shelled by
Big Berthas, besieged, attacked by gas and fire, cut off from France,
with nothing more imposing than machine guns for its defence,
it had held off the weight of the Crown Prince's army for a week.
Even after the Germans had actually penetrated the fort, they had
been able to advance no more than thirty or forty yards underground
in five days of fighting. Only thirst had conquered Vaux. What
wonders could not mighty Douaumont have achieved had it been
commanded by a Raynal!

Having made his decision, to Raynal late that night there came
a last flicker of hope when once again the French guns flared up.
Was Nivelle coming to save them after all? But by midnight a
strangely eery silence fell over the whole battlefield. There would
be no new relief attempt.

At 3.30 on the morning of June 7th, sleepy observers in Fort
Souville picked up the corrupted fragment of a last blinker message
from Vaux. '. . . *ne quittez pas* . . .' was all that could be de-
ciphered. A few hours later the fort surrendered amid scenes of pre-
twentieth century courtesy, an appropriate epilogue to what was
one of the most heroic isolated actions of the war. From behind
a barricade in the northwest corridor, Lieutenant Werner Müller
of the German Machine Gun Corps saw a French officer and two
men bearing a white flag. They handed over a formal letter addressed
'To The Commander of the German Forces Attacking Fort Vaux'.

518

Barely able to conceal his joy, Müller fetched his captain and together they were led to Raynal past a guard of French soldiers, standing rigidly to attention, 'like recruits', in the dimly-lit tunnel. The terms of surrender were formally signed, and then Raynal handed over to the Germans the highly ornamented bronze key of the Fort.

The evacuation of the captive garrison began. To one German war correspondent, its survivors presented 'the living image of desolation'. Nothing was more demanding of compassion than the spectacle of the captured, imitating Raynal's dog and crawling on their stomachs to drink frenetically of the putrid water from the very first shellhole. As they counted heads, the Germans were as surprised by the numbers of the garrison as they were by the sight of the cocker at Raynal's heels, bedraggled, battle-worn, but still alive. The garrison had suffered about a hundred casualties, including less than a score killed. To take Fort Vaux (which, but for thirst, could almost certainly have held out longer) the four German battalions (plus their Pioneers) directly concerned had alone expended 2,678 men and sixty-four officers. It was hardly surprising that French military thinkers would soon be making some far-reaching deductions about the value of underground forts.

Next day Raynal was taken to see the Crown Prince at Stenay. He was at once agreeably surprised to note that 'he is not the monkey our caricaturists have made him out to be . . . has none of that Prussian stiffness'. Speaking fluent French, the Crown Prince heaped praises on the French defenders, several times using the word '*admirable*'. He congratulated Raynal on being decorated by Joffre with one of the highest degrees of the *Légion d'Honneur*; a piece of news that had not reached him in the fort. Finally, observing that Raynal had lost his own sword, as a supreme token of military esteem he presented him with the captured sword of another French officer.

*   *   *

Though Raynal and his men were on their way to two-and-a-half years in a prisoner-of-war camp, there remained one more tragic scene to be played out at Fort Vaux. Since June 2nd, Nivelle had ordered five separate attempts to be made to relieve the fort. Each, inadequate to the task, had foundered with bloody losses. Following the failure of the attack on June 6th that had broken the heart of

Vaux's garrison, Nivelle had immediately ordered yet a sixth attack, this time to be carried out in brigade strength, by a special *'Brigade de Marche'* formed from crack units drawn from various parts of the Verdun front. It would be unleashed at dawn on June 8th. At a conference attended by some twenty of the generals under his command, vigorous protests were raised. Even Nivelle's evil genius, Major d'Alenson, seems to have been opposed to this new attempt. But Nivelle was adamant; his reputation was involved. When the German radio broadcast the news of the surrender of Fort Vaux the following day, he declared it to be a German hoax — just like the one in March.

The two regiments designated for the *'Brigade de Marche'* were the 2nd Zouaves and the *Régiment d'Infanterie Coloniale du Maroc*; both comprised of North African troops that were far from fresh. The commander, Colonel Savy, was told by Nivelle in person that they had been chosen.

for the finest mission that any French unit can have, that of going to the aid of comrades in arms who are valiantly performing their duty under tragic circumstances.

Hastily the North Africans were pushed up to the front, under an avalanche of rain. Meanwhile, at the identical moment that they were to go in, the German 50th Division was about to capitalise on the capture of Vaux by thrusting out towards Fort Tavannes. The two attacks met head on.

Thirty-two-year-old Sergeant-Major César Méléra had been detailed — to his evident annoyance — to take up the rear of his battalion of the Régiment Colonial, and stop stragglers falling back. He describes tersely the ensuing action as viewed from the immediate rear. Leaving for the front, a man committed suicide, ' tired of the war which he neither understood nor saw '. On the approach march :

The clay is so slippery and so difficult to climb that one marches as much on one's knees as one's feet. Arrived in a sweat at Souville Plateau where the Battalion is awaiting its rearguard. Lost the Machine-Gun Company. Found them again after half an hour. . . . Have to hold on to the coat of the man in front so as not to lose oneself. Fall into a hole. Arrive in a glade. Halt; the machine-gunners lost again. Three-quarters of an hour's pause.

At 4 a.m. Méléra reached Fort Tavannes, where he spent the day of the 8th. That night,

> runners bring news. The attack has miscarried . . . At the moment we were going to sortie, the Germans appeared at other points . . . the two infantries massacred by each other's artillery, obliged to return to their lines. 1st Battalion reaches Vaux. The Boche evacuate. Our own are forced to do the same. The Boche return. The 8th advances as far as the wood on the right. The Boche evacuate. Ours are again forced to do the same. As for the Zouaves, situation similar. Nothing to be gained by attacking. The German infantry has again diminished in quality. A pile of mediocre men supported by a fantastic artillery. The Vaux garrison has capitulated. Nothing is left in the attacking battalions but debris.

The Zouaves, in fact, had never left their point of departure. Caught in an annihilating barrage of 210 mm. howitzers designed to clear the way for the Germans' own attack, the C.O. and all but one of the Zouave officers were killed. The survivor, a second lieutenant, led what remained of the battalion back to its starting position. The Moroccans alone attacked. Of the centre battalion, seven out of eight officers fell, and companies were reduced to an average of twenty-five men apiece. Inside Fort Vaux, which Colonel Savy's force had been told was still in French hands, the embrasures were tenanted by German machine-gunners. They waited until what remained of the attackers were within a few yards, then mowed them down at almost point-blank range.

In all the ten months' battle it would be difficult to find an action that was both more futile and bloody. That day Pétain, enraged at the slaughter, intervened in what was strictly his subordinate's prerogative, and ordered Nivelle to make no more attempts to retake Vaux.

In the course of the initial fighting for Thiaumont there occurred an episode that was to become one of the great French legends of the First War, the *Tranchée des Baïonnettes*. Guarding the Ravine de la Dame immediately below and to the north of Thiaumont were two regiments from the Vendée, traditionally the home of France's most stubborn fighters, and among whose officers was one destined many years later to become a Marshal of France; de Lattre de Tassigny. No. 3 Company of the 137th Infantry Regiment was holding a line of trenches on the northwestern slopes of the Ravine, tactically an ill-chosen position that was well observed by the German artillery. All through the night of June 10th and the succeeding day, the regiment was deluged by shells from the German 210s. At roll call on the evening of the 11th, there were only seventy men left out of 164 in 3 Company, and the bombardment continued with even greater ferocity that night — probably augmented by short-falling French 155s. By the following morning, the 137th no longer existed (its Colonel declared that all he saw of its remnants afterwards was one second lieutenant and one man), and de Lattre's regiment was moved up hastily to close the gap. It was not until after the war that French teams exploring the battlefield provided a clue as to the fate of 3 Company. The trench it had occupied was discovered completely filled in, but from a part of it at regular intervals protruded rifles, with bayonets still fixed to their twisted and rusty muzzles. On excavation, a corpse was found beneath each rifle. From that plus the testimony of survivors from nearby units, it was deduced that 3 Company had placed its rifles on the parapet ready to repel any attack and — rather than abandon their trench — had been buried alive to a man there by the German bombardment.

When the story of the *Tranchée des Baïonnettes* was told it caught the world's imagination, and an American benefactor preserved it for posterity by encasing the trench in a sombre concrete shrine. In the light of later research, however, it seems probable that the real story was somewhat different. To begin with, it is taxing probability to extremes to believe that a whole section of trench, some thirty yards long at least, could have been filled in on top of its occupants by simultaneously exploding shells, and that not one single soldier — seeing the fate of some of his comrades — was able to escape interment. A much more plausible explanation is that the men of 3 Company indeed died at their post, but that the advancing Germans, finding the trench full of corpses, buried them where they lay, planted a rifle above each in lieu of a cross. But whatever the truth of the *Tranchée des Baïonnettes* it detracts nothing from the gallantry of the *Vendéens*, and both in its circumstances and the fact that none survived to tell the tale, it testifies further to the new degree of intensity in the June fighting at Verdun.

With this intensification of the battle there came to Nivelle and Pétain daily more and more disquieting evidence of a slump in French morale. Because of Joffre's stubborn holding back of fresh units for the Somme offensive, both Pétain's *Noria* system and its beneficent effects were running down. During the June fighting, divisions forced to remain longer in the line were losing an average of 4,000 men each time they went into action. Many troops had now experienced the peculiar horror of Verdun for the second, and even third time.

On top of all that the men at Verdun had to endure, thirst was now superimposed as a new regular torment. Typical was the experience of a brigade holding the line at Fleury in mid-June. In a first abortive attempt to get water up to them, barrels and wagons had all been blown to pieces by the German artillery. During two more days of scorching heat the brigade had nothing to drink. Eventually 200 men were detailed to carry water up from La Fourche, over a mile away. When the thirst-crazed men reached the water supply, they became oblivious both to their orders and the German shelling, and a chaotic scramble ensued. After they had satisfied their own thirsts, they set off with what remained of the water in buckets for their comrades, but under the shellfire most of it slopped away en route. The brigade suffered yet another day of thirst. Physical conditions were getting to be more than human nerves could stand; added to which, the psychological effects of months of steady retreat, liberally sprinkled with disasters but not even a minor tangible triumph, were beginning to tell. No sooner had the Second Army got over the depression that followed the failure of the counter-attack on Douaumont than Fort Vaux was lost. Now the Germans were grinding ahead again, apparently supported by an even mightier artillery than ever before, and who could tell where it would end?

CHAPTER TWENTY-FOUR

THE CRISIS

One more effort, said the Commander, and we have it. They said it in March, April . . . and up to the middle of July, and then they said it no more.—ARNOLD ZWEIG, *Education Before Verdun*

In their minds there appeared a vision, pale and bloody, of the long procession of their dead brothers in *Feldgrau*. And they asked : Why? Why? And in their tormented hearts most of them found no answer.—*Reichs Archives*, Vol. 14

FORT SOUVILLE commanded the last of the major cross-ridges running down to the Meuse on which the Verdun defences had been based. Behind it lay only Belleville Ridge, with its two secondary forts which were not reckoned capable of any serious resistance. Otherwise from Souville it was downhill all the way to Verdun, less than two and a half miles away, and once the fort (which constituted part of Pétain's original 'Line of Panic') fell into enemy hands it would be but a matter of time before the city itself was rendered untenable. The approach to Souville in front lay along a connecting ridge, placed like the bar in a letter 'H', linking the Souville heights to those that ran from Froideterre to Douaumont. The distant end of the bar was commanded by the disputed *Ouvrage de Thiaumont*, currently in French hands, and astride it lay the important village of Fleury. Both these had to be captured before an assault on Souville could be made.

For the attack, Knobelsdorf had somehow scraped together 30,000 men — including General Krafft von Dellmensingen's recently arrived Alpine Corps, one of the most highly rated units in the German Army. Compressed within a frontage of attack of about three miles, the new effort represented a greater concentration of force than even the initial thrust of February. Despite Brusilov's interruption, von Knobelsdorf — in sharp contrast to his Army Commander — was brimming over with optimism. He would be in Verdun within three days. Already he had ordered up the colours and bands of the various regiments for the triumphal entry to follow, and invited the Kaiser to watch the administering of the *coup de grâce* from Fifth Army Headquarters. During the days before the attack, Colonel Bansi, commanding the German heavy guns, noted rapturously the joy of once again being able to gallop his horse from battery to battery, 'through the glorious summer weather, and fresh blooming fields. . . . That gave one heart and courage, a freer and fresher feeling.' The Germans' light-hearted confidence was not entirely braggadocio nor just wishful-thinking. Von Knobelsdorf had one last trick up his sleeve.

As the German storm-troops passed by the artillery emplacements on their way up to the line, their eyes fell upon great piles of shells all painted with bright-green crosses. There was a deliberate air of mystery and secrecy surrounding the unfamiliar markings, but it was widely sensed that it had something to do with the leaders' assurances that this time they were going to break through to Verdun, and no mistake.

*   *   *

On the evening of June 22nd, Lieutenant Marcel Bechu, an officer on the staff of the French 130th Division, was sitting down to supper with his general at his command post near Souville. It was a beautiful summer night without a breath of wind, spoilt only by the German bombardment that had raged all day. Abruptly all the German guns ceased. For the first time in days there was silence, total silence; a silence that seemed 'more terrible than the din of the cannonade'. The officers glanced at each other with suspicion in their eyes; for, as Bechu remarked, 'man is not afraid of fighting, but he is terrified of a trap.' The French guns went on battering away, but for once were unanswered. For minutes that seemed like hours the uncanny silence continued, while in the shelter disquiet mounted. Then there came a sound above, said Bechu poetically,

> of multitudinous soft whistlings, following each other without cessation, as if thousands and thousands of birds cleaving the air in dizzy flight were fleeing over our heads to be swallowed up in swarms in the Ravine des Hospices behind. It was something novel and incomprehensible. . . .

Suddenly a sergeant burst into the shelter, without knocking or saluting, his mouth trembling with agitation.

'*Mon Général*, there are shells -- thousands of shells -- passing overhead, that don't burst!'

'Let's go and have a look,' said the General.

Outside, Bechu could now hear the distant rumble of the German guns, but still no sound of exploding shells. Then, out of the ravine, as they stood listening, crept 'a pungent, sickening odour of putrefaction compounded with the mustiness of stale vinegar.'

Strangled voices whispered: 'Gas! It's gas!'

In the neighbouring 129th Division, Lieutenant Pierre de Mazenod heard the silent shells falling all round his battery of 75s. It was, he thought, just like 'thousands of beads falling upon a large carpet'. For a few moments of blissful delusion, his men believed that the Germans were firing duds. Then came the first strangling sensations of the vile-smelling gas. The pack-horses plunged and reared in frenzy, broke from their tethers and ran amuck among the battery. Swiftly the gunners whipped on their gasmasks and ran to man their cannon. The masked men struggling at their guns reminded de Mazenod of 'the Carnival of Death'. The crude gasmasks of those days so constrained breathing that every action required several times the normal effort, but at least they saved one from asphyxiation. Now, however, men with their masks on still coughed and retched and tore at their throats in a desperate struggle for air. In some ghastly way the gas seemed to be getting through the masks.

It was supposed to. For months German scientists had been experimenting with a new formula. At last they had produced a gas against which they discovered that captured French gasmasks were only partially effective, and now it was being tried out for the first time. Phosgene was its name — or 'Green Cross Gas' as the German Army called it, on account of its shell markings — and it was one of the deadliest gases ever used in war. Little wonder that the Germans had such confidence in this new attack.

The 'Green Cross Gas' attacked every living thing. Leaves withered and even snails died; as one minor blessing, the flies swarming over the corpse-infested battlefield also disappeared temporarily. Horses lay, frothy-mouthed and hideously contorted, along all the tracks leading up to Souville. The chaos was indescribable; abandoned mobile soup kitchens stood tangled up with artillery caissons and ambulances. None of the supplies of cartridges and water that the front-line infantry had been calling for frantically all the previous day could get through the gas curtain, which in the stillness of the night lingered undissipated. Its effects extended to the rear areas, and even behind Verdun. A wounded subaltern recalls being treated by a spectre-like surgeon and his team, all wearing gas masks, while nearby a 'faceless' Chaplain gave absolution to the dying. Occasionally the medicos clutched their throats and fell.

It was the French artillery that bore the brunt of the 'Green Cross'. In de Mazenod's battery, gun crews were reduced to one or two men each, many of them 'green like corpses'. One by one the French batteries on the Right Bank fell silent. As bad luck would have it, even the immensely useful 155 mm. gun in Fort Moulainville, which had stayed in action all through the battle and had not been affected by the gas, was at last knocked out that morning by a 'Big Bertha' shell exploding inside the fort. For the first time in the titanic, four-month-old artillery duel, one set of gunners had gained the upper hand over the other. By dawn on the 23rd, only a few scattered cannon were still firing. Then, as abruptly as it had begun, the 'Green Cross' shelling ended, replaced once more by the thunderous barrages of high explosive. At 5 a.m. the German infantry moved forward in the densest formations yet seen, the reserves following closely behind the first waves. Before de Mazenod could get his 75s back into action, the Germans were too close. Soon he and the survivors of his battery found themselves keeping them at bay with rifles.

*　　*　　*

The main German blow struck right between the French 129th and 130th divisions, both suffering acutely from thirst, short of ammunition and badly demoralised by the lack of artillery support. French listening posts gloomily overheard German patrols reporting back that they had reached the French forward posts, and found them abandoned. A deep hole was punched with alarming rapidity right through the centre of the French line. In their first rush, the Bavarians overran the *Ouvrage de Thiaumont* and reached and momentarily encircled the Froideterre fortification. Other Bavarian units broke through to the subterranean command post on the edge of the Ravine des Vignes called '*Quatre Cheminées*', which contained the HQs of no less than four separate French units. For several days the staffs remained besieged inside, with the Germans dropping hand-grenades on them down the ventilator shafts that constituted the 'Four Chimneys'.

To the left of the Bavarians, the greatest triumph of the day was won by von Dellmensingen's Alpine Corps, its spearhead the

Bavarian Leib Regiment and the Second Prussian Jägers. The Leib was commanded by Lt.-Col. Ritter von Epp, later to achieve fame in the early days of the Nazi Party; while the Regimental Adjutant of the Jägers was an *Oberleutnant* Paulus whose name would forever be associated with the ' Verdun ' of a generation later — Stalingrad. High above the battle, watching it as from a grandstand, a French observer in a captive balloon, Lieutenant Tourtay, saw von Epp's men storm into the village of Fleury. It was only 8.15, and the Germans had already covered nearly a mile since the attack began three hours earlier. A few minutes later, Tourtay saw twenty-four German field guns arrive at a gallop to support their tenancy of Fleury. Then the French defence began to crystallise, and shortly after 9 o'clock Lieutenant Tourtay was overjoyed to see the first French barrages of the resuscitated French artillery beginning to take effect. All that day fighting raged in Fleury, but by the evening of the 23rd it was firmly in German hands.

To the French there were moments when it looked as if, as one of the Brigadiers remarked, ' *tout allait craquer* '. Every telephone call to Pétain's HQ at Bar-le-Duc brought worse news. There were more reports of ' *défaillances* ', indicative of that physical and moral exhaustion which especially alarmed Pétain. At Thiaumont, it appeared that nearly half of the 121st Chasseurs and eighteen of its officers had been taken prisoner; it was a bad omen when distinguished units like the Chasseurs surrendered so easily. Before midday an orderly officer came with a report that Germans were now only two and a half miles from Verdun as the crow flies, and within 1,200 yards of the final ridge, the Côtes de Belleville. On his heels another arrived to tell Pétain that Ritter von Epp's men were firing their machine guns obliquely into the streets of Verdun itself, causing a minor panic. To his subordinates Pétain never revealed his alarm that day, displaying an apparent imperturbability worthy of Joffre himself and remarking only: ' We have not been lucky today, but we shall be tomorrow.'

At 3 p.m., however, he telephoned de Castelnau, gravely pessimistic, expressing fears for the safety of the great bulk of the French artillery that still lay on the Right Bank, and begging for the third time that Joffre get the Somme Offensive advanced.

Joffre and his supporters later cited this conversation as further evidence that Pétain was still contemplating a voluntary evacuation of the Right Bank, and was only forestalled by the resolution of

Joffre and Nivelle. It was not so. On the Right Bank were positioned one-third of all the French guns at Verdun, and it would take an estimated three days to move them. Pétain feared — with reason — that if the German offensive continued, the defenders would be physically hurled across the Meuse, thereby losing all these guns; a sacrifice which, for France, would be second only to the capture of Verdun itself. In fact, Nivelle himself — though afterwards he was quick to claim that he had never been daunted — obviously shared Pétain's fears. He had already ordered the withdrawal of some of the guns in the Bras-Froideterre sector; in Verdun itself, the Governor was set frantically to digging trenches in the streets, fortifying houses for street fighting and preparing Vauban's ancient citadel for siege. Even Joffre's own actions belied his subsequent claim ' I was never worried '; hastily he sent Pétain four of the divisions he so zealously had been hoarding for the Somme; in Paris, one of his officers admitted to Clemenceau that Joffre was ' prostrated ' — upon which ' the Tiger ' commented: ' These people will lose France! '

It was all very well for Joffre to write sanctimoniously in his Memoirs that ' Pétain had once more allowed himself to be too much impressed by the enemy.' Perhaps Pétain had fallen prey too readily to his ever-deepening pessimism. But without a shadow of doubt June 23rd was a frighteningly close-run thing. Who could tell that night that the lethal ' Green Cross ' bombardment would not be repeated that an equally potent thrust might not roll up the French defences on the morrow?

It was something only Knobelsdorf and his commanders knew. The course of German fortunes that day could hardly be better illustrated than by the letter of a twenty five-year-old former student of Munich University, Hans Forster (killed near Verdun later in the year). Forster was an NCO with the 24th Bavarian Regiment, detailed to advance between Fleury and Froideterre. Waiting in shell-holes early that morning, he had noted that hardly any enemy shells fell, a pleasant contrast to the two previous days. At 7 a.m., coloured Very lights were fired, and the regiment surged forward. Within a few minutes it had reached its first objective, a French redoubt referred to as the ' A ' Work.

Forward! The French are flooding back; on the order of an officer they halt and take position again. ' Hand-grenades ' is the shout among us. On all sides the defenders are falling — others

surrender. One more powerful blow — the '*A' Work* is ours!!!
We go on through a hollow. In front of us a railway embankment;
to the right a curve in it. There forty–fifty French are standing with
their hands up. One corporal is still shooting at them — I stop
him. An elderly Frenchman raises a slightly wounded left hand
and smiles and thanks me. . . . Over the railway. . . . In a shellhole ten yards to the left of me is our Company Commander,
Lt. A. He calls out: 'It's gone wonderfully!' and laughs; then
he becomes serious, for he sees that some men have gone ahead and
are in danger of getting into our own fire. He stands up to shout
— then — shreds of his map fly up, he clasps his hands to his breast
and falls forward. Some men run to him, but in a few minutes he
is dead. Forward again. No pause. Over the Fleury barbed wire;
in ten minutes it's ours. With rifles slung, cigarettes in our mouths,
laughing and chatting, we go on. Captured French are coming
back in hundreds. . . . [Though he must have been mistaken,
Forster then claims to have seen, at the end of a long valley —
probably the Ravine des Vignes — the suburbs of Verdun] Oh,
Verdun — what rapture! we shake each others' hands with glowing faces. To the right of Fleury village stands Prince Henry [of
Bavaria, later wounded in the battle], moved with joy. It is a sight
— so great and sublime; time 8.20 a.m. The sun is shining. . . .
At about midday, the enemy gets together a counter-attack, but we
overrun it and occupy a line of trenches one and a half kilometres
in front of Fleury. Gunfire is mounting. We can no longer remain
in the open, and we hunt for shelters. . . . That evening when we
creep out of our holes we notice, to our horror, that the position
was evacuated at 7 o'clock and that only our handful from the 24th
and a few from the 10th were holding a line 500 yards wide. That
was impossible. Lieutenant E. gave the order to move back under
cover of dark, as we had been forgotten. Then, as early as 7.30
our own artillery began shooting up our positions. . . . Until 3
a.m. we lay in a hole. Immense thirst. At last it rained, so we could
lick the brims of our helmets, and the sleeves of our jackets. . . .

Forster then headed back towards the German lines, half-carrying
an NCO of the Leib Regiment who had been severely wounded in
the groin. As it grew light he recognised the wounded man to have
been a fellow student at Munich. Together they got back safely to
Fort Douaumont.

A number of factors had contributed to the ebb of the German attack that day. The effects of the 'Green Cross Gas' had been a little disappointing. French gasmasks had on the whole proved more effective (the French in fact reported only 1,600 gas casualties) than expected, and the gas tended to settle heavily in the hollows, so that French batteries on high ground were relatively protected. There had also been only enough 'Green Cross' shells to blanket the centre of the line, but the French guns on either flank were not knocked out. Above all, in their mistrust of novelty the German commanders had committed an error typical of the 1914-18 military mind; just as a hesitant Haig was later to throw away the supreme surprise value of the tank, so Knobelsdorf had decided not to risk all on Phosgene. Thus, three or four hours before the infantry went in, the gunners had been ordered to cease the gas shelling and revert to normal ammunition, giving the French a vital respite to get their guns back into action.

Tactically, too, the Germans had made the error of attacking (once again) on too narrow a front with too few reserves. This was partly due to the failure, during the preliminary offensive which began on June 8th, to consolidate their flanks by capturing Thiaumont on one side and the 'High Battery' position at Damloup on the other. Again, on the 23rd, brilliant though the German success had been in the centre, the attack had completely failed to burst the French line at the seams. Thus the French had been able to concentrate on blocking the direct menace to Fort Souville via Fleury. By the afternoon of the 23rd, Ritter von Epp had to report that the Leib Regiment could make no further progress. It had already lost fourteen of its officers, and 550 men.

In the sultry midsummer heat of one of the hottest days of the year at Verdun, thirst set the final seal on German hopes. That afternoon, the C.O. of one of the Bavarian Leib battalions signalled back from Fleury: 'If no water can be brought up, the battalion will have to be taken out of the line.' His neighbour, Prince Henry, reported that without water he feared his battalion might suffer 'serious reverses'. During the night, Ritter von Epp sent ninety-five water carriers to the Leib Regiment from Fort Douaumont; only twenty-eight arrived. Under these conditions, the regiment was physically incapable of continuing the attack the next day.

The fact that Boelcke's newly formed 'Flying Circus' had been withdrawn from Verdun (following the death of Immelmann) just as it was proving highly effective, also contributed to the day's failure; insofar as the French had once more regained air superiority with all the disadvantages that entailed for the German gunners. But, basically, the foundering of the German attack all boiled down to the shortage of manpower. At the critical moment in the battle, the German *Reichs Archives* note that the French defence was stretched to such an extent that one regiment of Chasseurs were left holding 1,500 yards of line, and in their estimate the presence of just one more German unit would have led to a breakthrough. What would have happened if Knobelsdorf had had available one of the three divisions Falkenhayn had sent to Russia, or if he had not been forced to interrupt the early offensive on June 12th, can be all too readily imagined.

That evening Knobelsdorf knew that his supreme bid to take Verdun had failed. Some four thousand French prisoners were claimed (their total casualties during this battle amounted to about 13,000), but the German losses had also been depressingly high. The Fifth Army was exhausted, French resistance was stiffening, and soon the inevitable counter-attacks could be expected. There was not enough ' Green Cross ' ammunition left for a second effort; nevertheless the weary, thirsty troops would have to go on battling just to hold on to the gains of the 23rd. A disappointed Kaiser returned to his HQ at Charleville-Mézières, and surreptitiously the regimental colours and bandsmen were dispersed to their depots.

As night fell over the French lines, even Pétain's pessimism had lifted a little. Nivelle issued a dramatic Order of the Day, ending with the famous words:

' You will not let them pass! '

Mangin — who had returned from his temporary eclipse on the very eve of the battle, now promoted to command a whole sector on the Right Bank — was as impetuous as ever, and all for launching an immediate counter-attack. This time he was right. The German advance had led itself into a narrow, tongue-like salient, with its apex, at Fleury, on an exposed forward slope. The next day, French counter-attacks hacked into the salient from both sides, and massed artillery gave the thirst-craved Bavarians a taste of what the French in their larger salient around Verdun had been experiencing ever since February. For a week Mangin attacked almost incessantly,

making eight separate attempts to regain the *Ouvrage de Thiaumont,*
and with the Germans striking back hard all the time. Casualties
were heavy, one of Mangin's battalions losing thirteen out of fourteen officers in an abortive attack on Fleury, and the result in terms
of ground reconquered was nil.

But it hardly seemed to matter any longer.

* * *

For the past months British wall-scribblers had been busy chalking
up exhortations (so reminiscent of the 1942-4 'Second Front' slogans)
of 'SAVE VERDUN' and 'STRIKE NOW IN THE WEST'.
Unmoved by public opinion or pressure from the French, Haig had
stolidly adhered to his date of mid-August for the opening of the
Somme Offensive. Then on May 26th, Joffre (pushed by Pétain) had
come to see him in a state of uncharacteristic agitation. If the British
did nothing till August, 'the French Army could cease to exist,'
shouted Joffre. Haig (according to his Diaries) had soothed him with
some 1840 brandy, and subsequently agreed to have the offensive
advanced to the end of June. On June 24th, following the bad news
from Verdun, Premier Briand himself came to beg Haig to bring the
attack forward again. Haig said it was too late now, but he would
accelerate the preliminary bombardment, and start that very day.
The rumble of the British guns, which could be heard in the South
of England, at German Supreme Headquarters was accompanied
in the ears of Falkenhayn (who appears to have been about the only
German not certain even at the eleventh hour just where the Big
Push was going to be) with the sound of his whole war strategy
collapsing.

For seven days the bombardment raged, the longest yet known.
Then, on July 1st, the French and British infantry went over the top.
Whereas, in Joffre's original plan outlined at the Chantilly Conference the previous year, Foch was to have attacked with forty divisions
and Haig with twenty-five, the needs of Verdun had now whittled
down the French contribution to a mere fourteen. But it was Foch's
men — in the van, the famous 'Iron Corps', now recovered from
its mauling before Verdun in February — who were to mark up
the only real successes. They worked forward in small groups supported by machine guns, using the land with pronounced tactical
skill, in the way they had learned at Verdun, and emulating where
possible the German's own infiltration techniques there. On the first

day they overran most of the German first line before getting stuck, and with comparatively light casualties. It was otherwise with the British forces. Led into battle largely by inexperienced officers of the 'Kitchener Army', trained by generals who believed that what had been good enough for Wellington was good enough for them, commanded by a man who — in his insular contempt for the French Army — felt there was nothing to be gained from its experiences, and weighed down by sixty-six-pound packs, Haig's men advanced in a line that would have earned credit at Dettingen. At a steady walk (laden as they were it would have been impossible to run), spaced regularly — as ordered — with not more than 'two or three paces interval', they advanced across No-Man's-Land, into what Winston Churchill described as being 'undoubtedly the strongest and most perfectly defended position in the world'. The enemy machine guns (a weapon described by Haig as 'much overrated') had not been knocked out by the bombardment. Back and forth they swept across the precisely arrayed British line. As its men fell in rows, so other lines came on at regular 100-yard intervals, displaying courage that the Germans found almost unbelievable. The majority of the attackers never even reached the forward German posts.

By the night of July 1st, Haig's army alone had lost nearly 60,000 men; among them 20,000 dead.[1] Of the day, Haig's chronicler, Colonel Boraston, had the impertinence to write that it 'bore out the conclusions of the British higher command, and amply justified the tactical methods employed'. It would have been more accurate to call it, as did a recent British writer: 'probably the biggest disaster to British arms since Hastings'. Certainly never before, nor since, had such wanton, pointless carnage been seen; not even at Verdun, where in the worst month of all (June) the total French casualty list barely exceeded what Britain lost on that *one day*. For another five months the bull-headed fight continued. Later, in defence of his Verdun operation, Falkenhayn and his supporters claimed that by thus weakening the French Army there, the Germans had been saved from disaster on the Somme; in fact, all Verdun probably did was to save the Allies from still greater losses there.

---

[1] By comparison, the whole Battle of Alamein in twelve days cost only 13,500 British casualties, dead, wounded and missing, and — according to Second World War standards — it was not a 'cheap' battle.

*   *   *

The German tide receded with incomparable swiftness from its highwater mark that day. By July 14th — Bastille Day — Mangin's counter-attacks had pushed the attackers practically back to their starting-off positions of July 10th. The bid to take Verdun was finally at an end. Between February 21st and July 15th, the French had lost over 275,000 men (according to their official war history) and 6,563 officers. Of these somewhere between 65,000 and 70,000 had been killed; 64,000 men and 1,400 officers had been captured (according to the Crown Prince). Over 120,000 of the French casualties had been suffered in the last two months alone. On the German side, Falkenhayn's 'limited offensive' had already cost close on a quarter of a million men; equivalent to about twice the total complement of the nine divisions he had been willing to allocate for the battle in February. The German artillery had fired off approximately 22,000,000 rounds; the French perhaps 15,000,000. Out of their total of ninety-six divisions on the Western front, the French had sent seventy to Verdun; the Germans forty-six-and-a-half.

It was perhaps symptomatic of the whole tragedy of Verdun that this last attack need never have taken place. The Crown Prince tells us that on July 11th Falkenhayn had once more changed his mind and ordered that he should 'henceforward adopt a defensive attitude'. But it was far too late to pass on the message to the divisional staffs. The futile slaughter proceeded. And even after the German offensive was called off after July 14th, still the tragedy could not be halted; all through July, August and part of September the hideous struggle at Verdun continued, little abated. Again it seemed as if humans had lost their power to stop the battle they had started, which went on and on, sustained by its own momentum. The French, who could never be entirely sure that July 11th did represent the Germans' last effort against Verdun and who had been pushed back so dangerously close to the city that one more breach, one more mistake, could still bring about its fall, had to fight desperately to regain breathing room. The Germans were confronted by a terrible dilemma; once their forward impetus ceased and they were forced over to the defensive, tactically they should have abandoned most of the terrain they had conquered at such hideous cost. It was largely indefensible. The Crown Prince recognised this, but even he admitted that it was impossible, because, psychologically, it ' would have had an immeasurably disastrous effect '.

Such were the symbolic proportions that names of meaningless ruins like Thiaumont and Fleury — not just *Verdun* now — had assumed in German minds. So all through the summer the ding-dong battle ensued; with the French bitterly attacking, attacking, attacking; and the Germans contesting every inch of ground, occasionally themselves attacking to regain a lost fragment. Typical of this new, transitional phase of the battle was the prolonged struggle for PC 119 on Thiaumont Ridge; built as a command post for perhaps a dozen men, its recapture by the French required a whole battalion. Again and again Fleury and the Ouvrage de Thiaumont changed hands; until, by the end of the summer, all that remained of Fleury (once a village of 500 people) was a white smear visible only from the air — the sole recognisable object found on its site a silver chalice from the church.

There were alarms on both sides. On August 4th, Private Meyer was detailed off to sing at a concert organised for the music-loving Crown Prince. But the sudden threat of a French breakthrough at Thiaumont dispatched Private Meyer's unit to plug the hole; the concert was cancelled, and the budding tenor captured by the French. On July 19th, Lloyd George told Repington of *The Times* that he was still seriously worried that Verdun might fall and the Germans ' would then shift around 2,000 guns on to our front and hammer in '. At the beginning of September, President Poincaré was to bestow the *Légion d'Honneur* upon a triumphant Verdun, but a sharper German reaction than usual re-awoke French fears to such an extent that it was felt prudent to postpone the ceremony until the new crisis had passed.

With the fighting raging back and forth over the same narrow, corpse-saturated battlefield in the blazing summer heat, the screw of horror tightened (if such a thing were possible) yet another turn. A French officer, Major Roman, describes the scene at the entrance to his dugout in July:

On my arrival, the corpse of an infantryman in a blue cap partially emerges from this compound of earth, stones and unidentifiable debris. But a few hours later, it is no longer the same; he has disappeared and has been replaced by a *Tirailleur* in khaki. And successively there appear other corpses in other uniforms. The shell that buries one disinters another. One gets acclimatised, however, to this spectacle; one can bear the horrible odour of this charnel-house in which one lives, but one's *joie de vivre*, after the war, will be eternally poisoned by it.

Despite their continued subjection to these vile conditions, French morale at Verdun rose perceptibly during August. Everywhere — on the Somme, in Russia, in Italy, in the Near East — the Allies were attacking, and — best of all — Verdun was no longer seriously threatened. Correspondingly, German morale sagged. In August, owing to the brutally exposed ground it was bidden to defend, Fifth Army casualties for the first time exceeded those of the French.

*　　*　　*

CHAPTER TWENTY-EIGHT

AFTERMATH

It seemed to us then as if a quite exceptional bond linked us
with those few who had been with us at the time. It was not
the normal sensation of affinity that always binds together men
who have endured common hardships. . . . It derived from the
fact that Verdun transformed men's souls. Whoever floundered
through this morass full of the shrieking and the dying,
whoever shivered in those nights, had passed the last frontier
of life, and henceforth bore deep within him the leaden memory
of a place that lies between Life and Death, or perhaps beyond
either. . . .—*Reichs Archives*, Vol. I (WERNER BEUMELBURG,
Douaumont)

They will not be able to make us do it again another day;
that would be to misconstrue the price of our effort. They
will have to resort to those who have not lived out these
days. . . .—SECOND-LIEUTENANT RAYMOND JUBERT

To Corporal Robert Perreau of the 203rd Regiment, the summit
of the Mort Homme after the battle ebbed from it in the bitter
winter of 1916-17

resembled in places a rubbish dump in which there had accumulated shreds of clothing, smashed weapons, shattered helmets,
rotting rations, bleached bones and putrescent flesh.

The following year, Lieutenant Louis Hourticq, a former Inspector at the Paris Beaux Arts, back in the Verdun sector for the second
time, described the countryside around Douaumont with its ampu-
tated, blackened tree trunks as being 'a corpse with tortured
features'. But, superficially, the recuperative powers of Nature are
immense. Soon even the blasted trees began to put out new shoots.
Staff-Sergeant Fonsagrive of the Artillery on his return in the
summer of 1917 noted that the battlefield was carpeted with waving
poppies; still, however, there was that all-pervading smell of decomposition. Slowly the city of Verdun, perhaps half of its houses
destroyed or damaged to some extent, came back to life. The
Verdunois returned whence they had been evacuated to set their town
in order and retill the ravaged fields. To nine villages around Verdun,

like Fleury, Douaumont, Cumières, the inhabitants never returned. The villages had literally vanished. The deeper scars of Nature took longer, far longer to heal. At the tragic cost of still more peasant lives lost when ploughs detonated unexploded shells, Champagne, Artois, Picardy, Flanders and even the Somme eventually came back into cultivation, with little trace of the horrors that had been enacted there. But Verdun defied man's peaceful amends longer than all of them. In places the topsoil had simply disappeared, blasted and scorched away by the endless shellfire. Nothing would grow there any more. It seemed as if the Almighty wanted Verdun preserved to posterity as the supreme example of man's inhumanity to man.

And well it might be. It is probably no exaggeration to call Verdun the 'worst' battle in history; even taking in account man's subsequent endeavours in the Second World War. No battle has ever lasted quite so long; Stalingrad, from the moment of the German arrival on the Volga to Paulus' surrender, had a duration of only five months, compared with Verdun's ten. Though the Somme claimed more dead than Verdun, the proportion of casualties suffered to the numbers engaged was notably higher at Verdun than any other First War battle; as indeed were the numbers of dead in relation to the area of the battlefield. Verdun was the First War in microcosm; an intensification of all its horrors and glories, courage and futility.

Estimates on the total casualties inflicted at Verdun vary widely; the accounting in human lives was never meticulous in that war. France's Official War History (published in 1936) sets her losses at Verdun during the ten months of 1916 at 377,231, of which 162,208 were killed or missing,[1] though calculations based on Churchill's 'The World Crisis' (1929) would put them as high as 469,000. The most reliable assessment of German losses for the same period comes to roughly 337,000 (Churchill: just under 373,000), and contemporary German lists admitted to over 100,000 in dead and missing alone. Whatever set of figures one accepts, the combined casualties of both sides reach the staggering total of over 700,000. Nor is that all, for although strictly speaking the 'Battle of Verdun' was limited to the fighting of 1916, in fact a heavy toll of lives had been enacted there long before Falkenhayn's offensive, and bitter fighting continued on its blood-sodden ground through 1917. One recent

[1] Figures of 'missing' on both sides also included those taken prisoner.

French estimate that is probably not excessive places the total French and German losses on the Verdun battlefield at 420,000 dead, and 800,000 gassed or wounded; nearly a million and a quarter in all. Supporting this figure is the fact that after the war some 150,000 unidentified and unburied corpses — or fragments of corpses — alone were collected from the battlefield and interred in the huge, forbidding *Ossuaire*. Still to this day remains are being discovered. In comparison, it is perhaps worth recalling the overall British Empire casualties for the whole of the Second World War were: 1,246,025, of which 353,652 dead and 90,844 missing.

Who ' won ' the Battle of Verdun? Few campaigns have had more written about them (not a little of it bombastic nonsense) and accounts vary widely. The volumes of the *Reichs Archives* dealing with the battle are appropriately entitled ' The Tragedy of Verdun ', while to a whole generation of French writers it represented the summit of ' *La Gloire* '. The baneful results of France's immortalisation of Verdun will be seen later, meanwhile it suffices to say that it was a desperate tragedy for both nations. Before one considers what either side did achieve through the Battle of Verdun, what *could* they have achieved?

*　　*　　*

The consequences of the Battle of Verdun did not end with 1918. It is one of the singular ironies of History that although Falkenhayn failed to bring France to her knees, more than any isolated event of the First War, Verdun led to France's defeat in 1940.

As has already been seen, Verdun contributed to its share of ' firsts ' significant to the development of warfare. Flame-throwers and Phosgene gas made their debut as assault weapons on a large scale there; for the first time it was shown that an army could be supplied by road transport; above all, Verdun was the forge from which originated the conception of an air*force* in the truest meaning of the word. Tactically, at Verdun the Germans perfected their infantry infiltration techniques, which — on a much larger scale — they employed with devastating effect against Gough's Fifth Army in March 1918; the French perfected the ' creeping barrage ', tried a second time with dismal results in 1917. But the full weight of the lessons of Verdun was not felt until after 1918. When the full bill of casualties then became available, military thinkers the world over were united on one point: no future war could ever be fought again like the last

---

[1] In 1918.

one. They differed only in their approach to deciding how it would
be fought. The problem particularly concerned France, who, of all
the belligerents, had suffered easily the highest losses in proportion
to her total manpower, and the answer of that huge body of *anciens
combattants* who had fought before Verdun was unhesitating.
Already on August 23rd 1916, G.Q.G. had pointed to it in a remarkable recantation:

> One fact dominates the six-month struggle between concrete and
> cannon; that is the force of resistance offered by a permanent
> fortification, even the least solid, to the enormous projectiles of
> modern warfare.

After the war, France remained hypnotised by the way Douaumont
and the other forts at Verdun had stood up to the months of ham-
mering. Major Raynal is to be found writing prefaces for military
books, pointing to the lunacy of making men fight ' in the open
air ' and recalling how his Leonidean handful inside Fort Vaux had
checked the whole German advance.

In an annex to his book, *La Bataille de Verdun*, Pétain remarks
pointedly:

> If from the beginning we had had confidence in the skill of our
> military engineers, the struggle before Verdun would have taken
> a different course. Fort Douaumont, occupied as it ought to have
> been, would not have been taken . . . from the first it would have
> discouraged German ambitions. Fortification, what little there was
> of it, played a very large rôle in the victory. . . .

It was Pétain who systematised the new thinking. After the war,
of the leaders that had emerged Marshals of France, none enjoyed
more widespread prestige and affection throughout the Army than
he who had entered the war as a superannuated colonel. Old age
soon removed Foch from the public arena, leaving a still virile Pétain
the principal arbiter of French military thought for the best part of
two decades. As Inspector General of the Army, and later Minister
of War, he harked back repeatedly to one of his favourite maxims:

> One does not fight with men against material; it is with material
> served by men that one makes war.

Never again, he promised, should such sacrifices be forced upon the youth of France. As early as 1922, he was calling for the creation of a ' Wall of France ' that would protect her permanently against the restive, traditional enemy. His idea of this ' Wall ' as it evolved was not of clusters, or even a line, of Douaumonts; for his 400's had proved that even a Douaumont was mortal. Instead it would consist chiefly of a continuous chain of retractable gun cupolas (similar to those mounted at Douaumont and Moulainville that had proved almost indestructible), linked by subterranean passages burrowed so deep as to be beyond the reach of any projectile. For years Pétain could not persuade the governments of an impoverished France to foot the huge cost of his Great Wall. It was no coincidence that the politician eventually giving his name to it was Maginot, the ex-Sergeant who had been seriously wounded at Verdun and had led the attack on Joffre at the first Secret Session in 1916. Nor was it a coincidence that the Chief of the Army General Staff under whom the Maginot Line materialised was a General Debeney, who had commanded a division through some of the worst fighting at Verdun, on the exposed and completely unfortified Mort Homme. Among existing works to be incorporated in the Maginot Line system were Forts Vaux and Douaumont, both to some extent repaired and augmented with additional flanking turrets. As the threat of a new war approached, one French military writer declared:

> The lessons of Verdun have not been lost; for the past fifteen years France has been working on her eastern frontier. . . . Be confident in this fortification with the most modern techniques.

As the *poilus* took up their posts deep in the bowels of the Maginot Line in 1939, the popular cries were ' *Ils ne passeront pas!* ' and ' *on les aura!* '

Thus, in France, since 1870 the wheel of military thinking had turned a fatal full cycle. In 1870 — in simplest terms — she had lost a war through adopting too defensive a posture and relying too much on permanent fortifications; in reaction against this calamitous defeat, she nearly lost the next war by being too aggressive-minded; and what resulted from the subsequent counter-reaction, the Maginot Line mentality, is almost too painful to recall.

★   ★   ★

If the effects of Verdun did not confine themselves to the period of the First War, neither were they limited to strictly military and strategic considerations. As France in the inter-war period buried herself beneath the concrete of the new super-Douaumonts of the Maginot Line, so spiritually she sought refuge behind the 'miracle' of Verdun. Because of Pétain's '*Noria*' system and the sheer length of the battle, something like seven-tenths of the whole French Army had passed through Verdun. The list of names in Verdun's Book of Honour is an impressive one; President Lebrun, Major of Artillery; President Coty, Private First Class; President de Gaulle, Captain of Infantry; Marshal Pétain, Marshal de Lattre, Admiral Darlan. . . . A whole generation of French leaders passes before one's eyes. Of all the battles of the First War, Verdun was the one in which the most Frenchmen had taken part — as well as being the one that made the most profound and most painful impact. Year after year the veterans, '*Ceux de Verdun*', with their black berets, rosettes and *rubans rouges,* made the pilgrimage in their thousands to the shrines of Verdun; to Vaux and Douaumont and the towering new *Ossuaire* that straddles the Thiaumont Ridge, its revolving beacons restlessly scanning the battlefield by night. On the anniversaries of February 21st or of the recapture of Douaumont, on Jeanne d'Arc Day, Armistice Day or July 14th, the torch-light processions filed up from Verdun to the Meuse Heights to attend sombre and moving commemorations (as often as not addressed to the Glorious Dead in the vocative). Depicting the sacredness of one of these regular pilgrimages, Henri de Montherlant wrote:

> *Je marchais sur cette terre humaine comme sur le visage même de la patrie.*

And Anna de Noailles:

> *Passant, sois de récits et de geste économe,*
> *Contemple, adore, prie et tais ce que tu sens.*

With the passage of the years, the symbol of Verdun attained ever-increasing sanctity and at the same time it grew — more dangerously for France — to be a touchstone of national faith. This ex-Verdun generation of Frenchmen, to whom the political world since 1918 bafflingly seemed to have become more, not less, menacing, gradually arrived at the mystic belief that, since France had triumphed in this most terrible of all battles, somehow it would always be able to ' *se débrouiller* '. In that grim duel, France had proved her virility; finally and forever. (The attitude is not without its parallel in today's Micawberish Briton, who secretly reassures himself that, because of the Battle of Britain in 1940, there is bound to be another miracle somewhere round the corner that will save Britain from economic disaster, without any further undue personal effort on his part.)

Hand in hand with the mystique of the Eternal Glory of Verdun went another influence, less perceptible but infinitely more pernicious.

This war has marked us for generations. It has left its imprint upon our souls [wrote Artillery Lieutenant de Mazenod from Verdun in June 1916]. All those inflamed nights of Verdun we shall rediscover one day in the eyes of our children.

Peter Bowman's *Beach Red* (1945) is an impression-
istic novel, in free verse form, of an American attack
on a Japanese-held beach in World War II. It gives a
vivid impression of modern war from the viewpoint of
the individual soldier.

BEACH RED

Oh, say, can you see by the dawn's early light
the glimmering haze squatting on its moist gray haunches and
guarding the waters with a battleship resting across its knees,
searching in diminishing circles until it challenges its own eyes?

The transport heaves at anchor and you sit on deck
with your combat pack harnessed, your rifle cleaned and ready
and your steel helmet claiming identity with those surrounding you—
assigned to its proper cluster in a field of mushrooms.

The stars that had pinned up the curtain of darkness
are beginning to loosen and fall spinning into the sea,
and there are sucking waves and there are creaking hawsers
and the smell of sweat and gun oil and leather
and clothes in which men have tried to capture sleep.

You lounge with intense casualness, waiting for the company commander
to emerge from the wardroom where lights burned all night
and low voices had planned and exhorted and said Amen.

It's all finished now; the briefing, the study of maps,
the review of reconnaissance reports from the various landing beaches,
the forecasts as to the probable condition of the surf,
the distribution of airphotos showing high and low tide views,
the marking of passages and points navigable by small craft,
the calculation of wind direction for laying down smoke screens,
the division into boat groups, the arrangement of assault schedules,
the elaborate checking and tabulation of supply and control facilities
and the selection of suitable assembly points in forward areas.

Unit meetings were held and innumerable small conferences took place.
Excitement transmitted itself from man to man in little shocks
and all during the early hours rumors were snatched at
and fierce arguments over nothing in particular rose and subsided.
Then came the last quiet waiting, and chill, fluttering wisps
of hushed tension smothered your gaping senses. This is it . . .

ı ı ı ı ı

Men on the righthand side of the landing craft disembark
over the front corner of the ramp and step off
to the right oblique, while those on the opposite side
move similarly to the left. The coxswain keeps the engines
purring in order to prevent the boat from turning sideways.

Here you go. The sea accepts you with stoic indifference,
investigating your hips with routine efficiency and a practiced touch
and emptying the warmth from the pockets of your body.

Draw in your breath. Hold your piece at high port.
Keep moving. Churn through the foam. Don't try to run
or the drag of the waves will upset your balance.
Proceed diagonally to the swirling surf with feet wide apart.

The overhead barrage covering the landing sounds like the screech
of a jalopy's brakes before it crashes into a barn.
Shell bursts stride across the atoll roof with awkward boots
and towers of orange flame spring up in their footprints.
A fifty-pound projectile from a five-inch Navy gun swoops down
and a leaping tree smears its green across the sky.

You see the men of the first two attacking waves
swarming up on the beach, digging in or creeping ahead.
Mortar units go forward to blast pathways through the strongpoints,
and the supporting fire of rifle squads can be heard
crackling like the stiff pages of newspapers bearing death notices.

Walk out your life from one step to the next
because that's all you can be sure of. Oh, Christ,
wouldn't it be nice to lie in the gurgling tide,
limp, cool and unknowing like the simple end of everything?

You wonder why there is no fire from the defenders.
Where is the spew of 37-mm. cannon raking the boats,
the heavy machine guns, the howitzers and small arms fire,

        ▪   ▪   ▪   ▪   ▪

547

The platoon reforms and gets set to move inland again.
The trail has become full of haphazard twists and turns,
with holes bulging with rain and unexpected rises and declines
and mud that tries to suck the bottoms from shoes.
It has narrowed perceptibly and grown more lush and untidy
as though wearied of the constant chore of keeping house
against the encroachments of a careless and unruly jungle family.

You doubt if there will be danger from snipers now,
because an overhead maze of leafage shuts out the light
and visibility is reduced to the scrubby gorse under foot
and to the slim bamboo shoots striking at your face.

Your hearing is dimmed, for the dense vegetation absorbs sound,
but you are aware of the smells of rotting plants,
the odor of game and the musky aroma of earth.

This is the home of the wallaby, phalanger and echidna
and other fauna you have never even heard of before.
There is a bird that sounds like a demented man
banging two blocks of wood together in a moronic cacophony,
and there is another that cries like a dog barking.
Here's where fruit-bats and reptiles of all shapes and sizes
establish a free government for themselves and for their posterity . . .
And did you know that a cassowary resembles an emu?

A man five yards ahead halts and raises his arm.
The soldier in front of you performs a similar gesture
and you carry the signal back in the same way.
You turn to Ivey and ask him what's going on
and he says that he is a stranger here himself.

The men stand in a single column, at close intervals,
patiently, as though they had all the time there is.
Close your eyes and you might be in line anywhere.
It might be a chow formation or a supply line

ı   ı   ı   ı   ı

The latest fashion notes for the well dressed jungle scout
prescribe that the helmet be wound about with splotch cloth
so that it does not scrape loudly against overhanging twigs,
and that the stiff canvas leggins be unlaced and removed
to guard against noise caused by their brush against shrubbery.
The trouser cuffs are then wrapped tightly around the ankles
and are tucked into the sock tops to prevent snagging.

Anything that jangles must be muffled or left behind entirely.
The canteen cup is removed from the carrier and temporarily
set aside so the loosely fitting canteen will not rattle.
Dogtags are taped around the edges so they won't clink,
and beltbuckle, knife, buttons, bayonet, machete and all metal surfaces
that might attract enemy attention by glinting in the sunlight
are covered with a drab coating of rich mud.
Nothing white or out of harmony with jungle color schemes
must be visibly evident, and the face, neck and hands
are treated with a liberal application of G.I. blackface cream.

Lindstrom has moved down to confer with a supply sergeant
who has been able to set up shop, and he
draws two machetes and some grenades, and some chocolate bars,
ammo clips, mosquito repellant, sulfa powder and pills, jungle kits,
halazone tablets to purify water, and a vial of brandy.

Empty your pockets of all the things that might be
of value to the enemy in case you are captured,
and above all, don't take any letters you might have,
orders, sketches or any other bits of stray printed matter
which might give the Japs a clue to American strength.
or the composition and identity of the units opposing them.

Take out your wallet and look at the random scraps
stuffed into the two leather compartments along its worn fold.
There are the souvenirs of your odd moments of memorabilia,
a pocket cemetery for the things you once thought important.

Here is the address of a girl living in Atlanta.
You met her at a party for soldiers and she
said you reminded her of her brother in the Navy
so she let you walk her home and kissed you.

Here is the key to the door of your house.
If ever you verged on idolatry, this bit of metal
was holy God and guardian angel and patron saint combined.
Don't look at it so long. Put it away quickly.

Here's a sales slip from a store selling military goods.
You did not find out that you had been overcharged
until the following morning, and you kept delaying your return
till you finally forgot what you wanted to complain about.

Here is one of those little ten cent store photographs
of an unregenerate brat you had a date with once,
and which you kept because the girl was undeniably photogenic.

Here's a calendar for the year of our war 1945,
printed in two colors and issued by the Moody Institute,
with various dates encircled for reasons long dead and buried.

Here's a receipt for a money order bearing number 13965
which you made out in the amount of six dollars
and sent on November tenth to someone you can't recall
for a purpose about which you haven't the slightest recollection.

Here are the words to a popular song, seasons old,
called "I'll Be Seeing You in All the Old Familiar
Places," which you copied out on a piece of paper
and wanted to memorize (but which you never did) because
you got sick and tired of merely humming the tune.

And here's a frayed, smudged item. It's your draft card.

᛫ ᛫ ᛫ ᛫ ᛫

When I consider Thy heavens, the work of Thy fingers,
the moon and the stars which Thou hast ordained, what
is man that Thou art mindful of him? (You are
going through the jungle and you see that there are
no paved sidewalks or curbstones or sewer gratings or automobiles
and there is nothing for the comfort and convenience of
creatures such as you. Everything here and elsewhere on earth
was made for the perpetuation of animals—dull, physical animals—
and this means animals eating and animals sleeping and animals
giving birth to more animals. The chicken was intended to
eat and be eaten, not by men but by animals,
and there is nothing in nature's cookbook that says it
is supposed to be roasted and served with browned potatoes
and stuffed with sliced apples and put on a dish.)

For Thou hast made him a little lower than the
angels and has crowned him with glory and honor (Everything
men have done to improve themselves has been a perversion
of original purpose. They have made buildings out of dust.
They have made apparel from a sheep's coat of hair.
They have chopped down trees and inscribed their histories thereon.
And all that they have accomplished has been the product
of an accidental intellect for which God was not responsible
because His work was finished with creation. Jungle law was
the only legislation laid down in the beginning, and that
is the root they will stumble over in the end.)

The lines are fallen unto me in pleasant places (So
here is your inheritance, your legacy, your residue of gain
after deductions have been made under jungle law. By continued
exposure to insects you may manage to contract malaria, filariasis,
yellow fever, dengue fever, relapsing fever, pappataci, espundia, oriental sore,
typhus, trench fever, bubonic plague, tularemia, dumdum fever or loa-loa.

If your supply of drinking water happens to become contaminated,
you may look forward with confidence to an impending attack
of dysentery, cholera, typhoid fever, helminthic infection or undulant fever.

ı   ı   ı   ı   ı

You look at your watch. "Now!" you whisper, "Now!" Whitney
takes hold of a slender bamboo stalk and shakes it
and the noise seems like a clap of piercing thunder.
The Jap whirls at the sound and instantly leaps to
a position of readiness, with legs spread wide and rifle
thrust out sideways as though to stand off an attack.
You see Lindstrom reach out with his left hand and
pick up a fistful of dirt which he will probably
use to throw in the Nip's eyes if he should
happen to turn around accidentally. He starts forward, slowly at
first, hoping to get within striking distance before being discovered.

Your breath is smothered with tension. He takes one step,
then another. Five or six more and he'll be able
to leap on the enemy and dig his trench knife
into the sentry's back. Stealthily he is narrowing the gap.

Suddenly, there is a crash of brittle underbrush behind him
and your head jerks at the sound and you see
another Jap running out from behind the rock pile, heading
straight for Lindstrom with his rifle distended and his bayonet
held high for a jab at the throat. The sentry
in the foreground wheels around and is momentarily stupefied at
the situation. Then he, too, raises his piece and charges.

Quick! Get on your feet! Smash through the restraining barrier
of brush. You see a look of consternation on Lindstrom's
face. He is standing there with his knife frozen in
his hand. You are free of the tangled vines now
and the butt of the Tommy gun is pressed against
your ribs. The first Jap reaches him and lunges with
a short, upward stab. Lindstrom sidesteps, throws the dirt in
his face and with the same motion grabs hold of
the rifle barrel. His other hand is raised to drive
the knife into the Nip's exposed body, but the sentry
closes in to aid his comrade and parries the blow,

catching the blade in a hook near the hilt of
his bayonet. You can't shoot now! You can't! You're sure
to hit your own man. Whitney and Egan are up.
Let's get 'em! Let's get 'em! Let's get 'em with
our knives or bayonets or bare hands. Let's get 'em!

You throw aside the submachine gun and run for the
struggling group, drawing your knife from its sheath at your
hip. Lindstrom has lost his footing and falls to the
earth. The knife is sprung from his hand and slithers
crazily along the ground. The Jap standing over him is
drawn back for a stroke. You jump with your fingers
outstretched and catch the front part of his throat, jerking
his head back. You can feel the muscles in his
neck convulsing and you can see the look of surprise
and immediate terror in his eyes. You twist the knife
into his back, putting all your strength behind its penetration.

You feel his gasping breath on your wrist and it
is mixed with saliva and the rifle drops from his
hands and blood bursts from his mouth and trickles down
his chin and he shivers. Then all at once he
becomes limp and you know he is dead. You withdraw
your stained knife and lower the carcass to the grass.

Egan and Whitney have already felled the other enemy soldier
and he lies with his knees retracted to his stomach
and his eyes bulging and sightless and his bony hands
pressed to the Imperial seal engraved on his rifle receiver.

They closed his life's book and sat on the cover.

ı   ı   ı   ı   ı

You swing your body around so that you face the
source of the Japanese fire, and you lift up the
Tommy gun and level it at a clump of bushes
that are still oscillating from enemy muzzle blasts. You are
angry. You are more angry now than you have ever
been in your life, and in your furious energy you
press the trigger until you feel that it has pierced
the skin of your forefinger. You are firing in a
single, continuous burst and you spray the treetrunks and the
rocks and the rises in the ground with a wild
whiplash of lead. The gun is getting hot and your
flesh becomes prickly and your shoulder is throbbing with the
recoil, but you keep on shooting until the ammunition drum
gives out and there is only the dull click of
the breeching mechanism. The noise is cleft and there is
gaping silence. That's all, brother. That's all. No more ammo.
You've had your fling and now they can come and
ring your doorbell and tell you that the men are
here to remove the corpses. You look toward Egan and
you see him twisted into an agonized posture, inflexible and
stony, like a personal monument to pain. He is in
blood an inch deep and it has darkened the earth
in an irregular blotch. You roll over into a small
depression next to him. See if he's alive. See if
anything can be done for him. Even if it's only
a gesture. Even if it's the last thing you do.

You stretch out your hand and place it over his
heart and you flatten your palm against his shirt, hoping
to catch a beat, a flutter, a vibration, a throb.
But there is only the sodden dampness of his sweat
and the thin tingle of human warmth turning to coldness.

He is dead in his own blood and in his
own shadow. This is light to pallor and flame to
cinder and fruit to dry core. You liked this man.

ı   ı   ı   ı   ı

The looping ribbon of memory is coiling itself around you,
drawing closer and closer and ever more pressing until it
feels like a woman's warm hand resting on your cheek.

What is thy beloved more than another beloved? My beloved
is unto me as a bundle of myrrh. Honey and
milk are under her tongue. Her lips are like a
thread of scarlet and her mouth is comely. The joints
of her thighs are like jewels. Her belly is like
a heap of wheat set about with lilies. And I
will make mention of my love more than of wine.

Let your heart make a recording of all the lovelinesses
that she has given you, and let it play them
back to you slowly, and let the needle stick occasionally
so that you may hear her say hello again and
again and again and touch your name to her lips.

Always she is waiting for your mind. Always your thoughts
run up the same path and burst through the same
door. Always at the end of thinking her soft fingers
smooth away distraction and the white image of her face
is a cushion for your weariness. How much of hell
you have put away to turn to her. How much
of desolation and sorrow and loneliness she helped you overcome.

Do you remember the last time you saw her on
that final furlough when you didn't have time to tell
her that you would be arriving, and you let yourself
into the house and you sat there waiting like an
empty glass for the bright, bubbly champagne of her coming?
Do you remember the hat she wore and the way
her hair was combed and how the room seemed to
fill up when she entered it, and the look in
her eyes when she saw you and how you had
to tell her to go wipe her face .

· · · · ·

When there was only one man in the world there
were problems, and when there were two men in the
world there were twice as many problems, and when another
man came along the problems were multiplied by three. But
now there are many more men and there are many
more problems and they've reproduced and spread themselves all over
the earth in a great, crawling germ. Wherever you go
you find men and their problems and they are built
one on top of the other in an opulent, spongy
congealment that asphyxiates the mind in a tangled anarchy of
ideas. It is a jungle of the spirit, and there
are trails that lead nowhere and the chunky, unshepherded growth
flowers into a sickly phantasm. And just as there are
scientific names for grasses and shrubs and vines and ferns
and trees, so too there are labels for these equivalent
flora, like Planning and Power and Competitive Systems and Centralization
and Interdependence and Liberals and Conservatives and Reactionaries and
        Radicals
and Standards of Living and Economic Control and Security and
Resources and Geography and Profit and Classes and National Honor.
It's a cumulative canker that keeps on adding to itself
in a frenzied orgasm of incarnation, and you'd have to
deduct one man from another all the way back to
the first man before you could discover what it means.

The mind came before words and the mind came before
ideas and the mind was the pursuer and not the
pursued. But now it's a turnabout chase and the mind
is the harried quarry and it cringes and is afraid.
Living is an empty pot and thinking is a can-opener
hanging from a pantry shelf and all the ingredients that
you mix into your life are taken from classified tins
with printed directions. You cannot improvise a recipe or escape
from the formula or deviate from accepted preparations. And it
is only when circumstance has swept the cupboard bare that

you learn the pudding's proof is not how a man
has spent his life but how he has ended it.

You are striving to recall a pattern. Surely, you know
how to die. Your father did it and his father
did it and so did his and his. There must
be something inside of you that will tell you what
procedure to follow, what last gesture you must make, what
music of the muscles, design of nerve and movement and
reflex. Listen for a cue. It will come. And your
whole face will light up with knowledge. Yes, you will
know how it is done, and you will do it
directly and unhesitatingly, just as it was done before you.

This is the animated earth that goes busily among stars.
Grass in the breeze. Breeze tugging at leaves. Leaves falling
in mud. Mud sustaining grass. All this in six days
with rest on the seventh. It's been a short week.

Well, you have eaten of its food and you have
drunk its water and you have warmed yourself by its
heat. You have walked on its surface, you have dug
into its being, you have felt of it when you
had need of strength. It has sheltered you from danger and
it has hidden you from the sight of your enemies
and taken you to its breast and given you a
couch to lie upon in your large exhaustion. And now
it asks you to repay the debt, and you can
do no more than give back what you have taken.

So toss the world over your shoulder for good luck.

Home is the hunter, home from the hill, and all
that you have hunted you bring in your arms, and
all that you bring is nothing. It is languorously quiet
and you feel enervated into the future and thought is
a burden you would like to put down somewhere and
run away from. Solitude is the only thing you are
conscious of and you are surprised that loneliness can become
a presence. It's like seeing a hand outstretched and grasping
it and unaccountably finding that it is your own. And
in the intimacy of self encountering self at long last,
all other awarenesses withdraw as though they had tactlessly intruded.

Advance, friend. Advance and be recognized. Salute and pass on
and take your place in ranks in a position of
rest. It's easy to sleep when you know you won't
have to get up again, but it's not so deep
a slumber nor so still a silence that it will
not break when your name is being called once more.

You cannot see the war because of all the fighting
and you cannot see its ugliness because of the stinking
horror and you cannot see humanity because of the people.
Everybody is born with an umbilical cord sticking out of
his navel and its purpose is not wholly the binding
of mother to son but the knotting together of man
to man. You walked through the jungle and Lindstrom and
Egan and Whitney were in front of you and you
were behind them, and between you there was connecting tissue.
It was not because of any similarity you may have
had in thought or behavior or habit or belief, but
because you had groped for it and found it and
it had drawn you close. One of you fell down
and another picked him up and carried him in the
simple compulsion of linked survival, and that is the parallel
transcending tribe and race in the utter need of existence.

There are symbols that remain unsearched and secrets that are
locked in miracles and elusive equations that cannot be solved
merely by turning to the back of the book. But
the sun is standing still and the sands are heated
and the hill is floating up to embrace you and
the trees are hoisting their shimmering green banners of hope.
And the sound of Taps ends on a high note . . .

You do not hear the continuing noise of battle from
the beach where the Jap counterattacking force is rapidly being
annihilated, or the clamor and disorder of retreat directly below
where the enemy has lost his positions and now streams
wildly back to join with reinforcements in the rear. You
do not see the bending bushes yielding to the press
of stampeding brown bodies, some transporting wounded and others cradling
machine guns and none looking back. You do not hear
the Americans shouting orders and regrouping in skirmish lines and
bringing up mortars and ammunition and calling for a medic.

You do not see the unwashed face of Private Whitney
poke itself through the grass and survey the ground in
clinical analysis, then wave to the other members of your
squad emerging from the brush. You do not see him
approach you at a crouch and look down at the
hole in your side and lift up your left wrist
and press his finger against it to detect a pulse.
You do not hear Lieutenant Nixon come forward to the
group and ask Whitney whether or not you're still alive.

"Lieutenant," he replies, "there is nothing moving but his watch."

9

Laotse, BOOK OF TAO
and Chuangtse, Commentaries
(Trans. & Ed. by Lin Yutang)

William James, "THE MORAL EQUIVALENT OF WAR"

E. L. Woodward, SOME POLITICAL CONSEQUENCES OF
THE ATOMIC BOMB

Dwight D. Eisenhower, "THE CHANCE FOR PEACE"

"FAREWELL RADIO AND TELEVISION
ADDRESS TO THE AMERICAN PEOPLE"

1. Compare and contrast the views of Laotse with
those of James on the desirability of peace and
the means for achieving peace.

2. How does James analyze the problem of war?

3. What does James say about the possibility of dis-
couraging war by dwelling on the horrors of war?

4. In what way does Woodward's attitude about the
future change in 1945? To what does he attribute
this change?

5. What "clear-cut solutions" does Woodward offer for
the control of the atomic bomb, and what prospect
of success does he see for each solution?

6. How does Eisenhower's notion of a "new kind of war"
relate to William James' concept of the need for a
"moral equivalent of war"?

7. What is Eisenhower's solution to the problem of
war?

8. Explain Eisenhower's warning about the "military
industrial complex."

Laotse, a great Chinese thinker of the sixth century B.C., was the founder of the Taoist religion. In his quest for "The Way" for man to live in harmony in the universe, he warned against the use of force and emphasized the need and the hope for world peace.

30. WARNING AGAINST
THE USE OF FORCE

He who by Tao purposes to help the ruler of men
Will oppose all conquest by force of arms.[13]
For such things are wont to rebound.
Where armies are, thorns and brambles grow.
The raising of a great host
Is followed by a year of dearth.[14]

Therefore a good general effects his purpose and stops.
    He dares not rely upon the strength of arms;
Effects his purpose and does not glory in it;
Effects his purpose and does not boast of it;
Effects his purpose and does not take pride in it;
    Effects his purpose as a regrettable necessity;
    Effects his purpose but does not love violence.
(For) things age after reaching their prime.
That (violence) would be against the Tao.
And he who is against the Tao perishes young.

    [13] The Chinese character for "military" is composed of two parts: "stop" and "arms." Chinese pacifists interpret this as meaning disapproval of arms ("stop armament"), whereas it may just as well mean to "stop" the enemy "by force." Etymologically, however, the word for "stop" is a picture of a footprint, so the whole is a picture of a "spear" over "footprints."
    [14] These six lines are by Waley, for they cannot be improved upon.

31. WEAPONS OF EVIL

Of all things, soldiers[15] are instruments of evil,
  Hated by men.
Therefore the religious man (possessed of Tao) avoids
  them.
The gentleman favors the left in civilian life,
But on military occasions favors the right.[16]

Soldiers are weapons of evil.
  They are not the weapons of the gentleman.
When the use of soldiers cannot be helped,
  The best policy is calm restraint.

Even in victory, there is no beauty,[17]
And who calls it beautiful
  Is one who delights in slaughter.
He who delights in slaughter
  Will not succeed in his ambition to rule the world.

[The things of good omen favor the left.
The things of ill omen favor the right.
The lieutenant-general stands on the left,
The general stands on the right.
That is to say, it is celebrated as a Funeral Rite.]

[15] Another reading, "fine weapons." *Ping* can mean both "soldiers" and "weapons."

[16] These are ceremonial arrangements. The left is a symbol of good omen, the creative; the right is a symbol of bad omen, the destructive.

[17] Another equally good reading: "no boasting," "and who boasts of victory."

The slaying of multitudes should be mourned with sorrow.

A victory should be celebrated with the Funeral Rite.[18]

30.1. THE DANGER OF RELYING ON AN ARMY. The Sage is never sure of what others regard as sure; hence, he does not rely on an army. The common men are sure of what one cannot be sure about; hence, a big army. When an army is there, it is against human nature not to try to get what one wants. And when one relies on the army, one perishes. (8:13)

31.1. ON THE EMPTINESS OF VICTORY.

"I have long wanted to meet you," said Duke Wu of Wei (known for his war exploits, speaking to Hsü Wukuei). "I love my people and follow righteousness. I am thinking of disarmament. What do you think?"

"You cannot do it," replied Hsü Wukuei. "To love the people is the beginning of hurting them. To plan disarmament in the cause of righteousness is the beginning of rearmament. If you start from there, you will never accomplish anything. The love of a good name is an instrument of an evil. Although Your Highness wishes to follow the doctrine of humanity and justice, I am afraid you are going to end in hypocrisy. The material leads to the material; pride comes with accom-

[18] One of the five Cardinal Rites of *Chou-li*. The last five lines but two read like a commentary, interpolated in the text by mistake. The evidence is conclusive: (1) The terms "lieutenant general" and "general" are the only ones in the whole text that are anachronisms, for these terms did not exist till Han times. (2) The commentary by Wang Pi is missing in this chapter, so it must have slipped into the text by a copyist's mistake. See also Ch. 69. Cf. Mencius, "The best fighter should receive the supreme punishment"; again, "Only he who does not love slaughter can unify the empire."

plishment, and war comes with the change of circumstances. Do not parade your soldiers before the Towers
of Lich'iao; do not display your infantry and cavalry in
the palace of Chut'an. Do not obtain things by immoral
means. Do not gain your end by astuteness, by strategy, or
by war. For to slaughter the people of another country,
take their territory in order to increase one's private
possessions and please oneself—what good will such a
war do? In what does such a victory consist? You should
leave it alone, and search within yourself, and let things
fulfil their nature without your interference. Thus the
people will already have escaped death. What need
will there be for disarmament?" (6:11)

*Chuangtse's argument against disarmament may appear
fallacious on the surface, but is fundamentally correct.
When it becomes necessary to talk of disarmament, all
plans of disarmament must fail, as man has learned today
His argument is essentially that of moral rearmament.*

*In the following selection, the dilemma of war or
peace is presented even more forcefully. The situation
of two thousand years ago, when preparedness for war
and unpreparedness for war seemed equally reckless,
is reminiscent of today.*

31.2. THE DILEMMA OF WAR AND PEACE. Wei Yung (King
Huei of Wei) signed a treaty with T'ien Houmou (King
Wei of Ch'i, a powerful state) and T'ien broke it. Wei
Yung was angry and was going to send someone to
assassinate him. His lion-head (a general's title) felt
ashamed when he heard of it, and said to him, "You
are a ruler of a country with ten thousand chariots and
you are thinking of revenge by assassination. If you will

give me an army of two hundred thousand men, I am going to attack them. I shall capture his people as slaves and drive away his cattle and horses and make him burn with shame and chagrin. And then, we shall raze his city. When Chi (T'ien) flees his country, I shall smash his back and break his spine."

Chitse felt ashamed when he heard of this and said, "Somebody built a city wall of ten *jen* and then you want to tear it down. What a waste of human labor! Now there has been no war for seven years and this seems a good beginning for building up a strong country. Yen (the officer) is a reckless fellow. Don't listen to him."

Huatse felt ashamed when he heard of this and said, "The man who talks about invading Ch'i is a reckless person. The man who talks about not invading Ch'i is also a reckless person. The man who calls them both reckless persons is also a reckless person himself."

"Then what am I going to do?" said the King.

"Just seek the Tao," replied Huatse.

Hueitse (Chuangtse's friend, a great sophist) heard about this and went to see Tai Chinjen (and told him how to speak to the King).

(Following Hueitse's advice) Tai Chinjen said to the King, "Have you ever heard of a thing called the snail?"

"Yes."

"There is a kingdom at the tip of the left feeler of the snail. Its people are called the Ch'us. And there is a kingdom at the tip of the right feeler of the snail, and its people are called the Mans. The Ch'us and the Mans have constant wars with one another, fighting about their territories. When a battle takes place, the dead lie about the field in tens of thousands. The defeated army runs for fifteen days before it returns to its own territory."

"Indeed," said the King. "Are you telling me a tall tale?"

"It isn't a tall tale at all. Let me ask you, do you think there is a limit to space in the universe?"

"No limit," replied the King.

"If you could let your mind roam about in infinity, and arrive in the Country of Understanding, would not your country seem to exist and yet not to exist?"

"It seems so," replied the King.

"In the center of the Country of Understanding, there is your country, Wei, and in the country of Wei there is the city of Liang, and in the center of the city of Liang, there is the king. Do you think there is any difference between that king and the king of the Mans?"

"No difference," replied the King.

The interviewer withdrew and the King felt lost. (7:2)

37. WORLD PEACE

The Tao never does,
　Yet through it everything is done,
If princes and dukes can keep the Tao,
　The world will of its own accord be reformed.
When reformed and rising to action,
　Let it be restrained by the Nameless pristine sim-
　　plicity.
The Nameless pristine simplicity
　Is stripped of desire (for contention).
By stripping of desire quiescence is achieved,
And the world arrives at peace of its own accord.

*From the preceding chapters, there is a kind of running
argument that quiescence and inaction represent the
state of unspoiled nature, the source of all power. It has
also become clear that as we live in the human world,
total abstention from activities is impossible, and so one
comes to the resultant attitude of a mild passivity and in-
dulgent quietness as the wisest mode of life. In the
following selection, we have probably the most complete
description of the doctrine of inaction, based on the
imitation of nature and the silent workings of the
universe, and recommending calm passivity and a mild
and mellow attitude as the wise man's way of life.*

37.1. THE DOCTRINE OF INACTION AND QUIETUDE. The heaven revolves and does not accumulate; hence the things of the creation are formed. The ruler of a state lets things run their course and does not accumulate; therefore the world follows and obeys him. The sage's influence circulates everywhere and does not accumulate; therefore the world pays him homage. To understand the way of nature and of the sage and to see the changes of the elements in time and space and apply them to the way of a ruler is to realize that each thing runs its own course and there is a state of quietude amidst all the activities. The sage is calm not because he says to himself, 'It is good to be calm,' and therefore chooses to be so. He is naturally calm because nothing in the world can disturb his mind. When water is at repose, it is so clear that it can reflect a man's beard; it maintains absolute level and is used by the carpenter for establishing the level. If water is clear when it is at rest, how much more so is the human spirit? When the mind of the sage is calm, it becomes the mirror of the universe, reflecting all within it.

Passivity, calm, mellowness, detachment and inaction characterize the things of the universe at peace and represent the height of development of Tao and character. Therefore the ruler and the sage take their rest therein To take rest is to be passive; passivity means having reserve power, and having reserve power implies order. Passivity means calm and when calm reverts to action, every action is right. Calm means inaction, and when the principle of inaction prevails, each man does his duty. Inaction means being at peace with oneself, and when one is at peace with oneself, sorrows and fears cannot disturb him and he enjoys long life.

Passivity, calm, mellowness, detachment and inaction

represent the root of all things. By understanding them Yao became an emperor, and Shun a good minister. In the position of power, these become the attributes of the emperor, the son of heaven; in the position of the common man, these become the attributes of the sage and philosopher-king. One retires with these virtues, and all the scholars at leisure in the hills and forests and rivers and seas admire him. One assumes office to put the world in order, and he accomplishes great results and the world becomes unified. He keeps quiet and becomes a sage, he acts and becomes a king. If he does nothing and guards carefully his original simplicity, no one in the entire world can compete with him in beauty of character. For such a one understands the character of the universe. This is called the great foundation and the great source of all being. That is to be in harmony with God. To bring the world into order, that is to achieve harmony with men. To be in harmony with men is the music of man, and to be in harmony with God is the music of God. Chuangtse says "Ah! my Master, my Master! He trims down all created things, and does not account it justice. He causes all created things to thrive and does not account it kindness. Dating back further than the remotest antiquity, He does not account himself old. Covering heaven, supporting earth, and fashioning various forms of things, He does not account himself skilled." This is called the music of heaven. Therefore, it is said, "He who understands the music of heaven lives in accordance with nature in his life and takes part in the process of change of things in his death." In repose, his character is in harmony with the *yin* principle; in activity, his movement is in harmony with the *yang* principle. Therefore he who understands the music of heaven is not blamed by heaven or criticized by men.

or burdened with material affairs or punished by the ghosts. Therefore it is said, "In action he is like heaven. In repose he is like the earth. Because his mind has found repose he becomes the king of the world. His departed ghost does not appear to disturb others, and his spirit does not know fatigue. Because his mind has found repose, therefore ɪhe creation pays homage to him." That is to say, passivity and calm are principles that run through the heaven and earth and all creation. That is the music of heaven. The music of heaven is that by which the sage nourishes all living things. (4:1)

37.2. "THE WORLD ARRIVES AT PEACE OF ITS OWN ACCORD." THE IMITATION OF NATURE. Though heaven and earth are great, they act impartially on all things. Though the things of the creation are many, the principle of peace is the same. Though the people in a nation are many, their sovereign is the king. The king imitates Teh (the character of Tao) and lets things be completed according to nature. Therefore it is said, "The kings of primitive times did nothing." In that, they were only following the character of nature. By judging the names of titles and ranks in the light of Tao, the king's position becomes established. By judging the distinction of position in the light of Tao, the duties of the king and his ministers become clear. By judging ability in the light of Tao, the officials of the country carry out their duties. By judging everything in the light of Tao, all things respond to our needs. Therefore character is that which is related to heaven and earth, and Tao is that which pervades all creation. . . . Therefore it is said, "In ancient times, those who helped in sustaining the life of the people had no desires themselves and the world lived in plenty, did nothing, and all things were reformed, remained deep at rest and the people lived at peace." (3:9)

54. THE INDIVIDUAL AND THE STATE

Who is firmly established is not easily shaken.
Who has a firm grasp does not easily let go.
From generation to generation his ancestral sacrifices
   Shall be continued without fail.

Cultivated in the individual, character will become
      genuine;
Cultivated in the family, character will become
      abundant;
Cultivated in the village, character will multiply;
Cultivated in the state, character will prosper;
Cultivated in the world, character will become uni-
      versal.

Therefore:
   According to (the character of) the individual,
      judge the individual;
   According to (the character of) the family, judge
      the family;
   According to (the character of) the village, judge
      the village;
   According to (the character of) the state, judge
      the state;

According to (the character of) the world, judge
the world.
How do I know the world is so.
By this.[11]

*The idea behind the first two lines is essential distrust
of visible devices, stated more clearly in the beginning
of chapter 27.* "The precaution taken against thieves who
open trunks, search bags, or ransack cabinets consists in
securing with cord and fastening with bolts and locks.
This is what the world calls wit. But a big thief comes
along and carries off the cabinet on his shoulders, with
box and bag, and runs away with them. His only fear is
that the bolts and locks should not be strong enough."
See selection 19.1.

54.1. THE NINE TESTS OF CONFUCIUS FOR JUDGING MEN.
"Man's mind," says Confucius, "is more treacherous than
mountains and rivers, and more difficult to know than
the sky. For with the sky you know what to expect in
respect of the coming of spring, summer, autumn and
winter, and the alternation of day and night. But man
hides his character behind an inscrutable appearance.
There are those who appear tame and self-effacing, but
conceal a terrible pride. There are those who have some
special ability but appear to be stupid. There are those
who are compliant and yielding but always get their
objective. Some are hard outside but soft inside, and
some are slow without but impatient within. Therefore
those who rush forward to do the righteous thing as if
they were craving for it, drop it like something hot.

[11] From within myself; or the meaning could be very well
developed in the following chapter, since the chapter division
is arbitrary.

Therefore (in the judgment of men) a gentleman sends a man to a distant mission in order to test his loyalty. He employs him near by in order to observe his manners. He gives him a lot to do in order to judge his ability. He suddenly puts a question to him in order to test his knowledge and makes a commitment with him under difficult circumstances to test his ability to live up to his word. He trusts him with money in order to test his heart, and announces to him the coming of a crisis to test his integrity. He makes him drunk in order to see the inside of his character, and puts him in female company to see his attitude toward women. Submitted to these nine tests, a fool always reveals himself" (8:14).

In this noted essay published in 1910, William James, leading psychologist and philosopher of pragmatism, dwelt on what he saw as the necessity of finding some other kind of emotional outlet for that provided by war.

THE MORAL EQUIVALENT OF WAR[1]

THE war against war is going to be no holiday
excursion or camping party. The military feelings are too deeply grounded to abdicate their
place among our ideals until better substitutes
are offered than the glory and shame that come
to nations as well as to individuals from the
ups and downs of politics and the vicissitudes
of trade. There is something highly para-
doxical in the modern man's relation to war.
Ask all our millions, north and south, whether
they would vote now (were such a thing possible) to have our war for the Union expunged
from history, and the record of a peaceful transition to the present time substituted for that
of its marches and battles, and probably hardly
a handful of eccentrics would say yes. Those

[1] Written for and first published by the Association
for International Conciliation (Leaflet No. 27) and
also published in *McClure's Magazine,* August, 1910,
and *The Popular Science Monthly*, October, 1910.

ancestors, those efforts, those memories and legends, are the most ideal part of what we now own together, a sacred spiritual possession worth more than all the blood poured out. Yet ask those same people whether they would be willing in cold blood to start another civil war now to gain another similar possession, and not one man or women would vote for the proposition. In modern eyes, precious though wars may be, they must not be waged solely for the sake of the ideal harvest. Only when forced upon one, only when an enemy's injustice leaves us no alternative, is a war now thought permissible.

It was not thus in ancient times. The earlier men were hunting men, and to hunt a neighboring tribe, kill the males, loot the village and possess the females, was the most profitable, as well as the most exciting, way of living. Thus were the more martial tribes selected, and in chiefs and peoples a pure pugnacity and love of glory came to mingle with the more fundamental appetite for plunder.

Modern war is so expensive that we feel trade to be a better avenue to plunder; but modern man inherits all the innate pugnacity and all the love of glory of his ancestors. Showing war's irrationality and horror is of no effect upon him. The horrors make the fascination. War is the *strong* life; it is life *in extremis;* war-taxes are the only ones men never hesitate to pay, as the budgets of all nations show us.

History is a bath of blood. The Iliad is one long recital of how Diomedes and Ajax, Sarpedon and Hector *killed.* No detail of the wounds they made is spared us, and the Greek mind fed upon the story. Greek history is a panorama of jingoism and imperialism — war for war's sake, all the citizens being warriors. It is horrible reading, because of the irrationality of it all — save for the purpose of making "history" — and the history is that of the utter ruin of a civilization in intellectual respects perhaps the highest the earth has ever seen.

Those wars were purely piratical. Pride,

gold, women, slaves, excitement, were their only motives. In the Peloponnesian war for example, the Athenians ask the inhabitants of Melos (the island where the "Venus of Milo" was found), hitherto neutral, to own their lordship. The envoys meet, and hold a debate which Thucydides gives in full, and which, for sweet reasonableness of form, would have satisfied Matthew Arnold. "The powerful exact what they can," said the Athenians, "and the weak grant what they must." When the Meleans say that sooner than be slaves they will appeal to the gods, the Athenians reply: "Of the gods we believe and of men we know that, by a law of their nature, wherever they can rule they will. This law was not made by us, and we are not the first to have acted upon it; we did but inherit it, and we know that you and all mankind, if you were as strong as we are, would do as we do. So much for the gods; we have told you why we expect to stand as high in their good opinion as you." Well, the Meleans still refused, and their town was taken. "The Athenians," Thucydides quietly says, "thereupon put to death all who were of military age and made slaves of the women and children. They then colonized the island, sending thither five hundred settlers of their own."

Such was the gory nurse that trained societies to cohesiveness. We inherit the warlike
type; and for most of the capacities of heroism
that the human race is full of we have to thank
this cruel history. Dead men tell no tales,
and if there were any tribes of other type than
this they have left no survivors. Our ancestors have bred pugnacity into our bone and
marrow, and thousands of years of peace won't
breed it out of us. The popular imagination
fairly fattens on the thought of wars. Let
public opinion once reach a certain fighting
pitch, and no ruler can withstand it. In the
Boer war both governments began with bluff
but could n't stay there, the military tension
was too much for them. In 1898 our people
had read the word " war " in letters three
inches high for three months in every newspaper. The pliant politician McKinley was
swept away by their eagerness, and our squalid
war with Spain became a necessity.

At the present day, civilized opinion is a

curious mental mixture. The military instincts and ideals are as strong as ever, but are confronted by reflective criticisms which sorely curb their ancient freedom. Innumerable writers are showing up the bestial side of military service. Pure loot and mastery seem no longer morally avowable motives, and pretexts must be found for attributing them solely to the enemy. England and we, our army and navy authorities repeat without ceasing, arm solely for "peace," Germany and Japan it is who are bent on loot and glory. "Peace" in military mouths to-day is a synonym for "war expected." The word has become a pure provocative, and no government wishing peace sincerely should allow it ever to be printed in a newspaper. Every up-to-date dictionary should say that "peace" and "war" mean the same thing, now *in posse*, now *in actu*. It may even reasonably be said that the intensely sharp competitive *preparation* for war by the nations *is the real war*, permanent, unceasing; and that the battles are only a sort of public verification of the mastery gained during the "peace"-interval.

It is plain that on this subject civilized man has developed a sort of double personality. If we take European nations, no legitimate interest of any one of them would seem to justify the tremendous destructions which a war to compass it would necessarily entail. It would seem as though common sense and reason ought to find a way to reach agreement in every conflict of honest interests. I myself think it our bounden duty to believe in such international rationality as possible. But, as things stand, I see how desperately hard it is to bring the peace-party and the war-party together, and I believe that the difficulty is due to certain deficiencies in the program of pacificism which set the militarist imagination strongly, and to a certain extent justifiably, against it. In the whole discussion both sides are on imaginative and sentimental ground. It is but one utopia against another, and everything one says must be abstract and hypothetical. Subject to this criticism and caution, I will try to characterize in abstract strokes the opposite imaginative forces, and point out what to my own very fallible mind seems the best utopian hypothesis, the most promising line of conciliation.

In my remarks, pacificist though I am, I will refuse to speak of the bestial side of the war-*régime* (already done justice to by many writers) and consider only the higher aspects of militaristic sentiment. Patriotism no one thinks discreditable; nor does any one deny that war is the romance of history. But inordinate ambitions are the soul of every patriotism, and the possibility of violent death the soul of all romance. The militarily patriotic and romantic-minded everywhere, and especially the professional military class, refuse to admit for a moment that war may be a transitory phenomenon in social evolution. The notion of a sheep's paradise like that revolts, they say, our higher imagination. Where then would be the steeps of life? If war had ever stopped, we should have to re-invent it, on this view, to redeem life from flat degeneration.

Reflective apologists for war at the present day all take it religiously. It is a sort of sacrament. Its profits are to the vanquished as well as to the victor; and quite apart from any question of profit, it is an absolute good, we are told, for it is human nature at its highest dynamic. Its "horrors" are a cheap price to pay for rescue from the only alternative supposed, of a world of clerks and teachers, of co-education and zo-ophily, of "consumer's leagues " and "associated charities," of industrialism unlimited, and femininism unabashed. No scorn, no hardness, no valor any more! Fie upon such a cattleyard of a planet!

So far as the central essence of this feeling goes, no healthy minded person, it seems to me, can help to some degree partaking of it. Militarism is the great preserver of our ideals of hardihood, and human life with no use for hardihood would be contemptible. Without risks or prizes for the darer, history would be insipid indeed; and there is a type of military character which every one feels that the race should never cease to breed, for every one is sensitive to its superiority. The duty is incumbent on mankind, of keeping military characters in stock — of keeping them, if not for use, then as ends in themselves and as pure pieces of perfection, — so that Roosevelt's weaklings and mollycoddles may not end by making everything else disappear from the face of nature.

This natural sort of feeling forms, I think, the innermost soul of army-writings. Without any exception known to me, militarist authors take a highly mystical view of their subject, and regard war as a biological or sociological necessity, uncontrolled by ordinary psychological checks and motives. When the time of development is ripe the war must come, reason or no reason, for the justifications pleaded are invariably fictitious. War is, in short, a permanent human *obligation*. General Homer Lea, in his recent book "The Valor of Ignorance," plants himself squarely on this ground. Readiness for war is for him

the essence of nationality, and ability in
it the supreme measure of the health of
nations.

Nations, General Lea says, are never sta-
tionary — they must necessarily expand or
shrink, according to their vitality or decrepi-
tude. Japan now is culminating; and by the
fatal law in question it is impossible that her
statesmen should not long since have entered,
with extraordinary foresight, upon a vast policy of conquest — the game in which the first
moves were her wars with China and Russia
and her treaty with England, and of which the
final objective is the capture of the Philip-
pines, the Hawaiian Islands, Alaska, and the
whole of our Coast west of the Sierra Passes.
This will give Japan what her ineluctable
vocation as a state absolutely forces her to
claim, the possession of the entire Pacific
Ocean; and to oppose these deep designs we
Americans have, according to our author,
nothing but our conceit, our ignorance, our
commercialism, our corruption, and our fem-
inism. General Lea makes a minute technical

comparison of the military strength which we at present could oppose to the strength of Japan, and concludes that the islands, Alaska, Oregon, and Southern California, would fall almost without resistance, that San Francisco must surrender in a fortnight to a Japanese investment, that in three or four months the war would be over, and our republic, unable to regain what it had heedlessly neglected to protect sufficiently, would then "disintegrate," until perhaps some Cæsar should arise to weld us again into a nation.

A dismal forecast indeed! Yet not unplausible, if the mentality of Japan's statesmen be of the Cæsarian type of which history shows so many examples, and which is all that General Lea seems able to imagine. But there is no reason to think that women can no longer be the mothers of Napoleonic or Alexandrian characters; and if these come in Japan and find their opportunity, just such surprises as "The Valor of Ignorance " paints may lurk in ambush for us. Ignorant as we still are of the innermost recesses of Japanese mentality, we may be foolhardy to disregard such possibilities.

Other militarists are more complex and more moral in their considerations. The "Philosophie des Krieges," by S. R. Steinmetz is a good example. War, according to this author, is an ordeal instituted by God, who weighs the nations in its balance. It is the essential form of the State, and the only function in which peoples can employ all their powers at once and convergently. No victory is possible save as the resultant of a totality of virtues, no defeat for which some vice or weakness is not responsible. Fidelity, cohesiveness, tenacity, heroism, conscience, education, inventiveness, economy, wealth, physical health and vigor — there is n't a moral or intellectual point of superiority that does n't tell, when God holds his assizes and hurls the peoples upon one another. *Die Weltgeschichte ist das Weltgericht;* and Dr. Steinmetz does not believe that in the long run chance and luck play any part in apportioning the issues.

The virtues that prevail, it must be noted,

are virtues anyhow, superiorities that count in peaceful as well as in military competition; but the strain on them, being infinitely intenser in the latter case, makes war infinitely more searching as a trial. No ordeal is comparable to its winnowings. Its dread hammer is the welder of men into cohesive states, and nowhere but in such states can human nature adequately develop its capacity. The only alternative is "degeneration."

Dr. Steinmetz is a conscientious thinker, and his book, short as it is, takes much into account. Its upshot can, it seems to me, be summed up in Simon Patten's word, that mankind was nursed in pain and fear, and that the transition to a "pleasure-economy" may be fatal to a being wielding no powers of defence against its disintegrative influences. If we speak of the *fear of emancipation from the fear-régime,* we put the whole situation into a single phrase; fear regarding ourselves now taking the place of the ancient fear of the enemy.

Turn the fear over as I will in my mind, it

all seems to lead back to two unwillingnesses of the imagination, one æsthetic, and the other moral; unwillingness, first to envisage a future in which army-life, with its many elements of charm, shall be forever impossible, and in which the destinies of peoples shall nevermore be decided quickly, thrillingly, and tragically, by force, but only gradually and insipidly by "evolution"; and, secondly, unwillingness to see the supreme theatre of human strenuousness closed, and the splendid military. aptitudes of men doomed to keep always in a state of latency and never show themselves in action. These insistent unwillingnesses, no less than other æsthetic and ethical insistencies, have, it seems to me, to be listened to and respected. One cannot meet them effectively by mere counter-insistency on war's expensiveness and horror. The horror makes the thrill; and when the question is of getting the extremest and supremest out of human nature, talk of expense sounds ignominious. The weakness of so much merely negative criticism is evident — pacificism makes no converts from the military party. The military party denies neither the bestiality nor the horror, nor the expense; it only says that these things tell but half the story. It only says that war is *worth* them; that, taking human nature as a whole, its wars are its best protection against its weaker and more cowardly self, and that mankind cannot *afford* to adopt a peace-economy.

Pacificists ought to enter more deeply into the æsthetical and ethical point of view of their opponents. Do that first in any controversy, says J. J. Chapman, *then move the point,* and your opponent will follow. So long as anti-militarists propose no substitute for war's disciplinary function, no *moral equivalent* of war, analogous, as one might say, to the mechanical equivalent of heat, so long they fail to realize the full inwardness of the situation. And as a rule they do fail. The duties, penalties, and sanctions pictured in the utopias they paint are all too weak and tame to touch the military-minded. Tolstoi's pacificism is the only exception to this rule, for it is profoundly pessimistic as regards all this world's values, and makes the fear of the Lord furnish the moral spur provided elsewhere by the fear of the enemy. But our socialistic peace-advocates all believe absolutely in this world's values; and instead of the fear of the Lord and the fear of the enemy, the only fear they reckon with is the fear of poverty if one be lazy. This weakness pervades all the socialistic literature with which I am acquainted. Even in Lowes Dickinson's exquisite dialogue,[1] high wages and short hours are the only forces invoked for overcoming man's distaste for repulsive kinds of labor. Meanwhile men at large still live as they always have lived, under a pain-and-fear economy — for those of us who live in an ease-economy are but an island in the stormy ocean — and the whole atmosphere of present-day utopian literature tastes mawkish and dishwatery to people who still keep a sense for life's more bitter flavors. It suggests, in truth, ubiquitous inferiority.

Inferiority is always with us, and merciless

[1] "Justice and Liberty," N. Y., 1909.

scorn of it is the keynote of the military temper. "Dogs, would you live forever?" shouted Frederick the Great. "Yes," say our utopians, "let us live forever, and raise our level gradually." The best thing about our "inferiors" to-day is that they are as tough as nails, and physically and morally almost as insensitive. Utopianism would see them soft and squeamish, while militarism would keep their callousness, but transfigure it into a meritorious characteristic, needed by "the service," and redeemed by that from the suspicion of inferiority. All the qualities of a man acquire dignity when he knows that the service of the collectivity that owns him needs them. If proud of the collectivity, his own pride rises in proportion. No collectivity is like an army for nourishing such pride; but it has to be confessed that the only sentiment which the image of pacific cosmopolitan industrialism is capable of arousing in countless worthy breasts is shame at the idea of belonging to *such* a collectivity. It is obvious that the United States of America as they exist to-day impress a mind like General Lea's as so much human blubber. Where is the sharpness and precipitousness, the contempt for life, whether one's own, or another's? Where is the savage "yes" and "no," the unconditional duty? Where is the conscription? Where is the blood-tax? Where is anything that one feels honored by belonging to?

Having said thus much in preparation, I will now confess my own utopia. I devoutly believe in the reign of peace and in the gradual advent of some sort of a socialistic equilibrium. The fatalistic view of the war-function is to me nonsense, for I know that war-making is due to definite motives and subject to prudential checks and reasonable criticisms, just like any other form of enterprise. And when whole nations are the armies, and the science of destruction vies in intellectual refinement with the sciences of production, I see that war becomes absurd and impossible from its own monstrosity. Extravagant ambitions will have to be replaced by reasonable claims, and nations must make common cause against them. I see no reason why all this should not apply to yellow as well as to white countries, and I look forward to a future when acts of war shall be formally outlawed as between civilized peoples.

All these beliefs of mine put me squarely into the anti-militarist party. But I do not believe that peace either ought to be or will be permanent on this globe, unless the states pacifically organized preserve some of the old elements of army-discipline. A permanently successful peace-economy cannot be a simple pleasure-economy. In the more or less socialistic future towards which mankind seems drifting we must still subject ourselves collectively to those severities which answer to our real position upon this only partly hospitable globe. We must make new energies and hardihoods continue the manliness to which the military mind so faithfully clings. Martial virtues must be the enduring cement; intrepidity, contempt of softness, surrender of private interest, obedience to command, must still remain the rock upon which states are built — unless, indeed, we wish for dangerous reactions against commonwealths fit only for contempt, and liable to invite attack whenever a centre of crystallization for military-minded enterprise gets formed anywhere in their neighborhood.

The war-party is assuredly right in affirming and reaffirming that the martial virtues, although originally gained by the race through war, are absolute and permanent human goods. Patriotic pride and ambition in their military form are, after all, only specifications of a more general competitive passion. They are its first form, but that is no reason for supposing them to be its last form. Men now are proud of belonging to a conquering nation, and without a murmur they lay down their persons and their wealth, if by so doing they may fend off subjection. But who can be sure that *other aspects of one's country* may not, with time and education and suggestion enough, come to be regarded with similarly effective feelings of pride and shame? Why should men not some day feel that it is worth a blood-tax to belong to a collectivity superior in *any* ideal respect? Why should they not blush with indignant shame if the community that owns them is vile in any way whatsoever? Individuals, daily more numerous, now feel this civic passion. It is only a question of blowing on the spark till the whole population gets incandescent, and on the ruins of the old morals of military honor, a stable system of morals of civic honor builds itself up. What the whole community comes to believe in grasps the individual as in a vise. The war-function has grasped us so far; but constructive interests may some day seem no less imperative, and impose on the individual a hardly lighter burden.

Wells adds[1] that he thinks that the conceptions of order and discipline, the tradition of service and devotion, of physical fitness, unstinted exertion, and universal responsibility, which universal military duty is now teaching European nations, will remain a permanent acquisition, when the last ammunition has been used in the fireworks that celebrate the final peace. I believe as he does. It would be simply preposterous if the only force that could work ideals of honor and standards of efficiency into English or American natures should be the fear of being killed by the Germans or the Japanese. Great indeed is Fear; but it is not, as our military enthusiasts believe and try to make us believe, the only stimulus known for awakening the higher ranges of men's spiritual energy. The amount of alteration in public opinion which my utopia postulates is vastly less than the difference between the mentality of those black warriors who pursued Stanley's party on the Congo with their cannibal war-cry of "Meat! Meat!" and that of the "general-staff" of any civilized nation. History has seen the latter interval bridged over: the former one can be bridged over much more easily.

[1] "First and Last Things," 1908, p, 226.

A leading historian and professor of International
Relations at Oxford, E. L. Woodward was moved to some
serious thinking on the consequences of the atomic bomb
almost immediately on the news of Hiroshima and Naga-
saki in 1945.

SOME POLITICAL CONSEQUENCES
OF THE ATOMIC BOMB

LESS than a year ago, in an inaugural lecture[1] delivered
before this University, I said two things which have since
come back again and again to my mind. One of them was about
the scope of a chair of international relations; the other was
about myself. I suggested that the holder of my chair need not
be afraid of asking the question 'What should be?' as well as
the question 'What is?' Of myself I said that I had always been
interested in ends and beginnings, and that in order to understand my own age I had felt it necessary to go back in history
to other ends and beginnings, and particularly to the transition
from the Roman Empire through the dark centuries to the high
middle age; the transition, if you like, from the *Aeneid* to the
Divine Comedy, or from the mosaics in the Roman dining-room
at Chedworth to the windows of Chartres Cathedral.

When I thought of these earlier ends and beginnings, when
I took heart from the toughness with which the frail creature
man persists in holding on to his conquests over nature and over
himself as part of nature, it seemed to me that we might still
have confidence in the future of western civilization. I was unwilling to allow this civilization to be described in terms of a
danse macabre. I was bold enough to reject the image—which
I had seen in a remarkable modern painting—of a fool leading
a child against a background of the ruin of cities.

I chose my words after much reflection. I remember now
that, while I was speaking in this noble room which was built
centuries ago for the use of scholars in Divinity, I wondered
whether I ought not to qualify my hopes, and to do so by quoting
another judgement which has haunted me since I first read it
some time before 1930; a noble epitaph passed on a lost cause
by one of the French Jansenists:

'Il me semble que je suis né dans une Église éclairée de diverses
lampes et divers flambeaux, et que Dieu permet que je les voie
éteindre les uns après les autres, sans qu'il paraisse qu'on y en
substitue de nouveaux. Ainsi il me semble que l'air s'obscurcit de

[1] *The Study of International Relations at a University.* Clarendon Press.
February 1945.

plus en plus, parce que nous ne méritons pas que Dieu répare les vides qu'il fait lui-même dans son Église.'

I have re-read my lecture of last February. I have asked myself: What should I say now? Should I reaffirm my confidence in the future, or should I too speak in terms of a darkening church? Should I also feel bound to say, 'Parce que nous ne méritons pas . . .'? I must admit, frankly, that, if I had then known as I know now of the terrible instrument which human knowledge has placed in human hands, I should not have ventured to speak so hopefully of western civilization.

My change of mood has not come from our lamentable failure to solve, in company with our Allies, any one of the immediate problems of resettlement and rehabilitation in Europe. I never expected these problems to be settled easily, at once, and according to plan. No historian can be surprised at the dissensions of Allies after a great war. It is enough to mention the fact that, at the Congress of Vienna, the unity of the four Powers, Great Britain, Austria, Russia, and Prussia, was broken almost at once. These Powers, after forming an alliance for twenty years, had come together to decide the territorial and political shape of central Europe. They met in September 1814. On 3 January 1815 two of the four Powers, Great Britain and Austria, signed a treaty with their former enemy France that they would go to war to resist the claims of Russia and Prussia.

The end of a great war has always meant the emergence of separatist interests, a struggle for position while the situation is still fluid and before boundaries are laid down. Similarly no historian would expect harmonious collaboration in the economic sphere. One has only to remember the chain of mistakes made after the war of 1914–18 or indeed to see that many of these mistakes which seem egregious in the light of after-events could hardly have been avoided at the time; so large in appearance, and so small in fact is the sphere of free action open to the plenipotentiaries at a peace conference.

The change in my mood, and since I am only quoting myself as illustrating an average, I might say the change in every one's mood has come, of course, from reflection upon the discovery of the atomic bomb. I use this term for convenience. It would be presumptuous of me to attempt to describe in more precise language the technical result of scientific experiments which represent an astonishing co-ordination of mind, imagination, and will. I do not underrate this achievement. Fortunately it has been the work of our own countrymen and of our friends, and not of our enemies. In German hands such a discovery would have ended certainly for a long time, perhaps for many centuries, perhaps for ever, any hope of civilization as we know it. The husks of civilization would have remained; the life-giving seed would have been blasted. As things are, we have a respite. We have time to think. We still have before us the choice between good and evil.

The choice is between good and evil. Although such a choice should be easy, no one who has given any care to the study of man will feel sure that man will not choose evil. Or rather, and this is what is meant by the tragic interpretation of history, it is impossible to feel sure that men will not bring this evil upon themselves against their will and even by the means which they may take in order to avert it. There is a danger lest, in our time of respite, which may be very short, we forget that the tragic interpretation of history is still valid. A few weeks ago a professor of physics at an English university, speaking to an audience in Birmingham, made a glowing forecast of the advance in comfort and ease which we might expect from the application of these new discoveries to peaceful ends. In his enthusiasm over the luxuries which he was offering, the professor seems to have swept aside the fears of students of the humanities by telling them that their minds were prejudiced because they studied the classics and the classics were all about war. Leaving aside this bland ignorance of what the classics are about, can it be said that philosophers, historians, and, for that matter, poets, have their vision so much clouded by the past that they cannot see the shapes of the future? There is some truth in a judgement of this kind. Every step forward in human history has been accompanied by laments that it could not be made, and that, if made, it would have bad results leading perhaps to catastrophe. The abandonment of the custom that every gentleman should carry a sword was once regarded by many people as fatal to the survival of a sense of honour.

Nevertheless, if there be a danger that too much occupation with the past may lead to the belief that 'as things have been, they remain', it is not less foolish to ignore the accumulated political wisdom of mankind. This experience, of which, in a sense, scholars in the humanities are the trustees, is not great, but it is enough to warn us that the *tempo* of adaptation to change is very slow. The rate of adjustment has quickened a little in modern times because there is a greater awareness of the social and political problems set by material change. On the other hand, the problem itself is much more serious because changes in the environment have come so quickly that the need of immediate adjustment is greater and not less than it once was. The first cannon were made in Europe before the battle of Crécy, but the decisive effects of artillery were not felt until over a century and a half later. Copernicus' *De Revolutionibus Orbium Coelestium* was published in 1543; a hundred years later the new astronomy had scarcely reached beyond a few specialists.

Above all, an increase in comfort, even an increase in artistic sensibility, cannot be said to fortify men against the temptations of power. The historian and the philosopher thus have a right to say to the scientist *sutor ne supra crepidam* and to point out that science has a social responsibility. It is presumptuous folly to assume that no gifts are too dangerous, or that there is no breaking-point in the strain to which human societies may be subject. The 'so-called' economic man imagined by abstract thinkers about a century ago is now out of fashion. There is equal folly in the hypothesis of a human creature infinitely and immediately amenable to successive revolutions in technology. The first duty, therefore, of students of the humanities at this present time is to recall our generation to the Greek sense of limits, or, if you like, to the Greek sense of fate and the historical connotation of Nemesis.

This duty is the more urgent because there is little analogy between our most recent achievement of power and earlier discoveries unless we go back far beyond recorded history to the invention of the wheel or the control of fire. Such discoveries in the remote past again offer no basis of political comparison because they did not carry with them immediate potentialities of general destruction through misuse. Let me be clear about this term 'general destruction'. I do not mean the universal annihilation of the human race. We may accept the physicists' assurance that there is, at least as far as can be foreseen, no risk of a general explosion in which all organic life above the deep

603

sea level would be destroyed. The misuse of the atomic bomb is likely to bring local, not universal destruction. It will bring this destruction to cities, and at all events for the critical period of adjustment immediately ahead of us—our time of respite— the basis of our civilization will remain urban. As our polities are now organized and as they must remain organized during the next twenty-five years, the destruction of cities would be enough to dislocate beyond hope of recovery the political and economic framework of our lives. The proportion of the killed to the survivors might be no more than in the Black Death, which in the fourteenth century destroyed about one-third of the population of western Europe. It might even be less, in relation to society as a whole, than the infantile death-rate in the eighteenth century. Nevertheless, the question is not one of numbers; all Africa might remain physically untouched by a shock which wrecked the highly complicated and interlocked machinery of civilization in Europe and in North America. We do not always realize how much depends upon this machinery. The instruments used by a symphony orchestra, the paper on which a poem is printed, the paints out of which a picture is made postulate a certain organization of society, a series of entries in ledgers, a legal system, and a thousand other requirements each one of which is linked with others like the rings in a coat of chain armour.

The destruction of cities, the centres of integration in civilized life, has happened before, and has resulted in anarchy and darkness. The process was mainly one of slow decay, and, just because it was slow, the possibilities of recovery were never entirely removed. The danger now is that we should be plunged into anarchy at once, and that we could no more organize recovery than a finely bred dog could long fend for himself if he were turned loose in the jungle. Europe at this moment is much nearer to dislocation beyond recovery than we in England can imagine, but we may still hope for betterment because the area of dislocation—the number of cities destroyed—can be regarded as small in comparison with the area which still stands. We are, however, very near to the edge of an abyss, and at least for a generation to come—a longer time than our period of respite—we cannot risk a greater strain. A war in which atomic bombs were employed to destroy within as many days the twelve most important cities in the North American Continent or the twelve most important cities now remaining in Europe might be too much for us. Human life would not disappear, but human beings would revert, helpless, without counsel, and without the physical means of recovery, to something like the culture of the late bronze age. Let us not delude ourselves on this point. We cannot just lower by a numerical percentage our standard of living. We are playing for the highest stakes: all or nothing.

If we are clear to ourselves what we mean by saying that the choice before us is between good and evil, we should also be clear why we cannot be sure that men will not choose evil. In the first place we must remember that for some people the destruction of western civilization would seem not evil but good. There is a type of revolutionary nihilism which can envisage destruction on a gigantic scale and which, in a way which seems to us perverted, regards this destruction as a necessary prelude to any lasting improvement. Until our own time we might have dismissed such revolutionary nihilism as confined to a few fanatics. We have now seen that these fanatics can control a government and that under the impulse of their fanaticism they can drive a nation into political madness. Who, with the examples of Germany and Japan before him, would now dare to say that a repetition of this ruthless attack upon civilization as we understand it will never be repeated? The philosophy of revolutionary violence reads a little odd to-day, and writings such as those of Sorel stand out in their absurdity as an invitation to the workers of the world to unite in committing suicide, but we still have as a stark political fact the existence of many thousands of Germans and Japanese conditioned from childhood so that they can hardly do otherwise than regard vengeance by destruction as a good in itself.

For myself, although I think that we must be on our guard against those who may deliberately choose evil, I regard as even more sinister—because more likely—the danger that men may bring destruction upon themselves against their will. If there were or ever could be an equal balance of power between nations, if the chances of successful aggression could be assessed mathematically, if the aggressor could not hope to avoid retaliation on a scale equal to his aggression, it is improbable that the atomic bomb would ever be used again in war. The trouble is that, hitherto, nations which have taken the initiative in war and have been guilty of aggression have been persuaded that they could succeed easily and quickly; that they could inflict far more damage than they were likely to receive, or that the results of victory would be so overwhelmingly great that the sufferings of war were worth enduring. History is filled, century after century, with mistakes of this kind; again and again over-confidence has been followed by defeat, and yet the mistakes are repeated. Once more, who will dare to say that this type of error will not recur? It is not inconceivable that by sudden and unannounced aggression a nation may think that it can make retaliation impossible. Public opinion in the aggressing country, driven on by propaganda, frightened lest it may itself be taken unawares, may acquiesce in such a lightning stroke. Or again, with the appalling prospect of warfare under these new conditions, the world may tolerate, as it tolerated in the case of Germany, minor acts of aggression until another Hitler or another Mussolini develop the insolence which the gods punish, but punish through the sufferings of others.

These errors of calculation may be made more easily because, although in some respects the atomic bomb will bring about a rise in the status of certain small or middle Powers, differences in degree of vulnerability to attack are and will remain so obvious that they must occur to everyone. Nations with less to lose may well find it easier to think that the risks are worth taking. A nation with a low standard of life, without wishing to destroy civilization, may think that it has something to gain from a general levelling down of other nations to its own level. Furthermore, there will be new ways—entirely new ways—of exercising a threat of war. It may not be impossible to smuggle atomic bombs into a country in peace-time, and to threaten to touch them off at long range. If such a procedure were adopted, for example, in London or in New York, if five or six of these bombs were hidden in either city at the instance of a hostile Power, and if this hostile Power gave notice, open and broadcast notice, that unless its demands were accepted within a few hours, the bombs would be exploded, what would be the attitude of opinion in the threatened cities?

I need not multiply these instances. I have said enough to explain why the choice between good and evil does not come before nations in a simple and obvious way. Most of the great choices of history have been made, as it were, blindfold. The Teutonic barbarians never wished to destroy the Roman Empire. I repeat that a new catastrophe might well begin from the action of a Power which reckoned that it could call a halt before destruction became universal, or that it was choosing evil in order to avert worse evil from itself, or even that by threats it could get what it wanted.

Here perhaps I may allow myself a short digression. I have assumed that an increase in comfort, a general raising of standards of life will not remove all incentive to war. This assumption may be wrong for the future, but, as far as the past is concerned, it is merely a statement of fact. For the last nine hundred years, in spite of temporary and local set-backs, the standard of life generally in western Europe has been rising, and yet we have seen in the twentieth century, at the end of this cycle of material improvement, two great wars. In a sense it may be said that war is a luxury which only rich nations can afford. The truth is, however, that we know the occasions out of which wars have arisen but that we can make very few generalizations about the cause of war. It may be that no more than these few generalizations are possible. Nevertheless, it is at least worth while trying to see whether we cannot find out a little more about one of the main social activities of man. Some attempt has been made in the United States to inquire into the matter; there has been little co-ordinated effort in England or indeed anywhere in Europe. It seems to me that it would repay our Government—if no private benefaction can be found for the purpose—to spend, say, £30,000 merely on seeing whether properly directed research into the cause or rather causes of war leads to valuable results. I should suggest getting together a small group of people, including a psychologist, an historian, a philosopher, a lawyer, an anthropologist, a business man, a civil servant. I should give these people such research assistance as they might need, and ask them to produce, after two years' study, a report in which they would set out the prolegomena for an inquiry into a matter of such vital importance to everyone. Until an inquiry of this kind has been made, we are in the dark about the value of any political arrangements which we may make for security.

Meanwhile, here and now, we have to do what we can to make

607

some provisional arrangements for security. We have indeed established an organization of a kind in which we have tried to avoid some of the mistakes made a quarter of a century ago when in a moment of high hopes the Covenant of the League of Nations was proclaimed to the world. How does the invention of the atomic bomb affect the plans which we have made? We may, perhaps, take certain considerations for granted. First, we may assume that no effective antidote to this bomb is likely to be found. Even if it were found, we should not be sure that within a short time the antidote itself could not be neutralized and deprived of its salutary effect. Secondly, we can assume that the secret devices used in the production of the bomb will not long remain secret. We can, I think, make this assumption irrespective of the intentions or wishes of those who now hold the secret. Thirdly, we may assume that, within a short time, the cost of producing the bomb will be reduced but that it will continue to require plant and apparatus on a scale which will limit its manufacture to governments or at all events make it possible for governments to prevent private persons or companies from manufacturing bombs. Fourthly, we may assume that the governments of all Powers capable of maintaining and working the necessary plant will wish to do so not merely from the point of view of defence but also in order not to be left behind in the possible adaptation of this new source of power to commercial uses. Finally, we must recognize that any arrangements which we may now try to make for controlling the production of the bomb may be upset later by the application of this power to peaceful purposes. Such application will bring with it immense problems of social, economic, and political adjustment, but we have problems enough on our hands without considering those which we have not to solve at once.

Let us come back, then, to our question: How does the atomic bomb affect our plans for security? Broadly speaking, there are four clear-cut types of answer to this question. We may say that no control is feasible. We may accept control by one nation. We may attempt control by a world government. We may set up a special international organization to deal with the manufacture, storage, and ultimate use of atomic bombs.

I do not think that any one of these four clear-cut answers will take us very far. We have already seen that a policy of *laisser faire* would not bring about such an equilibrium of power between nations that aggression would lose all chance of success and therefore cease to be a temptation. It is also unsafe to infer that no Power will use the atomic bomb through fear of reprisals because no Power used poison gas during the war now ended. The Germans and the Japanese would have used poison gas on a large scale if they had thought that it was the most effective weapon for their purposes. In fact it is not a very effective weapon against an enemy who has taken careful counter-measures against it. It would be still more unsafe to suppose that a promise not to use the atomic bomb in war would certainly be kept. The fate of the Kellogg Pact, and indeed of a dozen other pacts, should be warning enough for us. If therefore we do nothing at all, we shall merely run into calamity.

The second 'clear-cut solution'—control by a single Power—is impracticable. Theoretically it is not impossible. As things are, the controlling Power would be the United States, since it is out of the question that they would hand over the control to any other single government or nation. The United States could say, here and now, that no one else shall make this bomb; that any attempt to make it by any other government would be considered as an act of war against the United States and would be met by instant action against the offender. This plan would, of course, give to the United States complete world sovereignty and put their government into the position of Hobbes's *Leviathan*. All other States would have agreed to surrender their rights; the United States would retain all rights in full. This plan is impracticable because other Great Powers—Russia, for example—would not accept it and the Government and people of the United States would not themselves accept the corollaries; that is to say, they would not declare, here and now, that they would go to war with any other Power attempting to manufacture the bomb or that they required all other countries to accept inspection as a safeguard (for the United States) against secret manufacture.

The third 'clear-cut solution', a world government, is also impracticable. A world government may well come in the future, and when it comes, it may turn out to be a gross and fearful tyranny. This future world government may not even prevent war; it may only make all war into civil war. There is, however, no need to discuss whether a world government would be a good thing or a bad thing. It seems clear that within the next ten years there is not much possibility of getting it, since there is not the slightest chance that either the United States or Russia will surrender to it the powers which each now exercises in full sovereignty. Moreover there is no safe resting-place half-way between the present system of sovereign states and a single world-State. A new division of the world into two or three large federations would only increase our danger.

What then of the fourth 'clear-cut solution'? Can we envisage the control of the atomic bomb by a special international organization? Could we entrust this control to the Security Council of the United Nations? A solution on these lines is likely to appeal to harassed politicians, especially in Great Britain. It looks well. It is a convenient way of shelving the real problems, at least temporarily. It would satisfy, for the time, a large section of British opinion. It might save us, for the time, a good deal of money.

What does this solution mean? Does it mean that an international organization—the Security Council or some other body—will have the sole right to produce these bombs, to store them, and to decide, if need be, upon their employment in case of the imposition of sanctions against an aggressor? If this be what we mean by international control, let us ask what such control implies. We must begin with a convention, signed by all States in a position to produce bombs, and binding them to resign their right to do so. It is asking a good deal of independent States to expect them to sign a self-denying order of this kind, especially since, as I have pointed out, they will want to conduct experiments with a view to the profitable exploitation of this new source of energy in peaceful directions. In the light of recent experience, can we be sure that the convention, if signed, will be observed by all the signatories? Even the most hopeful supporters of the solution of international control, remembering the history of German rearmament, will admit the need to inspect the industrial plant of every country in order to make sure that the convention is being observed and that there is no clandestine manufacture of the bomb. If it should remain possible to produce the bombs only in a single plant of immense size, easily detected because it occupied a large area of surface and could be used solely for this production, inspection might not be unworkable, though it would require ceaseless vigilance over a great part of the world. Or again, if it could be said for certain that the materials for production were localized in a very few areas and that these areas could be closely watched and every scrap of material extracted from them kept under observation and notice taken of it as it was moved from place to place and country to country, the strictest supervision, though difficult, would not be entirely impossible. If, however, within a few years, there are means of dispersing the production over a number of separate installations, some of them underground, and none of them of immense size or recognizable at once as places intended for a single purpose, then inspection becomes impracticable. Similarly, if it be impossible to keep track of every fragment of precious material necessary for the process of manufacture, control at the source also becomes impracticable. In any case inspection is a very difficult matter against a government determined to acquire the bombs and using every ruse to avoid detection. All the necessary plant can be prepared in secret and assembled with speed as soon as the inspectors, who cannot be everywhere at the same time, have left the scene of operations. There are all manner of ways of diverting inspection from crucial sites or explaining why such-and-such an installation is required at this or that place. There can be factories or power stations within factories as well as factories underneath factories. A prearranged fire can be used to keep inspectors out of buildings on the plea of danger. An epidemic of disease may be invented in order to put a particular area under quarantine, and so on. Even with goodwill close inspection would give reason to ill feeling on the ground that the inspectors were commercial spies, and without close inspection there might as well be no scrutiny at all. This inspection would have to include all industrialized countries, great or small, since it would not be safe to overlook the possibility that one country might make a corrupt bargain with another country less suspect, may be, of political aggression.

With all these hazards, a system of inspection does not seem to provide adequate safeguards against deliberate breaches of a covenant by one or more States. Moreover, so far we have considered the matter only from one side. Let us look at the international organization itself. On the negative side, it will have to keep in being an army of inspectors ceaselessly at work from the Sahara to the North Cape, from Land's End to Kamchatka, and across the ocean from Alaska to Patagonia. How is this vast corps to be recruited and paid? Will the minds of its members be emptied of national feelings? Who is to be the inspector-general of this body, and how is he to be chosen?

There are difficulties enough here, but they are nothing to the practical problems involved in the positive side of the work of the international organization. Where is this organization to fix the site on which it will itself produce atomic bombs and carry out experiments in the peaceful application of the knowledge under its charge? What will happen at the sessions of the United Nations if a site is proposed in North America, or in Siberia, or in Australia, or even in Great Britain? Where are the bombs to be stored once they have been produced? We have had these problems before us in previous discussions of an international force. They are not insoluble problems, but it would be rash indeed to hope that they could be settled in the present atmosphere of suspicion and unrest throughout the world. Nevertheless, we should have to solve them because the international organization would have to be given something more than a few policemen or a token bodyguard. It will be necessary to protect the installations and storehouses of the bombs against a raid from a would-be aggressor unless we can be sure that we are about to enter a period of universal disarmament in all weapons other than atomic bombs under international control. Finally, we have to consider the international organization as a body or as the instrument of another body with the powers of binding and loosing, of deciding whether this fearful sanction shall or shall not be employed. This power of decision must be given to it if its inspectors are not to be flouted by the street arabs of an aggressor nation. Any body of persons, any organization to whom such power is entrusted has in fact the mastery of the world. There were intrigues enough at Geneva, but the League had not one lead bullet of its own. Unless men have changed since yesterday, and we know that they have not changed, what can we expect of the fate of this international body holding the greatest of prizes? Either it becomes at once, and almost by definition, a world government, or it is the battleground of rival Powers. We have already seen that, as things are, there is no likelihood that the strong Powers of the world will accept the Hobbesian solution and recognize *Leviathan*. They will not in present circumstances surrender their sovereignty to a world government whatever name may be given to it. Then we can be certain that they will struggle to dominate the international organization until this body, towering theoretically over all other bodies political, shrinks in stature like its humbler predecessor the League of Nations, or, as in far-off Merovingian times, becomes a *roi fainéant* to some Mayor of the Palace. Meanwhile the sovereign States, whatever verbal surrender they may make of their rights, will also ensure themselves, or some of them will ensure themselves, by seeing to it that they have the means of self-protection in the event of a breakdown of an international organ of control.

It would thus appear that, unless we are willing to be drugged once more by comfortable words, we have no hope of safety in any one of these 'clear-cut' plans. A policy of *laisser faire* could succeed, if at all, only on the hypothesis that a user of the atomic bomb will suffer as much damage as he inflicts. Even if such an hypothesis were valid, we must remember that human beings do not act on calculations of this kind. Hitler was prepared to sacrifice a whole generation for the sake of an imagined German future. Lenin was prepared to make a similar sacrifice of the Russian people. It is to our lasting credit that we ourselves did not flinch from an ordeal of this kind in 1940. The opposite policy to *laisser faire*, control by a single Power, namely, the United States, is not a practical policy; neither is the immediate establishment of a world government. It is also very hard to see how we could surmount or know that we had surmounted the difficulties in the way of giving a monopoly in the atomic bomb and the further exploration of this new knowledge to an international organization.

Is there then no hope of safety? Must we drift into a position in which we are at the mercy of any evilly disposed group of men who can win control of a powerful nation, and exact obedience from it? Again I return to my first conclusions about this bomb. There is no way of eluding the fact that we have lost the conditions of security which we suppose our grandfathers to have enjoyed, but I do not think that we need despair just because we cannot find any foolproof safety device against destruction.

We are more likely to get some measure of security if we do not attempt too much. We must accept the fact that, as the last ill-fated Disarmament Conference showed us, nations believe they are more secure if they are fully armed, and suspect any attempt to deprive them of a protection which is more comforting, perhaps, than real. We must recognize that, however easy it is to demonstrate the insufficiency and even the grave danger of closed national sovereignties, nationalism is still a living force of immense strength, and that the combination of factors giving it so strong an emotional appeal has become more and not less potent as a result of the last two wars. We must assume that public opinion in the great national sovereign States will support governmental opinion in regarding the acquisition of these new instruments as the best form of insurance. We must acknowledge the futility of trying, by inspection or any other means, to prevent such separate acquisition. We must not allow our own wishes, or for that matter, our English habit of moralizing our own national interests, to lead us into thinking that in the present state of world opinion we shall find it possible to entrust this instrument to any form of international organization possessing a monopoly of power. We must not forget that, certainly in the case of Germany and almost certainly in the case of Japan, we shall have to apply the closest system of supervision; fortunately the problem of inspection here, though not at all easy, ought not to be outside the range of possibility.

If we take for granted, on one side, the shortcomings, the jealousies and fears, I might say the ancestral fears of our fellow men, if we remember that other people are not much wiser than we in moments of honesty know ourselves to be, we can also recognize that the political animal man would not be where he now is in relation to other gregarious creatures if he had no glimmer of sense. His imagination is limited, but it exists. His willingness to change his ideas and habits has brought him through hazards which must have seemed insuperable. The general will, in Rousseau's phrase, is towards life and not death, or, if we prefer Hobbes, we can say that 'reason suggesteth convenient articles of peace'. Reason has already dictated certain articles of peace. We have an association of United Nations; we have a Security Council. The powers of the Council are limited; the United Nations have not moved very far towards unity, but there is something upon which we can build. Already, for example, the members of the Association are pledged to use their national air forces for an international purpose. It is clear, however, that the arrangements reached a few months ago for keeping the peace and for coercing offenders are now out of date. Since these arrangements must be modified, could we not also reinforce them by a simple pact that if any Power used the atomic bomb without the unanimous approval of other members of the Security Council, the Association as a whole would join in immediate retaliation?[1] This retaliation would be effected by the national forces of each member, in other words, by the bombs which each member possessed. The retaliation must be immediate. We cannot wait for a long discussion about the definition of aggression or send commissions of inquiry to establish the facts. There will be no doubt whether the bombs have or have not been employed.

This pact would admit the national possession but try to secure some form of general control of atomic bombs. Such a pact will not, of course, stand alone. It must be buttressed by agreements, which we already possess, for the peaceful settlement of disputes and for mutual aid. Even so, we cannot be sure that the pact will work. We cannot provide any guarantee that governments and peoples, knowing the ordeal to which they may have to submit, will not at a crisis look for a loophole of escape from their obligations or merely refuse to honour them. We may have another *dégringolade* such as we witnessed in the case of the League. On the other hand, although the lessons of the years 1933 to 1941 may be soon forgotten, public opinion in every country may realize that the best chance of safety lies in providing an overwhelming concentration of power against a transgressor. In the last resort, also, if the pact should break down, and once again a single country has to stand alone, as we stood alone against attack in 1940, such a country will itself possess some means of retaliation, if, as we are assuming, it is allowed to make and keep its own supply of bombs.

I should add one further consideration which seems to me to

[1] There would be a certain analogy between a pact of this kind and the proposals discussed in 1935–6 for an Air Pact. In the earlier case the proposals were put forward to meet the situation resulting from the rapid development of air power since the conclusion of the Locarno treaties.

favour the chances of a pact on the lines I have suggested. I have already reminded you that within a short time the man-power and capital necessary for the manufacture of this bomb may well be only one-fifth or even one-tenth of the outlay required for bringing the recent experiments to a success. We should therefore remember that this new invention, like others which have lessened the importance of numbers in war, will not be solely at the disposal of two or three great Powers. As I have suggested, the Powers of middle standing will certainly carry a greater displacement in world affairs than was imagined even a few months ago. This consideration is relevant to the general position of the Members of the British Commonwealth. If the invention of the atomic bomb, like most military inventions of recent years, is to the disadvantage of Great Britain, it is—speaking simply from the point of view of striking power or retaliatory power—much more to the advantage of the Dominions. It seems to me that the kind of pact which I have in mind is likely to appeal strongly to these Powers of middle rank; that they are likely to give life and effect to it, and that, taken together, they can exercise through it a much greater influence than has hitherto been thought possible.[1]

I have said that a pact for instant action against aggressive use of the atomic bomb cannot stand alone and that it must be supported by sensible arrangements for the peaceful settlement of disputes. I should also ask the question whether all other instruments of warfare are now out of date. The answer to this question requires technical knowledge which I do not possess, but I should suggest that we must not assume too quickly that we can discard every other means of armed protection. It is clear, for example, that if it ever came to the employment of sanctions against an aggressor State, that is to say, if atomic bombs were used in retaliation, we might still need a trained and disciplined force for the purpose of entering and occupying the territory of the aggressor. It is also clear that the range and character of other weapons—rocket bombs for example—must bring them qualitatively near to the atomic bomb itself, and that the next

---

[1] These considerations are enough to dispose of the idea that it would be safe to leave the bombs under the joint control of Great Britain, the United States, and the U.S.S.R. There are, of course, other obvious objections against a triumvirate of this kind.

stage in international discussions should be the extension of the pact covering the use of the atomic bomb to the employment of these other instruments of large-scale destruction. I do not think I need discuss this question here because it is secondary in the sense that any Power meditating aggression will obviously plan it in terms of the most deadly weapons available, and until we have done all that it is possible to do to prevent the worst catastrophe, we can leave the consideration of lesser evils.

So far I have considered this bomb from the point of view of maximum danger—the total ruin of the high civilization which we have inherited from our ancestors and which we have defended at terrible cost in two recent wars. Assuming that we avoid bringing such a catastrophe on ourselves, there are other problems upon which it would be wise for us to reflect. There is, for example, the bearing of this invention upon the future of political liberty as we understand it: liberty to criticize authority, to choose our avocations and mode of livelihood, to change our laws and institutions. Whether it remains for years to come only a potential source of destruction or whether it can be turned to peaceful ends, this new source of energy must remain under State control and therefore must increase enormously the power of the State over the citizen. Hitherto, a great increase in State power has rarely made for liberty of any kind. This fact is perhaps blurred to-day. For large masses of the population much of the content of political liberty in the past has been theoretical only, since in fact they have been under economic constraints and fears which have prevented the enjoyment of freedom in a large sense. Hence for the average man to-day an increase of State power has actually meant an increase in liberty and has brought with it a sense of emancipation. If past history (which the average man does not know) is of any guidance, this *interim* stage is unlikely to last very long. It therefore becomes of first importance to us to avoid the line of development which has been followed so often in human societies where the tendency has been to return from contract back to status after advancing from status to contract. This question is of greater significance now because every new instrument of force under State control lessens the chances of successful revolution—the last safeguard against a perpetual tyranny. The invention of railways, allowing a rapid concentration of troops, even more than the building of wide roads broke the localized power of the Paris mob in the nineteenth century. In the twentieth century the machine-gun, the armoured car, the aeroplane, and the tank in the control of authority have destroyed the possibility of any revolution which is not a hundred per cent. totalitarian (and therefore unlikely to favour liberty) or does not, as recently in Spain, develop into a fearful civil war. Even so the success of the Spanish revolution, and for that matter of the three major revolutions of our time, in Russia, Italy, and Germany, was due to special circumstances unlikely to recur. We might do well to think over this matter and to ask ourselves what domestic safeguards, if any, may be available to us against the misuse of this tremendous concentration of power henceforward in the hands of the State.

There is another danger less measurable but not less real. Perhaps the term danger is in some respects too narrow and in others not comprehensive enough. At present there is a melo-dramatic element about this new bomb. In spite of the evidence, few of us have taken its measure in human misery. We think of it much as we thought in the past, when, for example, we knew but did not comprehend the measure of suffering caused by inundations of the great Chinese rivers. Although we are consciously yet vaguely uneasy, a sense of total insecurity has not affected our people as a whole. Indeed we are still convalescent from the shocks of war, and our nerves cannot respond, for a time, to any new danger. What will be the effect upon public opinion in a few years time when governments in possession of these bombs are not just manœuvring for position—this is what they are doing to-day—but when the first grave international crisis arises or there are signs, in one or more nations, of the whipping up of animosities on a scale all too familiar to us? Above all, what will be the effect upon literature and art of this shadow creeping across the surface of the sun? Will it chill all creative energy? Will there be nothing but these images of the darkening church, of the fool and the child? Will the *Dies Irae* be chanted by a generation without faith and without hope? It is, of course, impossible to answer these questions. It is impossible to forecast even roughly the reaction of the artist and the poet to their environment. I can say only one thing, and what I have to say is perhaps a fitting end to an inquiry which has shown little more than my own perplexity. Throughout the last twelve years I have found myself repeating the words:

> Tomorrow, and tomorrow, and tomorrow, . . .
> And all our yesterdays have lighted fools
> The way to dusty death.

Nothing could express more clearly the mood in which we now face the consequences of our own deliberate acts; our own choice among the many choices open to us. And yet these words, which might also summarize the judgement of the gods upon us, were written over three centuries ago, not in the twilight or gathering darkness of a civilization but at the beginning of a cycle of European achievement without parallel in history. It may be that our mood to-day is not less out of relation with the future.

OXFORD

3 November, 1945.

Although he won his greatest fame as leader of the Allied forces in Western Europe in World War II, Dwight D. Eisenhower held out for himself the quest for peace as his major mission. These two addresses, one given at the beginning of his presidency in April 1953, and the other a farewell address at its termination in January 1961, give eloquent expression to those concerns.

50 ¶ Address "The Chance for Peace" Delivered Before the American Society of Newspaper Editors. *April* 16, 1953

IN THIS SPRING of 1953 the free world weighs one question above all others: the chance for a just peace for all peoples.

To weigh this chance is to summon instantly to mind another recent moment of great decision. It came with that yet more hopeful spring of 1945, bright with the promise of victory and of freedom. The hope of all just men in that moment too was a just and lasting peace.

The 8 years that have passed have seen that hope waver, grow dim, and almost die. And the shadow of fear again has darkly lengthened across the world.

Today the hope of free men remains stubborn and brave, but it is sternly disciplined by experience. It shuns not only all crude counsel of despair but also the self-deceit of easy illusion. It

weighs the chance for peace with sure, clear knowledge of what
happened to the vain hope of 1945.

In that spring of victory the soldiers of the Western Allies met
the soldiers of Russia in the center of Europe.   They were triumphant comrades in arms.   Their peoples shared the joyous
prospect of building, in honor of their dead, the only fitting monument—an age of just peace.   All these war-weary peoples shared
too this concrete, decent purpose: to guard vigilantly against the
domination ever again of any part of the world by a single,
unbridled aggressive power.

This common purpose lasted an instant and perished.   The
nations of the world divided to follow two distinct roads.

The United States and our valued friends, the other free nations, chose one road.

The leaders of the Soviet Union chose another.

The way chosen by the United States was plainly marked by a
few clear precepts, which govern its conduct in world affairs.

First: No people on earth can be held, as a people, to be an
enemy, for all humanity shares the common hunger for peace and
fellowship and justice.

Second: No nation's security and well-being can be lastingly
achieved in isolation but only in effective cooperation with fellow-
nations.

Third: Any nation's right to a form of government and an economic system of its own choosing is *inalienable.*

Fourth: Any nation's attempt to dictate to other nations their
form of government is *indefensible.*

And fifth: A nation's hope of lasting peace cannot be firmly
based upon any race in armaments but rather upon just relations
and honest understanding with all other nations.

In the light of these principles the citizens of the United States
defined the way they proposed to follow, through the aftermath
of war, toward true peace.

This way was faithful to the spirit that inspired the United Nations: to prohibit strife, to relieve tensions, to banish fears.   This

way was to control and to reduce armaments. This way was to allow all nations to devote their energies and resources to the great and good tasks of healing the war's wounds, of clothing and feeding and housing the needy, of perfecting a just political life, of enjoying the fruits of their own free toil.

The Soviet government held a vastly different vision of the future.

In the world of its design, security was to be found, not in mutual trust and mutual aid but in *force:* huge armies, subversion, rule of neighbor nations. The goal was power superiority at all cost. Security was to be sought by denying it to all others.

The result has been tragic for the world and, for the Soviet Union, it has also been ironic.

The amassing of Soviet power alerted free nations to a new danger of aggression. It compelled them in self-defense to spend unprecedented money and energy for armaments. It forced them to develop weapons of war now capable of inflicting instant and terrible punishment upon any aggressor.

It instilled in the free nations—and let none doubt this—the unshakable conviction that, as long as there persists a threat to freedom, they must, at any cost, remain armed, strong, and ready for the risk of war.

It inspired them—and let none doubt this—to attain a unity of purpose and will beyond the power of propaganda or pressure to break, now or ever.

There remained, however, one thing essentially unchanged and unaffected by Soviet conduct: the readiness of the free nations to welcome sincerely any genuine evidence of peaceful purpose enabling all peoples again to resume their common quest of just peace.

The free nations, most solemnly and repeatedly, have assured the Soviet Union that their firm association has never had any aggressive purpose whatsoever. Soviet leaders, however, have seemed to persuade themselves, or tried to persuade their people, otherwise.

And so it has come to pass that the Soviet Union itself has shared and suffered the very fears it has fostered in the rest of the world.

This has been the way of life forged by 8 years of fear and force.

ᵒWhat can the world, or any nation in it, hope for if no turning is found on this dread road?

The worst to be feared and the best to be expected can be simply stated.

The *worst* is atomic war.

The *best* would be this: a life of perpetual fear and tension; a burden of arms draining the wealth and the labor of all peoples; a wasting of strength that defies the American system or the Soviet system or any system to achieve true abundance and happiness for the peoples of this earth.

Every gun that is made, every warship launched, every rocket fired signifies, in the final sense, a theft from those who hunger and are not fed, those who are cold and are not clothed.

This world in arms is not spending money alone.

It is spending the sweat of its laborers, the genius of its scientists, the hopes of its children.

The cost of one modern heavy bomber is this: a modern brick school in more than 30 cities.

It is two electric power plants, each serving a town of 60,000 population.

It is two fine, fully equipped hospitals.

It is some 50 miles of concrete highway.

We pay for a single fighter plane with a half million bushels of wheat.

We pay for a single destroyer with new homes that could have housed more than 8,000 people.

This, I repeat, is the best way of life to be found on the road the world has been **taking**.

This is not a way of life at all, in any true sense. Under the cloud of threatening war, it is humanity hanging from a cross of iron.

These plain and cruel truths define the peril and point the hope that come with this spring of 1953.

This is one of those times in the affairs of nations when the gravest choices must be made, if there is to be a turning toward a just and lasting peace.

It is a moment that calls upon the governments of the world to speak their intentions with simplicity and with honesty.

It calls upon them to answer the question that stirs the hearts of all sane men: *is there no other way the world may live?*

The world knows that an era ended with the death of Joseph Stalin. The extraordinary 30-year span of his rule saw the Soviet Empire expand to reach from the Baltic Sea to the Sea of Japan, finally to dominate 800 million souls.

The Soviet system shaped by Stalin and his predecessors was born of one World War. It survived with stubborn and often amazing courage a second World War. It has lived to threaten a third.

Now a new leadership has assumed power in the Soviet Union. Its links to the past, however strong, cannot bind it completely. Its future is, in great part, its own to make.

This new leadership confronts a free world aroused, as rarely in its history, by the will to stay free.

This free world knows, out of the bitter wisdom of experience, that vigilance and sacrifice are the price of liberty.

It knows that the defense of Western Europe imperatively demands the unity of purpose and action made possible by the North Atlantic Treaty Organization, embracing a European Defense Community.

It knows that Western Germany deserves to be a free and equal partner in this community and that this, for Germany, is the only safe way to full, final unity.

It knows that aggression in Korea and in southeast Asia are threats to the whole free community to be met by united action.

This is the kind of free world which the new Soviet leadership confronts. It is a world that demands and expects the fullest respect of its rights and interests. It is a world that will always accord the same respect to all others.

So the new Soviet leadership now has a precious opportunity to awaken, with the rest of the world, to the point of peril reached and to help turn the tide of history.

Will it do this?

We do not yet know. Recent statements and gestures of Soviet leaders give some evidence that they may recognize this critical moment.

We welcome every honest act of peace.

We care nothing for mere rhetoric.

We are only for sincerity of peaceful purpose attested by deeds. The opportunities for such deeds are many. The performance of a great number of them waits upon no complex protocol but upon the simple will to do them. Even a few such clear and specific acts, such as the Soviet Union's signature upon an Austrian treaty or its release of thousands of prisoners still held from World War II, would be impressive signs of sincere intent. They would carry a power of persuasion not to be matched by any amount of oratory.

This we do know: a world that begins to witness the rebirth of trust among nations *can* find its way to a peace that is neither partial nor punitive.

With all who will work in good faith toward such a peace, we are ready, with renewed resolve, to strive to redeem the near-lost hopes of our day.

The first great step along this way must be the conclusion of an honorable armistice in Korea.

This means the immediate cessation of hostilities and the prompt initiation of political discussions leading to the holding of free elections in a united Korea.

It should mean, no less importantly, an end to the direct and indirect attacks upon the security of Indochina and Malaya. For any armistice in Korea that merely released aggressive armies to attack elsewhere would be a fraud.

We seek, throughout Asia as throughout the world, a peace that is true and total.

Out of this can grow a still wider task—the achieving of just political settlements for the other serious and specific issues between the free world and the Soviet Union.

None of these issues, great or small, is insoluble—given only the will to respect the rights of all nations.

Again we say: the United States is ready to assume its just part.

We have already done all within our power to speed conclusion of a treaty with Austria, which will free that country from economic exploitation and from occupation by foreign troops.

We are ready not only to press forward with the present plans for closer unity of the nations of Western Europe but also, upon that foundation, to strive to foster a broader European community, conducive to the free movement of persons, of trade, and of ideas.

This community would include a free and united Germany, with a government based upon free and secret elections.

This free community and the full independence of the East European nations could mean the end of the present unnatural division of Europe.

As progress in all these areas strengthens world trust, we could proceed concurrently with the next great work—the reduction of the burden of armaments now weighing upon the world. To this end we would welcome and enter into the most solemn agreements. These could properly include:

1. The limitation, by absolute numbers or by an agreed international ratio, of the sizes of the military and security forces of all nations.

2. A commitment by all nations to set an agreed limit upon that proportion of total production of certain strategic materials to be devoted to military purposes.

3. International control of atomic energy to promote its use for peaceful purposes only and to insure the prohibition of atomic weapons.

° 4. A limitation or prohibition of other categories of weapons of great destructiveness.

5. The enforcement of all these agreed limitations and prohibitions by adequate safeguards, including a practical system of inspection under the United Nations.

The details of such disarmament programs are manifestly critical and complex. Neither the United States nor any other nation can properly claim to possess a perfect, immutable formula. But the formula matters less than the faith—the good faith without which no formula can work justly and effectively.

The fruit of success in all these tasks would present the world with the greatest task, and the greatest opportunity, of all. It is this: the dedication of the energies, the resources, and the imaginations of all peaceful nations to a new kind of war. This would be a declared total war, not upon any human enemy but upon the brute forces of poverty and need.

The peace we seek, founded upon decent trust and cooperative effort among nations, can be fortified, not by weapons of war but by wheat and by cotton, by milk and by wool, by meat and by timber and by rice. These are words that translate into every language on earth. These are needs that challenge this world in arms.

This idea of a just and peaceful world is not new or strange to us. It inspired the people of the United States to initiate the European Recovery Program in 1947. That program was prepared to treat, with like and equal concern, the needs of Eastern and Western Europe.

We are prepared to reaffirm, with the most concrete evidence, our readiness to help build a world in which all peoples can be productive and prosperous.

This Government is ready to ask its people to join with all nations in devoting a substantial percentage of the savings achieved by disarmament to a fund for world aid and reconstruction. The purposes of this great work would be to help other peoples to develop the undeveloped areas of the world, to stimulate profitable and fair world trade, to assist all peoples to know the blessings of productive freedom.

The monuments to this new kind of war would be these: roads and schools, hospitals and homes, food and health.

We are ready, in short, to dedicate our strength to serving the *needs,* rather than the *fears,* of the world.

We are ready, by these and all such actions, to make of the United Nations an institution that can effectively guard the peace and security of all peoples.

I know of nothing I can add to make plainer the sincere purpose of the United States.

I know of no course, other than that marked by these and similar actions, that can be called the highway of peace.

I know of only one question upon which progress waits. It is this:

What is the Soviet Union ready to do?

Whatever the answer be, let it be plainly spoken.

Again we say: the hunger for peace is too great, the hour in history too late, for any government to mock men's hopes with mere words and promises and gestures.

The test of truth is simple. There can be no persuasion but by deeds.

Is the new leadership of the Soviet Union prepared to use its decisive influence in the Communist world, including control of the flow of arms, to bring not merely an expedient truce in Korea but genuine peace in Asia?

Is it prepared to allow other nations, including those of Eastern Europe, the free choice of their own forms of government?

Is it prepared to act in concert with others upon serious disarmament proposals to be made firmly effective by stringent U.N. control and inspection?

If not, where then is the concrete evidence of the Soviet Union's concern for peace?

The test is clear.

There is, before all peoples, a precious chance to turn the black tide of events.   If we failed to strive to seize this chance, the judgment of future ages would be harsh and just.

If we strive but fail and the world remains armed against itself, it at least need be divided no longer in its clear knowledge of who has condemned humankind to this fate.

The purpose of the United States, in stating these proposals, is simple and clear.

These proposals spring, without ulterior purpose or political passion, from our calm conviction that the hunger for peace is in the hearts of all peoples—those of Russia and of China no less than of our own country.

They conform to our firm faith that God created men to enjoy, not destroy, the fruits of the earth and of their own toil.

They aspire to this: the lifting, from the backs and from the hearts of men, of their burden of arms and of fears, so that they may find before them a golden age of freedom and of peace.

NOTE: The President's address was broadcast over television and radio from the Statler Hotel in Washington.

421   ¶ Farewell Radio and Television Address to the American People.   *January* 17, 1961

[Delivered from the President's Office at 8:30 p.m.]

My fellow Americans:

Three days from now, after half a century in the service of our country, I shall lay down the responsibilities of office as, in traditional and solemn ceremony, the authority of the Presidency is vested in my successor.

This evening I come to you with a message of leave-taking and farewell, and to share a few final thoughts with you, my countrymen.

Like every other citizen, I wish the new President, and all who will labor with him, Godspeed. I pray that the coming years will be blessed with peace and prosperity for all.

Our people expect their President and the Congress to find essential agreement on issues of great moment, the wise resolution of which will better shape the future of the Nation.

My own relations with the Congress, which began on a remote and tenuous basis when, long ago, a member of the Senate appointed me to West Point, have since ranged to the intimate during the war and immediate post-war period, and, finally, to the mutually interdependent during these past eight years.

In this final relationship, the Congress and the Administration have, on most vital issues, cooperated well, to serve the national good rather than mere partisanship, and so have assured that the business of the Nation should go forward. So, my official relationship with the Congress ends in a feeling, on my part, of gratitude that we have been able to do so much together.

II.

We now stand ten years past the midpoint of a century that has witnessed four major wars among great nations. Three of these involved our own country. Despite these holocausts America is today the strongest, the most influential and most productive nation in the world. Understandably proud of this pre-eminence, we yet realize that America's leadership and prestige depend, not merely upon our unmatched material progress, riches and military strength, but on how we use our power in the interests of world peace and human betterment.

III.

Throughout America's adventure in free government, our basic purposes have been to keep the peace; to foster progress in human achievement, and to enhance liberty, dignity and integrity among people and among nations. To strive for less would be unworthy of a free and religious people. Any failure traceable to arrogance, or our lack of comprehension or readiness to sacrifice would inflict upon us grievous hurt both at home and abroad.

Progress toward these noble goals is persistently threatened by the conflict now engulfing the world. It commands our whole attention, absorbs our very beings. We face a hostile ideology—global in scope, atheistic in character, ruthless in purpose, and insidious in method. Unhappily the danger it poses promises to be of indefinite duration. To meet it successfully, there is called for, not so much the emotional and transitory sacrifices of crisis, but rather those which enable us to carry forward steadily, surely, and without complaint the burdens of a prolonged and complex struggle—with liberty the stake. Only thus shall we remain, despite every provocation, on our charted course toward permanent peace and human betterment.

Crises there will continue to be. In meeting them, whether foreign or domestic, great or small, there is a recurring temptation to feel that some spectacular and costly action could become the miraculous solution to all current difficulties. A huge increase in newer elements of our defense; development of unrealistic programs to cure every ill in agriculture; a dramatic expansion in basic and applied research—these and many other possibilities, each possibly promising in itself, may be suggested as the only way to the road we wish to travel.

But each proposal must be weighed in the light of a broader consideration: the need to maintain balance in and among national programs—balance between the private and the public economy, balance between cost and hoped for advantage—balance between the clearly necessary and the comfortably desirable; balance between our essential requirements as a nation and the duties imposed by the nation upon the individual; balance between actions of the moment and the national welfare of the future. Good judgment seeks balance and progress; lack of it eventually finds imbalance and frustration.

The record of many decades stands as proof that our people and their government have, in the main, understood these truths and have responded to them well, in the face of stress and threat. But threats, new in kind or degree, constantly arise. I mention two only.

IV.

A vital element in keeping the peace is our military establishment. Our arms must be mighty, ready for instant action, so that no potential aggressor may be tempted to risk his own destruction.

Our military organization today bears little relation to that known by any of my predecessors in peacetime, or indeed by the fighting men of World War II or Korea.

Until the latest of our world conflicts, the United States had no armaments industry. American makers of plowshares could, with time and as required, make swords as well. But now we can no longer risk emergency improvisation of national defense; we have been compelled to create a permanent armaments industry of vast proportions. Added to this, three and a half million men and women are directly engaged in the defense establishment. We annually spend on military security more than the net income of all United States corporations.

This conjunction of an immense military establishment and a large arms industry is new in the American experience. The total influence—economic, political, even spiritual—is felt in every city, every State house, every office of the Federal government. We recognize the imperative need for this development. Yet we must not fail to comprehend its grave implications. Our toil, resources and livelihood are all involved; so is the very structure of our society.

In the councils of government, we must guard against the acquisition of unwarranted influence, whether sought or unsought, by the military-industrial complex. The potential for the disastrous rise of misplaced power exists and will persist.

We must never let the weight of this combination endanger our liberties or democratic processes. We should take nothing for granted. Only an alert and knowledgeable citizenry can compel the proper meshing of the huge industrial and military machinery of defense with our peaceful methods and goals, so that security and liberty may prosper together.

Akin to, and largely responsible for the sweeping changes in our industrial-military posture, has been the technological revolution during recent decades.

In this revolution, research has become central; it also becomes more formalized, complex, and costly. A steadily increasing share is conducted for, by, or at the direction of, the Federal government.

Today, the solitary inventor, tinkering in his shop, has been overshadowed by task forces of scientists in laboratories and testing fields. In the same fashion, the free university, historically the fountainhead of free ideas and scientific discovery, has experienced a revolution in the conduct of research. Partly because of the huge costs involved, a government contract becomes virtually a substitute for intellectual curiosity. For every old blackboard there are now hundreds of new electronic computers.

The prospect of domination of the nation's scholars by Federal employment, project allocations, and the power of money is ever present—and is gravely to be regarded.

Yet, in holding scientific research and discovery in respect, as we should, we must also be alert to the equal and opposite danger that public policy could itself become the captive of a scientific-technological elite.

It is the task of statesmanship to mold, to balance, and to integrate these and other forces, new and old, within the principles of our democratic system—ever aiming toward the supreme goals of our free society.

V.

Another factor in maintaining balance involves the element of time. As we peer into society's future, we—you and I, and our government—must avoid the impulse to live only for today, plundering, for our own ease and convenience, the precious resources of tomorrow. We cannot mortgage the material assets of our grandchildren without risking the loss also of their political and spiritual heritage. We want democracy to survive for all generations to come, not to become the insolvent phantom of tomorrow.

VI.

Down the long lane of the history yet to be written America knows that this world of ours, ever growing smaller, must avoid becoming a community of dreadful fear and hate, and be, instead, a proud confederation of mutual trust and respect.

Such a confederation must be one of equals. The weakest must come to the conference table with the same confidence as do we, protected as we are by our moral, economic, and military strength. That table, though scarred by many past frustrations, cannot be abandoned for the certain agony of the battlefield.

Disarmament, with mutual honor and confidence, is a continuing imperative. Together we must learn how to compose differences, not with arms, but with intellect and decent purpose. Because this need is so sharp and apparent I confess that I lay down my official responsibilities in this field with a definite sense of disappointment. As one who has witnessed the horror and the lingering sadness of war—as one who knows that another war could utterly destroy this civilization which has been so slowly and painfully built over thousands of years—I wish I could say tonight that a lasting peace is in sight.

Happily, I can say that war has been avoided. Steady progress toward our ultimate goal has been made. But, so much remains to be done. As a private citizen, I shall never cease to do what little I can to help the world advance along that road.

VII.

So—in this my last good night to you as your President—I thank you for the many opportunities you have given me for public service in war and peace. I trust that in that service you find some things worthy; as for the rest of it, I know you will find ways to improve performance in the future.

You and I—my fellow citizens—need to be strong in our faith that all nations, under God, will reach the goal of peace with justice. May we be ever unswerving in devotion to principle, confident but humble with power, diligent in pursuit of the Nation's great goals.

To all the peoples of the world, I once more give expression to America's prayerful and continuing aspiration:

We pray that peoples of all faiths, all races, all nations, may have their great human needs satisfied; that those now denied opportunity shall come to enjoy it to the full; that all who yearn for freedom may experience its spiritual blessings; that those who have freedom will understand, also, its heavy responsibilities; that all who are insensitive to the needs of others will learn charity; that the scourges of poverty, disease and ignorance will be made to disappear from the earth, and that, in the goodness of time, all peoples will come to live together in a peace guaranteed by the binding force of mutual respect and love.